지텔프 [공식] 기출문제집 | LEVEL 2

200[%] 활용법

G-TELP 교재 동영상강의

해커스인강(HackersIngang.com) 접속 ▶ 상단 메뉴의
[G-TELP → 수강신청] 클릭 ▶ 본 교재의 인강
[수강신청] 클릭하여 이용하기

바로가기 ▶

지텔프 기출 단어암기장(PDF)

해커스인강(HackersIngang.com) 접속 ▶
상단 메뉴의 **[G-TELP → MP3/자료 → 무료 MP3/자료] 클릭** ▶
본 교재의 **[지텔프 기출 단어암기장]**
글릭하어 이용하기

[무료 MP3/자료] 바로가기 ▶

문제풀이 MP3

해커스인강(HackersIngang.com) 접속 ▶
상단 메뉴의 **[G-TELP → MP3/자료 → 문제풀이 MP3] 클릭** ▶
본 교재의 **[문제풀이 MP3]** 클릭하여 이용하기

[문제풀이 MP3] 바로가기 ▶

무료 자동 채점 및 성적 분석 서비스

교재 내 수록되어 있는 실전 TEST의
채점 및 성적 분석 서비스를 제공합니다.

[무료 자동 채점 및 성적 분석 서비스]
바로 이용하기 ▶

"딱 한 장에 담은 지텔프 문법 총정리" 무료 강의

딱 한 장에 담았다! 지텔프 문법 총정리 QR 강의!
1. 6개 문법 포인트 총정리!
2. 해커스 G-TELP 전문 선생님의 상세한 해설
3. G-TELP 최신 출제 경향을 반영한 강의

[지텔프 문법 총정리강의] 바로가기 ▶

G-TELP 무료 학습 콘텐츠

지텔프 정답 실시간 확인	지텔프 단기고득점 비법강의	지텔프 무료 모의고사	지텔프 무료 학습자료

방법 **해커스영어**(Hackers.co.kr) 접속 ▶ **[공무원/지텔프]** 메뉴 클릭하여 이용하기

* QR코드로 [해커스영어] 바로가기 ▶

지텔프 공식 기출문제집 7회분 LEVEL 2

문제집

기출문제 7회분 + 정답 한눈에 보기
(OMR 답안지 수록)

지텔프 공식 기출문제집 | 7회분 LEVEL 2

문제집

해커스

지텔프코리아 제공 공식 기출문제를 완벽 해석 · 해설한

『지텔프 공식 기출문제집 7회분 Level 2』를 내면서

해커스에서 지텔프코리아가 제공한 지텔프 Level 2 공식 기출문제 7회분을 담은 『지텔프 공식 기출문제집 7회분 Level 2』를 출간하게 되었습니다.

영어 교재 분야에서 항상 베스트셀러의 자리를 지키는 해커스의 독보적인 노하우와 더 좋은 책을 만들겠다는 정성을 담아, 그 어떤 교재보다 완벽하게 지텔프 Level 2 시험에 대비할 수 있도록 하였습니다.

공식 기출문제를 수록한 실전서!

『지텔프 공식 기출문제집 7회분 Level 2』는 출제 기관으로부터 기출문제와 음성 7회분을 제공받아 교재에 수록하였습니다. 또한, 실제 지텔프와 동일한 구성의 문제지와 Answer Sheet을 함께 제공하여 실전 감각을 더욱 높일 수 있도록 하였습니다.

실전서 한 권으로 끝내는 지텔프 고득점 전략 학습!

출제 경향을 통해 지텔프만의 공식과 패턴을 완벽 분석하고, 영역별 고득점 전략을 제시하였습니다. 지텔프 입문자도 이 교재 한 권만으로 핵심 전략을 학습하고 문제풀이를 연습하면 목표하는 점수를 달성할 수 있습니다.

정확한 해석과 상세하고 이해하기 쉬운 해설로 문제풀이 실력 상승!

고득점 전략을 적용하는 방법을 익힐 수 있도록 모든 문제에 정확한 해석과 상세한 해설을 중요 어휘와 함께 수록하였습니다. 또한, 단순히 정답에 대한 해설만을 제공하는 것이 아니라 헷갈릴 수 있는 오답에 대한 상세한 분석을 함께 수록하여, 틀린 문제의 원인을 파악하고 문제풀이 실력을 향상시킬 수 있도록 하였습니다.

『지텔프 공식 기출문제집 7회분 Level 2』가 여러분의 지텔프 목표 점수 달성에 확실한 해결책이 되고, 영어 실력의 향상은 물론 여러분의 꿈을 향한 길에 믿음직한 동반자가 되기를 소망합니다.

해커스 지텔프연구소

목차

실제 시험으로 완벽 실전 대비! 실전완성 문제집 [책 속의 책]

명쾌한 해설로 점수 상승! 약점보완 **해설집**

 무료 문제풀이 MP3

 무료 자동 채점 및 성적 분석 서비스

 <딱 한 장에 담은 지텔프 문법 총정리> 및 총정리강의

 <지텔프 기출 단어암기장> PDF

교재 구성 및 특징

공식 기출문제 7회분으로 실전 감각 완성!

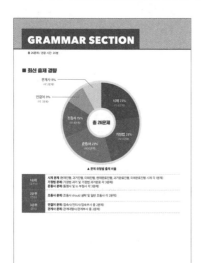

공식 기출문제 7회분 수록

풍부한 실전 경험을 쌓을 수 있도록, 지텔프코리아에서 제공한 공식 기출문제 7회분을 수록하였습니다.

실제 시험 음원 제공

실제 지텔프 시험 음원을 통해 음성의 구성 및 빠르기를 생생하게 체험함으로써 실전 감각을 키울 수 있습니다.

자동 채점 및 성적 분석 서비스

타이머, 모바일 OMR, 자동 채점, 정답률 및 취약 유형 분석까지 제공하는 자동 채점 및 성적 분석 서비스를 통해 실전 감각을 키울 수 있습니다.

영역별 핵심 전략으로 빠른 실력 향상!

최신 출제 경향

최신 지텔프 시험의 문제 유형별 출제 비율을 제공하고 유형별 출제 형태를 우선순위에 따라 정리하여 목표 점수 달성을 위해 효과적으로 학습할 수 있게 하였습니다.

핵심 전략

각 영역의 유형별/파트별 핵심 전략을 제공하여 영역별 출제 공식과 정답의 단서를 찾는 방법을 한눈에 확인할 수 있게 하였습니다.

취약 유형 분석과 명쾌한 해설로 확실한 점수 상승!

취약 유형 분석표
취약 유형 분석표를 통해 자신이 취약한 문제 유형을 스스로 확인할 수 있게 하였습니다.

지텔프 치트키
문제풀이의 핵심이 되는 지텔프 치트키를 통해 문제를 쉽고 빠르게 푸는 전략을 제공하였습니다.

해설 & 오답분석
모든 문제에 대한 정확한 해석, 상세한 해설과 필수 학습 어휘를 제공하였습니다. 해설과 오답분석을 통해 정답이 되는 이유와 오답이 되는 이유를 확실히 파악할 수 있습니다.

다양한 부가 학습자료로 목표 점수 달성!

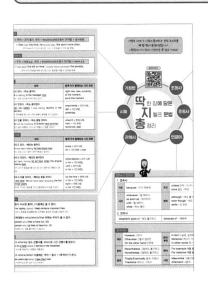

딱 한 장에 담은 지텔프 문법 총정리
지텔프 문법에서 출제되는 문법 포인트를 딱 한 장에 담은 총정리 자료를 통해 핵심만 빠르고 간단하게 정리할 수 있습니다.

복습용 MP3
각 테스트의 파트별 지문 음성을 분할한 복습용 MP3로 자신이 놓쳤던 부분을 확인하고 다시 듣는 연습을 하여 청취 실력을 향상시킬 수 있습니다.

지텔프 기출 단어암기장
지텔프 시험에 등장하는 빈출 어휘만 모은 단어암기장을 무료로 다운받아 이용할 수 있습니다.

* 지텔프 기출 단어암기장은 해커스인강(HackersIngang.com) 사이트에서 무료로 제공됩니다.

지텔프 시험 소개

■ 지텔프 시험은?

지텔프(G-TELP)란 General Tests of English Language Proficiency의 약자로 국제테스트 연구원(ITSC, International Testing Services Center)에서 주관하는 국제적 공인 영어시험이며, 한국에서는 1986년에 지텔프코리아가 설립되어 지텔프 시험을 운영 및 주관하고 있습니다. 현재 공무원, 군무원 등 각종 국가고시 영어 대체 시험, 기업체의 신입사원 채용 및 인사 · 승진 평가 시험, 대학교 · 대학원 졸업 자격 및 논문 심사 영어 대체 시험 등으로 널리 활용되고 있습니다.

■ 지텔프 Level별 시험 구성

지텔프는 Level 1부터 5까지 다섯 가지 Level의 시험으로 구분됩니다. 한국에서는 다섯 가지 Level 중 Level 2 정기시험 점수가 활용되고 있습니다. 그 외 Level은 현재 수시시험 접수만 가능하며, 공인 영어 성적으로 거의 활용되지 않습니다.

구분	출제 방식 및 시간	평가 기준	합격자의 영어 구사 능력	응시 자격
Level 1	청취 30문항(약 30분) 독해 및 어휘 60문항(70분) **총 90문항(약 100분)**	Native Speaker에 준하는 영어 능력: 상담, 토론 가능	외국인과 의사소통, 통역이 가능한 수준	Level 2 영역별 75점 이상 획득 시
Level 2	문법 26문항(20분) 청취 26문항(약 30분) 독해 및 어휘 28문항(40분) **총 80문항(약 90분)**	다양한 상황에서 대화 가능: 업무 상담 및 해외 연수 등 가능	일상생활 및 업무 상담, 세미나 참석, 해외 연수 등이 가능한 수준	제한 없음
Level 3	문법 22문항(20분) 청취 24문항(약 20분) 독해 및 어휘 24문항(40분) **총 70문항(약 80분)**	간단한 의사소통과 친숙한 상태에서의 단순 대화 가능	간단한 의사소통, 해외여행, 단순 업무 출장이 가능한 수준	제한 없음
Level 4	문법 20문항(20분) 청취 20문항(약 15분) 독해 및 어휘 20문항(25분) **총 60문항(약 60분)**	기본적인 문장을 통해 최소한의 의사소통 가능	기본적인 어휘의 짧은 문장을 통한 최소한의 의사소통이 가능한 수준	제한 없음
Level 5	문법 16문항(15분) 청취 16문항(약 15분) 독해 및 어휘 18문항(25분) **총 50문항(약 55분)**	극히 초보적인 수준의 의사소통 가능	영어 초보자로 일상의 인사, 소개 등을 듣고 이해 가능한 수준	제한 없음

■ 지텔프 Level 2의 구성

영역	내용	문항 수	시간	배점
문법	시제, 가정법, 준동사, 조동사, 연결어, 관계사	26문항 (1~26번)		100점
청취	PART 1 개인적인 이야기나 경험담에 관한 대화 PART 2 특정 주제에 대한 정보를 제공하는 공식적인 담화 PART 3 어떤 결정에 이르고자 하는 비공식적인 협상 등의 대화 PART 4 일반적인 어떤 일의 진행이나 과정에 대한 설명	7문항 (27~33번) 6문항 (34~39번) 6문항 (40~45번)* 7문항 (46~52번)*	영역별 시험 시간 제한 규정 폐지됨	100점
독해 및 어휘	PART 1 과거 역사 속의 인물이나 현시대 인물의 일대기 PART 2 최근의 사회적이고 기술적인 묘사에 초점을 맞춘 기사 PART 3 전문적인 것이 아닌 일반적인 내용의 백과사전 PART 4 어떤 것을 설명하거나 설득하는 상업 서신	7문항 (53~59번) 7문항 (60~66번) 7문항 (67~73번) 7문항 (74~80번)		100점
		80문항	약 90분	300점**

* 간혹 청취 PART 3에서 7문항, PART 4에서 6문항이 출제되는 경우도 있습니다.

** 각 영역 100점 만점으로 총 300점이며, 세 개 영역의 평균값이 공인 성적으로 활용되고 있습니다.

지텔프 시험 접수와 시험 당일 Tips

■ 시험 접수 방법

• **인터넷 접수 :** 지텔프 홈페이지(www.g-telp.co.kr)에서 회원가입 후 접수할 수 있습니다.
• **방문 접수 :** 접수 기간 내에 지텔프코리아 본사로 방문하여 접수할 수 있습니다.

■ 시험 당일 준비물

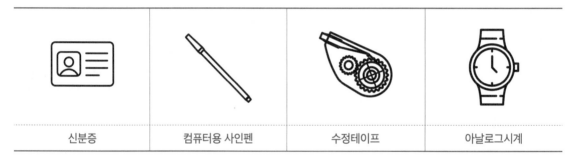

신분증	컴퓨터용 사인펜	수정테이프	아날로그시계

• 시험 당일 신분증이 없으면 시험에 응시할 수 없으므로, 반드시 신분증(주민등록증, 운전면허증, 공무원증 등)을 지참해야 합니다. 지텔프에서 인정하는 신분증 종류는 지텔프 홈페이지(www.g-telp.co.kr)에서 확인 가능합니다.

• 컴퓨터용 사인펜으로 마킹해야 하며 연필은 사용할 수 없습니다. 연필이나 볼펜으로 먼저 마킹한 후 사인펜으로 마킹하면 OMR 판독에 오류가 날 수 있으니 주의합니다.

• 마킹 수정 시, 수정테이프를 사용해야 하며 수정액은 사용할 수 없습니다. 다른 수험자의 수정테이프를 빌려 사용할 수 없으며, 본인의 것만 사용이 가능합니다.

• 대부분의 고사장에 시계가 준비되어 있지만, 자리에서 시계가 잘 보이지 않을 수도 있으니 개인 아날로그시계를 준비하면 좋습니다.

• 수험표는 별도로 준비하지 않아도 됩니다.

■ 시험 당일 Tips

① 고사장 가기 전
- 시험 장소를 미리 확인해 두고, 규정된 입실 시간에 늦지 않도록 유의합니다. 오후 2시 20분까지 입실해야 하며, 오후 2시 50분 이후에는 입실이 불가합니다.

② 고사장에서
- 1층 입구에 붙어 있는 고사실 배치표를 확인하여 자신이 배정된 고사실을 확인합니다.
- 고사실에는 각 응시자의 이름이 적힌 좌석표가 자리마다 놓여 있으므로, 자신이 배정된 자리에 앉으면 됩니다.

③ 시험 보기 직전
- 시험 도중에는 화장실에 다녀올 수 없고, 만약 화장실에 가면 다시 입실할 수 없으므로 미리 다녀오는 것이 좋습니다.
- 시험 시작 전에 OMR 카드의 정보 기입란에 올바른 정보를 기입해 둡니다.

④ 시험 시
- 답안을 따로 마킹할 시간이 없으므로 풀면서 바로 마킹하는 것이 좋습니다.
- 영역별 시험 시간 제한 규정이 폐지되었으므로, 본인이 취약한 영역과 강한 영역에 적절히 시간을 배분하여 자유롭게 풀 수 있습니다. 단, 청취 시간에는 다른 응시자에게 방해가 되지 않도록 주의해야 합니다.
- 시험지에 낙서를 하거나 다른 응시자들이 알아볼 수 있도록 큰 표시를 하는 것은 부정행위로 간주되므로 주의해야 합니다. 수험자 본인만 인지할 수 있는 작은 표시는 허용됩니다.
- OMR 카드의 정답 마킹란은 90번까지 제공되지만, 지텔프 Level 2의 문제는 80번까지만 있으므로 81~90번까지의 마킹란은 공란으로 비워두면 됩니다.

〈OMR 카드와 좌석표 미리보기〉

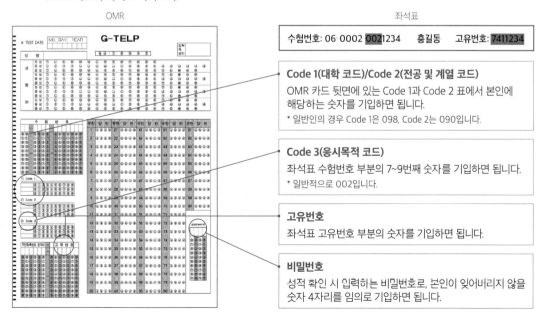

지텔프 시험 미리보기

문법 영역   GRAMMAR SECTION

- 빈칸에 알맞은 문법 사항을 4개의 보기 중에서 고르는 영역입니다.
- 시제, 가정법, 준동사, 조동사, 연결어, 관계사 문제가 출제됩니다.
- 1번부터 26번까지 총 26문제가 출제됩니다.

---

1.   In July, the James Webb telescope transmitted its first images back to Earth. According to the flight path, the telescope _____ the Sun when it takes the next set of photos.

   (a) will be orbiting
   (b) will orbit
   (c) is orbiting
   (d) orbits

해설 | 현재 동사로 미래의 의미를 나타내는 시간의 부사절 'when + 현재 동사'(when ~ takes)가 있고, 문맥상 미래 시점에 망원경이 다음 사진 세트를 찍을 때 그것(망원경)은 태양의 궤도를 돌고 있는 중일 것이라는 의미가 되어야 자연스럽다. 따라서 미래진행 시제 (a) will be orbiting이 정답이다.

---

2.   It was a beautiful Saturday afternoon, but Stanley was inside tidying up his room. Once he finishes _____, he will embark on an adventure with his friends.

   (a) to clean
   (b) to have cleaned
   (c) cleaning
   (d) having cleaned

해설 | 빈칸 앞 동사 finish는 동명사를 목적어로 취하므로, 동명사 (c) cleaning이 정답이다.

청취 영역 LISTENING SECTION

- 두 사람의 대화 혹은 한 사람의 담화를 듣고, 그와 관련된 6~7문제의 알맞은 정답을 4개의 보기 중에서 고르는 영역입니다.
- 4개 파트로 구성되며, PART 1/PART 3는 두 사람의 대화, PART 2/PART 4는 한 사람의 담화입니다.
- 27번부터 52번까지 총 26문제가 출제되며, 문제지에는 질문 없이 보기만 인쇄되어 있습니다.

PART 1. You will hear a conversation between two people. First you will hear questions 27 through 33. Then you will hear the conversation. Choose the best answer to each question in the time provided.

27. (a) the deadline of a signup period
    (b) the availability of an activity center
    (c) the problem with planning committees
    (d) the awards for a sports competition

28. (a) by purchasing the prizes himself
    (b) by sharing his own experience
    (c) by offering to teach badminton
    (d) by recruiting talented players

[음성]

Twenty-seven. What are Jasmine and Dustin discussing?
Twenty-eight. How can Dustin probably assist Jasmine?

M: Hello, Jasmine! How are preparations for the bowling tournament coming along?
F: Hi, Dustin. Everything is almost ready to go! We reserved the bowling alley and opened registration for players to join. I just need to think of what prizes to give the winners.
M: Oh, I can help you come up with some ideas. My badminton league always provides great gifts to its tournament champions.

Twenty-seven. What are Jasmine and Dustin discussing?
Twenty-eight. How can Dustin probably assist Jasmine?

해설 | 27. 남자가 'How are preparations for the bowling tournament coming along?'이라며 볼링 대회 준비가 어떻게 되어가고 있는지 묻자, 여자가 'I just need to think of what prizes to give the winners.'라며 우승자에게 무슨 상을 줄지 생각하기만 하면 된다고 한 뒤, 볼링 대회 우승자를 위한 상에 관해 이야기하는 내용이 이어지고 있다. 따라서 (d)가 정답이다.

28. 남자가 'I can help you come up with some ideas'라며 그가 아이디어 내는 것을 도와줄 수 있다고 한 뒤, 'My badminton league always provides great gifts to its tournament champions.'라며 그의 배드민턴 대회는 대회 우승자에게 항상 좋은 선물을 제공한다고 한 것을 통해, Dustin이 그의 경험을 공유함으로써 Jasmine을 도울 수 있을 것임을 추론할 수 있다. 따라서 (b)가 정답이다.

독해 및 어휘 영역   READING & VOCABULARY SECTION

- 지문을 읽고, 그와 관련된 7문제의 알맞은 정답을 4개의 보기 중에서 고르는 영역입니다. 7문제 중 마지막 2문제는 어휘 문제가 고정적으로 출제됩니다.
- 4개 파트로 구성되며, PART 1은 인물의 일대기, PART 2는 잡지 기사, PART 3는 지식 백과, PART 4는 비즈니스 편지 형태의 지문입니다.
- 53번부터 80번까지 총 28문제가 출제됩니다.

> **PART 1.** Read the following biography article and answer the questions. The underlined words in the article are for vocabulary questions.

CLAIRE DENIS

Claire Denis is a French filmmaker most famous for her artistic style which favors visual components over dialogue. Her most successful film *Beau Travail*, which captures the human condition, is considered a masterpiece of modern cinema.

Claire Denis was born on April 21, 1946, in Paris, France. She spent much of her childhood traveling through Africa. Because her father was employed as a civil servant there during the colonial era, the family moved to a different country every two years. To pass the time, the young Denis read detective novels and watched old war movies. These were her first exposure to the narrative form. Due to concerns about her health after contracting polio, Denis returned to France where she eventually enrolled in a prestigious film school. After graduating, she had the opportunity to <u>act</u> as a production assistant under many influential directors. During this time, she not only developed her understanding of the movie-making process from the bottom up but also began to fall in love with film as an expression of art.

53. What is Clare Denis best known for?

    (a) her preference for illustrative elements
    (b) her stunning film backgrounds
    (c) her successful documentary movies
    (d) her crafting of realistic dialogues

해설 | 1단락의 'Claire Denis is ~ most famous for her artistic style which favors visual components over dialogue.'에서 클레르 드니는 대사보다 시각적 요소를 선호하는 그녀의 예술 스타일로 가장 유명하다고 했다. 따라서 (a)가 정답이다.

54. Why did Denis move back to her home country?

    (a) so that she could work as a civil servant
    (b) so that she could receive better medical treatment
    (c) so that she could shoot the film version of her novel
    (d) so that she could enter the next phase of her schooling

해설 | 2단락의 'Due to concerns about her health after contracting polio, Denis returned to France'에서 소아마비에 걸린 후 건강에 대한 우려 때문에 드니가 프랑스로 돌아왔다고 했다. 따라서 (b)가 정답이다.

55. How most likely did Denis learn the fundamentals of film production?

    (a) She took a cinema class in high school.
    (b) She gained experience on movie sets.
    (c) She interviewed influential scriptwriters.
    (d) She analyzed many prestigious films.

해설 | 2단락의 'she had the opportunity to act as a production assistant under many influential directors'에서 드니가 많은 영향력 있는 감독들 밑에서 조연출로 활동할 기회를 가졌다고 한 뒤, 'During this time, she ~ developed her understanding of the movie-making process from the bottom up'에서 이 시기에 그녀는 영화 제작 과정에 대한 이해를 기초부터 착실히 증진시켰다고 한 것을 통해, 드니가 영화 촬영장에서 경험을 쌓음으로써 영화 제작의 기초를 배웠던 것임을 추론할 수 있다. 따라서 (b)가 정답이다.

58. In the context of the passage, act means _____.

    (a) suffice
    (b) profit
    (c) work
    (d) appear

해설 | 2단락의 'the opportunity to act as a production assistant'는 조연출로 활동할 기회라는 뜻이므로, act가 '활동하다'라는 의미로 사용된 것을 알 수 있다. 따라서 '활동하다'라는 같은 의미의 (c) work가 정답이다.

지텔프 시험 성적 확인 및 활용처

■ 지텔프 성적 확인 방법

성적표는 온라인으로 출력(1회 무료)하거나 우편으로 수령할 수 있으며, 수령 방법은 접수 시 선택할 수 있습니다. (성적 발표일도 시험 접수 시 확인 가능)

〈성적표 미리보기〉

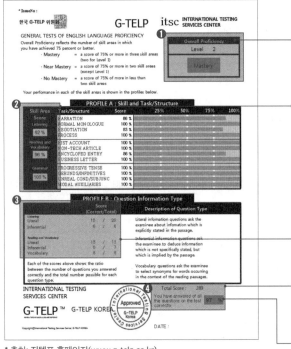

① **Mastery 등급의 합격·불합격 여부를 알려주는 항목**
각 영역 모두 75퍼센트 이상 획득한 경우 Mastery 등급을 받을 수 있습니다.
* 참고: 국가 자격 시험에서 활용되는 지텔프 성적은 Mastery 등급의 합격 여부와는 관계가 없고, 해당 시험에서 정한 기준 점수만 획득하면 인정됩니다.

② **PROFILE A: Skill and Task/Structure (영역별 능숙도)**
영역별로 맞은 문제에 대한 백분율이 표시됩니다.

③ **PROFILE B: Question Information Type**
(영역 내 질문 유형별 능숙도)
청취, 독해 및 어휘 두 영역에 관해서는 문제 유형별로 맞은 개수를 제공합니다. 문제 유형은 Literal(사실에 근거한 것), Inferential(추론 가능한 것), Vocabulary(유의어 파악)로 분류되어 있습니다.

④ **Total Score:**
세 영역의 총점이 표시되며, 총점 아래 백분율로 표시된 것이 세 영역의 평균 점수입니다.

※ 세 영역의 평균 점수(백분율)를 나타내며, 이 부분이 공인성적으로 활용되고 있는 점수입니다.

* 출처: 지텔프 홈페이지(www.g-telp.co.kr)

■ 지텔프 점수 계산법

점수는 아래의 공식으로 산출할 수 있습니다. 총점과 평균 점수의 경우, 소수점 이하 점수는 올림 처리합니다.

각 영역 점수 : 맞은 개수 × 3.75

평균 점수 : 각 영역 점수 합계 ÷ 3

예) 문법 12개, 청취 5개, 독해 및 어휘 10개 맞혔을 시,

　　문법 12 × 3.75 = 45점　　**청취** 5 × 3.75 = 18.75점　　**독해 및 어휘** 10 × 3.75 = 37.5점

　　→ **평균 점수** (45 + 18.75 + 37.5) ÷ 3 = 34점

■ 지텔프 성적 활용처

국가 자격 시험	기준 점수
경찰공무원(경사, 경장, 순경)	43점
경찰간부 후보생	50점
소방공무원(소방장, 소방교, 소방사)	43점
소방간부 후보생	50점
군무원 9급	32점
군무원 7급	47점
군무원 5급	65점
호텔서비스사	39점
박물관 및 미술관 준학예사	50점
국가공무원 5급	65점
외교관후보자	88점
국가공무원 7급	65점
국가공무원 7급 외무영사직렬	77점
입법고시	65점
법원행정고시	65점
카투사	73점
기상직 7급	65점
국가정보원	공인어학성적 제출 필수
변리사	77점
세무사	65점
공인노무사	65점
관광통역안내사	74점
호텔경영사	79점
호텔관리사	66점
감정평가사	65점
공인회계사	65점
보험계리사	65점
손해사정사	65점

* 그 외 공공기관 및 기업체에서도 지텔프 성적을 활용하고 있으며 지텔프 홈페이지에서 모든 활용처를 확인할 수 있습니다.

수준별 맞춤 학습 플랜

TEST 1을 풀어본 후 결과에 맞는 학습 플랜을 선택하여 공부합니다.

1주 완성 학습 플랜 60점 이상

• 1주 동안 매일 실전 TEST 1회분을 OMR 답안지를 활용하여 실전처럼 풀어본 후, 틀렸던 문제와 헷갈렸던 문제를 다시 한 번 풀어보며 완벽하게 이해합니다.

	Day 1	Day 2	Day 3	Day 4	Day 5	Day 6	Day 7
Week 1	TEST 1 문제풀이 및 오답분석	TEST 2 문제풀이 및 오답분석	TEST 3 문제풀이 및 오답분석	TEST 4 문제풀이 및 오답분석	TEST 5 문제풀이 및 오답분석	TEST 6 문제풀이 및 오답분석	TEST 7 문제풀이 및 오답분석

2주 완성 학습 플랜 40점 이상

• 2주 동안 이틀에 한 번 실전 TEST 1회분을 OMR 답안지를 활용하여 실전처럼 풀어본 후, 틀렸던 문제와 헷갈렸던 문제를 다시 한번 풀어보며 완벽하게 이해합니다.
• 둘째 날 취약한 문제 유형을 파악하여 각 유형에서 등장하는 단서 및 paraphrasing된 표현을 정리합니다.

	Day 1	Day 2	Day 3	Day 4	Day 5	Day 6	Day 7
Week 1	TEST 1 문제풀이 및 오답분석	TEST 1 취약 유형 분석 및 정리	TEST 2 문제풀이 및 오답분석	TEST 2 취약 유형 분석 및 정리	TEST 3 문제풀이 및 오답분석	TEST 3 취약 유형 분석 및 정리	TEST 4 문제풀이 및 오답분석
Week 2	TEST 4 취약 유형 분석 및 정리	TEST 5 문제풀이 및 오답분석	TEST 5 취약 유형 분석 및 정리	TEST 6 문제풀이 및 오답분석	TEST 6 취약 유형 분석 및 정리	TEST 7 문제풀이 및 오답분석	TEST 7 취약 유형 분석 및 정리

🔦 3주 완성 학습 플랜 40점 미만

- 3주 동안 3일에 한 번 실전 TEST 1회분을 OMR 답안지를 활용하여 실전처럼 풀어본 후, 틀렸던 문제와 헷갈렸던 문제를 다시 한번 풀어보며 완벽하게 이해합니다.
- 둘째 날 취약한 문제 유형을 파악하여 각 유형에서 등장하는 단서 및 paraphrasing된 표현을 정리합니다.
- 셋째 날 <박 한 상에 남은 지텔프 문법 총정리> 및 총정리강의를 통해 학습한 내용을 정리하고, <지텔프 기출 난어암기장>에 수록된 단어를 암기합니다.

	Day 1	Day 2	Day 3	Day 4	Day 5	Day 6	Day 7
Week 1	TEST 1 문제풀이 및 오답분석	TEST 1 취약 유형 분석 및 정리	TEST 1 총정리 및 어휘 암기	TEST 2 문제풀이 및 오답분석	TEST 2 취약 유형 분석 및 정리	TEST 2 총정리 및 어휘 암기	TEST 3 문제풀이 및 오답분석
Week 2	TEST 3 취약 유형 분석 및 정리	TEST 3 총정리 및 어휘 암기	TEST 4 문제풀이 및 오답분석	TEST 4 취약 유형 분석 및 정리	TEST 4 총정리 및 어휘 암기	TEST 5 문제풀이 및 오답분석	TEST 5 취약 유형 분석 및 정리
Week 3	TEST 5 총정리 및 어휘 암기	TEST 6 문제풀이 및 오답분석	TEST 6 취약 유형 분석 및 정리	TEST 6 총정리 및 어휘 암기	TEST 7 문제풀이 및 오답분석	TEST 7 취약 유형 분석 및 정리	TEST 7 총정리 및 어휘 암기

최신 출제 경향으로 보는

영역별 핵심 전략

GRAMMAR SECTION

LISTENING SECTION

READING & VOCABULARY SECTION

GRAMMAR SECTION

총 26문제 / 권장 시간: 20분

■ 최신 출제 경향

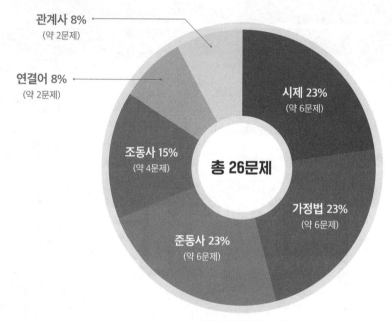

관계사 8%
(약 2문제)

연결어 8%
(약 2문제)

조동사 15%
(약 4문제)

총 26문제

시제 23%
(약 6문제)

가정법 23%
(약 6문제)

준동사 23%
(약 6문제)

▲ 문제 유형별 출제 비율

1순위 (23%)	**시제 문제** (현재진행, 과거진행, 미래진행, 현재완료진행, 과거완료진행, 미래완료진행 시제 각 1문제) **가정법 문제** (가정법 과거 및 가정법 과거완료 각 3문제) **준동사 문제** (동명사 및 to 부정사 각 3문제)
2순위 (15%)	**조동사 문제** (조동사 should 생략 및 일반 조동사 각 2문제)
3순위 (8%)	**연결어 문제** (접속사/전치사/접속부사 중 2문제) **관계사 문제** (관계대명사/관계부사 중 2문제)

■ 유형별 핵심 전략

보기의 구성이나 빈칸 문장을 통해 문제 유형을 확인한 후, 정답의 단서를 찾는다.

시제 유형	**핵심 전략** 빈칸 주변이나 보기에 포함된 시간 표현 관련 단서를 파악한다. **빈출 주제** [현재진행] right now, now 등 [과거진행] while + 과거 동사 등 [미래진행] when + 현재 동사 등 [현재완료진행] since + 과거 동사 or 과거 시점 + (for + 기간 표현) 등 [과거완료진행] before / when + 과거 동사 + (for + 기간 표현) 등 [미래완료진행] by the time + 현재 동사 + (for + 기간 표현) 등	6문제
가정법 유형	**핵심 전략** 빈칸이 if절에 있는 경우 주절의 시제, 빈칸이 주절에 있는 경우 if절의 시제를 파악한다. **빈출 주제** [가정법 과거] If + 주어 + 과거 동사, 주어 + would/could(조동사 과거형) + 동사원형 [가정법 과거완료] If + 주어 + had p.p., 주어 + would/could(조동사 과거형) + have p.p.	6문제
준동사 유형	**핵심 전략** 빈칸 앞 동사 또는 문장 구조를 파악한다. **빈출 주제** [동명사를 목적어로 취하는 동사] enjoy, recommend, avoid, consider, imagine, prevent, keep, dread 등 [to 부정사를 목적어로 취하는 동사] decide, need, intend, promise, expect, wish, plan, hope 등 [to 부정사를 목적격 보어로 취하는 동사] require, ask, encourage, allow 등 [to 부정사의 역할] 명사 역할(~하는 것), 형용사 역할(~하는, ~할), 부사 역할(~하기 위해, ~하게 되다)	6문제
조동사 유형	**핵심 전략** 빈칸 앞 당위성(주장·요구·명령·제안) 표현 또는 문맥을 파악한다. **빈출 주제** [조동사 should 생략] recommend, suggest, advise, essential, important, best, suggestion 등 [가능성/능력] can [허가] can, may [약한 추측] may, might [강한 확신] must [미래/예정] will [의지] will [의무/당위성] should, must [충고/조언] should	4문제
연결어 유형	**핵심 전략** 문장 해석을 통해 앞뒤 문장의 관계를 파악한다. **빈출 주제** [접속사] because, although, while 등 [접속 부사] However, In fact, For example, Otherwise 등	2문제
관계사 유형	**핵심 전략** 빈칸 앞 선행사와 그 선행사의 관계절 내 역할 및 콤마(,) 유무를 파악한다. **빈출 주제** [관계대명사] who, which, that 등 [관계부사] when, where 등	2문제

LISTENING SECTION

총 26문제 / 시험 시간: 약 30분

■ 최신 출제 경향

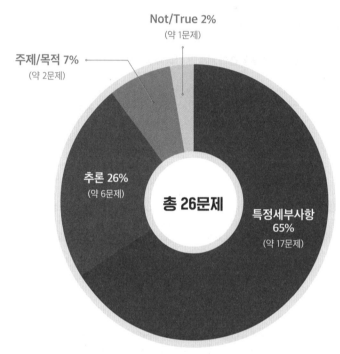

▲ 문제 유형별 출제 비율

1순위 (65%)	**특정세부사항 문제** (의문사를 이용해 특정한 정보를 묻는 문제) ex **What** caused the change in the city's air quality? ex **How** does exercise help improve one's overall health?
2순위 (26%)	**추론 문제** (화자가 다음에 할 일, 화자가 결정한 것, 추론 가능한 특정 사실 등을 묻는 문제) ex What is Mark **most likely** to do following the conversation? ex Why do people **probably** sleep less today than in the past?
3순위 (7%)	**주제/목적 문제** (대화 또는 담화의 주제나 목적을 묻는 문제) ex What is the talk **mainly** about? ex What is the **purpose** of the talk?
4순위 (2%)	**Not/True 문제** (대화 또는 담화에 언급된 것/언급되지 않은 것, 사실인 것/사실이 아닌 것을 묻는 문제) ex What is **not** a recognized benefit of using electric cars? ex Which is **true** about the recycling programs?

■ 파트별 핵심 전략

질문을 듣고 의문사와 키워드를 노트테이킹한 후 대화 또는 담화에서 키워드가 언급된 주변 내용을 주의 깊게 듣는다. 정답 단서가 그대로 언급되거나 올바르게 paraphrasing된 보기를 정답으로 선택한다.

PART 1 2인 대화	인사/안부 → 경험담 소개 → 몇 차례의 질문과 대답 → 마무리 인사 **핵심 전략** 실제로 경험한 사람의 발언에 주목한다. **빈출 주제** 파티 또는 행사에 다녀온 경험, 여행을 다녀온 경험, 동아리 활동 경험, 아르바이트 경험, 교환학생을 다녀온 경험, 취미 활동 소개 등	7문제
PART 2 1인 담화	인사/자기소개(소속·직책 등) → 대상 소개 → 세부사항 설명 → 마무리 인사 **핵심 전략** 소개/홍보 대상의 장점에 주목한다. **빈출 주제** 신기술을 접목한 신제품 홍보, 구독 서비스 홍보, 박람회·축제·이벤트 홍보, 기업 홍보 및 후원 요청 등	6문제
PART 3 2인 대화	인사/안부 → 두 가지 선택지 소개 → 장단점 비교 → 결정 및 추후 계획 암시 **핵심 전략** 최종 결정을 언급하는 마지막 발언에 주목한다. **빈출 주제** 아날로그 방식과 디지털 방식의 장단점 비교, 두 가지 전공의 장단점 비교, 두 가지 제품의 장단점 비교, 두 가지 주거 형태의 장단점 비교 등	6문제*
PART 4 1인 담화	인사/주의 환기 → 주제 소개 → 단계/항목별로 순차적 설명 **핵심 전략** 순서를 나타내는 말에 주목한다. **빈출 주제** 효율적인 업무 방법에 대한 조언, 환경을 보호하는 방법에 대한 조언, 건강을 관리하는 방법에 대한 조언, 동호회를 결성하는 절차 등	7문제*

* 간혹 청취 PART 3에서 7문제, PART 4에서 6문제가 출제되는 경우도 있다.

READING & VOCABULARY SECTION

총 28문제 / 권장 시간: 40분

■ 최신 출제 경향

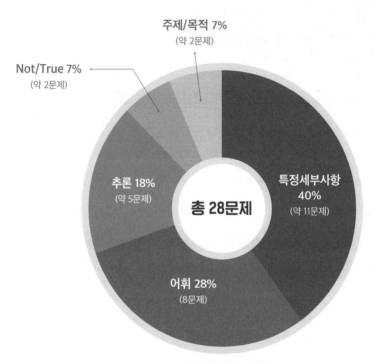

▲ 문제 유형별 출제 비율

1순위 (40%)	**특정세부사항 문제** (의문사를 이용해 특정한 정보를 묻는 문제) ex **How** did Bell come up with the idea for the telephone? ex **What** did Dr. Evans say caused the tsunami?
2순위 (28%)	**어휘 문제** (지문의 밑줄 친 어휘의 문맥상 유의어를 고르는 문제) ex In the context of the passage, <u>cherish</u> means _____.
3순위 (18%)	**추론 문제** (지문에 명시적으로 언급되지는 않았으나 추론 가능한 것을 묻는 문제) ex What will Greta and Joe **probably** do about the problem? ex Why **most likely** did the wildfire spread more quickly than previous burns?
4순위 (7%)	**주제/목적 문제** (지문의 주제나 목적을 묻는 문제) ex What is the article **mainly** about? ex **Why** did Lucas Berkley **write** a letter to Emily Nelson? **Not/True 문제** (지문에 언급된 것/언급되지 않은 것, 사실인 것/사실이 아닌 것을 묻는 문제) ex Which is **NOT** a part of the daily life of early settlers? ex According to the article, what is **true** about the Atkins diet?

■ 파트별 핵심 전략

질문을 읽고 의문사와 키워드를 파악한 후 지문에서 키워드가 언급된 주변 내용을 주의 깊게 읽는다. 정답 단서가 그대로 언급되거나 올바르게 paraphrasing된 보기를 정답으로 선택한다.

PART 1 인물의 일대기	인물 소개 → 어린 시절 및 진로 선택 계기 → 청년 시절 및 초기 활동 → 주요 업적 및 활동 → 근황 및 평가 **핵심 전략** 시기별로 인물에게 일어난 중요한 사건 및 업적에 주목한다. **빈출 주제** 예술가(가수·작곡가·화가 등)의 일대기 및 대표 작품들, 직업인(요리사·기업가 등)의 일대기 및 주요 업적 등	7문제
PART 2 잡지 기사	연구의 주제 → 연구의 계기 및 목적 → 연구의 결과 및 특징 → 연구의 의의 및 시사점 → 연구의 한계 및 추후 과제 **핵심 전략** 기사의 제목 및 기사에서 다루는 연구의 사회적 의의에 주목한다. **빈출 주제** 불치병의 치료법이나 신약 등의 발견 및 사회적 기대 효과, 첨단 기술의 발전 및 활용 방안, 새로운 동식물종의 발견 및 환경적 의의 등	7문제
PART 3 지식 백과	정의 → 기원/어원 → 여러 가지 특징 나열 → 현황 **핵심 전략** 소재의 정의 및 특징에 주목한다. **빈출 주제** 동물 혹은 식물의 종·생김새·서식 지역 소개, 최근 유행하고 있는 게임·SNS·취미 활동의 인기 요인 소개, 역사적으로 중요한 사건이나 장소의 의의 소개 등	7문제
PART 4 비즈니스 편지	편지의 목적 → 세부사항 → 요청 사항 → 끝인사 및 연락처 전달 **핵심 전략** 발신자가 편지를 쓴 목적에 주목한다. **빈출 주제** 불친절한 응대에 항의하거나 친절한 서비스에 감사함을 전하는 편지, 새로운 정책이나 변경된 규정을 공지 혹은 안내하는 편지, 입사를 지원하는 편지 등	7문제

TEST 1

GRAMMAR

LISTENING

READING & VOCABULARY

테스트 전 확인사항

1. OMR 답안지를 준비하셨나요? ☐
2. 컴퓨터용 사인펜, 수정 테이프를 준비하셨나요? ☐
3. 음성을 들을 준비를 하셨나요? ☐

TEST 1 음성 바로 듣기

🎧 **TEST 1.mp3**

해커스인강(HackersIngang.com)에서 무료 다운로드
상단 메뉴 [G-TELP → MP3/자료 → 문제풀이 MP3]

자동 채점 및 성적 분석
서비스 바로 이용하기

📋 **자동 채점 및 성적 분석 서비스**

∨ 타이머, 모바일 OMR, 자동 채점
∨ 정답률 및 취약 유형 분석

시험 시간 : 90분

목표 점수 : _____점
시작 시간 : _____시 _____분 ~ 종료 시간 : _____시 _____분

General Tests of English Language Proficiency
G-TELP

Level 2

GRAMMAR SECTION

TEST 1

TEST 2

TEST 3

TEST 4

TEST 5

TEST 6

TEST 7

지텔프 공식 기출문제집 7회분 Level 2

DIRECTIONS:

The following items need a word or words to complete the sentence. From the four choices for each item, choose the best answer. Then blacken in the correct circle on your answer sheet.

Example:

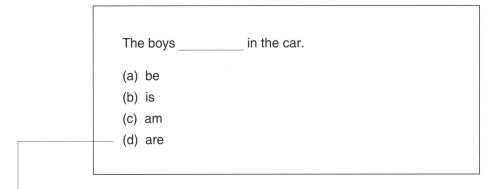

The boys _____ in the car.

(a) be

(b) is

(c) am

(d) are

The correct answer is (d), so the circle with the letter (d) has been blackened.

NOW TURN THE PAGE AND BEGIN

1. Though typically thought of as a hot, sandy area, a desert is merely defined by how little precipitation it receives. For example, Antarctica is considered a desert _____ it receives only eight inches of rain annually.

   (a) even though
   (b) in case
   (c) because
   (d) after

2. The music club president was supposed to lead the new member orientation today, but the vice president will give the introductory speech instead. Apparently, the president _____ a college interview at the time of the orientation.

   (a) was attending
   (b) will be attending
   (c) has been attending
   (d) attends

3. MVC Sports Shop suffered from low sales in the first quarter of the year. An employee suggested that they _____ their social media presence to improve their numbers and attract more young customers.

   (a) increase
   (b) will increase
   (c) are increasing
   (d) increased

4. For three years, Alpha Highlands was the top-grossing apartment rental company in San Francisco. However, its record was recently surpassed. Had a new competitor not appeared, Alpha Highlands _____ in the top spot.

   (a) will probably have stayed
   (b) would probably stay
   (c) will probably stay
   (d) would probably have stayed

5. The invention of perfume is usually associated with ancient Egyptians. Although their exact recipes were kept secret, it is known that the Egyptians used spices, herbs, and flowers _____ their fragrances.

   (a) having made
   (b) making
   (c) to make
   (d) to be making

6. Justin is hesitant about accepting a job offer that requires him to move to New York City. He worries that if he were to move there, he _____ financially due to the high cost of living.

   (a) will suffer
   (b) would have suffered
   (c) would suffer
   (d) will have suffered

7. Gloria just watched a singing competition on television. At first, she _____ the defending champion, but when she saw the opponent's performance, she immediately knew that the challenger deserved to win.

(a) would root for
(b) is rooting for
(c) has been rooting for
(d) was rooting for

8. Despite looking fluffy and light, clouds can weigh up to a million pounds because of the condensed water they carry. If a whole cloud were to fall from the sky, it _____ whatever was underneath it.

(a) would have crushed
(b) will have crushed
(c) will crush
(d) would crush

9. Engineering graduates who took the latest board exams are currently waiting for the results. They are excited and nervous at the same time, as the results are expected _____ any minute now.

(a) to be released
(b) having been released
(c) to have been released
(d) being released

10. Bauhaus was a highly influential art movement that started at the Staatliches Bauhaus design school in Germany. The movement is known for combining "rational" art, _____, with functionality.

(a) what uses geometric patterns
(b) which uses geometric patterns
(c) who uses geometric patterns
(d) that uses geometric patterns

11. Hannah noticed that the red bump on her arm has been there for three days now. Her husband recommended _____ ointment on it, but she decided to contact her doctor first.

(a) to have put
(b) having put
(c) putting
(d) to put

12. The small, family-owned market at Gomez Plaza has reopened to the public after a year of community-funded renovations. The business _____ for three decades before it caught fire last year due to faulty wiring.

(a) is operating
(b) has been operating
(c) will have operated
(d) had been operating

13. Jenny started living in Milan after accepting a scholarship to study fashion design. By the time she finishes her program, she _____ in the city for four years.

(a) will have been living
(b) has been living
(c) will be living
(d) is living

14. If dogs are taken on daily walks, their claws tend to naturally wear down due to friction from the concrete. So, walking on sidewalks is a useful strategy for owners who dislike _____ their dogs' nails.

(a) having trimmed
(b) trimming
(c) to trim
(d) to have trimmed

15. Bananas contain potassium, which is known to be a radioactive element. However, the amount of radiation is so negligible that if one were to eat several bananas at once, nothing _____ except a stomachache.

(a) would have happened
(b) will have happened
(c) will happen
(d) would happen

16. When one does not take antibiotics for the prescribed number of days, bacteria may become resistant to the medicine. The antibiotics _____ to kill the bacteria then lose their effectiveness as the resistant bacteria multiply.

(a) who were intended
(b) when were intended
(c) that were intended
(d) what were intended

17. A company-wide meeting was called to discuss current corporate social responsibility practices. The CEO wants a firm CSR policy that _____ clarify the company's stance on environmental conservation.

(a) may
(b) must
(c) will
(d) could

18. Everyone prefers the teaching assistant over Professor Smith, who is strict and grumpy at times. Students are always more inclined _____ to a lecture if the TA is the one delivering it.

(a) to listen
(b) having listened
(c) listening
(d) to have listened

19. Kevin decided to cut back on his coffee consumption this week. He skipped his morning cup of coffee today and, at the moment, he _____ extreme fatigue, a common symptom of caffeine withdrawal.

(a) experiences
(b) has experienced
(c) is experiencing
(d) will be experiencing

20. Barry is known as the artist of the family. He can draw, paint, sculpt, and take beautiful photos. He even performs in community plays. However, he considers _____ photographs his strongest talent.

(a) to take
(b) having taken
(c) taking
(d) to have taken

21. During World War II, Switzerland avoided conflict by remaining neutral and actively defending its territories from foreign invasion. If Switzerland had chosen a side, it _____ the devastation that much of the European continent experienced.

(a) will not have escaped
(b) might not have escaped
(c) may not escape
(d) might not escape

22. Ten years after discontinuing their special orange chicken sandwich, Ella's Diner is putting it back on the menu. Some of the longtime patrons have been requesting that the diner _____ back the classic dish.

(a) is bringing
(b) brought
(c) will bring
(d) bring

23. Debbie wants to adopt a cat, but she also wants to make sure she will be a good owner. For the past month, she _____ her weekends reading about tips and strategies for cat care.

(a) will have been spending
(b) had been spending
(c) is spending
(d) has been spending

24. In bowling, a set of three consecutive strikes is called a "turkey." In the late 1700s, food baskets containing turkeys were actually given to tournament winners. _____, "bowling a turkey" became a common saying in bowling.

(a) Eventually
(b) In addition
(c) Similarly
(d) By contrast

TEST 1

TEST 2

TEST 3

TEST 4

TEST 5

TEST 6

TEST 7

지텔프 공식 기출문제집 7회분 Level 2

25. Josh just finished his laundry.
    Unfortunately, the dye in his new red shirt
    bled into his other clothes and turned
    them slightly pink. Had he known that
    the color would bleed, he _____ the
    shirt separately.

    (a) will have washed
    (b) would have washed
    (c) would wash
    (d) will wash

26. In order to reproduce, plants need
    pollinators like bees and butterflies. Bats
    are also some of the best pollinators.
    Since they are bigger than the average
    insect, they _____ carry much more
    pollen.

    (a) can
    (b) must
    (c) should
    (d) shall

THIS IS THE END OF THE GRAMMAR SECTION
DO NOT GO ON UNTIL TOLD TO DO SO

LISTENING SECTION

DIRECTIONS:

The Listening Section has four parts. In each part you will hear a spoken passage and a number of questions about the passage. First you will hear the questions. Then you will hear the passage. From the four choices for each question, choose the best answer. Then blacken in the correct circle on your answer sheet.

Now you will hear an example question. Then you will hear an example passage.

Now listen to the example question.

(a) one
(b) two
(c) three
(d) four

Bill Johnson has four brothers, so the best answer is (d). The circle with the letter (d) has been blackened.

NOW TURN THE PAGE AND BEGIN

27. (a) searching for a lost pet
    (b) looking for a new pet
    (c) going to the dog shelter
    (d) walking a friend's dog

28. (a) put on her collar
    (b) attach her leash
    (c) tighten her collar
    (d) bring her leash

29. (a) She notices a moving figure.
    (b) She checks inside a house.
    (c) She looks in the nearby woods.
    (d) She hears barking noises.

30. (a) by shaking her favorite toy
    (b) by calling out her name
    (c) by using his special whistle
    (d) by offering her a snack

31. (a) He accidentally knocked Sara over.
    (b) He has made this mistake before.
    (c) He fell down while running.
    (d) He always asks Sara for help.

32. (a) locating one in his town
    (b) being around the other dogs
    (c) affording the price of classes
    (d) finding one with open spots

33. (a) visit the pet store
    (b) contact the training school
    (c) get some lunch
    (d) head to the dog park

TEST 1

TEST 2

TEST 3

TEST 4

TEST 5

TEST 6

TEST 7

지텔프 공식 기출문제집 7회분 Level 2

PART 2. *You will hear a presentation by one person to a group of people. First you will hear questions 34 through 39. Then you will hear the talk. Choose the best answer to each question in the time provided.*

34. (a) a modern art website
    (b) a popular art school
    (c) a famous art museum
    (d) a new art gallery

35. (a) He led a local art movement.
    (b) He hosts an annual art festival.
    (c) He painted a famous mural.
    (d) He is a public art educator.

36. (a) to incorporate live music
    (b) to showcase the trendiest art
    (c) to focus on visual input
    (d) to enhance visitors' experiences

37. (a) by buying photos of wildlife
    (b) by donating to a climate fund
    (c) by purchasing animal paintings
    (d) by joining an environmental group

38. (a) by attending daily performances
    (b) by watching cartoons about art
    (c) by meeting famous artists
    (d) by making their own art

39. (a) make a website purchase
    (b) buy an item at the café
    (c) win the online raffle
    (d) shop at the gift store

40. (a) He has been living off campus.
    (b) He has been sick for a long time.
    (c) He has been taking exams.
    (d) He has been busy studying.

41. (a) He can meet new people.
    (b) He can improve his work ethic.
    (c) He can gain valuable skills.
    (d) He can enhance his resume.

42. (a) because he finds classes boring
    (b) because he is in high-level courses
    (c) because he has difficult teachers
    (d) because he has changed majors

43. (a) work at the tutoring center
    (b) get some help with studying
    (c) do research at the library
    (d) go for walks around campus

44. (a) by getting some fresh air
    (b) by relaxing with music
    (c) by doing some exercise
    (d) by taking a snack break

45. (a) work at the supermarket
    (b) focus only on his studies
    (c) accept the office job
    (d) start learning to cook

TEST 1

TEST 2

TEST 3

TEST 4

TEST 5

TEST 6

TEST 7

PART 4. *You will hear an explanation of a process. First you will hear questions 46 through 52. Then you will hear the explanation. Choose the best answer to each question in the time provided.*

46. (a) preparing for a work retreat
    (b) throwing a holiday party
    (c) organizing a farewell event
    (d) planning a party for new staff

47. (a) by handing out an office poll
    (b) by inviting people to vote online
    (c) by asking around the office
    (d) by checking the office calendar

48. (a) They are too risky.
    (b) They are too hard to plan.
    (c) They can be frightening.
    (d) They can upset people.

49. (a) by staying overnight at a hotel
    (b) by inviting everyone from work
    (c) by choosing a clever theme
    (d) by renting a nearby venue

50. (a) He had a small budget.
    (b) It was poorly attended.
    (c) He received few donations.
    (d) It had to be canceled.

51. (a) sample a range of dishes
    (b) discuss it with colleagues
    (c) research common allergies
    (d) find a good caterer

52. (a) because she had asked for it
    (b) because she was a regular customer
    (c) because she found it thoughtful
    (d) because she was able to save money

THIS IS THE END OF THE LISTENING SECTION
DO NOT GO ON UNTIL TOLD TO DO SO

READING AND VOCABULARY SECTION

DIRECTIONS:

You will now read four different passages. Each passage is followed by comprehension and vocabulary questions. From the four choices for each item, choose the best answer. Then blacken in the correct circle on your answer sheet.

Read the following example passage and example question.

Example:

> Bill Johnson lives in New York. He is 25 years old. He has four brothers and two sisters.
>
> How many brothers does Bill Johnson have?
>
> (a) one
> (b) two
> (c) three
> (d) four

The correct answer is (d), so the circle with the letter (d) has been blackened.

NOW TURN THE PAGE AND BEGIN

PART 1. *Read the following biography article and answer the questions. The underlined words in the article are for vocabulary questions.*

BRUCE LEE

Bruce Lee was an actor, filmmaker, and martial arts expert. He is best known for exhibiting his unique fighting style in popular films that drew international attention to the budding Hong Kong action cinema scene. Lee reshaped the portrayal of Asian culture in the West by breaking down racial barriers in the film industry.

Jun-fan "Bruce" Lee was born on November 27, 1940, in San Francisco, California, while his parents were touring the US with the Chinese Opera. He was raised in Hong Kong, where his father was a famous singer. Lee was involved in show business from an early age, appearing in numerous films as a child actor.

As a teenager in Hong Kong, Lee was bullied due to his Chinese heritage. After street fighting landed him in trouble, his parents decided that he needed proper martial arts training. He began studying Wing Chun kung fu, a style of self-defense that focuses on using natural and scientific laws to generate strength.

Lee returned to the US at the age of eighteen. While in school, he taught his style of kung fu to friends and other students. He <u>founded</u> his own martial arts school in Seattle and, soon after, a second one in Los Angeles. Lee's reputation exploded as he participated in tournaments and widely discussed private matches. Around this time, he also became concerned about the restrictiveness of traditional fighting techniques. He developed Jeet Kune Do, a hybrid martial art philosophy that prioritizes freedom and self-expression over organized style.

Lee was noticed by a television producer at a karate tournament in 1964 and soon landed a prominent role in the show *The Green Hornet*. Still, he struggled to find other acting opportunities and soon came to terms with the fact that there were no lead roles available for Asian actors in Hollywood. He returned to Hong Kong and quickly became an action movie star, <u>showcasing</u> his theatrical fighting style and setting box office records.

Lee was on the brink of reaching international stardom with the release of his film *Enter the Dragon* when he died suddenly in Hong Kong in 1973. The film was a success and cemented his status as a cultural icon. Lee's legacy opened new pathways for Asian representation in Hollywood films. His life and philosophy continue to inspire people worldwide.

53. What is Bruce Lee best known for?

(a) founding martial arts studios around the world
(b) promoting the importance of self-defense through film
(c) becoming the first Asian actor to star in a Hollywood movie
(d) sparking viewers' interest in a specific type of movie

54. How did Lee start performing for audiences?

(a) He starred in movies as a young child.
(b) He appeared in films alongside his father.
(c) He toured opera halls with his parents.
(d) He sang onstage with a famous band.

55. How did Lee's parents respond to his street fighting?

(a) by encouraging him to focus on his schoolwork
(b) by teaching him about various fighting styles
(c) by discouraging him from engaging in fights
(d) by urging him to practice in a formal setting

56. Why did Lee establish his own martial arts philosophy?

(a) He was in conflict with other practitioners.
(b) He thought the discipline should have more flexibility.
(c) He noticed that traditional methods were losing popularity.
(d) He had already mastered the other styles.

57. Why, most likely, did Lee have trouble finding roles in Hollywood?

(a) because he lacked acting experience
(b) because his fighting style was difficult to film
(c) because action movies were unpopular at the time
(d) because he looked different from other movie stars

58. In the context of the passage, founded means _____.

(a) discovered
(b) attended
(c) created
(d) defended

59. In the context of the passage, showcasing means _____.

(a) winning
(b) displaying
(c) proving
(d) expressing

TEST 1

TEST 2

TEST 3

TEST 4

TEST 5

TEST 6

TEST 7

지텔프 공식 기출문제집 7회분 Level 2

ROBOTIC FALCON SUGGESTS EVIDENCE AGAINST SELFISH HERD HYPOTHESIS

The "selfish herd" hypothesis was first proposed by W.D. Hamilton in 1971 to explain why animals move in groups. For decades, scientists have believed that when a flock of pigeons in flight is under attack, individual birds will attempt to move to the middle of the group to shield themselves, leaving other birds <u>vulnerable</u> to attack. However, an innovative experiment using a robotic predator has provided evidence against this hypothesis.

The study on pigeons was led by behavioral ecologist Daniel Sankey at Royal Holloway University. Employing innovations in robotics to conduct their experiment, Sankey and his team used a robotic falcon, or RoboFalcon, to attack various flocks of pigeons. The scientists used tracking technology to observe each pigeon's movements as the RoboFalcon approached. Because the RoboFalcon could be programmed to follow precise orders, the experiment was repeated a number of times to ensure consistent results.

Although the "selfish herd" hypothesis suggests that each pigeon would try to fly to the center of the flock in order to avoid being attacked, Sankey found that the birds instead worked together to make a group escape. By relying on each other, the birds were relieved of the responsibility of tracking and avoiding the predator individually. The experiment was repeated with pigeon flocks of different sizes, with each trial providing similar results.

The pigeons further demonstrated their selflessness by moving in a flock, or a loosely organized group, rather than the more aerodynamic V-formation, which reduces the drag from the wind that birds face while flying. Despite needing to put eighteen percent more energy into flying as a result of the less efficient flight path, the pigeons demonstrated a willingness to take on added individual effort for the sake of the group's safety.

Sankey believes that the study highlights the importance of cooperation and escape mechanisms among prey and is planning to study the patterns of various animal species using similar technology. And, although the technology is still being <u>refined</u>, it has many potential uses. For instance, it could be used to herd birds away from potential danger and prevent problems that can arise when birds collide with passenger planes.

60. What is the article mainly about?

(a) a tendency among birds to protect one another
(b) tho ovolution of a εpocioε of flying predator
(c) an invention for scaring off unwanted birds
(d) the results of a study about bird migration

61. How did the researchers gather data from the trials?

(a) by calculating the distance flown by the flocks
(b) by observing changes in the robotic bird's behavior
(c) by noting the actions of individual flock members
(d) by counting the number of birds that disappeared

62. What were the pigeons probably doing during the attack?

(a) flying to different sections of the flock
(b) looking for protection in a different flock
(c) coordinating with the others to attack the predator
(d) keeping track of the attacker's location together

63. Why, most likely, did the birds need to put additional effort into flying?

(a) They had more obstacles in their flight path.
(b) They were lending support to struggling group members.
(c) They were facing extra wind resistance.
(d) They had to focus on staying in a tight formation.

64. According to the article, which is NOT a possible application of the technology used in the experiment?

(a) understanding the behavior of animal populations
(b) protecting animals from unsafe encounters
(c) ensuring smoother flights for commercial planes
(d) studying the effects of weather on flight patterns

65. In the context of the passage, vulnerable means _____.

(a) open
(b) scared
(c) ready
(d) pushed

66. In the context of the passage, refined means _____.

(a) filtered
(b) improved
(c) fixed
(d) decided

지텔프 공식 기출문제집 7회분 Level 2

THE DIABOLICAL IRONCLAD BEETLE

The diabolical ironclad beetle, or *Nosoderma diabolicum*, is a part of the wider ironclad beetle family. It can grow up to twenty-five millimeters in size. Native to California, this beetle can be found in woodland habitats and often gathers near trunks of large trees to feed on fungi and rotting bark.

At first glance, an observer might mistake the diabolical ironclad beetle for a rock. It is black or dark gray in color and has a rough outer texture, enabling the creature to blend into its natural environment. The diabolical ironclad beetle is also quite flat and prefers to stay close to the ground. Unlike many other beetle species, it is incapable of flying and instead moves by crawling from place to place.

As its name suggests, the diabolical ironclad beetle relies on an "ironclad" shell to protect itself from predators. The sturdy insect's body can withstand nearly 40,000 times its own body weight, twice as much as other beetles of the same family. This means that it can survive being run over by a car.

Based on microscopic studies, scientists attribute the nearly indestructible nature of this beetle's body to its exoskeleton, a hard outer shell made up of pieces that wrap around its organs in an interlocking structure. Small connective sutures—lines that link together different sections of the exoskeleton—fill in the gaps in the beetle's tough armor.

Patience is another key element to the diabolical ironclad beetle's survival. Researchers have observed that when it senses a predator nearby, such as an animal or a larger insect, the beetle will play dead by tucking its legs underneath its body and lying flat on the ground, remaining in this position until the threat is no longer detected.

These factors contribute to the diabolical ironclad beetle's abnormally long lifespan. Whereas many beetle species live for an average of a few weeks, the diabolical ironclad beetle can live for up to seven or eight years. In more ways than one, this beetle is among the most resilient insects of its kind.

67. What is the subject of the article?

    (a) a beetle that is native to the eastern US
    (b) an insect that feeds on decaying materials
    (c) an insect that lives primarily in the jungle
    (d) a beetle that is found in the California desert

68. How does the beetle blend into its environment?

    (a) by changing colors to match its surroundings
    (b) by looking like an object found in nature
    (c) by moving at an undetectable speed
    (d) by crawling underneath nearby rocks

69. According to the article, what differentiates the diabolical ironclad beetle from others in its family?

    (a) its ability to endure intense impact
    (b) its surprisingly heavy body weight
    (c) its potential to survive in high heat
    (d) its metallic-looking outer shell

70. Which is NOT true about the beetle's body?

    (a) It has strong bonds that hold together its exoskeleton.
    (b) It has a tough external layer that protects its organs.
    (c) It has multiple parts that make up its shell.
    (d) It has strong armor that quickly grows back.

71. Why, most likely, does the beetle tuck its legs underneath its body when it senses a predator?

    (a) so that it cannot be lifted up
    (b) so that it cannot be flipped over
    (c) so that its limbs will be protected
    (d) so that its presence goes unnoticed

72. In the context of the passage, attribute means _____.

    (a) credit
    (b) leave
    (c) expect
    (d) compare

73. In the context of the passage, abnormally means _____.

    (a) unusually
    (b) rarely
    (c) painfully
    (d) equally

TEST 1

TEST 2

TEST 3

TEST 4

TEST 5

TEST 6

TEST 7

지텔프 공식 기출문제집 7회분 Level 2

Jonathan Nottingham
Principal
Forest Road Elementary School

Dear Mr. Nottingham:

I want to express many thanks for your ongoing support of our zoo over the past several years. As you know, Safari Funland Zoo is <u>committed</u> to providing educational opportunities for community members of all ages. To this end, I am pleased to inform you about a new series that will be hosted in our facilities.

When you last visited us, your science teacher, Mr. Singh, expressed an interest in having your students spend more time studying our animals and their habitats. Inspired by this idea, I worked with my administrative team to develop a summer series called Wild Wonders, specifically for elementary school students.

Students in the program will participate in a series of hands-on workshops led by our incredible educators, providing students with unique opportunities to interact with our animals up close, including petting bottlenose dolphins from the Gulf of Mexico. Our program will also incorporate virtual reality technology, giving participants the chance to travel millions of years back in time to when dinosaurs roamed the earth.

Forest Road Elementary is known for <u>championing</u> the importance of studying the natural world. As an educator myself, I can assure you that learning about our zoo's conservation efforts for the many animal species that inhabit our facilities will help to ready the students for the natural science courses that they will take later in their schooling.

Should you have any inquiries, you can contact our events coordinator, Harry Buehler, at 555-0111. Meanwhile, if you have ideas for how to further develop the program, please reach out to my office—I would be happy to meet with you to discuss them.

Liza Lombardi
Liza Lombardi
Director
Safari Funland Zoo

74. What is the purpose of Liza Lombardi's letter to Principal Nottingham?

(a) to announce the creation of a new volunteer program
(b) to advertise an educational program developed by the zoo
(c) to inform him about the opening of a family-friendly exhibit
(d) to thank him for bringing his students to the zoo

75. According to the letter, how did Liza get the idea for Wild Wonders?

(a) by asking students about their interests
(b) by seeking advice from a natural scientist
(c) by speaking with a visiting educator
(d) by chatting with the school principal

76. What will students who join the program be able to do?

(a) explore exhibits under the guidance of experts
(b) study dolphin fossils using advanced technology
(c) travel to see animals in tropical locations
(d) conduct hands-on laboratory experiments

77. According to Liza, what can students gain from attending the event?

(a) They will learn how to care for various animal species.
(b) They will be better prepared for their future studies.
(c) They will get extra credit toward their science courses.
(d) They will learn about zoo management.

78. Why, most likely, would Principal Nottingham contact the events coordinator?

(a) to gather more information about the event
(b) to schedule a meeting with the program instructors
(c) to provide feedback on the proposal
(d) to report the number of students attending

79. In the context of the passage, committed means _____.

(a) opposed
(b) dedicated
(c) suited
(d) limited

80. In the context of the passage, championing means _____.

(a) winning
(b) promoting
(c) fighting
(d) awarding

THIS IS THE END OF THE TEST

TEST 2

GRAMMAR

LISTENING

READING & VOCABULARY

테스트 전 확인사항

1. OMR 답안지를 준비하셨나요? ☐
2. 컴퓨터용 사인펜, 수정 테이프를 준비하셨나요? ☐
3. 음성을 들을 준비를 하셨나요? ☐

🎧 **TEST 2.mp3**

해커스인강(HackersIngang.com)에서 무료 다운로드
상단 메뉴 [G-TELP → MP3/자료 → 문제풀이 MP3]

TEST 2 음성 바로 듣기

▤ **자동 채점 및 성적 분석 서비스**

ⅴ 타이머, 모바일 OMR, 자동 채점
ⅴ 정답률 및 취약 유형 분석

자동 채점 및 성적 분석
서비스 바로 이용하기

시험 시간 : 90분

목표 점수 : _____점
시작 시간 : _____시 _____분 ~ 종료 시간 : _____시 _____분

General Tests of English Language Proficiency
G-TELP

Level 2

GRAMMAR SECTION

TEST 1
TEST 2
TEST 3
TEST 4
TEST 5
TEST 6
TEST 7

지텔프 공식 기출문제집 7회분 Level 2

DIRECTIONS:

The following items need a word or words to complete the sentence. From the four choices for each item, choose the best answer. Then blacken in the correct circle on your answer sheet.

Example:

The boys _____ in the car.

(a) be
(b) is
(c) am
(d) are

The correct answer is (d), so the circle with the letter (d) has been blackened.

NOW TURN THE PAGE AND BEGIN

1. Molly will drive six hours to Upstate New York to attend her brother's wedding tomorrow. It is best that she _____ the house early so she can get there on time.

   (a) left
   (b) will leave
   (c) has left
   (d) leave

2. According to the dictionary definition of a "selfie," this type of photo cannot be taken by another person. The picture _____ include oneself and also be taken by oneself to qualify as a selfie.

   (a) must
   (b) might
   (c) will
   (d) can

3. Mr. Harris will be attending a business conference in Madrid this week. His plane leaves tonight, so he took the day off and _____ for the trip right now.

   (a) has been packing
   (b) packs
   (c) was packing
   (d) is packing

4. Citrus fruits are great for managing various health issues because of their fiber content. For example, oranges, _____, can help stabilize blood sugar levels and lower cholesterol.

   (a) which are high in fiber
   (b) what are high in fiber
   (c) who are high in fiber
   (d) that are high in fiber

5. Basketball players should be able to dribble well, as that skill enables them to make a variety of plays on the court. For this reason, it is important that players practice _____ frequently during training.

   (a) to dribble
   (b) having dribbled
   (c) dribbling
   (d) to have dribbled

6. Logan went grocery shopping yesterday, but he forgot to buy a few things because his shopping list was in his other bag. If he had not switched bags before leaving, he _____ everything on his list.

   (a) will get
   (b) would have gotten
   (c) would get
   (d) will have gotten

7. Pam's laundromat opened for business for the first time this afternoon, but very few people came. The neighboring store owner advised that Pam _____ flyers around town to get the word out to potential customers.

(a) posted
(b) will post
(c) posts
(d) post

8. The Molinere Bay Underwater Sculpture Park is the first of its kind. The park guides, _____, teach visitors to use scuba equipment so they can explore the park safely.

(a) who are all trained divers
(b) when are all trained divers
(c) where are all trained divers
(d) that are all trained divers

9. I just reminded my brother to take his keys with him when he leaves for his friend's party tonight. I _____ by the time he gets home, so I won't be able to let him in.

(a) had most likely been sleeping
(b) am most likely sleeping
(c) have most likely been sleeping
(d) will most likely be sleeping

10. The true number of coffee drinkers in the world is difficult to estimate. However, it's safe to say that if extreme coffee shortages were to occur, millions of people _____ elsewhere for their daily caffeine intake.

(a) would have had to turn
(b) will have had to turn
(c) would have to turn
(d) will have to turn

11. Kathleen was lucky to escape unscathed from the fire at the library last night. She _____ toward the exit when the fire alarm started blaring, so she managed to run right out of the building.

(a) has already walked
(b) was already walking
(c) is already walking
(d) would already be walking

12. When hiking in a wooded area, you may lose cellphone service because of interference caused by the thick canopy of trees overhead. To get the signal back, keep _____ until you reach a clearing.

(a) hiking
(b) to have hiked
(c) having hiked
(d) to hike

13. I was alone at home when the power suddenly went out around 6 p.m. Scared that the outage _____ last all night, I asked my friend Jill to come keep me company until the power returned.

    (a) can
    (b) shall
    (c) should
    (d) might

14. The parent–teacher conference was scheduled for today, but there was an unexpected thunderstorm that would've made it difficult for everyone to attend. To ensure everyone's safety, the principal urged parents not _____ to the school.

    (a) to go
    (b) going
    (c) to have gone
    (d) having gone

15. Dennis borrowed my *Vampire Arcadia* books last month, but he still hasn't gotten past the second one. He says he _____ to finish the series for a while, but he has trouble finding time to read.

    (a) will be meaning
    (b) is meaning
    (c) has been meaning
    (d) would mean

16. Many painters gravitate toward traditional watercolor paint because of the bright, "happy" colors it produces. _____, many artists like *gouache*, a different type of water-based paint that is favored for its light and reflective colors.

    (a) In fact
    (b) For example
    (c) Similarly
    (d) Otherwise

17. There is currently no known cure for asthma, though there are respiratory devices like inhalers that make it manageable. If a cure were to be invented today, it _____ such treatments obsolete.

    (a) will immediately make
    (b) would immediately make
    (c) will have immediately made
    (d) would have immediately made

18. This morning, Finn's professors were so impressed with his thesis manuscript that they recommended it for publication in an online journal. Immediately afterward, he was excited _____ his parents about his latest academic achievement.

    (a) to call
    (b) to have called
    (c) having called
    (d) calling

19. When I visited my hometown, I discovered that the bookstore I frequented back in high school had gone out of business. If it hadn't closed, I _____ again for old times' sake and said hello.

    (a) will have dropped by
    (b) would have dropped by
    (c) would drop by
    (d) will drop by

20. Harold's parents finally gave him their blessing to leave the family catering business and pursue a career in architecture. Before deciding to study in Oslo, he _____ his family run the business for seven years.

    (a) is helping
    (b) has been helping
    (c) had been helping
    (d) will have been helping

21. Cats were highly treasured in ancient Egypt, where they were believed to be magical creatures that warded off bad luck. Some ancient Egyptians even chose _____ the animals with jewelry as a sign of respect.

    (a) to have lavished
    (b) lavishing
    (c) having lavished
    (d) to lavish

22. Eagle Travel Agency is expanding to several southwestern states in the first quarter of next year. They've already hired a new manager for their Arizona branch, which is set to open _____ the holidays have ended.

    (a) although
    (b) until
    (c) as long as
    (d) as soon as

23. Seascapes is a landmark resort that has gained attention around the world for its private beaches. By the end of next month, the long-admired resort _____ tourists for thirty years.

    (a) has been serving
    (b) is serving
    (c) will be serving
    (d) will have been serving

24. Artificial ice rinks were invented in the 1840s so that people could ice skate all year round. If ice rinks didn't exist today, people _____ until winter to skate, when bodies of water naturally freeze over.

    (a) would have to wait
    (b) would have had to wait
    (c) will have had to wait
    (d) will have to wait

지텔프 공식 기출문제집 7회분 Level 2

25. Melissa had to have her car towed after her rear wheels got stuck in the mud by the lake. If she had parked farther away from the water's edge, she _____ to call for roadside assistance.

    (a) would not need
    (b) would not have needed
    (c) had not needed
    (d) will not have needed

26. Seth overslept and missed his friend Gina's singing recital last Thursday. He considered _____ her a gift in the hope that she would forgive him but ultimately decided to cook her a nice meal instead.

    (a) to have bought
    (b) buying
    (c) having bought
    (d) to buy

THIS IS THE END OF THE GRAMMAR SECTION
DO NOT GO ON UNTIL TOLD TO DO SO

LISTENING SECTION

TEST 1
TEST 2
TEST 3
TEST 4
TEST 5
TEST 6
TEST 7

DIRECTIONS:

The Listening Section has four parts. In each part you will hear a spoken passage and a number of questions about the passage. First you will hear the questions. Then you will hear the passage. From the four choices for each question, choose the best answer. Then blacken in the correct circle on your answer sheet.

Now you will hear an example question. Then you will hear an example passage.

Now listen to the example question.

```
(a) one
(b) two
(c) three
(d) four
```

Bill Johnson has four brothers, so the best answer is (d). The circle with the letter (d) has been blackened.

NOW TURN THE PAGE AND BEGIN

27. (a) so she can help a local shelter
    (b) so her older cat will have a friend
    (c) so she can feel less lonely
    (d) so her home will be free of mice

28. (a) He had a bad experience with cats.
    (b) He was worried about the cost.
    (c) He was not very familiar with cats.
    (d) He had never cared for a pet.

29. (a) by visiting the vet often
    (b) by giving her allergy medicine
    (c) by feeding her special cat food
    (d) by buying the finest cat treats

30. (a) her lack of money
    (b) her need for a reliable vehicle
    (c) her distance from the hospital
    (d) her limited free time

31. (a) because cats might be homesick
    (b) because cats might be ill
    (c) because cats can be violent
    (d) because cats can be frightened

32. (a) the exotic breed she wants
    (b) cats that have lived outdoors
    (c) the common breed she prefers
    (d) cats that are very active

33. (a) learn more about cats
    (b) bring a pet home
    (c) visit the animal shelter
    (d) schedule a vet consultation

34. (a) to welcome back university students
    (b) to invite freshmen to a series of events
    (c) to give high school students a campus tour
    (d) to share tips for adjusting to college life

35. (a) He will discuss his college experiences.
    (b) He will give a closing speech.
    (c) He will perform in a stage production.
    (d) He will give a lecture on the arts.

36. (a) getting to know the staff
    (b) learning more about the school
    (c) winning a valuable prize
    (d) enjoying the scenic campus

37. (a) because they are not allowed in the quad
    (b) because they would make the event too noisy
    (c) because there would not be enough food
    (d) because they have other events to attend

38. (a) meet student club members
    (b) join exclusive club activities
    (c) submit a club registration form
    (d) sign up to be a student leader

39. (a) by joining a seminar on health
    (b) by attending a dance workout
    (c) by participating in a raffle event
    (d) by competing in a singing contest

40. (a) to practice better eating habits
    (b) to allow for a longer break
    (c) to follow new rules at work
    (d) to adjust to a change of jobs

41. (a) by snacking on junk food
    (b) by having a large lunch
    (c) by distracting himself with work
    (d) by drinking plenty of water

42. (a) waking up early in the morning
    (b) using discounts from the paper
    (c) feeling grumpy all the time
    (d) being so good at cooking

43. (a) by going out with them after work
    (b) by having lunch with them
    (c) by joining them for activities
    (d) by eating with them in the office

44. (a) They serve healthy food.
    (b) They offer lunch specials.
    (c) They are limited in number.
    (d) They draw out-of-town visitors.

45. (a) look for more salad bars to visit
    (b) try ordering takeout food
    (c) continue bringing food to work
    (d) eat out with his coworkers

TEST 1

TEST 2

TEST 3

TEST 4

TEST 5

TEST 6

TEST 7

지텔프 공식 기출문제집 7회분 Level 2

PART 4. *You will hear an explanation of a process. First you will hear questions 46 through 52. Then you will hear the explanation. Choose the best answer to each question in the time provided.*

46. (a) how to make a home more comfortable
    (b) how to strengthen one's home security
    (c) how to avoid dangerous areas when traveling
    (d) how to protect a community from crime

47. (a) They can keep curtains closed.
    (b) They can ask someone to stay over.
    (c) They can leave electronics on.
    (d) They can leave a car in the driveway.

48. (a) to take advantage of a sale
    (b) to replace the original windows
    (c) to prevent another break-in
    (d) to give the illusion of protection

49. (a) by putting them inside clothing
    (b) by keeping them in a desk
    (c) by placing them in a nightstand
    (d) by tucking them under the bed

50. (a) police working around the clock
    (b) people living in the same area
    (c) a smart home security system
    (d) motion-activated lights

51. (a) to test how well the set-up performs
    (b) to experience how scary a break-in is
    (c) to see which products will work best
    (d) to show others that the home is protected

52. (a) feel safe going outside
    (b) leave the house at night
    (c) go away for a few days
    (d) rest with more ease

THIS IS THE END OF THE LISTENING SECTION
DO NOT GO ON UNTIL TOLD TO DO SO

READING AND VOCABULARY SECTION

DIRECTIONS:

You will now read four different passages. Each passage is followed by comprehension and vocabulary questions. From the four choices for each item, choose the best answer. Then blacken in the correct circle on your answer sheet.

Read the following example passage and example question.

Example:

Bill Johnson lives in New York. He is 25 years old. He has four brothers and two sisters.

How many brothers does Bill Johnson have?

(a) one
(b) two
(c) three
(d) four

The correct answer is (d), so the circle with the letter (d) has been blackened.

ⓐ ⓑ ⓒ ●

NOW TURN THE PAGE AND BEGIN

지텔프 공식 기출문제집 7회분 Level 2

RENÉ MAGRITTE

René Magritte was a Belgian artist in the twentieth century. He was a prominent figure of the Surrealism art movement, which included works depicting dreamlike, irrational imagery. Magritte often painted everyday objects in unsettling situations to make viewers question their understanding of reality, such as in his most famous work *The Treachery of Images*, which features an image of a tobacco pipe and the caption "This is not a pipe."

René François Ghislain Magritte was born on November 21, 1898. His mother died when he was thirteen, so he started drawing and painting to cope with the loss, an endeavor encouraged by his father. His works during this time were mostly abstract, but he began to experiment with different styles after enrolling in art school at age eighteen.

Later, Magritte found work as a poster and advertisement designer but carried on painting in his spare time. One day, he was shown a book containing a picture of the collage-like painting *The Song of Love* by early surrealist Giorgio de Chirico. Moved to tears by being able to "see thought" portrayed on canvas, Magritte began to <u>incorporate</u> aspects of the surrealist art style into his own work.

Magritte held his first art exhibition at a Brussels gallery in 1927 to lukewarm critical reception. Dismayed by his exhibition's lack of success, he moved to Paris a year later, where he continued to develop his art style and befriended popular surrealist painters. During this time, Magritte produced some of his most notable surrealist pieces, including *The Treachery of Images*. The painting's seemingly <u>contradictory</u> caption is meant to remind viewers that the painting is not actually a real pipe but simply an image of a pipe. These thought-provoking words and their connection to visual imagery would be a recurring theme in Magritte's future works.

Despite gaining some popularity in Paris, Magritte's exhibits were still unprofitable. He moved back to Brussels in 1930 to run an ad agency with his brother, during which time he created very little art. However, his paintings eventually started selling well enough for him to return to focusing on his own artwork full-time.

Magritte enjoyed significant recognition for his surrealist works until he passed away in 1967. His signature style influenced several art movements in the decades that followed, including pop and conceptual art, and his works are still featured in major exhibits today.

53. Who was René Magritte?

(a) a highly controversial artist
(b) a founder of a new art movement
(c) a creator of realistic portraits
(d) a painter of puzzling artwork

54. Why did Magritte start painting?

(a) He wanted to take a break from schoolwork.
(b) His father encouraged him to explore his creativity.
(c) He needed to find a way to overcome his grief.
(d) His mother wanted him to try a new hobby.

55. What inspired Magritte to make surrealist art?

(a) a work that presented ideas in a visual way
(b) a criticism of the style of his earlier works
(c) a painting done by one of his artist friends
(d) an art show that he saw while traveling

56. How did *The Treachery of Images* reflect Magritte's overall art style?

(a) by showcasing an inventive painting technique
(b) by displaying a motivational saying above the image
(c) by challenging the viewer's assumptions about the image
(d) by inviting the viewer to question the value of certain objects

57. Why, most likely, did Magritte help run an ad agency?

(a) to gain recognition in a different field
(b) to give himself a break from producing art
(c) to help his brother's business turn a profit
(d) to earn more of an income for himself

58. In the context of the passage, incorporate means _____.

(a) adjust
(b) follow
(c) organize
(d) mix

59. In the context of the passage, contradictory means _____.

(a) convenient
(b) conflicting
(c) uncertain
(d) meaningless

PART 2. Read the following magazine article and answer the questions. The underlined words in the article are for vocabulary questions.

HOW AN INJURED ARM CAN BE STRENGTHENED BY EXERCISING THE ARM ON THE OTHER SIDE

A recent study has shown that if one arm is injured, exercising the uninjured arm can significantly strengthen its weaker counterpart. This can be explained by "mirror activity," a previously established phenomenon in which moving one limb will cause the muscles in the opposite limb to activate.

The collaborative study was conducted by researchers in Chile, France, and Australia, who wanted to test whether mirror activity could be effective in preventing loss of muscle tissue. A broken or injured limb often needs to be immobilized in a cast for several weeks until it is ready for rehabilitative exercise. However, the lack of physical activity causes the muscles to shrink. Researchers hypothesized that exercising the uninjured arm might be able to prevent muscle loss in the injured arm, even if it is still in a cast.

For the experiment, thirty participants were asked to wear a sling on one arm, keeping it immobilized for eight hours a day for a month. Ten participants did not exercise either arm, while the remaining participants used their unrestricted arm to lift weights.

As expected, participants who exercised only experienced around two percent muscle loss in the immobilized arm, while the others experienced nearly twenty-eight percent muscle loss. Moreover, muscle strength in the injured arm actually increased for the participants who exercised, proving that mirror activity can not only successfully prevent muscle loss, but also tone and strengthen muscles in immobilized arms.

Scientists have long debated how mirror activity works. One theory is that if one side of the body is experiencing physical exertion, the brain will automatically activate the corresponding muscles on the opposite side of the body. The effect is unnoticeable to the naked eye, but the triggered muscles will give off slight electric signals.

The study's results can be used to improve rehabilitation methods. Being able to keep an injured arm strong while it is still in a cast will lessen time spent on rebuilding shrunken muscles later. In the future, researchers hope to study methods that will improve not just muscle strength but also movement and fine muscle control.

60. What is the article all about?

    (a) a way to prevent serious arm injuries
    (b) a way to avoid rehabilitation for an injury
    (c) a way to reduce the amount of pain from an injury
    (d) a way to improve the healing process for an injury

61. Why did researchers carry out the study?

    (a) to see if the amount of post-injury muscle loss would decrease
    (b) to investigate the psychological effects of having an injury
    (c) to explore ways to safely exercise an injured limb
    (d) to test the strength of a limb that has been repeatedly injured

62. What happened to the participants who exercised in the experiment?

    (a) They maintained the same level of strength in both of their arms.
    (b) They increased strength in their injured arm.
    (c) They experienced a faster healing time for their injured arm.
    (d) They gained flexibility in both of their arms.

63. Based on the article, what can be said about how mirror activity works?

    (a) that it is not related to brain activity
    (b) that it is not fully understood by scientists
    (c) that it only affects one side of the body
    (d) that it only applies to upper body muscles

64. How will this research benefit patients who are recovering from an injury?

    (a) It will give them greater control over movement.
    (b) It will eliminate the need for them to wear a cast.
    (c) It will reduce the duration of their recovery.
    (d) It will strengthen them against future injuries.

65. In the context of the passage, collaborative means _____.

    (a) additional
    (b) previous
    (c) consistent
    (d) cooperative

66. In the context of the passage, unrestricted means _____.

    (a) lower
    (b) free
    (c) clear
    (d) single

SNOW WHITE AND THE SEVEN DWARFS

Snow White and the Seven Dwarfs is a 1937 animated American film produced by Walt Disney. Based on a nineteenth-century German fairy tale about a queen who secretly <u>orders</u> her stepdaughter's death out of jealousy, it was the first ever full-length animated film in English. It is also considered one of Disney's greatest works for its innovations in animation.

When Disney first proposed the film in 1934, his ideas were met with doubt. The country was in the midst of the Great Depression, and this severe economic downturn weighed heavily on the minds of film producers and moviegoers. The public seemed to prefer films that addressed the decay of American society or live-action comedies that <u>appeased</u> their everyday anxieties. Consequently, skeptics in the movie industry called *Snow White* "Disney's folly," predicting its failure even before its release.

However, Disney remained optimistic. His animated short films had already been well-received by critics, and he wanted to bring his work to a larger audience. He borrowed considerable sums of money to fund production, knowing that he could lose his reputation, his studio, and even his house if the film did not do well.

Upon its release, *Snow White and the Seven Dwarfs* became a box-office hit. The film's elaborate storytelling and unique blend of fantasy and reality captivated audiences. Before *Snow White*, many believed that the public would not be interested in watching longer animations because of the absence of real people or places in them. To compensate for this, Disney's team worked hard to make the film more realistic than the traditional, exaggerated cartoon style, studying and replicating the real-life movements of hair, clothing, and hired actors.

The film's success highlighted the potential of animated features, paving the way not just for future Disney films, but also for the entire animation industry. In 1939, Disney received an Honorary Academy Award for *Snow White*, which was recognized as a "significant screen innovation which has charmed millions and pioneered a great new entertainment field for the motion picture cartoon." The film remains one of Disney's most popular films, ranking first on the American Film Institute's list of greatest American animations.

67. What is the article all about?

(a) the first American feature-length animation
(b) tho firct ovor full-length film in English
(c) the oldest cartoon produced by Disney
(d) a German adaptation of a classic fairy tale

68. Why, most likely, was *Snow White* expected to fail?

(a) because many people could not afford to go to the cinema
(b) because the movie did not follow the trends of the time
(c) because the public was not interested in movies
(d) because a film producer was not confident about the movie

69. Why did Walt Disney push to make the film despite criticism?

(a) He needed an uplifting project to focus on.
(b) He needed to revive his failing studio.
(c) He wanted to branch out from making short films.
(d) He wanted to restore his good reputation.

70. According to the article, how did Disney's animators make the film appealing to its audience?

(a) by hiring famous actors to voice the characters
(b) by setting the story in familiar locations
(c) by using an exaggerated cartoon style
(d) by creating highly realistic-looking characters

71. Based on the article, how did the film's success affect the animation genre?

(a) It motivated studios to be more competitive with Disney.
(b) It inspired a special award category for animated films.
(c) It introduced new animation technology into the industry.
(d) It raised expectations for cartoon entertainment.

72. In the context of the passage, orders means _____.

(a) buys
(b) demands
(c) approves
(d) rules

73. In the context of the passage, appeased means _____.

(a) favored
(b) satisfied
(c) calmed
(d) filled

PART 4. *Read the following business letter and answer the questions. The underlined words in the letter are for vocabulary questions.*

Donna Stewart
c/o Velvet Records
516 Rhubarb Ave.
San Jose, CA

Dear Ms. Stewart:

We at the Do Wonders Foundation would like to thank you for supporting our organization. Your annual donations have helped <u>advance</u> our mission to fund different charities over the past few years, and we hope we can count on your continued generosity.

This year, to celebrate Do Wonders' fifteenth anniversary, we will be hosting a benefit concert to raise funds for expansion of the Ellis Cancer Institute. We are inviting local artists and would like to know if you are interested in being the main <u>act</u>. Considering your past contributions to Do Wonders, we believe that you are the perfect choice to headline the event. As an acclaimed singer-songwriter, your presence will inspire the audience and help draw attention to our mission. The concert will not only celebrate our years of service but also raise funds for research into cancer treatment and prevention.

All proceeds from ticket sales will go to the Ellis Cancer Institute. Musical artists will also be encouraged to share donation links on their social media pages for fans who want to contribute to the cause. In addition, musicians may choose to waive their performance fee, instead donating the money they would have received to the institute.

Should you have any questions or concerns, we would be glad to address them with you or your agent. I will be out of the office for the next few weeks, but please feel welcome to contact our office manager for more information.

Best regards,

Tom Denver
Head of External Affairs
Do Wonders Foundation

74. Why did Tom Denver write to Donna Stewart?

(a) to thank her for donating money to charity
(b) to request that she sponsor a fundraising event
(c) to ask her to headline a nonprofit concert
(d) to invite her to host a benefit concert

75. What is the purpose of the event?

(a) to gather donations for a research center
(b) to urge people to contribute to different charities
(c) to raise money to support local artists
(d) to fund the opening of a new institute

76. Why, most likely, is Donna being invited to the event?

(a) She has supported the foundation in the past.
(b) She is known as an inspiring guest speaker.
(c) She has hosted a similar event.
(d) She is a cancer survivor herself.

77. What is NOT a way that the concert organizers plan to raise funds?

(a) by asking artists to perform for free
(h) by selling merchandise during the event
(c) by soliciting online contributions from fans
(d) by making tickets available for purchase

78. According to the letter, how can Donna find out more about the event?

(a) by inquiring with her manager
(b) by asking her booking agent
(c) by getting in touch with Tom
(d) by contacting an administrator

79. In the context of the passage, advance means _____.

(a) release
(b) confirm
(c) promote
(d) provide

80. In the context of the passage, act means _____.

(a) performer
(b) character
(c) reason
(d) issue

THIS IS THE END OF THE TEST

[해설집] 정답·스크립트·해석·해설 p.54 / 자동 채점 및 성적 분석 서비스 ▶

TEST 1 TEST 2 TEST 3 TEST 4 TEST 5 TEST 6 TEST 7

지텔프 공식 기출문제집 7회분 Level 2

TEST 3

GRAMMAR

LISTENING

READING & VOCABULARY

테스트 전 확인사항

1. OMR 답안지를 준비하셨나요? ☐
2. 컴퓨터용 사인펜, 수정 테이프를 준비하셨나요? ☐
3. 음성을 들을 준비를 하셨나요? ☐

TEST 3 음성 바로 듣기

🎧 **TEST 3.mp3**

해커스인강(HackersIngang.com)에서 무료 다운로드
상단 메뉴 [G-TELP → MP3/자료 → 문제풀이 MP3]

자동 채점 및 성적 분석
서비스 바로 이용하기

▤ **자동 채점 및 성적 분석 서비스**

∨ 타이머, 모바일 OMR, 자동 채점
∨ 정답률 및 취약 유형 분석

시험 시간 : 90분

목표 점수 : _____점
시작 시간 : _____시 _____분 ~ 종료 시간 : _____시 _____분

General Tests of English Language Proficiency
G-TELP

Level 2

GRAMMAR SECTION

DIRECTIONS:

The following items need a word or words to complete the sentence. From the four choices for each item, choose the best answer. Then blacken in the correct circle on your answer sheet.

Example:

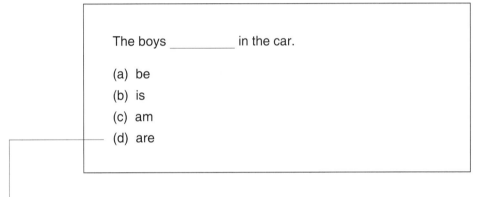

The boys _____ in the car.

(a) be
(b) is
(c) am
(d) are

The correct answer is (d), so the circle with the letter (d) has been blackened.

ⓐ ⓑ ⓒ ●

NOW TURN THE PAGE AND BEGIN

1. Jerry is now the head chef at Ciao Bella, the finest Italian restaurant in the city. He _____ as a sous-chef there for two years before he was promoted to the top position last week.

    (a) had been serving
    (b) has been serving
    (c) would serve
    (d) will have served

2. Hawaii is one of the only US states that can grow coffee commercially because of the islands' tropical climate. For coffee trees to flourish, an area _____ have warm temperatures and plentiful rainfall all year round.

    (a) will
    (b) can
    (c) may
    (d) must

3. The local cotton mill has been operating since long before Susan was born. By the end of this year, the company that employs both of her parents _____ quality cotton fabric for five decades.

    (a) will be producing
    (b) produces
    (c) had been producing
    (d) will have been producing

4. Melanie expects to keep tossing and turning later because her neighbors are having another noisy party. If they were more considerate, Melanie _____ soundly tonight, but it seems unlikely.

    (a) will have slept
    (b) will sleep
    (c) would sleep
    (d) would have slept

5. A woman just walked into Delia's Beauty Shop claiming that a lotion bottle was half empty when purchased. She wants the store _____ it, but she is unable to prove that she never opened the lotion.

    (a) to replace
    (b) replacing
    (c) having replaced
    (d) to have replaced

6. At nearly seventy feet long, the megalodon was one of the largest fish to have existed. If this gigantic shark were still alive today, it _____ the whale shark, which is currently the largest living fish.

    (a) would dwarf
    (b) would have dwarfed
    (c) will dwarf
    (d) will have dwarfed

7. Michaela developed a fear of spiders because of a traumatic childhood experience. When she was eight, a large brown spider bit her knee while she _____ in the yard, causing it to swell and itch.

(a) has been playing
(b) was playing
(c) is playing
(d) had been playing

8. Jack the Ripper, an infamous London serial killer, evaded justice and was never officially identified. _____, the Zodiac Killer from California was never caught after going on a brutal 1960s crime spree.

(a) Therefore
(b) Finally
(c) Similarly
(d) However

9. There has been a surge in the theft of packages delivered to our neighborhood. Just yesterday, a tall man, _____, was caught on a security camera stealing a box from our neighbor's porch.

(a) who was wearing a black hoodie
(b) what was wearing a black hoodie
(c) that was wearing a black hoodie
(d) which was wearing a black hoodie

10. Worried about the high cost of repairs, Eric tried fixing his broken phone himself, but the phone stopped working entirely. Had he hired a technician instead, his phone _____ before it sustained any further damage.

(a) would likely be fixed
(b) will likely be fixed
(c) would likely have been fixed
(d) will likely have been fixed

11. Diamond Knoll School just installed a new digital public announcement system for better campus communication. The new PA system uses wireless technology and can be set _____ the whole school or just specific buildings and classrooms.

(a) addressing
(b) to have addressed
(c) having addressed
(d) to address

12. Phrenology is the study of the cranial structure as it is related to mental function. Phrenologists once claimed they _____ determine someone's intelligence by the shape of their skull, but that theory lacked scientific support.

(a) might
(b) could
(c) would
(d) should

13. When sales of Simple Scents perfume skyrocketed, the marketing team attributed the increase to their new celebrity spokesperson. If they had not made the deal with the superstar, sales _____ all last quarter.

    (a) will have remained flat
    (b) would have remained flat
    (c) will remain flat
    (d) would remain flat

14. Lawrence asked his mother if he could paint the doghouse she built. She agreed, but since it was Lawrence's very first painting project, she insisted that he _____ the floor with newspapers to avoid splatter marks.

    (a) covered
    (b) will cover
    (c) was covering
    (d) cover

15. Rita saw a social media post that claimed her favorite granola bar contained dangerous traces of pesticides and could cause health problems when ingested. Now, she _____ the internet to see if the post is fake.

    (a) is scouring
    (b) has been scouring
    (c) will be scouring
    (d) would scour

16. One reason fingernails generally grow faster than toenails is that hands are exposed to more sunlight. This extra exposure allows the fingernails to produce a nutrient _____ for them to outpace toenails in terms of growth.

    (a) where is necessary
    (b) what is necessary
    (c) that is necessary
    (d) who is necessary

17. There are many beautiful places to visit in the Chicago area, but Matthew's favorite is the Brookfield Zoo. He _____ the zoo ever since he got to feed a giraffe there as a child.

    (a) had been frequenting
    (b) has been frequenting
    (c) will frequent
    (d) is frequenting

18. The Chupa Chups lollipop logo was designed by famous surrealist artist Salvador Dalí. He suggested that the logo _____ to the top of the wrapper instead of its original placement on the side.

    (a) will be moved
    (b) be moved
    (c) would move
    (d) has been moved

19. Daphne is tired of her quiet office job at the insurance company. When she is not busy, she daydreams about escaping and imagines _____ on a tropical beach with a cocktail in hand.

(a) having relaxed
(b) to relax
(c) relaxing
(d) to have relaxed

20. Joey has been excited ever since he was accepted into his school's two-month foreign exchange program. Later this afternoon, he _____ for his flight to Germany next week.

(a) packs
(b) has packed
(c) will be packing
(d) will have been packing

21. The word *orange* was initially only used as the name of the citrus fruit. _____ it was used to describe the color in the 1500s, most people used *red* or *yellow* to describe the hue.

(a) Until
(b) Because
(c) Given that
(d) In case

22. Most of the bank's employees refused to transfer to a new branch in another city. However, Shane welcomed _____ at another branch just so he could enjoy a change of scenery and meet new people.

(a) having worked
(b) to work
(c) working
(d) to be working

23. The sun is important for all life forms on Earth. Plants rely on sunlight for photosynthesis, while animals are dependent on plants for food. If the sun were to suddenly vanish, living things _____ very long.

(a) will not have survived
(b) will not survive
(c) would not survive
(d) would not have survived

24. The southern counterpart to the aurora borealis is called the aurora australis. The best time _____ both of these amazing displays of northern and southern lights is in the winter season.

(a) to witness
(b) having witnessed
(c) to have witnessed
(d) witnessing

지텔프 공식 기출문제집 7회분 Level 2

25. My sister tried a recipe that she saw in an online video: a potato chip omelet made inside the chips' bag. It took a while to cook, but she appreciated _____ an unusual new culinary technique.

(a) to learn
(b) having learned
(c) to have learned
(d) learning

26. After four years of development, the mumps vaccine was released in 1967. At the time, this was the fastest development of a vaccine. Had the vaccine taken longer to produce, more people _____ by the virus.

(a) will be infected
(b) would have been infected
(c) will have been infected
(d) would be infected

THIS IS THE END OF THE GRAMMAR SECTION
DO NOT GO ON UNTIL TOLD TO DO SO

LISTENING SECTION

DIRECTIONS:

The Listening Section has four parts. In each part you will hear a spoken passage and a number of questions about the passage. First you will hear the questions. Then you will hear the passage. From the four choices for each question, choose the best answer. Then blacken in the correct circle on your answer sheet.

Now you will hear an example question. Then you will hear an example passage.

Now listen to the example question.

> (a) one
> (b) two
> (c) three
> (d) four

Bill Johnson has four brothers, so the best answer is (d). The circle with the letter (d) has been blackened.

NOW TURN THE PAGE AND BEGIN

지텔프 공식 기출문제집 7회분 Level 2

27. (a) enjoying a peaceful picnic
    (b) working on a school project
    (c) celebrating a special occasion
    (d) looking for a specific bird

28. (a) It offers discounts for locals.
    (b) It allows them to breathe clean air.
    (c) It can lower their anxiety.
    (d) It gives them a place to walk.

29. (a) feeding the birds by hand
    (b) touring the bird enclosures
    (c) watching the birds fly around
    (d) seeing an exciting bird show

30. (a) because they are trained by the volunteers
    (b) because they were raised in a pet store
    (c) because they are used to being around people
    (d) because they were previously kept in a zoo

31. (a) by reading a story about its history
    (b) by talking with the rescue workers
    (c) by seeing pictures in the bird museum
    (d) by looking around the visitor center

32. (a) the process for bird adoption
    (b) how people can donate their time
    (c) the souvenir items for sale
    (d) how the facility is maintained

33. (a) take photos by the bird statue
    (b) look at the pictures they took
    (c) shake hands with the mascot
    (d) ask someone for directions

34. (a) a guide for emergency preparation
    (b) an interactive alarm system
    (c) a system for detecting intrusion
    (d) a device for preventing fires

35. (a) by listening for different sounds
    (b) by calling the tech company
    (c) by watching for flashing lights
    (d) by checking in with firefighters

36. (a) to evaluate the threat level
    (b) to show to the insurance company
    (c) to add to a photo database
    (d) to keep a record for researchers

37. (a) They can call the fire department.
    (b) They can check on anyone in the house.
    (c) They can alert people in nearby houses.
    (d) They can contact the homeowner.

38. (a) having a prepared escape plan
    (b) having the voice alert function
    (c) seeing accurate visual maps
    (d) wearing a protective mask

39. (a) by visiting a local branch
    (b) by living in a certain area
    (c) by downloading an application
    (d) by attending the talk

지텔프 공식 기출문제집 7회분 Level 2

PART 3. *You will hear a conversation between two people. First you will hear questions 40 through 45. Then you will hear the conversation. Choose the best answer to each question in the time provided.*

40. (a) because they want to reorganize their space
    (b) because they have changed houses
    (c) because they dislike sharing things
    (d) because they have their own rooms

41. (a) She wants to have room for overnight guests.
    (b) She wants to leave room for a study area.
    (c) The room is not as big as before.
    (d) The room is still not very spacious.

42. (a) getting hurt while using the ladder
    (b) having their sleep interrupted
    (c) falling off in the middle of the night
    (d) being afraid of heights

43. (a) She could have more storage space.
    (b) She could get to the kids more quickly.
    (c) She could do chores more comfortably.
    (d) She could have more options for decorating.

44. (a) to have a better window view
    (b) to have more room to stretch out
    (c) to be closest to the door
    (d) to avoid a scary spot

45. (a) give her sons separate rooms
    (b) get the least expensive bed
    (c) buy each of her sons a bed
    (d) let the boys choose their beds

PART 4. *You will hear an explanation of a process. First you will hear questions 46 through 52. Then you will hear the talk. Choose the best answer to each question in the time provided.*

46. (a) learning to navigate social media
    (b) managing social media anxiety
    (c) choosing the best social media site
    (d) limiting time on social media

47. (a) those who provide meaningful content
    (b) those who value their appearance
    (c) those who are satisfied with their lives
    (d) those who make reasonable posts

48. (a) by filtering out the less important content
    (b) by reminding one to communicate quickly
    (c) by removing one from the site after a while
    (d) by setting a limit on social interaction

49. (a) alerts about new uploads
    (b) updates posted by friends
    (c) messages from loved ones
    (d) news about urgent situations

50. (a) by deleting one's web browsers
    (b) by temporarily removing access
    (c) by planning an all-day outing
    (d) by turning off one's phone

51. (a) He no longer enjoyed social media.
    (b) He was bored of other activities.
    (c) He was looking for friends with common interests.
    (d) He wanted to use his time more wisely.

52. (a) check social media on a computer
    (b) use specialized phone settings
    (c) delete all social media accounts
    (d) stop posting from public spaces

THIS IS THE END OF THE LISTENING SECTION
DO NOT GO ON UNTIL TOLD TO DO SO

READING AND VOCABULARY SECTION

DIRECTIONS:

You will now read four different passages. Each passage is followed by comprehension and vocabulary questions. From the four choices for each item, choose the best answer. Then blacken in the correct circle on your answer sheet.

Read the following example passage and example question.

Example:

> Bill Johnson lives in New York. He is 25 years old. He has four brothers and two sisters.
>
> How many brothers does Bill Johnson have?
>
> (a) one
> (b) two
> (c) three
> (d) four

The correct answer is (d), so the circle with the letter (d) has been blackened.

NOW TURN THE PAGE AND BEGIN

PART 1. *Read the following biography article and answer the questions. The underlined words in the article are for vocabulary questions.*

SAUL BASS

Saul Bass was an American graphic designer and filmmaker. He produced some of the world's most recognizable brand logos and film posters. However, Bass is most known for revolutionizing title sequences for films by using eye-catching graphics and animation.

Saul Bass was born on May 8, 1920, in the Bronx, New York, to Jewish immigrant parents. Bass acquired an interest in visual arts as a boy and frequented the Metropolitan Museum of Art to study famous artworks. After high school, he went to a prominent art school, the Art Students League of New York, on a fellowship. He also worked as a freelance graphic artist to fund his studies.

Bass then went to Brooklyn College, where he was mentored by György Kepes, a well-known graphic designer and art theorist. There, his artistic expression was further influenced by the Bauhaus art movement, which focused on minimalist yet functional designs.

In 1946, Bass moved to California and designed print advertisements for films, as well as magazine covers, <u>corporate</u> logos, and other works. Director Otto Preminger hired him to produce the poster for the film *Carmen Jones* in 1954. The work impressed Preminger so much that he also asked Bass to create the movie's title sequence—the introductory clip in which the title, cast members, and production credits appear before the film starts. His work was an iconic success.

Traditional opening sequences were often stationary lists too plain to draw viewers' interest. Bass took an entirely different approach by adding movement and sound to an otherwise unremarkable introduction to a movie. This led to the development of kinetic typography, in which letters moved across the screen. Combined with striking color contrast and cut-out animation, Bass's title sequences served as a visual reflection of a film's story.

Bass received commissions from the film industry's top directors, including Alfred Hitchcock, Stanley Kubrick, and Martin Scorsese. Bass's innovative style was also adopted by other designers, making title sequences an important part of films. Among Bass's last title sequence credits were the Scorsese films *Goodfellas* and *Casino*.

Bass died in 1996, but his legacy lives on. His entire body of work, consisting of 2,700 items, is stored at the Academy Film Archive. His designs are still <u>featured</u> as the logos of renowned companies such as AT&T and Kleenex.

53. What is Saul Bass best known for?

(a) directing award-winning movies
(b) designing famous brand logos
(c) inventing tho film titlo sequence
(d) creating appealing opening credits

54. What helped influence Bass's creative expression?

(a) the theories he formed with a famous designer
(b) the experiences he gained as a mentor
(c) an art class he attended in his childhood
(d) an artistic trend he learned about in college

55. Why did Otto Preminger hire Bass to create the title sequence for *Carmen Jones*?

(a) because he needed someone on relatively short notice
(b) because he wanted his most trusted designer on board
(c) because he liked Bass's promotional art for the film
(d) because he admired Bass's work on previous credits

56. How did Bass's opening sequences differ from traditional sequences?

(a) They appeared after the movie's first scene.
(b) They presented information in an unusual format.
(c) They offered mysterious clues to the film's plot.
(d) They showed a clip of the film in animated form.

57. How, most likely, did Bass's contributions change the film industry?

(a) Title sequences are now produced in color.
(b) Audiences now pay more attention to title sequences.
(c) Audiences now arrive early to avoid missing title sequences.
(d) Title sequences have now become longer.

58. In the context of the passage, corporate means _____.

(a) business
(b) worker
(c) management
(d) financial

59. In the context of the passage, featured means _____.

(a) faced
(b) reported
(c) used
(d) recommended

HOW THE WORD "OK" ORIGINATED

The word "OK" is one of the most common abbreviations in the English language. Signifying agreement or acceptance, it is alternatively spelled as "okay." The word is often used as an interjection, as in "OK, I understand."

There are several theories about the word's origins. These include the word being shorthand for a German phrase that means "no changes," or being derived from the Native American Choctaw language's word for "it is so." However, a story involving the *Boston Morning Post* is the most widely accepted.

In the 1830s, young intellectuals in Boston would create language fads by coming up with abbreviations for intentionally misspelled words. The practice resulted in such expressions as "KC" for "knuff ced," which is slang for "enough said," and "OW" for "oll wright," meaning "all right." Most of these acronyms faded over time, but one remained. "OK" is believed to have first surfaced in 1839, when the *Boston Morning Post* editor ended an article with "OK," for "oll korrect." Indicating that the content was "all correct," the abbreviation was picked up by other newspapers and used often in publishing.

"OK" further spread through the United States during the 1840 presidential elections. President Martin Van Buren, who hailed from Kinderhook, New York, used "Old Kinderhook," or "OK," as his 1840 re-election campaign nickname. He coined "Vote for OK" as his campaign slogan. Van Buren lost the presidential race, but "OK" endured and became part of Americans' everyday speech.

The word later gained worldwide popularity with the invention of the telegraph. Telegram messages became more expensive to send when more letters were used. Thus, "OK" became the code used by telegraph operators to acknowledge receipt of a message. This was how "OK" traveled to Great Britain and, eventually, to the rest of the world.

"OK" has been adopted into most of the world's languages with variations in spelling and pronunciation. It is also expressed as a hand signal formed by touching the thumb and index finger to form a circle while holding the other fingers straight. The word itself can serve as an adjective, adverb, noun, or verb, making it highly versatile and useful in many situations.

60. What is mainly being discussed in the article?

(a) the world's most common word
(b) the declining use of a word
(c) the benefits of abbreviated words
(d) the origin of a popular word

61. How was the abbreviation "OK" used in the late 1830s?

(a) as a slang expression in spoken conversation
(b) as a short version of an editorial phrase
(c) as a printer's stamp indicating that newsprint was dry
(d) as a way to describe young intellectuals

62. When did "OK" become widely used in America?

(a) when the president made a nickname using his initials
(b) when it played a role in a presidential campaign
(c) when it became a symbol for the president's hometown
(d) when a re-elected president said it in his victory speech

63. Why, most likely, did "OK" become popular when sending telegrams?

(a) It was easily understood by operators worldwide.
(b) It served as a positive way to end a message.
(c) It allowed operators to type a reply quickly.
(d) It cost less to use when sending confirmation.

64. How has "OK" further evolved in the present times?

(a) by being useful in many language situations
(b) by showing up mostly as a hand signal
(c) by taking the place of traditional words for agreement
(d) by being able to express any kind of meaning

65. In the context of the passage, surfaced means _____.

(a) declared
(b) landed
(c) appeared
(d) hidden

66. In the context of the passage, versatile means _____.

(a) inventive
(b) skillful
(c) flexible
(d) realistic

ASIAN AROWANA

The Asian arowana is a fish species found primarily in the fresh waters of Southeast Asia. It is one of the most sought-after and expensive ornamental fish in the world. The Asian arowana is highly prized for its beauty and cultural significance.

With a long, narrow body that can grow up to three feet in the wild, the Asian arowana comes in many colors, but solid red, silver, and gold are the most common. Arowanas have whisker-like appendages called "barbels" that jut out of their chins and are used to detect prey. The fish are also covered in shiny, coin-like scales resembling those of mythical Asian dragons. The Asian arowana can live for over sixty years in captivity.

In the wild, arowanas are carnivorous. Classified as surface feeders, their diet includes insects, spiders, frogs, and lizards that sit on vegetation close to the water. Arowanas are also able to jump out of the water to catch their prey. They hunt their food discreetly, often hiding in the shade before jumping on their meal.

Reproduction for the Asian arowana involves a process called "paternal mouthbrooding." The male arowana, whose mouth is wider than the female's, keeps the eggs in its mouth, protecting them until they hatch. Then, the hatchlings remain in the mouth for a few months before being released into the water.

Another trait of the Asian arowana is its graceful swimming motion. The movement is said to resemble that of a dragon as the fish glides through the water, earning it the "dragon fish" nickname. Because dragons symbolize good luck in Chinese culture, the arowana is particularly coveted as an aquarium pet because it is also believed to bring its owner money and good fortune.

Due to its popularity as a pet and the destruction of its habitats, the Asian arowana has become critically endangered. Import and trade of the fish is now banned in many countries, including the US. However, this protected status reinforces the arowana's reputation as a rare and prized fish, raising its market value considerably. Reports say that a single fish was once bought for $300,000.

67. Which is NOT true of the Asian arowana?

    (a) that it has a life expectancy of more than half a century
    (b) that it has a body that can change colors over time
    (c) that it has a long and slender body of about three feet
    (d) that it has a facial feature that senses nearby prey

68. How does the Asian arowana get its food?

    (a) by eating plants that grow at the water's edge
    (b) by hunting only in the shaded parts of the water
    (c) by jumping out of the water to hunt on land
    (d) by pouncing on prey that lingers near the water

69. Why are young arowanas kept in the male arowana's mouth and not in the female's?

    (a) The temperature of a male's mouth is warmer.
    (b) The male's mouth has a larger capacity.
    (c) The teeth in a male's mouth are not as sharp.
    (d) The male's mouth has multiple compartments.

70. What is the connection between dragons and the Asian arowana in Chinese culture?

    (a) They are both popular in children's stories.
    (b) They are both believed to bring good luck.
    (c) They are both used in religious symbolism.
    (d) They are both used in major celebrations.

71. Based on the article, what has probably contributed to the high price of Asian arowanas?

    (a) the limitations on where it can be sold
    (b) the laws against entering its habitats
    (c) the absence of any populations in the wild
    (d) the difficulty of breeding it in captivity

72. In the context of the passage, coveted means _____.

    (a) desired
    (b) needed
    (c) accepted
    (d) envied

73. In the context of the passage, reputation means _____.

    (a) knowledge
    (b) journey
    (c) link
    (d) place

Barbara West
Manager, White Plains Hotel
52 Hartland Ave.
Atlantic City, NJ

Dear Mrs. West,

I am writing this letter to express my gratitude to you for being my mentor for the past few years. As you already know, I will be moving to a different branch of the hotel. The newly opened location on Mammoth Avenue needs staff, and I have been assigned to be its branch manager.

I believe that working as your assistant manager here at the White Plains Hotel has helped shape me for my new position. I would therefore like to thank you for your training and guidance over the last three years. Through you, I learned how to effectively meet the many demands of hotel management. I became skilled at accommodating guests, hosting events, and ensuring the hotel's overall upkeep. You also taught me how to successfully handle customer complaints.

Another important lesson I learned from you is how to keep my presence of mind and stay focused in times of emergency. I admired how professionally you acted when the adjacent building caught fire last year. You managed to reassure the guests who were panicking and guide them to a safer place. I was honored to have witnessed your dedication to serve and protect our clients that day.

I am confident that the experience and knowledge I have gained while working with you will help me manage the Mammoth Avenue branch effectively. Moreover, I am certain that the person who will replace me as your assistant manager will be lucky to be working with you.

Thank you once again for everything. I look forward to seeing you again at the managers' monthly strategy meeting.

Sincerely,

Andy Johnson
Andy Johnson

74. Why is Andy Johnson writing a letter to Barbara West?

(a) to show appreciation for her recent recommendation
(b) to thank her for aiding his professional development
(c) to express his gratitude for promoting him to manager
(d) to let her know that he is leaving for a different company

75. Why did the hotel decide to transfer Andy to another branch?

(a) The manager of the branch has been dismissed.
(b) The branch has been recently launched in a new area.
(c) The branch has grown steadily for several years.
(d) The hotel is closing its current location.

76. According to the letter, what is NOT true about Andy's work experience with Barbara?

(a) She familiarized him with the hotel's maintenance needs.
(b) She showed him how to make customers a priority.
(c) She taught him how to deal with difficult employees.
(d) She gave him skills for managing hotel activities.

77. What did Andy learn from Barbara's actions when a major mishap occurred at work?

(a) the value of staying calm in the face of a crisis
(b) the trick to distracting worried guests
(c) the importance of being ready for sudden disasters
(d) the best ways to handle minor injuries

78. How, most likely, will Andy be interacting with Barbara in the future?

(a) by collaborating together as managers
(b) by helping her train his replacement
(c) by interviewing people for staff positions
(d) by meeting at regular social occasions

79. In the context of the passage, shape means _____.

(a) adjust
(b) consider
(c) pattern
(d) prepare

80. In the context of the passage, reassure means _____.

(a) satisfy
(b) silence
(c) question
(d) comfort

THIS IS THE END OF THE TEST

지텔프 공식 기출문제집 7회분 Level 2

TEST 4

GRAMMAR

LISTENING

READING & VOCABULARY

테스트 전 확인사항

1. OMR 답안지를 준비하셨나요? ☐
2. 컴퓨터용 사인펜, 수정 테이프를 준비하셨나요? ☐
3. 음성을 들을 준비를 하셨나요? ☐

TEST 4 음성 바로 듣기

🎧 **TEST 4.mp3**

해커스인강(HackersIngang.com)에서 무료 다운로드
상단 메뉴 [G-TELP → MP3/자료 → 문제풀이 MP3]

자동 채점 및 성적 분석
서비스 바로 이용하기

📋 **자동 채점 및 성적 분석 서비스**

∨ 타이머, 모바일 OMR, 자동 채점
∨ 정답률 및 취약 유형 분석

시험 시간 : 90분

목표 점수 : _____점
시작 시간 : _____시 _____분 ~ 종료 시간 : _____시 _____분

General Tests of English Language Proficiency
G-TELP

Level 2

GRAMMAR SECTION

DIRECTIONS:

The following items need a word or words to complete the sentence. From the four choices for each item, choose the best answer. Then blacken in the correct circle on your answer sheet.

Example:

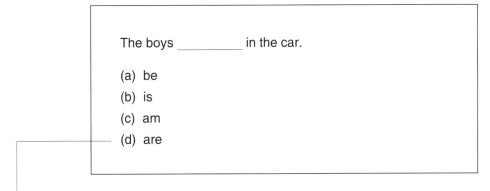

The boys _____ in the car.

(a) be

(b) is

(c) am

(d) are

The correct answer is (d), so the circle with the letter (d) has been blackened.

NOW TURN THE PAGE AND BEGIN

1. Derrick has been hired to audit the finances of Landsdale Security Company. Right now, he _____ the company's invoices to their financial records to check for fraudulent spending and calculation errors.

   (a) is comparing
   (b) was comparing
   (c) would compare
   (d) has been comparing

2. Bees are an important part of the natural ecosystem, as they pollinate many plants. Ecologists believe that if bees were to suddenly disappear, entire ecosystems _____ immediately.

   (a) would collapse
   (b) will have collapsed
   (c) would have collapsed
   (d) will collapse

3. Radio XCZR has a promo for the summer music festival. The first caller _____ the entire festival lineup will be given a free festival ticket and a meet-and-greet pass for an artist of their choice.

   (a) what can recite
   (b) when can recite
   (c) who can recite
   (d) which can recite

4. Frequent hydration in hot weather is important because it keeps the body cool and replaces fluids lost through sweating. Therefore, it is advisable _____ a water bottle along when going outside on a hot day.

   (a) bringing
   (b) having brought
   (c) to have brought
   (d) to bring

5. Lisa wants to be a full-time college professor, for which she needs a PhD. Her adviser suggests that she _____ applying for doctoral programs as soon as the final year of her master's program begins.

   (a) started
   (b) has started
   (c) will start
   (d) start

6. There are several things that need to be done regularly to keep a violin in optimal condition. For example, strings _____ be changed at least once per year so that the violin's sound does not deteriorate.

   (a) must
   (b) might
   (c) can
   (d) will

7. Miranda landed her first leading role on a sitcom when she was just nineteen. By the time she turns thirty next month, she _____ in a major TV show for over a decade.

   (a) will have been starring
   (b) will be starring
   (c) has been starring
   (d) would star

8. During the 1920s Prohibition era, bars were forced to close because of government laws that prohibited the sale of alcohol. Whenever bar owners were caught _____ alcohol to the public, they were heavily fined.

   (a) having sold
   (b) to sell
   (c) selling
   (d) to have sold

9. My cousin tends to make impulsive decisions that she often regrets afterward. When she asks me for advice, I say that if I were her, I _____ a pros and cons list before making major decisions.

   (a) will write
   (b) will have written
   (c) would have written
   (d) would write

10. Many people believe that goldfish have a short memory span. _____, this assumption has been proven false, as studies show that goldfish can remember their owners' faces and even distinguish them from other people.

    (a) Thus
    (b) In other words
    (c) In addition
    (d) However

11. The sky was beautiful this morning, so Kyle decided to take the day off from work. He asked his friends _____ boating on the lake for a few hours so they could all relax together.

    (a) going
    (b) to go
    (c) to have gone
    (d) having gone

12. Matt and his girlfriend Katie were going to visit his hometown last Saturday, but their flight was canceled due to engine problems. If their plane hadn't broken down, Matt _____ Katie to his parents that night.

    (a) would have introduced
    (b) would introduce
    (c) will introduce
    (d) will have introduced

지텔프 공식 기출문제집 7회분 Level 2

13. *Black Swan* is a 2010 psychological horror movie about rival ballerinas competing for the lead role in *Swan Lake*. _____, the competition is so intense that it slowly drives the main character insane.

   (a) After all
   (b) Nonetheless
   (c) In fact
   (d) Therefore

14. To stay productive while working from home, one should minimize distractions. It is best that one _____ a workspace separate from one's other living areas so that keeping out distractions is easier.

   (a) create
   (b) will create
   (c) has created
   (d) created

15. The Browns go on a family vacation together every summer. This year, the kids _____ summer camp around the same time that their family trip is usually scheduled, so their parents will probably just stay home.

   (a) have been attending
   (b) will have attended
   (c) attended
   (d) will be attending

16. In 1775, the French helped the Americans win the Revolutionary War by supplying them with money and military forces. Had France refused to give its support, the US _____ its independence from Britain.

   (a) will not win
   (b) might not win
   (c) might not have won
   (d) will not have won

17. When Elijah was accepted to an out-of-state university, he moved into a campus dorm. He was initially excited to be on his own but, after a few months, he realized that he missed _____ at home.

   (a) to have lived
   (b) living
   (c) having lived
   (d) to live

18. Based on the 1982 movie of the same name, *E.T. the Extra-Terrestrial* is one of the worst-selling video games in history. In fact, the game, _____, did so poorly that it bankrupted its creators.

   (a) that was released by Atari
   (b) which was released by Atari
   (c) who was released by Atari
   (d) what was released by Atari

19. In the 1800s, poor farmers were occasionally allowed to live on a nobleman's lands. In exchange, these sharecroppers were required to farm the land, and the nobleman _____ take some of their crops as payment.

(a) would
(b) can
(c) should
(d) might

20. Mary went to the hospital because she fractured her left foot. When asked how it happened, she told the doctor that she _____ the floor when she suddenly became dizzy and slipped on the slick tiles.

(a) will have mopped
(b) mopped
(c) has been mopping
(d) had been mopping

21. Sitting in front of a computer all day can increase the risk of cardiovascular problems and other health concerns. If one wishes _____ this, one should stand up and walk around every thirty minutes.

(a) to avoid
(b) to have avoided
(c) having avoided
(d) avoiding

22. Christina found a lost puppy under her back porch three months ago. After making sure it didn't belong to anyone else, she decided to keep the dog and _____ of it ever since.

(a) takes care
(b) will have taken care
(c) has been taking care
(d) had been taking care

23. Laminated glass is a type of glass that does not shatter. The inventor accidentally discovered this while he _____ a glass flask covered with chemicals. After dropping the flask by mistake, he found it surprisingly intact.

(a) would use
(b) has been using
(c) was using
(d) had used

24. Mike put off writing his final research paper and lost points for turning it in two days past the deadline. If he had started his paper earlier, he _____ a better grade on the assignment.

(a) would have earned
(b) will earn
(c) will have earned
(d) would earn

25. My favorite restaurant changed management recently, and the new owners have announced that they will change the menu completely. If I were them, I _____ at least a few of the dishes from the old menu.

(a) would have kept
(b) will have kept
(c) will keep
(d) would keep

26. Leo has locked himself in his dorm room so he can focus on studying for finals. He refuses to check social media or even meet his friends at the cafeteria until he finishes _____ his notes.

(a) having reviewed
(b) reviewing
(c) to have reviewed
(d) to review

THIS IS THE END OF THE GRAMMAR SECTION
DO NOT GO ON UNTIL TOLD TO DO SO

LISTENING SECTION

DIRECTIONS:

The Listening Section has four parts. In each part you will hear a spoken passage and a number of questions about the passage. First you will hear the questions. Then you will hear the passage. From the four choices for each question, choose the best answer. Then blacken in the correct circle on your answer sheet.

Now you will hear an example question. Then you will hear an example passage.

Now listen to the example question.

    (a) one
    (b) two
    (c) three
    (d) four

Bill Johnson has four brothers, so the best answer is (d). The circle with the letter (d) has been blackened.

NOW TURN THE PAGE AND BEGIN

지텔프 공식 기출문제집 7회분 Level 2

27. (a) touring a modern art museum
    (b) visiting a historic landmark
    (c) exploring a culture of the past
    (d) watching a tribal ceremony

28. (a) the documentary on royal families
    (b) the narration of major exhibits
    (c) the film about building design
    (d) the showcase of an artist's works

29. (a) because of their outfits
    (b) because of their weapons
    (c) because of their movement
    (d) because of their size

30. (a) He was nervous about getting lost.
    (b) He was frightened of skeletons.
    (c) He was afraid of the dark.
    (d) He was in a cold place.

31. (a) because they were skillfully made
    (b) because they looked realistic
    (c) because they were massive
    (d) because they seemed peaceful

32. (a) by asking the staff directly
    (b) by looking at a brochure
    (c) by hearing an announcement
    (d) by checking the message board

33. (a) attend a museum opening
    (b) view a special exhibit
    (c) visit a new art gallery
    (d) take a pottery class

You will hear a presentation by one person to a group of people. First you will hear questions 34 through 39. Then you will hear the talk. Choose the best answer to each question in the time provided.

34. (a) to share information about healthy eating
    (b) to promote a gardening festival
    (c) to provide tips for successful dieting
    (d) to support local farming projects

35. (a) how to adopt an active lifestyle
    (b) how to lose weight quickly
    (c) how to better one's physical health
    (d) how to protect the environment

36. (a) an opportunity to watch artists work
    (b) an opportunity to order custom footwear
    (c) a chance to make a leather bag
    (d) a chance to buy handcrafted shoes

37. (a) by highlighting its versatility
    (b) by highlighting its affordability
    (c) by showing that it is easy to cook
    (d) by showing that it is tasty

38. (a) They can sign up for a free giveaway.
    (b) They can apply to be an event judge.
    (c) They can take part in eating competitions.
    (d) They can participate in a cooking contest.

39. (a) to be entered into a contest
    (b) to receive an event T-shirt
    (c) to access additional discounts
    (d) to get them before they sell out

40. (a) He has researched publishing.
    (b) He is a well-known publisher.
    (c) He is working for a publisher.
    (d) He has published books before.

41. (a) She can experiment with narration.
    (b) She can create her own language.
    (c) She can try out various genres.
    (d) She can focus on darker themes.

42. (a) because of the marketing expenses
    (b) because of the printing costs
    (c) because of the equipment costs
    (d) because of the illustrator expenses

43. (a) by outlining her ideas first
    (b) by having a good editor
    (c) by getting tips from other writers
    (d) by writing multiple drafts

44. (a) getting repeatedly turned down
    (b) being misled by publishers
    (c) having to wait for feedback
    (d) losing her publishing rights

45. (a) hire a professional agent
    (b) launch her book on her own
    (c) seek funds for self-publication
    (d) pitch her book to publishers

You will hear an explanation of a process. First you will hear questions 46 through 52. Then you will hear the explanation. Choose the best answer to each question in the time provided.

46. (a) managing stress on a long trip
    (b) overcoming a fear of small spaces
    (c) entertaining oneself on a plane
    (d) handling anxiety about flying

47. (a) by choosing an aisle seat
    (b) by talking to others during takeoff
    (c) by lowering the window shade
    (d) by watching a film as a distraction

48. (a) to remind themselves that pilots are experts
    (b) to know what to do during turbulence
    (c) to understand that planes are reliable
    (d) to learn about emergency procedures

49. (a) to protect their ears from engine noises
    (b) to tune out loud conversations
    (c) to block worrisome mechanical sounds
    (d) to listen to guided meditations

50. (a) It eases his anxiety.
    (b) It keeps him from being bothered.
    (c) It takes his mind off work.
    (d) It helps him stay off social media.

51. (a) do some breathing exercises
    (b) avoid consuming too much food
    (c) take motion sickness medicine
    (d) refrain from drinking caffeine

52. (a) ask the flight staff for help
    (b) thank the pilot personally
    (c) be patient with the attendants
    (d) bring gifts for the cabin crew

THIS IS THE END OF THE LISTENING SECTION
DO NOT GO ON UNTIL TOLD TO DO SO

READING AND VOCABULARY SECTION

DIRECTIONS:

You will now read four different passages. Each passage is followed by comprehension and vocabulary questions. From the four choices for each item, choose the best answer. Then blacken in the correct circle on your answer sheet.

Read the following example passage and example question.

Example:

Bill Johnson lives in New York. He is 25 years old. He has four brothers and two sisters.

How many brothers does Bill Johnson have?

(a) one
(b) two
(c) three
(d) four

The correct answer is (d), so the circle with the letter (d) has been blackened.

NOW TURN THE PAGE AND BEGIN

TERRY PRATCHETT

Terry Pratchett was a critically acclaimed English author most famous for his humorous take on popular fantasy and science fiction plot lines. He was the United Kingdom's bestselling author of the '90s, and his best-known work is the science fiction series Discworld.

Terence David John Pratchett was born on April 28, 1948, in Buckinghamshire, England. At a young age, he was already a fan of science fiction and would often attend sci-fi fan conventions. He was also an avid writer, publishing many articles for his school newspaper. At thirteen, Pratchett published his first science fiction short story, "The Hades Business," in a school magazine.

After high school, Pratchett decided to work as a journalist for his local newspaper. There he met a publisher named Colin Smythe, who was intrigued when Pratchett mentioned that he was writing a science fiction novel. After reading the draft, Smythe praised the unique concept and agreed to publish it. *The Carpet People* was released in 1971 and was well received, marking the beginning of Pratchett's career as a novelist. He published two more novels shortly afterward, both of which received mostly positive reviews.

In 1983, Pratchett released the first book of the Discworld series, *The Colour of Magic*. Set on a disc-like planet being carried through space by four elephants and a giant turtle, the novel is an absurd fantasy comedy that made fun of common science fiction plot lines. Pratchett's humorous tone received considerable praise and became a trademark of the Discworld series. *The Colour of Magic* was later adapted into a television show, a video game, and a graphic novel.

Pratchett continued to write the Discworld series for the next three decades, with most of the books landing on the UK bestseller list. He also wrote several sci-fi novels for children. In 2007, he was diagnosed with Alzheimer's disease, which somewhat affected his reading and writing abilities. Nevertheless, he continued to write books and even accepted a teaching position at a university. Two years later, he was knighted by Queen Elizabeth II for his contributions to English literature.

Pratchett died on March 12, 2015, and his last Discworld novel was published later that year. Comprising forty-one novels, the series has sold more than 80 million copies worldwide. His works remain among the most popular fantasy novels.

53. What is Pratchett best known for?

(a) his comedic approach to common fictional storylines
(b) his status as the bestselling fantasy author of all time
(c) his literary contributions as a popular nonfiction novelist
(d) his direction of a groundbreaking sci-fi film series

54. Why, most likely, did Pratchett decide against continuing his education after high school?

(a) because his school grades were below average
(b) because he wanted to gain professional experience
(c) because he got a job offer from a national newspaper
(d) because his family was unable to support him financially

55. Why did Smythe agree to release Pratchett's first book?

(a) because Pratchett asked him to do so as a personal favor
(b) because he thought Pratchett's ideas were original
(c) because he and Pratchett had worked together as journalists
(d) because Pratchett agreed to add more novels to the series

56. Which of the following is NOT true about *The Colour of Magic*?

(a) that it features animals in the story
(b) that it established the series' tone
(c) that it is set in a fictional city on planet Earth
(d) that it inspired other forms of media

57. What was Pratchett's career like after his Alzheimer's diagnosis?

(a) He quit writing to become a university professor.
(b) He started writing books geared toward children.
(c) He was able to keep working on new projects.
(d) He accepted a position working for Queen Elizabeth II.

58. In the context of the passage, marking means _____.

(a) indicating
(b) recording
(c) accepting
(d) grading

59. In the context of the passage, comprising means _____.

(a) taking in
(b) including
(c) extending
(d) setting up

EXTREME INDOOR HEAT CAN REDUCE COGNITIVE PERFORMANCE

Heat waves—periods of extremely high temperatures during the summer season—are proven to have many harmful physical effects, such as heatstroke and dehydration. However, not much is known about the effects of high indoor temperatures on cognition. To find out more about how extreme heat can affect cognitive ability, researchers from the Harvard T.H. Chan School of Public Health tested a group of university students.

Cognitive abilities are skills required for completing mental tasks. The sharper one's cognitive abilities, the faster one can solve problems. For this study, the researchers tested the cognitive skills of twenty-four students who lived in a dormitory with central air conditioning and another twenty who lived in a dormitory without air conditioning. The study took place over twelve days, during which time the researchers placed devices in the students' rooms to record daily indoor temperatures.

For the first five days of the study, indoor temperatures in each building were average for the season. Then, a five-day heat wave occurred, followed by two days where the weather gradually cooled. For each day, the participants were required to take two cognitive tests on their smartphone, right after waking up. For the first test, the participants had to quickly and correctly identify the color of the displayed words to test their cognitive speed. The second test consisted of basic arithmetic problems to assess the students' working memory.

The researchers observed that during the heat wave, students who lived in the building without air conditioning performed about thirteen percent worse than their peers living in the air-conditioned building. The most significant difference came during the two-day period after the heat wave. In the air-conditioned building, temperatures somewhat decreased, but in the non-air-conditioned building, temperatures stayed relatively high. Even when the heat wave had passed, its effects could still be experienced indoors.

In their discussion of the study's findings, researchers stressed the importance of designing buildings with proper safeguards against extreme temperatures so that occupants can stay healthy and productive, even in hot weather.

60. Why did researchers perform the study?

 (a) to find out how heat affects students' moods
 (b) to establish a link between temperature and mental health
 (c) to explore a correlation between heat waves and motivation
 (d) to test the impact of extreme heat on brain function

61. What is true about the participants in the study?

 (a) They lived on the same floor of a dormitory.
 (b) They completed tasks for almost two weeks.
 (c) They were equally divided into two groups.
 (d) They came from many different age groups.

62. What were participants tested on to measure their cognitive speed?

 (a) their skill at identifying a word's meaning
 (b) their skill at spelling color names correctly
 (c) their ability to quickly solve basic math problems
 (d) their ability to rapidly choose the correct color of a word

63. What probably happened to the students' cognitive performance right after the heat wave subsided?

 (a) Both groups showed signs of improvement.
 (b) Students without air conditioning still did worse.
 (c) Students with air conditioning fell behind slightly.
 (d) Neither group showed any significant change.

64. Based on the final paragraph, how might building designers contribute to improving health and productivity?

 (a) by engineering a new cooling device
 (b) by paying special attention to temperature control
 (c) by checking in regularly with residents
 (d) by evaluating recent weather patterns

65. In the context of the passage, observed means _____.

 (a) noticed
 (b) guaranteed
 (c) repeated
 (d) confessed

66. In the context of the passage, stressed means _____.

 (a) featured
 (b) listed
 (c) emphasized
 (d) enlarged

BOROBUDUR TEMPLE

The Borobudur Temple is located in central Java, Indonesia. It is known as the largest Buddhist temple in the world, covering an area of 27,125 square feet and reaching nearly 115 feet in height.

There are no precise records of Borobudur's construction, but most historians estimate that it occurred sometime during the eighth or ninth century. The temple was initially a site for Buddhist pilgrimage and rituals, but it was abandoned for nearly 400 years, beginning around the time Islam became the dominant religion in Indonesia. In 1814, the temple was rediscovered by British explorers. However, it was almost completely hidden by ash from a nearby volcano and needed major rebuilding.

In 1907, a team began restoring the temple but ran into several costly architectural problems and had to contend with artifacts being frequently stolen from the site. The project was <u>suspended</u>, and it was only in 1983 that a second restoration project was completed, with the help of monetary donations from five other countries.

The temple was rebuilt with many of its original stones. It is shaped like a pyramid and contains several levels: a square base with five square terraces and three circular platforms, all stacked on top of each other. There is a large, dome-shaped structure at the top called a "stupa," a Buddhist place of burial that typically contains religious objects.

Each level of the temple represents a step on the journey to enlightenment. The lowest level features carved depictions of human desires, while the next few levels show the life of Buddha and Buddhist writings. Farther up, the circular platforms have several smaller stupas, many with a hidden Buddha statue still inside. The lack of decoration in the upper levels signifies detachment from the material world.

Visitors can go through each of the nine levels, starting at the bottom and gradually walking clockwise around the monument to the last stupa at the highest level, which represents enlightenment. Today, the Borobudur Temple is once again a popular site of pilgrimage. It <u>holds</u> cultural and religious significance and is recognized by UNESCO as a World Heritage Site.

67. What is most significant about the Borobudur Temple?

(a) its status as a sizeable religious monument
(b) its standing as the oldest temple in the world
(c) its history of mysterious construction
(d) its ranking as the world's most beautiful temple

68. Why, most likely, was the Borobudur Temple abandoned?

(a) because its primary caregiver passed away
(b) because religious practices became forbidden
(c) because its visitors converted to a different faith
(d) because a volcanic eruption led to evacuations

69. Why, most likely, was the initial restoration project discontinued?

(a) It made the construction team vulnerable to injury.
(b) It made the site vulnerable to severe weather.
(c) The damage was too severe to fix.
(d) The damage was too costly to fix.

70. What CANNOT be found at the temple?

(a) carvings illustrating human desires
(b) images representing religious scenes
(c) figures inside domed structures
(d) texts praising benefits of the physical world

71. How does the temple embody the Buddhist concept of movement toward spiritual insight?

(a) by having visitors progress upward
(b) by welcoming visitors with a message of inclusion
(c) by guiding visitors in a circular path
(d) by leading visitors deeper into the monument

72. In the context of the passage, suspended means _____.

(a) hung
(b) paused
(c) punished
(d) born

73. In the context of the passage, holds means _____.

(a) conducts
(b) finds
(c) takes
(d) carries

Leia Summerhold
Funding Manager
American Literary Research Society
728 Oak Lawn
Cook County, IL

Dear Ms. Summerhold:

I am an American Studies PhD student specializing in American literature, art, and culture at Longmore University. I am writing this letter to apply for a one-time research grant of $5,000 for my dissertation. My research is titled "Working-Class Narratives in American Music."

My research is about how the American working class influences certain pieces of music. From rhythmic folk songs to more radical modern anthems, music has historically been a valuable reflection of workers' lives. My dissertation aims to examine how certain songs can be used to trace the experiences of the working class to as far back as the late 1800s.

I believe my dissertation is in line with your institution's mission to document and expand understanding of different American literary movements. Throughout history, music has been closely linked to poetry, in particular. Given that strong connection between literature and music, my dissertation will allow for greater understanding of the role of the working class in the evolution of both types of art over the years.

Many of the resources related to my research are unavailable through online databases and require paid access. With the help of your grant, I would be able to research the history of music in working-class communities more thoroughly. I have attached my complete research proposal to this letter, which includes details about the methods I will use and the resources I would like to access. I hope that you will consider my application, and I eagerly await your response.

Sincerely,

Mike Graves

Mike Graves

74. Why is Mike Graves writing a letter to Leia Summerhold?

(a) to apply for admission to a doctoral program
(b) to submit his dissertation for approval
(c) to ask for necessary research materials
(d) to request financial support for a project

75. What is the aim of Mike's research?

(a) to compare different American music genres
(b) to explore the way music is affected by society
(c) to investigate the effects of playing music while working
(d) to trace the origins of American folk music

76. How is Mike's research objective related to the American Literary Research Society's goal?

(a) Both encourage better understanding of an art form.
(b) Both emphasize the impact of literature on music.
(c) Both honor the contributions of workers to the performing arts.
(d) Both focus on analyzing modern music.

77. According to the letter, why, most likely, does Mike need funding?

(a) so he can view some important resources
(b) so he can visit working-class communities
(c) so he can afford to hire a research assistant
(d) so he can publish his findings independently

78. What did Mike attach to the letter?

(a) a proposal for a second research study
(b) a detailed overview of his research plan
(c) a copy of his completed dissertation
(d) a list of resources he has already consulted

79. In the context of the passage, trace means _____.

(a) find
(b) chase
(c) follow
(d) draw

80. In the context of the passage, connection means _____.

(a) limit
(b) balance
(c) agreement
(d) relationship

지텔프 공식 기출문제집 7회분 Level 2

THIS IS THE END OF THE TEST

지텔프 공식 기출문제집
7회분 Level 2

TEST 5

GRAMMAR

LISTENING

READING & VOCABULARY

테스트 전 확인사항

1. OMR 답안지를 준비하셨나요? ☐
2. 컴퓨터용 사인펜, 수정 테이프를 준비하셨나요? ☐
3. 음성을 들을 준비를 하셨나요? ☐

TEST 5 음성 바로 듣기

🎧 **TEST 5.mp3**

해커스인강(HackersIngang.com)에서 무료 다운로드
상단 메뉴 [G-TELP → MP3/자료 → 문제풀이 MP3]

자동 채점 및 성적 분석
서비스 바로 이용하기

📋 **자동 채점 및 성적 분석 서비스**

∨ 타이머, 모바일 OMR, 자동 채점
∨ 정답률 및 취약 유형 분석

시험 시간 : 90분

목표 점수 : _____점
시작 시간 : _____시 _____분 ~ 종료 시간 : _____시 _____분

General Tests of English Language Proficiency
G-TELP

Level 2

GRAMMAR SECTION

DIRECTIONS:

The following items need a word or words to complete the sentence. From the four choices for each item, choose the best answer. Then blacken in the correct circle on your answer sheet.

Example:

The boys _____ in the car.

(a) be

(b) is

(c) am

(d) are

The correct answer is (d), so the circle with the letter (d) has been blackened.

ⓐ ⓑ ⓒ ●

NOW TURN THE PAGE AND BEGIN

1. Power outages can result from calamities such as thunderstorms and even car crashes. But amusingly, squirrels, _____, are behind many outages in the US, even outnumbering those caused by storms.

   (a) who are fond of climbing electric posts
   (b) which are fond of climbing electric posts
   (c) what are fond of climbing electric posts
   (d) that are fond of climbing electric posts

2. Harriet's dentist says that wisdom tooth extraction can cause pain and soreness for several days after the procedure. He says that it will be best _____ only soft foods after the minor surgery.

   (a) having consumed
   (b) to consume
   (c) consuming
   (d) to have consumed

3. Professor Wiley saw Chelsea texting six times during his lecture. He became so frustrated when he caught her for the seventh time that he demanded she _____ her phone on his desk until class ended.

   (a) leave
   (b) will leave
   (c) left
   (d) had left

4. Contrary to popular belief, the color red doesn't make the bulls used in bullfighting angry; bulls are actually colorblind. Rather, they can't resist _____ the matador's cape because of its waving motion.

   (a) having attacked
   (b) to have attacked
   (c) to attack
   (d) attacking

5. When Carl goes on vacation next week, he will be traveling by boat rather than by plane, even though boats are much slower. If he were not afraid of heights, Carl _____ by plane instead.

   (a) would have traveled
   (b) will travel
   (c) would travel
   (d) will have traveled

6. Jennifer fell asleep on the couch in the middle of the afternoon. She _____ when a moderately strong earthquake started, and she woke up to find that all the books on her shelves were shaking.

   (a) would nap
   (b) had napped
   (c) has been napping
   (d) was napping

7. Poaching has grown so severe in Africa that elephants may be adapting to the situation. Some researchers believe that African elephants _____ to be tuskless since the 1990s to give themselves a better chance of survival.

   (a) will have evolved
   (b) are evolving
   (c) had been evolving
   (d) have been evolving

8. While Gary was swimming, he developed a muscle cramp in his thigh and began sinking into the pool. Fortunately, a lifeguard noticed and rescued him. If it had not been for that lifeguard, Gary _____.

   (a) will drown
   (b) could drown
   (c) could have drowned
   (d) will have drowned

9. The blue whale is the largest animal ever to have lived. There are reports of individuals up to thirty-three meters in length, and the blue whale's tongue _____ weigh as much as an elephant.

   (a) should
   (b) must
   (c) can
   (d) will

10. The oldest computer virus, called Creeper, was created as an experiment to prove that it was possible to make self-replicating applications. _____ modern computer viruses are harmful, Creeper never actually damaged any computers.

    (a) Although
    (b) Because
    (c) In case
    (d) Unless

11. In Longyearbyen, Norway, the climate is so cold that conditions are impractical for burial. That's why locals who pass away are sent _____ in cemeteries on the mainland.

    (a) having been buried
    (b) to be buried
    (c) to have been buried
    (d) being buried

12. In addition to being a rich source of potassium, bananas provide much of the vitamin B6 and fiber we need in our diets. So, people who enjoy _____ bananas receive many health benefits.

    (a) to have eaten
    (b) to eat
    (c) having eaten
    (d) eating

13. After months of hesitation, Eugene finally asked his officemate Sherry out for dinner. He finishes before her today, but he _____ for her by the building's entrance when her work shift ends at 7:30 p.m.

(a) waits
(b) would wait
(c) will be waiting
(d) was waiting

14. The theme of nature reclaiming Earth's cities is prevalent in apocalyptic science fiction. According to the book *The World Without Us*, if humans were to disappear, vegetation _____ manmade structures as plants re-establish their dominance.

(a) would replace
(b) will replace
(c) will have replaced
(d) would have replaced

15. The commercially successful cellphone game *Flappy Bird* was once criticized for some of its unoriginal features. _____, the game was rumored to have been taken down because of plagiarism. That accusation was later proven false.

(a) Meanwhile
(b) However
(c) In fact
(d) In other words

16. Samantha fully understands the responsibilities outlined in her new contract. The only detail _____ is how many weeks of paid vacation she will be entitled to each year.

(a) where is still unclear
(b) that is still unclear
(c) who is still unclear
(d) what is still unclear

17. When Steve Irwin died from a stingray attack in 2006, shock could be felt around the globe. The seemingly fearless zookeeper, known as "The Crocodile Hunter," _____ exotic animals since 1992.

(a) had been documenting
(b) documented
(c) has been documenting
(d) would document

18. Wallace's Alehouse burned down last night. Wallace's girlfriend, who just returned from a trip, is coming to stay with him. If it weren't for her support, he _____ difficulty handling his grief in the days ahead.

(a) would have
(b) will have
(c) will have had
(d) would have had

19. Due to insomnia, Nathaniel hasn't been able to sleep since going to bed around 11 p.m. If he remains awake for thirty more minutes, he _____ unsuccessfully to sleep for almost three hours.

(a) had tried
(b) will have been trying
(c) has been trying
(d) will be trying

20. In 2007, PepsiCo showed responsibility in practicing "corporate citizenship." When an ex-employee of Coca-Cola offered _____ confidential documents to PepsiCo, they notified their rival company, which led to an FBI investigation and the suspect's arrest.

(a) having sold
(b) to sell
(c) selling
(d) to have sold

21. Margaret has been allergic to peanut butter since she was a baby. If she were to try eating it today as an adult, the same rash _____ again. This time, it might even be worse.

(a) will probably have occurred
(b) would probably occur
(c) will probably occur
(d) would probably have occurred

22. When having guests over, Mrs. Rogers's priority is to make the visitors feel at home. She lets her guests know that they _____ help themselves to any of the snacks they find in her kitchen.

(a) shall
(b) will
(c) must
(d) may

23. Eleanor has just come out of a five-year relationship and has been feeling down lately. Her best friend advises that she _____ a new hobby so she can keep her mind off the breakup.

(a) will find
(b) found
(c) has found
(d) find

24. The earliest record players, called phonographs, did not need electricity in order to play music. Operation of the machine involved _____ a crank until the motor had enough power to keep the turntable spinning.

(a) turning
(b) to turn
(c) having turned
(d) to have turned

지텔프 공식 기출문제집 7회분 Level 2

25. Tess will be late for her friend's wedding procession because the car broke down on the way to the church. Her husband _____ their car, and they'll try to catch up before the exchange of vows.

   (a) now fixed
   (b) was now fixing
   (c) is now fixing
   (d) would now fix

26. Political writer Jose Rizal was instrumental in hastening the Philippines' independence from Spanish rule. If it hadn't been for Rizal's patriotic writings, the Filipinos _____ against their colonizers in the 1890s.

   (a) would not revolt
   (b) will not revolt
   (c) will not have revolted
   (d) would not have revolted

THIS IS THE END OF THE GRAMMAR SECTION
DO NOT GO ON UNTIL TOLD TO DO SO

LISTENING SECTION

TEST 1

TEST 2

TEST 3

TEST 4

TEST 5

TEST 6

TEST 7

지텔프 공식 기출문제집 7회분 Level 2

DIRECTIONS:

The Listening Section has four parts. In each part you will hear a spoken passage and a number of questions about the passage. First you will hear the questions. Then you will hear the passage. From the four choices for each question, choose the best answer. Then blacken in the correct circle on your answer sheet.

Now you will hear an example question. Then you will hear an example passage.

Now listen to the example question.

> (a) one
> (b) two
> (c) three
> (d) four

Bill Johnson has four brothers, so the best answer is (d). The circle with the letter (d) has been blackened.

NOW TURN THE PAGE AND BEGIN

27. (a) because they both work for the same company
    (b) because their work schedules are flexible
    (c) because their workplaces are near each other
    (d) because they are clients of the same company

28. (a) that he was returning to college
    (b) that he just ended a relationship
    (c) that he was enjoying his work
    (d) that he found his girlfriend a job

29. (a) to tell her about a friend's special occasion
    (b) to congratulate her for getting engaged
    (c) to ask her advice about wedding decorations
    (d) to invite her to a party he is planning

30. (a) that they owned the same T-shirt
    (b) that they had the same friends
    (c) that they loved the same movie
    (d) that they liked the same series

31. (a) by dancing with her at a party
    (b) by accepting the help of his friend
    (c) by serving her at his coffee shop
    (d) by running into her at the park

32. (a) He seemed confused.
    (b) He felt uncomfortable.
    (c) He started laughing.
    (d) He became furious.

33. (a) order some food for lunch
    (b) go to a college reunion
    (c) return to his workplace
    (d) attend his friend's wedding

34. (a) introducing a device for cycling
    (b) promoting a smart bicycle
    (c) announcing a bicycle race
    (d) launching a company for cyclists

35. (a) by giving them voice prompts
    (b) by suggesting multiple routes
    (c) by showing the turns on a map
    (d) by finding the most scenic route

36. (a) when someone tries to remove the lock
    (b) when the owner walks away too quickly
    (c) when the owner is far from the moving bike
    (d) when someone gets too close to the bike

37. (a) ask for help from the authorities
    (b) download a special locator app
    (c) activate an alarm on the phone
    (d) use the map in the application

38. (a) It suggests ways to burn more calories.
    (b) It sends the rider reminders to exercise.
    (c) It records the rider's weight changes.
    (d) It measures the rider's activity levels.

39. (a) purchase a lighting accessory
    (b) subscribe to paid content
    (c) visit a nearby store location
    (d) agree to receive news updates

40. (a) because she takes care of cats
    (b) because she is working at a cat shelter
    (c) because she recently adopted a cat
    (d) because she is considering getting cats

41. (a) the way they sleep
    (b) the way they fit in one hand
    (c) the way they look
    (d) the way they play together

42. (a) by hiding plants away from it
    (b) by keeping a close eye on it
    (c) by getting fake plants for it
    (d) by spraying a scent on the plants

43. (a) They tend to be overly aggressive.
    (b) They are less popular than kittens.
    (c) They are less friendly than kittens.
    (d) They tend to hide from strangers.

44. (a) spending extra money on its care
    (b) teaching it to break bad habits
    (c) having it for such a short time
    (d) trying to keep it more active

45. (a) choose a kitten as a pet
    (b) purchase some new houseplants
    (c) adopt a more mature cat
    (d) convince his wife to get a dog

46. (a) how to balance work and school
    (b) how to prevent exam stress
    (c) how to study effectively in college
    (d) how to find a job on campus

47. (a) by hiring students with the fewest courses
    (b) by working around student availability
    (c) by advising students about their class schedules
    (d) by letting students study during work hours

48. (a) catch up on social media
    (b) relax and text with friends
    (c) take care of personal errands
    (d) go over class materials

49. (a) so their work does not interfere with their studies
    (b) so they can do their job without distractions
    (c) so their study time is always on weekends
    (d) so they can avoid working overtime

50. (a) to work more hours
    (b) to socialize more often
    (c) to get more sleep
    (d) to do more reading

51. (a) It introduces them to support groups.
    (b) It provides them with job opportunities.
    (c) It forces them to get out more.
    (d) It helps them release stress.

52. (a) talk to management
    (b) give up the job
    (c) take fewer classes
    (d) speak with professors

THIS IS THE END OF THE LISTENING SECTION
DO NOT GO ON UNTIL TOLD TO DO SO

READING AND VOCABULARY SECTION

DIRECTIONS:

You will now read four different passages. Each passage is followed by comprehension and vocabulary questions. From the four choices for each item, choose the best answer. Then blacken in the correct circle on your answer sheet.

Read the following example passage and example question.

Example:

Bill Johnson lives in New York. He is 25 years old. He has four brothers and two sisters.

How many brothers does Bill Johnson have?

(a) one
(b) two
(c) three
(d) four

The correct answer is (d), so the circle with the letter (d) has been blackened.

NOW TURN THE PAGE AND BEGIN

BESSIE COLEMAN

Bessie Coleman was an aviator best known for being the first African American woman to hold a pilot's license. Having succeeded to do so in the 1920s, Coleman inspired other women, as well as African Americans in general, to pursue careers in aviation, despite the limited opportunities for minorities at the time.

Bessie Coleman was born on January 26, 1892, in Atlanta, Texas. Her mother was a housekeeper, and her father was a poor tenant farmer. As a child, Coleman helped her mother harvest cotton in the fields and do laundry to save money for college. Coleman was able to study at a "colored" university but, due to financial difficulties, did not complete her education.

In 1915, Coleman was working in Chicago as a beautician when she heard stories of French women serving as aircraft pilots during the First World War. Her brother teased her about French women being able to do something that she could not, and Coleman, who had always been ambitious, took the joke as a challenge. She developed an interest in flying and attempted to enroll at aviation schools. However, no school would accept her because at the time, working in American aviation was only open to white men.

Coleman's friend Robert Abbott, a newspaper publisher, advised her to go to France, where aviation schools were more integrated. After studying French, she moved to France in 1920 and was accepted at the Caudron Brothers' School of Aviation in Le Crotoy. She received her pilot's license in 1921. Coleman's achievements attracted worldwide interest, and her return to the US was met by a great deal of press coverage.

Coleman performed remarkable feats in air shows and became a celebrity in early aviation exhibitions, earning the nickname "Brave Bess." She wanted to make enough money to open an aviation school for women and African Americans. Having worked so hard to overcome discrimination, she refused to appear in shows that reinforced racist beliefs, such as barring black audiences from using the same entrance white people used.

During a test flight for an air show in 1926, Coleman was killed when her plane spun out of control due to a mechanical failure. Her dream of building an aviation school was realized, however, when her fellow pilots founded the Bessie Coleman Aero Club in 1929. Her many accolades include being inducted into the National Aviation Hall of Fame.

53. What is Bessie Coleman most known for?

(a) being the first African American aviator
(b) being the first woman to earn a pilot's license
(c) being the first female African American pilot
(d) being the first advocate for racial equality

54. Why did Coleman decide to start applying to flight schools?

(a) to prove that her brother was wrong
(b) to be like the French women she admired
(c) to get away from her hometown of Chicago
(d) to overcome her lifelong fear of heights

55. How was Coleman able to obtain her pilot's license?

(a) by writing to the aviation board
(b) by asking a friend to train her
(c) by studying in a different country
(d) by taking a special examination

56. Why, most likely, did Coleman earn the nickname "Brave Bess"?

(a) because she performed dangerous stunts
(b) because she fought against discrimination
(c) because she refused to work without equal pay
(d) because she fought hard to open a school

57. What role did the Aero Club play in Coleman's story?

(a) It donated a plane while hers was being repaired.
(b) It provided training for her fellow pilots.
(c) It funded a scholarship in her name.
(d) It was established by friends after her death.

58. In the context of the passage, harvest means _____.

(a) save
(b) make
(c) lose
(d) pick

59. In the context of the passage, reinforced means _____.

(a) managed
(b) supported
(c) stretched
(d) guarded

PART 2. Read the following magazine article and answer the questions. The underlined words in the article are for vocabulary questions.

"RICKROLLING": THE INTERNET JOKE THAT BECAME A CULTURAL PHENOMENON

"Rickrolling" is an Internet meme that involves tricking someone into watching a video of the 1987 hit song "Never Gonna Give You Up" by Rick Astley. The trend started as an Internet prank in which people were tricked into clicking the video's link, which was disguised as an interesting—but different—hyperlink.

The first well-known appearance of the prank came in 2007 when a user from the forum website 4chan posted a link of what was claimed to be a trailer for *Grand Theft Auto IV*, a much-anticipated video game. When clicked, however, the link brought people to a music video of "Never Gonna Give You Up" instead. While some people were dismayed, most took the joke lightheartedly. The prank was given the name "rickrolling," with "rick" taken from Rick Astley's name. It then became trendy among the site users to rickroll more people, and the practice spread throughout the US.

Outside the Internet, people sought other ways to rickroll: stadiums suddenly played the song during sports events, a flash mob sang the song at a train station, and students rickrolled during class presentations. Rickrolling even made its way into politics. During an Oregon House of Representatives session, members snuck snippets of the song's lyrics into their speeches. While the lawmakers secretly had a little fun, their joke did not affect legislation, and their proposed laws were ultimately <u>passed</u>. An edited video of the speeches was later released for April Fools' Day.

The most frequently used Internet upload of the music video has been removed twice for terms-of-use violations: once in 2010 and again in 2014. It has since been unblocked and has gained over one billion views. Rickrolling continues to be relevant today, mostly appearing on social media and at gatherings. The catchy lyrics and classic '80s vibe of the song used, as well as its retro music video make it ideal for pranks.

When Astley himself was asked about his thoughts regarding rickrolling, he replied that he found it hilarious and <u>recognized</u> it as a harmless way for people to have fun. Astley even thanked 4chan's founder for the rickrolling phenomenon.

60. What is mainly being discussed in the article?

   (a) how an online practical joke became widespread
   (b) how a popular country song was revived
   (c) how using memes can bring people together
   (d) how harmless pranks influence people's lives

61. How did the first rickrollers entice people to click the link to Rick Astley's music video?

   (a) by claiming it would show them a car ad
   (b) by suggesting it would lead to a movie trailer
   (c) by saying it was about a popular game
   (d) by insisting it was an important message

62. Which of the following is NOT an example of how rickrolling was done outside the Internet?

   (a) people performing the song in a train station
   (b) politicians using the song in their campaign ads
   (c) students playing the song while presenting in school
   (d) lawmakers using the song's words in their address

63. Why, most likely, was the original Astley video taken down?

   (a) because the prank offended many people
   (b) because the video had been used without permission
   (c) because the entertainment company had closed
   (d) because the singer claimed copyright violations

64. Why might audiences still feel drawn to the song "Never Gonna Give You Up"?

   (a) People think the song is charmingly outdated.
   (b) The music video shows people getting pranked.
   (c) People think it carries a positive message.
   (d) The original artist still performs it regularly.

65. In the context of the passage, passed means _____.

   (a) saved
   (b) offered
   (c) ignored
   (d) approved

66. In the context of the passage, recognized means _____.

   (a) tolerated
   (b) noticed
   (c) accepted
   (d) signaled

PART 3. Read the following encyclopedia article and answer the questions. The underlined words in the article are for vocabulary questions.

PASSENGER PIGEON

The passenger pigeon is an extinct species of pigeon native to and once abundant in North America. Because of the birds' extremely dense population, they had been reported to blacken the skies when they flew in flocks. The pigeons went extinct in 1914.

Passenger pigeons were medium-sized birds, measuring about 15 to 16 inches in length and weighing about 9 to 12 ounces. The male had blue-gray feathers on its body and red on its breast, while the female had a brownish body, gray breast, and white belly. The bird was notable for being compact and streamlined for prolonged flight.

A unique trait of passenger pigeons was the way they congregated in order to breed. A colony of birds could cover hundreds of thousands of acres and have hundreds of nests per tree. One nesting site in Wisconsin was estimated to have about 136 million birds. Passenger pigeons may have numbered up to five billion at the height of their population. When searching for food, the pigeons were observed to fly by the millions, blotting out the sky and darkening it.

While many animals preyed on the pigeons, humans were the main <u>culprit</u> of the birds' extinction. Forests were cut down for farmlands, an act that destroyed the pigeons' home and primary food source. Mass hunting of the birds began in the 1800s. Farmers considered the birds to be pests and gunned them down to protect the grain fields. Pigeon meat was also sold for a cheap price.

The passenger pigeons' numbers were noticeably decreasing by the 1860s. When a bill was finally introduced in the Michigan legislature for a ten-year halt to hunting, it was too late to save the pigeons. The once-plentiful birds were now mostly living as individual survivors in the wild or in captivity. The remaining pigeons were not enough to repopulate the species.

On September 1, 1914, the last living passenger pigeon, Martha, died in the Cincinnati Zoo, <u>stirring</u> public concern for the conservation of animals. Since 2012, attempts have been made to revive the species. A wildlife conservation group called Revive and Restore hopes to use genetic cloning to return the passenger pigeon to the forests and fields of North America.

67. According to the text, what was noteworthy about passenger pigeons?

    (a) their ability to travel for extended periods
    (b) their unusual flock shape when flying
    (c) their tendency to migrate away from populated areas
    (d) their ability to fly at record-breaking speeds

68. Which of the following was NOT true about passenger pigeons before their population declined?

    (a) Their females formed small groups for breeding.
    (b) Their habitat was spread across wide areas.
    (c) Their population peaked at billions of birds.
    (d) Their flocks blocked sunlight when flying.

69. Why, most likely, did the pigeons become hunted?

    (a) because they were taking over the forests
    (b) because they were the main source of income for farmers
    (c) because they were feeding on valuable crops
    (d) because they attracted many other pests

70. Why was the law that outlawed pigeon hunting unable to save the species?

    (a) The period it covered was too short.
    (b) The birds were already too few in number.
    (c) The last of their kind had already been captured.
    (d) The majority of hunters refused to cooperate.

71. How have conservation groups been trying to bring back the species?

    (a) by rebuilding the pigeons' former habitat
    (b) by offering a reward for remaining specimens
    (c) by trying to breed the last two remaining birds
    (d) by carrying out experimental procedures

72. In the context of the passage, culprit means _____.

    (a) excuse
    (b) proof
    (c) solution
    (d) cause

73. In the context of the passage, stirring means _____.

    (a) touching
    (b) raising
    (c) beating
    (d) mixing

Jessica Florence
HR Representative
Justice Resource, Inc.
45 Oak Street
New York City, NY

Dear Ms. Florence,

I was scheduled for a job interview last Monday but was unable to attend due to an unforeseen event. I have already spoken with you about this matter, and I am now writing this letter to formally apologize and explain the situation behind my absence.

On the day of our interview, I received a call from my son's elementary school informing me that he was sick and had been admitted to the school's clinic. He needed to be fetched urgently, and since my wife is currently out of the country, I had no choice but to cancel our interview.

We went to see a doctor, who said my son was suffering from food poisoning. (I suspect the cause to be the school's drinking fountain, as my son asserted that the water "tasted funny.") In any case, my son's health is much better now. He knows that I missed my interview and feels guilty, and he even offered to somehow "fix" the situation, but I explained to him that family comes first. He will always be my top priority, and I hope that any potential employer can understand and perhaps even respect that sense of duty as a sign of good character.

I want to assure you that I take work-related responsibilities seriously, and I would never break a professional commitment without a pressing reason. I apologize for missing the interview. I would like to request another chance to prove my value to your team at Justice Resource, Inc.

Attached to this letter is a record of my son's medical visit. Thank you for your understanding.

Sincerely,

Brandon Smith
Brandon Smith

74. What is the purpose of Brandon Smith's letter?

(a) to request feedback on his job interview
(b) to apologize for his absence at a client meeting
(c) to establish why he cannot attend employee training
(d) to explain why he missed an appointment

75. Why did Brandon have to cancel his plans?

(a) His international flight was delayed.
(b) He was the only one able to handle the emergency.
(c) He needed to take care of his wife who was ill.
(d) His son's school needed to close suddenly.

76. How did Brandon's son probably get sick?

(a) from problems with the school's water supply
(b) from someone in his class who was running a fever
(c) from outdated food served in the school's lunchroom
(d) from an allergy to an item packed in his lunch

77. Why, most likely, does Brandon explain to Jessica that family is the most important thing in his life?

(a) so she can see that he maintains a happy household
(b) so she understands that he can only work limited hours
(c) so she will assign him fewer duties as an employee
(d) so she will admire his loyalty as a potential worker

78. Why does Brandon think he deserves another chance for an interview?

(a) because he openly admitted his mistake
(b) because he is ordinarily more reliable
(c) because he demonstrated his value to the company
(d) because he has never missed an interview before

79. In the context of the passage, unforeseen means _____.

(a) unexpected
(b) unlikely
(c) unpopular
(d) unsafe

80. In the context of the passage, assure means _____.

(a) teach
(b) concern
(c) ask
(d) promise

THIS IS THE END OF THE TEST

지텔프 공식 기출문제집
7회분 Level 2

TEST 6

GRAMMAR

LISTENING

READING & VOCABULARY

테스트 전 확인사항

1. OMR 답안지를 준비하셨나요? ☐
2. 컴퓨터용 사인펜, 수정 테이프를 준비하셨나요? ☐
3. 음성을 들을 준비를 하셨나요? ☐

TEST 6 음성 바로 듣기

🎧 **TEST 6.mp3**

해커스인강(HackersIngang.com)에서 무료 다운로드
상단 메뉴 [G-TELP → MP3/자료 → 문제풀이 MP3]

**자동 채점 및 성적 분석
서비스 바로 이용하기**

📑 **자동 채점 및 성적 분석 서비스**

ⅴ 타이머, 모바일 OMR, 자동 채점
ⅴ 정답률 및 취약 유형 분석

시험 시간 : 90분

목표 점수 : _____점

시작 시간 : _____시 _____분 ~ 종료 시간 : _____시 _____분

General Tests of English Language Proficiency
G-TELP

Level 2

GRAMMAR SECTION

DIRECTIONS:

The following items need a word or words to complete the sentence. From the four choices for each item, choose the best answer. Then blacken in the correct circle on your answer sheet.

Example:

The boys _____ in the car.

(a) be
(b) is
(c) am
(d) are

The correct answer is (d), so the circle with the letter (d) has been blackened.

NOW TURN THE PAGE AND BEGIN

1. Research shows that many adults are still afraid of the dark. Among those who admit to having the fear, however, nearly 70% said they dislike _____ the issue to others.

   (a) mentioning
   (b) to mention
   (c) having mentioned
   (d) to have mentioned

2. After a grueling admissions process, Lea was finally accepted into a prestigious arts school in the United Kingdom. Starting this semester, she _____ in London with a relative while she goes to school.

   (a) stayed
   (b) has been staying
   (c) will be staying
   (d) will have stayed

3. My brothers are arguing with each other over who should retrieve the ball that got kicked into the yard of the abandoned house next door. The house, _____, is believed by local kids to be haunted.

   (a) that has been vacant for years
   (b) which has been vacant for years
   (c) who has been vacant for years
   (d) what has been vacant for years

4. The hiring manager rejected a job candidate this morning saying, "He had impressive qualifications, but he couldn't recall anything about our mission. If he had researched our company, he _____ the job on the spot."

   (a) would get
   (b) will have gotten
   (c) will get
   (d) would have gotten

5. Movie previews are called "trailers" because they were originally shown after the movie, not before. _____, this proved rather ineffective, as the audience did not stay around after the film to watch them.

   (a) However
   (b) In particular
   (c) In addition
   (d) Meanwhile

6. Patrick is not even halfway through his flight, yet he has been in the air since his 6 a.m. departure from Chicago. By the time he reaches Melbourne tomorrow, he _____ for sixteen hours!

   (a) would fly
   (b) will have been flying
   (c) will be flying
   (d) has been flying

7. Clyde is organizing the company's annual talent competition, which is set for three months from now. To ensure smooth planning for the event, he is encouraging interested performers _____ their applications on time.

(a) to have submitted
(b) submitting
(c) to submit
(d) having submitted

8. Despite being a highly paid software developer at a multinational company, Sheila still dreams of quitting her job someday. In fact, if money were no longer a factor, she _____ a full-time illustrator of children's books.

(a) will have become
(b) will become
(c) would become
(d) would have become

9. While visiting the set of *Game of Thrones*, Queen Elizabeth II declined to sit on the Iron Throne. The queen, _____ to not sit on a foreign throne, refused to even sit on a fictional one.

(a) that may have been following a royal rule
(b) which may have been following a royal rule
(c) what may have been following a royal rule
(d) who may have been following a royal rule

10. Globally, there is a growing initiative to plant more trees. Some countries even put tree planting into their legislation. In the Philippines, for instance, all students _____ plant at least ten trees before they can graduate.

(a) must
(b) would
(c) might
(d) can

11. Richard's prized collection of vintage baseball cards was stolen from his house last night. According to him, nobody was home, as he _____ when the robbery took place.

(a) was grocery shopping
(b) grocery shopped
(c) is grocery shopping
(d) has grocery shopped

12. During the Great Plague, people had little understanding of how the disease spread. Even so, business owners who did not want to risk _____ the plague asked customers to clean coins in vinegar before paying.

(a) having contracted
(b) to contract
(c) to have contracted
(d) contracting

13. The Great Red Spot is the most
    noticeable feature on the planet Jupiter.
    The reddish dot is actually a giant storm
    that _____ on Jupiter's surface for
    at least 150 years.

    (a) had been raging
    (b) raged
    (c) is raging
    (d) has been raging

14. Carla is finding it easy to get back into
    her exercise routine, even after a two-
    week break. Before that, she somewhat
    struggled to hold a two-minute plank.
    Now, surprisingly, she _____ do it
    with relative ease.

    (a) should
    (b) would
    (c) can
    (d) might

15. During Daryl's birthday dinner, two of
    his friends started arguing loudly in the
    restaurant. It got so bad that the manager
    demanded that the friends _____
    the restaurant immediately.

    (a) leave
    (b) were leaving
    (c) will leave
    (d) left

16. My brother was under some stress at
    work, so I suggested watercolor painting
    as a way to help him relax. He had
    anticipated _____ the hobby, but he
    was surprised by how soothing it actually
    was.

    (a) to have enjoyed
    (b) enjoying
    (c) to enjoy
    (d) having enjoyed

17. In 1979, Elvita Adams jumped from the
    86th floor of the Empire State Building
    and survived. If she had not been blown
    by a gust of wind, she _____ instead
    of landing on the 85th floor.

    (a) will likely have perished
    (b) would likely perish
    (c) would likely have perished
    (d) will likely perish

18. Last week, a designer outlet store
    announced that it was having a big sale
    the next day. _____, hundreds of
    eager shoppers lined up outside the store
    before it opened. The lines stretched for
    two blocks!

    (a) As a result
    (b) On the contrary
    (c) In other words
    (d) For example

19. In 1928, Alexander Fleming noticed *Penicillium* mold on a half-finished experiment when he returned from vacation. Had it not been for the petri dish that he left lying around, he _____ penicillin.

    (a) would probably not have discovered
    (b) would probably not discover
    (c) will probably not discover
    (d) will probably not have discovered

20. Jenna recently moved to Buffalo and was warmly welcomed by her new housemates. Before the move, she _____ in Albany alone, so having companions was a refreshing change from her solitary living situation.

    (a) is living
    (b) had been living
    (c) will live
    (d) has been living

21. St. Jerome earned a place in religious history with the Vulgate, the first official Latin translation of the Bible from the original Hebrew and Greek. It took St. Jerome twenty-two years _____ the translation.

    (a) to have completed
    (b) to complete
    (c) completing
    (d) having completed

22. Jake will be given an "Employee of the Month" certificate at next week's meeting for being such a talented salesperson. If I were his manager, I _____ him with a raise or an all-expense-paid vacation instead.

    (a) will have rewarded
    (b) will reward
    (c) would reward
    (d) would have rewarded

23. From a startup of just three employees, ARB, Inc. has scaled up to over 200 employees in five years. Currently, the company executives _____ for a new office, as their building is already packed to capacity.

    (a) look
    (b) are looking
    (c) will look
    (d) have been looking

24. The government has been alerting the public to an ongoing flu outbreak. They advise that everyone _____ the strict health and sanitation guidelines put in place to stop the spread of the disease.

    (a) has followed
    (b) is following
    (c) will follow
    (d) follow

25. Fred has been an editor with YJ Communications for only six months, but he is already job hunting. He works long hours for unfair pay. Even if he were to be offered a promotion, he _____ it.

(a) would not have taken
(b) will not take
(c) will not have taken
(d) would not take

26. Mr. and Mrs. Simmons were filled with joy when they found out that their son was going to graduate *summa cum laude*. All they ever wanted was for him _____ college, but he exceeded their expectations.

(a) finishing
(b) to be finishing
(c) to finish
(d) having finished

THIS IS THE END OF THE GRAMMAR SECTION
DO NOT GO ON UNTIL TOLD TO DO SO

LISTENING SECTION

DIRECTIONS:

The Listening Section has four parts. In each part you will hear a spoken passage and a number of questions about the passage. First you will hear the questions. Then you will hear the passage. From the four choices for each question, choose the best answer. Then blacken in the correct circle on your answer sheet.

Now you will hear an example question. Then you will hear an example passage.

Now listen to the example question.

> (a) one
> (b) two
> (c) three
> (d) four

Bill Johnson has four brothers, so the best answer is (d). The circle with the letter (d) has been blackened.

NOW TURN THE PAGE AND BEGIN

27. (a) attending a viewing of a rare phenomenon
    (b) watching a live stream about astronomy
    (c) organizing a total eclipse watch party
    (d) going to her parents' place to stargaze

28. (a) that he was actually in Russia
    (b) that he watched with a global audience
    (c) that he live streamed it for his viewers
    (d) that he saw it from his home

29. (a) She learned a lot from them.
    (b) They brought delicious food.
    (c) She made many new friends.
    (d) They played enjoyable music.

30. (a) by benefiting from clear weather
    (b) by getting advice from a teacher
    (c) by hiking to the top of a mountain
    (d) by living within the right area

31. (a) He did not have protective glasses.
    (b) He tuned into the event late.
    (c) He was busy adjusting his camera.
    (d) He could not attend in person.

32. (a) covering up against the cold
    (b) taking pictures of the sky
    (c) watching the event quietly
    (d) rushing to get a better view

33. (a) look at photos of the event online
    (b) make plans to visit his cousin
    (c) view a recording of the event
    (d) join a local stargazing club

34. (a) to inform people about a surprise party
    (b) to invite people to a charity event
    (c) to celebrate a coworker's birthday
    (d) to announce an event in honor of a colleague

35. (a) to participate in a fun contest
    (b) to appear more professional
    (c) to surprise him with a prank
    (d) to be more comfortable

36. (a) He developed new treatments.
    (b) He made a major donation.
    (c) He kept it from closing down.
    (d) He set up the organization.

37. (a) by guessing the ingredients in the special dessert
    (b) by knowing facts about the guest of honor's life
    (c) by remembering the words to popular songs
    (d) by answering questions about the hospital correctly

38. (a) a dance competition
    (b) a special performance
    (c) a farewell speech
    (d) a gift presentation

39. (a) to receive directions to the event
    (b) to figure out seating arrangements
    (c) to find the right-sized venue
    (d) to make sure there is enough food

40. (a) living in a spacious home
    (b) seeing houses with big yards
    (c) having a different climate
    (d) living in a coastal region

41. (a) that it brings back good memories of her childhood
    (b) that it gives her a feeling of well-being
    (c) that it reminds her of her father's love for nature
    (d) that it gives her a sense of pride in her hard work

42. (a) because it grows too slowly
    (b) because it damages easily
    (c) because it attracts insects
    (d) because it has too many weeds

43. (a) by being easy for her to install
    (b) by not needing to be watered
    (c) by being easy for her to repair
    (d) by not needing to be cleaned

44. (a) She would dislike the smell.
    (b) Her kids like to play in the yard.
    (c) She enjoys being without shoes.
    (d) Her dog likes to run outside.

45. (a) allow a natural lawn to grow
    (b) hire professional landscapers
    (c) plant trees and flowers outside
    (d) settle for an artificial backyard

46. (a) how to teach an online class
    (b) how to choose the right course
    (c) how to get good grades
    (d) how to behave in a virtual class

47. (a) that they are hard to follow
    (b) that they depend on the group size
    (c) that they apply to all classrooms
    (d) that they vary between classes

48. (a) by maintaining eye contact
    (b) by using careful language
    (c) by helping to answer questions
    (d) by refraining from talking too much

49. (a) to avoid coming off as impolite
    (b) to avoid facing penalties
    (c) to keep from disrupting class
    (d) to appear more professional

50. (a) They can correct others' grammar.
    (b) They can make formal speeches.
    (c) They can use a professional tone.
    (d) They can keep conversations short.

51. (a) ask for extra credit
    (b) offer a good excuse
    (c) submit an incomplete assignment
    (d) let the teacher know ahead of time

52. (a) by asking an outsider to join class discussions
    (b) by posting information without permission
    (c) by sending a private message to the entire group
    (d) by making their student profiles public

THIS IS THE END OF THE LISTENING SECTION
DO NOT GO ON UNTIL TOLD TO DO SO

READING AND VOCABULARY SECTION

DIRECTIONS:

You will now read four different passages. Each passage is followed by comprehension and vocabulary questions. From the four choices for each item, choose the best answer. Then blacken in the correct circle on your answer sheet.

Read the following example passage and example question.

Example:

> Bill Johnson lives in New York. He is 25 years old. He has four brothers and two sisters.
>
> How many brothers does Bill Johnson have?
>
> (a) one
> (b) two
> (c) three
> (d) four

The correct answer is (d), so the circle with the letter (d) has been blackened.

NOW TURN THE PAGE AND BEGIN

PART 1. Read the following biography article and answer the questions. The underlined words in the article are for vocabulary questions.

CLAUDE MONET

Claude Monet was a French painter best known for developing Impressionism, a nineteenth-century art movement that aimed to capture the artist's "impression" or experience of a moment rather than an accurate depiction. Monet was one of the movement's founders, along with several other French painters.

Oscar-Claude Monet was born on November 14, 1840, in Paris, France, but the family moved to Normandy when he was five. As a child, Monet loved to draw and wanted to become an artist. With his mother's support, fifteen-year-old Monet enrolled in Le Havre secondary school of the arts. His talent in charcoal drawing was acknowledged by his neighbors, who often bought his works. However, it was the landscape painter Eugène Boudin who urged him to try painting. Monet soon joined Boudin in painting outdoors, a practice that would eventually become the foundation of Monet's work.

At the age of nineteen, Monet moved back to Paris to study art. He was disappointed with the traditional art methods being taught there, but he met fellow artists who shared his new approach to art by painting pictures that were not exact representations of real life. Instead, they were interpretations of what the painter sees. Often working outdoors, Monet and his fellow artists used small brushstrokes that emphasized fleeting moments in time—particularly the changing light and colors—rather than the subject matter's details.

In 1872, Monet painted *Impression, Sunrise*, which portrayed the port in his hometown during a morning fog. It was exhibited in Paris, where art critics used the title of his work to discredit him and his fellow artists by calling them "impressionists" because their paintings looked more like sketches than finished works. The name stuck, and the exhibition later became known as the First Impressionist Exhibition.

Monet gained critical and financial success during the 1890s with his series of paintings on a single subject. The most notable of these was *Water Lilies*. The series consisted of approximately 250 large-scale water lily paintings that depicted the flower garden at his home in Giverny, where he spent the last thirty years of his life.

Monet died on December 5, 1926. Considered the greatest Impressionist painter, he continues to influence modern art styles, including abstract art, through his work. His paintings are displayed in museums worldwide, and a single painting can sell for tens of millions of dollars.

53. What is Claude Monet best known for?

   (a) helping to introduce a new style of art
   (b) producing more work than any other painter
   (c) founding a school for promising artists
   (d) creating highly realistic landscape paintings

54. Why did Monet start to take an interest in painting?

   (a) because he was encouraged by another artist
   (b) because he became bored with charcoal drawing
   (c) because he was urged by his teachers
   (d) because he was influenced by his mother

55. What probably distinguished Monet's artwork from the typical style at the time?

   (a) a focus on capturing objects while they were completely still
   (b) an emphasis on particular color schemes to create a modern look
   (c) a focus on the way the scene changed while he was painting
   (d) an emphasis on the finest details of the subject matter

56. What is the significance of Monet's *Impression, Sunrise*?

   (a) It was his most well-received creation.
   (b) It inspired the name for an entire movement.
   (c) It captured the scene in his own backyard.
   (d) It was the first painting to be sold at auction.

57. How does Monet continue to impact the world of art?

   (a) by altering the direction of all art forms
   (b) by making painting profitable for artists
   (c) by providing inspiration for other art styles
   (d) by calling attention to the struggles of aspiring artists

58. In the context of the passage, practice means _____.

   (a) field
   (b) rehearsal
   (c) business
   (d) habit

59. In the context of the passage, discredit means _____.

   (a) examine
   (b) imitate
   (c) fool
   (d) insult

WHY WE GET GOOSEBUMPS

Do you ever wonder why the hairs at the back of your neck stand up when you are cold, listening to a scary story, or feeling intense emotions? This sensation, where the base of the hair involuntarily springs up and causes tiny, raised bumps to appear on the skin, is called goosebumps.

The term "goosebumps" derives its name from how the raised skin resembles the skin of a goose after its feathers have been plucked. Although hair rises all over the body when goosebumps occur, the bumps are most visible in places where hair is thinner, such as the arms and back of one's neck.

Goosebumps have no clear practical use for modern humans. Rather, they appear as an indication that someone is scared or wowed by something beautiful, like a song. However, scientists think that goosebumps were useful to early humans. First, back when humans were still covered in thick hair, goosebumps provided added insulation from the cold. That is, when the hair stood up, it fluffed up. This action trapped air close to the skin, which allowed early humans to retain body heat.

Second, goosebumps are a by-product of the human "fight or flight" response, the involuntary reaction to a perceived danger or threat that prepares one to either fight or withdraw from a dangerous situation. Sensing danger automatically triggers the reflexes, which contract the small muscles at the base of the hairs, causing the hairs to stand up. With their hair puffed up, early humans appeared bigger, which would have caused their enemy— perhaps a bear or a snake—to back off.

Although humans stopped growing fur a long time ago, goosebumps remain as a leftover survival instinct. When people hear a scary story, their brains register the situation as life-threatening and react accordingly. The same can be said about a reaction to something aesthetically pleasing, like good music. Unexpectedly strong emotional input can trigger the sympathetic nervous system, causing tiny muscles to contract and the hairs to stand up in response.

60. What is the article all about?

(a) a human's automatic response to external stimulation
(b) an emotional response that occurs when humans receive bad news
(c) a human's controlled response to changes in the weather
(d) a natural response no longer experienced by humans

61. Which of the following is NOT true about goosebumps?

(a) They only occur in areas of the body that have thick hair.
(b) They have little practical use to humans nowadays.
(c) They are most noticeable in areas of the body with thin hair.
(d) Their appearance mimics the look of real goose skin.

62. According to the article, how did having goosebumps help early humans survive harsh environments?

(a) by preventing the skin from absorbing moisture
(b) by keeping them cool in the summer months
(c) by protecting them in low temperatures
(d) by alerting them to upcoming storms

63. Why was it probably helpful for early humans to have goosebumps around predators?

(a) because it helped them blend in with their environment
(b) because it made their bodies look more intimidating
(c) because it strengthened their skin's resistance to injury
(d) because it signaled a need for lightning-fast reflexes

64. Why, most likely, do people have goosebumps when they experience something good?

(a) because they want other people to share in their excitement
(b) because they are surprised by the effect of certain input
(c) because they are preparing themselves to be let down
(d) because they want to show their appreciation for positive input

65. In the context of the passage, trapped means _____.

(a) held
(b) produced
(c) imprisoned
(d) packed

66. In the context of the passage, register means _____.

(a) enroll
(b) express
(c) include
(d) recognize

지텔프 공식 기출문제집 7회분 Level 2

PAGERS

Pagers are portable telecommunication devices that receive and display alphanumeric messages. Also known as beepers, pagers either vibrate or make a beeping sound to <u>notify</u> the user that a message has been received. Pagers are usually worn hanging from a belt loop or clipped to one's pocket.

Devices similar to pagers were in use by some US police stations as early as 1921, but it was only in 1949 that a patent for the telephone pager was <u>secured</u>. World War II veteran, Al Gross, had modified the technology used in radio-controlled bomb detonators to send signals to pagers instead. Originally intended to aid communication among hospital doctors during emergencies, the pager was demonstrated at a medical convention that same year. A year later, it was being used in US hospitals.

The technology is simple. One uses a telephone or email to send a message, which is then forwarded to the pager of the intended recipient. The incoming message is then displayed on the pager's screen. The simplest pagers can only receive and display numbers, which function like a code, while some pagers show a combination of numbers and text.

Pagers became widely used in the 1980s and reached their cultural heyday in the mid-1990s, with over 60 million users. Wearing a pager on one's belt became a status symbol that meant one was essential enough to need to be reachable at a moment's notice.

Paging networks have more broadcast power than cellular networks. Paging signals can penetrate walls of almost any material and are thus more reliable. However, pagers also have disadvantages. One of their main downsides is the difficulty of replying. When a pager receives a message, the user needs to either send the reply on a network's website or find a phone and contact the sender.

Toward the late 1990s, cell phones, which use two-way communication, became widely affordable. The pager was unable to compete with the cell phone's multiple features and ease of replying, so the number of pager subscribers soon dropped.

Nevertheless, many doctors, police officers, and other emergency responders still use paging systems today due to the devices' broadcast power and reliability in emergencies.

67. What was the initial purpose of the telephone pager?

(a) to be a radio system for soldiers in times of war
(b) to be a bomb detonation device for the military
(c) to be a warning device for police officers
(d) to be a communication device for medical professionals

68. According to the third paragraph, which of the following is true about the most basic type of pagers?

(a) They can only receive local messages.
(b) They can only display special characters.
(c) They can only receive numeric characters.
(d) They can only display short messages.

69. Based on the text, why, most likely, did many people wear pagers during the '90s?

(a) so they could show off their ability to afford the device
(b) so they could communicate with friends more easily
(c) so they could feel a sense of belonging
(d) so they could appear important to others

70. According to the fifth paragraph, how are pagers better than cell phones?

(a) They have more dependable signals.
(b) They are more reliable for tracking location.
(c) They are made of more durable materials.
(d) They can broadcast across more networks.

71. When, most likely, did pagers start to decline in popularity?

(a) when responding to pagers became more difficult
(b) when a more versatile form of communication appeared
(c) when certain features were updated
(d) when hospitals banned use of the devices

72. In the context of the passage, notify means _____.

(a) warn
(b) guide
(c) inform
(d) identify

73. In the context of the passage, secured means _____.

(a) obtained
(b) taken
(c) withheld
(d) known

Evelyn Harding
Editor-in-Chief
The Traveling Post
8788 Main St.
Pikesville, MD

Dear Ms. Harding:

I have been a long-time reader of your literary magazine, and some of my past professors are regular contributors. Recently, I saw a call for articles on your website on the topic of "home," and I am pleased to submit my essay entitled "The Heart of the Metro" for your publication.

I know that you mainly <u>feature</u> published authors in your magazine. I am pleased to share that my creative nonfiction has appeared in the *Observer Chronicles*, *Pinnacle Magazine*, and *The Daily Illustrated*. I teach creative nonfiction writing at Glengarry University. When I'm not writing or teaching, I volunteer for an organization that promotes adolescent literacy.

In a nutshell, my essay talks about moving from my hometown of Burton, Ohio, to New York City. Growing up in a small town, I was equally frightened and amazed by NYC, with its skyscrapers, crowds, and busy streets. I was used to the laid-back <u>atmosphere</u> of my hometown, where everyone was relaxed, and time seemed to pass slowly. I was unsure if I would ever adapt to my new environment.

Five years later, I have grown to love NYC, with its diverse cultures and opportunities for adventure. Through my essay, I hope to inspire newcomers who want to thrive wherever they decide to live. Likewise, I wish to encourage other people who might be anxious about leaving their hometown to not be afraid of new opportunities.

I have attached the full essay here for your reference. Thank you for considering my submission.

Sincerely yours,

Lewis Bell
New York City, NY

74. How did Lewis Bell know about the magazine's call for submissions?

 (a) He read about it in the newspaper.
 (b) He heard about it from a former professor.
 (c) He saw a post on their webpage.
 (d) He regularly contributes to the publication.

75. Why, most likely, did Bell mention several publications to Evelyn Harding?

 (a) to demonstrate to her that he understands many topics
 (b) to prove to her that he has a diverse writing portfolio
 (c) to encourage her to read his recently published work
 (d) to show her that he is already an established author

76. What is Lewis Bell's essay mainly about?

 (a) his fear of crowded places
 (b) his experience as a newcomer
 (c) his decision to move back home
 (d) his search for new opportunities

77. Based on the letter, what does Bell probably want his essay to do?

 (a) encourage others who are adjusting to a new home
 (b) inspire city dwellers to write about their experiences
 (c) encourage people in rural areas to move to a city
 (d) inspire new writers who wish to get published

78. Aside from the letter, what else did Bell include in his correspondence with Harding?

 (a) a published piece of writing
 (b) a recommendation letter
 (c) a copy of his submission
 (d) a list of character references

79. In the context of the passage, <u>feature</u> means _____.

 (a) announce
 (b) contain
 (c) imagine
 (d) present

80. In the context of the passage, <u>atmosphere</u> means _____.

 (a) approach
 (b) feeling
 (c) movement
 (d) surface

THIS IS THE END OF THE TEST

지텔프 공식 기출문제집
7회분 Level 2

TEST 7

GRAMMAR

LISTENING

READING & VOCABULARY

테스트 전 확인사항

1. OMR 답안지를 준비하셨나요? ☐
2. 컴퓨터용 사인펜, 수정 테이프를 준비하셨나요? ☐
3. 음성을 들을 준비를 하셨나요? ☐

TEST 7 음성 바로 듣기

🎧 **TEST 7.mp3**

해커스인강(HackersIngang.com)에서 무료 다운로드
상단 메뉴 [G-TELP → MP3/자료 → 문제풀이 MP3]

자동 채점 및 성적 분석
서비스 바로 이용하기

자동 채점 및 성적 분석 서비스

∨ 타이머, 모바일 OMR, 자동 채점
∨ 정답률 및 취약 유형 분석

시험 시간 : 90분

목표 점수 : _____점
시작 시간 : _____시 _____분 ~ 종료 시간 : _____시 _____분

General Tests of English Language Proficiency
G-TELP

Level 2

GRAMMAR SECTION

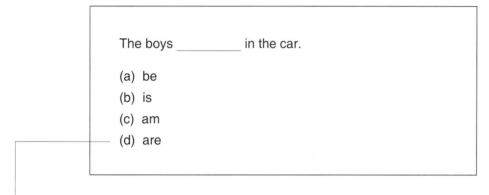

DIRECTIONS:

The following items need a word or words to complete the sentence. From the four choices for each item, choose the best answer. Then blacken in the correct circle on your answer sheet.

Example:

> The boys _____ in the car.
>
> (a) be
> (b) is
> (c) am
> (d) are

The correct answer is (d), so the circle with the letter (d) has been blackened.

ⓐ ⓑ ⓒ ●

NOW TURN THE PAGE AND BEGIN

1. Kenneth misplaced his reading glasses somewhere in the house and is trying to find them by retracing his steps. The last place he remembers _____ them is the kitchen, where he read the morning paper.

   (a) to use
   (b) to have used
   (c) using
   (d) having been using

2. Young artists should try out different creative exercises to develop their drawing skills. For example, they _____ turn a photograph upside down and draw the lines they see instead of thinking about the whole picture.

   (a) can
   (b) would
   (c) shall
   (d) will

3. Last week, my train was delayed for several hours, so it was late at night when I finally arrived home. If I had not been so exhausted, I _____ my brother's barbecue the next day.

   (a) would attend
   (b) will have attended
   (c) will attend
   (d) would have attended

4. James's daughter wants to start taking the bus to school soon. He _____ her to school every morning since she started kindergarten, so he will miss their routine.

   (a) had been driving
   (b) will drive
   (c) was driving
   (d) has been driving

5. Andrew is flying to Chicago for the first time to attend a physics conference. He is usually bad with directions, so he is relieved that a driver _____ for him when he arrives at the airport.

   (a) waits
   (b) will be waiting
   (c) was waiting
   (d) has waited

6. About 800 people attempt to climb Mount Everest every year. If expeditions up the mountain were made easier, more people _____ to do it, just to say they climbed the tallest mountain in the world.

   (a) will have probably tried
   (b) will probably try
   (c) would probably try
   (d) would have probably tried

7. For tonight's dessert, Harriet has chosen to make a famously difficult dish: the soufflé. Her chef sister advises that she _____ the recipe exactly, or her soufflé will collapse.

(a) followed
(b) will follow
(c) has followed
(d) follow

8. The Lowells are excited to become foster parents, but the licensing process has been intense. By the time they earn their license, they _____ rigorous background checks, first-aid training, and home assessments for almost six months.

(a) are undergoing
(b) will undergo
(c) will have been undergoing
(d) had been undergoing

9. No one is certain what caused the dancing plague of 1518, in which roughly 400 people danced uncontrollably for days. _____, several theories have emerged to explain the phenomenon, including food poisoning and mass hysteria.

(a) Similarly
(b) Likewise
(c) Instead
(d) However

10. Gail has been knitting for a month and is ready to try some more advanced techniques. So, she is taking the time _____ a few different types of stitches, including her mother's favorite: the herringbone stitch.

(a) to have learned
(b) having learned
(c) learning
(d) to learn

11. Painting one's nails can be a complex process requiring several steps. For the first step, beauty experts recommend that a base coat _____ to prevent darker-colored nail polish from staining the nails.

(a) is being applied
(b) be applied
(c) has been applied
(d) will be applied

12. Katherine has finally arrived in Paris and can't wait to tour all the famous sites. However, she has acrophobia, or fear of heights. If she weren't acrophobic, she _____ the Eiffel Tower right away.

(a) would climb
(b) will have climbed
(c) would have climbed
(d) will climb

13. Roger was not going to let a broken toe stop him from attending the yearly arts and crafts fair. He stayed at the fair all day, _____ his foot was causing him extreme pain.

(a) unless
(b) even though
(c) whereas
(d) in case

14. Rebecca moved away from home three years ago, and she often craves her mother's chocolate chip cookies. She is considering _____ an oven just so she can make the recipe for herself.

(a) buying
(b) to have bought
(c) having bought
(d) to buy

15. Margaret Atwood is a prolific Canadian author and environmental activist. She grew up spending time in the woods with her father, _____. Those experiences sparked her interest in environmental issues at a young age.

(a) that studied forest insects
(b) who studied forest insects
(c) which studied forest insects
(d) what studied forest insects

16. Watching previews is Matthew's favorite part of going to the movie theater, which is why he was annoyed when he arrived twenty minutes late. If he had not gotten stuck in traffic, he _____ the previews.

(a) would not miss
(b) will not miss
(c) would not have missed
(d) will not have missed

17. My father and I rarely have dinner together because of our different meal schedules. He is determined _____ right when he gets home from work at 5 p.m., while I usually wait until at least 7.

(a) having eaten
(b) eating
(c) to eat
(d) to have eaten

18. A beluga whale named Noc learned to mimic human speech while in captivity. A diver _____ Noc's tank when he heard someone say "out," realizing later that Noc was the one who had said it.

(a) will check
(b) was checking
(c) is checking
(d) has checked

19. The bootlace worm, a creature that lives along the coast of Great Britain, excretes a toxic substance that is fatal to crabs and roaches. The worm, _____, can grow up to 200 feet long.

(a) which spends most of its time tangled
(b) what spends most of its time tangled
(c) that spends most of its time tangled
(d) who spends most of its time tangled

20. Kristen used to be very knowledgeable about her city's rock music scene. She _____ music reviews for the local paper until she got so busy with work that she could no longer go to live concerts.

(a) is writing
(b) had been writing
(c) has been writing
(d) will have written

21. Chris wants to start a business selling kitchen utensils, but he isn't sure how to navigate the legal issues. His friends are suggesting that he _____ a lawyer to make sure his business follows all regulations.

(a) hire
(b) will hire
(c) has hired
(d) is hiring

22. After retirement, Gina took up woodworking. She hoped that it would be a satisfying hobby, but she soon gave up. Had she known how complex and expensive woodworking would be, she _____ in the first place.

(a) will never start
(b) will never have started
(c) would never have started
(d) would never start

23. In Roald Dahl's "The Wonderful Story of Henry Sugar," a man becomes rich after he gains the ability to see through playing cards. He wears disguises to avoid _____ by casino authorities.

(a) being detected
(b) to have been detected
(c) to be detected
(d) having been detected

24. In spite of her piercing eyes and stern demeanor, students should not be afraid of Mrs. Hawke. She _____ look intimidating, but she is actually the kindest teacher at the school.

(a) must
(b) should
(c) will
(d) may

25. Deep sea fish don't typically have air bladders, which help other fish float or sink. If deep sea fish had these air sacs, the enormous water pressure at the bottom of the ocean _____ them immediately.

(a) will have crushed
(b) would have crushed
(c) will crush
(d) would crush

26. Max has drawn up detailed plans showing how he wants his bathroom to look after remodeling. Now he _____ all of the supplies he will need when he begins the project next month.

(a) is ordering
(b) has been ordering
(c) had ordered
(d) will have ordered

THIS IS THE END OF THE GRAMMAR SECTION
DO NOT GO ON UNTIL TOLD TO DO SO

LISTENING SECTION

DIRECTIONS:

The Listening Section has four parts. In each part you will hear a spoken passage and a number of questions about the passage. First you will hear the questions. Then you will hear the passage. From the four choices for each question, choose the best answer. Then blacken in the correct circle on your answer sheet.

Now you will hear an example question. Then you will hear an example passage.

Now listen to the example question.

(a) one
(b) two
(c) three
(d) four

Bill Johnson has four brothers, so the best answer is (d). The circle with the letter (d) has been blackened.

NOW TURN THE PAGE AND BEGIN

27. (a) to organize her anniversary party
    (b) to find a location for a town meeting
    (c) to plan for an upcoming local event
    (d) to sign up as a community volunteer

28. (a) her special recipe
    (b) her invitation to the event
    (c) her favorite foods
    (d) her invitation to enter a contest

29. (a) The goal is to surprise the audience with familiar faces.
    (b) The organizers found famous singers too costly.
    (c) The goal is to highlight community members.
    (d) The organizers failed to secure talent in advance.

30. (a) hosting group art lessons
    (b) involving a local dance club
    (c) holding writing workshops
    (d) having someone draw portraits

31. (a) He could gain recognition as an artist.
    (b) He could advertise his painting business.
    (c) He could recruit new club members.
    (d) He could find sponsors for his upcoming show.

32. (a) by uploading photos to the website
    (b) by showing them in the town hall
    (c) by applying for an available booth
    (d) by displaying them at a restaurant

33. (a) meet one of Troy's club members
    (b) help Troy with an application form
    (c) head home to get some more rest
    (d) work on setup plans for the event

PART 2. *You will hear a presentation by one person to a group of people. First you will hear questions 34 through 39. Then you will hear the talk. Choose the best answer to each question in the time provided.*

34. (a) a luxury outdoor restaurant
    (b) a place to eat with a special theme
    (c) a place to stay with medieval decor
    (d) a restaurant with a modern menu

35. (a) the kind that was typically served to travelers
    (b) the kind that was commonly eaten by knights
    (c) the kind that was often served to royalty
    (d) the kind that was normally eaten by farmers

36. (a) attend a special audition
    (b) sign up on a special list
    (c) show up wearing a costume
    (d) email the director

37. (a) One must outscore other players.
    (b) One must participate every week.
    (c) One must secure a sponsor.
    (d) One must pay an entry fee.

38. (a) to encourage people to dance
    (b) to appeal to young guests
    (c) to create a festive atmosphere
    (d) to accurately reflect history

39. (a) by bringing a family member
    (b) by showing identification
    (c) by ordering a special dinner
    (d) by dressing in medieval clothing

PART 3. *You will hear a conversation between two people. First you will hear questions 40 through 45. Then you will hear the conversation. Choose the best answer to each question in the time provided.*

40. (a) picking a location for her wedding
    (b) choosing a planner for her wedding
    (c) selecting a theme for her wedding
    (d) deciding on guests for her wedding

41. (a) because it can handle large groups
    (b) because it is connected to a chapel
    (c) because it offers a dinner package
    (d) because it includes a dance DJ

42. (a) It is only open on weekdays.
    (b) It is a popular location.
    (c) It is out of her budget.
    (d) It is often closed in the spring.

43. (a) There is free parking for guests nearby.
    (b) There is very little traffic in the area.
    (c) It is ideal for taking wedding photos.
    (d) It is close to the ceremony location.

44. (a) the size of the rain shelter
    (b) a flood of uninvited guests
    (c) the presence of annoying bugs
    (d) a lack of proper security

45. (a) reserve the ballroom space
    (b) find a wedding consultant
    (c) call her fiancé for advice
    (d) book the garden venue

TEST 1
TEST 2
TEST 3
TEST 4
TEST 5
TEST 6
TEST 7

지텔프 공시 기출문제집 7회분 Level 2

PART 4. *You will hear an explanation of a process. First you will hear questions 46 through 52. Then you will hear the explanation. Choose the best answer to each question in the time provided.*

46. (a) picking a place to stay on vacation
    (b) finding a special hotel deal
    (c) choosing the perfect vacation spot
    (d) booking an overseas flight

47. (a) so they can save their money
    (b) so they can meet other guests
    (c) so they can entertain friends
    (d) so they can enjoy staying in

48. (a) by staying away from tourist attractions
    (b) by sticking to the quiet part of town
    (c) by asking fellow travelers
    (d) by choosing a populated area

49. (a) It will keep one from getting lost.
    (b) It will be easier to visit local attractions.
    (c) It will be easier to travel to and from the airport.
    (d) It will reduce the risk of danger.

50. (a) to avoid asking directions
    (b) to find affordable restaurants
    (c) to locate important services
    (d) to make a detailed itinerary

51. (a) ask for a special rate
    (b) take a shorter vacation
    (c) share a room with a friend
    (d) decide what is most important

52. (a) to pack as lightly as possible
    (b) to read about other people's experiences
    (c) to make reservations well in advance
    (d) to consult online travel blogs

THIS IS THE END OF THE LISTENING SECTION
DO NOT GO ON UNTIL TOLD TO DO SO

READING AND VOCABULARY SECTION

DIRECTIONS:

You will now read four different passages. Each passage is followed by comprehension and vocabulary questions. From the four choices for each item, choose the best answer. Then blacken in the correct circle on your answer sheet.

Read the following example passage and example question.

Example:

Bill Johnson lives in New York. He is 25 years old. He has four brothers and two sisters.

How many brothers does Bill Johnson have?

(a) one
(b) two
(c) three
(d) four

The correct answer is (d), so the circle with the letter (d) has been blackened.

NOW TURN THE PAGE AND BEGIN

Read the following biography article and answer the questions. The underlined words in the article are for vocabulary questions.

URSULA K. LE GUIN

Ursula K. Le Guin was an American author celebrated for her novels in the fantasy and science fiction genres. She is best known for creating far-flung, unfamiliar worlds, and for using these distant landscapes to explore complex social issues that hit close to home for her many readers.

Born Ursula Kroeber on October 21, 1929, in Berkeley, California, Le Guin grew up surrounded by books due to the influence of her parents Theodora and Alfred Kroeber, a best-selling writer and a well-known anthropologist, respectively. As a young girl, Le Guin was fascinated by the Native American myths that her father often told her. She was especially intrigued by the fantastical elements they contained, which soon led her to develop an interest in books that combined fantasy with reality.

In 1953, Le Guin earned her master's degree in literature from Columbia University and settled in Oregon with her husband soon after. While raising her children at home, she started writing seriously, publishing several poems early on and focusing on fantasy and science fiction stories later. Her first book to attract significant public attention was *A Wizard of Earthsea*, a young adult novel about a boy who joins a school of wizardry and struggles to control his burgeoning power.

Her next book, *The Left Hand of Darkness*, introduced an alien planet in which gender and gender norms do not exist. The book was considered a groundbreaking work of science fiction for its complex analysis of human gender and sexuality. It won Le Guin both the Hugo and Nebula Awards, two prestigious awards for the fantasy and science fiction genres, making her the first female author to receive both prizes for the same novel.

In contrast to most science fiction writers at the time, who tended to speculate on the future of natural and physical sciences, Le Guin liked to explore the so-called "softer sciences," like psychology and sociology, in order to confront different aspects of contemporary human behavior. Her father's anthropology career was most likely influential in the approach she took with her fiction. She continually tackled sensitive issues such as sexism and racism through her different literary works.

Le Guin died on January 22, 2018. She earned many awards and other distinctions, and her work continues to influence writers both inside and outside the fantasy and science fiction genres.

53. What is Ursula K. Le Guin famous for?

   (a) her novels based on explorers' lives
   (b) her books set in strange worlds
   (c) her articles on social behavior
   (d) her illustrations of beautiful
       landscapes

54. How did Le Guin probably develop her
    specific taste in reading?

   (a) from the myths her father often
       shared
   (b) from the books her mother had
       written
   (c) from the stories her grandparents
       often told
   (d) from the books her teachers had
       assigned

55. When did Le Guin first start attracting
    mainstream attention for her writing?

   (a) after releasing her first nonfiction
       book
   (b) before moving to a new state with her
       husband
   (c) after publishing several shorter works
   (d) before she earned her master's
       degree

56. According to the article, what was
    innovative about *The Left Hand of
    Darkness*?

   (a) It challenged views of the time
       regarding gender.
   (b) It was written as an analytical essay.
   (c) It took place on multiple alien planets.
   (d) It explored complex human
       relationships.

57. Why was Le Guin considered different
    from other writers at the time?

   (a) She published works in every genre.
   (b) She resisted writing about human
       behavior.
   (c) She was heavily influenced by her
       time spent in nature.
   (d) She focused on different branches of
       science.

58. In the context of the passage, tackled
    means _____.

   (a) blocked
   (b) addressed
   (c) ignored
   (d) solved

59. In the context of the passage, distinctions
    means _____.

   (a) contracts
   (b) elections
   (c) approvals
   (d) achievements

지텔프 공식 기출문제집 7회분 Level 2

INDONESIA REDUCES DEFORESTATION THROUGH CASH INCENTIVES

Indonesia is home to the third largest rainforest in the world. However, it also has one of the highest deforestation rates, mainly due to rural farmers who routinely clear the forest for agriculture. Farmers whose harvest is too small, perhaps due to pests or unexpected storms, will often remove trees from the surrounding land so they can plant more crops.

Recently, researchers from Johns Hopkins University have found that Indonesia's average deforestation rate has consistently decreased since 2008. Evidence suggests that the recent reduction in deforestation can be <u>attributed</u> to the Indonesian government's conditional cash transfer (CCT) program.

The program, which started in 2008, is meant to give additional money to families living in poverty. Under the program, the government subsidizes $45 to $90 per family each year as long as registered individuals fulfill a few conditions, such as receiving yearly medical checkups and keeping children in school until junior high. CCTs are given only to Indonesia's poorest, with the aim of improving the economic condition of over six million residents.

In a 2020 study that examined the environmental impact of the program, researchers analyzed 7,468 rural Indonesian villages where families had received CCTs from 2008 until 2012. It was discovered that deforestation rates in the surrounding areas were 30% lower on average for that time period than they had been in previous years. Further research showed that deforestation rates remained low even after extreme weather events, when strong winds or rains damaged crops and lowered yield for farmers.

Based on these results, researchers theorized that farmers stopped clearing surrounding forestland due to the subsidies they had received under the CCT program. The low deforestation rate even during inclement weather suggested that farmers no longer had to rely on a big harvest for <u>sufficient</u> income, as they now had extra money to support their families.

Indonesia's CCT program has provided some evidence that attempting to reduce poverty may positively affect the environment, despite many policymakers' beliefs to the contrary. Researchers hope that the successful implementation of CCTs in Indonesia and its unexpected influence on the country's high deforestation rate will lead to similar results in other countries with large tropical rainforests.

60. What is the main reason for Indonesia's high deforestation rate?

(a) the need to plant different kinds of crops
(b) the illegal logging done by large companies
(c) the frequent clearings of wooded areas by locals
(d) the tourists that hike through the area every year

61. Why, most likely, was the CCT program implemented?

(a) to help students who were failing their classes
(b) to discourage illegal clearing of land
(c) to provide support to struggling schools
(d) to decrease poverty among the country's citizens

62. How were rural villages in the study affected by the CCT program?

(a) They attained the lowest unemployment rates.
(b) They preserved more of their local land.
(c) They increased the sale of natural resources.
(d) They became more resistant to severe weather events.

63. According to the study, how did the CCT program help farmers?

(a) by enabling them to plant crops in larger areas
(b) by ensuring their crops would survive bad weather
(c) by giving them the means to buy their harvest back
(d) by providing more income during smaller harvests

64. According to the article, what belief about poverty reduction is most likely held by many policymakers?

(a) that it will positively affect population growth
(b) that it can only be achieved through government aid
(c) that it will negatively affect the environment
(d) that it is impossible to manage effectively

65. In the context of the passage, attributed means _____.

(a) returned
(b) released
(c) gifted
(d) credited

66. In the context of the passage, sufficient means _____.

(a) valid
(b) enough
(c) enjoyable
(d) taxable

PART 3. *Read the following encyclopedia article and answer the questions. The underlined words in the article are for vocabulary questions.*

MARDI GRAS

Mardi Gras is a holiday most famously held in New Orleans, Louisiana. The celebration features big float parades and an abundance of "throws," trinkets that are traditionally tossed to parade attendees. Due to its festive atmosphere, Mardi Gras is one of the most well-attended events in New Orleans, drawing thousands of tourists every year.

One theory about Mardi Gras's origin claims that the holiday evolved from the ancient Roman festival that honored Saturn, the god of agriculture. Called Saturnalia, it included extravagant partying and feasting. When Christianity spread to Rome, the festival was incorporated into traditional Christian rituals as a new holiday. It became a way to indulge oneself before Lent, when fasting and silence were commonly observed in religious households.

The tradition spread throughout Europe where it eventually became known as *Mardi Gras*, *Mardi* being the French word for "Tuesday" and *gras* for "fat." The first Mardi Gras celebration in the US was on March 3, 1699, when French explorers camped at a site close to New Orleans. Though the holiday is now celebrated all over the US, New Orleans still hosts some of the most popular Mardi Gras festivities in the world.

Mardi Gras celebrations in New Orleans start two weeks before the Christian holiday of Ash Wednesday, with the main events of the festival happening during the final week. The exact date of Mardi Gras changes every year, but it always falls between February 3 and March 9. The biggest events are the parades, where festival organizers showcase elaborate floats based on themes like "Famous Lovers" or "Equality for All."

During the parade, individuals riding the floats give away trinkets called "throws," generally inexpensive plastic items, to attendees. Throws are usually bead necklaces, souvenir coins, or small toys, and some are even considered collectible items. Eager onlookers can sometimes become very competitive about trying to catch these prized trinkets.

Much like Saturnalia, Mardi Gras is also known as an opportunity for partying and excessive drinking. Mardi Gras tourism has contributed hundreds of billions of dollars to New Orleans' economy, significantly boosting local businesses, especially clubs and bars.

67. According to the article, what draws large crowds to New Orleans every year?

    (a) a traditional celebration with ancient origins
    (b) a chance for an exclusive tour of city landmarks
    (c) a nationwide contest for best parade float
    (d) a re-enactment of a famous Roman feast

68. Why is Mardi Gras celebrated before Lent?

    (a) to encourage fun before a period of self-control
    (b) to avoid conflict with other religious holidays
    (c) to limit the amount of traffic in the city
    (d) to allow tourists to observe both traditions

69. How did Mardi Gras end up being celebrated in New Orleans?

    (a) It was promoted by a major church in the city.
    (b) It spread from other major cities in the US.
    (c) It was brought over by world travelers.
    (d) It aligned with the state's founding day.

70. According to the article, what is a main feature of Mardi Gras?

    (a) the chance to wear elaborate costumes
    (b) the opportunity to buy collectible items
    (c) the concerts organized by festival volunteers
    (d) the floats created to reflect certain themes

71. According to the final paragraph, what does Mardi Gras have in common with Saturnalia?

    (a) the negative effect it has on the economy
    (b) the time of year it typically takes place
    (c) the way it is traditionally celebrated
    (d) the contribution it has to local history

72. In the context of the passage, observed means _____.

    (a) practiced
    (b) serviced
    (c) supervised
    (d) recorded

73. In the context of the passage, prized means _____.

    (a) useful
    (b) expensive
    (c) desired
    (d) rare

Erwin Todd
839 Park Avenue
Delaware, OH

Dear Mr. Todd:

I am sending this warning letter in response to your multiple <u>occasions</u> of public disturbance to our community. The behavior of your guests during your frequent late-night parties has resulted in property damage and noise complaints from your neighbors, several of whom have already approached you on this matter. While your parties temporarily stop after such discussions, they often start up again after a few weeks.

Reports from the community show that this problem does not solely affect your next-door neighbors. Just this week, the Greenbrook Homeowners Association has received six separate complaints from other residents on your street. Each one reported loud music coming from your house from dusk until dawn. Several passersby have also noticed the noise and alerted us to broken bottles and other trash littering the sidewalk in front of your residence.

Just last night, some of your guests sent a baseball flying into the neighbor's house, shattering her window. The neighbor called us shortly afterward to file a complaint. She will be contacting you soon regarding compensation, though I cannot speak to the likelihood of charges being filed against you for destruction of property.

The association believes that this recent event, on top of a consistent record of public disturbance, <u>entails</u> serious action on our part. We can no longer let this pass. Please consider this a formal request to stop disturbing your neighbors and other members of our community. If we receive another complaint, we will be forced to take this matter to the police.

Sincerely,

Catherine Williams

Catherine Williams
President
Greenbrook Homeowners Association

74. Why did Catherine Williams send Erwin Todd a letter?

    (a) to inform him of a lawsuit against him
    (b) to complain about him destroying her property
    (c) to warn him about his behavior toward her
    (d) to ask him to stop disturbing his neighbors

75. How did Erwin's neighbors first try to resolve the issue?

    (a) by sending him letters of complaint
    (b) by speaking with him in person
    (c) by contacting an attorney
    (d) by pressing charges with the police

76. Why does Catherine believe that Erwin has created a widespread problem?

    (a) because guests have destroyed public property
    (b) because a number of complaints have been received
    (c) because some neighbors have chosen to move away
    (d) because people will no longer pass by the house

77. What finally prompted the association to take action?

    (a) a report of people trespassing on private property
    (b) a call from a concerned community business
    (c) a complaint about damage to a residence
    (d) a formal request from law enforcement

78. What will probably happen if Erwin does not stop holding loud parties?

    (a) The local authorities will get involved.
    (b) The association will strip him of community privileges.
    (c) The police will evict him from his house.
    (d) He will be banned from entertaining guests.

79. In the context of the passage, occasions means _____.

    (a) incidents
    (b) affairs
    (c) points
    (d) goals

80. In the context of the passage, entails means _____.

    (a) prevents
    (b) requires
    (c) limits
    (d) protects

THIS IS THE END OF THE TEST

정답 한눈에 보기
& OMR 답안지

정답 한눈에 보기

TEST 1

1	c	11	c	21	b	31	b	41	d	51	b	61	c	71	d
2	b	12	d	22	d	32	c	42	b	52	c	62	d	72	a
3	a	13	a	23	d	33	b	43	b	53	d	63	c	73	a
4	d	14	b	24	a	34	d	44	c	54	a	64	d	74	b
5	c	15	d	25	b	35	a	45	c	55	d	65	a	75	c
6	c	16	c	26	a	36	d	46	c	56	b	66	b	76	a
7	d	17	c	27	a	37	a	47	b	57	d	67	b	77	b
8	d	18	a	28	c	38	d	48	a	58	c	68	b	78	a
9	a	19	c	29	a	39	a	49	d	59	b	69	a	79	b
10	b	20	c	30	d	40	d	50	c	60	a	70	d	80	b

TEST 2

1	d	11	b	21	d	31	d	41	b	51	a	61	a	71	d
2	a	12	a	22	d	32	a	42	b	52	d	62	b	72	b
3	d	13	d	23	d	33	a	43	b	53	d	63	b	73	c
4	a	14	a	24	a	34	b	44	d	54	c	64	c	74	c
5	c	15	c	25	b	35	a	45	d	55	a	65	d	75	a
6	b	16	c	26	b	36	b	46	b	56	c	66	b	76	a
7	d	17	b	27	c	37	c	47	c	57	d	67	a	77	b
8	a	18	a	28	c	38	a	48	c	58	d	68	b	78	d
9	d	19	b	29	c	39	c	49	a	59	b	69	c	79	c
10	c	20	c	30	a	40	d	50	b	60	d	70	d	80	a

TEST 3

1	a	11	d	21	a	31	d	41	d	51	d	61	b	71	a
2	d	12	b	22	c	32	b	42	a	52	a	62	b	72	a
3	d	13	b	23	c	33	a	43	c	53	d	63	d	73	d
4	c	14	d	24	a	34	b	44	d	54	d	64	a	74	b
5	a	15	a	25	d	35	a	45	c	55	c	65	c	75	b
6	a	16	c	26	b	36	a	46	d	56	b	66	c	76	c
7	b	17	b	27	c	37	b	47	a	57	b	67	b	77	a
8	c	18	b	28	c	38	b	48	c	58	a	68	d	78	a
9	a	19	c	29	a	39	d	49	c	59	c	69	b	79	d
10	c	20	c	30	c	40	b	50	b	60	d	70	b	80	d

TEST 4

#		#		#		#		#		#		#		#	
1	a	11	b	21	a	31	a	41	c	51	d	61	b	71	a
2	a	12	a	22	c	32	b	42	b	52	a	62	d	72	b
3	c	13	c	23	c	33	b	43	b	53	a	63	b	73	d
4	d	14	a	24	a	34	a	44	a	54	b	64	b	74	d
5	d	15	d	25	d	35	c	45	b	55	b	65	a	75	b
6	a	16	c	26	b	36	d	46	d	56	c	66	c	76	a
7	a	17	b	27	c	37	d	47	a	57	c	67	a	77	a
8	c	18	b	28	c	38	d	48	c	58	a	68	c	78	b
9	d	19	a	29	a	39	c	49	c	59	b	69	d	79	c
10	d	20	d	30	d	40	a	50	a	60	d	70	d	80	d

TEST 5

#		#		#		#		#		#		#		#	
1	b	11	b	21	b	31	b	41	c	51	d	61	c	71	d
2	b	12	d	22	d	32	b	42	b	52	b	62	b	72	d
3	a	13	c	23	d	33	c	43	b	53	c	63	b	73	b
4	d	14	a	24	a	34	a	44	c	54	a	64	a	74	d
5	c	15	c	25	c	35	a	45	c	55	c	65	d	75	b
6	d	16	b	26	d	36	c	46	a	56	a	66	c	76	a
7	d	17	a	27	c	37	d	47	b	57	d	67	a	77	d
8	c	18	a	28	c	38	d	48	d	58	d	68	a	78	b
9	c	19	b	29	a	39	d	49	a	59	b	69	c	79	a
10	a	20	b	30	d	40	a	50	c	60	a	70	b	80	d

TEST 6

#		#		#		#		#		#		#		#	
1	a	11	a	21	b	31	d	41	a	51	d	61	a	71	b
2	c	12	d	22	c	32	c	42	b	52	b	62	c	72	c
3	b	13	d	23	b	33	c	43	b	53	a	63	b	73	a
4	d	14	c	24	d	34	d	44	c	54	a	64	b	74	c
5	a	15	a	25	d	35	a	45	a	55	c	65	a	75	d
6	b	16	b	26	c	36	d	46	d	56	b	66	d	76	b
7	c	17	c	27	a	37	b	47	d	57	c	67	d	77	a
8	c	18	a	28	b	38	b	48	b	58	d	68	c	78	c
9	d	19	a	29	a	39	d	49	a	59	d	69	d	79	d
10	a	20	b	30	d	40	c	50	c	60	a	70	a	80	b

TEST 7

#		#		#		#		#		#		#		#	
1	c	11	b	21	a	31	c	41	a	51	d	61	d	71	c
2	a	12	a	22	c	32	c	42	b	52	b	62	b	72	a
3	d	13	b	23	a	33	d	43	d	53	b	63	d	73	c
4	d	14	a	24	d	34	b	44	c	54	a	64	c	74	d
5	b	15	b	25	d	35	c	45	a	55	c	65	d	75	b
6	c	16	c	26	a	36	b	46	a	56	a	66	b	76	b
7	d	17	c	27	c	37	a	47	d	57	d	67	a	77	c
8	c	18	b	28	a	38	d	48	d	58	b	68	a	78	a
9	d	19	a	29	c	39	b	49	b	59	d	69	c	79	a
10	d	20	b	30	a	40	a	50	c	60	c	70	d	80	b

G-TELP

※ TEST DATE

MO.	DAY	YEAR

성 명

등급 ① ② ③ ④ ⑤

감독관인 / 확인

성명란

	초 성	ㄱ ㄴ ㄷ ㄹ ㅁ ㅂ ㅅ ㅇ ㅈ ㅊ ㅋ ㅌ ㅍ ㅎ
성	중 성	ㅏ ㅑ ㅓ ㅕ ㅗ ㅛ ㅜ ㅠ ㅡ ㅣ ㅐ ㅒ ㅔ ㅖ ㅘ ㅙ ㅚ ㅝ ㅞ ㅟ ㅢ
	종 성	ㄱ ㄴ ㄷ ㄹ ㅁ ㅂ ㅅ ㅇ ㅈ ㅊ ㅋ ㅌ ㅍ ㅎ ㄲ ㄸ ㅃ ㅆ ㅉ

(Korean name entry grid with 초성/중성/종성 rows repeated)

수 험 번 호

(Numbered bubble grid 0–9)

1) Code 1.
(0 1 2 3 4 5 6 7 8 9) ×3

2) Code 2.
(0 1 2 3 4 5 6 7 8 9) ×3

3) Code 3.
(0 1 2 3 4 5 6 7 8 9) ×3

주민등록번호 앞자리 / 고 유 번 호
(Numbered bubble grid 0–9)

문항	답 란	문항	답 란	문항	답 란	문항	답 란	문항	답 란	문항	답 란
1	ⓐⓑⓒⓓ	21	ⓐⓑⓒⓓ	41	ⓐⓑⓒⓓ	61	ⓐⓑⓒⓓ	81	ⓐⓑⓒⓓ		
2	ⓐⓑⓒⓓ	22	ⓐⓑⓒⓓ	42	ⓐⓑⓒⓓ	62	ⓐⓑⓒⓓ	82	ⓐⓑⓒⓓ		
3	ⓐⓑⓒⓓ	23	ⓐⓑⓒⓓ	43	ⓐⓑⓒⓓ	63	ⓐⓑⓒⓓ	83	ⓐⓑⓒⓓ		
4	ⓐⓑⓒⓓ	24	ⓐⓑⓒⓓ	44	ⓐⓑⓒⓓ	64	ⓐⓑⓒⓓ	84	ⓐⓑⓒⓓ		
5	ⓐⓑⓒⓓ	25	ⓐⓑⓒⓓ	45	ⓐⓑⓒⓓ	65	ⓐⓑⓒⓓ	85	ⓐⓑⓒⓓ		
6	ⓐⓑⓒⓓ	26	ⓐⓑⓒⓓ	46	ⓐⓑⓒⓓ	66	ⓐⓑⓒⓓ	86	ⓐⓑⓒⓓ		
7	ⓐⓑⓒⓓ	27	ⓐⓑⓒⓓ	47	ⓐⓑⓒⓓ	67	ⓐⓑⓒⓓ	87	ⓐⓑⓒⓓ		
8	ⓐⓑⓒⓓ	28	ⓐⓑⓒⓓ	48	ⓐⓑⓒⓓ	68	ⓐⓑⓒⓓ	88	ⓐⓑⓒⓓ		
9	ⓐⓑⓒⓓ	29	ⓐⓑⓒⓓ	49	ⓐⓑⓒⓓ	69	ⓐⓑⓒⓓ	89	ⓐⓑⓒⓓ		
10	ⓐⓑⓒⓓ	30	ⓐⓑⓒⓓ	50	ⓐⓑⓒⓓ	70	ⓐⓑⓒⓓ	90	ⓐⓑⓒⓓ		
11	ⓐⓑⓒⓓ	31	ⓐⓑⓒⓓ	51	ⓐⓑⓒⓓ	71	ⓐⓑⓒⓓ				
12	ⓐⓑⓒⓓ	32	ⓐⓑⓒⓓ	52	ⓐⓑⓒⓓ	72	ⓐⓑⓒⓓ				
13	ⓐⓑⓒⓓ	33	ⓐⓑⓒⓓ	53	ⓐⓑⓒⓓ	73	ⓐⓑⓒⓓ		password	
14	ⓐⓑⓒⓓ	34	ⓐⓑⓒⓓ	54	ⓐⓑⓒⓓ	74	ⓐⓑⓒⓓ			
15	ⓐⓑⓒⓓ	35	ⓐⓑⓒⓓ	55	ⓐⓑⓒⓓ	75	ⓐⓑⓒⓓ			
16	ⓐⓑⓒⓓ	36	ⓐⓑⓒⓓ	56	ⓐⓑⓒⓓ	76	ⓐⓑⓒⓓ			
17	ⓐⓑⓒⓓ	37	ⓐⓑⓒⓓ	57	ⓐⓑⓒⓓ	77	ⓐⓑⓒⓓ			
18	ⓐⓑⓒⓓ	38	ⓐⓑⓒⓓ	58	ⓐⓑⓒⓓ	78	ⓐⓑⓒⓓ			
19	ⓐⓑⓒⓓ	39	ⓐⓑⓒⓓ	59	ⓐⓑⓒⓓ	79	ⓐⓑⓒⓓ			
20	ⓐⓑⓒⓓ	40	ⓐⓑⓒⓓ	60	ⓐⓑⓒⓓ	80	ⓐⓑⓒⓓ			

password
(0 1 2 3 4 5 6 7 8 9) ×4

절취선

G-TELP

※ TEST DATE

MO.		DAY		YEAR			

감독 확인	

성 명	

등급	① ② ③ ④ ⑤

성명란		
성	초 성	㉠ ㉡ ㉢ ㉣ ㉤ ㉥ ㉦ ㉧ ㉨ ㉩ ㉪ ㉫ ㉬ ㉭
	중 성	ㅏ ㅑ ㅓ ㅕ ㅗ ㅛ ㅜ ㅠ ㅡ ㅣ ㅔ ㅐ ㅖ ㅒ ㅘ ㅚ ㅢ ㅝ ㅟ ㅙ
	종 성	㉠ ㉡ ㉢ ㉣ ㉤ ㉥ ㉦ ㉧ ㉨ ㉩ ㉪ ㉫ ㉬ ㉭ ㄲ ㄸ ㅃ ㅆ ㅉ
명	초 성	㉠ ㉡ ㉢ ㉣ ㉤ ㉥ ㉦ ㉧ ㉨ ㉩ ㉪ ㉫ ㉬ ㉭
	중 성	ㅏ ㅑ ㅓ ㅕ ㅗ ㅛ ㅜ ㅠ ㅡ ㅣ ㅔ ㅐ ㅖ ㅒ ㅘ ㅚ ㅢ ㅝ ㅟ ㅙ
	종 성	㉠ ㉡ ㉢ ㉣ ㉤ ㉥ ㉦ ㉧ ㉨ ㉩ ㉪ ㉫ ㉬ ㉭ ㄲ ㄸ ㅃ ㅆ ㅉ
	초 성	㉠ ㉡ ㉢ ㉣ ㉤ ㉥ ㉦ ㉧ ㉨ ㉩ ㉪ ㉫ ㉬ ㉭
	중 성	ㅏ ㅑ ㅓ ㅕ ㅗ ㅛ ㅜ ㅠ ㅡ ㅣ ㅔ ㅐ ㅖ ㅒ ㅘ ㅚ ㅢ ㅝ ㅟ ㅙ
	종 성	㉠ ㉡ ㉢ ㉣ ㉤ ㉥ ㉦ ㉧ ㉨ ㉩ ㉪ ㉫ ㉬ ㉭ ㄲ ㄸ ㅃ ㅆ ㅉ
란	초 성	㉠ ㉡ ㉢ ㉣ ㉤ ㉥ ㉦ ㉧ ㉨ ㉩ ㉪ ㉫ ㉬ ㉭
	중 성	ㅏ ㅑ ㅓ ㅕ ㅗ ㅛ ㅜ ㅠ ㅡ ㅣ ㅔ ㅐ ㅖ ㅒ ㅘ ㅚ ㅢ ㅝ ㅟ ㅙ
	종 성	㉠ ㉡ ㉢ ㉣ ㉤ ㉥ ㉦ ㉧ ㉨ ㉩ ㉪ ㉫ ㉬ ㉭ ㄲ ㄸ ㅃ ㅆ ㅉ

수 험 번 호
⓪ ① ② ③ ④ ⑤ ⑥ ⑦ ⑧ ⑨ (2자리) – (4자리) – (7자리)

1) Code 1.

	⓪ ① ② ③ ④ ⑤ ⑥ ⑦ ⑧ ⑨
	⓪ ① ② ③ ④ ⑤ ⑥ ⑦ ⑧ ⑨
	⓪ ① ② ③ ④ ⑤ ⑥ ⑦ ⑧ ⑨

2) Code 2.

	⓪ ① ② ③ ④ ⑤ ⑥ ⑦ ⑧ ⑨
	⓪ ① ② ③ ④ ⑤ ⑥ ⑦ ⑧ ⑨
	⓪ ① ② ③ ④ ⑤ ⑥ ⑦ ⑧ ⑨

3) Code 3.

	⓪ ① ② ③ ④ ⑤ ⑥ ⑦ ⑧ ⑨
	⓪ ① ② ③ ④ ⑤ ⑥ ⑦ ⑧ ⑨
	⓪ ① ② ③ ④ ⑤ ⑥ ⑦ ⑧ ⑨

주민등록번호 앞자리		고 유 번 호
⓪ ① ② ③ ④ ⑤ ⑥ ⑦ ⑧ ⑨ (6자리)	–	⓪ ① ② ③ ④ ⑤ ⑥ ⑦ ⑧ ⑨ (7자리)

문항	답 란	문항	답 란	문항	답 란	문항	답 란	문항	답 란
1	ⓐ ⓑ ⓒ ⓓ	21	ⓐ ⓑ ⓒ ⓓ	41	ⓐ ⓑ ⓒ ⓓ	61	ⓐ ⓑ ⓒ ⓓ	81	ⓐ ⓑ ⓒ ⓓ
2	ⓐ ⓑ ⓒ ⓓ	22	ⓐ ⓑ ⓒ ⓓ	42	ⓐ ⓑ ⓒ ⓓ	62	ⓐ ⓑ ⓒ ⓓ	82	ⓐ ⓑ ⓒ ⓓ
3	ⓐ ⓑ ⓒ ⓓ	23	ⓐ ⓑ ⓒ ⓓ	43	ⓐ ⓑ ⓒ ⓓ	63	ⓐ ⓑ ⓒ ⓓ	83	ⓐ ⓑ ⓒ ⓓ
4	ⓐ ⓑ ⓒ ⓓ	24	ⓐ ⓑ ⓒ ⓓ	44	ⓐ ⓑ ⓒ ⓓ	64	ⓐ ⓑ ⓒ ⓓ	84	ⓐ ⓑ ⓒ ⓓ
5	ⓐ ⓑ ⓒ ⓓ	25	ⓐ ⓑ ⓒ ⓓ	45	ⓐ ⓑ ⓒ ⓓ	65	ⓐ ⓑ ⓒ ⓓ	85	ⓐ ⓑ ⓒ ⓓ
6	ⓐ ⓑ ⓒ ⓓ	26	ⓐ ⓑ ⓒ ⓓ	46	ⓐ ⓑ ⓒ ⓓ	66	ⓐ ⓑ ⓒ ⓓ	86	ⓐ ⓑ ⓒ ⓓ
7	ⓐ ⓑ ⓒ ⓓ	27	ⓐ ⓑ ⓒ ⓓ	47	ⓐ ⓑ ⓒ ⓓ	67	ⓐ ⓑ ⓒ ⓓ	87	ⓐ ⓑ ⓒ ⓓ
8	ⓐ ⓑ ⓒ ⓓ	28	ⓐ ⓑ ⓒ ⓓ	48	ⓐ ⓑ ⓒ ⓓ	68	ⓐ ⓑ ⓒ ⓓ	88	ⓐ ⓑ ⓒ ⓓ
9	ⓐ ⓑ ⓒ ⓓ	29	ⓐ ⓑ ⓒ ⓓ	49	ⓐ ⓑ ⓒ ⓓ	69	ⓐ ⓑ ⓒ ⓓ	89	ⓐ ⓑ ⓒ ⓓ
10	ⓐ ⓑ ⓒ ⓓ	30	ⓐ ⓑ ⓒ ⓓ	50	ⓐ ⓑ ⓒ ⓓ	70	ⓐ ⓑ ⓒ ⓓ	90	ⓐ ⓑ ⓒ ⓓ
11	ⓐ ⓑ ⓒ ⓓ	31	ⓐ ⓑ ⓒ ⓓ	51	ⓐ ⓑ ⓒ ⓓ	71	ⓐ ⓑ ⓒ ⓓ		
12	ⓐ ⓑ ⓒ ⓓ	32	ⓐ ⓑ ⓒ ⓓ	52	ⓐ ⓑ ⓒ ⓓ	72	ⓐ ⓑ ⓒ ⓓ		
13	ⓐ ⓑ ⓒ ⓓ	33	ⓐ ⓑ ⓒ ⓓ	53	ⓐ ⓑ ⓒ ⓓ	73	ⓐ ⓑ ⓒ ⓓ		
14	ⓐ ⓑ ⓒ ⓓ	34	ⓐ ⓑ ⓒ ⓓ	54	ⓐ ⓑ ⓒ ⓓ	74	ⓐ ⓑ ⓒ ⓓ		
15	ⓐ ⓑ ⓒ ⓓ	35	ⓐ ⓑ ⓒ ⓓ	55	ⓐ ⓑ ⓒ ⓓ	75	ⓐ ⓑ ⓒ ⓓ		
16	ⓐ ⓑ ⓒ ⓓ	36	ⓐ ⓑ ⓒ ⓓ	56	ⓐ ⓑ ⓒ ⓓ	76	ⓐ ⓑ ⓒ ⓓ		
17	ⓐ ⓑ ⓒ ⓓ	37	ⓐ ⓑ ⓒ ⓓ	57	ⓐ ⓑ ⓒ ⓓ	77	ⓐ ⓑ ⓒ ⓓ		
18	ⓐ ⓑ ⓒ ⓓ	38	ⓐ ⓑ ⓒ ⓓ	58	ⓐ ⓑ ⓒ ⓓ	78	ⓐ ⓑ ⓒ ⓓ		
19	ⓐ ⓑ ⓒ ⓓ	39	ⓐ ⓑ ⓒ ⓓ	59	ⓐ ⓑ ⓒ ⓓ	79	ⓐ ⓑ ⓒ ⓓ		
20	ⓐ ⓑ ⓒ ⓓ	40	ⓐ ⓑ ⓒ ⓓ	60	ⓐ ⓑ ⓒ ⓓ	80	ⓐ ⓑ ⓒ ⓓ		

password

⓪ ① ② ③ ④ ⑤ ⑥ ⑦ ⑧ ⑨	⓪ ① ② ③ ④ ⑤ ⑥ ⑦ ⑧ ⑨	⓪ ① ② ③ ④ ⑤ ⑥ ⑦ ⑧ ⑨	⓪ ① ② ③ ④ ⑤ ⑥ ⑦ ⑧ ⑨

절취선

G-TELP

※ TEST DATE

MO.	DAY	YEAR

감독
관인

성 명	

등급 ① ② ③ ④ ⑤

성 명 란	초 성	㉠ ㉡ ㉢ ㉣ ㉤ ㉥ ㉦ ㉧ ㉨ ㉩ ㉪ ㉫ ㉬ ㉭
	중 성	ㅏ ㅑ ㅓ ㅕ ㅗ ㅛ ㅜ ㅠ ㅡ ㅣ ㅐ ㅒ ㅔ ㅖ ㅚ ㅟ ㅢ ㅘ ㅝ ㅙ ㅞ
	종 성	ㄱ ㄴ ㄷ ㄹ ㅁ ㅂ ㅅ ㅇ ㅈ ㅊ ㅋ ㅌ ㅍ ㅎ ㄲ ㄳ ㄵ ㄶ ㄺ

수 험 번 호

0 1 2 3 4 5 6 7 8 9 (repeated for each column)

1) Code 1.
0 1 2 3 4 5 6 7 8 9
0 1 2 3 4 5 6 7 8 9
0 1 2 3 4 5 6 7 8 9

2) Code 2.
0 1 2 3 4 5 6 7 8 9
0 1 2 3 4 5 6 7 8 9
0 1 2 3 4 5 6 7 8 9

3) Code 3.
0 1 2 3 4 5 6 7 8 9
0 1 2 3 4 5 6 7 8 9
0 1 2 3 4 5 6 7 8 9

주민등록번호 앞자리	고 유 번 호

0 1 2 3 4 5 6 7 8 9 (repeated for each column)

문항	답 란	문항	답 란	문항	답 란	문항	답 란	문항	답 란	문항	답 란
1	ⓐⓑⓒⓓ	21	ⓐⓑⓒⓓ	41	ⓐⓑⓒⓓ	61	ⓐⓑⓒⓓ	81	ⓐⓑⓒⓓ		
2	ⓐⓑⓒⓓ	22	ⓐⓑⓒⓓ	42	ⓐⓑⓒⓓ	62	ⓐⓑⓒⓓ	82	ⓐⓑⓒⓓ		
3	ⓐⓑⓒⓓ	23	ⓐⓑⓒⓓ	43	ⓐⓑⓒⓓ	63	ⓐⓑⓒⓓ	83	ⓐⓑⓒⓓ		
4	ⓐⓑⓒⓓ	24	ⓐⓑⓒⓓ	44	ⓐⓑⓒⓓ	64	ⓐⓑⓒⓓ	84	ⓐⓑⓒⓓ		
5	ⓐⓑⓒⓓ	25	ⓐⓑⓒⓓ	45	ⓐⓑⓒⓓ	65	ⓐⓑⓒⓓ	85	ⓐⓑⓒⓓ		
6	ⓐⓑⓒⓓ	26	ⓐⓑⓒⓓ	46	ⓐⓑⓒⓓ	66	ⓐⓑⓒⓓ	86	ⓐⓑⓒⓓ		
7	ⓐⓑⓒⓓ	27	ⓐⓑⓒⓓ	47	ⓐⓑⓒⓓ	67	ⓐⓑⓒⓓ	87	ⓐⓑⓒⓓ		
8	ⓐⓑⓒⓓ	28	ⓐⓑⓒⓓ	48	ⓐⓑⓒⓓ	68	ⓐⓑⓒⓓ	88	ⓐⓑⓒⓓ		
9	ⓐⓑⓒⓓ	29	ⓐⓑⓒⓓ	49	ⓐⓑⓒⓓ	69	ⓐⓑⓒⓓ	89	ⓐⓑⓒⓓ		
10	ⓐⓑⓒⓓ	30	ⓐⓑⓒⓓ	50	ⓐⓑⓒⓓ	70	ⓐⓑⓒⓓ	90	ⓐⓑⓒⓓ		
11	ⓐⓑⓒⓓ	31	ⓐⓑⓒⓓ	51	ⓐⓑⓒⓓ	71	ⓐⓑⓒⓓ				
12	ⓐⓑⓒⓓ	32	ⓐⓑⓒⓓ	52	ⓐⓑⓒⓓ	72	ⓐⓑⓒⓓ		password		
13	ⓐⓑⓒⓓ	33	ⓐⓑⓒⓓ	53	ⓐⓑⓒⓓ	73	ⓐⓑⓒⓓ				
14	ⓐⓑⓒⓓ	34	ⓐⓑⓒⓓ	54	ⓐⓑⓒⓓ	74	ⓐⓑⓒⓓ				
15	ⓐⓑⓒⓓ	35	ⓐⓑⓒⓓ	55	ⓐⓑⓒⓓ	75	ⓐⓑⓒⓓ				
16	ⓐⓑⓒⓓ	36	ⓐⓑⓒⓓ	56	ⓐⓑⓒⓓ	76	ⓐⓑⓒⓓ				
17	ⓐⓑⓒⓓ	37	ⓐⓑⓒⓓ	57	ⓐⓑⓒⓓ	77	ⓐⓑⓒⓓ				
18	ⓐⓑⓒⓓ	38	ⓐⓑⓒⓓ	58	ⓐⓑⓒⓓ	78	ⓐⓑⓒⓓ				
19	ⓐⓑⓒⓓ	39	ⓐⓑⓒⓓ	59	ⓐⓑⓒⓓ	79	ⓐⓑⓒⓓ				
20	ⓐⓑⓒⓓ	40	ⓐⓑⓒⓓ	60	ⓐⓑⓒⓓ	80	ⓐⓑⓒⓓ				

password
0 1 2 3 4 5 6 7 8 9 (repeated for each column)

절취선

G-TELP

※ TEST DATE

MO.	DAY	YEAR

감독
확인
관인

성 명	

등급 ① ② ③ ④ ⑤

성 명 란

	초성	ㄱ ㄴ ㄷ ㄹ ㅁ ㅂ ㅅ ㅇ ㅈ ㅊ ㅋ ㅌ ㅍ ㅎ
성	중성	ㅏ ㅑ ㅓ ㅕ ㅗ ㅛ ㅜ ㅠ ㅡ ㅣ ㅐ ㅒ ㅔ ㅖ ㅚ ㅟ ㅢ ㅘ ㅝ ㅙ
	종성	ㄱ ㄴ ㄷ ㄹ ㅁ ㅂ ㅅ ㅇ ㅈ ㅊ ㅋ ㅌ ㅍ ㅎ ㄲ ㄸ ㅃ ㅆ ㅉ
	초성	ㄱ ㄴ ㄷ ㄹ ㅁ ㅂ ㅅ ㅇ ㅈ ㅊ ㅋ ㅌ ㅍ ㅎ
명	중성	ㅏ ㅑ ㅓ ㅕ ㅗ ㅛ ㅜ ㅠ ㅡ ㅣ ㅐ ㅒ ㅔ ㅖ ㅚ ㅟ ㅢ ㅘ ㅝ ㅙ
	종성	ㄱ ㄴ ㄷ ㄹ ㅁ ㅂ ㅅ ㅇ ㅈ ㅊ ㅋ ㅌ ㅍ ㅎ ㄲ ㄸ ㅃ ㅆ ㅉ
	초성	ㄱ ㄴ ㄷ ㄹ ㅁ ㅂ ㅅ ㅇ ㅈ ㅊ ㅋ ㅌ ㅍ ㅎ
란	중성	ㅏ ㅑ ㅓ ㅕ ㅗ ㅛ ㅜ ㅠ ㅡ ㅣ ㅐ ㅒ ㅔ ㅖ ㅚ ㅟ ㅢ ㅘ ㅝ ㅙ
	종성	ㄱ ㄴ ㄷ ㄹ ㅁ ㅂ ㅅ ㅇ ㅈ ㅊ ㅋ ㅌ ㅍ ㅎ ㄲ ㄸ ㅃ ㅆ ㅉ
	초성	ㄱ ㄴ ㄷ ㄹ ㅁ ㅂ ㅅ ㅇ ㅈ ㅊ ㅋ ㅌ ㅍ ㅎ
	중성	ㅏ ㅑ ㅓ ㅕ ㅗ ㅛ ㅜ ㅠ ㅡ ㅣ ㅐ ㅒ ㅔ ㅖ ㅚ ㅟ ㅢ ㅘ ㅝ ㅙ
	종성	ㄱ ㄴ ㄷ ㄹ ㅁ ㅂ ㅅ ㅇ ㅈ ㅊ ㅋ ㅌ ㅍ ㅎ ㄲ ㄸ ㅃ ㅆ

수 험 번 호

(0 1 2 3 4 5 6 7 8 9 number grids)

1) Code 1.
	0 1 2 3 4 5 6 7 8 9
	0 1 2 3 4 5 6 7 8 9
	0 1 2 3 4 5 6 7 8 9

2) Code 2.
	0 1 2 3 4 5 6 7 8 9
	0 1 2 3 4 5 6 7 8 9
	0 1 2 3 4 5 6 7 8 9

3) Code 3.
	0 1 2 3 4 5 6 7 8 9
	0 1 2 3 4 5 6 7 8 9
	0 1 2 3 4 5 6 7 8 9

주민등록번호 앞자리 | 고 유 번 호

(0 1 2 3 4 5 6 7 8 9 number grids)

답 란

문항	답 란	문항	답 란	문항	답 란	문항	답 란	문항	답 란	문항	답 란
1	ⓐⓑⓒⓓ	21	ⓐⓑⓒⓓ	41	ⓐⓑⓒⓓ	61	ⓐⓑⓒⓓ	81	ⓐⓑⓒⓓ		
2	ⓐⓑⓒⓓ	22	ⓐⓑⓒⓓ	42	ⓐⓑⓒⓓ	62	ⓐⓑⓒⓓ	82	ⓐⓑⓒⓓ		
3	ⓐⓑⓒⓓ	23	ⓐⓑⓒⓓ	43	ⓐⓑⓒⓓ	63	ⓐⓑⓒⓓ	83	ⓐⓑⓒⓓ		
4	ⓐⓑⓒⓓ	24	ⓐⓑⓒⓓ	44	ⓐⓑⓒⓓ	64	ⓐⓑⓒⓓ	84	ⓐⓑⓒⓓ		
5	ⓐⓑⓒⓓ	25	ⓐⓑⓒⓓ	45	ⓐⓑⓒⓓ	65	ⓐⓑⓒⓓ	85	ⓐⓑⓒⓓ		
6	ⓐⓑⓒⓓ	26	ⓐⓑⓒⓓ	46	ⓐⓑⓒⓓ	66	ⓐⓑⓒⓓ	86	ⓐⓑⓒⓓ		
7	ⓐⓑⓒⓓ	27	ⓐⓑⓒⓓ	47	ⓐⓑⓒⓓ	67	ⓐⓑⓒⓓ	87	ⓐⓑⓒⓓ		
8	ⓐⓑⓒⓓ	28	ⓐⓑⓒⓓ	48	ⓐⓑⓒⓓ	68	ⓐⓑⓒⓓ	88	ⓐⓑⓒⓓ		
9	ⓐⓑⓒⓓ	29	ⓐⓑⓒⓓ	49	ⓐⓑⓒⓓ	69	ⓐⓑⓒⓓ	89	ⓐⓑⓒⓓ		
10	ⓐⓑⓒⓓ	30	ⓐⓑⓒⓓ	50	ⓐⓑⓒⓓ	70	ⓐⓑⓒⓓ	90	ⓐⓑⓒⓓ		
11	ⓐⓑⓒⓓ	31	ⓐⓑⓒⓓ	51	ⓐⓑⓒⓓ	71	ⓐⓑⓒⓓ				
12	ⓐⓑⓒⓓ	32	ⓐⓑⓒⓓ	52	ⓐⓑⓒⓓ	72	ⓐⓑⓒⓓ				
13	ⓐⓑⓒⓓ	33	ⓐⓑⓒⓓ	53	ⓐⓑⓒⓓ	73	ⓐⓑⓒⓓ				
14	ⓐⓑⓒⓓ	34	ⓐⓑⓒⓓ	54	ⓐⓑⓒⓓ	74	ⓐⓑⓒⓓ				
15	ⓐⓑⓒⓓ	35	ⓐⓑⓒⓓ	55	ⓐⓑⓒⓓ	75	ⓐⓑⓒⓓ				
16	ⓐⓑⓒⓓ	36	ⓐⓑⓒⓓ	56	ⓐⓑⓒⓓ	76	ⓐⓑⓒⓓ				
17	ⓐⓑⓒⓓ	37	ⓐⓑⓒⓓ	57	ⓐⓑⓒⓓ	77	ⓐⓑⓒⓓ				
18	ⓐⓑⓒⓓ	38	ⓐⓑⓒⓓ	58	ⓐⓑⓒⓓ	78	ⓐⓑⓒⓓ				
19	ⓐⓑⓒⓓ	39	ⓐⓑⓒⓓ	59	ⓐⓑⓒⓓ	79	ⓐⓑⓒⓓ				
20	ⓐⓑⓒⓓ	40	ⓐⓑⓒⓓ	60	ⓐⓑⓒⓓ	80	ⓐⓑⓒⓓ				

password

(0 1 2 3 4 5 6 7 8 9 number grids)

절취선

G-TELP

※ TEST DATE

MO.	DAY	YEAR

감독확인관인

성 명		

등급 ① ② ③ ④ ⑤

성명란	초성	ㄱ ㄴ ㄷ ㄹ ㅁ ㅂ ㅅ ㅇ ㅈ ㅊ ㅋ ㅌ ㅍ ㅎ
	중성	ㅏ ㅑ ㅓ ㅕ ㅗ ㅛ ㅜ ㅠ ㅡ ㅣ ㅐ ㅒ ㅔ ㅖ ㅘ ㅙ ㅚ ㅝ ㅞ ㅟ ㅢ
	종성	ㄱ ㄴ ㄷ ㄹ ㅁ ㅂ ㅅ ㅇ ㅈ ㅊ ㅋ ㅌ ㅍ ㅎ ㄲ ㄸ ㅃ ㅆ ㅉ

수 험 번 호

| 0 1 2 3 4 5 6 7 8 9 |

1) Code 1.
| 0 1 2 3 4 5 6 7 8 9 |
| 0 1 2 3 4 5 6 7 8 9 |
| 0 1 2 3 4 5 6 7 8 9 |

2) Code 2.
| 0 1 2 3 4 5 6 7 8 9 |
| 0 1 2 3 4 5 6 7 8 9 |
| 0 1 2 3 4 5 6 7 8 9 |

3) Code 3.
| 0 1 2 3 4 5 6 7 8 9 |
| 0 1 2 3 4 5 6 7 8 9 |
| 0 1 2 3 4 5 6 7 8 9 |

주민등록번호 앞자리 / 고 유 번 호

문항	답란	문항	답란	문항	답란	문항	답란	문항	답란	문항	답란
1	ⓐⓑⓒⓓ	21	ⓐⓑⓒⓓ	41	ⓐⓑⓒⓓ	61	ⓐⓑⓒⓓ	81	ⓐⓑⓒⓓ		
2	ⓐⓑⓒⓓ	22	ⓐⓑⓒⓓ	42	ⓐⓑⓒⓓ	62	ⓐⓑⓒⓓ	82	ⓐⓑⓒⓓ		
3	ⓐⓑⓒⓓ	23	ⓐⓑⓒⓓ	43	ⓐⓑⓒⓓ	63	ⓐⓑⓒⓓ	83	ⓐⓑⓒⓓ		
4	ⓐⓑⓒⓓ	24	ⓐⓑⓒⓓ	44	ⓐⓑⓒⓓ	64	ⓐⓑⓒⓓ	84	ⓐⓑⓒⓓ		
5	ⓐⓑⓒⓓ	25	ⓐⓑⓒⓓ	45	ⓐⓑⓒⓓ	65	ⓐⓑⓒⓓ	85	ⓐⓑⓒⓓ		
6	ⓐⓑⓒⓓ	26	ⓐⓑⓒⓓ	46	ⓐⓑⓒⓓ	66	ⓐⓑⓒⓓ	86	ⓐⓑⓒⓓ		
7	ⓐⓑⓒⓓ	27	ⓐⓑⓒⓓ	47	ⓐⓑⓒⓓ	67	ⓐⓑⓒⓓ	87	ⓐⓑⓒⓓ		
8	ⓐⓑⓒⓓ	28	ⓐⓑⓒⓓ	48	ⓐⓑⓒⓓ	68	ⓐⓑⓒⓓ	88	ⓐⓑⓒⓓ		
9	ⓐⓑⓒⓓ	29	ⓐⓑⓒⓓ	49	ⓐⓑⓒⓓ	69	ⓐⓑⓒⓓ	89	ⓐⓑⓒⓓ		
10	ⓐⓑⓒⓓ	30	ⓐⓑⓒⓓ	50	ⓐⓑⓒⓓ	70	ⓐⓑⓒⓓ	90	ⓐⓑⓒⓓ		
11	ⓐⓑⓒⓓ	31	ⓐⓑⓒⓓ	51	ⓐⓑⓒⓓ	71	ⓐⓑⓒⓓ				
12	ⓐⓑⓒⓓ	32	ⓐⓑⓒⓓ	52	ⓐⓑⓒⓓ	72	ⓐⓑⓒⓓ				
13	ⓐⓑⓒⓓ	33	ⓐⓑⓒⓓ	53	ⓐⓑⓒⓓ	73	ⓐⓑⓒⓓ	password			
14	ⓐⓑⓒⓓ	34	ⓐⓑⓒⓓ	54	ⓐⓑⓒⓓ	74	ⓐⓑⓒⓓ				
15	ⓐⓑⓒⓓ	35	ⓐⓑⓒⓓ	55	ⓐⓑⓒⓓ	75	ⓐⓑⓒⓓ				
16	ⓐⓑⓒⓓ	36	ⓐⓑⓒⓓ	56	ⓐⓑⓒⓓ	76	ⓐⓑⓒⓓ	0 1 2 3 4 5 6 7 8 9			
17	ⓐⓑⓒⓓ	37	ⓐⓑⓒⓓ	57	ⓐⓑⓒⓓ	77	ⓐⓑⓒⓓ				
18	ⓐⓑⓒⓓ	38	ⓐⓑⓒⓓ	58	ⓐⓑⓒⓓ	78	ⓐⓑⓒⓓ				
19	ⓐⓑⓒⓓ	39	ⓐⓑⓒⓓ	59	ⓐⓑⓒⓓ	79	ⓐⓑⓒⓓ				
20	ⓐⓑⓒⓓ	40	ⓐⓑⓒⓓ	60	ⓐⓑⓒⓓ	80	ⓐⓑⓒⓓ				

절취선

G-TELP

※ TEST DATE

MO.	DAY	YEAR

감독확인
관인

성 명		

등급　① ② ③ ④ ⑤

성명란		초 성 / 중 성 / 종 성

(한글 자모 표기란: ㄱ ㄴ ㄷ ㄹ ㅁ ㅂ ㅅ ㅇ ㅈ ㅊ ㅋ ㅌ ㅍ ㅎ / ㅏ ㅑ ㅓ ㅕ ㅗ ㅛ ㅜ ㅠ ㅡ ㅣ ㅐ ㅒ ㅔ ㅖ ㅚ ㅘ ㅝ ㅟ ㅢ ㅙ ㅞ / ㄱ ㄴ ㄷ ㄹ ㅁ ㅂ ㅅ ㅇ ㅈ ㅊ ㅋ ㅌ ㅍ ㅎ ㄲ ㄸ ㅃ ㅆ ㅉ)

수 험 번 호

0 1 2 3 4 5 6 7 8 9

1) Code 1.

0 1 2 3 4 5 6 7 8 9
0 1 2 3 4 5 6 7 8 9
0 1 2 3 4 5 6 7 8 9

2) Code 2.

0 1 2 3 4 5 6 7 8 9
0 1 2 3 4 5 6 7 8 9
0 1 2 3 4 5 6 7 8 9

3) Code 3.

0 1 2 3 4 5 6 7 8 9
0 1 2 3 4 5 6 7 8 9
0 1 2 3 4 5 6 7 8 9

주민등록번호 앞자리 / 고 유 번 호

0 1 2 3 4 5 6 7 8 9

문항	답 란	문항	답 란	문항	답 란	문항	답 란	문항	답 란	문항	답 란
1	ⓐⓑⓒⓓ	21	ⓐⓑⓒⓓ	41	ⓐⓑⓒⓓ	61	ⓐⓑⓒⓓ	81	ⓐⓑⓒⓓ		
2	ⓐⓑⓒⓓ	22	ⓐⓑⓒⓓ	42	ⓐⓑⓒⓓ	62	ⓐⓑⓒⓓ	82	ⓐⓑⓒⓓ		
3	ⓐⓑⓒⓓ	23	ⓐⓑⓒⓓ	43	ⓐⓑⓒⓓ	63	ⓐⓑⓒⓓ	83	ⓐⓑⓒⓓ		
4	ⓐⓑⓒⓓ	24	ⓐⓑⓒⓓ	44	ⓐⓑⓒⓓ	64	ⓐⓑⓒⓓ	84	ⓐⓑⓒⓓ		
5	ⓐⓑⓒⓓ	25	ⓐⓑⓒⓓ	45	ⓐⓑⓒⓓ	65	ⓐⓑⓒⓓ	85	ⓐⓑⓒⓓ		
6	ⓐⓑⓒⓓ	26	ⓐⓑⓒⓓ	46	ⓐⓑⓒⓓ	66	ⓐⓑⓒⓓ	86	ⓐⓑⓒⓓ		
7	ⓐⓑⓒⓓ	27	ⓐⓑⓒⓓ	47	ⓐⓑⓒⓓ	67	ⓐⓑⓒⓓ	87	ⓐⓑⓒⓓ		
8	ⓐⓑⓒⓓ	28	ⓐⓑⓒⓓ	48	ⓐⓑⓒⓓ	68	ⓐⓑⓒⓓ	88	ⓐⓑⓒⓓ		
9	ⓐⓑⓒⓓ	29	ⓐⓑⓒⓓ	49	ⓐⓑⓒⓓ	69	ⓐⓑⓒⓓ	89	ⓐⓑⓒⓓ		
10	ⓐⓑⓒⓓ	30	ⓐⓑⓒⓓ	50	ⓐⓑⓒⓓ	70	ⓐⓑⓒⓓ	90	ⓐⓑⓒⓓ		
11	ⓐⓑⓒⓓ	31	ⓐⓑⓒⓓ	51	ⓐⓑⓒⓓ	71	ⓐⓑⓒⓓ				
12	ⓐⓑⓒⓓ	32	ⓐⓑⓒⓓ	52	ⓐⓑⓒⓓ	72	ⓐⓑⓒⓓ				
13	ⓐⓑⓒⓓ	33	ⓐⓑⓒⓓ	53	ⓐⓑⓒⓓ	73	ⓐⓑⓒⓓ	password			
14	ⓐⓑⓒⓓ	34	ⓐⓑⓒⓓ	54	ⓐⓑⓒⓓ	74	ⓐⓑⓒⓓ				
15	ⓐⓑⓒⓓ	35	ⓐⓑⓒⓓ	55	ⓐⓑⓒⓓ	75	ⓐⓑⓒⓓ	0 1 2 3 4 5 6 7 8 9			
16	ⓐⓑⓒⓓ	36	ⓐⓑⓒⓓ	56	ⓐⓑⓒⓓ	76	ⓐⓑⓒⓓ				
17	ⓐⓑⓒⓓ	37	ⓐⓑⓒⓓ	57	ⓐⓑⓒⓓ	77	ⓐⓑⓒⓓ				
18	ⓐⓑⓒⓓ	38	ⓐⓑⓒⓓ	58	ⓐⓑⓒⓓ	78	ⓐⓑⓒⓓ				
19	ⓐⓑⓒⓓ	39	ⓐⓑⓒⓓ	59	ⓐⓑⓒⓓ	79	ⓐⓑⓒⓓ				
20	ⓐⓑⓒⓓ	40	ⓐⓑⓒⓓ	60	ⓐⓑⓒⓓ	80	ⓐⓑⓒⓓ				

절취선

G-TELP

※ TEST DATE

MO.	DAY	YEAR

감독확인
관인

성 명	

등급 ① ② ③ ④ ⑤

성명란	초성 중성 종성 (반복)	ㄱ ㄴ ㄷ ㄹ ㅁ ㅂ ㅅ ㅇ ㅈ ㅊ ㅋ ㅌ ㅍ ㅎ ㄲ ㄸ ㅃ ㅆ ㅉ / ㅏ ㅑ ㅓ ㅕ ㅗ ㅛ ㅜ ㅠ ㅡ ㅣ ㅐ ㅒ ㅔ ㅖ ㅘ ㅙ ㅚ ㅝ ㅞ ㅟ ㅢ

수 험 번 호

(숫자 0~9 마킹란)

1) Code 1.
| 0 1 2 3 4 5 6 7 8 9 |
| 0 1 2 3 4 5 6 7 8 9 |
| 0 1 2 3 4 5 6 7 8 9 |

2) Code 2.
| 0 1 2 3 4 5 6 7 8 9 |
| 0 1 2 3 4 5 6 7 8 9 |
| 0 1 2 3 4 5 6 7 8 9 |

3) Code 3.
| 0 1 2 3 4 5 6 7 8 9 |
| 0 1 2 3 4 5 6 7 8 9 |
| 0 1 2 3 4 5 6 7 8 9 |

주민등록번호 앞자리	고 유 번 호
(0~9 마킹란)	(0~9 마킹란)

문항	답 란	문항	답 란	문항	답 란	문항	답 란	문항	답 란	문항	답 란
1	ⓐ ⓑ ⓒ ⓓ	21	ⓐ ⓑ ⓒ ⓓ	41	ⓐ ⓑ ⓒ ⓓ	61	ⓐ ⓑ ⓒ ⓓ	81	ⓐ ⓑ ⓒ ⓓ		
2	ⓐ ⓑ ⓒ ⓓ	22	ⓐ ⓑ ⓒ ⓓ	42	ⓐ ⓑ ⓒ ⓓ	62	ⓐ ⓑ ⓒ ⓓ	82	ⓐ ⓑ ⓒ ⓓ		
3	ⓐ ⓑ ⓒ ⓓ	23	ⓐ ⓑ ⓒ ⓓ	43	ⓐ ⓑ ⓒ ⓓ	63	ⓐ ⓑ ⓒ ⓓ	83	ⓐ ⓑ ⓒ ⓓ		
4	ⓐ ⓑ ⓒ ⓓ	24	ⓐ ⓑ ⓒ ⓓ	44	ⓐ ⓑ ⓒ ⓓ	64	ⓐ ⓑ ⓒ ⓓ	84	ⓐ ⓑ ⓒ ⓓ		
5	ⓐ ⓑ ⓒ ⓓ	25	ⓐ ⓑ ⓒ ⓓ	45	ⓐ ⓑ ⓒ ⓓ	65	ⓐ ⓑ ⓒ ⓓ	85	ⓐ ⓑ ⓒ ⓓ		
6	ⓐ ⓑ ⓒ ⓓ	26	ⓐ ⓑ ⓒ ⓓ	46	ⓐ ⓑ ⓒ ⓓ	66	ⓐ ⓑ ⓒ ⓓ	86	ⓐ ⓑ ⓒ ⓓ		
7	ⓐ ⓑ ⓒ ⓓ	27	ⓐ ⓑ ⓒ ⓓ	47	ⓐ ⓑ ⓒ ⓓ	67	ⓐ ⓑ ⓒ ⓓ	87	ⓐ ⓑ ⓒ ⓓ		
8	ⓐ ⓑ ⓒ ⓓ	28	ⓐ ⓑ ⓒ ⓓ	48	ⓐ ⓑ ⓒ ⓓ	68	ⓐ ⓑ ⓒ ⓓ	88	ⓐ ⓑ ⓒ ⓓ		
9	ⓐ ⓑ ⓒ ⓓ	29	ⓐ ⓑ ⓒ ⓓ	49	ⓐ ⓑ ⓒ ⓓ	69	ⓐ ⓑ ⓒ ⓓ	89	ⓐ ⓑ ⓒ ⓓ		
10	ⓐ ⓑ ⓒ ⓓ	30	ⓐ ⓑ ⓒ ⓓ	50	ⓐ ⓑ ⓒ ⓓ	70	ⓐ ⓑ ⓒ ⓓ	90	ⓐ ⓑ ⓒ ⓓ		
11	ⓐ ⓑ ⓒ ⓓ	31	ⓐ ⓑ ⓒ ⓓ	51	ⓐ ⓑ ⓒ ⓓ	71	ⓐ ⓑ ⓒ ⓓ				
12	ⓐ ⓑ ⓒ ⓓ	32	ⓐ ⓑ ⓒ ⓓ	52	ⓐ ⓑ ⓒ ⓓ	72	ⓐ ⓑ ⓒ ⓓ	password			
13	ⓐ ⓑ ⓒ ⓓ	33	ⓐ ⓑ ⓒ ⓓ	53	ⓐ ⓑ ⓒ ⓓ	73	ⓐ ⓑ ⓒ ⓓ				
14	ⓐ ⓑ ⓒ ⓓ	34	ⓐ ⓑ ⓒ ⓓ	54	ⓐ ⓑ ⓒ ⓓ	74	ⓐ ⓑ ⓒ ⓓ	(0~9 마킹란)			
15	ⓐ ⓑ ⓒ ⓓ	35	ⓐ ⓑ ⓒ ⓓ	55	ⓐ ⓑ ⓒ ⓓ	75	ⓐ ⓑ ⓒ ⓓ				
16	ⓐ ⓑ ⓒ ⓓ	36	ⓐ ⓑ ⓒ ⓓ	56	ⓐ ⓑ ⓒ ⓓ	76	ⓐ ⓑ ⓒ ⓓ				
17	ⓐ ⓑ ⓒ ⓓ	37	ⓐ ⓑ ⓒ ⓓ	57	ⓐ ⓑ ⓒ ⓓ	77	ⓐ ⓑ ⓒ ⓓ				
18	ⓐ ⓑ ⓒ ⓓ	38	ⓐ ⓑ ⓒ ⓓ	58	ⓐ ⓑ ⓒ ⓓ	78	ⓐ ⓑ ⓒ ⓓ				
19	ⓐ ⓑ ⓒ ⓓ	39	ⓐ ⓑ ⓒ ⓓ	59	ⓐ ⓑ ⓒ ⓓ	79	ⓐ ⓑ ⓒ ⓓ				
20	ⓐ ⓑ ⓒ ⓓ	40	ⓐ ⓑ ⓒ ⓓ	60	ⓐ ⓑ ⓒ ⓓ	80	ⓐ ⓑ ⓒ ⓓ				

절취선

MEMO

MEMO

지텔프 목표 점수 달성을 완료했다면?
공무원 단기 합격도 역시 1위 해커스다!

공무원

서울시 / 국가직 일반행정
최종 합격 2관왕!

신*연 합격생

수 십 번의 회독 끝에 높은 점수를 받았습니다!

행정법은 함수민 선생님 강의를 들었습니다. 처음에는 엄청난 양의 문제에 당황스러웠지만
점차 내용이 반복됨을 알게 되었고, 그 후 **모르는 내용과 외워야 할 내용을 정확히 구분하여
정리하면서 수 십 번을 반복해 암기**하였습니다. 결국 수 십 번의 회독 끝에 시험에서는
국가직 100점, 서울시에서는 95점이라는 높은 점수를 받았습니다.

군무원

컴퓨터공학 전공,
10개월 만에 사이버직 합격!

김*근 합격생

비문학 독해력이 늘어나는 신비한 체험!

비문학 연습 교재는 해커스의 국어 비문학 독해 333이라는 교재인데
하루 3개의 지문씩 30일 동안 풀 수 있도록 구성되어 있어 매우 연습하기 좋더라고요.
저는 **3개 지문을 6분 안에 풀도록 꾸준히 연습**을 했어요.

경찰

완전 노베이스로 시작,
8개월 만에 인천청 합격!

강*혁 합격생

형사법 부족한 부분은 모의고사로 채우기!

기본부터 기출문제집과 같이 병행해서 좋았던 것 같습니다. 그리고 1차 시험 보기 전까지
심화 강의를 끝냈는데 **개인적으로 심화강의 추천**드립니다. 안정적인 실력이 아니라
생각해서 기출 후 **전범위 모의고사에서 부족한 부분들을 많이 채워** 나간 것 같습니다.

소방

특전사 출신 노베이스,
6개월 만에 특채 합격!

이*영 합격생

후반에는 모의고사로 실전감각 UP!

수험기간 후반에는 시간을 정해놓고 **매일 모의고사를 풀면서 실전감각을 익혔고,**
틀린 부분에 대해서는 **다시 개념을 복습**하는 시간을 가졌습니다.

교재 확인 및 수강신청은 여기서!

해커스공무원
gosi.Hackers.com

공무원

해커스군무원
army.Hackers.com

군무원

해커스경찰
police.Hackers.com

경찰공무원

해커스소방
fire.Hackers.com

소방공무원

지텔프 공식
기출문제집 | 7회분
LEVEL 2

해커스

공식기출
TEST 1
정답 · 스크립트 · 해석 · 해설

GRAMMAR

LISTENING

READING & VOCABULARY

GRAMMAR _____ / 26 (점수 : _____ 점)
LISTENING _____ / 26 (점수 : _____ 점)
READING & VOCABULARY _____ / 28 (점수 : _____ 점)

TOTAL _____ / 80 (평균 점수 : _____ 점)

*각 영역 점수: 맞은 개수 × 3.75
*평균 점수: 각 영역 점수 합계 ÷ 3

정답 및 취약 유형 분석표

GRAMMAR

번호	정답	유형
01	c	연결어
02	b	시제
03	a	조동사
04	d	가정법
05	c	준동사
06	c	가정법
07	d	시제
08	d	가정법
09	a	준동사
10	b	관계사
11	c	준동사
12	d	시제
13	a	시제
14	b	준동사
15	d	가정법
16	c	관계사
17	c	조동사
18	a	준동사
19	c	시제
20	c	준동사
21	b	가정법
22	d	조동사
23	d	시제
24	a	연결어
25	b	가정법
26	a	조동사

LISTENING

PART	번호	정답	유형
PART 1	27	a	특정세부사항
	28	c	특정세부사항
	29	a	특정세부사항
	30	d	특정세부사항
	31	b	추론
	32	c	특정세부사항
PART 2	33	b	추론
	34	d	주제/목적
	35	a	추론
	36	d	특정세부사항
	37	a	특정세부사항
	38	d	특정세부사항
	39	a	특정세부사항
PART 3	40	d	특정세부사항
	41	d	특정세부사항
	42	b	특정세부사항
	43	b	추론
	44	c	특정세부사항
	45	c	추론
	46	c	주제/목적
	47	b	특정세부사항
	48	a	추론
PART 4	49	d	특정세부사항
	50	c	특정세부사항
	51	b	특정세부사항
	52	c	특정세부사항

READING & VOCABULARY

PART	번호	정답	유형
PART 1	53	d	특정세부사항
	54	a	특정세부사항
	55	d	특정세부사항
	56	b	특정세부사항
	57	d	추론
	58	c	어휘
	59	b	어휘
	60	a	주제/목적
	61	c	특정세부사항
PART 2	62	d	추론
	63	c	추론
	64	d	Not/True
	65	a	어휘
	66	b	어휘
	67	b	주제/목적
	68	b	특정세부사항
	69	a	특정세부사항
PART 3	70	d	Not/True
	71	d	추론
	72	a	어휘
	73	a	어휘
	74	b	주제/목적
	75	c	특정세부사항
	76	a	특정세부사항
PART 4	77	b	특정세부사항
	78	a	추론
	79	b	어휘
	80	b	어휘

유형	맞힌 개수
시제	/ 6
가정법	/ 6
준동사	/ 6
조동사	/ 4
연결어	/ 2
관계사	/ 2
TOTAL	/ 26

유형	맞힌 개수
주제/목적	/ 2
특정세부사항	/ 18
Not/True	/ 0
추론	/ 6
TOTAL	/ 26

유형	맞힌 개수
주제/목적	/ 3
특정세부사항	/ 10
Not/True	/ 2
추론	/ 5
어휘	/ 8
TOTAL	/ 28

공식기출
TEST 1

01 연결어   접속사   난이도 ●○○

Though typically thought of as a hot, sandy area, a desert is merely defined by how little precipitation it receives. For example, Antarctica is considered a desert _____ it receives only eight inches of rain annually.

(a) even though
(b) in case
(c) because
(d) after

일반적으로 뜨겁고 모래로 뒤덮인 지역으로 여겨지지만, 사막은 단순히 강수량이 얼마나 적은지에 따라 정의된다. 예를 들어, 남극대륙은 연간 강수량이 8인치에 불과하기 때문에 사막으로 여겨진다.

─○ 지텔프 치트키

'~이기 때문에'라는 의미의 이유를 나타낼 때는 because를 쓴다.

> 💡 **이유를 나타내는 빈출 접속사**
> because ~이기 때문에   since ~이기 때문에   as ~이기 때문에

해설 | 문맥상 남극대륙은 연간 강수량이 8인치에 불과하기 때문에 사막으로 여겨진다는 의미가 되어야 자연스럽다. 따라서 '~이기 때문에'라는 의미의 이유를 나타내는 부사절 접속사 (c) because가 정답이다.

> 오답분석
> (a) even though는 '~에도 불구하고', (b) in case는 '~할 경우에 대비하여', (d) after는 '~한 이후에'라는 의미로, 문맥에 적합하지 않아 오답이다.

어휘 | typically adv. 일반적으로   sandy adj. 모래로 뒤덮인, 모래투성이의   merely adv. 단순히, 단지   define v. (단어·구의 뜻을) 정의하다 precipitation n. 강수량, 강우   Antarctica n. 남극대륙   annually adv. 연간, 매년

02 시제   미래진행   난이도 ●●○

The music club president was supposed to lead the new member orientation today, but the vice president will give the introductory speech instead. Apparently, the president _____ a college interview at the time of the orientation.

(a) was attending
(b) will be attending
(c) has been attending
(d) attends

음악 동아리 회장이 오늘 신입 회원 오리엔테이션을 이끌기로 되어 있었는데, 부회장이 대신 소개 연설을 할 것이다. 듣자 하니, 오리엔테이션 시간에 회장은 대학 면접에 참석하고 있는 중일 것이다.

─○ 지텔프 치트키

'for + 기간 표현' 없이 특정 미래 시점을 나타내는 표현만 있으면 미래진행 시제가 정답이다.

> 💡 **미래진행과 자주 함께 쓰이는 시간 표현**
> • when / if + 현재 동사 ~할 때 / 만약 ~한다면   • until / by + 미래 시점 ~까지
> • next + 시간 표현 다음 ~에   • starting + 미래 시점 / tomorrow ~부터 / 내일

해설 | 미래진행 시제와 함께 자주 쓰이는 특정 미래 시점을 나타내는 시간 표현 'at the time of + 미래에 일어날 일'(at the time of the orientation)이 있고, 문맥상 오리엔테이션이 있는 미래 시점에 회장이 대학 면접에 참석하고 있는 중일 것이라는 의미를 만드는 미래진행 시제 (b) will be attending이 정답이다.

어휘 | be supposed to phr. ~하기로 되어 있다 vice president phr. 부회장 introductory speech phr. 소개 연설 apparently adv. 듣자 하니

---

03 조동사   조동사 should 생략   난이도 ●●○

MVC Sports Shop suffered from low sales in the first quarter of the year. An employee suggested that they _____ their social media presence to improve their numbers and attract more young customers.

(a) increase
(b) will increase
(c) are increasing
(d) increased

━○ **지텔프 치트키**

suggest 다음에는 that절에 동사원형이 온다.

💡 **주장·요구·명령·제안을 나타내는 빈출 동사**
suggest 제안하다 request 요청하다 recommend 권고하다 demand 요구하다 order 명령하다 urge 강력히 촉구하다 ask 요청하다 propose 제안하다 insist 주장하다 advise 권고하다

해설 | 주절에 제안을 나타내는 동사 suggest가 있으므로 that절에는 '(should +) 동사원형'이 와야 한다. 따라서 동사원형 (a) increase가 정답이다.

어휘 | suffer from phr. ~으로 고통받다 quarter n. 분기, 3개월 presence n. 영향력, 존재

MVC 스포츠용품점은 올해 1분기에 저조한 매출로 고통받았다. 한 직원은 매출을 개선하고 더 많은 젊은 고객들을 끌어모으기 위해 그들의 소셜 미디어 영향력을 늘려야 한다고 제안했다.

---

04 가정법   가정법 과거완료   난이도 ●●○

For three years, Alpha Highlands was the top-grossing apartment rental company in San Francisco. However, its record was recently surpassed. Had a new competitor not appeared, Alpha Highlands _____ in the top spot.

(a) will probably have stayed
(b) would probably stay
(c) will probably stay
(d) would probably have stayed

━○ **지텔프 치트키**

Had p.p.가 있으면 'would/could + have p.p.'가 정답이다.

💡 **가정법 과거완료(도치)**
Had + 주어 + p.p., 주어 + would/could(조동사 과거형) + have p.p.

3년 동안, Alpha Highlands사는 샌프란시스코에서 최고의 수익을 내는 아파트 임대 회사였다. 그러나, 최근에 그 기록은 깨졌다. 새로운 경쟁자가 나타나지 않았다면, Alpha Highlands사는 아마 1위를 지켰을 것이다.

해설 | if가 생략되어 도치된 절에 'had p.p.' 형태의 Had ~ not appeared가 있으므로, 주절에는 이와 짝을 이루어 가정법 과거완료를 만드는 'would(조동사 과거형) + have p.p.'가 와야 한다. 따라서 (d) would probably have stayed가 정답이다. 참고로, 'Had a new competitor not appeared ~'는 'If a new competitor had not appeared ~'로 바꿔 쓸 수 있다.

어휘 | top-grossing adj. 최고의 수익을 내는 rental adj. 임대의; n. 임대, 임차 surpass v. 넘어서다, 능가하다 top spot phr. 1위

---

05 준동사   to 부정사의 부사 역할   난이도 ●●●

The invention of perfume is usually associated with ancient Egyptians. Although their exact recipes were kept secret, it is known that the Egyptians used spices, herbs, and flowers _____ their fragrances.

(a) having made
(b) making
(c) to make
(d) to be making

지텔프 치트키

'~하기 위해'라고 말할 때는 to 부정사를 쓴다.

해설 | 빈칸 앞에 주어(Egyptians), 동사(used), 목적어(spices, herbs, and flowers)가 갖춰진 완전한 절이 있으므로, 빈칸 이하는 문장의 필수 성분이 아닌 수식어구이다. 따라서 목적을 나타내며 수식어구를 이끌 수 있는 to 부정사 (c) to make가 정답이다.

어휘 | be associated with phr. ~과 관련되다 recipe n. 비결 keep secret phr. ~을 비밀로 해두다 spice n. 향신료 fragrance n. 향수, 향기

향수의 발명은 일반적으로 고대 이집트인들과 관련된다. 비록 그들의 정확한 비결은 비밀에 부쳐졌지만, 이집트인들은 향수를 만들기 위해 향신료, 허브, 꽃을 사용했다고 알려져 있다.

---

06 가정법   가정법 과거   난이도 ●●○

Justin is hesitant about accepting a job offer that requires him to move to New York City. He worries that if he were to move there, he _____ financially due to the high cost of living.

(a) will suffer
(b) would have suffered
(c) would suffer
(d) will have suffered

Justin은 뉴욕시로 이사해야 하는 일자리 제안을 수락하는 것에 대해서 망설이고 있다. 그는 만약 그곳으로 이사하게 된다면, 높은 생활비 때문에 재정적으로 어려움을 겪을 것이라고 걱정한다.

지텔프 치트키

'if + were to + 동사원형'이 있으면 'would/could + 동사원형'이 정답이다.

> 💡 **가정법 과거(were to)**
> If + 주어 + were to + 동사원형, 주어 + would/could(조동사 과거형) + 동사원형

해설 | if절에 과거 동사(were to move)가 있으므로, 주절에는 이와 짝을 이루어 가정법 과거를 만드는 'would(조동사 과거형) + 동사원형'이 와야 한다. 따라서 (c) would suffer가 정답이다.

어휘 | be hesitant about phr. ~에 대해서 망설이다 accept v. 수락하다, 받아들이다 financially adv. 재정적으로, 경제적으로 cost of living phr. 생활비

07 시제 과거진행 난이도 ●●○

Gloria just watched a singing competition on television. At first, she _____ the defending champion, but when she saw the opponent's performance, she immediately knew that the challenger deserved to win.

(a) would root for
(b) is rooting for
(c) has been rooting for
(d) was rooting for

Gloria는 방금 텔레비전에서 노래 대회를 보았다. 처음에, 그녀는 전년도 우승자를 응원하고 있던 중이었지만, 경쟁자의 공연을 보았을 때, 그녀는 도전자가 우승할 자격이 있다는 것을 바로 알아차렸다.

지텔프 치트키

'for + 기간 표현' 없이 'when + 과거 동사'만 있으면 과거진행 시제가 정답이다.

💡 **과거진행과 자주 함께 쓰이는 시간 표현**
- when / while + 과거 동사 ~했을 때 / ~하던 도중에
- last + 시간 표현 / yesterday 지난 ~에 / 어제

해설 | 과거진행 시제와 함께 쓰이는 시간 표현 'when + 과거 동사'(when ~ saw)가 있고, 문맥상 노래 대회에서 경쟁자의 공연을 보기 전까지 전년도 우승자를 응원하고 있던 중이었다는 의미가 되어야 자연스럽다. 따라서 과거진행 시제 (d) was rooting for가 정답이다.

어휘 | defending champion phr. 전년도 우승자, 타이틀 방어자 opponent n. 경쟁자, 상대 challenger n. 도전자 deserve v. ~할 자격이 있다 root for phr. ~을 응원하다

08 가정법 가정법 과거 난이도 ●●○

Despite looking fluffy and light, clouds can weigh up to a million pounds because of the condensed water they carry. If a whole cloud were to fall from the sky, it _____ whatever was underneath it.

(a) would have crushed
(b) will have crushed
(c) will crush
(d) would crush

폭신폭신하고 가벼워 보임에도 불구하고, 구름은 운반하는 응축된 수분 때문에 100만 파운드까지 무게가 나갈 수 있다. 만약 구름 전체가 하늘에서 떨어진다면, 그것은 그 아래에 있는 것이 무엇이든 눌러 부술 것이다.

지텔프 치트키

'if + were to + 동사원형'이 있으면 'would/could + 동사원형'이 정답이다.

해설 | If절에 과거 동사(were to fall)가 있으므로, 주절에는 이와 짝을 이루어 가정법 과거를 만드는 'would(조동사 과거형) + 동사원형'이 와야 한다. 따라서 (d) would crush가 정답이다.

어휘 | fluffy adj. 폭신폭신한, 솜털 같은 weigh v. 무게가 나가다 condensed adj. 응축된, 압축된 underneath prep. ~의 아래에 crush v. 눌러 부수다, 뭉개다

Engineering graduates who took the latest board exams are currently waiting for the results. They are excited and nervous at the same time, as the results are expected _____ any minute now.

(a) **to be released**
(b) having been released
(c) to have been released
(d) being released

최근의 자격시험을 치른 공학 졸업생들은 현재 결과를 기다리고 있는 중이다. 이제 곧 결과가 <u>발표될 것</u>으로 예상되는 만큼 흥분과 긴장을 동시에 하고 있다.

⊶○ 지텔프 치트키

expect는 to 부정사를 목적격 보어로 취한다.

> 💡 **to 부정사를 목적격 보어로 취하는 빈출 동사**
> expect 예상하다 determine 결심하다 encourage 권장하다 require 요구하다 urge 강력히 촉구하다 allow 허락하다 ask 요청하다 want 원하다

해설 | 빈칸 앞 동사 expect는 'expect + 목적어 + 목적격 보어'의 형태로 쓰일 때 to 부정사를 목적격 보어로 취하여, '-이 ~하는 것을 예상하다'라는 의미로 사용된다. 참고로, 'the results are expected to be released'는 'expect(동사) + the results(목적어) + to be released (목적격 보어)'에서 변형된 수동태 구문으로, 수동태가 되어도 목적격 보어인 to 부정사는 그대로 유지된다. 따라서 to 부정사 (a) to be released가 정답이다.

> **오답분석**
> (c) to have been released도 to 부정사이기는 하지만, 완료부정사(to have been released)로 쓰일 경우 '예상되는' 시점보다 '발표되는' 시점이 앞선다는 것을 나타내므로 문맥에 적합하지 않아 오답이다.

어휘 | graduate n. 졸업생; v. 졸업하다 board exam phr. 자격시험 release v. 발표하다, 공개하다

Bauhaus was a highly influential art movement that started at the Staatliches Bauhaus design school in Germany. The movement is known for combining "rational" art, _____, with functionality.

(a) what uses geometric patterns
(b) **which uses geometric patterns**
(c) who uses geometric patterns
(d) that uses geometric patterns

Bauhaus는 독일의 Staatliches Bauhaus 디자인 학교에서 시작된 매우 영향력 있는 예술 운동이었다. 이 운동은 "합리적" 예술인, <u>기하학적 무늬를 사용하는</u> 것과, 기능성을 결합한 것으로 알려져 있다.

⊶○ 지텔프 치트키

사물 선행사가 관계절 안에서 주어 역할을 하고, 빈칸 앞에 콤마(,)가 있으면 주격 관계대명사 which가 정답이다.

해설 | 사물 선행사 "rational" art를 받으면서 콤마(,) 뒤에 올 수 있는 주격 관계대명사가 필요하므로, (b) which uses geometric patterns가 정답이다.

> **오답분석**
> (d) 관계대명사 that도 사물 선행사를 받을 수 있지만, 콤마 뒤에 올 수 없으므로 오답이다.

11 준동사   동명사를 목적어로 취하는 동사   난이도 ●●○

Hannah noticed that the red bump on her arm has been there for three days now. Her husband recommended _____ ointment on it, but she decided to contact her doctor first.

(a) to have put
(b) having put
(c) putting
(d) to put

Hannah는 자기 팔에 있는 빨간 혹이 이제 3일째라는 것을 알아챘다. 그녀의 남편이 거기에 연고를 바르는 것을 권했지만, 그녀는 의사에게 먼저 연락하기로 결정했다.

○ 지텔프 치트키

recommend는 동명사를 목적어로 취한다.

☼ **동명사를 목적어로 취하는 빈출 동사**
recommend 권하다 discuss 논의하다 avoid 피하다 imagine 상상하다 mind 개의하다 keep 계속하다 consider 고려하다
prevent 방지하다 enjoy 즐기다 risk 위험을 무릅쓰다 involve 포함하다

해설 | 빈칸 앞 동사 recommend는 동명사를 목적어로 취하므로, 동명사 (c) putting이 정답이다.

오답분석
(b) having put도 동명사이기는 하지만, 완료동명사(having put)로 쓰일 경우 '권하는' 시점보다 '(연고를) 바르는' 시점이 앞선다는 것을 나타내므로 문맥에 적합하지 않아 오답이다.

어휘 | bump n. 혹, 타박상 ointment n. 연고, 바르는 약

12 시제   과거완료진행   난이도 ●●○

The small, family-owned market at Gomez Plaza has reopened to the public after a year of community-funded renovations. The business _____ for three decades before it caught fire last year due to faulty wiring.

(a) is operating
(b) has been operating
(c) will have operated
(d) had been operating

Gomez 광장에 있는 가족에 의해 운영되는 작은 가게가 1년간의 지역 주민들이 자금을 댄 개조 공사 후에 대중에게 다시 개방되었다. 이 가게는 지난해 배선 결함으로 인해 불이 나기 전에 30년 동안 운영되어 오고 있던 중이었다.

○ 지텔프 치트키

'for + 기간 표현'과 'before + 과거 동사'가 함께 오면 과거완료진행 시제가 정답이다.

☼ **과거완료진행과 자주 함께 쓰이는 시간 표현**
• before / when / since + 과거 동사 + (for + 기간 표현) ~하기 전에 / ~했을 때 / ~ 이래로 (~ 동안)
• (for + 기간 표현) + (up) until + 과거 동사 (~ 동안) ~했을 때까지

해설 | 과거완료진행 시제와 함께 쓰이는 시간 표현 'for + 기간 표현'(for three decades)과 'before + 과거 동사'(before ~ caught)가 있고, 문맥상 가게가 대과거(운영되기 시작한 시점)부터 과거(지난해 불이 난 시점)까지 30년 동안 계속해서 운영되어 오고 있던 중이었다는 의미가 되어야 자연스럽다. 따라서 과거완료진행 시제 (d) had been operating이 정답이다.

어휘 | family-owned adj. 가족에 의해 운영되는 renovation n. 개조, 보수 catch fire phr. 불이 붙다 faulty wiring phr. 배선 결함

13 시제   미래완료진행   난이도 ●●○

Jenny started living in Milan after accepting a scholarship to study fashion design. By the time she finishes her program, she _____ in the city for four years.

(a) will have been living
(b) has been living
(c) will be living
(d) is living

Jenny는 패션 디자인을 공부하기 위한 장학금을 받은 후 밀라노에서 살기 시작했다. 프로그램이 끝날 무렵이면, 그녀는 4년 동안 그 도시에 살아오고 있는 중일 것이다.

지텔프 치트키

'by the time + 현재 동사'와 'for + 기간 표현'이 함께 오면 미래완료진행 시제가 정답이다.

💡 미래완료진행과 자주 함께 쓰이는 시간 표현
• by the time / when / if + 현재 동사 + (for + 기간 표현) ~할 무렵이면 / ~할 때 / 만약 ~한다면 (~ 동안)
• by / in + 미래 시점 + (for + 기간 표현) ~ 즈음에는 / ~에 (~ 동안)

해설 | 현재 동사로 미래의 의미를 나타내는 시간의 부사절 'by the time + 현재 동사'(By the time ~ finishes)가 사용되었고, 미래완료진행 시제와 함께 쓰이는 시간 표현 'for + 기간 표현'(for four years)이 있다. 또한, 문맥상 미래 시점인 Jenny의 프로그램이 끝날 무렵이면 그녀는 4년 동안 계속해서 그 도시에 살아오고 있는 중일 것이라는 의미가 되어야 자연스럽다. 따라서 미래완료진행 시제 (a) will have been living이 정답이다.

오답분석
(c) 미래진행 시제는 특정 미래 시점에 한창 진행 중일 일을 나타내므로, 과거 또는 현재에 시작해서 특정 미래 시점까지 계속해서 진행되고 있을 일을 표현할 수 없어 오답이다.

어휘 | scholarship n. 장학금

14 준동사   동명사를 목적어로 취하는 동사   난이도 ●●○

If dogs are taken on daily walks, their claws tend to naturally wear down due to friction from the concrete. So, walking on sidewalks is a useful strategy for owners who dislike _____ their dogs' nails.

(a) having trimmed
(b) trimming
(c) to trim
(d) to have trimmed

개는 매일 산책시키면, 그들의 발톱이 콘크리트로부터의 마찰로 인해 자연스럽게 마모되는 경향이 있다. 그래서, 보도를 걷는 것은 개의 발톱을 다듬는 것을 싫어하는 견주들에게 유용한 전략이다.

dislike는 동명사를 목적어로 취한다.

☀ 동명사를 목적어로 취하는 빈출 동사
dislike 싫어하다 avoid 피하다 imagine 상상하다 mind 개의하다 keep 계속하다 consider 고려하다 prevent 방지하다
enjoy 즐기다 recommend 권장하다 risk 위험을 무릅쓰다 involve 포함하다

해설 | 빈칸 앞 동사 dislike는 동명사를 목적어로 취하므로, 동명사 (b) trimming이 정답이다.

오답분석
(a) having trimmed도 동명사이기는 하지만, 완료동명사(having trimmed)로 쓰일 경우 '싫어하는' 시점보다 '(발톱을) 다듬는' 시점이
앞선다는 것을 나타내므로 문맥에 적합하지 않아 오답이다.

어휘 | take a walk phr. 산책하다 claw n. 발톱 wear down phr. 마모되다 friction n. 마찰 sidewalk n. 보도, 인도 strategy n. 전략
trim v. (깎아서 곱게) 다듬다, 손질을 하다

15 가정법   가정법 과거   난이도 ●●○

Bananas contain potassium, which is known to be a
radioactive element. However, the amount of radiation is so
negligible that if one were to eat several bananas at once,
nothing _____ except a stomachache.

(a) would have happened
(b) will have happened
(c) will happen
(d) would happen

바나나는 칼륨이 함유되어 있는데, 이것은 방사성 원
소로 알려져 있다. 하지만, 방사선량은 무시할 만한 정
도여서 만약 한 번에 여러 개의 바나나를 먹는다면, 복
통 외에는 아무 일도 안 일어날 것이다.

■─○ 지텔프 치트키

'if + were to + 동사원형'이 있으면 'would/could + 동사원형'이 정답이다.

해설 | if절에 과거 동사(were to eat)가 있으므로, 주절에는 이와 짝을 이루어 가정법 과거를 만드는 'would(조동사 과거형) + 동사원형'이 와야
한다. 따라서 (d) would happen이 정답이다.

어휘 | contain v. ~이 함유되어 있다, 포함하다 potassium n. 칼륨 radioactive element phr. 방사성 원소 radiation n. 방사선, 방사능
negligible adj. 무시할 만한, 하찮은 at once phr. 한 번에, 동시에 stomachache n. 복통, 배탈

16 관계사   주격 관계대명사 that   난이도 ●●○

When one does not take antibiotics for the prescribed
number of days, bacteria may become resistant to the
medicine. The antibiotics _____ to kill the bacteria
then lose their effectiveness as the resistant bacteria
multiply.

(a) who were intended
(b) when were intended

항생제를 미리 정해진 일수 동안 복용하지 않으면, 박
테리아가 약에 내성이 생기게 될 수도 있다. 박테리
아를 죽일 목적이었던 항생제는 내성균이 증식하면
서 효능을 잃는다.

(c) that were intended

(d) what were intended

해설 | 사물 선행사 The antibiotics를 받으면서 보기의 관계절 내에서 동사 were intended의 주어가 될 수 있는 주격 관계대명사가 필요하므로, (c) that were intended가 정답이다.

어휘 | antibiotic n. 항생제, 항바이러스 prescribed adj. 미리 정해진, 규정된 become resistant to phr. ~에 내성이 생기다 effectiveness n. 효능 resistant bacteria phr. 내성균 multiply v. 증식시키다, 번식하다 be intended to phr. ~할 목적이다

---

17 조동사   조동사 will   난이도 ●●●

A company-wide meeting was called to discuss current corporate social responsibility practices. The CEO wants a firm CSR policy that _____ clarify the company's stance on environmental conservation.

현재 기업의 사회적 책임 실천을 논의하기 위해 전사적 회의가 소집되었다. 최고 경영자는 환경 보호에 관한 회사의 입장을 명확하게 할 확고한 CSR 정책을 원한다.

(a) may
(b) must
(c) will
(d) could

해설 | 문맥상 최고 경영자는 환경 보호에 관한 회사의 입장을 명확하게 할 확고한 CSR 정책을 원한다는 내용이 되어야 자연스러우므로, '~할 것이다'를 뜻하면서 의지를 나타내는 조동사 (c) will이 정답이다.

어휘 | company-wide adj. 전사적인 corporate social responsibility phr. 기업의 사회적 책임 practice n. 실천, 실행 firm adj. 확고한, 강경한 clarify v. 명확하게 하다, 분명히 말하다 stance n. 입장, 자세 conservation n. 보호, 보전

---

18 준동사   to 부정사를 목적격 보어로 취하는 동사   난이도 ●●○

Everyone prefers the teaching assistant over Professor Smith, who is strict and grumpy at times. Students are always more inclined _____ to a lecture if the TA is the one delivering it.

누구나 Smith 교수보다 조교를 선호하는데, Smith 교수는 때로는 엄격하고 성미가 까다롭다. 조교가 강의하는 사람이면 학생들은 항상 강의에 더 귀 기울이는 경향이 있다.

(a) to listen
(b) having listened
(c) listening
(d) to have listened

TEST 1
TEST 2
TEST 3
TEST 4
TEST 5
TEST 6
TEST 7

지텔프 공식 기출문제집 7회분 Level 2

incline은 to 부정사를 목적격 보어로 취한다.

해설 | 빈칸 앞 동사 incline은 'incline + 목적어 + 목적격 보어'의 형태로 쓰일 때 to 부정사를 목적격 보어로 취하여, '~에게 ~하는 경향이 생기게 하다'라는 의미로 사용된다. 참고로, 'Students are inclined to listen'은 'incline(동사) + students(목적어) + to listen(목적격 보어)' 에서 변형된 수동태 구문으로, 수동태가 되어도 목적격 보어인 to 부정사는 그대로 유지된다. 따라서 to 부정사 (a) to listen이 정답이다.

오답분석
(d) to have listened도 to 부정사이기는 하지만, 완료부정사(to have listened)로 쓰일 경우 '경향이 있는' 시점보다 '귀 기울이는' 시점 이 앞선다는 것을 나타내므로 문맥에 적합하지 않아 오답이다.

어휘 | teaching assistant phr. 조교 strict adj. 엄격한 grumpy adj. 성미가 까다로운, 기분이 언짢은 deliver a lecture phr. 강의를 하다

19 시제   현재진행
난이도 ●●○

Kevin decided to cut back on his coffee consumption this week. He skipped his morning cup of coffee today and, at the moment, he _____ extreme fatigue, a common symptom of caffeine withdrawal.

(a) experiences
(b) has experienced
(c) is experiencing
(d) will be experiencing

Kevin은 이번 주에 커피 섭취량을 줄이기로 결심했다. 그는 오늘 아침 커피를 걸렀고, 바로 지금, 카페인 금 단의 흔한 증상인 극심한 피로를 겪고 있는 중이다.

at the moment가 있으면 현재진행 시제가 정답이다.

☼ 현재진행과 자주 함께 쓰이는 시간 표현
• right now / now / currently / at the moment 바로 지금 / 지금 / 현재 / 바로 지금
• these days / nowadays 요즘

해설 | 현재진행 시제와 함께 쓰이는 시간 표현 at the moment가 있고, 문맥상 말하고 있는 시점인 바로 지금 Kevin이 극심한 피로를 겪고 있는 중이라는 의미가 되어야 자연스럽다. 따라서 현재진행 시제 (c) is experiencing이 정답이다.

어휘 | cut back phr. 줄이다, 축소하다 consumption n. 음식 섭취량 skip v. 거르다, 생략하다 extreme adj. 극심한, 극도의 fatigue n. 피로, 피곤 symptom n. 증상, 증세 withdrawal n. 금단 (증상)

20 준동사   동명사를 목적어로 취하는 동사
난이도 ●●○

Barry is known as the artist of the family. He can draw, paint, sculpt, and take beautiful photos. He even performs in community plays. However, he considers _____ photographs his strongest talent.

(a) to take
(b) having taken

Barry는 가족 중에서 예술가로 알려져 있다. 그는 그 림을 그리고, 채색하고, 조각하고, 아름다운 사진을 찍 을 수 있다. 그는 심지어 지역사회 연극에서 공연도 한 다. 하지만, 그는 사진 찍는 것을 자기의 가장 큰 재능 이라고 생각한다.

(c) taking

(d) to have taken

consider는 동명사를 목적어로 취한다.

해설 | 빈칸 앞 동사 consider는 동명사를 목적어로 취하므로, 동명사 (c) taking이 정답이다.

오답분석

(b) having taken도 동명사이기는 하지만, 완료동명사(having taken)로 쓰일 경우 '생각하는' 시점보다 '(사진을) 찍는' 시점이 앞선다는 것을 나타내므로 문맥에 적합하지 않아 오답이다.

어휘 | sculpt v. 조각하다 talent n. 재능, 재주

---

21 가정법　　가정법 과거완료　　　　　　　　　　　난이도 ●●○

During World War II, Switzerland avoided conflict by remaining neutral and actively defending its territories from foreign invasion. If Switzerland had chosen a side, it _____ the devastation that much of the European continent experienced.

(a) will not have escaped

(b) might not have escaped

(c) may not escape

(d) might not escape

제2차 세계대전 동안, 스위스는 중립을 지키고 외국의 침략으로부터 자국의 영토를 적극적으로 방어함으로써 분쟁을 피했다. 만약 스위스가 한 편을 택했었다면, 유럽 대륙의 많은 곳이 겪은 참화를 <u>피하지 못했을지도 모른다</u>.

'if + had p.p.'가 있으면 'would/could/might + have p.p.'가 정답이다.

💡 **가정법 과거완료**
If + 주어 + had p.p., 주어 + would/could/might(조동사 과거형) + have p.p.

해설 | If절에 'had p.p.' 형태의 had chosen이 있으므로, 주절에는 이와 짝을 이루어 가정법 과거완료를 만드는 'might(조동사 과거형) + have p.p.'가 와야 한다. 따라서 (b) might not have escaped가 정답이다.

어휘 | conflict n. 분쟁, 전쟁 neutral adj. 중립의 defend v. 방어하다, 지키다 territory n. 영토, 영역 invasion n. 침략, 침공
side n. 편, (대립하는 사람·그룹의) 한쪽 devastation n. 참화, 참상 continent n. 대륙 escape v. 피하다

---

22 조동사　　조동사 should 생략　　　　　　　　　　난이도 ●●○

Ten years after discontinuing their special orange chicken sandwich, Ella's Diner is putting it back on the menu. Some of the longtime patrons have been requesting that the diner _____ back the classic dish.

(a) is bringing

특별한 오렌지 치킨샌드위치 판매를 중단한 지 10년이 지나서, Ella's Diner는 그것을 메뉴에 되돌려놓고 있다. 오랜 고객 중 몇 명은 식당이 그 대표적인 음식을 다시 <u>도입해야 한다</u>고 요청해 오고 있는 중이다.

(b) brought
(c) will bring
(d) bring

request 다음에는 that절에 동사원형이 온다.

해설 | 주절에 요구를 나타내는 동사 request가 있으므로 that절에는 '(should +) 동사원형'이 와야 한다. 따라서 동사원형 (d) bring이 정답이다.

어휘 | discontinue v. 중단하다 put back phr. 되돌려놓다 longtime adj. 오랜 patron n. 고객 diner n. 작은 식당 classic adj. 대표적인

---

23 시제 현재완료진행   난이도 ●●○

Debbie wants to adopt a cat, but she also wants to make sure she will be a good owner. For the past month, she _____ her weekends reading about tips and strategies for cat care.

(a) will have been spending
(b) had been spending
(c) is spending
(d) has been spending

Debbie는 고양이를 입양하기를 원하지만, 자기가 좋은 주인이 될지도 확실하게 하고 싶어 한다. 지난 한 달 동안, 그녀는 고양이를 돌보는 것에 관한 조언과 방법을 읽으며 주말을 <u>보내오고 있는 중이다.</u>

'for the past + 기간 표현'이 있으면 현재완료진행 시제가 정답이다.

> 💡 **현재완료진행과 자주 함께 쓰이는 시간 표현**
> • (ever) since + 과거 시점 + (for + 기간 표현) ~한 이래로 (줄곧) (~ 동안)
> • lately / for + 기간 표현 + now 최근에 / 현재 ~ 동안

해설 | 현재완료진행 시제와 함께 쓰이는 시간 표현 'for the past + 기간 표현'(For the past month)이 있고, 문맥상 Debbie는 지난 한 달 동안 계속해서 고양이를 돌보는 것에 관한 조언과 방법을 읽으며 주말을 보내오고 있는 중이라는 의미가 되어야 자연스럽다. 따라서 현재완료진행 시제 (d) has been spending이 정답이다.

오답분석
(c) 현재진행 시제는 특정 현재 시점에 한창 진행 중인 일을 나타내므로, 과거에 시작해서 현재 시점까지 계속해서 진행되고 있는 일을 표현할 수 없어 오답이다.

어휘 | adopt v. 입양하다 make sure phr. 확실하게 하다 strategy n. 방법, 전략

---

24 연결어 접속부사   난이도 ●○○

In bowling, a set of three consecutive strikes is called a "turkey." In the late 1700s, food baskets containing turkeys were actually given to tournament winners. _____,

볼링에서는, 한 세트의 세 번 연속되는 스트라이크를 "turkey"라고 한다. 1700년대 후반에는, 실제로 칠면조가 담긴 음식 바구니가 토너먼트 우승자들에게 주어지기도 했다. 결국, "bowling a turkey"는 볼링에서

"bowling a turkey" became a common saying in bowling.

(a) **Eventually**
(b) In addition
(c) Similarly
(d) By contrast

흔히 쓰이는 말이 되었다.

'결국'이라는 의미의 결과를 나타낼 때는 Eventually를 쓴다.

해설 | 문맥상 볼링에서는 한 세트의 세 번 연속되는 스트라이크를 "turkey"라고 부르고, 실제로 칠면조가 담긴 음식 바구니가 토너먼트 우승자들에게 주어지기도 해서, 결국 "bowling a turkey"가 볼링에서 흔히 쓰이는 말이 되었다는 의미가 되어야 자연스럽다. 따라서 '결국'이라는 의미의 결과를 나타내는 접속부사 (a) Eventually가 정답이다.

오답분석
(b) In addition은 '게다가', (c) Similarly는 '비슷하게', (d) By contrast는 '그에 반해서'라는 의미로, 문맥에 적합하지 않아 오답이다.

어휘 | consecutive adj. 연속되는, 연속적인 strike n. 스트라이크(첫 번째 던진 공으로 핀을 전부 쓰러뜨리는 것) contain v. 담다, 들어있다
tournament n. 토너먼트, 시합

---

25 가정법   가정법 과거완료   난이도 ●●○

Josh just finished his laundry. Unfortunately, the dye in his new red shirt bled into his other clothes and turned them slightly pink. Had he known that the color would bleed, he _____ the shirt separately.

(a) will have washed
(b) **would have washed**
(c) would wash
(d) will wash

Josh는 방금 세탁을 끝냈다. 불행하게도, 새로 산 빨간색 셔츠의 염료가 그의 다른 옷들에 번져서 다른 옷들이 약간 분홍색으로 변했다. 그가 그 색이 번질 줄 알았다면, 그는 셔츠를 따로 세탁했을 것이다.

Had p.p.가 있으면 'would/could + have p.p.'가 정답이다.

해설 | if가 생략되어 도치된 절에 'had p.p.' 형태의 Had ~ known이 있으므로, 주절에는 이와 짝을 이루어 가정법 과거완료를 만드는 'would (조동사 과거형) + have p.p.'가 와야 한다. 따라서 (b) would have washed가 정답이다. 참고로, 'Had he known ~'은 'If he had known ~'으로 바꿔 쓸 수 있다.

어휘 | laundry n. 세탁, 빨래 dye n. 염료(액), 물감 bleed v. 번지다 slightly adv. 약간, 조금 separately adv. 따로, 별도로

---

26 조동사   조동사 can   난이도 ●○○

In order to reproduce, plants need pollinators like bees and butterflies. Bats are also some of the best pollinators. Since they are bigger than the average insect, they _____

번식을 하기 위해, 식물은 벌이나 나비와 같은 수분 매개체가 필요하다. 박쥐도 최고의 수분 매개체의 일부이다. 박쥐는 평균적인 곤충보다 더 크기 때문에, 훨씬

carry much more pollen.

(a) **can**
(b) must
(c) should
(d) shall

━●─ 지텔프 치트키

'~할 수 있다'라고 말할 때는 can을 쓴다.

해설 | 문맥상 수분 매개체의 일부인 박쥐는 평균적인 곤충보다 더 크기 때문에, 훨씬 더 많은 꽃가루를 옮길 수 있다는 의미가 되어야 자연스럽다. 따라서 '~할 수 있다'를 뜻하면서 능력을 나타내는 조동사 (a) can이 정답이다.

어휘 | reproduce v. 번식하다 pollinator n. 수분 매개체 pollen n. 꽃가루

더 많은 꽃가루를 옮길 수 있다.

LISTENING

PART 1 (27-33) 일상 대화 도망간 개를 찾는 두 친구의 대화

음성 바로 듣기

안부 인사	M: Hey, Sara. ²⁷Can you help me find my dog Peanut? She escaped from her leash about five minutes ago.
주제 제시: 반려견 도망	F: Oh, no, James! Your dog escaped again? M: Yeah. I'm starting to feel bad that this keeps happening. It's the second time this week.
도망의 원인	F: How does Peanut keep escaping? Is her collar too loose? M: I guess so, Sara. ²⁸I loosen her collar so she can breathe more easily when she sleeps, but sometimes I forget to tighten it before taking her for a walk. F: I know you're trying to be nice to Peanut, James. But you need to be careful. Your dog should always be on a leash. M: I know, I know. I take full responsibility for messing up. I just hope we can find—
반려견 발견	F: Oh! ²⁹I just saw a dark streak running across the road. I bet that was Peanut! M: Where? Can you point me in the right direction? F: There, by those trees in front of the white house. M: By the white house? Yes, I see Peanut! You're a lifesaver, Sara. I owe you one.
목줄을 다시 채우 려는 시도	F: I'm following right behind you. Let's get Peanut back on her leash. M: Thanks. She keeps running away from me because she thinks this is a game. Can you help me catch her? F: Sure. Peanut! Peanut! Come here, girl. James, do you have a special call or whistle she might respond to? M: I haven't tried anything like that. Oh—³⁰I did bring her favorite treats with me. I'll shake the package now and see if that gets her attention . . . F: Wow, ³⁰it's working! She's coming back this way. M: She really loves these treats. Good girl, Peanut. You're panting; see how tired you are. You've got to stop running off like that. F: ³⁰I'm so relieved that you got her back on her leash and she's safe. Peanut, did you hear me? I said I'm happy you're safe!
도움을 요청한 것에 관해 사과	M: Sorry I dragged you into this, Sara. I just happened to run into you when Peanut got off her leash.

남: 안녕, Sara. ²⁷내 개 Peanut을 찾는 걸 도와줄 수 있어? 5분 전쯤에 목줄을 풀고 달아났어.

여: 오, 안돼, James! 너희 개가 또 도망갔니?
남: 응. 자꾸 이런 일이 생겨서 기분이 안 좋아지기 시작하고 있어. 이번 주에만 벌써 두 번째야.

여: Peanut은 어떻게 계속 도망가는 거야? 목줄이 너무 느슨해?
남: 그런 것 같아, Sara. ²⁸나는 Peanut이 잘 때 더 편하게 숨 쉴 수 있도록 목줄을 느슨하게 해주는데, 가끔 산책을 데리고 나가기 전에 목줄을 조이는 걸 잊어버려.
여: 네가 Peanut에게 친절하게 하려는 건 알아, James. 하지만 너는 조심해야 해. 너희 개는 항상 목줄을 매고 있어야 해.
남: 알아, 알아. 내가 엉망으로 만든 건 전적으로 책임 져야지. 우리가 찾을 수 있기를 바랄 뿐이야...

여: 오! ²⁹방금 검은 줄무늬가 길을 가로질러 뛰어가는 걸 봤어. 분명 Peanut이었을 거야!
남: 어디? 정확한 방향을 알려줄래?
여: 저기, 하얀 집 앞에 있는 저 나무들 옆이야.
남: 하얀 집 옆? 응, Peanut이 보여! 넌 구세주야, Sara. 내가 너에게 신세 졌어.

여: 내가 네 뒤에 바로 따라가고 있어. Peanut에게 다시 목줄을 채우자.
남: 고마워. Peanut이 이게 게임인 줄 알고 자꾸 나한테서 도망쳐. Peanut을 잡는 걸 도와줄 수 있어?
여: 물론이지. Peanut! Peanut! 이리와, 얘야. James, Peanut이 반응할 만한 특별한 신호나 휘파람이 있어?
남: 그런 건 아무것도 안 해봤어. 오, ³⁰Peanut이 좋아하는 간식을 가져왔어. 내가 지금 포장을 흔들어보고 관심을 끌 수 있는지 볼게...
여: 와, ³⁰효과가 있네! 이쪽으로 돌아오고 있어.
남: Peanut이 이 간식을 정말 좋아해. 잘했어, Peanut. 헐떡거리고 있네, 얼마나 피곤한지 봐. 그렇게 도망치는 거 그만둬야지.
여: ³⁰네가 Peanut의 목줄을 다시 채우고 Peanut이 무사해서 정말 다행이야. Peanut, 내 말 들었어? 네가 무사해서 기쁘다고 했어!

남: 이런 일에 끌어들여서 미안해, Sara. Peanut이 목줄을 풀었을 때 우연히 너를 마주쳤네.

F: Ha-ha. ³¹I'm laughing because you ran into me the last time this happened as well.	여: 하하. ³¹지난번에도 이런 일이 일어났을 때 우연히 마주쳐서 웃음이 나네.
M: I know. Please don't remind me. ³¹It's getting to be embarrassing.	남: 알아. 제발 상기시키지 마. ³¹점점 당황스러워지잖아.

훈련학교 제안

F: Don't be embarrassed, James. You know I'm happy to help anytime. Peanut is such a good dog. But . . . have you considered sending her to obedience school?	여: 당황하지 마, James. 내가 언제든 기꺼이 도와줄게. Peanut은 정말 좋은 개야. 하지만... 훈련학교에 보내는 건 생각해 봤어?
M: Actually, ³²I have considered obedience school. They offer sessions at a pet shop in the center of town. But ³²I heard they're pretty expensive. The high cost is my biggest concern.	남: 사실, ³²훈련학교도 생각해 봤어. 시내 중심가에 있는 반려동물 가게에서 수업하거든. 근데 ³²꽤 비싸다고 들었어. 비싼 게 제일 큰 걱정이야.
F: It might be worth looking into. Peanut can be hard to control at times.	여: 알아볼 가치가 있을 것 같아. Peanut은 때때로 통제하기 어려울 수 있거든.

남자가 다음에 할 일

M: You're right, Sara. ³³I'll call today about getting her some training.	남: 네 말이 맞아, Sara. ³³Peanut에게 훈련받게 하는 것 관련해서 오늘 전화해 볼게.
F: I'm glad to hear it, James. Meanwhile, are you sure you're going to make it home without Peanut running away again? Ha-ha.	여: 다행이네, James. 그나저나, Peanut이 또 도망가지 않고 집에 갈 수 있을 거라고 확신해? 하하.
M: Ha-ha. Yes, I'm confident that I have the situation under control. Thanks again, Sara. You were such a big help today. Well, ³³I'll go make that phone call now.	남: 하하. 응, 내가 상황을 통제하고 있다고 확신해. 다시 한번 고마워, Sara. 오늘 정말 큰 도움이 되었어. 음, ³³지금 바로 전화를 해볼게.
F: You're welcome, James. I'm off to get some lunch, so I'll see you later. And I'll see you too, Peanut!	여: 천만에, James. 나는 점심 먹으러 갈 테니까, 나중에 봐. 너도 이따 봐, Peanut!

어휘 | escape from ~에서 달아나다   leash[liːʃ] 목줄, 밧줄   collar[kálər] 목줄, 목걸이   loose[luːs] 느슨한, 헐거운   breathe[briːð] 숨 쉬다, 호흡하다   tighten[taitn] 조이다, 줄이다   take a walk 산책하러 나가다   take responsibility for ~을 책임지다   mess up 엉망으로 만들다   streak[striːk] 줄무늬   lifesaver[láifsèivər] 구세주   owe[ou] 신세 지다, 빚지다   whistle[hwisl] 휘파람, 호각   treat[triːt] 간식   pant[pænt] 헐떡거리다   drag into ~에 끌어들이다   run into 우연히 마주치다   remind[rimáind] 상기시키다, 떠올리게 하다   obedience school 훈련학교   concern[kənsə́ːrn] 걱정, 문제   worth[wəːrθ] ~의 가치가 있는   control[kəntróul] 통제하다, 관리하다; 통제   confident[kánfədənt] 확신하는, 자신 있는

---

27 **특정세부사항**   What   난이도 ●○○

What was James doing before meeting Sara?	James는 Sara를 만나기 전에 무엇을 하고 있었는가?
(a) searching for a lost pet	**(a) 잃어버린 반려동물을 찾는 것**
(b) looking for a new pet	(b) 새로운 반려동물을 찾는 것
(c) going to the dog shelter	(c) 유기견 보호소에 가는 것
(d) walking a friend's dog	(d) 친구의 개를 산책시키는 것

⟲ 정답 잡는 치트키

질문의 키워드 before meeting Sara와 관련된 주변 내용을 주의 깊게 듣는다.

해설 | 남자가 'Can you help me find my dog Peanut?'이라며 자기의 개 Peanut을 찾는 걸 도와줄 수 있는지 물었다. 따라서 (a)가 정답이다.

어휘 | dog shelter 유기견 보호소

---

28 특정세부사항   What   난이도 ●●○

What does James sometimes forget to do before walking Peanut?	James는 Peanut을 산책시키기 전에 가끔 무엇을 하는 것을 잊는가?
(a) put on her collar	(a) 목줄을 착용시킨다
(b) attach her leash	(b) 목줄을 부착한다
(c) tighten her collar	**(c) 목줄을 조인다**
(d) bring her leash	(d) 목줄을 가져온다

━○ 정답 잡는 치트키

질문의 키워드 forget이 그대로 언급되고, walking이 taking ~ for a walk로 paraphrasing되어 언급된 주변 내용을 주의 깊게 듣는다.

해설 | 남자가 'I loosen her collar ~ when she sleeps, but sometimes I forget to tighten it before taking her for a walk.'라며 Peanut이 잘 때 목줄을 느슨하게 해주는데, 가끔 산책을 데리고 나가기 전에 목줄을 조이는 걸 잊어버린다고 했다. 따라서 (c)가 정답이다.

어휘 | attach [ətǽtʃ] 부착하다

---

29 특정세부사항   How   난이도 ●●○

How is Sara able to locate Peanut?	Sara는 어떻게 Peanut을 찾을 수 있는가?
(a) She notices a moving figure.	**(a) 움직이는 형태를 주목한다.**
(b) She checks inside a house.	(b) 집 안을 점검한다.
(c) She looks in the nearby woods.	(c) 근처의 숲을 살핀다.
(d) She hears barking noises.	(d) 짖는 소리를 듣는다.

━○ 정답 잡는 치트키

질문의 키워드 locate가 saw로 paraphrasing되어 언급된 주변 내용을 주의 깊게 듣는다.

해설 | 여자가 'I just saw a dark streak running across the road. I bet that was Peanut!'이라며 방금 검은 줄무늬가 길을 가로질러 뛰어가는 걸 봤는데, 분명 Peanut이었을 거라고 했다. 따라서 (a)가 정답이다.

어휘 | figure [fígjər] 형태, 모습   barking [báːrkiŋ] 짖는

TEST 1
TEST 2
TEST 3
TEST 4
TEST 5
TEST 6
TEST 7

30 특정세부사항 　　How

난이도 ●●○

How does James finally catch Peanut?

(a) by shaking her favorite toy
(b) by calling out her name
(c) by using his special whistle
(d) by offering her a snack

James는 어떻게 마침내 Peanut을 잡는가?

(a) 좋아하는 장난감을 흔듦으로써
(b) 이름을 부름으로써
(c) 특별한 휘파람을 활용함으로써
(d) 간식을 줌으로써

─○ 정답 잡는 치트키

질문의 키워드 catch와 관련된 주변 내용을 주의 깊게 듣는다.

해설 | 남자가 'I did bring her favorite treats with me. I'll shake the package now and see if that gets her attention . . .'이라 며 Peanut이 좋아하는 간식을 가져왔는데, 지금 포장을 흔들어 보고 관심을 끌 수 있는지 보겠다고 하자, 여자가 'it's working! She's coming back this way.'라며 효과가 있고, Peanut이 이쪽으로 돌아오고 있다고 한 뒤, 'I'm so relieved that you got her back on her leash'라며 남자가 Peanut의 목줄을 다시 채워서 정말 다행이라고 했다. 따라서 (d)가 정답이다.

⇄ **Paraphrasing**
treats 간식 → a snack 간식

어휘 | call out ~을 부르다

31 추론 　　특정사실

난이도 ●●●

Why, most likely, does James feel embarrassed?

(a) He accidentally knocked Sara over.
(b) He has made this mistake before.
(c) He fell down while running.
(d) He always asks Sara for help.

James는 왜 당황한 것 같은가?

(a) 잘못하여 Sara를 치어 넘어뜨렸다.
(b) 전에 이런 실수를 한 적이 있다.
(c) 뛰다가 넘어졌다.
(d) 항상 Sara에게 도움을 요청한다.

─○ 정답 잡는 치트키

질문의 키워드 feel embarrassed가 be embarrassing으로 paraphrasing되어 언급된 주변 내용을 주의 깊게 듣는다.

해설 | 여자가 'I'm laughing because you ran into me the last time this happened as well.'이라며 지난번에도 이런 일이 일어났을 때 우연히 마주쳐서 웃음이 난다고 하자, 남자가 'It's getting to be embarrassing.'이라며 점점 당황스러워진다고 한 것을 통해, James가 전에도 개를 잃어버리는 실수를 했을 때 Sara를 마주쳐서 당황한 것임을 추론할 수 있다. 따라서 (b)가 정답이다.

어휘 | accidentally[æksədéntəli] 잘못하여, 우연히　knock over 치어 넘어뜨리다　fall down 넘어지다

32 특정세부사항 　　What

난이도 ●●○

What is James's biggest concern about obedience school?

(a) locating one in his town
(b) being around the other dogs
(c) affording the price of classes
(d) finding one with open spots

훈련학교에 관한 James의 가장 큰 걱정은 무엇인가?

(a) 마을에 있는 곳의 위치를 찾는 것
(b) 다른 개들 주위에 있는 것
(c) 수업료를 감당하는 것
(d) 빈자리가 있는 곳을 찾는 것

질문의 키워드 biggest concern과 obedience school이 그대로 언급된 주변 내용을 주의 깊게 듣는다.

해설 | 남자가 'I have considered obedience school'이라며 훈련학교도 생각해 봤다고 한 뒤, 'I heard they're pretty expensive. The high cost is my biggest concern.'이라며 꽤 비싸다고 들어서 비싼 게 제일 큰 걱정이라고 했다. 따라서 (c)가 정답이다.

어휘 | locate[lóukeit] 위치를 찾다 spot[spɑːt] 자리, 장소

---

33 추론 다음에 할 일 난이도 ●○○

What will James probably do right after the conversation?	James는 대화 직후에 무엇을 할 것 같은가?
(a) visit the pet store	(a) 반려동물 가게를 방문한다
(b) contact the training school	**(b) 훈련학교에 연락한다**
(c) get some lunch	(c) 점심을 먹는다
(d) head to the dog park	(d) 반려견 공원으로 향한다

다음에 할 일을 언급하는 후반을 주의 깊게 듣는다.

해설 | 남자가 'I'll call today about getting her some training.'이라며 Peanut에게 훈련받게 하는 것 관련해서 오늘 전화해 보겠다고 한 뒤, 'I'll go make that phone call now'라며 지금 바로 전화를 해보겠다고 한 것을 통해, James는 훈련학교에 연락해서 상담받을 것임을 추론할 수 있다. 따라서 (b)가 정답이다.

⇄ **Paraphrasing**
call 전화하다 → contact 연락하다

PART 2 [34~39] 발표 새로운 현대 미술관 개관 홍보

음성 바로 듣기

주제
제시:
현대
미술관
개관

Hello, everyone. ³⁴I'm excited to announce the opening of our new modern art gallery. Once we saw the interest people had in buying art on our website, we decided we needed a physical space where we could hold exhibits and more. And today, we open our doors to the public. Welcome to Creative Endeavors.

초청
연사

Creative Endeavors is honored to be hosting a series of guest speakers. ³⁵Our first speaker is Andy Wells, who will be discussing the public art project he set in motion to bring beauty and wonder to our community. You've probably seen the painted statues of robots all around town that were made by Andy and a group of other local artists. I know that all of you will enjoy his talk. You can purchase tickets for Andy Wells and all our future

안녕하세요, 여러분. ³⁴새로운 현대 미술관의 개관을 발표하게 되어 기쁩니다. 웹사이트에서 사람들이 미술품을 사는 것에 관심이 있음을 확인한 후, 전시회 등을 열 수 있는 물리적인 공간이 필요하다고 결정했습니다. 그리고 오늘, 저희는 대중에게 문을 엽니다. Creative Endeavors에 오신 것을 환영합니다.

Creative Endeavors는 일련의 초청 연사들을 모시게 되어 영광입니다. ³⁵첫 번째 연사는 Andy Wells인데, 그는 공동체에 아름다움과 경이를 선사하기 위해 그가 추진했던 공공 예술 프로젝트에 관해 이야기할 것입니다. 여러분은 아마 Andy와 다른 지역 예술가 단체가 만든 로봇 동상을 마을 곳곳에서 본 적이 있을 것입니다. 저는 여러분 모두가 그의 강연을 좋아할 것임을 알고 있습니다. 여러분은 최대 한 달 전에 미리 안내대나 온라인에서 Andy Wells와 모든 향후 연사들의 티켓을

speakers at the front desk or online up to a month in advance. It is always best to purchase tickets early in case they sell out.

In our largest exhibition hall, we will be hosting a show called Artistic Sensations. [36]The main goal of Artistic Sensations is to incorporate media and sound into our shows and really activate the senses of art lovers like yourselves. Sight, sound, and touch will be part of the Artistic Sensations experience. And in the weeks to come, we even plan to add some artwork that will incorporate the sense of smell!

In our smaller exhibition space, [37]we are showing work from photographers who venture into the wild to take photos of endangered species. A percentage of every purchase will go to a wildlife preservation fund. That's right, folks. We're not just here to make a profit; we aim to make a difference and welcome you to join us in our mission. [37]All the photos in the main exhibit will celebrate nature and the betterment of our planet.

Because we are passionate about ensuring a bright future for children, we will be offering weekend classes where kids from as young as five can learn the basics of drawing and painting. Older children ages ten and up can learn about animation. Also, [38]we have 3D printers, so your youngsters can print creative objects that they design with the help of our talented staff.

We have put careful thought into our gallery's interior, which includes about 5,000 feet of exhibition space. It's a lot of ground to cover! When you're ready for a break, you can grab a seat at the Creative Café and sip a hot coffee or dine on a light meal. The café is enclosed by a garden, giving our visitors a sense of privacy. Many consider the garden a work of art in itself! The café also includes a gift shop that sells a variety of posters and art books.

We are delighted that you have come to the opening of Creative Endeavors. We'll be sharing more news online in the coming weeks, when we will be hosting raffles and other promotions. And [39]be on the lookout for discounted art on our website. Because of today's grand opening, several amazing art pieces are available online at fifty percent off.

Thanks for coming, everyone, and we hope you enjoy the artwork.

구매할 수 있습니다. 티켓이 매진될 경우를 대비해 항상 일찍 구매하는 것이 가장 좋습니다.

가장 큰 전시장에서, Artistic Sensations라고 불리는 쇼를 개최할 것입니다. [36]Artistic Sensations의 주요 목표는 미디어와 소리를 쇼에 통합하여 여러분과 같은 예술 애호가들의 감각을 실제로 활성화하는 것입니다. 시각, 청각, 촉각이 Artistic Sensations 경험의 일부가 될 것입니다. 그리고 몇 주 후에는, 심지어 후각을 통합한 예술작품도 추가할 계획입니다!

소규모 전시 공간에서는, [37]멸종 위기에 처한 종의 사진을 찍기 위해 야생으로 모험을 떠나는 사진작가들의 작품을 전시하고 있습니다. 모든 구매 금액이 일부는 야생동물 보호 기금으로 기부됩니다. 맞습니다, 여러분. 저희는 단순히 이윤을 내기 위해 여기에 있는 것이 아니라, 변화를 만드는 것을 목표로 하며 여러분도 저희의 사명에 동참해 주기 바랍니다. [37]주 전시회에 있는 모든 사진은 자연과 지구의 개선을 기념할 것입니다.

저희는 어린이들에게 밝은 미래를 보장하는 것에 열정적이기 때문에, 다섯 살 정도의 어린아이들이 그림 그리기의 기초를 배울 수 있는 주말 수업을 제공할 것입니다. 10세 이상의 좀 더 나이가 많은 어린이는 애니메이션에 관해 배울 수 있습니다. 또한, [38]3D 프린터를 갖추고 있어, 어린이들이 재능 있는 직원의 도움을 받아 자기가 디자인한 창의적인 물체들을 출력할 수 있습니다.

약 5,000피트의 전시 공간을 포함하는 미술관의 인테리어에도 세심한 주의를 기울였습니다. 그것은 정말 넓은 공간입니다! 휴식을 취할 준비가 되었다면, Creative Café에 자리를 잡고 따뜻한 커피를 마시거나 가벼운 식사를 할 수 있습니다. 카페는 정원으로 둘러싸여 있어, 방문객들에게 프라이버시를 제공합니다. 많은 사람이 정원을 그 자체로 하나의 예술 작품이라고 생각합니다! 카페는 다양한 포스터와 화집을 판매하는 선물 가게도 포함합니다.

Creative Endeavors의 개관식에 오시게 되어 기쁩니다. 앞으로 몇 주 동안 온라인에서 더 많은 소식을 공유할 것이며, 추첨 판매 및 기타 판촉이 진행될 것입니다. 그리고 [39]저희 웹사이트에서 할인된 예술작품이 있는지 세심히 살펴봐 주세요. 오늘의 개관식을 기념하여, 여러 가지 멋진 예술 작품을 온라인에서 50% 할인된 가격에 구매할 수 있습니다.

모두 와주셔서 감사드리며, 작품을 즐기시기 바랍니다.

어휘 | physical[fízikəl] 물리적인 a series of 일련의 set in motion 추진하다 wonder[wʌ́ndər] 경이; 놀라다 statue[stǽtʃuː] 동상, 조각상
in advance 미리 incorporate into ~에 통합시키다 activate[ǽktəvèit] 활성화하다 venture[véntʃər] 모험하다; (사업상의) 모험
endangered species 멸종 위기에 처한 동식물의 종 preservation[prèzərvéiʃən] 보호, 보존 folk[fouk] 여러분, 사람들
make a profit 이윤을 내다 aim to ~하는 것을 목표로 하다 mission[míʃən] 사명, 임무 betterment[bétərmənt] 개선, 향상
passionate[pǽʃənət] 열정적인 ensure[inʃúər] 보장하다 youngster[jʌ́ŋstər] 어린이 talented[tǽləntid] 재능 있는, 뛰어난
grab[græb] 이용하다, (기회를) 붙잡다 sip[sip] 마시다 dine[dain] 식사를 하다 enclose[inklóuz] 둘러싸다, 에워싸다 art book 화집, 아트북
raffle[rǽfl] 추첨 판매, 제비뽑기 promotion[prəmóuʃən] 판촉 be on the lookout for ~이 있는지 세심히 살피다

| **34** | **주제/목적** | 담화의 주제 | 난이도 ●●○ |

What is the talk all about?	담화의 주제는 무엇인가?
(a) a modern art website	(a) 현대 미술 웹사이트
(b) a popular art school	(b) 인기 있는 미술 학교
(c) a famous art museum	(c) 유명한 미술관
(d) a new art gallery	**(d) 새로운 미술관**

━○ 정답 잡는 치트키

담화의 주제를 언급하는 초반을 주의 깊게 듣고 전체 맥락을 파악한다.

해설 | 화자가 'I'm excited to announce the opening of our new modern art gallery.'라며 새로운 현대 미술관의 개관을 발표하게 되어 기쁘다고 한 뒤, 담화 전반에 걸쳐 새로운 미술관인 Creative Endeavors를 홍보하는 내용이 이어지고 있다. 따라서 (d)가 정답이다.

| **35** | **추론** | 특정사실 | 난이도 ●●○ |

Why, most likely, has Andy Wells been invited to speak?	Andy Wells는 왜 연설하도록 초대된 것 같은가?
(a) He led a local art movement.	**(a) 지역 예술 운동을 이끌었다.**
(b) He hosts an annual art festival.	(b) 연례 미술 축제를 개최한다.
(c) He painted a famous mural.	(c) 유명한 벽화를 그렸다.
(d) He is a public art educator.	(d) 공공 미술 교육자이다.

━○ 정답 잡는 치트키

질문의 키워드 Andy Wells가 그대로 언급된 주변 내용을 주의 깊게 듣는다.

해설 | 화자가 'Our first speaker is Andy Wells, who will be discussing the public art project he set in motion to bring beauty and wonder to our community.'라며 첫 번째 연사는 Andy Wells인데, 그는 공동체에 아름다움과 경이를 선사하기 위해 그가 추진했던 공공 예술 프로젝트에 관해 이야기할 것이라고 한 것을 통해, Andy Wells가 공공 예술 프로젝트인 지역 예술 운동을 이끌어서 연설하도록 초대된 것임을 추론할 수 있다. 따라서 (a)가 정답이다.

↻ **Paraphrasing**
set in motion 추진했다 → led 이끌었다
the public art project 공공 예술 프로젝트 → a local art movement 지역 예술 운동

어휘 | mural[mjúrəl] 벽화

TEST 1
TEST 2
TEST 3
TEST 4
TEST 5
TEST 6
TEST 7

지텔프 공식 기출문제집 7회분 Level 2

36 특정세부사항 What

난이도 ●●●

What is the main goal of Artistic Sensations?

(a) to incorporate live music
(b) to showcase the trendiest art
(c) to focus on visual input
(d) to enhance visitors' experiences

Artistic Sensations의 주요 목표는 무엇인가?

(a) 라이브 음악을 통합한다
(b) 최신 유행의 예술을 소개한다
(c) 시각적 자극에 초점을 맞춘다
(d) 방문객들의 경험을 향상시킨다

정답 잡는 치트키

질문의 키워드 main goal of Artistic Sensations가 그대로 언급된 주변 내용을 주의 깊게 듣는다.

해설 | 화자가 'The main goal of Artistic Sensations is to incorporate media and sound into our shows and really activate the senses of art lovers like yourselves.'라며 Artistic Sensations의 주요 목표는 미디어와 소리를 쇼에 통합하여 청자들과 같은 예술 애호가들의 감각을 실제로 활성화하는 것이라고 했으므로, 미디어와 소리를 쇼에 통합함으로써 방문객들의 경험을 향상시키는 것이 주요 목표임을 알 수 있다. 따라서 (d)가 정답이다.

↻ Paraphrasing
activate the senses 감각을 활성화하다 → enhance ~ experiences 경험을 향상시키다

어휘 | showcase[ʃóukeis] 소개하다 trendy[tréndi] 최신 유행의 visual[víʒuəl] 시각적인 enhance[inhǽns] 향상하다, 개선하다

37 특정세부사항 How

난이도 ●●○

According to the talk, how can visitors to Creative Endeavors support the planet?

(a) by buying photos of wildlife
(b) by donating to a climate fund
(c) by purchasing animal paintings
(d) by joining an environmental group

담화에 따르면, Creative Endeavors의 방문객들은 어떻게 지구를 도울 수 있는가?

(a) 야생동물의 사진을 구매함으로써
(b) 기후 기금에 기부함으로써
(c) 동물 그림을 구매함으로써
(d) 환경 보호 단체에 가입함으로써

정답 잡는 치트키

질문의 키워드 planet이 그대로 언급된 주변 내용을 주의 깊게 듣는다.

해설 | 화자가 'we are showing work from photographers who venture into the wild to take photos of endangered species. A percentage of every purchase will go to a wildlife preservation fund.'라며 멸종 위기에 처한 종의 사진을 찍기 위해 야생으로 모험을 떠나는 사진작가들의 작품을 전시하고 있으며, 모든 구매 금액의 일부는 야생동물 보호 기금으로 기부된다고 한 뒤, 'All the photos in the main exhibit will celebrate nature and the betterment of our planet.'이라며 주 전시회에 있는 모든 사진은 자연과 지구의 개선을 기념할 것이라고 했다. 따라서 (a)가 정답이다.

어휘 | support[səpɔ́ːrt] 돕다, 지원하다 donate[dóuneit] 기부하다, 기증하다 environmental group 환경 보호 단체

38 특정세부사항 How

난이도 ●●○

How can children enjoy a day at Creative Endeavors?

아이들은 어떻게 Creative Endeavors에서 하루를 즐길 수 있는가?

(a) by attending daily performances
(b) by watching cartoons about art
(c) by meeting famous artists
(d) by making their own art

(a)ʳ 매일의 공연에 참석함으로써
(b) 미술에 관한 만화를 봄으로써
(c) 유명한 예술가들을 만남으로써
(d) 그들만의 미술품을 만듦으로써

🔵━○ **정답 잡는 치트키**

질문의 키워드 children이 youngsters로 paraphrasing되어 언급된 주변 내용을 주의 깊게 듣는다.

해설 | 화자가 'we have 3D printers, so your youngsters can print creative objects that they design'이라며 3D 프린터를 갖추고 있어, 어린이들이 자기가 디자인한 창의적인 물체들을 출력할 수 있다고 했다. 따라서 (d)가 정답이다.

오답분석

(b) 화자가 10세 이상의 어린이는 애니메이션에 관해 배울 수 있다고 언급하기는 했지만, 미술에 관한 만화를 보는 것은 아니므로 오답이다.

어휘 | cartoon[kɑːrtúːn] 만화, 만평

---

39 **특정세부사항** What 난이도 ●●●

What can visitors do to get discounted art?

(a) make a website purchase
(b) buy an item at the café
(c) win the online raffle
(d) shop at the gift store

방문객들이 할인된 예술품을 사기 위해 할 수 있는 것은 무엇인가?

(a) 웹사이트에서 구입한다
(b) 카페에서 물건을 산다
(c) 온라인 추첨 판매에 당첨된다
(d) 선물 가게에서 쇼핑한다

🔵━○ **정답 잡는 치트키**

질문의 키워드 discounted art가 그대로 언급된 주변 내용을 주의 깊게 듣는다.

해설 | 화자가 'be on the lookout for discounted art on our website. Because of today's grand opening, several amazing art pieces are available online at fifty percent off.'라며 웹사이트에서 할인된 예술품이 있는지 세심히 살펴봐 주기 바라며, 오늘의 개관식을 기념하여 여러 가지 멋진 예술 작품을 온라인에서 50% 할인된 가격에 구매할 수 있다고 했다. 따라서 (a)가 정답이다.

오답분석

(c) 화자가 추첨 판매가 진행될 것이라고 언급하기는 했지만, 예술품을 사기 위한 추첨 판매인지는 언급되지 않았으므로 오답이다.

PART 3 [40~45] **장단점 논의** 아르바이트하는 것과 공부에 집중하는 것의 장단점

음성 바로 듣기

| 안부 인사 | F: | Hey, Chris. ⁴⁰You must be studying a lot, because I haven't seen you in a while. |

여: 안녕, Chris. ⁴⁰한동안 너를 못 봤는데, 공부를 많이 하고 있나 봐.

| 주제 제시: 장단점 비교 | M: | Hi Jenny. ⁴⁰You're right, I have been studying. I was also offered a part-time job in the admissions office. But I'm not sure if I should take it, since I have so many big exams coming up. |

남: 안녕 Jenny. ⁴⁰네 말이 맞아, 공부하고 있었어. 입학처에서 아르바이트 제안도 받았어. 그런데 앞으로 중요한 시험이 너무 많아서 그 일을 해야 할지 잘 모르겠어.

아르
바이트
하는
것의
장점

F: That's a tough choice, Chris. Maybe we can talk about the pros and cons to help you decide?

M: Thanks! One advantage of taking the job is that I could really use the extra income for food.

F: Right. My own food budget for the month is running low. The life of a student can be tough!

M: Exactly. It's definitely not fun being hungry all the time. Well, [41]another advantage is the work experience. I haven't had any jobs or internships yet, and I think this experience in the admissions office will look good when I apply for full-time jobs in the future.

F: Yeah, jobs at the university usually look great on paper. So what're the downsides?

아르
바이트
하는
것의
단점

M: Well, one downside is that I won't be able to get as much help from my teachers because I'll have to leave for work right after class. [42]I'm already struggling this semester because I'm taking a lot of upper-level math classes as part of my engineering major.

F: Right. Also, jobs in the admissions office don't extend into the summertime. So if you plan to work in the summer, you'll have to find another job.

공부에
집중
하는
것의
장점

M: Good point. Okay, now let's talk about the advantages of focusing on my classes. The biggest advantage is that I'll be able to spend more time in the library. Finals are right around the corner!

F: Exactly. If there was ever a time to stay hunkered down in the library, it's these last few weeks before final exams. Also, [43]you would have some extra time to visit the new tutoring center that just opened up.

M: I didn't think about that. I've heard really good things about the new tutoring center.

F: Yes, but one disadvantage is that both the tutoring center and the library are on the other side of campus. And you live right next door to the admissions office!

공부에
집중
하는
것의
단점

M: I know. That's why I applied for the job. Another disadvantage is that I don't want to study *too* much and get burned out. Sometimes I just find myself staring at the page . . . and I'm not sure if I'm really understanding anything.

F: Oh, you can definitely study too much. [44]Burnout is a real thing. Sometimes I find that I actually do better on tests if I force myself to stop studying and do other things, like jogging on the treadmill while I listen to music. It helps my mind feel fresher and sharper.

여: 힘든 선택이네, Chris. 결정하는 데 도움이 되도록 장단점에 관해 이야기해 볼 수 있을까?

남: 고마워! 그 일을 맡는 것의 한 가지 장점은 여분의 수입을 식비로 사용할 수 있다는 거야.

여: 맞아. 내 한 달 식비 예산이 떨어져 가고 있어. 학생의 삶은 힘들 수 있어!

남: 맞아. 항상 배고프면 분명 재미없지. 음, [41]또 하나의 장점은 업무 경험이야. 나는 아직 직장이나 인턴십 경험이 없는데, 입학처에서의 경험이 나중에 정규직에 지원할 때 도움이 될 거야.

여: 응, 대학교에서의 일자리는 보통 서류상으로 좋아 보여. 그렇다면 부정적인 면은 뭐야?

남: 음, 한 가지 부정적인 면은 수업 후에 바로 일하러 가야 하기 때문에 선생님들의 도움을 많이 받을 수 없을 거란 거야. [42]이번 학기에는 공학 전공과목의 일부로 상위 수준의 수학 수업을 많이 듣고 있어서 벌써 허덕이고 있어.

여: 맞아. 그리고, 입학처 일은 여름까지 이어지지 않아. 그래서 여름에 일할 계획이 있다면, 다른 일을 찾아야 할 거야.

남: 좋은 지적이야. 자, 이제 수업에 집중하는 것의 장점에 대해 말해보자. 가장 큰 장점은 도서관에서 더 많은 시간을 보낼 수 있을 거란 거야. 기말시험이 바로 코앞에 와 있어!

여: 맞아. 도서관에 쪼그리고 앉아 지낼 때가 있었다면, 바로 기말시험 전 마지막 몇 주야. 또한, [43]너는 얼마 전에 문을 연 새로운 개인교습 센터를 방문할 시간도 가질 수 있을 거야.

남: 그런 건 생각 못 했어. 새로운 개인교습 센터에 관해서 좋은 얘기를 많이 들었어.

여: 응, 하지만 한 가지 단점은 개인교습 센터와 도서관 모두 캠퍼스 반대편에 있다는 거야. 그리고 넌 입학처 바로 옆에 살잖아!

남: 알아. 그래서 그 일자리에 지원했던 거야. 또 하나의 단점은 나는 공부를 *너무* 많이 해서 기진맥진해지는 걸 원하지 않는다는 거야. 가끔은 내가 그냥 페이지를 응시하고 있는 걸 발견하곤 하는데... 정말 이해하고 있는 건지 모르겠어.

여: 오, 넌 확실히 공부를 너무 많이 할 수도 있겠네. [44]번아웃은 실제로 있는 거야. 가끔 나는 억지로 공부를 멈추고 음악을 들으면서 러닝머신 위에서 조깅하는 것과 같은 다른 것들을 하면 실제로 시험을 더 잘 본다는 것을 알게 돼. 그건 내 마음을 더 상쾌하고 예리하게 느끼게 도와줘.

	M: Well, Jenny, you've been a lot of help. Thanks.	남: 음, Jenny, 많은 도움이 됐어. 고마워.
남자의 결정	F: So, I'm curious: Are you going to take the job or focus solely on your studies? M: Well, Jenny, I don't know if you heard it, but that was my stomach answering for me. ⁴⁵I need to take a trip to the supermarket soon, and shopping will be much nicer with more money for food in my pocket. F: Wise decision, Chris. Maybe I'll see you there!	여: 그래서, 그 일을 할 건지, 아니면 오로지 공부에 집중할 건지 궁금해. 남: 음, Jenny, 네가 들었는지는 모르겠지만, 그건 내 배가 대신 대답한 거였어. ⁴⁵나는 곧 슈퍼마켓에 가야하는데, 주머니에 식료품 살 돈이 더 있다면 쇼핑이 훨씬 더 즐거울 거야. 여: 현명한 결정이야, Chris. 거기서 볼 수도 있겠네!

어휘 | admissions office 입학처 tough[tʌf] 힘든, 어려운 income[ínkʌm] 수입, 소득 food budget 식비 예산 run low 떨어져 가다, 고갈되다
definitely[défənitli] 분명히, 확실히 on paper 서류상으로 downside[dáunsaid] 부정적인 면 struggle[strʌ́gl] 허덕이다, 어려움을 겪다
semester[siméstər] 학기 major[méidʒər] 전공과목 extend into ~까지 이어지다 summertime[sʌ́mərtaim] 여름
final[fáinl] 기말시험; 최종의 around the corner 코 앞에 와 있는 hunker down 쪼그리고 앉다 burned out 기진맥진한
stare[ster] 응시하다, 쳐다보다 burnout[bə́rnàut] 번아웃(극도의 피로) treadmill[trédmil] 러닝머신 solely[sóulli] 오로지, 단지

---

40 특정세부사항   Why   난이도 ●○○

Why has Jenny not seen Chris for a while?	Jenny는 왜 한동안 Chris를 보지 못했는가?
(a) He has been living off campus. (b) He has been sick for a long time. (c) He has been taking exams. **(d) He has been busy studying.**	(a) 캠퍼스 밖에서 생활해 오고 있다. (b) 오랫동안 아팠다. (c) 시험을 보고 있다. **(d) 공부하느라 바빴다.**

━○ 정답 잡는 치트키

질문의 키워드 has ~ not seen ~ for a while이 haven't seen ~ in a while로 paraphrasing되어 언급된 주변 내용을 주의 깊게 듣는다.

해설 | 여자가 'You must be studying a lot, because I haven't seen you in a while.'이라며 한동안 남자를 못 봤는데 공부를 많이 하고 있는 것 같다고 하자, 남자가 'You're right, I have been studying.'이라며 여자의 말대로 자기는 공부하고 있었다고 했다. 따라서 (d)가 정답이다.

어휘 | off campus 캠퍼스 밖의

---

41 특정세부사항   장·단점   난이도 ●●●

How does Chris think he can benefit from some work experience?	Chris는 어떻게 업무 경험으로부터 이익을 얻을 수 있다고 생각하는가?
(a) He can meet new people. (b) He can improve his work ethic. (c) He can gain valuable skills. **(d) He can enhance his resume.**	(a) 새로운 사람들을 만날 수 있다. (b) 근로 윤리를 향상할 수 있다. (c) 귀중한 기술을 얻을 수 있다. **(d) 경력을 향상할 수 있다.**

━○ 정답 잡는 치트키

질문의 키워드 some work experience와 관련된 긍정적인 흐름을 파악한다.

해설 | 남자가 'another advantage is the work experience. I haven't had any jobs or internships yet, and I think this experience in the admissions office will look good when I apply for full-time jobs in the future.'라며 또 하나의 장점은 업무 경험인데, 아직 직장이나 인턴십 경험이 없어서 입학처에서의 경험이 나중에 정규직에 지원할 때 도움이 될 거라고 했다. 따라서 (d)가 정답이다.

어휘 | work ethic 근로 윤리 gain[gein] 얻다 resume[rizú:m] 경력; 다시 시작하다

---

42 특정세부사항   Why
난이도 ●●○

Why is Chris struggling with some classes this semester?

(a) because he finds classes boring
(b) because he is in high-level courses
(c) because he has difficult teachers
(d) because he has changed majors

Chris는 왜 이번 학기에 수업에 허덕이고 있는가?

(a) 수업이 지루하다고 생각하기 때문에
(b) 고급 과정에 있기 때문에
(c) 까다로운 선생님들이 있기 때문에
(d) 전공을 바꾸었기 때문에

──○ 정답 잡는 치트키

질문의 키워드 struggling이 그대로 언급된 주변 내용을 주의 깊게 듣는다.

해설 | 남자가 'I'm already struggling this semester because I'm taking a lot of upper-level math classes'라며 이번 학기에는 상위 수준의 수학 수업을 많이 듣고 있어서 벌써 허덕이고 있다고 했다. 따라서 (b)가 정답이다.

⇄ **Paraphrasing**
upper-level ~ classes 상위 수준의 수업 → high-level courses 고급 과정

---

43 추론   특정사실
난이도 ●●●

According to Jenny, what could Chris do with his extra time?

(a) work at the tutoring center
(b) get some help with studying
(c) do research at the library
(d) go for walks around campus

Jenny에 따르면, Chris가 추가시간으로 무엇을 할 수 있는가?

(a) 개인교습 센터에서 일하다
(b) 공부에 도움을 받는다
(c) 도서관에서 조사한다
(d) 캠퍼스 주변에 산책하러 간다

──○ 정답 잡는 치트키

질문의 키워드 extra time이 그대로 언급된 주변 내용을 주의 깊게 듣는다.

해설 | 여자가 'you would have some extra time to visit the new tutoring center that just opened up'이라며 얼마 전에 문을 연 새로운 개인교습 센터를 방문할 시간도 가질 수 있을 것이라고 한 것을 통해, Chris가 추가시간에 개인교습 센터를 방문해서 공부에 도움을 받을 수 있음을 추론할 수 있다. 따라서 (b)가 정답이다.

오답분석
(a) 여자가 공부에 집중하는 것의 장점으로 새로운 개인교습 센터를 방문하는 것을 언급했지만, 개인교습 센터에서 일하는 것을 언급한 것은 아니므로 오답이다.

어휘 | go for a walk 산책하러 가다

44 특정세부사항　How

난이도 ●●○

How is Jenny able to avoid feeling burned out?

(a) by getting some fresh air
(b) by relaxing with music
(c) by doing some exercise
(d) by taking a snack break

Jenny는 어떻게 기진맥진한 느낌을 피할 수 있는가?

(a) 맑은 공기를 접함으로써
(b) 음악을 들으며 편안히 쉼으로써
(c) 운동을 함으로써
(d) 간식 시간을 가짐으로써

─○ 정답 잡는 치트키

질문의 키워드 feeling burned out이 Burnout으로 paraphrasing되어 언급된 주변 내용을 주의 깊게 듣는다.

해설 | 여자가 'Burnout is a real thing. Sometimes I find that I actually do better on tests if I force myself to stop studying and do other things, like jogging on the treadmill'이라며 번아웃은 실제로 있는 것이고, 가끔 억지로 공부를 멈추고 러닝머신 위에서 조깅하는 것과 같은 다른 것들을 하면 실제로 시험을 더 잘 본다는 것을 알게 된다고 했다. 따라서 (c)가 정답이다.

⇄ **Paraphrasing**
jogging 조깅 → exercise 운동

오답분석
(b) 여자가 음악을 듣는 것을 언급했지만, 음악을 듣는 것이 기진맥진한 느낌을 피하게 할 수 있다고 한 것은 아니므로 오답이다.

45 추론　다음에 할 일

난이도 ●●○

What has Chris most likely decided to do after the conversation?

(a) work at the supermarket
(b) focus only on his studies
(c) accept the office job
(d) start learning to cook

Chris는 대화 이후에 무엇을 하기로 결정했을 것 같은가?

(a) 슈퍼마켓에서 일한다
(b) 그의 연구에만 집중한다
(c) 사무직을 맡는다
(d) 요리하는 것을 배우기 시작한다

─○ 정답 잡는 치트키

다음에 할 일을 언급하는 후반을 주의 깊게 듣는다.

해설 | 남자가 'I need to take a trip to the supermarket soon, and shopping will be much nicer with more money for food in my pocket.'이라며 곧 슈퍼마켓에 가야 하는데, 주머니에 식료품 살 돈이 더 있다면 쇼핑이 훨씬 더 즐거울 거라고 한 것을 통해, Chris는 사무직인 입학처 일을 맡아서 할 것임을 추론할 수 있다. 따라서 (c)가 정답이다.

어휘 | office job 사무직

인사
+
주제
제시

Welcome to the *Work Wise* podcast. Every year, it seems like a few coworkers retire or move on to other things, and so we have to say goodbye. [46]On today's episode, we're going to help you say goodbye in style by throwing a farewell party for your coworker. Let's get started!

조언1:
시간
고려
하기

The first point to account for is timing. Will you hold the party during the workday or after hours? [47]An office poll will help you determine the ideal time for everyone to attend. You wouldn't want to hold a weekend party only to discover that family obligations end up interfering with attendance. [47]I usually put together an office poll online, and it never takes more than a few minutes for my coworkers to fill out.

조언2:
깜짝
파티
피하기

The second point is that [48]it's best to avoid surprises. Your coworker might want to dress nicely and would appreciate some advance notice if you're hosting a celebration in their honor. Also, it would be a letdown if you organized a great party only to have it be on a day when your coworker has other plans. I once organized a surprise farewell event for a coworker who had a doctor's appointment. He ended up missing his own party! [48]I learned the hard way that surprise parties are seldom worth the risk.

조언3:
파티
장소
정하기

The third point concerns the party location. If you hold a party in the office, employees from different departments can swing by and say their farewells in familiar surroundings. Since they work in the same building, it's easy to drop in and say goodbye. Then again, [49]if you really want this to be a special occasion, you can reserve a private party space. I once reserved a conference room at a nearby hotel, and everyone was happy to leave work early and celebrate their coworker's last day in a festive atmosphere.

조언4:
예산
고려
하기

Point number four concerns your budget. Does your office have a fund reserved for events? Do you need to ask for employee donations? If so, how much should each person give? Make sure you find out what both your coworkers and your company are willing to give. [50]Last time, I was a bit disappointed when only a few employees gave money toward their coworker's party. However, after a brief chat with human resources, the company supplied some extra funds that we could use to hold a great party.

Work Wise 팟캐스트에 오신 것을 환영합니다. 매년, 몇몇 동료들이 은퇴하거나 다른 곳으로 이직하는 것처럼 보여서, 작별 인사를 해야 합니다. [46]오늘 에피소드에서는, 동료를 위해 송별회를 열어 멋지게 작별 인사를 하도록 도와드리겠습니다. 시작해 봅시다!

첫 번째로 고려해야 할 점은 시간입니다. 파티를 근무 시간 중에 열 것인가요, 아니면 근무 시간 후에 열 것인가요? [47]사무실 여론조사는 모든 사람이 참석하기에 이상적인 시간을 정하는 데 도움이 될 것입니다. 주말 파티를 열어서 가족 사정으로 참석에 지장을 주게 되는 상황을 보게 되는 것은 원치 않으실 겁니다. [47]저는 보통 온라인으로 사무실 여론조사를 준비하는데, 동료들이 작성하는 데 몇 분도 채 걸리지 않습니다.

두 번째 요점은 [48]깜짝 파티를 피하는 것이 최선이라는 것입니다. 동료는 멋지게 옷을 입고 싶을 수도 있고 그들을 축하하여 축하 행사를 열게 된다면 사전 공지를 고맙게 생각할 것입니다. 또한, 멋진 파티를 준비했다가 동료가 다른 계획이 있는 날에 파티를 열게 된다면 실망스러울 것입니다. 저는 이전에 진료 예약이 있는 동료를 위해 깜짝 작별 행사를 준비한 적이 있습니다. 그는 결국 파티를 놓쳤습니다! [48]저는 깜짝 파티가 위험을 무릅쓸 가치가 거의 없다는 것을 어렵게 배웠습니다.

세 번째 요점은 파티 장소에 관한 것입니다. 사무실에서 파티를 열면, 서로 다른 부서의 직원들이 들러 익숙한 환경에서 작별 인사를 할 수 있습니다. 같은 건물에 근무하기 때문에, 쉽게 잠깐 들러 작별 인사를 나눌 수 있습니다. 또 한편으로는, [49]특별한 행사가 되기를 정말 바란다면, 개인 파티 공간을 예약할 수도 있습니다. 저는 이전에 근처 호텔에 있는 회의실을 예약한 적이 있는데, 모두가 기꺼이 일찍 퇴근해 축제 분위기 속에서 동료의 마지막 날을 축하했습니다.

네 번째 요점은 예산에 관한 것입니다. 사무실에 행사를 위한 기금이 마련되어 있나요? 직원들에게 기부금을 요청해야 하나요? 그렇다면, 한 사람당 얼마를 내야 하나요? 동료들과 회사 모두 기꺼이 낼 수 있는 금액이 얼마인지 알아보세요. [50]저번에, 소수의 직원만 동료의 파티를 위해 돈을 냈을 때 저는 조금 실망했습니다. 하지만, 인사팀과 짧은 대화 후에, 회사는 멋진 파티를 열 수 있도록 여분의 자금을 제공했습니다.

조언5: 음식 알레 르기나 특별 식단 고려	Point number five concerns food. Are there any food allergies or special diets you need to account for as you plan the menu? Make sure to order food items that everyone is familiar with and can enjoy. My office typically uses the same caterer and orders a range of meat and vegetable dishes, which seems to satisfy everyone's appetite. But [51]don't forget to check with your coworkers before planning the menu.	다섯 번째 요점은 음식에 관한 것입니다. 메뉴를 계획할 때 고려해야 할 음식 알레르기나 특별 식단이 있나요? 모두가 친숙하고 즐길 수 있는 음식을 주문해야 합니다. 제 사무실은 보통 같은 음식 공급업체를 쓰고 모든 사람의 입맛을 만족시키는 것으로 보이는 다양한 고기와 야채 요리를 주문합니다. 하지만 [51]메뉴를 계획하기 전에 동료들에게 문의하는 것을 잊지 마세요.
조언6: 작별 선물 준비	Point number six concerns the farewell gift. Don't worry too much about purchasing the perfect gift. We've all heard the expression, "It's the thought that counts." If you can't decide what to get, a gift card is perfectly acceptable. [52]When I presented my coworker with a farewell gift card to Coffee Chalet, she was happy that we had all thought of her. The sentiment meant more to her than the present, she later told me, although she did appreciate the pumpkin spice lattes!	여섯 번째 요점은 작별 선물에 관한 것입니다. 완벽한 선물을 사는 것에 대해서 너무 걱정하지 마세요. 우리는 모두 "중요한 것은 마음이다"라는 표현을 들어본 적이 있습니다. 무엇을 살지 결정할 수 없다면, 기프트 카드는 완벽하게 만족스러울 만합니다. [52]제가 동료에게 작별 선물로 Coffee Chalet 기프트 카드를 줬을 때, 그녀는 우리가 모두 그녀를 생각해 준 것에 기뻐했습니다. 비록 호박 스파이스 라테를 맛있게 먹었지만, 그 감정은 그녀에게 선물보다 더 의미가 있었다고 나중에 그녀가 제게 말했습니다.
끝인사	Well, time to start planning that party. Thanks for listening to *Work Wise*!	음, 파티 계획을 시작할 시간이네요. *Work Wise*를 들어주셔서 감사합니다!

어휘 | move on 더 좋은 일자리로 옮기다 in style 멋지게 farewell party 송별회 workday[wə́rkdei] 근무일 after hours 근무 시간 후에 only to 그 결과는 ~뿐 family obligation 가족의 의무 end up ~게 되다, 결국 ~되다 interfere with ~에 지장을 주다, ~을 방해하다 put together 준비하다, 만들다 poll[poul] 여론조사, 투표 fill out 작성하다, 기입하다 surprise[sərpráiz] 뜻밖의 파티 appreciate[əprí:ʃièit] 고맙게 생각하다, (음식 따위를) 맛있게 먹다 advance[ædvǽns] 사전의 in a person's honor ~을 축하하여 letdown[létdàun] 실망, 의기소침 doctor's appointment 진료 예약 worth[wə:rθ] ~의 가치가 있는 concern[kənsə́:rn] ~에 관한 것이다 swing by 들르다 surrounding[səráundiŋ] 환경; 주변의 drop in 잠깐 들르다 occasion[əkéiʒən] 행사, 경우 festive atmosphere 축제 분위기 donation[dounéiʃən] 기부(금), 기증 chat[tʃæt] 대화, 이야기; 이야기를 나누다 supply[səplái] 제공하다, 지급하다 a range of 다양한 appetite[ǽpətàit] 입맛 gift card 기프트 카드(상품권의 기능과 신용카드의 편리함을 합친 선불 카드) acceptable[ækséptəbl] 만족스러운, 받아들일 만한 sentiment[séntəmənt] 감정, 심리

46 주제/목적 담화의 주제

난이도 ●○○

What is the talk mainly about?

(a) preparing for a work retreat
(b) throwing a holiday party
(c) **organizing a farewell event**
(d) planning a party for new staff

담화의 주제는 무엇인가?

(a) 직장 야유회를 준비하는 것
(b) 휴가 파티를 여는 것
(c) **송별회를 준비하는 것**
(d) 새로운 직원을 위한 파티를 계획하는 것

◁─○ 정답 잡는 치트키

담화의 주제를 언급하는 초반을 주의 깊게 듣고 전체 맥락을 파악한다.

해설 | 화자가 'On today's episode, we're going to help you say goodbye in style by throwing a farewell party for your coworker.'라며 오늘 에피소드에서는 동료를 위해 송별회를 열어 멋지게 작별 인사를 하도록 도와주겠다고 한 뒤, 담화 전반에 걸쳐 송별회를 준비할 때 고려해야 하는 사항에 관해 설명하는 내용이 이어지고 있다. 따라서 (c)가 정답이다.

32 본 교재 인강·무료 지텔프 문법 총정리강의 HackersIngang.com

⇄ **Paraphrasing**

a farewell party 송별회 → a farewell event 송별회

어휘 | retreat[ritríːt] 야유회

---

47 특정세부사항   How   난이도 ●●○

How does the speaker determine the ideal time for a party?

(a) by handing out an office poll
(b) by inviting people to vote online
(c) by asking around the office
(d) by checking the office calendar

화자는 파티에 이상적인 시간을 어떻게 결정하는가?

(a) 사무실 여론조사를 나눠줌으로써
(b) 온라인에서 투표하도록 사람들에게 요청함으로써
(c) 사무실 여기저기에 물어봄으로써
(d) 사무실 달력을 확인함으로써

→○ 정답 잡는 치트키

질문의 키워드 ideal time이 그대로 언급된 주변 내용을 주의 깊게 듣는다.

해설 | 화자가 'An office poll will help you determine the ideal time for everyone to attend.'라며 사무실 여론조사는 모든 사람이 참석하기에 이상적인 시간을 정하는 데 도움이 될 것이라고 한 뒤, 'I usually put together an office poll online, and it never takes more than a few minutes for my coworkers to fill out.'이라며 자기는 보통 온라인으로 사무실 여론조사를 준비하는데, 동료들이 작성하는 데 몇 분도 채 걸리지 않는다고 했다. 따라서 (b)가 정답이다.

오답분석

(a) 화자가 사무실 여론조사를 한다고 언급하기는 했지만, 이것은 온라인 여론조사를 의미하는 것으로, 여론조사를 나눠주는 것은 화자가 언급한 온라인 여론조사 방식이 아니므로 오답이다.

어휘 | hand out 나눠주다, 배포하다

---

48 추론   특정사실   난이도 ●●●

Why, most likely, does the speaker consider it best to avoid surprises?

(a) They are too risky.
(b) They are too hard to plan.
(c) They can be frightening.
(d) They can upset people.

화자는 왜 깜짝 파티를 피하는 것이 최선이라고 생각하는 것 같은가?

(a) 너무 위험하다.
(b) 계획하기가 너무 어렵다.
(c) 깜짝 놀라게 할 수 있다.
(d) 사람들을 당황하게 할 수 있다.

→○ 정답 잡는 치트키

질문의 키워드 best to avoid surprises가 그대로 언급된 주변 내용을 주의 깊게 듣는다.

해설 | 화자가 'it's best to avoid surprises'라며 깜짝 파티를 피하는 것이 최선이라고 한 뒤, 'I learned the hard way that surprise parties are seldom worth the risk.'라며 깜짝 파티가 위험을 무릅쓸 가치가 거의 없다는 것을 어렵게 배웠다고 한 것을 통해, 화자는 깜짝 파티가 다른 일정과 겹칠 수도 있는 등 너무 위험해서 피하는 것이 최선이라고 생각하고 있음을 추론할 수 있다. 따라서 (a)가 정답이다.

어휘 | risky[ríski] 위험한, 무서운   frightening[fráitniŋ] 깜짝 놀라게 하는, 위협적인

49 특정세부사항 How

난이도 ●●○

According to the talk, how can the organizer make the event more of a special occasion?

(a) by staying overnight at a hotel
(b) by inviting everyone from work
(c) by choosing a clever theme
(d) by renting a nearby venue

담화에 따르면, 주최자는 어떻게 행사를 더 특별한 행사로 만들 수 있는가?

(a) 호텔에서 하룻밤 동안 묵음으로써
(b) 직장의 모든 사람을 초대함으로써
(c) 기발한 테마를 선택함으로써
(d) 가까운 장소를 빌림으로써

━○ 정답 잡는 치트키

질문의 키워드 special occasion이 그대로 언급된 주변 내용을 주의 깊게 듣는다.

해설 | 화자가 'if you really want this to be a special occasion, you can reserve a private party space'라며 특별한 행사가 되기를 정말 바란다면 개인 파티 공간을 예약할 수도 있다고 했다. 따라서 (d)가 정답이다.

⇄ **Paraphrasing**
reserve a ~ space 공간을 예약하다 → renting a ~ venue 장소를 빌림

어휘 | organizer[ɔ́ːrɡənàizər] 주최자 overnight[óuvərnait] 하룻밤 동안 clever[klévər] 기발한

50 특정세부사항 Why

난이도 ●●○

Why was the speaker disappointed by his last work party?

(a) He had a small budget.
(b) It was poorly attended.
(c) He received few donations.
(d) It had to be canceled.

화자는 왜 그의 지난 직장 파티에 실망했는가?

(a) 예산이 적었다.
(b) 사람이 별로 모이지 않았다.
(c) 거의 모금을 받지 못했다.
(d) 취소되어야 했다.

━○ 정답 잡는 치트키

질문의 키워드 disappointed가 그대로 언급된 주변 내용을 주의 깊게 듣는다.

해설 | 화자가 'Last time, I was a bit disappointed when only a few employees gave money toward their coworker's party.'라며 저번에 소수의 직원만 동료의 파티를 위해 돈을 냈을 때 조금 실망했다고 했다. 따라서 (c)가 정답이다.

어휘 | poorly attended 사람이 별로 모이지 않은

51 특정세부사항 What

난이도 ●○○

What does the speaker recommend that one do before planning the menu?

(a) sample a range of dishes
(b) discuss it with colleagues
(c) research common allergies
(d) find a good caterer

화자는 메뉴를 계획하기 전에 무엇을 할 것을 추천하는가?

(a) 다양한 요리를 시식한다
(b) 동료들과 의논한다
(c) 공통의 알레르기를 조사하다
(d) 좋은 음식 공급업체를 찾는다

질문의 키워드 before planning the menu가 그대로 언급된 주변 내용을 주의 깊게 듣는다.

해설 | 화자가 'don't forget to check with your coworkers before planning the menu'라며 메뉴를 계획하기 전에 동료들에게 문의하는 것을 잊지 말라고 했다. 따라서 (b)가 정답이다.

↻ **Paraphrasing**

check with ~ coworkers 동료들에게 문의하다 → discuss ~ with colleagues 동료들과 의논하다

어휘 | sample[sǽmpl] ~을 시식하다; 샘플, 표본

52 특정세부사항 Why

난이도 ●●○

Why was the speaker's coworker happy with her café gift card?

(a) because she had asked for it
(b) because she was a regular customer
(c) **because she found it thoughtful**
(d) because she was able to save money

화자의 동료는 왜 카페 기프트 카드에 만족했는가?

(a) 그것을 요구했기 때문에
(b) 단골이었기 때문에
(c) **마음을 써주었다고 생각했기 때문에**
(d) 돈을 절약할 수 있었기 때문에

질문의 키워드 gift card가 그대로 언급된 주변 내용을 주의 깊게 듣는다.

해설 | 화자가 'When I presented my coworker with a farewell gift card ~, she was happy that we had all thought of her.'라며 동료에게 작별 선물로 기프트 카드를 줬을 때, 모두가 그녀를 생각해 준 것에 기뻐했다고 했다. 따라서 (c)가 정답이다.

어휘 | regular customer 단골, 정기 고객   thoughtful[θɔ́ːtfəl] 마음 쓰는, 사려 깊은

READING & VOCABULARY

PART 1 (53~59) 인물의 일대기 무술 영화에 큰 영향을 미친 브루스 리

인물 이름	**BRUCE LEE**	**브루스 리**
소개 + 유명한 이유	Bruce Lee was an actor, filmmaker, and martial arts expert. [53]He is best known for exhibiting his unique fighting style in popular films that drew international attention to the budding Hong Kong action cinema scene. Lee reshaped the portrayal of Asian culture in the West by breaking down racial barriers in the film industry.	브루스 리는 배우이자, 영화제작자이자, 무술 전문가였다. [53]그는 신진 홍콩 액션 영화계에 국제적인 관심을 끌었던 인기 영화들에서 독특한 격투 스타일을 보여준 것으로 가장 잘 알려져 있다. 리는 영화계에서 인종 간의 장벽을 허물면서 서구에서 아시아 문화의 묘사를 새 형태로 만들었다.
출생 및 어린 시절	Jun-fan "Bruce" Lee was born on November 27, 1940, in San Francisco, California, while his parents were touring the US with the Chinese Opera. He was raised in Hong Kong, where his father was a famous singer. [54]Lee was involved in show business from an early age, appearing in numerous films as a child actor.	전 팬 "브루스" 리는 1940년 11월 27일에 캘리포니아 샌프란시스코에서 부모님이 중국 오페라단과 함께 미국을 순회하던 중에 태어났다. 그는 홍콩에서 자랐는데, 그의 아버지는 유명한 가수였다. [54]리는 아역 배우로서 수많은 영화에 출연하며, 어릴 때부터 쇼 비즈니스에 종사했다.
10대 시절 + 업적 시작 계기	As a teenager in Hong Kong, Lee was bullied due to his Chinese heritage. [55]After street fighting landed him in trouble, his parents decided that he needed proper martial arts training. He began studying Wing Chun kung fu, a style of self-defense that focuses on using natural and scientific laws to generate strength.	홍콩에서 10대 시절, 리는 중국계라는 이유로 괴롭힘을 당했다. [55]길거리 싸움으로 곤경에 빠지자, 그의 부모는 그에게 적절한 무술 훈련이 필요하다고 결정했다. 그는 자연과 과학의 법칙을 이용해 힘을 생기게 하는 데 중점을 둔 호신술인 영춘권을 배우기 시작했다.
주요 업적1: 무술 학교 설립 및 절권도 개발	Lee returned to the US at the age of eighteen. While in school, he taught his style of kung fu to friends and other students. He [58]founded his own martial arts school in Seattle and, soon after, a second one in Los Angeles. Lee's reputation exploded as he participated in tournaments and widely discussed private matches. Around this time, he also became concerned about the restrictiveness of traditional fighting techniques. [56]He developed Jeet Kune Do, a hybrid martial art philosophy that prioritizes freedom and self-expression over organized style.	리는 18세에 미국으로 돌아왔다. 학교에 있는 동안, 그는 친구들과 다른 학생들에게 그의 쿵후 스타일을 가르쳤다. 그는 시애틀에 [58]그만의 무술학교를, 곧이어, 로스앤젤레스에 두 번째 무술학교를 설립했다. 리의 명성은 그가 토너먼트에 참가하고 개인 경기를 널리 알리면서 폭발적으로 증가했다. 이 시기쯤에, 그는 전통적인 격투 기술의 제한성에 대해서도 고민하게 되었다. [56]그는 절권도를 개발했는데, 이것은 체계적인 스타일보다 자유와 자기표현을 우선시하는 종합적인 무술 철학이었다.
주요 업적2: 배우로서의 활약	Lee was noticed by a television producer at a karate tournament in 1964 and soon landed a prominent role in the show *The Green Hornet*. Still, [57]he struggled to find other acting opportunities and soon came to terms with the fact that there were no lead roles available for Asian actors in Hollywood. He returned to Hong Kong and quickly became an action movie star, [59]showcasing his theatrical fighting style and setting box office records.	리는 1964년에 가라테 대회에서 텔레비전 프로그램 제작자에 의해 눈에 띄었고 곧 *The Green Hornet*이라는 쇼에서 중요한 역할을 얻었다. 하지만, [57]그는 다른 연기 기회를 찾는데 분투했고 할리우드에서 아시아 배우에게 주어지는 주연급 배역이 없다는 사실을 곧 받아들이게 되었다. 그는 홍콩으로 돌아와서 [59]과장된 격투 스타일을 선보이며 흥행 기록을 세우면서 빠르게 유명 액션 영화배우가 되었다.

죽음
+
후기
업적

Lee was on the brink of reaching international stardom with the release of his film *Enter the Dragon* when he died suddenly in Hong Kong in 1973. The film was a success and cemented his status as a cultural icon. Lee's legacy opened new pathways for Asian representation in Hollywood films. His life and philosophy continue to inspire people worldwide.

리가 1973년 홍콩에서 갑작스럽게 사망했을 때, 그의 영화 *Enter the Dragon*의 개봉으로 국제적인 스타의 반열에 오르기 직전이었다. 그 영화는 성공적이었고 문화적 아이콘으로서의 그의 지위를 굳혔다. 리의 유산은 할리우드 영화에서 아시아를 대표하는 새로운 길을 열었다. 그의 삶과 철학은 전 세계 사람들에게 계속해서 영감을 주고 있다.

어휘 | martial arts phr. 무술 expert n. 전문가 attention n. 관심, 주목 budding adj. 신진의, 나타나기 시작한
reshape v. 새 형태로 만들다, 고치다 portrayal n. 묘사 racial barrier phr. 인종 간의 장벽 show business phr. 쇼 비즈니스, 연예 공연업
child actor phr. 아역 배우 teenager n. 10대, 청소년 bully v. 괴롭히다 heritage n. 혈통, 유산 land in trouble phr. 곤경에 빠지다
Wing Chun phr. 영춘권 self-defense n. 호신(술) generate v. 생기게 하다, 기르다 reputation n. 명성, 평판
explode v. 폭발적으로 증가하다 tournament n. 토너먼트, 승자 진출권 restrictiveness n. 제한적임 Jeet Kune Do phr. 절권도
hybrid adj. 혼성의, 혼종의 philosophy n. 철학 prioritize v. 우선시하다 self-expression n. 자기표현
organized adj. 체계적인, 조직적인 karate n. 가라데(손발을 이용해서 싸우는 일본 권법) land v. 얻다, 치지히다
prominent adj. 중요한, 현지된 struggle v. 분투하다 come to terms with phr. (안 좋은 일을) 받아들이다 lead role phr. 주연
star n. 유명 영화배우, 주연; v. 주연을 맡다, 주역을 맡아 연기하다 theatrical adj. 과장된, 일부러 꾸미는 box office record phr. 흥행 기록
on the brink of phr. ~의 직전에 stardom n. 스타의 반열, 스타덤 cement v. 굳히다, 다지다 status n. 지위
cultural icon phr. 문화적 아이콘 legacy n. 유산, 업적 pathway n. 길, 방향 inspire v. 영감을 주다

---

53 **특정세부사항** 유명한 이유 난이도 ●●●○

What is Bruce Lee best known for?

(a) founding martial arts studios around the world
(b) promoting the importance of self-defense through film
(c) becoming the first Asian actor to star in a Hollywood movie
(d) sparking viewers' interest in a specific type of movie

브루스 리는 무엇으로 가장 잘 알려져 있는가?

(a) 전 세계에 무술 스튜디오를 설립한 것
(b) 영화를 통해 호신술의 중요성을 알린 것
(c) 할리우드 영화에서 주연을 맡은 최초의 아시아 배우가 된 것
(d) 특정 유형의 영화에 관한 시청자들의 관심을 불러일으킨 것

▶━━○ **정답 잡는 치트키**

질문의 키워드 best known이 그대로 언급된 주변 내용을 주의 깊게 읽는다.

해설 | 1단락의 'He is best known for exhibiting his unique fighting style in popular films that drew international attention to the budding Hong Kong action cinema scene.'에서 브루스 리는 신진 홍콩 액션 영화계에 국제적인 관심을 끌었던 인기 영화들에서 독특한 격투 스타일을 보여준 것으로 가장 잘 알려져 있다고 했다. 따라서 (d)가 정답이다.

⇄ **Paraphrasing**
drew ~ attention 관심을 끌었다 → sparking ~ interest 관심을 불러일으킨 것

어휘 | spark interest phr. 관심을 불러일으키다

---

54 **특정세부사항** How 난이도 ●●●○

How did Lee start performing for audiences?

리는 이렇게 관중들을 위한 공연을 시작했는가?

(a) **He starred in movies as a young child.**
(b) He appeared in films alongside his father.
(c) He toured opera halls with his parents.
(d) He sang onstage with a famous band.

(a) 어린 시절에 영화에 출연했다.
(b) 아버지와 함께 영화에 출연했다.
(c) 부모님과 함께 오페라 홀을 순회했다.
(d) 유명한 밴드와 함께 무대 위에서 노래를 불렀다.

○ 정답 잡는 치트키

질문의 키워드 performing for audiences가 appearing in ~ films로 paraphrasing되어 언급된 주변 내용을 주의 깊게 읽는다.

해설 | 2단락의 'Lee was involved in show business from an early age, appearing in numerous films as a child actor.'에서 리는 아역 배우로서 수많은 영화에 출연하며, 어릴 때부터 쇼 비즈니스에 종사했다고 했다. 따라서 (a)가 정답이다.

⇄ **Paraphrasing**
appearing in ~ films 영화에 출연하며 → starred in movies 영화에 출연했다

어휘 | audience n. 관중 alongside prep. ~과 함께 onstage adv. 무대 위에서

---

55 특정세부사항   How   난이도 ●●○

How did Lee's parents respond to his street fighting?

(a) by encouraging him to focus on his schoolwork
(b) by teaching him about various fighting styles
(c) by discouraging him from engaging in fights
(d) **by urging him to practice in a formal setting**

리의 부모는 어떻게 그의 길거리 싸움에 대응했는가?

(a) 그가 학업에 집중하도록 격려함으로써
(b) 그에게 다양한 격투 스타일에 대해 가르쳐줌으로써
(c) 그에게 싸움에 관여하지 못하게 함으로써
(d) **그에게 정식으로 연습하도록 설득함으로써**

○ 정답 잡는 치트키

질문의 키워드 street fighting이 그대로 언급된 주변 내용을 주의 깊게 읽는다.

해설 | 3단락의 'After street fighting landed him in trouble, his parents decided that he needed proper martial arts training. He began studying Wing Chun kung fu'에서 길거리 싸움으로 곤경에 빠지자, 리의 부모는 그에게 적절한 무술 훈련이 필요하다고 결정했고, 그는 영춘권을 배우기 시작했다고 했다. 따라서 (d)가 정답이다.

오답분석
(b) 3단락에서 리의 부모가 리에게 적절한 무술 훈련이 필요하다고 결정했다고는 했지만, 리의 부모가 리에게 다양한 격투 스타일에 대해 가르쳐준 것은 아니므로 오답이다.

어휘 | respond to phr. ~에 대응하다 schoolwork n. 학업 discourage from phr. ~을 못 하게 말리다, 단념하게 하다
engage in phr. ~에 관여하다 in a formal setting phr. 정식으로

---

56 특정세부사항   Why   난이도 ●●●

Why did Lee establish his own martial arts philosophy?

(a) He was in conflict with other practitioners.
(b) **He thought the discipline should have more flexibility.**

리는 왜 자기만의 무술 철학을 세웠는가?

(a) 다른 사람들과 충돌했다.
(b) **규율이 좀 더 유연성을 가져야 한다고 생각했다.**

(c) He noticed that traditional methods were losing popularity.

(d) He had already mastered the other styles.

(c) 전통적인 방식이 인기를 잃어가고 있음을 알아차렸다.

(d) 이미 다른 스타일에 숙달했다.

➤─○ 정답 잡는 치트키

질문의 키워드 martial arts philosophy가 그대로 언급된 주변 내용을 주의 깊게 읽는다.

해설 | 4단락의 'He developed Jeet Kune Do, a hybrid martial art philosophy that prioritizes freedom and self-expression over organized style.'에서 그는 절권도를 개발했는데, 이것은 체계적인 스타일보다 자유와 자기표현을 우선시하는 종합적인 무술 철학이었다고 했다. 따라서 (b)가 정답이다.

어휘 | in conflict with phr. ~과 충돌하다 practitioner n. (특정 종교·철학 등을) 실천하는 사람 discipline n. 규율 flexibility n. 유연성, 융통성 popularity n. 인기 master v. ~을 숙달하다, 터득하다

---

57 추론 특정사실 난이도 ●●●

Why, most likely, did Lee have trouble finding roles in Hollywood?

(a) because he lacked acting experience
(b) because his fighting style was difficult to film
(c) because action movies were unpopular at the time
(d) because he looked different from other movie stars

리는 왜 할리우드에서 배역을 찾는 데 어려움을 겪었을 것 같은가?

(a) 연기 경험이 부족했기 때문에
(b) 그의 격투 스타일은 촬영하기 어려웠기 때문에
(c) 그 당시에는 액션 영화가 인기가 없었기 때문에
(d) 다른 유명 영화배우들과 다르게 보였기 때문에

➤─○ 정답 잡는 치트키

질문의 키워드 Hollywood가 그대로 언급된 주변 내용을 주의 깊게 읽는다.

해설 | 5단락의 'he struggled to find other acting opportunities and soon came to terms with the fact that there were no lead roles available for Asian actors in Hollywood'에서 리는 다른 연기 기회를 찾는데 분투했고 할리우드에서 아시아 배우에게 주어지는 주연급 배역이 없다는 사실을 곧 받아들이게 되었다고 한 것을 통해, 리는 인종으로 인해 다른 유명 영화배우들과 다르게 보였기 때문에 할리우드에서 배역을 찾는 데 어려움을 겪었음을 추론할 수 있다. 따라서 (d)가 정답이다.

어휘 | lack v. ~이 부족하다

---

58 어휘 유의어 난이도 ●●○

In the context of the passage, <u>founded</u> means _____.

(a) discovered
(b) attended
(c) created
(d) defended

지문의 문맥에서, 'founded'는 -을 의미한다.

(a) 발견했다
(b) 참석했다
(c) 설립했다
(d) 지켰다

➤─○ 정답 잡는 치트키

밑줄 친 어휘의 유의어를 찾는 문제이므로, founded가 포함된 구절을 읽고 문맥을 파악한다.

해설 | 4단락의 'founded his own martial arts school'은 그만의 무술학교를 설립했다는 뜻이므로, founded가 '설립했다'라는 의미로 사용된 것을 알 수 있다. 따라서 '설립했다'라는 같은 의미의 (c) created가 정답이다.

59 어휘 유의어

In the context of the passage, <u>showcasing</u> means _____.

(a) winning
(b) displaying
(c) proving
(d) expressing

지문의 문맥에서, 'showcasing'은 -을 의미한다.

(a) 얻으며
(b) 선보이며
(c) 증명하며
(d) 표현하며

○ 정답 잡는 치트키

밑줄 친 어휘의 유의어를 찾는 문제이므로, showcasing이 포함된 구절을 읽고 문맥을 파악한다.

해설 | 5단락의 'showcasing his theatrical fighting style'은 과장된 격투 스타일을 선보인다는 뜻이므로, showcasing이 '선보이며'라는 의미로 사용된 것을 알 수 있다. 따라서 '선보이며'라는 같은 의미의 (b) displaying이 정답이다.

PART 2 (60~66) 잡지 기사   새들이 함께 협력하여 위기를 극복한다는 증거 발견

연구결과

ROBOTIC FALCON SUGGESTS EVIDENCE AGAINST SELFISH HERD HYPOTHESIS

로봇 매가 이기적인 무리 가설에 반대하는 증거를 제공하다

연구소개

The "selfish herd" hypothesis was first proposed by W.D. Hamilton in 1971 to explain why animals move in groups. For decades, [60]scientists have believed that when a flock of pigeons in flight is under attack, individual birds will attempt to move to the middle of the group to shield themselves, [65]leaving other birds <u>vulnerable</u> to attack. [60]However, an innovative experiment using a robotic predator has provided evidence against this hypothesis.

"이기적인 무리" 가설은 동물들이 무리를 지어 이동하는 이유를 설명하기 위해 1971년 W.D. Hamilton에 의해 처음으로 제안되었다. 수십 년 동안, [60]과학자들은 비행 중인 비둘기 무리가 공격을 받을 때, 개별 새들이 자기를 보호하기 위해 무리의 중앙으로 이동하려고 시도하면서, [65]다른 새들을 공격에 취약한 채로 내버려 둘 것이라고 믿어 왔다. [60]그러나, 로봇 포식자를 이용한 혁신적인 실험은 이 가설에 반대하는 증거를 제시했다.

연구방법

The study on pigeons was led by behavioral ecologist Daniel Sankey at Royal Holloway University. Employing innovations in robotics to conduct their experiment, Sankey and his team used a robotic falcon, or RoboFalcon, to attack various flocks of pigeons. [61]The scientists used tracking technology to observe each pigeon's movements as the RoboFalcon approached. Because the RoboFalcon could be programmed to follow precise orders, the experiment was repeated a number of times to ensure consistent results.

비둘기들에 관한 연구는 Royal Holloway 대학교의 행동 생태학자 Daniel Sankey에 의해 주도되었다. 그들의 실험을 수행하기 위해 로봇공학의 혁신을 이용하여, Sankey와 그의 팀은 다양한 비둘기 무리를 공격하기 위해 로봇 매, 즉 RoboFalcon을 사용했다. [61]과학자들은 RoboFalcon이 접근할 때 각각의 비둘기의 움직임을 관찰하기 위해 추적 기술을 사용했다. RoboFalcon이 정확한 명령을 따르도록 프로그래밍이 될 수 있었기 때문에, 일관된 결과를 보장하기 위해 실험은 여러 번 반복되었다.

근거1
[62]Although the "selfish herd" hypothesis suggests that each pigeon would try to fly to the center of the flock in order to avoid being attacked, Sankey found that the birds instead worked together to make a group escape. By relying on each other, the birds were relieved of the responsibility of tracking and avoiding the predator individually. The experiment was repeated with pigeon flocks of different sizes, with each trial providing similar results.

근거2
[63]The pigeons further demonstrated their selflessness by moving in a flock, or a loosely organized group, rather than the more aerodynamic V-formation, which reduces the drag from the wind that birds face while flying. Despite needing to put eighteen percent more energy into flying as a result of the less efficient flight path, the pigeons demonstrated a willingness to take on added individual effort for the sake of the group's safety.

시사점
Sankey believes that the study highlights the importance of cooperation and escape mechanisms among prey and [64(a)]is planning to study the patterns of various animal species using similar technology. And, although [66]the technology is still being refined, it has many potential uses. For instance, [64(b)]it could be used to herd birds away from potential danger and [64(c)]prevent problems that can arise when birds collide with passenger planes.

[63]비록 "이기적인 무리" 가설은 각 비둘기가 공격받는 것을 피하기 위해 무리의 중앙으로 날아가려고 하는 것을 제시하지만, Sankey는 새들이 그 대신 집단 탈출하기 위해 함께 협력한다는 사실을 발견했다. 서로 의지함으로써 그 새들은 개별적으로 포식자를 추적하고 피해야 하는 부담을 덜었다. 이 실험은 다양한 규모의 비둘기 무리를 대상으로 반복되었으며, 각 실험에서 비슷한 결과가 나왔다.

[63]비둘기들은 날 때 직면하는 공기의 저항을 줄여주는 더 공기역학적인 V자 형태가 아니라, 무리를 짓거나 느슨하게 조직된 집단을 이루어 이동함으로써 그들의 이타적인 모습을 보여주었다. 덜 효율적인 비행경로의 결과로 비행에 18% 더 많은 에너지를 투입할 필요가 있음에도 불구하고, 비둘기들은 십난의 안전을 위해 기꺼이 개별적인 노력을 더 기울이는 모습을 보여주었다.

Sankey는 이 연구가 먹잇감 간의 협력과 탈출 메커니즘의 중요성을 강조한다고 믿고 있으며, [64(a)]유사한 기술을 사용하여 다양한 동물 종들의 패턴을 연구할 계획이다. 그리고, 비록 [66]이 기술은 아직도 개선되고 있지만, 많은 잠재적인 용도가 있다. 예를 들어, [64(b)]새들을 잠재적인 위험으로부터 멀리 이동하게 하고 [64(c)]새들이 여객기와 충돌할 때 발생할 수 있는 문제를 방지하는 데 사용될 수 있다.

어휘 | falcon n. 매 a flock of phr. ~의 무리, 떼 pigeon n. 비둘기 shield v. 보호하다 predator n. 포식자, 천적 behavioral ecologist phr. 행동 생태학자 employ v. 이용하다 innovation n. 혁신 conduct v. 수행하다, 실시하다 observe v. 관찰하다 approach v. 접근하다, 다가가다 precise adj. 정확한 repeat v. 반복하다 consistent adj. 일관된 escape n. 탈출, 도피 rely on phr. ~에 의지하다, 의존하다 relieve of phr. ~을 덜어 주다 responsibility n. 부담, 책무 trial n. 실험, 시험 demonstrate v. 보여주다, 입증하다 selflessness n. 이타심 loosely adv. 느슨하게 aerodynamic adj. 공기역학적인 drag n. 항력, 장애물 flight path phr. 비행경로 willingness n. 기꺼이 하기 for the sake of phr. ~을 위해 highlight v. 강조하다 cooperation n. 협력 prey n. 먹이 potential adj. 잠재적인 herd v. 이동하게 하다 collide with phr. ~과 충돌하다 passenger plane phr. 여객기, 비행기

60 주제/목적 기사의 주제

난이도 ●●○

What is the article mainly about?

(a) **a tendency among birds to protect one another**
(b) the evolution of a species of flying predator
(c) an invention for scaring off unwanted birds
(d) the results of a study about bird migration

기사의 주제는 무엇인가?

(a) 새들 간에 서로를 보호하려는 경향
(b) 날아다니는 포식자 종의 진화
(c) 원치 않는 새들을 겁주어 쫓아내기 위한 발명품
(d) 새의 이주에 관한 연구 결과

지문의 초반을 주의 깊게 읽고 전체 맥락을 파악한다.

해설 | 1단락의 'scientists have believed that when a flock of pigeons in flight is under attack, individual birds will attempt ~ to shield themselves, leaving other birds vulnerable to attack. However, an innovative experiment ~ has provided evidence against this hypothesis.'에서 과학자들은 비행 중인 비둘기 무리가 공격을 받을 때, 개별 새들이 자기를 보호하려고 하면서, 다른 새들을 공격에 취약한 채로 내버려 둘 것이라고 믿어 왔지만, 혁신적인 실험은 이 가설에 반대하는 증거를 제시했다고 한 뒤, 지문 전반에 걸쳐 위험한 상황에서 새들이 서로 보호하려는 경향을 가지는 것을 설명하는 내용이 이어지고 있다. 따라서 (a)가 정답이다.

어휘 | tendency n. 경향 evolution n. 진화 scare off phr. 겁주어 쫓아내다 migration n. 이주, 이동

---

61 특정세부사항 How
난이도 ●●○

How did the researchers gather data from the trials?

(a) by calculating the distance flown by the flocks
(b) by observing changes in the robotic bird's behavior
(c) by noting the actions of individual flock members
(d) by counting the number of birds that disappeared

연구자들은 어떻게 실험에서 자료를 모았는가?

(a) 새 떼가 날아간 거리를 계산함으로써
(b) 로봇 새의 행동 변화를 관찰함으로써
(c) 개별 무리 구성원들의 행동에 주목함으로써
(d) 사라진 새들의 수를 세어 봄으로써

질문의 키워드 researchers가 scientists로 paraphrasing되어 언급된 주변 내용을 주의 깊게 읽는다.

해설 | 2단락의 'The scientists used tracking technology to observe each pigeon's movements as the RoboFalcon approached.'에서 과학자들은 RoboFalcon이 접근할 때 각각의 비둘기의 움직임을 관찰하기 위해 추적 기술을 사용했다고 했다. 따라서 (c)가 정답이다.

⇄ **Paraphrasing**
each pigeon's movements 각각의 비둘기의 움직임 → the actions of individual flock members 개별 무리 구성원들의 행동

어휘 | calculate v. 계산하다 distance n. 거리 behavior n. 행동 note v. ~에 주목하다 count v. (숫자를) 세다 disappear v. 사라지다

---

62 추론 특정사실
난이도 ●●●

What were the pigeons probably doing during the attack?

(a) flying to different sections of the flock
(b) looking for protection in a different flock
(c) coordinating with the others to attack the predator
(d) keeping track of the attacker's location together

비둘기들은 공격받는 동안 무엇을 하고 있었을 것 같은가?

(a) 무리의 다른 구역으로 날아가는 것
(b) 다른 무리에서 보호받으려는 것
(c) 포식자를 공격하기 위해 다른 새들과 협력하는 것
(d) 공격자의 위치를 함께 추적하는 것

질문의 키워드 attack이 그대로 언급된 주변 내용을 주의 깊게 읽는다.

해설 | 3단락의 'Although the ~ hypothesis suggests that each pigeon would try to fly to the center of the flock in order to avoid being attacked, Sankey found that the birds instead worked together ~. By relying on each other, the birds were relieved of the responsibility of tracking ~ the predator individually.'에서 비록 가설은 각 비둘기가 공격받는 것을 피하

기 위해 무리의 중앙으로 날아가려고 하는 것을 제시하지만, Sankey는 새들이 그 대신 함께 협력하고 서로 의지함으로써, 새들이 개별적으로 포식자를 추적해야 하는 부담을 덜었다고 한 것을 통해, 비둘기들은 공격받는 동안 함께 협력하여 공격자의 위치를 추적함을 추론할 수 있다. 따라서 (d)가 정답이다.

⇄ **Paraphrasing**
the predator 포식사 → the attacker 공격사

오답분석
(a) 3단락에서 가설은 각 비둘기가 공격받는 것을 피하기 위해 무리의 중앙으로 날아가려고 하는 것을 제시한다고 했지만, 이는 가설에 불과한 것으로 실제 비둘기들이 취한 행동은 아니므로 오답이다.
(c) 3단락에서 새들이 공격받는 동안 함께 협력한다고는 했지만, 포식자를 공격하기 위해 협력하는 것은 아니므로 오답이다.

어휘 | section n. 구역 protection n. 보호 coordinate with phr. ~과 협력하다 keep track of phr. ~을 추적하다 attacker n. 공격자

63 추론 특정사실 난이도 ●●○

Why, most likely, did the birds need to put additional effort into flying?

(a) They had more obstacles in their flight path.
(b) They were lending support to struggling group members.
(c) They were facing extra wind resistance.
(d) They had to focus on staying in a tight formation.

새들은 왜 나는 데 추가적인 노력을 해야 했을 것 같은가?

(a) 비행경로에 더 많은 장애물이 있었다.
(b) 어려움을 겪고 있는 무리 구성원들을 돕고 있었다.
(c) 더 많은 공기 저항에 직면해 있었다.
(d) 빽빽한 대형을 유지하는 데 집중해야 했다.

━O 정답 잡는 치트키
질문의 키워드 additional effort into flying이 more energy into flying으로 paraphrasing되어 언급된 주변 내용을 주의 깊게 읽는다.

해설 | 4단락의 'The pigeons further demonstrated their selflessness by moving in a flock, or a loosely organized group, rather than the more aerodynamic V-formation, which reduces the drag from the wind ~. Despite needing to put eighteen percent more energy into flying as a result of the less efficient flight path'에서 비둘기들은 공기의 저항을 줄여주는 더 공기역학적인 V자 형태가 아니라, 무리를 짓거나 느슨하게 조직된 집단을 이루어 이동함으로써 그들의 이타적인 모습을 보여주었고, 덜 효율적인 비행경로의 결과로 비행에 18% 더 많은 에너지를 투입할 필요가 있었다고 한 것을 통해, 새들은 무리 지어 이동함으로 인해 더 많은 공기 저항에 직면해서 나는 데 추가적인 노력을 해야 했음을 추론할 수 있다. 따라서 (c)가 정답이다.

⇄ **Paraphrasing**
the drag from the wind 공기의 저항 → wind resistance 공기 저항

어휘 | obstacle n. 장애물 lend support to phr. ~을 지원하다 wind resistance phr. 공기 저항 formation n. 대형

64 Not/True Not 문제 난이도 ●●●

According to the article, which is NOT a possible application of the technology used in the experiment?

(a) understanding the behavior of animal populations
(b) protecting animals from unsafe encounters
(c) ensuring smoother flights for commercial planes
(d) studying the effects of weather on flight patterns

기사에 따르면, 실험에 사용된 기술의 잠재적인 활용이 아닌 것은 무엇인가?

(a) 동물 개체군의 행동을 이해하는 것
(b) 안전하지 않은 마주침으로부터 동물들을 보호하는 것
(c) 상용 비행기의 원활한 비행을 보장하는 것
(d) 비행 패턴에 관한 날씨의 영향을 연구하는 것

TEST 1
TEST 2
TEST 3
TEST 4
TEST 5
TEST 6
TEST 7

지텔프 공식 기출문제집 7회분 Level 2

질문의 키워드 possible application과 관련된 지문의 후반을 주의 깊게 읽고, 보기의 키워드와 지문 내용을 대조하며 언급되는 것을 하나씩 소거한다.

해설 | (d)는 지문에 언급되지 않았으므로, (d)가 정답이다.

오답분석

(a) 보기의 키워드 behavior가 patterns로 paraphrasing되어 언급된 5단락에서 유사한 기술을 사용하여 다양한 동물 종들의 패턴을 연구할 계획이라고 언급되었다.

(b) 보기의 키워드 unsafe encounters가 danger로 paraphrasing되어 언급된 5단락에서 새들을 잠재적인 위험으로부터 멀리 이동하게 할 수 있다고 언급되었다.

(c) 보기의 키워드 commercial planes가 passenger planes로 paraphrasing되어 언급된 5단락에서 새들이 여객기와 충돌할 때 발생할 수 있는 문제를 방지하는 데 사용될 수 있다고 언급되었다.

어휘 | application n. 활용, 적용 population n. 개체군, 집단 encounter n. 마주침, 조우 ensure v. 보장하다 smoother adj. 원활한, 매끄러운 commercial plane phr. 상용 비행기

---

65 어휘   유의어   난이도 ●●○

In the context of the passage, <u>vulnerable</u> means _____.

(a) open
(b) scared
(c) ready
(d) pushed

지문의 문맥에서, 'vulnerable'은 –을 의미한다.

(a) 무방비한
(b) 두려워하는
(c) 준비된
(d) 힘든

밑줄 친 어휘의 유의어를 찾는 문제이므로, vulnerable이 포함된 구절을 읽고 문맥을 파악한다.

해설 | 1단락의 'leaving other birds vulnerable to attack'은 다른 새들을 공격에 취약한 채로 내버려 두었다는 뜻이므로, vulnerable이 '취약한'이라는 의미로 사용된 것을 알 수 있다. 따라서 '무방비한'이라는 비슷한 의미의 (a) open이 정답이다.

---

66 어휘   유의어   난이도 ●●○

In the context of the passage, <u>refined</u> means _____.

(a) filtered
(b) improved
(c) fixed
(d) decided

지문의 문맥에서, 'refined'는 –을 의미한다.

(a) 여과된
(b) 개선된
(c) 고쳐진
(d) 결정된

밑줄 친 어휘의 유의어를 찾는 문제이므로, refined가 포함된 구절을 읽고 문맥을 파악한다.

해설 | 5단락의 'the technology is still being refined'는 이 기술이 아직도 개선되고 있다는 뜻이므로, refined가 '개선된'이라는 의미로 사용된 것을 알 수 있다. 따라서 '개선된'이라는 같은 의미의 (b) improved가 정답이다.

표제어

THE DIABOLICAL IRONCLAD BEETLE

정의

The diabolical ironclad beetle, or *Nosoderma diabolicum*, is a part of the wider ironclad beetle family. It can grow up to twenty-five millimeters in size. [67]Native to California, this beetle can be found in woodland habitats and often gathers near trunks of large trees to feed on fungi and rotting bark.

특징1:
겉모습
및
움직임

[68]At first glance, an observer might mistake the diabolical ironclad beetle for a rock. It is black or dark gray in color and has a rough outer texture, enabling the creature to blend into its natural environment. **The diabolical ironclad beetle is also quite flat and prefers to stay close to the ground. Unlike many other beetle species, it is incapable of flying and instead moves by crawling from place to place.**

특징2:
튼튼한
껍데기

As its name suggests, the diabolical ironclad beetle relies on an "ironclad" shell to protect itself from predators. [69]The sturdy insect's body can withstand nearly 40,000 times its own body weight, twice as much as other beetles of the same family. **This means that it can survive being run over by a car.**

특징3:
단단한
외골격

Based on microscopic studies, [72]scientists attribute the nearly indestructible nature of this beetle's body to its exoskeleton, [70(a)/(b)]a hard outer shell made up of pieces that wrap around its organs in an interlocking structure. [70(c)]Small connective sutures—lines that link together different sections of the exoskeleton—fill in the gaps in the beetle's tough armor.

특징4:
인내심

Patience is another key element to the diabolical ironclad beetle's survival. Researchers have observed that [71]when it senses a predator nearby, such as an animal or a larger insect, the beetle will play dead by tucking its legs underneath its body and lying flat on the ground, remaining in this position until the threat is no longer detected.

특징5:
긴
수명

These factors contribute to the diabolical ironclad beetle's [73]abnormally long lifespan. Whereas many beetle species live for an average of a few weeks, the diabolical ironclad beetle can live for up to seven or eight years. In more ways than one, this beetle is among the most resilient insects of its kind.

악마의 철갑 딱정벌레

악마의 철갑 딱정벌레, 즉 *Nosoderma diabolicum* 는 더 넓은 철갑 딱정벌렛과의 일부이나. 최대 25밀리미터까지 자랄 수 있다. [67]캘리포니아 토종인, 이 딱정벌레는 삼림지대 서식지에서 볼 수 있으며 곰팡이와 썩은 나무껍질을 먹고 살기 위해 종종 큰 나무줄기 근처에 모인다.

[68]힐끗 보기에, 관찰자는 악마의 철갑 딱정벌레를 돌로 착각할 수도 있다. 그것은 검은색 또는 짙은 회색이고 거친 겉면을 가지고 있어서, 그 생물이 자연환경과 잘 뒤섞이게 한다. 악마의 철갑 딱정벌레는 또한 꽤 납작하고 땅에 가까이 머무는 것을 선호한다. 다른 많은 딱정벌레 종과 달리, 날지 못하며 대신 이곳저곳을 기어다니며 움직인다.

이름이 보여주듯이, 이 악마의 철갑 딱정벌레는 포식자들로부터 자신을 보호하기 위해 "철갑" 껍데기에 의존한다. [69]이 튼튼한 곤충의 몸은 자기 몸무게의 거의 40,000배에 달하는 하중을 견딜 수 있으며, 이는 같은 딱정벌렛과에 속하는 다른 딱정벌레보다 두 배나 많은 무게이다. 이는 이것이 차에 치여도 살아남을 수 있다는 것을 의미한다.

현미경 연구에 따르면, [72]과학자들은 이 딱정벌레 몸의 거의 파괴할 수 없는 특성을 외골격, 즉 [70(a)/(b)]기관을 서로 맞물린 구조로 감싸는 조각들로 구성된 단단한 외피 덕분으로 본다. [70(c)]외골격의 여러 부분을 연결하는 작은 연결 봉합선이 딱정벌레의 튼튼한 철갑의 틈새를 메워준다.

인내심은 이 악마의 철갑 딱정벌레의 생존을 위한 또 다른 핵심 요소이다. 연구자들은 [71]이 딱정벌레가 동물이나 더 큰 곤충과 같은 포식자가 근처에 있음을 감지할 때, 다리를 몸 아래로 집어넣고 바닥에 납작 엎드려 죽은 척하며 위협이 더 이상 감지되지 않을 때까지 이 자세를 유지하는 것을 관찰했다.

이러한 요인들은 악마의 철갑 딱정벌레의 [73]비정상적으로 긴 수명에 기여한다. 많은 딱정벌레 종이 평균 몇 주를 사는 반면, 악마의 철갑 딱정벌레는 7년 또는 8년까지 살 수 있다. 여러 가지 면에서, 이 딱정벌레는 같은 종류의 가장 회복력이 있는 곤충 중 하나이다.

어휘 | **diabolical ironclad beetle** phr. 악마의 철갑 딱정벌레 **native to** phr. ~ 토종의 **woodland habitat** phr. 삼림지대 서식지
trunk n. 나무줄기 **fungi** n. 곰팡이 **rot** v. 썩다, 부패하다 **bark** n. 나무껍질 **glance** n. 힐끗 보기 **observer** n. 관찰자, 관측자

blend into phr. ~과 뒤섞이다 crawl v. 기어가다 withstand v. 견디다 be run over by phr. (차에) 치이다
microscopic study phr. 현미경 연구 indestructible adj. 파괴할 수 없는 exoskeleton n. 외골격 made up of phr. ~으로 구성된
wrap v. 감싸다 interlock v. 서로 맞물리다 armor n. 철갑, 갑옷 patience n. 인내심 sense v. 감지하다; n. 감각 tuck v. 집어넣다
threat n. 위협 lifespan n. 수명 resilient adj. 회복력 있는

---

67 주제/목적 　기사의 주제   난이도 ●●○

What is the subject of the article?

(a) a beetle that is native to the eastern US
(b) **an insect that feeds on decaying materials**
(c) an insect that lives primarily in the jungle
(d) a beetle that is found in the California desert

기사의 주제는 무엇인가?

(a) 미국 동부 토종의 딱정벌레
(b) **부패한 물질을 먹고 사는 곤충**
(c) 주로 정글에 서식하는 곤충
(d) 캘리포니아 사막에서 발견되는 딱정벌레

━○ 정답 잡는 치트키

지문의 초반을 주의 깊게 읽고 전체 맥락을 파악한다.

해설 | 1단락의 'Native to California, this beetle can be found in woodland habitats and often gathers near trunks of large trees to feed on fungi and rotting bark.'에서 캘리포니아 토종인, 이 딱정벌레는 삼림지대 서식지에서 볼 수 있으며 곰팡이와 썩은 나무껍질을 먹고 살기 위해 종종 큰 나무줄기 근처에 모인다고 한 뒤, 지문 전반에 걸쳐 악마의 철갑 딱정벌레의 특징을 설명하는 내용이 이어지고 있다. 따라서 (b)가 정답이다.

⇄ Paraphrasing
fungi and rotting bark 곰팡이와 썩은 나무껍질 → decaying materials 부패한 물질

오답분석
(a) 1단락에서 악마의 철갑 딱정벌레가 캘리포니아, 즉 미국 서부 지역 토종이라고 했으므로 오답이다.

어휘 | decay v. 부패하다, 썩다 primarily adv. 주로 desert n. 사막

---

68 특정세부사항 　How   난이도 ●○○

How does the beetle blend into its environment?

(a) by changing colors to match its surroundings
(b) **by looking like an object found in nature**
(c) by moving at an undetectable speed
(d) by crawling underneath nearby rocks

딱정벌레는 어떻게 주변 환경과 뒤섞이는가?

(a) 환경에 맞게 색을 바꿈으로써
(b) **자연에서 발견되는 물체처럼 보이게 함으로써**
(c) 감지할 수 없는 속도로 움직임으로써
(d) 근처 돌 밑을 기어다님으로써

━○ 정답 잡는 치트키

질문의 키워드 blend into its environment가 그대로 언급된 주변 내용을 주의 깊게 읽는다.

해설 | 2단락의 'At first glance, an observer might mistake the diabolical ironclad beetle for a rock. It is black or dark gray in color and has a rough outer texture, enabling the creature to blend into its natural environment.'에서 힐끗 보기에, 관찰자는 악마의 철갑 딱정벌레를 돌로 착각할 수도 있다고 하면서, 딱정벌레는 검은색 또는 짙은 회색이고 거친 겉면을 가지고 있어서 자연 환경과 잘 뒤섞이게 한다고 했다. 따라서 (b)가 정답이다.

⇄ **Paraphrasing**

a rock 돌 → an object found in nature 자연에서 발견되는 물체

어휘 | surrounding n. 환경, 주위 undetectable adj. 감지할 수 없는

---

69 특정세부사항 What

난이도 ●●○

According to the article, what differentiates the diabolical ironclad beetle from others in its family?

(a) its ability to endure intense impact
(b) its surprisingly heavy body weight
(c) its potential to survive in high heat
(d) its metallic-looking outer shell

기사에 따르면, 악마의 철갑 딱정벌레가 같은 과의 다른 딱정벌레들과 구별되는 것은 무엇인가?

(a) 강한 충격을 견디는 능력
(b) 의외로 무거운 체중
(c) 고열에서 살아남는 가능성
(d) 금속처럼 생긴 외피

⟶○ 정답 잡는 치트키

질문의 키워드 family가 그대로 언급된 주변 내용을 주의 깊게 읽는다.

해설 | 3단락의 'The sturdy insect's body can withstand nearly 40,000 times its own body weight, twice as much as other beetles of the same family.'에서 이 튼튼한 곤충의 몸은 자기 몸무게의 거의 40,000배에 달하는 하중을 견딜 수 있으며, 이는 같은 딱정벌렛과에 속하는 다른 딱정벌레보다 두 배나 많은 무게라고 했다. 따라서 (a)가 정답이다.

⇄ **Paraphrasing**

withstand 견디다 → endure 견디다

어휘 | differentiate from phr. ~과 구별하다 endure v. 견디다 intense adj. 강한 surprisingly adv. 의외로, 놀랄 만큼
body weight phr. 체중 potential n. 가능성, 잠재력

---

70 Not/True Not 문제

난이도 ●●●

Which is NOT true about the beetle's body?

(a) It has strong bonds that hold together its exoskeleton.
(b) It has a tough external layer that protects its organs.
(c) It has multiple parts that make up its shell.
(d) It has strong armor that quickly grows back.

딱정벌레의 몸에 관해 사실이 아닌 것은 무엇인가?

(a) 외골격을 지탱하는 강한 결합력을 가지고 있다.
(b) 기관을 보호하는 단단한 외피를 가지고 있다.
(c) 껍데기를 구성하는 여러 부분을 가지고 있다.
(d) 빠르게 다시 자라나는 강한 철갑을 가지고 있다.

⟶○ 정답 잡는 치트키

질문의 키워드 beetle's body가 그대로 언급된 주변 내용을 주의 깊게 읽고, 보기의 키워드와 지문 내용을 대조하며 언급되는 것을 하나씩 소거한다.

해설 | (d)는 지문에 언급되지 않았으므로, (d)가 정답이다.

오답분석

(a) 보기의 키워드 strong bonds가 interlocking structure로 paraphrasing되어 언급된 4단락에서 기관을 서로 맞물린 구조로 감싸는 조각들로 구성된 단단한 외피가 있다고 언급되었다.
(b) 보기이 키워드 tough external layer가 hard outer shell로 paraphrasing되어 언급된 4단락에서 기관을 서로 맞물린 구조로 감싸는 조각들로 구성된 단단한 외피가 있다고 언급되었다.

(c) 보기의 키워드 multiple parts가 different sections로 paraphrasing되어 언급된 4단락에서 외골격의 여러 부분을 연결하는 작은 연결 봉합선이 있다고 언급되었다.

어휘 | bond n. 결합력 hold together phr. 지탱하다 grow back phr. 다시 자라다

---

71 추론 특정사실 난이도 ●●○

Why, most likely, does the beetle tuck its legs underneath its body when it senses a predator?

(a) so that it cannot be lifted up
(b) so that it cannot be flipped over
(c) so that its limbs will be protected
(d) so that its presence goes unnoticed

딱정벌레는 왜 포식자를 감지할 때 다리를 몸 아래로 집어넣는 것 같은가?

(a) 들어 올려질 수 없도록 하기 위해서
(b) 뒤집힐 수 없도록 하기 위해서
(c) 팔다리가 보호되도록 하기 위해서
(d) 존재가 눈에 띄지 않도록 하기 위해서

🔑 정답 잡는 치트키
질문의 키워드 tuck its legs와 predator가 그대로 언급된 주변 내용을 주의 깊게 읽는다.

해설 | 5단락의 'when it senses a predator nearby, ~, the beetle will play dead by tucking its legs underneath its body ~, remaining in this position until the threat is no longer detected'에서 이 딱정벌레는 포식자가 근처에 있음을 감지할 때, 다리를 몸 아래로 집어넣고 죽은 척하며 위협이 더 이상 감지되지 않을 때까지 이 자세를 유지한다고 한 것을 통해, 딱정벌레는 포식자를 감지하면 눈에 띄지 않도록 하기 위해서 다리를 몸 아래로 집어넣고 죽은 척하는 것임을 추론할 수 있다. 따라서 (d)가 정답이다.

어휘 | flip over phr. 뒤집다 limb n. 팔다리 presence n. 존재, 영향력 unnoticed adj. 눈에 띄지 않는

---

72 어휘 유의어 난이도 ●●○

In the context of the passage, <u>attribute</u> means _____.

(a) credit
(b) leave
(c) expect
(d) compare

지문의 문맥에서, 'attribute'는 -을 의미한다.

(a) 덕분이다
(b) 남기다
(c) 예상하다
(d) 비교하다

🔑 정답 잡는 치트키
밑줄 친 어휘의 유의어를 찾는 문제이므로, attribute가 포함된 구절을 읽고 문맥을 파악한다.

해설 | 4단락의 'scientists attribute the ~ nature of this beetle's body to its exoskeleton'은 과학자들이 이 딱정벌레 몸의 특성을 외골격 덕분으로 본다는 뜻이므로, attribute가 '덕분으로 본다'라는 의미로 사용된 것을 알 수 있다. 따라서 '덕분이다'라는 같은 의미의 (a) credit이 정답이다.

In the context of the passage, <u>abnormally</u> means _____.

(a) unusually
(b) rarely
(c) painfully
(d) equally

지문의 문맥에서, 'abnormally'는 -을 의미한다.

(a) 비정상적으로
(h) 드물게
(c) 가슴 아프게
(d) 똑같이

◯ 정답 잡는 치트키

밑줄 친 어휘의 유의어를 찾는 문제이므로, abnormally가 포함된 구절을 읽고 문맥을 파악한다.

해설 | 6단락의 'abnormally long lifespan'은 비정상적으로 긴 수명이라는 뜻이므로, abnormally가 '비정상적으로'라는 의미로 사용된 것을 알 수 있다. 따라서 '비정상적으로'라는 같은 의미의 (a) unusually가 정답이다.

PART 4 (74~80) 비즈니스 편지 동물원의 새 프로그램을 홍보하는 편지

수신인 정보	Jonathan Nottingham Principal Forest Road Elementary School	Jonathan Nottingham 교장 Forest Road 초등학교

Dear Mr. Nottingham:

Mr. Nottingham께:

편지의 목적: 새로운 시리즈 소개

I want to express many thanks for your ongoing support of our zoo over the past several years. As you know, [79]Safari Funland Zoo is <u>committed</u> to providing educational opportunities for community members of all ages. To this end, [74]I am pleased to inform you about a new series that will be hosted in our facilities.

지난 몇 년간 우리 동물원에 대해 계속되는 지원에 많은 감사를 표하고 싶습니다. 아시다시피, [79]Safari Funland 동물원은 모든 연령대의 지역사회 구성원들에게 교육 기회를 제공하기 위해 <u>전념하고</u> 있습니다. 이것을 위하여, [74]우리 시설에서 개최될 새로운 시리즈에 관해 알려드리게 되어 기쁩니다.

프로그램의 개발 배경

[75]When you last visited us, your science teacher, Mr. Singh, expressed an interest in having your students spend more time studying our animals and their habitats. Inspired by this idea, I worked with my administrative team to develop a summer series called Wild Wonders, specifically for elementary school students.

[75]지난번에 방문하셨을 때, 과학 선생님인 Mr. Singh이 학생들이 우리의 동물과 그들의 서식지를 살펴보는데 더 많은 시간을 쓰도록 하는 것에 관심을 표했습니다. 이 아이디어에서 영감을 받아, 저는 행정팀과 협력하여 특히 초등학생들을 위한 Wild Wonders라는 여름 시리즈를 개발했습니다.

프로그램의 특징

[76]Students in the program will participate in a series of hands-on workshops led by our incredible educators, providing students with unique opportunities to interact with our animals up close, including petting bottlenose dolphins from the Gulf of Mexico. Our program will also incorporate virtual reality technology, giving participants the chance to travel millions of years back in time to when dinosaurs roamed the earth.

[76]프로그램에 소속된 학생들은 훌륭한 교육자들이 이끄는 일련의 체험 워크숍에 참가할 것이며, 학생들에게 멕시코만에서 온 병코돌고래를 쓰다듬는 것을 포함하여, 동물들과 바로 가까이에서 교감할 독특한 기회를 제공할 것입니다. 프로그램은 또한 가상 현실 기술을 통합하여, 참가자들에게 공룡이 지구를 돌아다녔던 수백만 년 전으로 거슬러 이동할 기회를 제공할 것입니다.

프로그램의 효과

Forest Road Elementary [80]is known for championing the importance of studying the natural world. As an educator

Forest Road 초등학교는 [80]자연 학습의 중요성을 <u>옹호하는 것</u>으로 잘 알려져 있습니다. 교육자로서, [77]저는

myself, [77]I can assure you that learning about our zoo's conservation efforts for the many animal species that inhabit our facilities will help to ready the students for the natural science courses that they will take later in their schooling.

| 끝인사 | [78]Should you have any inquiries, you can contact our events coordinator, Harry Buehler, at 555-0111. Meanwhile, if you have ideas for how to further develop the program, please reach out to my office—I would be happy to meet with you to discuss them. |

| 발신인 정보 | *Liza Lombardi*
Liza Lombardi
Director
Safari Funland Zoo |

우리 시설에 서식하는 많은 동물 종에 대한 동물원의 보존 노력에 관해 배우는 것은 학생들이 나중에 수업에서 들을 자연과학 과목을 대비하는 데 도움이 될 것이라고 확신할 수 있습니다.

[78]문의 사항이 있으시면, 행사 진행자인 Harry Buehler에게 555-0111로 연락하시면 됩니다. 한편, 프로그램을 더 발전시킬 방법에 대해 의견이 있으시면, 제 사무실로 연락해 주시면 기꺼이 만나서 논의해 보겠습니다.

Liza Lombardi 드림
책임자
Safari Funland 동물원

어휘 | ongoing adj. 계속 진행중인　facility n. 시설　habitat n. 서식지　inspire v. 영감을 주다　administrative adj. 행정의, 사무의　hands-on adj. 실체험 목적의, 직접 해보는　incredible adj. 훌륭한, 대단한　interact with phr. ~과 교감하다, 상호작용하다　up close phr. 바로 가까이에(서)　pet v. 쓰다듬다, 어루만지다　bottlenose dolphin phr. 병코돌고래　gulf n. 만　incorporate v. 통합하다　virtual reality phr. 가상 현실　roam v. 돌아다니다, 배회하다　assure v. 확신시키다, 보장하다　conservation n. 보존, 보호　inhabit v. 서식하다, 거주하다　schooling n. 수업, 학교 교육　coordinator n. 진행자　reach out phr. 연락을 취하다

74　주제/목적　편지의 목적　　　　　　　　　　　　난이도 ●●○

What is the purpose of Liza Lombardi's letter to Principal Nottingham?	Nottingham 교장에게 보낸 Liza Lombardi의 편지의 목적은 무엇인가?
(a) to announce the creation of a new volunteer program **(b) to advertise an educational program developed by the zoo** (c) to inform him about the opening of a family-friendly exhibit (d) to thank him for bringing his students to the zoo	(a) 새로운 자원봉사 프로그램의 창설을 발표하기 위해서 **(b) 동물원에서 개발한 교육 프로그램을 알리기 위해서** (c) 가정 친화적인 전시회의 개막을 알리기 위해서 (d) 학생들을 동물원에 데리고 와 준 것에 감사하기 위해서

＞━○ 정답 잡는 치트키

지문의 초반을 주의 깊게 읽고 전체 맥락을 파악한다.

해설 | 1단락의 'I am pleased to inform you about a new series that will be hosted in our facilities'에서 시설에서 개최될 새로운 시리즈에 관해 알려주게 되어 기쁘다고 한 뒤, 동물원에서 개발한 새로운 교육 프로그램인 Wild Wonders에 관해 홍보하는 내용이 이어지고 있다. 따라서 (b)가 정답이다.

어휘 | creation n. 창설　family-friendly adj. 가정 친화적인

---

75 특정세부사항 How

난이도 ●○○

According to the letter, how did Liza get the idea for Wild Wonders?

(a) by asking students about their interests
(b) by seeking advice from a natural scientist
(c) by speaking with a visiting educator
(d) by chatting with the school principal

편지에 따르면, Liza는 어떻게 Wild Wonders에 관한 아이디어를 얻었는가?

(a) 학생들에게 그들이 관심사를 물어봄으로써
(b) 자연 과학자로부터 조언을 구함으로써
(c) 방문한 교육자와 이야기함으로써
(d) 학교장과 이야기를 나눔으로써

━○ 정답 잡는 치트키

질문의 키워드 idea와 Wild Wonders가 그대로 언급된 주변 내용을 주의 깊게 읽는다.

해설 | 2단락의 'When you last visited us, your science teacher, Mr. Singh, expressed an interest in having your students spend more time studying our animals and their habitats. Inspired by this idea, I worked · to develop a summer series called Wild Wonders'에서 지난번에 방문했을 때 과학 선생님인 Mr. Singh이 학생들이 동물과 그들의 서식지를 살펴보는데 더 많은 시간을 쓰도록 하는 것에 관심을 표했고, 이 아이디어에서 영감을 받아, Wild Wonders라는 여름 시리즈를 개발했다고 했다. 따라서 (c)가 정답이다.

⇄ **Paraphrasing**
science teacher 과학 선생님 → educator 교육자

어휘 | natural scientist phr. 자연 과학자 educator n. 교육자 school principal phr. 학교장

76 특정세부사항 What

난이도 ●●○

What will students who join the program be able to do?

(a) explore exhibits under the guidance of experts
(b) study dolphin fossils using advanced technology
(c) travel to see animals in tropical locations
(d) conduct hands-on laboratory experiments

이 프로그램에 참여하는 학생들은 무엇을 할 수 있을 것인가?

(a) 전문가들의 지도하에 동물들을 탐구한다
(b) 첨단 기술을 이용하여 돌고래 화석을 살펴본다
(c) 열대지방에 있는 동물들을 보러 여행한다
(d) 직접 해보는 실험실 실험을 한다

━○ 정답 잡는 치트키

질문의 키워드 students who join the program이 Students in the program으로 paraphrasing되어 언급된 주변 내용을 주의 깊게 읽는다.

해설 | 3단락의 'Students in the program will participate in a series of hands-on workshops led by our incredible educators, providing students with unique opportunities to interact with our animals up close, including petting bottlenose dolphins from the Gulf of Mexico.'에서 프로그램에 소속된 학생들은 훌륭한 교육자들이 이끄는 일련의 체험 워크숍에 참가할 것이며, 학생들에게 멕시코만에서 온 병코돌고래를 쓰다듬는 것을 포함하여, 동물들과 바로 가까이에서 교감할 독특한 기회를 제공할 것이라고 했다. 따라서 (a)가 정답이다.

⇄ **Paraphrasing**
led by ~ educators 교육자들이 이끄는 → under the guidance of experts 전문가들의 지도하에

어휘 | explore v. 탐구하다 guidance n. 지도 fossil n. 화석 tropical adj. 열대(지방)의

According to Liza, what can students gain from attending the event?

(a) They will learn how to care for various animal species.
(b) They will be better prepared for their future studies.
(c) They will get extra credit toward their science courses.
(d) They will learn about zoo management.

Liza에 따르면, 학생들이 이 행사에 참여함으로써 얻을 수 있는 것은 무엇인가?

(a) 다양한 동물 종을 돌보는 방법을 배울 것이다.
(b) 향후의 공부를 위해 더 나은 준비를 할 것이다.
(c) 과학 과목에서 추가 학점을 받을 것이다.
(d) 동물원 관리에 관해 배울 것이다.

🔑 정답 잡는 치트키

질문의 키워드 students gain과 관련된 주변 내용을 주의 깊게 읽는다.

해설 | 4단락의 'I can assure you that learning about our zoo's conservation efforts for the many animal species ~ will help to ready the students for the natural science courses that they will take later in their schooling'에서 많은 동물 종에 대한 동물원의 보존 노력에 관해 배우는 것은 학생들이 나중에 수업에서 들을 자연과학 과목을 대비하는 데 도움이 될 것이라고 확신할 수 있다고 했다. 따라서 (b)가 정답이다.

어휘 | credit n. 학점; v. ~ 덕분으로 돌리다 management n. 관리

Why, most likely, would Principal Nottingham contact the events coordinator?

(a) to gather more information about the event
(b) to schedule a meeting with the program instructors
(c) to provide feedback on the proposal
(d) to report the number of students attending

Nottingham 교장은 왜 행사 진행자에게 연락할 것 같은가?

(a) 행사에 관한 더 많은 정보를 얻기 위해서
(b) 프로그램 강사들과의 회의 일정을 잡기 위해서
(c) 제안에 관한 피드백을 제공하기 위해서
(d) 참석하는 학생 수를 보고하기 위해서

🔑 정답 잡는 치트키

질문의 키워드 events coordinator가 그대로 언급된 주변 내용을 주의 깊게 읽는다.

해설 | 5단락의 'Should you have any inquiries, you can contact our events coordinator, Harry Buehler'에서 문의 사항이 있으면 행사 진행자인 Harry Buehler에게 연락하라고 한 것을 통해, Nottingham 교장이 문의 사항이 있으면 행사 진행자에게 연락할 것임을 추론할 수 있다. 따라서 (a)가 정답이다.

어휘 | gather v. 얻다, 모으다

In the context of the passage, <u>committed</u> means _____.

(a) opposed
(b) dedicated
(c) suited
(d) limited

지문의 문맥에서, 'committed'는 -을 의미한다.

(a) 반대하는
(b) 전념하는
(c) 적당한
(d) 제한되는

TEST 1

TEST 2

TEST 3

TEST 4

TEST 5

TEST 6

TEST 7

지텔프 공식 기출문제집 7회분 Level 2

밑줄 친 어휘의 유의어를 찾는 문제이므로, committed가 포함된 구절을 읽고 문맥을 파악한다.

해설 | 1단락의 'Safari Funland Zoo is committed to providing educational opportunities'는 Safari Funland 동물원이 교육 기회를 제공하기 위해 전념하고 있다는 뜻이므로, committed가 '전념하는'이라는 의미로 사용된 것을 알 수 있다. 따라서 '전념하는'이라는 같은 의미의 (b) dedicated가 정답이다.

80 어휘   유의어   난이도 ●●●

In the context of the passage, <u>championing</u> means _____.

(a) winning
(b) promoting
(c) fighting
(d) awarding

지문의 문맥에서, 'championing'은 -을 의미한다.

(a) 획득하는 것
(b) 장려하는 것
(c) 논쟁하는 것
(d) 수여하는 것

밑줄 친 어휘의 유의어를 찾는 문제이므로, championing이 포함된 구절을 읽고 문맥을 파악한다.

해설 | 4단락의 'is known for championing the importance of studying the natural world'는 자연 학습의 중요성을 옹호하는 것으로 잘 알려져 있다는 뜻이므로, championing이 '옹호하는 것'이라는 의미로 사용된 것을 알 수 있다. 따라서 '장려하는 것'이라는 비슷한 의미의 (b) promoting이 정답이다.

공식기출
TEST 2
정답·스크립트·해석·해설

GRAMMAR

LISTENING

READING & VOCABULARY

GRAMMAR	_____ / 26	(점수 : _____	점)
LISTENING	_____ / 26	(점수 : _____	점)
READING & VOCABULARY	_____ / 28	(점수 : _____	점)

TOTAL _____ / 80 **(평균 점수 : _____ 점)**

*각 영역 점수: 맞은 개수 × 3.75
*평균 점수: 각 영역 점수 합계 ÷ 3

정답 및 취약 유형 분석표

GRAMMAR

번호	정답	유형
01	d	조동사
02	a	조동사
03	d	시제
04	a	관계사
05	c	준동사
06	b	가정법
07	d	조동사
08	a	관계사
09	d	시제
10	c	가정법
11	b	시제
12	a	준동사
13	d	조동사
14	a	준동사
15	c	시제
16	c	연결어
17	b	가정법
18	a	준동사
19	b	가정법
20	c	시제
21	d	준동사
22	d	연결어
23	d	시제
24	a	가정법
25	b	가정법
26	b	준동사

LISTENING

PART	번호	정답	유형
PART 1	27	c	특정세부사항
	28	c	특정세부사항
	29	c	특정세부사항
	30	a	추론
	31	d	특정세부사항
	32	a	추론
PART 2	33	a	추론
	34	b	주제/목적
	35	a	특정세부사항
	36	b	특정세부사항
	37	c	추론
	38	a	특정세부사항
	39	c	특정세부사항
PART 3	40	d	특정세부사항
	41	a	특정세부사항
	42	b	특정세부사항
	43	b	특정세부사항
	44	b	특정세부사항
	45	d	추론
	46	b	주제/목적
	47	c	특정세부사항
	48	c	특정세부사항
PART 4	49	a	특정세부사항
	50	b	추론
	51	a	특정세부사항
	52	d	특정세부사항

READING & VOCABULARY

PART	번호	정답	유형
PART 1	53	d	특정세부사항
	54	c	특정세부사항
	55	a	특정세부사항
	56	c	특정세부사항
	57	d	추론
	58	d	어휘
	59	b	어휘
	60	d	주제/목적
PART 2	61	a	특정세부사항
	62	b	특정세부사항
	63	b	추론
	64	c	특정세부사항
	65	d	어휘
	66	b	어휘
PART 3	67	a	주제/목적
	68	b	추론
	69	c	특정세부사항
	70	d	특정세부사항
	71	d	특정세부사항
	72	b	어휘
	73	c	어휘
PART 4	74	c	주제/목적
	75	a	특정세부사항
	76	a	추론
	77	b	Not/True
	78	d	특정세부사항
	79	c	어휘
	80	a	어휘

유형	맞힌 개수
시제	/ 6
가정법	/ 6
준동사	/ 6
조동사	/ 4
연결어	/ 2
관계사	/ 2
TOTAL	/ 26

유형	맞힌 개수
주제/목적	/ 2
특정세부사항	/ 18
Not/True	/ 0
추론	/ 6
TOTAL	/ 26

유형	맞힌 개수
주제/목적	/ 3
특정세부사항	/ 12
Not/True	/ 1
추론	/ 4
어휘	/ 8
TOTAL	/ 28

GRAMMAR

01 조동사   조동사 should 생략   난이도 ●●○

Molly will drive six hours to Upstate New York to attend her brother's wedding tomorrow. It is best that she _____ the house early so she can get there on time.

(a) left
(b) will leave
(c) has left
(d) leave

Molly는 내일 오빠의 결혼식에 참석하기 위해 뉴욕주 북부 지방까지 여섯 시간을 운전할 것이다. 그녀는 제 때 도착할 수 있도록 일찍 집을 <u>나서는</u> 것이 최선이다.

○ 지텔프 치트키

best 다음에는 that절에 동사원형이 온다.

🔅 **주장·요구·명령·제안을 나타내는 빈출 형용사**
best 최선인   essential 필수적인   important 중요한   necessary 필요한   mandatory 의무적인

해설 | 주절에 주장을 나타내는 형용사 best가 있으므로 that절에는 '(should +) 동사원형'이 와야 한다. 따라서 동사원형 (d) leave가 정답이다.

어휘 | upstate adj. 주 북부의   on time phr. 제때

02 조동사   조동사 must   난이도 ●○○

According to the dictionary definition of a "selfie," this type of photo cannot be taken by another person. The picture _____ include oneself and also be taken by oneself to qualify as a selfie.

(a) must
(b) might
(c) will
(d) can

"셀피"의 사전적 정의에 따르면, 이러한 유형의 사진 은 타인에 의해 촬영될 수 없다. 셀피로 간주하려면 사 진은 자기 자신을 포함해야 하고 또한 자기 자신에 의 해 촬영되어야 한다.

○ 지텔프 치트키

'~해야 한다'라고 말할 때는 must를 쓴다.

해설 | 문맥상 셀피로 간주하려면 사진은 자기 자신을 포함해야 하고 또한 자기 자신에 의해 촬영되어야 한다는 의미가 되어야 자연스러우므로, '~해야 한다'를 뜻하면서 의무를 나타내는 조동사 (a) must가 정답이다. 참고로, must와 should 모두 '~해야 한다'를 뜻하지만, must는 should보다 강한 어조로 조언하거나 의무를 나타낼 때 쓴다.

어휘 | definition n. 정의, 개념   selfie n. 셀피, 셀카(셀프카메라)   qualify as phr. ~이라 간주하다

03 시제 현재진행

Mr. Harris will be attending a business conference in Madrid this week. His plane leaves tonight, so he took the day off and _____ for the trip right now.

(a) has been packing
(b) packs
(c) was packing
(d) is packing

Mr. Harris는 이번 주에 마드리드에서 열리는 비즈니스 콘퍼런스에 참석하고 있는 중일 것이다. 그의 비행기가 오늘 밤에 출발하므로, 그는 휴가를 내고 바로 지금 출장을 위해 짐을 싸고 있는 중이나.

➤─○ 지텔프 치트키

right now가 있으면 현재진행 시제가 정답이다

> 💡 **현재진행과 자주 함께 쓰이는 시간 표현**
> • right now / now / currently / at the moment 바로 지금 / 지금 / 현재 / 바로 지금
> • these days / nowadays 요즘

해설 | 현재진행 시제와 함께 쓰이는 시간 표현 right now가 있고, 문맥상 말하고 있는 현재 시점에 Mr. Harris가 짐을 싸고 있는 중이라는 의미가 되어야 자연스럽다. 따라서 현재진행 시제 (d) is packing이 정답이다.

> **오답분석**
> (b) 현재 시제는 반복되는 일이나 습관, 일반적인 사실을 나타내므로, 현재 시점에 한창 진행 중인 일을 표현하기에는 현재진행 시제보다 부적절하므로 오답이다.

어휘 | day off phr. 휴가, 휴일 pack v. 짐을 싸다

04 관계사 주격 관계대명사 which

Citrus fruits are great for managing various health issues because of their fiber content. For example, oranges, _____, can help stabilize blood sugar levels and lower cholesterol.

(a) which are high in fiber
(b) what are high in fiber
(c) who are high in fiber
(d) that are high in fiber

감귤류는 섬유질 함량 때문에 다양한 건강 문제를 관리하는 데 좋다. 예를 들면, 오렌지는, 섬유질이 풍부해서, 혈당을 안정시키고 콜레스테롤을 낮추는 데 도움을 줄 수 있다.

➤─○ 지텔프 치트키

사물 선행사가 관계절 안에서 주어 역할을 하고, 빈칸 앞에 콤마(,)가 있으면 주격 관계대명사 which가 정답이다.

해설 | 사물 선행사 oranges를 받으면서 콤마(,) 뒤에 올 수 있는 주격 관계대명사가 필요하므로, (a) which are high in fiber가 정답이다.

> **오답분석**
> (d) 관계대명사 that도 사물 선행사를 받을 수 있지만, 콤마 뒤에 올 수 없으므로 오답이다.

어휘 | citrus fruits phr. 감귤류 manage v. 관리하다 fiber n. 섬유질 content n. 함량 stabilize v. 안정시키다 blood sugar level phr. 혈당
cholesterol n. 콜레스테롤

Basketball players should be able to dribble well, as that skill enables them to make a variety of plays on the court. For this reason, it is important that players practice _____ frequently during training.

(a) to dribble
(b) having dribbled
(c) dribbling
(d) to have dribbled

농구 선수들은 드리블을 잘할 수 있어야 하는데, 그 기술이 코트에서 다양한 경기를 할 수 있게 하기 때문이다. 이런 이유로, 선수들이 훈련 중에 <u>드리블하는 것을</u> 자주 연습하는 것이 중요하다.

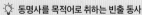 지텔프 치트키

practice는 동명사를 목적어로 취한다.

💡 **동명사를 목적어로 취하는 빈출 동사**
practice 연습하다   dislike 싫어하다   avoid 피하다   imagine 상상하다   mind 개의하다   keep 계속하다   consider 고려하다
prevent 방지하다   enjoy 즐기다   recommend 권장하다   risk 위험을 무릅쓰다   involve 포함하다

해설 | 빈칸 앞 동사 practice는 동명사를 목적어로 취하므로, 동명사 (c) dribbling이 정답이다.

오답분석
(b) having dribbled도 동명사이기는 하지만, 완료동명사(having dribbled)로 쓰일 경우 '연습하는' 시점보다 '드리블하는' 시점이 앞선 다는 것을 나타내므로 문맥에 적합하지 않아 오답이다.

어휘 | dribble v. 드리블하다, 튕기다; n. 드리블   court n. (테니스·배구 등의) 코트   for this reason phr. 이런 이유로

Logan went grocery shopping yesterday, but he forgot to buy a few things because his shopping list was in his other bag. If he had not switched bags before leaving, he _____ everything on his list.

(a) will get
(b) would have gotten
(c) would get
(d) will have gotten

Logan은 어제 장을 보러 갔지만, 구입 품목 목록이 다른 가방에 들어 있었기 때문에 몇 가지를 사는 것을 잊었다. 만약 그가 출발하기 전에 가방을 바꾸지 않았었다면, 그는 목록에 있는 모든 것을 <u>샀을 것이다.</u>

🔑 지텔프 치트키

'if + had p.p.'가 있으면 'would/could + have p.p.'가 정답이다.

💡 **가정법 과거완료**
If + 주어 + had p.p., 주어 + would/could(조동사 과거형) + have p.p.

해설 | If절에 'had p.p.' 형태의 had not switched가 있으므로, 주절에는 이와 짝을 이루어 가정법 과거완료를 만드는 'would(조동사 과거형) + have p.p.'가 와야 한다. 따라서 (b) would have gotten이 정답이다.

어휘 | shopping list phr. 구입 품목 목록   switch v. 바꾸다, 교체하다

07 조동사 　조동사 should 생략
난이도 ●●○

Pam's laundromat opened for business for the first time this afternoon, but very few people came. The neighboring store owner advised that Pam _____ flyers around town to get the word out to potential customers.

(a) posted
(b) will post
(c) posts
(d) post

Pam의 빨래방은 오늘 오후에 처음으로 개업했지만, 거의 사람들이 오지 않았다. 인근 가게 주인은 Pam이 잠재 고객들에게 소문을 내기 위해 마을 주변에 전단을 붙여야 한다고 조언했다.

○── 지텔프 치트키

advise 다음에는 that절에 동사원형이 온다.

💡 **주장·요구·명령·제안을 나타내는 빈출 동사**
advise 조언하다　suggest 제안하다　request 요청하다　recommend 권고하다　demand 요구하다　order 명령하다
urge 강력히 촉구하다　ask 요청하다　propose 제안하다　insist 주장하다

해설 | 주절에 제안을 나타내는 동사 advise가 있으므로 that절에는 '(should +) 동사원형'이 와야 한다. 따라서 동사원형 (d) post가 정답이다.

어휘 | laundromat n. 빨래방, 셀프서비스 세탁소　open for business phr. 개업하다, 영업을 하고 있다　neighboring adj. 인근의, 근처에 사는 flyer n. (광고·안내용) 전단　get the word out phr. 말을 퍼뜨리다

08 관계사 　주격 관계대명사 who
난이도 ●○○

The Molinere Bay Underwater Sculpture Park is the first of its kind. The park guides, _____, teach visitors to use scuba equipment so they can explore the park safely.

(a) who are all trained divers
(b) when are all trained divers
(c) where are all trained divers
(d) that are all trained divers

Molinere만 수중 조각 공원은 이러한 종류의 첫 번째 공원이다. 공원 안내인들은, 모두 훈련받은 다이빙 선수들로, 방문객들이 안전하게 공원을 탐험할 수 있도록 스쿠버 장비를 사용하는 것을 가르친다.

○── 지텔프 치트키

사람 선행사가 관계절 안에서 주어 역할을 하고, 빈칸 앞에 콤마(,)가 있으면 주격 관계대명사 who가 정답이다.

해설 | 사람 선행사 The park guides를 받으면서 보기의 관계절 내에서 주어 역할을 할 수 있는 주격 관계대명사가 필요하므로, (a) who are all trained divers가 정답이다.

오답분석
(d) 관계대명사 that도 사람 선행사를 받을 수 있지만, 콤마 뒤에 올 수 없으므로 오답이다.

어휘 | bay n. 만　underwater adj. 수중의, 물속의　sculpture n. 조각　trained adj. 훈련받은, 교육된　diver n. 다이빙 선수

09 시제　　미래진행

난이도 ●●○

I just reminded my brother to take his keys with him when he leaves for his friend's party tonight. I _____ by the time he gets home, so I won't be able to let him in.

(a) had most likely been sleeping
(b) am most likely sleeping
(c) have most likely been sleeping
(d) will most likely be sleeping

나는 방금 내 동생에게 오늘 밤 친구의 파티에 갈 때 열쇠를 가지고 가라고 상기시켰다. 동생이 집에 도착할 무렵에 나는 <u>자고 있는 중일 가능성이 높아서</u>, 동생을 집에 들어오게 할 수 없을 것이다.

> **지텔프 치트키**
>
> 'by the time + 현재 동사'가 있으면 미래진행 시제가 정답이다.

해설 | 미래진행 시제의 단서로 쓰이는 시간 표현 'by the time + 현재 동사'(by the time ~ gets)가 사용되었고, 문맥상 동생이 집에 도착할 무렵에 나는 자고 있는 중일 가능성이 높다는 의미가 되어야 자연스럽다. 따라서 미래진행 시제 (d) will most likely be sleeping이 정답이다.

어휘 | remind v. 상기시키다, 생각나게 하다

---

10 가정법　　가정법 과거

난이도 ●●○

The true number of coffee drinkers in the world is difficult to estimate. However, it's safe to say that if extreme coffee shortages were to occur, millions of people _____ elsewhere for their daily caffeine intake.

(a) would have had to turn
(b) will have had to turn
(c) would have to turn
(d) will have to turn

세계에서 커피를 마시는 사람들의 실제 수는 추정하기 어렵다. 그러나, 만약 심심한 커피 부족이 발생한다면, 수백만 명의 사람들이 매일 카페인 섭취를 위해 다른 곳으로 <u>눈길을 돌려야 할 것</u>이라고 해도 과언이 아니다.

> **지텔프 치트키**
>
> 'if + were to + 동사원형'이 있으면 'would/could + 동사원형'이 정답이다.
>
> 💡 **가정법 과거(were to)**
> If + 주어 + were to + 동사원형, 주어 + would/could(조동사 과거형) + 동사원형

해설 | if절에 과거 동사(were to occur)가 있으므로, 주절에는 이와 짝을 이루어 가정법 과거를 만드는 'would(조동사 과거형) + 동사원형'이 와야 한다. 따라서 (c) would have to turn이 정답이다.

어휘 | estimate v. 추정하다, 예상하다　it's safe to say phr. ~라고 해도 과언이 아니다　shortage n. 부족, 결핍　intake n. 섭취
turn v. 눈길을 돌리다

---

11 시제　　과거진행

난이도 ●●○

Kathleen was lucky to escape unscathed from the fire at the library last night. She _____ toward the exit when the

Kathleen은 지난밤 도서관에서의 화재에서 다행히도 다치지 않고 탈출했다. 화재경보기가 요란하게 울리

fire alarm started blaring, so she managed to run right out of the building.

(a) has already walked
(b) was already walking
(c) is already walking
(d) would already be walking

기 시작했을 때 그녀는 출구를 향해 <u>이미 걸어가고 있던 중이었기</u> 때문에, 바로 건물 밖으로 뛰쳐나올 수 있었다.

🔵○ **지텔프 치트키**

'for + 기간 표현' 없이 'when + 과거 동사'만 있으면 과거진행 시제가 정답이다.

> ☀️ **과거진행과 자주 함께 쓰이는 시간 표현**
> • when / while + 과거 동사 ~했을 때 / ~하던 도중에
> • last + 시간 표현 / yesterday 지난 ~에 / 어제

해설 | 과거진행 시제와 함께 쓰이는 시간 표현 'when + 과거 동사'(when ~ started)가 있고, 문맥상 과거 시점인 지난밤 도서관에서의 화재로 인해 화재경보기가 요란하게 울리기 시작했을 때 Kathleen은 출구를 향해 이미 걸어가고 있던 중이었다는 의미가 되어야 자연스럽다. 따라서 과거진행 시제 (b) was already walking이 정답이다.

어휘 | unscathed adj. 다치지 않은, 아무 탈 없는 exit n. 출구; v. 나가다 fire alarm phr. 화재경보기 blare v. 요란하게 울리다

---

12 준동사   동명사를 목적어로 취하는 동사   난이도 ●○○

When hiking in a wooded area, you may lose cellphone service because of interference caused by the thick canopy of trees overhead. To get the signal back, keep _____ until you reach a clearing.

(a) hiking
(b) to have hiked
(c) having hiked
(d) to hike

나무가 우거진 지역에서 도보 여행할 때, 머리 위에 빽빽하게 지붕 모양으로 우거진 나무들로 인해 야기되는 간섭으로 휴대전화 서비스가 끊길 수 있다. 신호를 다시 받으려면, 빈터에 도착할 때까지 <u>도보 여행하는 것</u>을 계속 해라.

🔵○ **지텔프 치트키**

keep은 동명사를 목적어로 취한다.

해설 | 빈칸 앞 동사 keep은 동명사를 목적어로 취하므로, 동명사 (a) hiking이 정답이다.

> 오답분석
> (c) having hiked도 동명사이기는 하지만, 완료동명사(having hiked)로 쓰일 경우 '계속하는' 시점보다 '도보 여행하는' 시점이 앞선다는 것을 나타내므로 문맥에 적합하지 않아 오답이다.

어휘 | wooded adj. 나무가 우거진 interference n. 간섭, 방해 canopy n. (숲의 나뭇가지들이) 지붕 모양으로 우거진 것 overhead adv. 머리 위에, 높이 signal n. 신호 clearing n. (숲속의) 빈터

13 조동사　조동사 might

I was alone at home when the power suddenly went out around 6 p.m. Scared that the outage _____ last all night, I asked my friend Jill to come keep me company until the power returned.

(a) can
(b) shall
(c) should
(d) might

나는 오후 6시쯤에 갑자기 전기가 나갔을 때 집에 혼자 있었다. 정전이 밤새 계속될지도 몰라 겁이 나서, 나는 친구 Jill에게 전기가 다시 들어올 때까지 내 곁에 있어 달라고 부탁했다.

━○ 지텔프 치트키

'~할지도 모른다'라고 말할 때는 might를 쓴다.

해설 | 문맥상 정전이 밤새 계속될지도 몰라 겁이 나서 친구 Jill에게 전기가 다시 들어올 때까지 곁에 있어 달라고 부탁했다는 의미가 되어야 자연스럽고, 실제로는 정전이 밤새 계속되지 않은 상황에서 일어날지도 모르는 일을 추측하고 있으므로 '~할지도 모른다'를 뜻하면서 약한 추측을 나타내는 조동사 (d) might가 정답이다. 참고로, might와 may 모두 '~할지도 모른다'를 뜻하지만, might는 may보다 일어날 가능성이 더 작은 경우에 쓴다.

어휘 | power n. 전기　go out phr. (불·전깃불이) 나가다　outage n. 정전　keep company phr. ~의 곁에 있어 주다

---

14 준동사　to 부정사를 목적격 보어로 취하는 동사

The parent–teacher conference was scheduled for today, but there was an unexpected thunderstorm that would've made it difficult for everyone to attend. To ensure everyone's safety, the principal urged parents not _____ to the school.

(a) to go
(b) going
(c) to have gone
(d) having gone

오늘 학부모-교사 회의가 예정되어 있었는데, 모두를 참석하기 어렵게 하는 예기치 않은 뇌우가 있었다. 모두의 안전을 보장하기 위해, 교장은 학부모들에게 학교에 안 갈 것을 강력히 촉구했다.

━○ 지텔프 치트키

urge는 to 부정사를 목적격 보어로 취한다.

> 💡 **to 부정사를 목적격 보어로 취하는 빈출 동사**
> urge 강력히 촉구하다　encourage 권장하다　require 요구하다　allow 허락하다　ask 요청하다

해설 | 빈칸 앞 동사 urge는 'urge+ 목적어 + 목적격 보어'의 형태로 쓰일 때 to 부정사를 목적격 보어로 취하여, '-에게 ~할 것을 촉구하다'라는 의미로 사용된다. 따라서 to 부정사 (a) to go가 정답이다.

오답분석

(c) to have gone도 to 부정사이기는 하지만, 완료부정사(to have gone)로 쓰일 경우 '강력히 촉구하는' 시점보다 '가는' 시점이 앞선다는 것을 나타내므로 문맥에 적합하지 않아 오답이다.

어휘 | thunderstorm n. 뇌우, 폭풍우　principal n. 교장

Dennis borrowed my *Vampire Arcadia* books last month, but he still hasn't gotten past the second one. He says he _____ to finish the series for a while, but he has trouble finding time to read.

(a) will be meaning
(b) is meaning
(c) has been meaning
(d) would mean

Dennis는 지난달에 나의 *Vampire Arcadia* 책들을 빌렸지만, 아직도 두 번째 책을 다 읽지 못했다. 그는 한동안 이 시리즈를 다 읽는 것을 목표해 오고 있는 중이시만, 책을 읽을 시간을 내는 데 어려움을 겪고 있다고 말한다.

지텔프 치트키

'for + 기간 표현'과 현재 동사가 함께 오면 현재완료진행 시제가 정답이다.

해설 | 빈칸 문장에 현재 동사가 사용되었고, 지속을 나타내는 시간 표현 'for + 기간 표현'(for a while)이 있다. 또한, 문맥상 Dennis기 지난달(책들을 빌린 시점)부터 현재까지 계속해서 이 시리즈를 다 읽는 것을 목표해 오고 있는 중이라는 의미가 되어야 자연스럽다. 따라서 현재완료진행 시제 (c) has been meaning이 정답이다.

오답분석

(b) 현재진행 시제는 특정 현재 시점에 한창 진행 중인 일을 나타내므로, 과거에 시작해서 현재 시점까지 계속해서 진행되고 있는 일을 표현할 수 없어 오답이다.

어휘 | for a while phr. 한동안   mean to phr. ~을 목표로 하다, ~할 작정이다

16 **연결어**   접속부사   난이도 ●●●

Many painters gravitate toward traditional watercolor paint because of the bright, "happy" colors it produces. _____, many artists like *gouache*, a different type of water-based paint that is favored for its light and reflective colors.

(a) In fact
(b) For example
(c) Similarly
(d) Otherwise

많은 화가는 전통적인 수채화 물감이 만들어 내는 밝고 "행복한" 색상 때문에 그것에 마음이 끌린다. 마찬가지로, 많은 예술가는 가볍고 빛을 반사하는 색상으로 인해 선호되는 또 다른 종류의 수성 물감인 *구아슈*를 좋아한다.

지텔프 치트키

'마찬가지로'라는 의미의 첨언을 나타낼 때는 Similarly를 쓴다.

해설 | 문맥상 많은 화가가 수채화 물감이 만들어 내는 밝고 "행복한" 색상 때문에 그것에 끌리고, 마찬가지로 많은 예술가는 가볍고 빛을 반사하는 색상으로 인해 선호되는 또 다른 종류의 수성 물감인 *구아슈*를 좋아한다는 의미가 되어야 자연스럽다. 따라서 '마찬가지로'라는 의미의 첨언을 나타내는 접속부사 (c) Similarly가 정답이다.

오답분석

(a) In fact는 '사실은', (b) For example은 '예를 들어', (d) Otherwise는 '그렇지 않으면'이라는 의미로, 문맥에 적합하지 않아 오답이다.

어휘 | gravitate toward phr. 마음이 끌려 ~으로 가다   watercolor n. 수채화   gouache n. 구아슈(불투명 수채화 물감으로 그리는 화법과 그 그림 물감)   favor v. 선호하다   reflective adj. 빛을 반사하는

17 가정법　가정법 과거

난이도 ●●○

There is currently no known cure for asthma, though there are respiratory devices like inhalers that make it manageable. If a cure were to be invented today, it _____ such treatments obsolete.

(a) will immediately make
(b) would immediately make
(c) will have immediately made
(d) would have immediately made

천식을 관리할 수 있게 해주는 흡입기와 같은 호흡용 장치는 있지만, 현재 천식에 대한 알려진 치료법은 없다. 만약 치료법이 오늘날 발명된다면, 그것은 그러한 치료법들을 <u>즉시</u> <u>쓸모없게 만들 것이다</u>.

해설 ┃ If절에 과거 동사(were to be invented)가 있으므로, 주절에는 이와 짝을 이루어 가정법 과거를 만드는 'would(조동사 과거형) + 동사원형'이 와야 한다. 따라서 (b) would immediately make가 정답이다.

어휘 ┃ cure n. 치료법　asthma n. 천식　respiratory adj. 호흡(용)의　inhaler n. 흡입기　manageable adj. 관리할 수 있는　treatment n. 치료법　obsolete adj. 쓸모없게 된

18 준동사　to 부정사의 부사 역할

난이도 ●●●

This morning, Finn's professors were so impressed with his thesis manuscript that they recommended it for publication in an online journal. Immediately afterward, he was excited _____ his parents about his latest academic achievement.

(a) to call
(b) to have called
(c) having called
(d) calling

오늘 아침에, Finn의 교수님들은 그의 학위 논문 원고에 매우 감명받아 온라인 잡지에 그것을 게재할 것을 추천했다. 그 직후, 그는 최근의 학문적 성취에 관해 부모님께 <u>전화하게 되어</u> 들떴다.

해설 ┃ 문맥상 Finn이 최근의 학문적 성취에 관해 부모님에게 전화하게 되어 들떴다는 의미로, 전화하게 되어서 들떴다는 감정의 원인을 나타내는 to 부정사가 와야 한다. 따라서 (a) to call이 정답이다.

오답분석

(b) to have called도 to 부정사이기는 하지만, 완료부정사(to have called)로 쓰일 경우 '들뜨는' 시점보다 '전화하는' 시점이 앞선다는 것을 나타내므로 문맥에 적합하지 않아 오답이다.

어휘 ┃ thesis n. 학위 논문　manuscript n. 원고　journal n. 잡지, 정기 간행물　achievement n. 성취

19 가정법　가정법 과거완료

When I visited my hometown, I discovered that the bookstore I frequented back in high school had gone out of business. If it hadn't closed, I _____ again for old times' sake and said hello.

(a) will have dropped by
(b) would have dropped by
(c) would drop by
(d) will drop by

내가 고향을 방문했을 때, 고등학교 시절에 자주 가던 서점이 폐업한 것을 발견했다. 만약 그곳이 문을 닫지 않았었다면, 나는 옛날을 생각해서 다시 들렀을 것이고 인사를 했을 것이다.

지텔프 치트키

'if + had p.p.'가 있으면 'would/could + have p.p.'가 정답이다.

해설 | If절에 'had p.p.' 형태의 hadn't closed가 있으므로, 주절에는 이와 짝을 이루어 가정법 과거완료를 만드는 'would(조동사 과거형) + have p.p.'가 와야 한다. 따라서 (b) would have dropped by가 정답이다.

어휘 | hometown n. 고향　frequent v. 자주 가다　out of business phr. 폐업하여, 망한　for old times' sake phr. 옛날을 생각해서

20 시제　과거완료진행

Harold's parents finally gave him their blessing to leave the family catering business and pursue a career in architecture. Before deciding to study in Oslo, he _____ his family run the business for seven years.

(a) is helping
(b) has been helping
(c) had been helping
(d) will have been helping

Harold의 부모님은 마침내 그가 가족 음식 공급 사업을 그만두고 건축 분야에서 경력을 추구하는 것을 축복해 주었다. 오슬로에서 공부하기로 결정하기 전에, 그는 자기 가족이 사업을 운영하는 것을 7년 동안 도와오고 있던 중이었다.

지텔프 치트키

'before + 과거 동사'와 'for + 기간 표현'이 함께 오면 과거완료진행 시제가 정답이다.

　💡 **과거완료진행과 자주 함께 쓰이는 시간 표현**
　　• before / when / since + 과거 동사 + (for + 기간 표현) ~하기 전에 / ~했을 때 / ~ 이래로 (~ 동안)
　　• (for + 기간 표현) + (up) until + 과거 동사 (~ 동안) ~했을 때까지

해설 | 과거완료진행 시제와 함께 쓰이는 시간 표현 'before + 과거 동사'(Before deciding)와 'for + 기간 표현'(for seven years)이 있고, 문맥상 Harold가 대과거(가족 음식 공급 사업을 돕기 시작했던 시점)부터 과거(오슬로에서 공부하기로 결정한 시점)까지 7년 동안 계속해서 가족이 사업을 운영하는 것을 도와오고 있던 중이었다는 의미가 되어야 자연스럽다. 따라서 과거완료진행 시제 (c) had been helping이 정답이다.

어휘 | give one's blessing phr. 축복하다　pursue a career phr. 경력을 추구하다

21 준동사   to 부정사를 목적어로 취하는 동사   난이도 ●●○

Cats were highly treasured in ancient Egypt, where they were believed to be magical creatures that warded off bad luck. Some ancient Egyptians even chose _____ the animals with jewelry as a sign of respect.

(a) to have lavished
(b) lavishing
(c) having lavished
(d) to lavish

고양이는 고대 이집트에서 매우 귀중하게 여겨졌는데, 이곳은 고양이가 불운을 물리치는 마법의 생명체로 믿어졌다. 일부 고대 이집트인들은 심지어 존중의 표시로 그 동물들을 보석으로 <u>호화롭게 하는 것을</u> 결정했다.

─○ 지텔프 치트키

choose는 to 부정사를 목적어로 취한다.

> 🔅 **to 부정사를 목적어로 취하는 빈출 동사**
> **choose** 결정하다   **decide** 결정하다   **promise** 약속하다   **expect** 예상하다   **vow** 맹세하다   **wish** 희망하다   **plan** 계획하다   **hope** 바라다
> **agree** 동의하다   **intend** 계획하다   **prepare** 준비하다

해설 | 빈칸 앞 동사 choose는 to 부정사를 목적어로 취하므로, to 부정사 (d) to lavish가 정답이다.

> **오답분석**
> (a) to have lavished도 to 부정사이기는 하지만, 완료부정사(to have lavished)로 쓰일 경우 '결정하는' 시점보다 '호화롭게 하는' 시점이 앞선다는 것을 나타내므로 문맥에 적합하지 않아 오답이다.

어휘 | treasure v. 귀중하게 여기다   creature n. 생명체   ward off phr. 물리치다   respect n. 존중, 경의   lavish v. 아낌없이 주다, 낭비하다

---

22 연결어   접속사   난이도 ●●○

Eagle Travel Agency is expanding to several southwestern states in the first quarter of next year. They've already hired a new manager for their Arizona branch, which is set to open _____ the holidays have ended.

(a) although
(b) until
(c) as long as
(d) as soon as

Eagle 여행사는 내년 1분기에 남서부의 여러 주로 확장할 것이다. 그들은 이미 애리조나 지점을 위한 새로운 관리자를 고용했는데, 그곳은 연휴가 <u>끝나자마자</u> 문을 열도록 예정되어 있다.

─○ 지텔프 치트키

'~하자마자'라는 의미를 나타낼 때는 as soon as를 쓴다.

해설 | 문맥상 여행사는 연휴가 끝나자마자 문을 열도록 예정되어 있다는 의미가 되어야 자연스럽다. 따라서 '~하자마자'라는 의미의 시간을 나타내는 부사절 접속사 (d) as soon as가 정답이다.

> **오답분석**
> (a) although는 '~이긴 하지만', (b) until은 '~할 때까지', (c) as long as는 '~하는 한'이라는 의미로, 문맥에 적합하지 않아 오답이다.

어휘 | branch n. 지점, 지사   be set to phr. ~하도록 예정되어 있다

23 시제   미래완료진행   난이도 ●●○

Seascapes is a landmark resort that has gained attention around the world for its private beaches. By the end of next month, the long-admired resort _____ tourists for thirty years.

(a) has been serving
(b) is serving
(c) will be serving
(d) will have been serving

Seascapes는 사유지 바닷가로 전 세계적으로 주의를 끌어온 랜드마크 리조트이다. 다음 달 말 즈음에는, 오랫동안 높이 평가된 그 리조트가 30년 동안 관광객들에게 <u>서비스를 제공해 오고 있는 중일 것이다.</u>

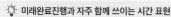 **지텔프 치트키**

'by + 미래 시점'과 'for + 기간 표현'이 함께 오면 미래완료진행 시제가 정답이다.

> 🔆 **미래완료진행과 자주 함께 쓰이는 시간 표현**
> • by the time / when / if + 현재 동사 + (for + 기간 표현) ~할 무렵이면 / ~할 때 / 만약 ~한다면 (~ 동안)
> • by / in + 미래 시점 + (for + 기간 표현) ~ 즈음에는 / ~에 (~ 동안)

해설 | 미래완료진행 시제와 함께 쓰이는 표현 'by + 미래 시점'(By the end of next month)과 'for + 기간 표현'(for thirty years)이 있고, 문맥상 미래 시점인 다음 달 말 즈음에는 Seascapes 리조트가 30년 동안 계속해서 관광객들에게 서비스를 제공해 오고 있는 중일 것이라는 의미가 되어야 자연스럽다. 따라서 미래완료진행 시제 (d) will have been serving이 정답이다.

> 오답분석
> (c) 미래진행 시제는 특정 미래 시점에 진행 중일 일을 나타내므로, 과거 또는 현재에 시작해서 특정 미래 시점까지 계속해서 진행되고 있을 일을 표현할 수 없어 오답이다.

어휘 | landmark n. 랜드마크(멀리서 보고 위치 파악에 도움이 되는 대형 건물 같은 것) gain attention phr. 주의를 끌다 admire v. 높이 평가하다

24 가정법   가정법 과거   난이도 ●●○

Artificial ice rinks were invented in the 1840s so that people could ice skate all year round. If ice rinks didn't exist today, people _____ until winter to skate, when bodies of water naturally freeze over.

(a) would have to wait
(b) would have had to wait
(c) will have had to wait
(d) will have to wait

사람들이 일 년 내내 아이스 스케이트를 탈 수 있도록 인공 아이스링크가 1840년대에 발명되었다. 만약 오늘날 아이스링크가 존재하지 않는다면, 사람들은 스케이트를 타기 위해 물이 자연적으로 완전히 얼음으로 뒤덮이는 겨울까지 <u>기다려야 할 것이다.</u>

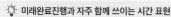 **지텔프 치트키**

'if + 과거 동사'가 있으면 'would/could + 동사원형'이 정답이다.

> 🔆 **가정법 과거**
> If + 주어 + 과거 동사, 주어 + would/could(조동사 과거형) + 동사원형

해설 | If절에 과거 동사(didn't exist)가 있으므로, 주절에는 이와 짝을 이루어 가정법 과거를 만드는 'would(조동사 과거형) + 동사원형'이 와야 한다. 따라서 (a) would have to wait이 정답이다.

어휘 | artificial adj. 인공의, 인위적인 all year round phr. 일 년 내내 naturally adv. 자연적으로, 저절로 freeze over phr. 완전히 얼음으로 뒤덮이다

가정법　가정법 과거완료　　　　　　　　　　　　　　　　난이도 ●●○

Melissa had to have her car towed after her rear wheels got stuck in the mud by the lake. If she had parked farther away from the water's edge, she _____ to call for roadside assistance.

(a) would not need
(b) would not have needed
(c) had not needed
(d) will not have needed

Melissa는 뒷바퀴가 호숫가 진흙에 꼼짝 못 하게 된 후에 차를 견인하게 해야 했다. 만약 그녀가 물가에서 더 멀리 주차했었다면, 그녀는 긴급출동 서비스를 요청할 필요가 없었을 것이다.

─○ 지텔프 치트키

'if + had p.p.'가 있으면 'would/could + have p.p.'가 정답이다.

해설 | If절에 'had p.p.' 형태의 had parked가 있으므로, 주절에는 이와 짝을 이루어 가정법 과거완료를 만드는 'would(조동사 과거형) + have p.p.'가 와야 한다. 따라서 (b) would not have needed가 정답이다.

어휘 | tow v. (자동차·보트를) 견인하다 **rear wheel** phr. 뒷바퀴 **get stuck** phr. 꼼짝 못 하게 되다 **mud** n. 진흙, 진창 **water's edge** phr. 물가 **roadside assistance** phr. 긴급출동 서비스

---

26 **준동사**　동명사를 목적어로 취하는 동사　　　　　　　　　　난이도 ●●○

Seth overslept and missed his friend Gina's singing recital last Thursday. He considered _____ her a gift in the hope that she would forgive him but ultimately decided to cook her a nice meal instead.

(a) to have bought
(b) buying
(c) having bought
(d) to buy

Seth는 늦잠을 자서 지난 목요일에 친구 Gina의 노래 발표회를 놓쳤다. 그는 그녀가 자신을 용서해 줄 것이라는 희망을 품고 그녀에게 선물을 사주는 것을 고려했지만, 결국 대신 그녀에게 맛있는 식사를 요리해주기로 결정했다.

─○ 지텔프 치트키

consider는 동명사를 목적어로 취한다.

해설 | 빈칸 앞 동사 consider는 동명사를 목적어로 취하므로, 동명사 (b) buying이 정답이다.

> **오답분석**
> (c) having bought도 동명사이기는 하지만, 완료동명사(having bought)로 쓰일 경우 '고려하는' 시점보다 '(선물을) 사주는' 시점이 앞선다는 것을 나타내므로 문맥에 적합하지 않아 오답이다.

어휘 | oversleep v. 늦잠 자다 **recital** n. 발표회, 독주회 **in the hope that** phr. 희망을 품고 **ultimately** adv. 결국, 마침내

LISTENING

PART 1 (27~33) 일상 내화   고양이 입양에 관한 두 친구의 대화

안부 인사	M: Hey, Grace! Out for a walk? F: Hello, Harry! I'm actually going to the animal shelter.
주제 제시: 고양이 입양	M: The shelter? Are you planning to adopt a pet? F: Yes, I am! [27]I live by myself, and I thought it'd be nice to adopt a pet to keep me company. M: I see. What kind of pet are you thinking of getting? F: Well, my friend Becca just got an adorable little Persian kitty. He's got a long fluffy coat and the cutest smushed-in face! As soon as I saw him, I knew I wanted one just like him.
남자의 고양이 입양 경험	M: Well, my cat is practically my best friend. But [28]I was so nervous when I first got her, since I didn't know much about cats back then. F: Nervous? Why? I've never had a cat before, but it seems like taking care of one is pretty easy. They just stay inside all the time and loaf around the house. M: Um . . . Well, in my case, it really helped to do some research before going through with the adoption process.
고려할 사항1: 필수품	F: What else is there to know? M: Well, first, you'll need supplies for the cat. A bed, a scratcher, a litter box, toys, and so on. F: Oh, right. I guess I'll need to buy some things.
고려할 사항2: 건강 관리	M: [29]Then you'll need to keep your cat healthy. My cat has food allergies, so she needs a special kind of cat food. She has a few other health conditions as well, so she takes medicine twice a week for those. F: I didn't think about all that.
고려할 사항3: 비용 문제	M: Taking care of my cat has been a lot of work—and expensive. I read that it's a good idea to put some money aside in case there's a medical emergency, since a trip to the animal hospital can be quite costly. So, [30]before adopting my cat, I saved up. F: Hmm. [30]For me, that could be the biggest problem. Money is pretty tight at the moment since I'm working part time and taking night classes. I doubt I'll be able to come up with much of an emergency fund.

남: 안녕, Grace! 산책하러 나왔어?
여: 안녕, Harry! 나는 사실 동물 보호소에 가고 있어.

남: 보호소? 반려동물을 입양할 계획이야?
여: 응, 그러려고! [27]나는 홀로 사는데, 내 곁에 있어줄 반려동물을 입양하면 좋을 것 같아.
남: 그렇구나. 어떤 종류의 반려동물을 키울 생각이야?
여: 음, 내 친구 Becca는 최근에 사랑스럽고 작은 페르시아고양이를 데려왔어. 그 고양이는 길고 폭신폭신한 털과 가장 귀여운 뭉개진 얼굴을 가지고 있었어! 그 고양이를 보자마자, 나는 그 고양이와 같은 고양이를 원한다는 걸 알게 됐어.
남: 음, 내 고양이는 실제로 나의 가장 친한 친구야. 하지만 [28]내가 그때는 고양이에 관해 잘 몰랐기 때문에, 처음 키울 때 너무 긴장했어.
여: 긴장했다고? 왜? 나는 이전에 고양이를 한 번도 키워본 적이 없는데, 고양이를 돌보는 건 꽤 쉬운 것 같아. 고양이들은 항상 그냥 집 안에 있으면서 집에서 빈둥거리잖아.
남: 음... 글쎄, 내 경우에는, 입양 절차를 밟기 전에 조사를 좀 하는 게 정말 도움이 됐어.

여: 그 밖에 알아야 할 게 있어?
남: 음, 우선, 고양이를 위한 필수품이 있어야 할 거야. 침대, 스크래처, 반려동물용 변기, 장난감 등 말이야.
여: 오, 맞아. 나는 물건을 좀 사야 할 것 같아.

남: [29]그러고 나서 고양이 건강도 챙겨야 할 거야. 우리 고양이는 음식 알레르기가 있어서, 특별한 종류의 고양이 사료가 필요해. 다른 건강 질환도 몇 가지 있어서, 그것 때문에 일주일에 두 번씩 약을 먹어.
여: 그런 건 전부 생각하지 못했어.

남: 우리 고양이를 돌보는 일은 손이 많이 가고 비용도 많이 들었어. 동물 병원에 가는 건 비용이 꽤 많이 들 수 있기 때문에, 응급 의료 상황에 대비해서 저축을 해두는 게 좋은 생각이라는 글을 읽었어. 그래서, [30]고양이를 입양하기 전에, 나는 저축을 했어.
여: 흠. [30]나에게는, 그게 가장 큰 문제일 수도 있어. 나는 아르바이트도 하고 야간 수업도 듣고 있어서 지금 돈이 좀 빠듯해. 비상금의 많은 부분을 내놓을 수 있을지 의문스러워.

고려할 사항4: 적응 기간	M: [31]You should also keep in mind that the first few weeks with a new cat tend to be rocky. **These days my cat almost never leaves my side, but** [31]at first, she hissed whenever I tried to pet her and rarely came out from under the bed.
	F: But [32]Becca's little Persian was such an angel . . .
고려할 사항5: 품종	M: Grace, there's something else you should know. [32]You probably won't find a Persian cat at the shelter. The shelter will have a lot of common, local breeds, like you see running around outside. But they're just as wonderful as any Persian.
	F: Oh. Wow. I guess . . . there's a lot I didn't know. You must think I'm pretty foolish.
여자가 다음에 할 일	M: Not at all, Grace! Lots of people adopt pets without knowing much about the process. I know you've got a big heart, and [33]I think the cat that joins your home one day will be very lucky indeed!
	F: One day, Harry. [33]But not today. I've got a lot of research to do first.

남: [31]새 고양이를 키우는 처음 몇 주는 험난하다는 점도 명심해야 해. 요즘은 우리 고양이가 내 곁을 거의 떠나지 않지만, [31]처음에는, 내가 고양이를 쓰다듬으려고 할 때마다 쉿 소리를 내고 침대 밑에서 거의 나오지 않았어.

여: 하지만 [32]Becca의 작은 페르시아고양이는 정말 천사였어...

남: Grace, 네가 알아야 할 다른 게 있어. [32]보호소에서는 페르시아고양이를 찾을 수 없을 거야. 보호소에는 밖에서 뛰어다니는 흔히 있는 지역 품종이 많을 거야. 하지만 그들도 페르시아고양이만큼이나 훌륭해.

여: 오. 와. 내가 생각하기에... 내가 몰랐던 게 많네. 너는 내가 꽤 바보 같다고 생각하겠구나.

남: 전혀 그렇지 않아, Grace! 많은 사람이 그 과정에 관해 잘 알지 못한 채로 반려동물을 입양해. 네가 넓은 마음을 가진 걸 알아서, [33]언젠가 너희 집에 올 고양이는 정말로 아주 운이 좋을 거로 생각해!

여: 언젠가 말이야, Harry. [33]하지만 오늘은 아니야. 난 먼저 조사해야 할 게 많아.

어휘 | animal shelter 동물 보호소 adopt[ədʌ́pt] 입양하다 pet[pet] 반려동물; 쓰다듬다, 어루만지다 live by oneself 홀로 살다
keep company ~의 곁에 있어 주다, 친구가 되어 주다 adorable[ədɔ́ːrəbl] 사랑스러운, 귀여운 fluffy[flʌ́fi] 폭신폭신한, 솜털 같은
coat[kout] 털 smush[smʌʃ] 으깨다, 부수다 practically[prǽktikəliː] 실제로, 사실상 take care of ~을 돌보다 loaf around 빈둥거리다
adoption[ədʌ́pʃən] 입양 supply[səplái] 필수품, 물품 scratcher[skrǽtʃər] 스크래쳐(고양이가 긁기 좋게 만든 가구)
litter box 반려동물용 변기 condition[kəndíʃən] 질환 put aside 저축하다 medical emergency 응급 의료 상황
tight[tait] 빠듯한, 여유가 없는 doubt[daut] 의문스럽게 생각하다, 의심하다 come up with (돈 등을) 내놓다 emergency fund 비상금
keep in mind ~을 명심하다 rocky[rɑ́ki] 험난한, 고난이 많은 hiss[his] 쉿 소리를 내다 breed[briːd] 품종; 기르다
foolish[fúːliʃ] 바보 같은, 어리석은

---

27 **특정세부사항**   Why   난이도 ●○○

Why does Grace want to get a cat?

(a) so she can help a local shelter
(b) so her older cat will have a friend
(c) so she can feel less lonely
(d) so her home will be free of mice

Grace는 왜 고양이를 키우고 싶어 하는가?

(a) 그녀가 지역 보호소를 도울 수 있기 위해서
(b) 그녀의 나이 든 고양이가 친구를 가지게 하기 위해서
(c) 그녀가 덜 외로울 수 있기 위해서
(d) 그녀의 집에 쥐가 없도록 하기 위해서

⟶○ 정답 잡는 치트키

질문의 키워드 get a cat이 adopt a pet으로 paraphrasing되어 언급된 주변 내용을 주의 깊게 듣는다.

해설 | 여자가 'I live by myself, and I thought it'd be nice to adopt a pet to keep me company.'라며 홀로 사는데, 자기 곁에 있어줄 반려동물을 입양하면 좋을 것 같다고 했다. 따라서 (c)가 정답이다.

어휘 | lonely[lóunli] 외로운, 고독한 free of ~이 없는

28 특정세부사항 Why

Why was Harry nervous before adopting his cat?

(a) He had a bad experience with cats.
(b) He was worried about the cost.
(c) He was not very familiar with cats.
(d) He had never cared for a pet.

Harry는 왜 고양이를 입양하기 전에 긴장했는가?

(a) 고양이와의 나쁜 경험이 있었다.
(b) 비용에 관해 걱정했다.
(c) 고양이에 관해 잘 알지 못했다.
(d) 반려동물을 돌본 적이 없었다.

🔘 **정답 잡는 치트키**

질문의 키워드 nervous가 그대로 언급된 주변 내용을 주의 깊게 듣는다.

해설 | 남자가 'I was so nervous when I first got her, since I didn't know much about cats back then'이라며 그때는 고양이에 관해 잘 몰랐기 때문에, 처음 키울 때 너무 긴장했다고 했다. 따라서 (c)가 정답이다.

⇄ **Paraphrasing**
didn't know much about cats 고양이에 관해 잘 몰랐다 → was not very familiar with cats 고양이에 관해 잘 알지 못했다

어휘 | care for ~을 돌보다, 보살피다

29 특정세부사항 How

How does Harry keep his cat healthy?

(a) by visiting the vet often
(b) by giving her allergy medicine
(c) by feeding her special cat food
(d) by buying the finest cat treats

Harry는 어떻게 그의 고양이를 건강하게 유지하는가?

(a) 수의사를 자주 방문함으로써
(b) 알레르기 약을 줌으로써
(c) 특별한 고양이 사료를 먹임으로써
(d) 최상의 고양이 간식을 구매함으로써

🔘 **정답 잡는 치트키**

질문의 키워드 cat healthy가 그대로 언급된 주변 내용을 주의 깊게 듣는다.

해설 | 남자가 'Then you'll need to keep your cat healthy. My cat has food allergies, so she needs a special kind of cat food.'라며 그리고 나서 고양이 건강도 챙겨야 하는데, 자기 고양이는 음식 알레르기가 있어서 특별한 종류의 고양이 사료가 필요하다고 했다. 따라서 (c)가 정답이다.

⇄ **Paraphrasing**
a special kind of cat food 특별한 종류의 고양이 사료 → special cat food 특별한 고양이 사료

오답분석
(b) 남자가 자기 고양이에게 다른 건강 질환도 몇 가지 있어서 일주일에 두 번씩 약을 먹인다고는 언급했지만, 알레르기 약을 준다고 한 것은 아니므로 오답이다.

어휘 | vet[vet] 수의사 feed[fi:d] 먹이다, 먹이를 주다 treat[tri:t] 간식

30 추론 특정사실

What would be the biggest problem for Grace if her pet had an emergency?

(a) her lack of money
(b) her need for a reliable vehicle
(c) her distance from the hospital
(d) her limited free time

Grace의 반려동물이 위급 상황에 처한다면 그녀에게 가장 큰 문제는 무엇일 것 같은가?

(a) 돈의 부족
(b) 신뢰할 만한 이동 수단의 필요
(c) 병원으로부터의 거리
(d) 한정된 자유 시간

➜─○ **정답 잡는 치트키**

질문의 키워드 biggest problem이 그대로 언급된 주변 내용을 주의 깊게 듣는다.

해설 | 남자가 'before adopting my cat, I saved up'이라며 고양이를 입양하기 전에 저축했다고 하자, 여자가 'For me, that could be the biggest problem. Money is pretty tight at the moment'라며 자기에게는 그게 가장 큰 문제일 수도 있다며, 지금 돈이 좀 빠듯하다고 한 것을 통해, Grace의 반려동물이 위급 상황에 처한다면 돈이 부족한 것이 가장 큰 문제가 될 것임을 추론할 수 있다. 따라서 (a)가 정답이다.

⇄ **Paraphrasing**
Money is pretty tight 돈이 좀 빠듯하다 → lack of money 돈의 부족

어휘 | reliable[riláiəbl] 신뢰할 만한, 믿음직한 vehicle[víː(h)ikl] 이동 수단, 차량 distance[dístəns] 거리, 간격 limited[límitid] 한정된

31 특정세부사항 Why

Why does Harry say the first few weeks of pet ownership can be rocky?

(a) because cats might be homesick
(b) because cats might be ill
(c) because cats can be violent
(d) because cats can be frightened

Harry는 왜 반려동물을 키우는 처음 몇 주가 험난할 수 있다고 말하는가?

(a) 고양이들이 향수병을 앓을지도 모르기 때문에
(b) 고양이들이 아플지도 모르기 때문에
(c) 고양이들이 폭력적일 수 있기 때문에
(d) 고양이들이 겁을 먹을 수 있기 때문에

➜─○ **정답 잡는 치트키**

질문의 키워드 first few weeks와 rocky가 그대로 언급된 주변 내용을 주의 깊게 듣는다.

해설 | 남자가 'You should also keep in mind that the first few weeks with a new cat tend to be rocky.'라며 새 고양이를 키우는 처음 몇 주는 험난하다는 점도 명심해야 한다고 한 뒤, 'at first, she hissed whenever I tried to pet her and rarely came out from under the bed'라며 처음에는 고양이를 쓰다듬으려고 할 때마다 쉿 소리를 내고 침대 밑에서 거의 나오지 않았다고 했다. 따라서 (d)가 정답이다.

어휘 | homesick[hóumsìk] 향수병을 앓는, 집을 그리워하는 violent[váiələnt] 폭력적인, 격렬한

32 추론 특정사실

According to Harry, what kind of cat will Grace probably not be able to find at the shelter?

Harry에 따르면, Grace가 보호소에서 찾을 수 없는 고양이는 어떤 종류일 것 같은가?

(a) **the exotic breed she wants**
(b) cats that have lived outdoors
(c) the common breed she prefers
(d) cats that are very active

(a) **그녀가 원하는 외래 품종**
(b) 야외에서 생활해 온 고양이들
(c) 그녀가 선호하는 일반적인 품종
(d) 아주 활동적인 고양이들

해설 | 여자가 'Becca's little Persian was such an angel'이라며 Becca의 작은 페르시아고양이가 정말 천사였다고 하자, 남자가 'You probably won't find a Persian cat at the shelter. The shelter will have a lot of common, local breeds, like you see running around outside.'라며 보호소에서는 페르시아고양이를 찾을 수 없을 것이고, 밖에서 뛰어다니는 흔히 있는 지역 품종이 많을 것이라고 한 것을 통해, Grace는 보호소에서 그녀가 원하는 외래 품종인 페르시아고양이를 찾을 수 없을 것임을 추론할 수 있다. 따라서 (a)가 정답이다.

⇄ **Paraphrasing**
a Persian cat 페르시아고양이 → the exotic breed 외래 품종

어휘 | exotic[igzátik] 외래의, 외국의 active[ǽktiv] 활동적인, 활발한

---

33 **추론**   다음에 할 일   난이도 ●○○

What will Grace probably do today?

(a) **learn more about cats**
(b) bring a pet home
(c) visit the animal shelter
(d) schedule a vet consultation

Grace는 오늘 무엇을 할 것 같은가?

(a) **고양이에 관해 더 알아본다**
(b) 반려동물을 집에 데려온다
(c) 동물 보호소를 방문한다
(d) 수의사의 진찰 일정을 잡는다

해설 | 남자가 'I think the cat that joins your home one day will be very lucky indeed'라며 언젠가 여자의 집에 올 고양이는 정말로 아주 운이 좋을 거로 생각한다고 하자, 여자가 'But not today. I've got a lot of research to do first.'라며 하지만 오늘은 아니고, 먼저 조사해야 할 게 많다고 한 것을 통해, Grace는 오늘 고양이에 관해 더 알아볼 것임을 추론할 수 있다. 따라서 (a)가 정답이다.

PART 2(34~39) **발표** 환영 주간 활동 및 행사 소개

음성 바로 듣기

34Greetings, Hawke University freshmen. It is my great pleasure to extend this invitation to Hawke University's Welcome Week. Held during the first week of fall semester, Welcome Week helps incoming freshmen transition to university life. The Office of Student Affairs has lots of exciting activities and events planned for you. Here are some of them!

주제
제시:
환영
주간
소개

34안녕하세요, Hawke 대학교 신입생 여러분. Hawke 대학교의 환영 주간에 초대하게 되어 매우 기쁩니다. 가을 학기 첫 주 동안 열리는, 환영 주간은 새로 온 신입생들이 대학 생활로 전환하는 것을 돕습니다. 학생처는 여러분을 위해 많은 흥미로운 활동과 행사를 계획하고 있습니다. 그중 몇 가지를 소개합니다!

월요일 활동 및 행사: 졸업생 연설

[35]On Monday, alumnus Jeffrey Teal will give a welcome speech in the campus quad. Since graduating from the Performing Arts program ten years ago, Jeffrey Teal has performed in several critically acclaimed stage productions. Now, [35]he has come back to give you a warm welcome to campus and share stories of his time at Hawke University and how it has influenced him. This is an opportunity to hear from one of the university's top graduates, so don't miss it.

화요일 활동 및 행사: 보물 찾기

On Tuesday, there will be a school-wide scavenger hunt. We'll give you a list of items which you'll have to find by searching around our school's most important landmarks. [36]An unexpected benefit of the scavenger hunt is that you'll get to learn more about Hawke University's history while exploring the campus. And the prize for finding the most items? A full year of free textbooks from the campus bookstore. Happy hunting!

수요일 활동 및 행사: 바비큐 파티

On Wednesday, there will be an all-day barbecue. Come hang out with your fellow freshmen while enjoying a burger or a tofu dog in the northwest corner of the quad. When you're lining up for food, make sure you show us your student ID. After we've confirmed your student number, you will be given two free food stubs, which you may use at the event. [37]The barbecue is only for freshmen, so don't forget to bring your ID for your food!

목요일 활동 및 행사: 학생 동아리 의 날

On Thursday, [38]we will be holding Student Club Day, where you can meet members of our various clubs. Hawke University encourages students to discover and explore their passions outside of school. From recreational groups to community service organizations, you're sure to find something you're interested in. [38]Each club will have its own booth in the quad. Feel free to approach any of them to talk to the members and learn more about their club activities. If you'd like to sign up for any clubs, take an application form from their booth and submit it to the Office of Student Affairs the following week.

금요일 활동 및 행사1: 야외 댄스 운동 세션

On Friday, Hawke University's Department of Physical Education will be holding outdoor dance workout sessions. Our instructors will lead students and faculty in a fun dance routine. At the end of each session, there will also be a seminar to help you learn about what resources are available on campus to keep you physically fit. Put on your best workout outfit and join us in the quad!

[35]월요일에는, 졸업생 Jeffrey Teal이 캠퍼스 쿼드에서 환영 연설을 할 것입니다. 10년 전에 Performing Arts 프로그램을 졸업한 후, Jeffrey Teal은 비평가들의 극찬을 받은 여러 연극 작품에서 연기했습니다. 이제, [35]그는 여러분에게 캠퍼스에 온 것을 따뜻하게 환영하고 Hawke 대학교에서의 시간과 그것이 그에게 어떤 영향을 미쳤는지에 대한 이야기를 나누기 위해 돌아왔습니다. 이것은 대학교의 최고 졸업생 중 한 명으로부터 이야기를 들을 기회이니, 놓치지 마세요.

화요일에는, 학교 전체에서 보물찾기가 열립니다. 우리 학교의 가장 중요한 주요 지형지물들을 탐색하며 여러분이 찾아야 할 물건들의 목록을 드릴 것입니다. [36]이 보물찾기의 뜻밖의 장점은 캠퍼스를 탐험하면서 Hawke 대학교의 역사에 관해 더 많이 배우게 될 것이라는 점입니다. 또 가장 많은 물건을 찾은 것에 대한 경품은요? 캠퍼스 서점에서 제공하는 1년 치 무료 교과서입니다. 즐거운 수색이죠!

수요일에는, 하루 종일 바비큐 파티가 있을 것입니다. 쿼드 북서쪽 코너에서 햄버거나 두부 핫도그를 즐기며 같은 신분의 신입생들과 어울려 보세요. 음식을 먹기 위해 줄을 설 때는, 반드시 학생증을 제시하세요. 학생 번호를 확인한 후에, 무료 식권 두 장을 받으실 것이며, 행사장에서 사용하실 수 있습니다. [37]바비큐 파티는 신입생들만을 위한 것이니, 음식을 받으려면 신분증을 지참하는 것을 잊지 마세요!

목요일에는, [38]학생 동아리의 날을 개최할 것인데, 여러분은 다양한 동아리 회원들을 만날 수 있습니다. Hawke 대학교는 학생들이 학교 밖에서 그들의 열정을 발견하고 탐구하도록 장려합니다. 레크리에이션 단체에서 지역사회 봉사 단체에 이르기까지, 여러분이 관심 있는 것을 분명히 찾을 수 있을 것입니다. [38]각 동아리는 쿼드에 각각의 부스가 있을 것입니다. 그것 중 어느 것에나 자유롭게 다가가 회원들과 이야기하고 동아리 활동에 대해 자세히 알아보세요. 만약 동아리에 가입하고 싶다면, 부스에서 신청서를 가져와서 다음 주에 학생처에 제출하세요.

금요일에는, Hawke 대학교 체육학과에서 야외 댄스 운동 세션을 개최합니다. 강사들이 학생과 교직원을 재미있는 댄스 루틴으로 이끌 것입니다. 각 세션 이후에는, 캠퍼스에서 신체 건강을 유지하기 위해 어떤 자원을 이용할 수 있는지 알아보는 것을 돕는 세미나도 있습니다. 가장 좋아하는 운동복을 입고 쿼드에서 참여해 보세요!

Lastly, on Friday, [39]we will be holding the annual Welcome Week Raffle. Prizes include Hawke University apparel and passes for various campus restaurants, as well as the grand prize of a brand-new laptop. To enter, all you have to do is attend the "Raffle Rap" in the main auditorium and write down the keyword given at the end of the song. Hint: I've heard this year's keyword rhymes with "spicy." Names of the winners will be posted outside the Office of Student Affairs by the end of the day. Good luck freshmen, and we hope to see you during Welcome Week!

금요일 활동 및 행사2: 추첨

마지막으로, 금요일에는, [39]연례 환영 주간 추첨이 열립니다. 경품으로는 최우수상에 신형 노트북이 주어지는 것뿐만 아니라, Hawke 대학교 옷과 다양한 캠퍼스 레스토랑 이용권을 포함합니다. 참가하려면, 대강당에서 열리는 "래플 랩"에 참여하여 노래 끝에 주어진 키워드를 적기만 하면 됩니다. 힌트는 올해의 키워드가 "spicy"와 운이 맞는다고 들었습니다. 우승자 명단은 그날 중으로 학생처 외부에 게시될 것입니다. 신입생 여러분, 행운을 빌며, 환영 주간 동안 뵙기를 바랍니다!

어휘 | extend an invitation 초대장을 보내다 incoming[ínkəmiŋ] 새로 온, 신입의 transition[trænzíʃən] 전환, 변화 alumnus[əlʎmnəs] 졸업생, 동창생 quad[kwad] 쿼드(사각형 안뜰) critically acclaimed 비평가들의 극찬을 받은 stage production 연극 작품 scavenger hunt 보물찾기 landmark[lǽndmà:rk] 주요 지형지물, 랜드마크 unexpected[ʌ́nikspèktid] 뜻밖의, 예기치 않은 explore[iksplɔ́:r] 탐험하다, 조사하다 hunting[hʎntiŋ] 수색, 사냥 hang out with ~와 어울리다, 시간을 보내다 fellow[félou] 같은 신분의, 동료의 tofu[tóufu:] 두부 food stub 식권 passions[pǽʃən] 열정, 흥미 approach[əpróutʃ] 다가가다, 접근하다 workout[wə́:rkàut] 운동 faculty[fǽkəlti] 교직원, 교수진 dance routine 댄스 루틴(정해진 춤 동작) keep fit 건강을 유지하다 physically[fízikəli] 신체적으로 outfit[áutfit] 복장, 옷 apparel[əpǽrəl] 옷, 의류, 의복 grand prize 최우수상 brand-new 신형의, 아주 새로운 main auditorium 대강당 write down ~을 적어두다, 기록하다 rhyme with ~과 운이 맞다

---

34 주제/목적 담화의 목적 난이도 ●●○

What is the purpose of the talk?

(a) to welcome back university students
(b) to invite freshmen to a series of events
(c) to give high school students a campus tour
(d) to share tips for adjusting to college life

담화의 목적은 무엇인가?

(a) 대학생들의 복귀를 환영하기 위해서
(b) 신입생들을 일련의 행사에 초대하기 위해서
(c) 고등학생들에게 캠퍼스 구경을 시켜주기 위해서
(d) 대학 생활에 적응하기 위한 조언을 공유하기 위해서

━○ 정답 잡는 치트키

담화의 목적을 언급하는 초반을 주의 깊게 듣고 전체 맥락을 파악한다.

해설 | 화자가 'Greetings, Hawke University freshmen. It is my great pleasure to extend this invitation to Hawke University's Welcome Week.'이라며 Hawke 대학교 신입생들에게 환영 주간에 초대하게 되어 매우 기쁘다고 한 뒤, 담화 전반에 걸쳐 환영 주간에 있을 활동과 행사를 소개하는 내용이 이어지고 있다. 따라서 (b)가 정답이다.

어휘 | adjust[ədʒʎst] 적응하다, 조절하다

---

35 특정세부사항 What 난이도 ●●○

What will graduate Jeffrey Teal do at the event?

(a) He will discuss his college experiences.
(b) He will give a closing speech.

졸업생 Jeffrey Teal은 행사에서 무엇을 할 것인가?

(a) 대학 경험을 이야기할 것이다.
(b) 폐회사를 할 것이다.

(c) He will perform in a stage production.
(d) He will give a lecture on the arts.

(c) 연극 작품에서 연기할 것이다.
(d) 미술에 관한 강의를 할 것이다.

◀─○ 정답 잡는 치트키

질문의 키워드 graduate Jeffrey Teal이 alumnus Jeffrey Teal로 paraphrasing되어 언급된 주변 내용을 주의 깊게 듣는다.

해설 | 화자가 'On Monday, alumnus Jeffrey Teal will give a welcome speech in the campus quad.'라며 월요일에는 졸업생 Jeffrey Teal이 캠퍼스 쿼드에서 환영 연설을 할 것이라고 한 뒤, 'he has come back to ~ share stories of his time at Hawke University and how it has influenced him'이라며 그는 Hawke 대학교에서의 시간과 그것이 그에게 어떤 영향을 미쳤는지에 대한 이야기를 나누기 위해 돌아왔다고 했다. 따라서 (a)가 정답이다.

어휘 | closing speech 폐회사

---

36 특정세부사항   What   난이도 ●○○

According to the speaker, what is an unexpected benefit of the scavenger hunt?

(a) getting to know the staff
(b) learning more about the school
(c) winning a valuable prize
(d) enjoying the scenic campus

화자에 따르면, 보물찾기의 뜻밖의 장점은 무엇인가?

(a) 직원을 알게 되는 것
(b) 학교에 관해 더 배우는 것
(c) 값진 경품을 받는 것
(d) 경치 좋은 캠퍼스를 즐기는 것

◀─○ 정답 잡는 치트키

질문의 키워드 unexpected benefit of the scavenger hunt가 그대로 언급된 주변 내용을 주의 깊게 듣는다.

해설 | 화자가 'An unexpected benefit of the scavenger hunt is that you'll get to learn more about Hawke University's history while exploring the campus.'라며 이 보물찾기의 뜻밖의 장점은 캠퍼스를 탐험하면서 Hawke 대학교의 역사에 관해 더 많이 배우게 될 것이라는 점이라고 했다. 따라서 (b)가 정답이다.

⇄ Paraphrasing
University 대학교 → the school 학교

어휘 | scenic[síːnik] 경치 좋은

---

37 추론   특정사실   난이도 ●●○

According to the talk, why, most likely, will non-freshmen be unable to join the barbecue?

(a) because they are not allowed in the quad
(b) because they would make the event too noisy
(c) because there would not be enough food
(d) because they have other events to attend

담화에 따르면, 신입생이 아닌 사람들은 왜 바비큐 파티에 참석할 수 없을 것 같은가?

(a) 그들은 쿼드에 들어갈 수 없기 때문에
(b) 그들은 행사를 너무 시끄럽게 만들 것이기 때문에
(c) 충분한 음식이 없을 것이기 때문에
(d) 그들은 참석해야 할 다른 행사가 있기 때문에

질문의 키워드 non-freshmen be unable to join the barbecue가 barbecue is only for freshmen으로 paraphrasing되어 언급된 주변 내용을 주의 깊게 듣는다.

해설 | 화자가 'The barbecue is only for freshmen, so don't forget to bring your ID for your food!'라며 바비큐 파티는 신입생들만을 위한 것이니, 음식을 받으려면 신분증을 지참하는 것을 잊지 말라고 한 것을 통해, 바비큐 파티에 충분한 음식이 없을 것이기 때문에 신입생이 아닌 사람들은 바비큐 파티에 참석할 수 없을 것임을 추론할 수 있다. 따라서 (c)가 정답이다.

38 특정세부사항 What
난이도 ●●○

What can one do at the booths on Student Club Day?

(a) **meet student club members**
(b) join exclusive club activities
(c) submit a club registration form
(d) sign up to be a student leader

학생 동아리의 날에 부스에서 무엇을 할 수 있는가?

(a) **학생 동아리 회원들을 만난다**
(b) 비 개방적인 동아리 활동에 참여한다
(c) 동아리 신청서를 제출한다
(d) 학생회장이 되기 위해 등록한다

질문의 키워드 booths와 Student Club Day가 그대로 언급된 주변 내용을 주의 깊게 듣는다.

해설 | 화자가 'we will be holding Student Club Day'라며 학생 동아리의 날을 개최할 것이라고 한 뒤, 'Each club will have its own booth in the quad. Feel free to approach any of them to talk to the members'라며 각 동아리는 쿼드에 각자의 부스가 있을 것인데, 그것 중 어느 것에나 자유롭게 다가가 회원들과 이야기하라고 했다. 따라서 (a)가 정답이다.

어휘 | exclusive[iksklúːsiv] 비 개방적인, 독점적인 registration form 신청서 student leader 학생회장

39 특정세부사항 How
난이도 ●●●

How can one get Hawke University apparel?

(a) by joining a seminar on health
(b) by attending a dance workout
(c) **by participating in a raffle event**
(d) by competing in a singing contest

Hawke 대학교 옷은 어떻게 받을 수 있는가?

(a) 건강에 관한 세미나에 참가함으로써
(b) 댄스 운동에 참여함으로써
(c) **추첨 행사에 참여함으로써**
(d) 노래 경연대회에서 경쟁함으로써

질문의 키워드 Hawke University apparel이 그대로 언급된 주변 내용을 주의 깊게 듣는다.

해설 | 화자가 'we will be holding the annual Welcome Week Raffle. Prizes include Hawke University apparel'이라며 연례 환영 주간 추첨이 열리고, 경품으로는 Hawke 대학교 옷을 포함한다고 했다. 따라서 (c)가 정답이다.

오답분석
(d) 화자가 "래플 랩"에 참여하는 것을 언급하기는 했지만, 이것은 노래 경연대회가 아니라 노래 끝에 주어진 키워드를 적는 것이므로 오답이다.

어휘 | singing contest 노래 경연대회

음성 바로 듣기

안부 인사	**F:** Hey, Adam! How's the new job? **M:** 40My new job is great so far, Rose. The only problem is my lunch routine.
주제 제시: 장단점 비교	**F:** Your lunch routine? **M:** Yeah. 40I used to pack my lunch every day at my old job. But now, I'm wondering if I should join my coworkers and eat out for lunch. **F:** Hmm. You sound pretty concerned about this. Want to go over the pros and cons?
도시락 싸는 것의 장점	**M:** Sure. You see, 41I like to eat heavy lunches because it keeps me full for the rest of the day. I don't need snacks to keep me going. That's why I usually pack a lot of food and bring it with me. **F:** Also, you can probably save quite a bit of money by preparing your own lunch every day. **M:** You bet! Plus—don't laugh—but I'm a coupon clipper. People don't read the newspapers much anymore, but 42I always get the local paper and go straight for the coupons. And no place has as many discounts as my local grocery store.
도시락 싸는 것의 단점	**F:** A coupon clipper! 42Just like my grandmother! Ha-ha. 42Grandma Beatrice checks the papers every day looking for bargains. However, we should also consider the disadvantages of preparing lunch in the morning. Like how much time it takes. **M:** Bingo. That's my biggest issue, Rose. I was waking up so early to cook that later in the day I'd feel kind of grumpy and exhausted. **F:** Aw, I know how that feels. Another disadvantage of packing your own lunch is the extra baggage. Lunch containers take up a lot of space in your work bag. **M:** Yup. I already bring a lot of things to work, like my laptop and paperwork. It gets pretty heavy carrying all that every day, plus my lunch.
외식 하는 것의 장점	**F:** Sounds tiring! Now, why don't we look at the advantages of eating out for lunch? **M:** Let's see. If I eat out for lunch, it's my chance to step out of the office. I could really use the break from work. **F:** Right. 43Eating lunch outside the office will help take your mind off work for a while. It'll be a nice change of pace. **M:** 43Another advantage is that I can join my coworkers for lunch. They all eat together, and I'm the only one who stays behind to eat at my desk.

여: 안녕, Adam! 새로운 직장은 어때?
남: 40새로운 직장은 지금까지 괜찮아, Rose. 유일한 문제는 점심 루틴뿐이야.

여: 점심 루틴?
남: 응. 40예전 직장에서는 매일 점심을 싸 오곤 했어. 그런데 지금은, 직장 동료들과 함께 외식해야 할지 고민이야.
여: 흠. 그게 상당히 마음에 걸리는 것 같네. 장단점을 검토해 볼까?

남: 물론이지. 너도 알다시피, 41나는 하루 종일 포만감을 유지할 수 있기 때문에 점심을 든든하게 먹는 걸 좋아해. 계속 활동하기 위해서 간식이 필요하지 않거든. 그래서 나는 평소에 음식을 많이 싸서 가지고 다녀.
여: 또한, 매일 점심을 직접 준비하면 아마 꽤 많은 돈을 절약할 수 있어.
남: 물론이지! 게다가, 웃지 말고, 그런데 난 쿠폰 클리퍼야. 사람들은 더 이상 신문을 잘 읽지 않지만, 42난 항상 지역 신문을 사서 쿠폰을 곧장 찾아. 그리고 우리 동네 식료품점만큼 할인을 많이 해주는 곳도 없어.

여: 쿠폰 클리퍼! 42우리 할머니 같네! 하하. 42할머니 Beatrice는 매일 신문을 보며 특가품을 찾으셔. 하지만, 우리는 아침에 점심을 준비하는 것의 단점도 고려해야 해. 시간이 얼마나 걸리는지 같은 것 말이야.
남: 맞었어. 그게 내 가장 큰 문제야, Rose. 요리하려고 너무 일찍 일어나서 그날 오후면 심술이 나고 기진맥진하곤 했어.
여: 아, 나도 그게 어떤 느낌인지 알아. 도시락을 직접 싸는 것의 또 다른 단점은 추가적인 짐이 생기는 거야. 도시락 용기는 업무용 가방에서 많은 공간을 차지해.
남: 응. 나는 이미 노트북이랑 서류 같은 많은 물건을 가지고 출근하거든. 매일 그렇게 다 들고 다니고, 거기에 점심 도시락까지 더해지면 꽤 무거워져.

여: 피곤할 것 같아! 이제, 점심에 외식하는 것의 장점을 살펴보는 게 어때?
남: 어디 보자. 점심에 외식하면, 사무실 밖으로 나갈 기회가 생겨. 업무로부터의 휴식이 정말 필요하거든.
여: 맞아. 43사무실 밖에서 점심을 먹는 건 잠시나마 업무를 잊는 데 도움이 될 거야. 좋은 기분 전환이 될 거야.
남: 43또 다른 장점은 직장 동료들과 점심을 같이 먹을 수 있다는 거야. 그들은 모두 함께 식사해서, 책상에서 점심을 먹기 위해 남아 있는 사람은 나뿐이거든.

외식하는 것의 단점	F: Aw, that must be so lonely! Well, since you're new to the office, it'll be a great way to get to know your coworkers. M: ⁴³It might even help me make friends. I can think of a few disadvantages to eating out, though. F: Like what, Adam? M: Well, ⁴⁴the restaurants around my office get very crowded around lunchtime. There are many tourists visiting the aquarium in the harbor district where I work, and it seems like everyone gets lunch at the same time. F: Yeah, I have to meet clients in the harbor district sometimes. And another disadvantage is that there are not a lot of healthy options in the area. M: True. I've really only seen one place with healthy food options—that new salad bar?

여: 아, 정말 외롭겠네! 음, 너는 사무실에 새로 왔으니, 동료들과 친해지는 좋은 방법이 될 거야.
남: ⁴³친구를 사귀는데도 도움이 될 거야. 그래도 외식하는 것의 단점이 몇 가지 생각나.

여: 어떤 것들이야, Adam?
남: 음, ⁴⁴점심시간쯤에 사무실 주변 식당들이 엄청나게 붐비더라. 내가 일하는 항만 지구에 있는 수족관을 방문하는 관광객들이 많은데, 다들 같은 시간에 점심을 먹는 것 같아.
여: 응, 나도 가끔 항만 지구에서 고객을 만나야 해. 그리고 또 다른 단점은 그 지역에 건강한 선택지가 많지 않다는 거야.
남: 맞아. 건강식 선택지가 있는 곳은 정말 딱 한 곳인 것 같은데, 그 새로운 샐러드 바 정도?

남자의 결정	F: I know it. So, ⁴⁵have you decided what to do? M: Yes, Rose. ⁴⁵I think I'd rather spend more time sleeping in before work. F: That's understandable, Adam. And who knows—maybe you can find a few coupons for the salad bar? M: Ha-ha—maybe!

여: 나도 알아. 그래서, ⁴⁵어떻게 할지 결정했어?
남: 응, Rose. ⁴⁵나는 차라리 출근 전에 잠을 자는 데 좀 더 많은 시간을 쓰는 게 나을 것 같아.
여: 그건 이해할 수 있어, Adam. 그리고 샐러드 바 쿠폰 몇 장을 찾을 수 있을지 혹시 알아?
남: 하하, 아마도!

어휘 | routine[ruːtíːn] 루틴, 일과 **eat out** 외식하다 concern[kənsə́ːrn] 마음에 걸리게 하다, 염려하다 **go over** ~을 검토하다
you bet 물론이지, 그렇고 말고 **coupon clipper** 쿠폰 클리퍼(쿠폰을 잘 활용하는 사람) **grocery store** 식료품점 bargain[báːrgən] 특가품
bingo[bíŋgou] 맞혔어 grumpy[grʌ́mpi] 심술이 난, 기분이 언짢은 exhausted[igzɔ́ːstid] 기진맥진한 baggage[bǽgidʒ] 짐, 가방
take up 차지하다, 걸리다 paperwork[péipərwə̀ːrk] 서류 **could use** 필요하다 **take one's mind off** ~을 잊다
change of pace 기분 전환 crowded[kráudid] 붐비는, 혼잡한 **harbor district** 항만 지구
understandable[ʌ̀ndərstǽndəbl] 이해할 수 있는, 이해할 만한

---

40 **특정세부사항** **Why** 난이도 ●●○

Why is Adam thinking about switching up his lunch routine?	Adam은 왜 점심 루틴을 바꾸는 것에 관해 생각하고 있는가?
(a) to practice better eating habits (b) to allow for a longer break (c) to follow new rules at work **(d) to adjust to a change of jobs**	(a) 더 나은 식습관을 실천하기 위해서 (b) 더 긴 휴식 시간을 고려하기 위해서 (c) 직장에서 새로운 규칙을 따르기 위해서 **(d) 직장을 바꾼 것에 적응하기 위해서**

→○ 정답 잡는 치트키

질문의 키워드 lunch routine이 그대로 언급된 주변 내용을 주의 깊게 듣는다.

해설 | 남자가 'My new job is great so far, Rose. The only problem is my lunch routine.'이라며 새로운 직장은 지금까지 괜찮은데 유일한 문제는 점심 루틴뿐이라고 한 뒤, 'I used to pack my lunch every day at my old job. But now, I'm wondering if I should join my coworkers and eat out for lunch.'라며 예전 직장에서는 매일 점심을 싸 오곤 했는데, 지금은 직장 동료들과 함께 외식해야 할지 고민이라고 했다. 따라서 (d)가 정답이다.

어휘 | **eating habits** 식습관 **allow for** ~을 고려하다, 참작하다

According to Adam, how does he avoid getting hungry after lunch?

(a) by snacking on junk food
(b) by having a large lunch
(c) by distracting himself with work
(d) by drinking plenty of water

Adam에 따르면, 그는 어떻게 점심 식사 후에 배가 고파지는 것을 피하는가?

(a) 간편식으로 간단히 식사함으로써
(b) 점심을 많이 먹음으로써
(c) 일을 해서 주의를 딴 데로 돌림으로써
(d) 물을 많이 마심으로써

⊶○ **정답 잡는 치트키**

질문의 키워드 avoid getting hungry가 keeps ~ full로 paraphrasing되어 언급된 주변 내용을 주의 깊게 듣는다.

해설 | 남자가 'I like to eat heavy lunches because it keeps me full for the rest of the day'라며 하루 종일 포만감을 유지할 수 있기 때문에 점심을 든든하게 먹는 걸 좋아한다고 했다. 따라서 (b)가 정답이다.

⇄ **Paraphrasing**
to eat heavy lunches 점심을 든든하게 먹는 것 → having a large lunch 점심을 많이 먹음

어휘 | snack[snæk] 간단히 식사하다, 간식을 먹다; 간식　junk food 간편식, 인스턴트 식품　distract[distrǽkt] (주의를) 딴 데로 돌리다

What does Adam have in common with Rose's grandmother?

(a) waking up early in the morning
(b) using discounts from the paper
(c) feeling grumpy all the time
(d) being so good at cooking

Adam과 Rose의 할머니의 공통점은 무엇인가?

(a) 아침에 일찍 일어나는 것
(b) 신문에서 할인을 이용하는 것
(c) 항상 심술이 난다고 느끼는 것
(d) 요리를 아주 잘하는 것

⊶○ **정답 잡는 치트키**

질문의 키워드 grandmother가 그대로 언급된 주변 내용을 주의 깊게 듣는다.

해설 | 남자가 'I always get the local paper and go straight for the coupons'라며 항상 지역 신문을 사서 쿠폰을 곧장 찾는다고 하자, 여자가 'Just like my grandmother!', 'Grandma Beatrice checks the papers every day looking for bargains.'라며 남자가 자기 할머니와 비슷한데, 할머니 Beatrice는 매일 신문을 보며 특가품을 찾는다고 했다. 따라서 (b)가 정답이다.

How can Adam befriend his coworkers?

(a) by going out with them after work
(b) by having lunch with them
(c) by joining them for activities
(d) by eating with them in the office

Adam은 어떻게 그의 동료들과 친구가 될 수 있는가?

(a) 퇴근 후에 그들과 사귐으로써
(b) 그들과 점심을 먹음으로써
(c) 활동을 위해 그들과 함께함으로써
(d) 사무실에서 그들과 식사함으로써

정답 잡는 치트키

질문의 키워드 coworkers가 그대로 언급되고, befriend가 make friends로 paraphrasing되어 언급된 주변 내용을 주의 깊게 듣는다.

해설ㅣ 여자가 'Eating lunch outside the office will help take your mind off work for a while.'이라며 사무실 밖에서 점심을 먹는 건 잠시나마 업무를 잊는 데 도움이 될 거라고 하자, 남자가 'Another advantage is that I can join my coworkers for lunch.', 'It might even help me make friends.'라며 또 다른 장점은 직장 동료들과 점심을 같이 먹을 수 있다는 것이고, 친구를 사귀는데도 도움이 될 것이라고 했다. 따라서 (b)가 정답이다.

⇄ **Paraphrasing**
Eating lunch 점심을 먹는 것 → having lunch 점심을 먹음

어휘ㅣ befriend[biférénd] 친구가 되다 go out with ~와 사귀다

44 특정세부사항   Why   난이도 ●●○

According to the conversation, why are restaurants in the harbor district busy during lunchtime?

(a) They serve healthy food.
(b) They offer lunch specials.
(c) They are limited in number.
(d) They draw out-of-town visitors.

대화에 따르면, 항만 지구의 식당들은 점심시간 동안 왜 바쁜가?

(a) 건강한 음식을 제공한다.
(b) 점심 특선을 제공한다.
(c) 수가 한정되어 있다.
(d) 다른 마을의 방문객들을 끌어들인다.

정답 잡는 치트키

질문의 키워드 harbor district와 lunchtime이 그대로 언급된 주변 내용을 주의 깊게 듣는다.

해설ㅣ 남자가 'the restaurants around my office get very crowded around lunchtime. There are many tourists visiting the aquarium in the harbor district where I work'라며 점심시간쯤에 사무실 주변 식당들이 엄청나게 붐비는데, 남자가 일하는 항만 지구에 있는 수족관을 방문하는 관광객들이 많다고 했다. 따라서 (d)가 정답이다.

⇄ **Paraphrasing**
tourists 관광객들 → visitors 방문객들

어휘ㅣ draw[drɔː] 끌어들이다 out-of-town 다른 마을의, 시외의

45 추론   다음에 할 일   난이도 ●●○

What has Adam most likely decided to do about his lunch?

(a) look for more salad bars to visit
(b) try ordering takeout food
(c) continue bringing food to work
(d) eat out with his coworkers

Adam은 점심 식사에 관해 무엇을 하기로 결정한 것 같은가?

(a) 갈 만한 샐러드 바를 더 찾는다
(b) 포장 음식을 주문해 본다
(c) 직장에 음식을 계속 가져간다
(d) 동료들과 외식한다

정답 잡는 치트키

다음에 할 일을 언급하는 후반을 주의 깊게 듣는다.

PART 4 (46~52) 설명 집을 안전하게 지키기 위한 5가지 조언

음성 바로 듣기

인사 + 주제 제시

Hello and welcome to *HomeLife*. I was asked to speak today about my years growing up in one of the most dangerous and crime-ridden cities in the world. ⁴⁶We all wish we could live in a secure apartment community or a gated residence, but the reality is that most of the world has to struggle with crime. Today's talk is meant to acknowledge these widespread problems and to help keep you and your family safe if you ever end up facing some of the same challenges.

조언1: 집에 사람이 있다는 인식 심어주기

First, ⁴⁷keep your house occupied. I know, I know—you can't *always* be in your house. But it is possible to give the impression that somebody is always at home. ⁴⁷When you need to go somewhere, you can make your house look occupied by keeping the television and a few lights turned on. If intruders see lights in your house or detect any noise inside, they'll be discouraged from breaking in.

조언2: 집 입구 튼튼하게 하기

Second, strengthen the entry points to your house. Make sure that the doors are solid and have functioning locks. Burglars often come in through windows, but you can deter unwanted visitors by installing security bars on your first-floor windows. Not all locks and security bars are created equal, however. I learned this the hard way many years ago, when ⁴⁸a burglar simply pried open my front door. After that, my family decided to invest in high-quality products. The better the quality, the more difficult it will be for intruders to get in through these entry points.

조언3: 귀중품 숨겨두기

Third, keep your valuables hidden in places that are not obvious. Burglars tend to search obvious areas like desk drawers and nightstands for valuable items. ⁴⁹I always kept my valuables hidden deep in the pockets of an old winter coat, which I hung in the back of the closet. The longer burglars take to find something to steal, the greater the chance of them getting frustrated and moving on. According to some statistics, burglars take an average of twelve minutes to search a house. Any longer than that and they get too scared to stick around.

*HomeLife*에 오신 것을 환영합니다. 저는 오늘 세계에서 가장 위험하고 범죄에 시달리는 도시 중 한 곳에서 성장한 경험에 대해 이야기해 달라는 요청을 받았습니다. ⁴⁶우리 모두는 안전한 아파트 단지나 외부인 출입을 통제하는 주택에 살고 싶지만, 현실은 전 세계 대부분이 범죄와 싸워야 한다는 것입니다. 오늘의 강연은 이러한 광범위한 문제를 인식하고 여러분과 여러분의 가족이 유사한 문제에 직면했을 때 안전하게 유지하는 데 도움을 드리기 위한 것입니다.

첫 번째로, ⁴⁷집을 사람이 살고 있는 상태로 유지하세요. *항상* 집에 있을 수는 없다는 것을 저도 잘 알고 있습니다. 하지만 누군가 항상 집에 있다는 인상을 줄 수는 있습니다. ⁴⁷어딘가에 가야 할 때는, 텔레비전과 몇 개의 조명을 켜둠으로써 집에 사람이 있는 것처럼 보이게 할 수 있습니다. 침입자들이 집안의 불빛을 보거나 내부에서 소음을 감지하면, 침입하기를 단념하게 될 것입니다.

두 번째로, 집으로 들어가는 입구를 더 튼튼하게 하세요. 문이 견고한지와 자물쇠가 제대로 작동하는지를 확인하세요. 빈집 털이들은 종종 창문을 통해 들어오지만, 여러분은 1층 창문에 보안 바를 설치함으로써 원치 않는 방문객들을 저지할 수 있습니다. 그러나 모든 자물쇠와 보안 바는 똑같이 만들어지지 않습니다. 저는 이것을 몇 년 전에 ⁴⁸빈집 털이가 현관문을 간단히 비집어 열었을 때 힘들게 배웠습니다. 그 후, 우리 가족은 고품질 제품에 투자하기로 결정했습니다. 품질이 좋을수록, 침입자들이 이 입구들을 통해 들어오는 것이 더 어려워질 것입니다.

세 번째로, 귀중품들을 잘 보이지 않는 곳에 숨겨두세요. 빈집 털이들은 귀중품을 찾기 위해 책상 서랍이나 침실용 탁자와 같이 잘 보이는 곳을 뒤지는 경향이 있습니다. ⁴⁹저는 항상 귀중품들을 옷장 뒤쪽에 걸어둔 낡은 겨울 코트 주머니 깊숙한 곳에 숨겨두었습니다. 빈집 털이들이 무언가 훔칠 것을 찾는데 시간이 오래 걸릴수록, 그들이 좌절하고 다른 곳으로 이동할 가능성이 커집니다. 일부 통계 자료에 따르면, 빈집 털이들은 집을 뒤지는데 평균 12분이 걸립니다. 그보다 더 오래 걸리면 그들은 겁을 먹고 더 이상 머물지 않습니다.

Fourth, take advantage of technology. Video cameras, video doorbells, and motion-activated lights will make even the boldest criminal think twice. ⁵⁰When I was growing up, we didn't have this sort of technological assistance! If we were lucky, some friendly neighbors would help keep an eye on things. But now there are "smart" home security systems that record and send any suspicious behavior right to your phone. This sort of round-the-clock surveillance is getting more common and affordable every year.

Finally, ⁵¹hold a burglary trial to test the security of your house. A burglary trial is a simulation where you or someone you trust attempts to break into your house to test the effectiveness of your security set-up. Now, many people have asked me if this step is really necessary. Well, let me tell you from experience: ⁵¹You'll never truly know how effective your set-up is unless it has been tested.

⁵²Ever since taking these precautions, I've been able to sleep much better at night. There is nothing better, in my opinion, than feeling safe and comfortable in your own home. If you are among the many who feel unsafe at home, then I hope you picked up a few useful tips from this episode of *HomeLife*.

조언4:
과학
기술
활용

조언5:
강도
시험해
보기

끝인사

네 번째로, 과학기술을 활용하세요. 영상 카메라, 영상 초인종, 동작 감지 조명은 가장 대담한 범죄자들조차도 다시 생각하게 만들 것입니다. ⁵⁰제가 성장할 때는, 이런 종류의 기술적인 지원이 없었습니다! 운이 좋다면 몇몇 친절한 이웃들이 감시를 도와줄 것입니다. 그러나 지금은 의심스러운 행동을 녹화하여 바로 여러분의 휴대전화로 전송하는 "스마트" 집 보안 시스템이 있습니다. 이런 종류의 24시간 감시는 매년 더 흔해지고 가격도 저렴해지고 있습니다.

마지막으로, ⁵¹집의 보안을 시험하기 위해 강도 시험을 진행하세요. 강도 시험은 보안 장치의 효과성을 시험하기 위해 당신이나 당신이 믿는 누군가가 당신의 집에 침입하려고 시도하는 모의실험입니다. 지금, 많은 분이 이 단계가 정말로 필요한지 제게 물어보셨습니다. 음, 제 경험으로 말씀드리자면, ⁵¹시험을 해보지 않으면 장치가 얼마나 효과적인지 진정으로 알 수 없습니다.

⁵²이러한 예방 조치를 취한 이후에, 저는 밤에 훨씬 잠을 잘 잘 수 있게 되었습니다. 제 생각에, 집에서 안전하고 편안하게 느끼는 것보다 더 좋은 것은 없습니다. 만약 여러분이 집에서 안전하지 않다고 느끼는 많은 분 중 한 분이라면, 이번 *HomeLife* 에피소드에서 몇 가지 유용한 조언을 얻으셨기를 바랍니다.

어휘 | crime-ridden 범죄에 시달리는 secure[sikjúər] 안전한 gated[géitid] 외부인 출입을 통제하는 residence[rézədəns] 주택, 거주지 struggle[strʌ́gl] 싸우다 crime[kraim] 범죄 challenge[tʃǽlindʒ] 문제, 도전 occupied[ákjupaid] 사람이 살고 있는, 사용(되는) 중인 impression[impréʃən] 인상, 생각 intruder[intrú:dər] 침입자, 강도 detect[ditékt] 감지하다, 발견하다 discourage from ~을 단념하게 하다 strengthen[stréŋθən] 더 튼튼하게 하다, 강화하다 entry point 입구 solid[sálid] 견고한, 튼튼한 burglar[bə́:rglər] 빈집 털이, 강도 deter[ditə́:r] 저지하다, 단념시키다 unwanted[ʌnwántid] 원치 않는, 반갑지 않은 pry open 비집어 열다 valuable[vǽljuəbl] 귀중품; 값비싼 obvious[ábviəs] 잘 보이는, 명백한 nightstand[náitstænd] 침실용 탁자 valuable item 귀중품 steal[sti:l] 훔치다; 절도 statistics[stətístiks] 통계 (자료) stick around 머무르다 take advantage of ~을 활용하다 bold[bould] 대담한, 용감한 criminal[kríminl] 범죄자, 범인 keep an eye on ~을 감시하다 suspicious[səspíʃəs] 의심스러운, 수상한 round-the-clock 24시간 계속의 surveillance[sərvéiləns] 감시 trial[tráiəl] 시험, 실험 simulation[sìmjuléiʃən] 모의실험 break into 침입하다 effectiveness[iféktivnis] 효과성, 유효성 set-up[sétʌp] 장치 precaution[prikɔ́:ʃən] 예방 조치

---

46 **주제/목적** 담화의 주제   난이도 ●●○

What is the talk all about?

(a) how to make a home more comfortable
(b) how to strengthen one's home security
(c) how to avoid dangerous areas when traveling
(d) how to protect a community from crime

담화의 주제는 무엇인가?

(a) 집을 좀 더 편안하게 만드는 방법
(b) 집 보안을 강화하는 방법
(c) 여행할 때 위험한 지역을 피하는 방법
(d) 범죄로부터 지역사회를 보호하는 방법

← ○ 정답 잡는 치트키

담화의 주제를 언급하는 초반을 주의 깊게 듣고 전체 맥락을 파악한다.

해설 | 화자가 'We all wish we could live in a secure apartment community or a gated residence, but the reality is that most of the world has to struggle with crime. Today's talk is meant ~ to help keep you and your family safe if you ever end up facing some of the same challenges.'라며 우리 모두는 안전한 아파트 단지나 외부인 출입을 통제하는 주택에 살고 싶지만, 현실은 전 세계 대부분이 범죄와 싸워야 하는데, 오늘의 강연은 자신과 가족이 유사한 문제에 직면했을 때 안전하게 유지하는 데 도움을 주기 위한 것이라고 한 뒤, 담화 전반에 걸쳐 집 보안을 강화하는 방법에 관한 내용이 이어지고 있다. 따라서 (b)가 정답이다.

오답분석

(a) 화자가 집에서 편안하게 느끼는 것이 중요하다고는 언급하였지만, 이는 집 보안을 강화했을 때 나타나는 결과로 언급된 것이므로 오답이다.

---

47 특정세부사항   How   난이도 ●○○

According to the talk, how can residents make sure that a house looks occupied?

(a) They can keep curtains closed.
(b) They can ask someone to stay over.
(c) They can leave electronics on.
(d) They can leave a car in the driveway.

담화에 따르면, 거주자들은 어떻게 집에 사람이 사는 것처럼 보이도록 확실히 할 수 있는가?

(a) 커튼을 닫아 놓을 수 있다.
(b) 누군가에게 자고 가도록 부탁할 수 있다.
(c) 전자 기기를 켜둘 수 있다.
(d) 진입로에 차를 주차해 둘 수 있다.

━○ 정답 잡는 치트키

질문의 키워드 occupied가 그대로 언급된 주변 내용을 주의 깊게 듣는다.

해설 | 화자가 'keep your house occupied'라며 집을 사람이 살고 있는 상태로 유지하라고 한 뒤, 'When you need to go somewhere, you can make your house look occupied by keeping the television and a few lights turned on.'이라며 어딘가에 가야 할 때는 텔레비전과 몇 개의 조명을 켜둠으로써 집에 사람이 있는 것처럼 보이게 할 수 있다고 했다. 따라서 (c)가 정답이다.

⇄ **Paraphrasing**
keeping the television and a few lights turned on 텔레비전과 몇 개의 조명을 켜둠 → leave electronics on 전자 기기를 켜두다

어휘 | stay over (남의 집에서 하룻밤) 자고 가다   driveway[dráivwei] 진입로, 차도

---

48 특정세부사항   Why   난이도 ●●○

Why did the speaker's family decide to invest in high-quality products?

(a) to take advantage of a sale
(b) to replace the original windows
(c) to prevent another break-in
(d) to give the illusion of protection

화자의 가족은 왜 고품질 제품에 투자하기로 결정했는가?

(a) 할인을 활용하기 위해서
(b) 원래의 창문을 교체하기 위해서
(c) 또 다른 침입을 막기 위해서
(d) 보호받는 듯한 착각을 주기 위해서

━○ 정답 잡는 치트키

질문의 키워드 invest in high-quality products가 그대로 언급된 주변 내용을 주의 깊게 듣는다.

해설 | 화자가 'a burglar simply pried open my front door. After that, my family decided to invest in high-quality products.'라며 빈집 털이가 현관문을 간단히 비집어 열었고, 그 후 가족은 고품질 제품에 투자하기로 결정했다고 했다. 따라서 (c)가 정답이다.

어휘 | break-in (불법) 침입 illusion[ilúːʒən] 착각, 환상

---

49 **특정세부사항**   **How**   난이도 ●●○

How did the speaker hide his valuable items?   화자는 어떻게 귀중품들을 숨겼는가?

(a) by putting them inside clothing   **(a) 옷 안에 넣음으로써**
(b) by keeping them in a desk   (b) 책상에 보관함으로써
(c) by placing them in a nightstand   (c) 침실용 탁자에 놓음으로써
(d) by tucking them under the bed   (d) 침대 밑에 숨겨둠으로써

←○ 정답 잡는 치트키

질문의 키워드 valuable items가 valuables로 paraphrasing되어 언급된 주변 내용을 주의 깊게 듣는다.

해설 | 화자가 'I always kept my valuables hidden deep in the pockets of an old winter coat, which I hung in the back of the closet.'이라며 항상 귀중품들을 옷장 뒤쪽에 걸어둔 낡은 겨울 코트 주머니 깊숙한 곳에 숨겨두었다고 했다. 따라서 (a)가 정답이다.

↻ **Paraphrasing**

an old winter coat 낡은 겨울 코트 → clothing 옷

어휘 | tuck[tʌk] ~을 숨기다, 쑤셔 넣다

---

50 **추론**   **특정사실**   난이도 ●●●

What sort of home surveillance did the speaker probably   화자가 성장하는 동안 어떤 종류의 집 감시 시스템이
have while growing up?   있었을 것 같은가?

(a) police working around the clock   (a) 24시간 내내 근무하는 경찰
(b) people living in the same area   **(b) 같은 지역에 사는 사람들**
(c) a smart home security system   (c) 스마트 집 보안 시스템
(d) motion-activated lights   (d) 동작 감지 조명

←○ 정답 잡는 치트키

질문의 키워드 growing up이 그대로 언급되고, surveillance가 keep an eye on things로 paraphrasing되어 언급된 주변 내용을 주의 깊게 듣는다.

해설 | 화자가 'When I was growing up, we didn't have ~ technological assistance! If we were lucky, some friendly neighbors would help keep an eye on things.'라며 자기가 성장할 때는 기술적인 지원이 없었고, 운이 좋다면 몇몇 친절한 이웃들이 감시를 도와줄 것이라고 한 것을 통해, 화자가 성장하는 동안 같은 지역에 사는 사람들이 집 감시 시스템의 역할을 했음을 추론할 수 있다. 따라서 (b)가 정답이다.

↻ **Paraphrasing**

neighbors 이웃들 → people living in the same area 같은 지역에 사는 사람들

어휘 | around the clock 24시간 내내, 밤낮으로 쉬지 않고

51

특정세부사항   Why   난이도 ●●○

According to the talk, why is a burglary trial necessary?	담화에 따르면, 강도 시험은 왜 필요한가?
(a) to test how well the set-up performs	**(a) 장치가 잘 작동하는지 시험하기 위해서**
(b) to experience how scary a break-in is	(b) 침입이 얼마나 무서운지 경험해 보기 위해서
(c) to see which products will work best	(c) 어떤 제품들이 가장 잘 작동할지 알아보기 위해서
(d) to show others that the home is protected	(d) 다른 사람들에게 집이 보호되고 있음을 보여주기 위해서

🔑 정답 잡는 치트키

질문의 키워드 burglary trial이 그대로 언급된 주변 내용을 주의 깊게 듣는다.

해설 | 화자가 'hold a burglary trial to test the security of your house'라며 집의 보안을 시험하기 위해 강도 시험을 진행하라고 한 뒤, 'You'll never truly know how effective your set-up is unless it has been tested'라며 시험을 해보지 않으면 장치가 얼마나 효과적인지 진정으로 알 수 없다고 했다. 따라서 (a)가 정답이다.

어휘 | scary[skéri] 무서운, 두려운

52

특정세부사항   What   난이도 ●●○

What has the speaker been able to do since taking extra precautions at home?	화자가 집에서 추가적인 예방 조치를 취한 이후에 할 수 있는 것은 무엇인가?
(a) feel safe going outside	(a) 밖에 나가서도 안심한다
(b) leave the house at night	(b) 밤에 집을 나선다
(c) go away for a few days	(c) 며칠간 떠나 있다
(d) rest with more ease	**(d) 더욱 편하게 쉰다**

🔑 정답 잡는 치트키

질문의 키워드 precautions가 그대로 언급된 주변 내용을 주의 깊게 듣는다.

해설 | 화자가 'Ever since taking these precautions, I've been able to sleep much better at night.'이라며 이러한 예방 조치를 취한 이후에, 밤에 훨씬 잠을 잘 잘 수 있게 되었다고 했다. 따라서 (d)가 정답이다.

     ↪ Paraphrasing
sleep much better 훨씬 잠을 잘 자다 → rest with more ease 더욱 편하게 쉬다

어휘 | go away 떠나다, 가버리다   with ease 편하게

READING & VOCABULARY

PART 1 (53~59) 인물의 일대기 조현실수의 화가로 유명한 르네 마그리트

인물 이름

RENÉ MAGRITTE

소개 + 유명한 이유

[53]René Magritte was a Belgian artist in the twentieth century. **He was a prominent figure of the Surrealism art movement, which included works depicting dreamlike, irrational imagery.** [53/56]Magritte often painted everyday objects in unsettling situations to make viewers question their understanding of reality, such as in his most famous work *The Treachery of Images*, which features an image of a tobacco pipe and the caption "This is not a pipe."

어린 시절 + 업적 시작 계기

René François Ghislain Magritte was born on November 21, 1898. [54]His mother died when he was thirteen, so he started drawing and painting to cope with the loss, an endeavor encouraged by his father. His works during this time were mostly abstract, but he began to experiment with different styles after enrolling in art school at age eighteen.

초기 활동

Later, Magritte found work as a poster and advertisement designer but carried on painting in his spare time. [55]One day, he was shown a book containing a picture of the collage-like painting *The Song of Love* by early surrealist Giorgio de Chirico. Moved to tears by being able to "see thought" portrayed on canvas, Magritte [58]began to incorporate aspects of the surrealist art style into his own work.

주요 작품

Magritte held his first art exhibition at a Brussels gallery in 1927 to lukewarm critical reception. Dismayed by his exhibition's lack of success, he moved to Paris a year later, where he continued to develop his art style and befriended popular surrealist painters. During this time, Magritte produced some of his most notable surrealist pieces, including *The Treachery of Images*. [56]The painting's [59]seemingly contradictory caption is meant to remind viewers that the painting is not actually a real pipe but simply an image of a pipe. These thought-provoking words and their connection to visual imagery would be a recurring theme in Magritte's future works.

전성기

Despite gaining some popularity in Paris, [57]Magritte's exhibits were still unprofitable. He moved back to Brussels in 1930 to run an ad agency with his brother, during which time he created very little art. However, his

르네 마그리트

[53]르네 마그리트는 20세기의 벨기에 예술가였다. 그는 몽롱하고 비이성적인 이미지를 묘사한 작품들을 포함한 초현실주의 예술 운동의 중요한 인물이었다. [53/56]마그리트는 담배 파이프의 이미지와 "이것은 파이프가 아니다"라는 캡션이 있는 가장 유명한 작품인 *이미지의 배반*에서와 같이, 일상적인 사물을 불안하게 만드는 상황에 부닥치게 하여 보는 사람들이 현실에 대한 이해에 의문을 품게 하는 그림을 자주 그렸다.

르네 프랑수아 길랭 마그리트는 1898년 11월 21일에 태어났다. [54]그의 어머니는 그가 13살일 때 사망했고, 그는 아버지의 권유로 상실을 극복하기 위해 그림 그리기를 시작했다. 이 시기 동안의 그의 작품들은 대부분 추상적이었지만, 그는 18세 때 미술 학교에 입학한 후에 다양한 스타일을 실험하기 시작했다.

이후, 마그리트는 포스터와 광고 디자이너의 일을 구했지만 여가 시간에는 그림을 계속 그렸다. [55]그러던 어느 날, 그는 초기 초현실주의자인 조르조 데 키리코의 콜라주 같은 그림인 *사랑의 노래* 사진이 담긴 책을 보게 되었다. 캔버스에 그려진 "생각을 보는 것"을 할 수 있어서 눈물을 흘린, 마그리트는 [58]초현실주의 화풍의 측면들을 그의 작품에 혼합하기 시작했다.

마그리트는 1927년 브뤼셀 미술관에서 그의 첫 번째 미술 전시회를 열었고 미지근한 비판적인 반응을 얻었다. 전시회가 성공하지 못한 것에 실망하여, 그는 1년 후 파리로 떠났고, 그곳에서 계속해서 자신의 화풍을 발전시켰고 인기 있는 초현실주의 화가들과 친구가 되었다. 이 시기 동안, 마그리트는 *이미지의 배반*을 포함하여, 그의 가장 주목할 만한 초현실주의 작품 중 일부를 제작했다. [56]그 그림의 [59]겉보기에 모순되는 캡션은 보는 사람들에게 그 그림이 실제로 진짜 파이프가 아니라 단지 파이프의 이미지라는 것을 상기시켜 주기 위한 것이다. 이러한 생각하게 하는 단어들과 시각적 이미지의 연결은 마그리트의 향후 작품들에서 반복되어 발생하는 주제가 된다.

파리에서 어느 정도 인기를 얻었음에도 불구하고, [57]마그리트의 전시는 여전히 수익을 못 냈다. 그는 1930년에 그의 형과 함께 광고 대행사를 운영하기 위해 브뤼셀로 돌아왔고, 그 동안 거의 작품을 제작하지

paintings eventually started selling well enough for him to return to focusing on his own artwork full-time.

Magritte enjoyed significant recognition for his surrealist works until he passed away in 1967. His signature style influenced several art movements in the decades that followed, including pop and conceptual art, and his works are still featured in major exhibits today.

죽음
+
후기
업적

않았다. 그러나, 그의 그림들은 마침내 그가 자기 작품에 전념할 수 있을 만큼 잘 팔리기 시작했다.

마그리트는 1967년에 사망하기 전까지 초현실주의 작품들로 상당한 인정을 받았다. 그의 대표적인 스타일은 팝과 개념 예술을 포함하여 그 이후 수십 년간 여러 미술 운동에 영향을 미쳤고, 그의 작품들은 오늘날에도 여전히 주요 전시회에 전시되어 있다.

어휘 | **prominent** adj. 중요한, 유명한 **figure** n. 인물 **Surrealism** n. 초현실주의(20세기에 일어난 문예·예술 운동) **depict** v. 묘사하다, 그리다
dreamlike adj. 몽롱한, 꿈과 같은 **irrational** adj. 비이성적인 **unsettling** adj. 불안하게 만드는 **reality** n. 현실
tobacco pipe phr. 담배 파이프 **caption** n. 캡션(사진·삽화 등에 붙인 설명) **cope with** phr. ~을 극복하다, ~에 대처하다 **loss** n. 상실
endeavor n. 노력, 시도, 애씀 **abstract** adj. 추상적인, 심오한 **enroll** v. 입학시키다, 등록하다 **carry on** phr. ~을 계속하다
spare time phr. 여가 시간 **collage** n. 콜라주(색종이나 사진 등의 조각들을 붙여 그림을 만드는 미술 기법) **surrealist** n. 초현실주의자
portray v. 그리다, 묘사하다 **aspect** n. 측면, 양상 **lukewarm** adj. 미지근한 **reception** n. 반응, 평판 **dismay** v. 실망시키다
befriend v. 친구가 되어주다 **seemingly** adv. 겉보기에는 **remind** v. 상기시키다, 생각나게 하다
thought-provoking adj. 생각하게 하는, 시사하는 바가 많은 **recurring** adj. 반복되어 발생하는, 순환하는 **unprofitable** adj. 수익을 못 내는
recognition n. 인정, 인식 **pass away** phr. 사망하다 **conceptual art** phr. 개념 예술(예술 작품이 구현하는 개념·사상을 가장 중요하게 보는 예술)

---

53 특정세부사항   Who

난이도 ●●○

Who was René Magritte?

(a) a highly controversial artist
(b) a founder of a new art movement
(c) a creator of realistic portraits
(d) a painter of puzzling artwork

르네 마그리트는 누구였는가?

(a) 대단히 논란의 소지가 큰 화가
(b) 새로운 예술 운동의 창시자
(c) 사실적 초상화의 창작자
(d) 당혹스러운 예술작품의 화가

⟶○ 정답 잡는 치트키

인물에 관해 소개하는 지문의 초반을 주의 깊게 읽는다.

해설 | 1단락의 'René Magritte was a Belgian artist in the twentieth century.'에서 르네 마그리트는 20세기의 벨기에 예술가였다고 한 뒤, 'Magritte often painted everyday objects in unsettling situations to make viewers question their understanding of reality'에서 마그리트는 일상적인 사물을 불안하게 만드는 상황에 부닥치게 하여 보는 사람들이 현실에 대한 이해에 의문을 품게 하는 그림을 자주 그렸다고 했다. 따라서 (d)가 정답이다.

⇄ Paraphrasing
artist 예술가 → a painter 화가

어휘 | **highly controversial** phr. 대단히 논란의 소지가 큰 **portrait** n. 초상화 **puzzling** adj. 당혹스러운, 당황하게 하는

---

54 특정세부사항   Why

난이도 ●●○

Why did Magritte start painting?

(a) He wanted to take a break from schoolwork.
(b) His father encouraged him to explore his creativity.

마그리트는 왜 그림을 그리기 시작했는가?

(a) 그는 학업으로부터 쉬고 싶어 했다.
(b) 그의 아버지는 그에게 창의성을 탐구하도록 권했다.

(c) He needed to find a way to overcome his grief.

(d) His mother wanted him to try a new hobby.

(c) 그는 슬픔을 극복할 방법을 찾아야 했다.

(d) 그의 어머니는 그가 새로운 취미를 시도하기를 원했다.

○ 정답 잡는 치트키

질문의 키워드 start painting이 그대로 언급된 주변 내용을 주의 깊게 읽는다.

해설 | 2단락의 'His mother died when he was thirteen, so he started drawing and painting to cope with the loss, an endeavor encouraged by his father.'에서 마그리트의 어머니는 그가 13살일 때 사망했고, 그는 아버지의 권유로 상실을 극복하기 위해 그림 그리기를 시작했다고 했다. 따라서 (c)가 정답이다.

⇄ Paraphrasing
cope with the loss 상실을 극복하다 → overcome ~ grief 슬픔을 극복하다

어휘 | schoolwork n. 학업, 학교 공부 explore v. 탐구하다, 탐색하다 creativity n. 창의성, 독창력 overcome v. 극복하다 grief n. 슬픔

---

55 특정세부사항   What   난이도 ●●○

What inspired Magritte to make surrealist art?

(a) a work that presented ideas in a visual way
(b) a criticism of the style of his earlier works
(c) a painting done by one of his artist friends
(d) an art show that he saw while traveling

마그리트가 초현실주의 작품을 만들도록 영감을 준 것은 무엇이었는가?

(a) 아이디어를 시각화하여 표현한 작품
(b) 그의 초기 작품 스타일에 대한 비평
(c) 그의 화가 친구들에 의해 그려진 그림
(d) 여행 중에 봤던 미술 전시회

○ 정답 잡는 치트키

질문의 키워드 surrealist art가 그대로 언급된 주변 내용을 주의 깊게 읽는다.

해설 | 3단락의 'One day, he was shown a book containing a picture of the collage-like painting *The Song of Love* by early surrealist Giorgio de Chirico. Moved to tears by being able to "see thought" portrayed on canvas, Magritte began to incorporate aspects of the surrealist art style into his own work.'에서 그러던 어느 날, 마그리트는 초기 초현실주의자인 조르조 데 키리코의 콜라주 같은 그림인 *사랑의 노래* 사진이 담긴 책을 보게 되었고, 캔버스에 그려진 "생각을 보는 것"을 할 수 있어서 눈물을 흘리던 마그리트는 초현실주의 화풍의 측면들을 그의 작품에 혼합하기 시작했다고 했다. 따라서 (a)가 정답이나.

---

56 특정세부사항   How   난이도 ●●●

How did *The Treachery of Images* reflect Magritte's overall art style?

(a) by showcasing an inventive painting technique
(b) by displaying a motivational saying above the image
(c) by challenging the viewer's assumptions about the image
(d) by inviting the viewer to question the value of certain objects

*이미지의 배반*은 어떻게 마그리트의 전반적인 화풍을 반영했는가?

(a) 독창적인 그림 기법을 선보임으로써
(b) 이미지 위에 동기를 주는 문구를 표시함으로써
(c) 이미지에 대한 보는 사람의 가정에 이의를 제기함으로써
(d) 보는 사람에게 특정 사물의 가치에 대해 의문을 품도록 유도함으로써

질문의 키워드 *The Treachery of Images*가 그대로 언급된 주변 내용을 주의 깊게 읽는다.

해설 | 1단락의 'Magritte often painted everyday objects in unsettling situations to make viewers question their understanding of reality, such as in his most famous work *The Treachery of Images*'에서 마그리트는 가장 유명한 작품인 *이미지의 배반*에서와 같이, 일상적인 사물을 불안하게 만드는 상황에 부닥치게 하여 보는 사람들이 현실에 대한 이해에 의문을 품게 하는 그림을 자주 그렸다고 한 뒤, 4단락의 'The painting's seemingly contradictory caption is meant to remind viewers that the painting is not actually a real pipe but simply an image of a pipe. These thought-provoking words and their connection to visual imagery would be a recurring theme in Magritte's future works.'에서 *이미지의 배반*의 겉보기에 모순되는 캡션은 보는 사람들에게 그 그림이 실제로 진짜 파이프가 아니라 단지 파이프의 이미지라는 것을 상기시켜 주기 위한 것이고, 이러한 생각하게 하는 단어들과 시각적 이미지의 연결은 마그리트의 향후 작품들에서 반복되어 발생하는 주제가 된다고 했다. 따라서 (c)가 정답이다.

오답분석

(d) 1단락에서 마그리트는 일상적인 사물을 불안하게 만드는 상황에 부닥치게 하여 보는 사람들이 현실에 대한 이해에 의문을 품게 하는 그림을 자주 그렸다고는 했지만, 특정 사물이 가치가 있는지에 의문을 품도록 유도한 것은 아니므로 오답이다.

어휘 | motivational adj. 동기를 주는 challenge v. 이의를 제기하다, 도전하다 assumption n. 가정 value n. 가치

---

57 추론 특정사실 난이도 ●●◯

Why, most likely, did Magritte help run an ad agency?	마그리트는 왜 광고 대행사 운영을 도왔을 것 같은가?
(a) to gain recognition in a different field	(a) 다른 분야에서 인정받기 위해서
(b) to give himself a break from producing art	(b) 예술 작품 제작에서 벗어나 자신에게 휴식을 주기 위해서
(c) to help his brother's business turn a profit	(c) 형의 사업이 이익을 내도록 돕기 위해서
(d) to earn more of an income for himself	**(d) 혼자 힘으로 더 많은 수입을 얻기 위해서**

질문의 키워드 run an ad agency가 그대로 언급된 주변 내용을 주의 깊게 읽는다.

해설 | 5단락의 'Magritte's exhibits were still unprofitable. He moved back to Brussels in 1930 to run an ad agency with his brother'에서 마그리트의 전시는 여전히 수익을 못 냈고, 그는 1930년에 그의 형과 함께 광고 대행사를 운영하기 위해 브뤼셀로 돌아왔다고 한 것을 통해, 마그리트는 전시로 수익을 못 내자 혼자 힘으로 더 많은 수입을 얻기 위해 광고 대행사 운영을 도왔음을 추론할 수 있다. 따라서 (d)가 정답이다.

어휘 | field n. 분야 turn a profit phr. 이익을 내다 income n. 수입 for oneself phr. 혼자 힘으로

---

58 어휘 유의어 난이도 ●●◯

In the context of the passage, incorporate means _____.	지문의 문맥에서, 'incorporate'는 -을 의미한다.
(a) adjust	(a) 조정하다
(b) follow	(b) 따르다
(c) organize	(c) 체계화하다
(d) mix	**(d) 혼합하다**

밑줄 친 어휘의 유의어를 찾는 문제이므로, incorporate가 포함된 구절을 읽고 문맥을 파악한다.

해설 | 3단락의 'began to incorporate aspects of the surrealist art style into his own work'는 초현실주의 화풍의 측면들을 작품에 혼합하기 시작했다는 뜻이므로, incorporate가 '혼합하다'라는 의미로 사용된 것을 알 수 있다. 따라서 '혼합하다'라는 같은 의미이 (d) mix 가 정답이다.

59 어휘 유의어 난이도 ●●○

In the context of the passage, <u>contradictory</u> means _____.

(a) convenient
(b) conflicting
(c) uncertain
(d) meaningless

지문의 문맥에서, 'contradictory'는 -을 의미한다.

(a) 편리한
(b) 모순되는
(c) 불확실한
(d) 무의미한

밑줄 친 어휘의 유의어를 찾는 문제이므로, contradictory가 포함된 구절을 읽고 문맥을 파악한다.

해설 | 4단락의 'seemingly contradictory caption'은 겉보기에 모순되는 캡션이라는 뜻이므로, contradictory가 '모순되는'이라는 의미로 사용된 것을 알 수 있다. 따라서 '모순되는'이라는 같은 의미의 (b) conflicting이 정답이다.

PART 2 [60~66] 잡지 기사 다치지 않은 팔을 운동하는 것이 다친 팔에 미치는 영향

연구 결과	[60]**HOW AN INJURED ARM CAN BE STRENGTHENED BY EXERCISING THE ARM ON THE OTHER SIDE**	[60]어떻게 다친 팔이 다른 쪽 팔을 운동시킴으로써 강화될 수 있는가
연구 소개	[60]A recent study has shown that if one arm is injured, exercising the uninjured arm can significantly strengthen its weaker counterpart. This can be explained by "mirror activity," a previously established phenomenon in which moving one limb will cause the muscles in the opposite limb to activate.	[60]최근의 한 연구는 만약 한쪽 팔을 다치면, 다치지 않은 팔을 운동하는 것이 더 약한 팔을 상당히 강화할 수 있다는 것을 보여주었다. 이것은 한쪽 팔을 움직이는 것이 반대쪽 팔의 근육을 활성화하게 한다는 이전에 확립된 현상인 "거울 활동"에 의해 설명될 수 있다.
가설	[61/65]The <u>collaborative</u> study was conducted by researchers in Chile, France, and Australia, who wanted to test whether mirror activity could be effective in preventing loss of muscle tissue. A broken or injured limb often needs to be immobilized in a cast for several weeks until it is ready for rehabilitative exercise. However, the lack of physical activity causes the muscles to shrink. [61]Researchers hypothesized that exercising the uninjured arm might be able to prevent muscle loss in the injured arm, even if it is still in a cast.	[61/65]이 공동의 연구는 거울 활동이 근육 조직의 손실을 예방하는 데 효과적일 수 있는지를 실험하기를 원했던 칠레, 프랑스, 호주의 연구자들에 의해 수행되었다. 부러지거나 다친 팔은 종종 재활 운동을 할 준비가 될 때까지 몇 주 동안 깁스를 하고 움직이지 못하게 되어야 한다. 그러나, 신체적 활동의 부족은 근육을 수축하게 만든다. [61]연구자들은 다치지 않은 팔을 운동하면 깁스를 한 상태에서도 다친 팔의 근육 손실을 예방할 수 있을 것이라는 가설을 세웠다.

For the experiment, thirty participants were asked to wear a sling on one arm, keeping it immobilized for eight hours a day for a month. Ten participants did not exercise either arm, while the remaining participants used [66]their unrestricted arm to lift weights.

실험을 위해, 30명의 참가자에게 한 팔에 팔걸이 붕대를 착용하도록 하고, 한 달간 하루에 여덟 시간씩 팔을 움직이지 못하게 했다. 10명의 참가자는 양쪽 팔을 운동하지 않았고, 나머지 참가자들은 [66]자유로운 팔을 사용하여 역기를 들어 올렸다.

As expected, participants who exercised only experienced around two percent muscle loss in the immobilized arm, while the others experienced nearly twenty-eight percent muscle loss. Moreover, [62]muscle strength in the injured arm actually increased for the participants who exercised, proving that mirror activity can not only successfully prevent muscle loss, but also tone and strengthen muscles in immobilized arms.

예상대로, 다른 참가자들이 거의 28%의 근육 손실을 경험했지만, 운동한 참가자들은 움직이지 않은 팔에서 약 2%의 근육 손실만을 경험했다. 게다가, [62]운동을 한 참가자들의 경우 다친 팔의 근력이 실제로 증가하여, 거울 활동이 성공적으로 근육 손실을 예방할 수 있을 뿐만 아니라, 움직이지 않은 팔에서 근육을 탄탄하게 만들고 강화할 수 있다는 것도 증명했다.

[63]Scientists have long debated how mirror activity works. One theory is that if one side of the body is experiencing physical exertion, the brain will automatically activate the corresponding muscles on the opposite side of the body. The effect is unnoticeable to the naked eye, but the triggered muscles will give off slight electric signals.

[63]과학자들은 거울 활동이 어떻게 작동하는지에 대해 오랫동안 논쟁을 벌여왔다. 한 가지 이론은 신체의 한쪽이 격렬한 신체 활동을 경험하면, 뇌가 자동으로 신체의 반대쪽에 있는 해당 근육을 활성화한다는 것이다. 이 효과는 맨눈으로는 눈에 띄지 않지만, 작동된 근육은 약간의 전기 신호를 방출할 것이다.

[64]The study's results can be used to improve rehabilitation methods. Being able to keep an injured arm strong while it is still in a cast will lessen time spent on rebuilding shrunken muscles later. In the future, researchers hope to study methods that will improve not just muscle strength but also movement and fine muscle control.

[64]이 연구의 결과는 재활 방법을 개선하는 데 사용될 수 있다. 다친 팔을 깁스한 상태에서 강하게 유지할 수 있게 되면 나중에 줄어든 근육을 회복하는 데 드는 시간을 줄일 것이다. 향후에, 연구자들은 근력뿐만 아니라 움직임과 미세한 근육 조절을 개선할 방법을 연구하기를 희망한다.

어휘 | strengthen v. 강화하다, 더 튼튼하게 하다 counterpart n. (한 쌍의) 한쪽, 상대 phenomenon n. 현상 limb n. 팔, 다리
activate v. 활성화하다, 작동시키다 loss n. 손실, 상실 muscle tissue phr. 근육 조직 immobilize v. 움직이지 못하게 하다, 고정시키다
cast n. 깁스(붕대) rehabilitative exercise phr. 재활 운동 shrink v. 수축하다, 줄다 hypothesize v. 가설을 세우다
sling n. (부러진 팔을 고정하는) 팔걸이 붕대 lift v. 들어 올리다 weight n. 역기 muscle strength phr. 근력
tone v. (근육·피부를) 탄탄하게 만들다 debate v. 논쟁을 벌이다; n. 논쟁, 논란 theory n. 이론 physical exertion phr. 격렬한 신체 활동
automatically adv. 자동으로 corresponding adj. (~에) 해당하는 unnoticeable adj. 눈에 띄지 않는 naked eye phr. 맨눈, 육안
trigger v. 작동시키다, 촉발시키다 electric signal phr. 전기 신호 rebuild v. 회복하다 fine adj. 미세한 muscle control phr. 근육 조절

---

60 주제/목적   기사의 주제   난이도 ●●○

What is the article all about?

(a) a way to prevent serious arm injuries
(b) a way to avoid rehabilitation for an injury
(c) a way to reduce the amount of pain from an injury
(d) **a way to improve the healing process for an injury**

기사의 주제는 무엇인가?

(a) 심각한 팔 부상을 방지하는 방법
(b) 부상에 대한 재활 치료를 피하는 방법
(c) 부상으로 인한 통증의 양을 줄이는 방법
(d) **부상의 치유 과정을 개선하는 방법**

▶○ 정답 잡는 치트키

제목과 지문의 초반을 주의 깊게 읽고 전체 맥락을 파악한다.

해설 | 기사의 제목 'How An Injured Arm Can Be Strengthened By Exercising The Arm On The Other Side'에서 어떻게 다친 팔이 다른 쪽 팔을 운동시킴으로써 강화될 수 있는가를 언급하였다. 그다음에, 1단락의 'A recent study has shown that if one arm is injured, exercising the uninjured arm can significantly strengthen its weaker counterpart.'에서 최근의 한 연구는 만약 한 쪽 팔을 다치면 다치지 않은 팔을 운동하는 것이 더 약한 팔을 상당히 강화할 수 있다는 것을 보여주었다고 한 뒤, 이것이 부상의 치유 과정을 개선하는 방법으로 활용될 수 있음을 설명하는 내용이 이어지고 있다. 따라서 (d)가 정답이다.

어휘 | healing process phr. 치유 과정

61 특정세부사항   Why   난이도 ●●○

Why did researchers carry out the study?

(a) to see if the amount of post-injury muscle loss would decrease
(b) to investigate the psychological effects of having an injury
(c) to explore ways to safely exercise an injured limb
(d) to test the strength of a limb that has been repeatedly injured

연구자들은 왜 연구를 수행했는가?

(a) 부상 후 근육 손실의 양이 감소하는지 확인하기 위해서
(b) 부상을 입는 것의 심리적 영향을 조사하기 위해서
(c) 다친 팔을 안전하게 운동하는 방법을 모색하기 위해서
(d) 반복적으로 다친 팔의 힘을 시험하기 위해서

━○ 정답 잡는 치트키

질문의 키워드 carry out the study가 study was conducted로 paraphrasing되어 언급된 주변 내용을 주의 깊게 읽는다.

해설 | 2단락의 'The collaborative study was conducted by researchers ~, who wanted to test whether mirror activity could be effective in preventing loss of muscle tissue.'에서 이 공동의 연구는 거울 활동이 근육 조직의 손실을 예방하는 데 효과적일 수 있는지를 실험하기를 원했던 연구자들에 의해 수행되었다고 한 뒤, 'Researchers hypothesized that exercising the uninjured arm might be able to prevent muscle loss in the injured arm, even if it is still in a cast.'에서 연구자들은 다치지 않은 팔을 운동하면 깁스를 한 상태에서도 다친 팔의 근육 손실을 예방할 수 있을 것이라는 가설을 세웠다고 했다. 따라서 (a)가 정답이다.

어휘 | investigate v. 조사하다 psychological adj. 심리적인, 정신의 repeatedly adv. 반복적으로

62 특정세부사항   What   난이도 ●●○

What happened to the participants who exercised in the experiment?

(a) They maintained the same level of strength in both of their arms.
(b) They increased strength in their injured arm.
(c) They experienced a faster healing time for their injured arm.
(d) They gained flexibility in both of their arms.

실험에서 운동한 참가자들에게 무슨 일이 있었는가?

(a) 양팔에 같은 수준의 힘을 유지했다.
(b) 다친 팔에 힘이 강화됐다.
(c) 다친 팔의 치유 시간이 더 빨라지는 것을 경험했다.
(d) 양팔에 유연성을 갖게 되었다.

━○ 정답 잡는 치트키

질문의 키워드 participants who exercised가 그대로 언급된 주변 내용을 주의 깊게 읽는다.

해설 | 4단락의 'muscle strength in the injured arm actually increased for the participants who exercised'에서 운동을 한 참가자들의 경우 다친 팔의 근력이 실제로 증가하였다고 했다. 따라서 (b)가 정답이다.

오답분석
(c) 6단락에서 다친 팔을 깁스한 상태에서 강하게 유지할 수 있게 되면 나중에 줄어든 근육을 회복하는 데 드는 시간을 줄일 것이라고는 했지만, 실제 실험에서 결과로 드러난 것은 아니므로 오답이다.

어휘 | flexibility n. 유연성, 적응성

---

63 추론 특정사실 　　　　　　　　　　　　　난이도 ●●○

Based on the article, what can be said about how mirror activity works?

(a) that it is not related to brain activity
(b) that it is not fully understood by scientists
(c) that it only affects one side of the body
(d) that it only applies to upper body muscles

기사에 따르면, 거울 활동이 어떻게 작동하는지에 관해 말해질 수 있는 것은 무엇인가?

(a) 뇌 활동과 관련이 없다는 것
(b) 과학자들에 의해 완전히 이해되지 않는다는 것
(c) 몸의 한쪽에만 영향을 준다는 것
(d) 상체 근육에만 적용된다는 것

○━ 정답 잡는 치트키

질문의 키워드 how mirror activity works가 그대로 언급된 주변 내용을 주의 깊게 읽는다.

해설 | 5단락의 'Scientists have long debated how mirror activity works.'에서 과학자들은 거울 활동이 어떻게 작동하는지에 대해 오랫동안 논쟁을 벌여왔다고 한 것을 통해, 거울 활동이 어떻게 작동하는지에 관해 과학자들에 의해 완전히 이해되지 않음을 추론할 수 있다. 따라서 (b)가 정답이다.

어휘 | brain activity phr. 뇌 활동　upper body phr. 상체, 상반신

---

64 특정세부사항 How 　　　　　　　　　　　　　난이도 ●●○

How will this research benefit patients who are recovering from an injury?

(a) It will give them greater control over movement.
(b) It will eliminate the need for them to wear a cast.
(c) It will reduce the duration of their recovery.
(d) It will strengthen them against future injuries.

연구는 부상으로부터 회복 중인 환자들에게 어떻게 도움이 될 것인가?

(a) 움직임을 더 잘 제어할 수 있게 할 것이다.
(b) 깁스할 필요를 없앨 것이다.
(c) 회복 기간을 줄일 것이다.
(d) 향후 부상에 대한 대비를 강화할 것이다.

○━ 정답 잡는 치트키

질문의 키워드 recovering from an injury가 rehabilitation으로 paraphrasing되어 언급된 주변 내용을 주의 깊게 읽는다.

해설 | 6단락의 'The study's results can be used to improve rehabilitation methods. Being able to keep an injured arm strong while it is still in a cast will lessen time spent on rebuilding shrunken muscles later.'에서 이 연구의 결과는 재활 방법을 개선하는 데 사용될 수 있고, 다친 팔을 깁스한 상태에서 강하게 유지할 수 있게 되면 나중에 줄어든 근육을 회복하는 데 드는 시간을 줄일 것이라고 했다. 따라서 (c)가 정답이다.

↻ **Paraphrasing**
lessen time 시간을 줄이다 → reduce the duration 기간을 줄이다

어휘 | control n. 제어, 억제 eliminate v. 없애다, 제거하다 recovery n. 회복

65 어휘 유의어 난이도 ●○○

In the context of the passage, <u>collaborative</u> means _____.

(a) additional
(b) previous
(c) consistent
(d) **cooperative**

지문의 문맥에서, 'collaborative'는 -을 의미한다.

(a) 추가의
(b) 이전의
(c) 일관된
(d) **협동하는**

─○ 정답 잡는 치트키

밑줄 친 어휘의 유의어를 찾는 문제이므로, collaborative가 포함된 구절을 읽고 문맥을 파악한다.

해설 | 2단락의 'The collaborative study'는 공동의 연구라는 뜻이므로, collaborative가 '공동의'라는 의미로 사용된 것을 알 수 있다. 따라서 '협동하는'이라는 비슷한 의미의 (d) cooperative가 정답이다.

66 어휘 유의어 난이도 ●○○

In the context of the passage, <u>unrestricted</u> means _____.

(a) lower
(b) **free**
(c) clear
(d) single

지문의 문맥에서, 'unrestricted'는 -을 의미한다.

(a) 더 아래쪽의
(b) **자유로운**
(c) 분명한
(d) 단 하나의

─○ 정답 잡는 치트키

밑줄 친 어휘의 유의어를 찾는 문제이므로, unrestricted가 포함된 구절을 읽고 문맥을 파악한다.

해설 | 3단락의 'their unrestricted arm'은 자유로운 팔이라는 뜻이므로, unrestricted가 '자유로운'이라는 의미로 사용된 것을 알 수 있다. 따라서 '자유로운'이라는 같은 의미의 (b) free가 정답이다.

PART 3[67~73] 지식 백과 애니메이션 영화 산업을 바꾼 백설 공주와 일곱 난쟁이

| 표제어 | **SNOW WHITE AND THE SEVEN DWARFS** | **백설 공주와 일곱 난쟁이** |

| 정의 | [67]*Snow White and the Seven Dwarfs* is a 1937 animated American film **produced by Walt Disney.** Based on a nineteenth-century German fairy tale about a queen who [72]secretly <u>orders</u> her stepdaughter's death out of jealousy, [67]it was the first ever full-length animated | [67]*백설 공주와 일곱 난쟁이*는 월트 디즈니에 의해 제작된 1937년 미국 애니메이션 영화이다. 질투심에 사로잡혀 [72]의붓딸의 죽음을 몰래 명령하는 여왕에 관한 19세기 독일 동화를 기반으로 한, [67]이것은 영어로 된 최초의 장편 애니메이션 영화였다. 이것은 또한 애 |

film in English. It is also considered one of Disney's greatest works for its innovations in animation.

개봉 전의 회의적인 반응

When Disney first proposed the film in 1934, his ideas were met with doubt. The country was in the midst of the Great Depression, and this severe economic downturn weighed heavily on the minds of film producers and moviegoers. [68]The public seemed to prefer films that addressed the decay of American society or [73]live-action comedies that appeased their everyday anxieties. Consequently, skeptics in the movie industry called *Snow White* "Disney's folly," predicting its failure even before its release.

대중의 반응에 상반된 디즈니

However, Disney remained optimistic. [69]His animated short films had already been well-received by critics, and he wanted to bring his work to a larger audience. He borrowed considerable sums of money to fund production, knowing that he could lose his reputation, his studio, and even his house if the film did not do well.

개봉 후의 긍정적인 반응

Upon its release, *Snow White and the Seven Dwarfs* became a box-office hit. [70]The film's elaborate storytelling and unique blend of fantasy and reality captivated audiences. Before *Snow White*, many believed that the public would not be interested in watching longer animations because of the absence of real people or places in them. To compensate for this, [70]Disney's team worked hard to make the film more realistic than the traditional, exaggerated cartoon style, studying and replicating the real-life movements of hair, clothing, and hired actors.

현황 + 시사점

[71]The film's success highlighted the potential of animated features, paving the way not just for future Disney films, but also for the entire animation industry. In 1939, Disney received an Honorary Academy Award for *Snow White*, which was recognized as a "significant screen innovation which has charmed millions and pioneered a great new entertainment field for the motion picture cartoon." The film remains one of Disney's most popular films, ranking first on the American Film Institute's list of greatest American animations.

니메이션의 혁신으로 디즈니의 가장 위대한 작품들 중 하나로 여겨진다.

1934년에 디즈니가 이 영화를 처음 제안했을 때, 그의 생각은 의심에 부닥쳤다. 미국은 대공황의 한가운데에 있었고, 이 극심한 경기 침체는 영화 제작자들과 영화 팬들의 마음을 무겁게 짓눌렀다. [68]대중은 미국 사회의 쇠퇴를 다룬 영화나 [73]그들의 일상적인 불안을 달랬던 실사 코미디를 선호하는 것처럼 보였다. 결과적으로, 영화 산업의 회의론자들은 백설 공주를 "디즈니의 어리석음"이라고 부르며, 개봉 전부터 그것의 실패를 예측했다.

그러나, 디즈니는 낙관적이었다. [69]그의 단편 애니메이션 영화는 이미 비평가들로부터 호평을 받았고, 그의 작품을 더 많은 관객에게 선보이고 싶어 했다. 영화가 흥행에 실패하면 자신의 명성과, 스튜디오, 심지어 집까지 잃을 수 있다는 것을 알면서도, [69]그는 제작에 자금을 대려고 상당한 액수의 돈을 빌렸다.

개봉과 동시에, 백설 공주와 일곱 난쟁이는 흥행에 성공했다. [70]이 영화의 정교한 스토리텔링과 더불어 환상과 현실의 독특한 조합이 관객들의 마음을 사로잡았다. 백설 공주 이전에, 많은 사람은 그것에 실제 사람이나 장소의 부재 때문에 대중이 더 긴 애니메이션을 보는 것에 관심이 없을 것이라고 믿었다. 이것을 보완하기 위해, [70]디즈니 팀은 머리카락, 옷, 고용된 배우들의 실제 움직임을 연구하고 복제하면서, 영화를 전통적이고 과장된 만화 스타일보다 더 사실적으로 만들기 위해 노력했다.

[71]이 영화의 성공은 애니메이션 작품의 잠재력을 부각했고, 이후의 디즈니 영화뿐 아니라, 전체 애니메이션 산업을 위해 길을 열어주었다. 1939년에, 디즈니는 백설 공주로 "수백만 명을 매료시키고 만화 영화의 훌륭한 새로운 엔터테인먼트 분야를 개척한 중요한 스크린 혁신"으로 인정받아 아카데미 명예상을 수상했다. 이 영화는 미국 영화 연구소의 위대한 미국 애니메이션 목록에서 1위를 차지하며, 디즈니의 가장 인기 있는 영화 중 하나로 남아 있다.

어휘 | fairy tale phr. 동화 secretly adv. 몰래 stepdaughter n. 의붓딸 jealousy n. 질투심, 시샘 full-length adj. 장편의 innovation n. 혁신 doubt n. 의심 in the midst of phr. ~의 한가운데에 Great Depression phr. (1929년 미국에서 비롯한) 대공황 economic downturn phr. 경기 침체 weigh v. 짓누르다 moviegoer n. 영화 팬 decay n. 쇠퇴, 퇴락 skeptic n. 회의론자 folly n. 어리석음, 판단력 부족 optimistic adj. 낙관적인 be well received by critics phr. 비평가들로부터 호평을 받다 audience n. 관객, 관중 sum n. 액수, 합 production n. (영화·연극 등의) 제작 reputation n. 명성 be a box-office hit phr. 흥행에 성공하다 elaborate adj. 정교한 blend n. 조합, 혼합 captivate v. ~의 마음을 사로잡다 compensate v. 보완하다 exaggerated adj. 과장된 replicate v. 복제하다 highlight v. ~을 부각하다 potential n. 잠재력 pave the way for phr. ~을 위해 길을 열다 charm v. 매료하다; n. 매력 pioneer v. 개척하다; n. 개척자 rank first phr. 1위를 차지하다

67 주제/목적　기사의 주제　난이도 ●●○

What is the article all about?

(a) the first American feature-length animation
(b) the first ever full-length film in English
(c) the oldest cartoon produced by Disney
(d) a German adaptation of a classic fairy tale

기사의 주제는 무엇인가?

(a) 미국 최초의 장편 애니메이션
(b) 영어로 된 최초의 장편 영화
(c) 디즈니가 제작한 가장 오래된 만화
(d) 고전 동화의 독일어 번안

▶━○ 정답 잡는 치트키

지문의 초반을 주의 깊게 읽고 전체 맥락을 파악한다.

해설 | 1단락의 'Snow White and the Seven Dwarfs is a 1937 animated American film'에서 백설 공주와 일곱 난쟁이는 1937년 미국 애니메이션 영화라고 했고, 'it was the first ever full-length animated film in English'에서 이것은 영어로 된 최초의 장편 애니메이션 영화였다고 한 뒤, 백설 공주와 일곱 난쟁이에 관해 설명하는 내용이 이어지고 있다. 따라서 (a)가 정답이다.

⇄ **Paraphrasing**
full-length animated film 장편 애니메이션 영화 → feature-length animation 장편 애니메이션

오답분석
(b) 1단락에서 백설 공주와 일곱 난쟁이가 영어로 된 최초의 장편 애니메이션 영화였다고 했지만, 최초의 장편 영화인지는 언급되지 않았으므로 오답이다.

어휘 | feature-length adj. 장편의　adaptation n. 번안, 개작

68 추론　특정사실　난이도 ●●○

Why, most likely, was Snow White expected to fail?

(a) because many people could not afford to go to the cinema
(b) because the movie did not follow the trends of the time
(c) because the public was not interested in movies
(d) because a film producer was not confident about the movie

백설 공주가 실패할 것으로 예상된 이유는 무엇이었을 것 같은가?

(a) 많은 사람이 영화관에 갈 여유가 없었기 때문에
(b) 영화가 시대의 흐름을 따르지 않았기 때문에
(c) 대중이 영화에 관심이 없었기 때문에
(d) 영화 제작자가 영화에 대해 자신감이 없었기 때문에

▶━○ 정답 잡는 치트키

질문의 키워드 expected to fail이 predicting ~ failure로 paraphrasing되어 언급된 주변 내용을 주의 깊게 읽는다.

해설 | 2단락의 'The public seemed to prefer films that addressed the decay of American society or live-action comedies that appeased their everyday anxieties. Consequently, skeptics in the movie industry called Snow White "Disney's folly," predicting its failure even before its release.'에서 대중은 미국 사회의 쇠퇴를 다룬 영화나 그들의 일상적인 불안을 달랬던 실사 코미디를 선호하는 것처럼 보였고, 결과적으로 영화 산업의 회의론자들은 백설 공주를 "디즈니의 어리석음"이라고 부르며, 개봉 전부터 그것의 실패를 예측했다고 한 것을 통해, 백설 공주는 당시 시대의 흐름이던 미국 사회의 쇠퇴를 다룬 영화나 실사 코미디가 아니었기 때문에 실패할 것으로 예상되었음을 추론할 수 있다. 따라서 (b)가 정답이다.

어휘 | afford v. (~을 살 금전적·시간적) 여유가 되다　confident adj. 자신감이 있는, 확신하는

특정세부사항   Why   난이도 ●●●

Why did Walt Disney push to make the film despite criticism?

(a) He needed an uplifting project to focus on.
(b) He needed to revive his failing studio.
(c) He wanted to branch out from making short films.
(d) He wanted to restore his good reputation.

월트 디즈니는 왜 비판에도 불구하고 영화 제작을 밀어붙였는가?

(a) 집중할 만한 희망을 주는 프로젝트가 필요했다.
(b) 실패한 스튜디오를 되살려야 했다.
(c) 단편 영화 제작에서 확장하고 싶어 했다.
(d) 좋은 평판을 회복하고 싶어 했다.

━━○ **정답 잡는 치트키**

질문의 키워드 make the film이 production으로 paraphrasing되어 언급된 주변 내용을 주의 깊게 읽는다.

해설 | 3단락의 'His animated short films had already been well-received by critics, and he wanted to bring his work to a larger audience. He borrowed considerable sums of money to fund production'에서 디즈니의 단편 애니메이션 영화는 이미 비평가들로부터 호평을 받았고, 작품을 더 많은 관객에게 선보이고 싶어 했으며, 제작에 자금을 대려고 상당한 액수의 돈을 빌렸다고 했다. 따라서 (c)가 정답이다.

어휘 | uplifting adj. 희망을 주는   revive v. 되살리다   branch out from phr. ~에서 확장하다   restore v. 회복하다

---

70 **특정세부사항**   How   난이도 ●●●

According to the article, how did Disney's animators make the film appealing to its audience?

(a) by hiring famous actors to voice the characters
(b) by setting the story in familiar locations
(c) by using an exaggerated cartoon style
(d) by creating highly realistic-looking characters

기사에 따르면, 디즈니의 만화 영화 제작자들은 어떻게 영화를 관객에게 매력적으로 만들었는가?

(a) 유명 배우들을 고용해서 등장인물의 목소리를 내게 함으로써
(b) 친숙한 장소를 배경으로 이야기를 설정함으로써
(c) 과장된 만화 스타일을 사용함으로써
(d) 아주 진짜처럼 보이는 등장인물들을 만듦으로써

━━○ **정답 잡는 치트키**

질문의 키워드 appealing to ~ audience가 captivated audiences로 paraphrasing되어 언급된 주변 내용을 주의 깊게 읽는다.

해설 | 4단락의 'The film's elaborate storytelling and unique blend of fantasy and reality captivated audiences.'에서 이 영화의 정교한 스토리텔링과 더불어 환상과 현실의 독특한 조합이 관객들의 마음을 사로잡았다고 한 뒤, 'Disney's team worked hard to make the film more realistic than the traditional, exaggerated cartoon style, studying and replicating the real-life movements of hair, clothing, and hired actors'에서 디즈니 팀은 머리카락, 옷, 고용된 배우들의 실제 움직임을 연구하고 복제하면서, 영화를 전통적이고 과장된 만화 스타일보다 더 사실적으로 만들기 위해 노력했다고 했다. 따라서 (d)가 정답이다.

어휘 | animator n. 만화 영화 제작자   appealing adj. 매력적인   realistic-looking adj. 진짜처럼 보이는

---

71 **특정세부사항**   How   난이도 ●●○

Based on the article, how did the film's success affect the animation genre?

(a) It motivated studios to be more competitive with Disney.

기사에 따르면, 영화의 성공이 어떻게 애니메이션 장르에 영향을 미쳤는가?

(a) 스튜디오들이 디즈니와 더 경쟁할 수 있도록 동기를 부여했다.

(b) It inspired a special award category for animated films.
(c) It introduced new animation technology into the industry.
(d) It raised expectations for cartoon entertainment.

(b) 애니메이션 영화에 대한 특별상 부문에 영감을 주었다.
(c) 새로운 애니메이션 기술을 업계에 도입했다.
(d) 만화 엔터테인먼트에 대한 기대를 높였다.

◁─○ 정답 잡는 치트키

질문의 키워드 film's success가 그대로 언급되고, animation genre가 animation industry로 paraphrasing되어 언급된 주변 내용을 주의 깊게 읽는다.

해설 | 5단락의 'The film's success highlighted the potential of animated features, paving the way not just for future Disney films, but also for the entire animation industry.'에서 이 영화의 성공이 애니메이션 작품의 잠재력을 부각했고, 이후의 디즈니 영화뿐 아니라 전체 애니메이션 산업을 위해 길을 열어주었다고 한 것을 통해, 영화의 성공이 애니메이션 장르에 대한 기대를 높였음을 알 수 있다. 따라서 (d)가 정답이다.

어휘 | motivate v. 동기를 부여하다 expectation n. 기대

---

72 어휘   유의어   난이도 ●●○

In the context of the passage, <u>orders</u> means _____.

(a) buys
(b) demands
(c) approves
(d) rules

지문의 문맥에서, 'orders'는 -을 의미한다.

(a) 산다
(b) 요구한다
(c) 찬성한다
(d) 통치한다

◁─○ 정답 잡는 치트키

밑줄 친 어휘의 유의어를 찾는 문제이므로, orders가 포함된 구절을 읽고 문맥을 파악한다.

해설 | 1단락의 'secretly orders her stepdaughter's death'는 의붓딸의 죽음을 몰래 명령한다는 뜻이므로, orders가 '명령한다'라는 의미로 사용된 것을 알 수 있다. 따라서 '요구한다'라는 비슷한 의미의 (b) demands가 정답이다.

---

73 어휘   유의어   난이도 ●●○

In the context of the passage, <u>appeased</u> means _____.

(a) favored
(b) satisfied
(c) calmed
(d) filled

지문의 문맥에서, 'appeased'는 -을 의미한다.

(a) 찬성했다
(b) 만족시켰다
(c) 안정시켰다
(d) 채웠다

◁─○ 정답 잡는 치트키

밑줄 친 어휘의 유의어를 찾는 문제이므로, appeased가 포함된 구절을 읽고 문맥을 파악한다.

해설 | 2단락의 'live-action comedies that appeased their everyday anxieties'는 일상적인 불안을 달랬던 실사 코미디라는 뜻이므로, appeased가 '달랬다'라는 의미로 사용된 것을 알 수 있다. 따라서 '안정시켰다'라는 비슷한 의미의 (c) calmed가 정답이다.

TEST 1 TEST 2 TEST 3 TEST 4 TEST 5 TEST 6 TEST 7

지텔프 공식 기출문제집 7회분 Level 2

TEST 2 READING & VOCABULARY 99

수신인 정보	Donna Stewart c/o Velvet Records 516 Rhubarb Ave. San Jose, CA Dear Ms. Stewart:	Donna Stewart c/o Velvet Records 루바브 가 516번지 캘리포니아주 산호세 Ms. Stewart께:

첫인사	We at the Do Wonders Foundation would like to thank you for supporting our organization. Your annual donations have helped [79]advance our mission to fund different charities over the past few years, and we hope we can count on your continued generosity.	Do Wonders 재단은 우리 단체를 후원해 주신 것에 대해 귀하께 감사드리고자 합니다. 귀하의 연간 기부금은 지난 몇 년 동안 여러 자선단체에 자금을 지원하는 [79]저희의 사명을 진척시키는 데 도움이 되었으며, 귀하의 지속적인 관대함을 기대할 수 있기를 바랍니다.
편지의 목적: 공연 제안	[74/75]This year, to celebrate Do Wonders' fifteenth anniversary, we will be hosting a benefit concert to raise funds for expansion of the Ellis Cancer Institute. [74/76]We are inviting local artists and would like to know if you are interested in being [80]the main act. [76]Considering your past contributions to Do Wonders, we believe that you are the perfect choice to headline the event. As an acclaimed singer-songwriter, your presence will inspire the audience and help draw attention to our mission. The concert will not only celebrate our years of service but also raise funds for research into cancer treatment and prevention.	[74/75]올해, Do Wonders의 15주년을 기념하여, Ellis 암 연구소의 확장을 위한 기금을 마련하기 위해 자선 콘서트를 열 것입니다. [74/76]지역 예술가들을 초대할 것이며 귀하께서 [80]주 공연자가 되는 것에 관심이 있으신지 알고 싶습니다. [76]Do Wonders에 대한 귀하의 과거 기부금을 고려할 때, 저희는 귀하께서 이 행사에 주 공연자로 나오기에 완벽한 선택이라고 믿습니다. 호평을 받는 싱어송라이터로서, 귀하의 참석은 청중에게 영감을 줄 것이고 저희의 사명에 관심을 끌도록 도울 것입니다. 이 콘서트는 저희의 수년간의 봉사를 기념할 뿐만 아니라, 암 치료 및 예방 연구를 위한 기금도 마련할 것입니다.
수익금 관련 세부 사항	[77(d)]All proceeds from ticket sales will go to the Ellis Cancer Institute. [77(c)]Musical artists will also be encouraged to share donation links on their social media pages for fans who want to contribute to the cause. In addition, [77(a)]musicians may choose to waive their performance fee, instead donating the money they would have received to the institute.	[77(d)]티켓 판매의 모든 수익금은 Ellis 암 연구소로 갈 것입니다. [77(c)]음악가들은 또한 대의에 기여하기를 원하는 팬들을 위해 그들의 소셜 미디어 페이지에 기부 링크를 공유하도록 권장될 것입니다. 게다가, [77(a)]음악가들은 그들이 받았을 수도 있는 돈을 연구소에 기부하는 대신, 그들의 출연료를 포기하기로 선택할 수도 있습니다.
끝인사	Should you have any questions or concerns, we would be glad to address them with you or your agent. I will be out of the office for the next few weeks, but [78]please feel welcome to contact our office manager for more information.	궁금한 점이나 우려 사항이 있으시면, 기꺼이 귀하 또는 귀하의 대리인과 함께 그것들을 이야기할 것입니다. 저는 앞으로 몇 주 동안 부재중일 것이지만, [78]더 많은 정보를 얻기 위해 언제든지 사무실 관리자에게 연락하세요.
발신인 정보	Best regards, Tom Denver Head of External Affairs Do Wonders Foundation	Tom Denver 드림 대외 업무 부장 Do Wonders 재단

어휘 | support v. 후원하다, 지지하다 donation n. 기부(금) mission n. 사명, 임무 count on phr. ~을 기대하다, ~에 의지하다
generosity n. 관대함, 아량 benefit concert phr. 자선 콘서트 raise fund phr. 기금을 마련하다 cancer n. 암
contribution n. 기부(금), 기여 headline v. 주 공연자로 나오다 acclaimed adj. 호평을 받는 presence n. 참석, 존재
treatment n. 치료 proceeds n. 수익금 cause n. 대의(명분), 운동 waive v. 포기하다, 적용하지 않다 performance fee phr. 출연료
agent n. 대리인 External Affairs phr. 대외 업무

TEST 1

TEST 2

TEST 3

TEST 4

TEST 5

TEST 6

TEST 7

지텔프 공식 기출문제집 7회분 Level 2

74 **주제/목적**　편지의 목적　　　　　　　　　　　난이도 ●●○

Why did Tom Denver write to Donna Stewart?

(a) to thank her for donating money to charity
(b) to request that she sponsor a fundraising event
(c) to ask her to headline a nonprofit concert
(d) to invite her to host a benefit concert

왜 Tom Denver는 Donna Stewart에게 편지를 썼는가?

(a) 자선 단체에 돈을 기부해 준 것에 감사하기 위해서
(b) 모금 행사를 후원해 달라고 요청하기 위해서
(c) 비영리 콘서트에 주 공연자로 나와달라고 요청하기 위해서
(d) 자선 콘서트의 진행자로 초대하기 위해서

⊶○ 정답 잡는 치트키

지문의 초반을 주의 깊게 읽고 전체 맥락을 파악한다.

해설 ┃ 2단락의 'This year, ~, we will be hosting a benefit concert to raise funds for expansion of the Ellis Cancer Institute. We ~ would like to know if you are interested in being the main act.'에서 올해, Ellis 암 연구소의 확장을 위한 기금을 마련하기 위해 자선 콘서트를 열 것이고, 주 공연자가 되는 것에 관심이 있는지 알고 싶다고 한 뒤, 자선 콘서트에 관해 설명하는 내용이 이어지고 있다. 따라서 (c)가 정답이다.

　⇄ Paraphrasing
　being the main act 주 공연자가 되는 것 → headline 주 공연자로 나오다
　a benefit concert 자선 콘서트 → a nonprofit concert 비영리 콘서트

　오답분석
　(a) 1단락에서 단체를 후원해 준 것에 대해 감사를 표하긴 했지만, 이것이 편지의 주목적은 아니므로 오답이다.

어휘 ┃ sponsor v. 후원하다　nonprofit adj. 비영리적인

75 **특정세부사항**　What　　　　　　　　　　　난이도 ●●○

What is the purpose of the event?

(a) to gather donations for a research center
(b) to urge people to contribute to different charities
(c) to raise money to support local artists
(d) to fund the opening of a new institute

행사의 목적은 무엇인가?

(a) 연구 센터를 위한 기부금을 모으기 위해서
(b) 사람들에게 다양한 자선 단체에 기부하도록 촉구하기 위해서
(c) 지역 예술가들을 지원하기 위한 돈을 모으기 위해서
(d) 새로운 연구소의 개관에 자금을 대기 위해서

⊶○ 정답 잡는 치트키

질문의 키워드 event가 benefit concert로 paraphrasing되어 언급된 주변 내용을 주의 깊게 읽는다.

해설 ┃ 2단락의 'This year, ~, we will be hosting a benefit concert to raise funds for expansion of the Ellis Cancer Institute.'에서 올해, Ellis 암 연구소의 확장을 위한 기금을 마련하기 위해 자선 콘서트를 열 것이라고 했다. 따라서 (a)가 정답이다.

　⇄ Paraphrasing
　raise funds 기금을 마련하다 → gather donations 기부금을 모으다

76 **추론**　특정사실　　　　　　　　　　　난이도 ●●○

Why, most likely, is Donna being invited to the event?

Donna는 왜 이 행사에 초대받은 것 같은가?

(a) **She has supported the foundation in the past.**
(b) She is known as an inspiring guest speaker.
(c) She has hosted a similar event.
(d) She is a cancer survivor herself.

(a) 과거에 재단을 후원한 적이 있다.
(b) 영감을 주는 초청 연사로 알려져 있다.
(c) 비슷한 행사를 주최한 적이 있다.
(d) 암을 극복해 낸 사람이다.

🔑 정답 잡는 치트키

질문의 키워드 invited가 그대로 언급된 주변 내용을 주의 깊게 읽는다.

해설 | 2단락의 'We are inviting local artists and would like to know if you are interested in being the main act. Considering your past contributions to Do Wonders, we believe that you are the perfect choice to headline the event.'에서 지역 예술가들을 초대할 것이며 주 공연자가 되는 것에 관심이 있는지 알고 싶고, Do Wonders에 대한 과거 기부금을 고려할 때, 이 행사에 주 공연자로 나오기에 완벽한 선택이라고 믿는다고 한 것을 통해, Donna가 이전에 Do Wonders 재단을 후원한 적이 있음을 추론할 수 있다. 따라서 (a)가 정답이다.

어휘 | inspiring adj. 영감을 주는, 고무하는 survivor n. 극복해 낸 사람, 생존자

77 Not/True   Not 문제

난이도 ●●●

What is NOT a way that the concert organizers plan to raise funds?

(a) by asking artists to perform for free
(b) **by selling merchandise during the event**
(c) by soliciting online contributions from fans
(d) by making tickets available for purchase

콘서트 주최자들이 기금을 마련하려고 계획하는 방법 이 아닌 것은 무엇인가?

(a) 예술가들에게 무료로 공연하도록 요청함으로써
(b) **행사 중에 상품을 판매함으로써**
(c) 팬들에게 온라인 기부를 요청함으로써
(d) 티켓을 구입할 수 있도록 함으로써

🔑 정답 잡는 치트키

질문의 키워드 raise funds와 관련된 주변 내용을 주의 깊게 읽고, 보기의 키워드와 지문 내용을 대조하며 언급되는 것을 하나씩 소거한다.

해설 | (b)는 지문에 언급되지 않았으므로, (b)가 정답이다.

오답분석
(a) 보기의 키워드 perform for free가 waive ~ performance fee로 paraphrasing되어 언급된 3단락에서 음악가들은 출연료를 포 기하기로 선택할 수도 있다고 언급되었다.
(c) 보기의 키워드 fans가 그대로 언급된 3단락에서 음악가들은 대의에 기여하기를 원하는 팬들을 위해 그들의 소셜 미디어 페이지에 기부 링크를 공유하도록 권장될 것이라고 언급되었다.
(d) 보기의 키워드 tickets가 그대로 언급된 3단락에서 티켓 판매의 모든 수익금은 Ellis 암 연구소로 갈 것이라고 언급되었다.

78 특정세부사항   How

난이도 ●○○

According to the letter, how can Donna find out more about the event?

(a) by inquiring with her manager
(b) by asking her booking agent

편지에 따르면, Donna는 어떻게 행사에 관해 더 많은 것을 알 수 있는가?

(a) 그녀의 관리자에게 문의함으로써
(b) 그녀의 출연 계약 담당자에게 문의함으로써

(c) by getting in touch with Tom
(d) by contacting an administrator

(c) Tom과 연락을 취함으로써
(d) 관계자에게 연락함으로써

O 정답 잡는 치트키

실문의 키워드 more about the event가 more information으로 paraphrasing되어 언급된 주변 내용을 주의 깊게 읽는다.

해설 | 4단락의 'please feel welcome to contact our office manager for more information'에서 더 많은 정보를 얻기 위해 언제든지 사무실 관리자에게 연락하라고 했다. 따라서 (d)가 정답이다.

⇄ **Paraphrasing**
office manager 사무실 관리자 → an administrator 관계자

오답분석
(a) 4단락에서 더 많은 정보를 얻기 위해 사무실 관리자에게 연락하라고는 했지만, 이는 Do Wonders 재단의 관리자를 의미하므로 오답이다.

어휘 | booking agent phr. 출연 계약 담당자 get in touch with phr. ~와 연락을 취하다 administrator n. 관계자, 관리자

---

79 어휘 유의어   난이도 ●●○

In the context of the passage, <u>advance</u> means _____.

(a) release
(b) confirm
(c) promote
(d) provide

지문의 문맥에서, 'advance'는 -을 의미한다.

(a) 공개하다
(b) 확인하다
(c) 진척시키다
(d) 제공하다

O 정답 잡는 치트키

밑줄 친 어휘의 유의어를 찾는 문제이므로, advance가 포함된 구절을 읽고 문맥을 파악한다.

해설 | 1단락의 'advance our mission'은 사명을 진척시킨다는 뜻이므로, advance가 '진척시키다'라는 의미로 사용된 것을 알 수 있다. 따라서 '진척시키다'라는 같은 의미의 (c) promote가 정답이다.

---

80 어휘 유의어   난이도 ●●○

In the context of the passage, <u>act</u> means _____.

(a) performer
(b) character
(c) reason
(d) issue

지문의 문맥에서, 'act'는 -을 의미한다.

(a) 공연자
(b) 인물
(c) 요인
(d) 사안

O 정답 잡는 치트키

밑줄 친 어휘의 유의어를 찾는 문제이므로, act가 포함된 구절을 읽고 문맥을 파악한다.

해설 | 2단락의 'the main act'는 주 공연자라는 뜻이므로, act가 '공연자'라는 의미로 사용된 것을 알 수 있다. 따라서 '공연자'라는 같은 의미의 (a) performer가 정답이다.

TEST 1 | TEST 2 | TEST 3 | TEST 4 | TEST 5 | TEST 6 | TEST 7

지텔프 공식 기출문제집 7회분 Level 2

공식기출
TEST 3
정답 · 스크립트 · 해석 · 해설

GRAMMAR

LISTENING

READING & VOCABULARY

GRAMMAR _____ / 26 (점수 : _____ 점)
LISTENING _____ / 26 (점수 : _____ 점)
READING & VOCABULARY _____ / 28 (점수 : _____ 점)

TOTAL _____ / 80 (평균 점수 : _____ 점)

*각 영역 점수: 맞은 개수 × 3.75
*평균 점수: 각 영역 점수 합계 ÷ 3

정답 및 취약 유형 분석표

자동 채점 및 성적 분석 서비스 ▶

GRAMMAR

번호	정답	유형
01	a	시제
02	d	조동사
03	d	시제
04	c	가정법
05	a	준동사
06	a	가정법
07	b	시제
08	c	연결어
09	a	관계사
10	c	가정법
11	d	준동사
12	b	조동사
13	b	가정법
14	d	조동사
15	a	시제
16	c	관계사
17	b	시제
18	c	조동사
19	c	준동사
20	c	시제
21	a	연결어
22	c	준동사
23	c	가정법
24	a	준동사
25	d	준동사
26	b	가정법

LISTENING

PART	번호	정답	유형
	27	c	특정세부사항
	28	c	추론
	29	a	특정세부사항
PART 1	30	c	특정세부사항
	31	d	특정세부사항
	32	b	특정세부사항
	33	a	추론
	34	b	주제/목적
	35	a	추론
	36	a	특정세부사항
PART 2	37	b	특정세부사항
	38	b	특정세부사항
	39	d	특정세부사항
	40	b	특정세부사항
	41	d	특정세부사항
	42	a	추론
PART 3	43	c	특정세부사항
	44	d	추론
	45	c	추론
	46	d	주제/목적
	47	a	특정세부사항
	48	c	특정세부사항
PART 4	49	c	특정세부사항
	50	b	특정세부사항
	51	d	특정세부사항
	52	a	추론

READING & VOCABULARY

PART	번호	정답	유형
	53	d	특정세부사항
	54	d	특정세부사항
	55	c	특정세부사항
PART 1	56	b	특정세부사항
	57	b	추론
	58	a	어휘
	59	c	어휘
	60	d	주제/목적
	61	b	특정세부사항
	62	b	특정세부사항
PART 2	63	d	추론
	64	a	특정세부사항
	65	c	어휘
	66	c	어휘
	67	b	Not/True
	68	d	특정세부사항
	69	b	특정세부사항
PART 3	70	b	특정세부사항
	71	a	추론
	72	a	어휘
	73	d	어휘
	74	b	주제/목적
	75	b	특정세부사항
	76	c	Not/True
PART 4	77	a	특정세부사항
	78	a	추론
	79	d	어휘
	80	d	어휘

유형	맞힌 개수
시제	/ 6
가정법	/ 6
준동사	/ 6
조동사	/ 4
연결어	/ 2
관계사	/ 2
TOTAL	/ 26

유형	맞힌 개수
주제/목적	/ 2
특정세부사항	/ 17
Not/True	/ 0
추론	/ 7
TOTAL	/ 26

유형	맞힌 개수
주제/목적	/ 2
특정세부사항	/ 12
Not/True	/ 2
추론	/ 4
어휘	/ 8
TOTAL	/ 28

GRAMMAR

01 시제　과거완료진행　　　　　　　　　　　난이도 ●●○

Jerry is now the head chef at Ciao Bella, the finest Italian restaurant in the city. He _____ as a sous-chef there for two years before he was promoted to the top position last week.

(a) **had been serving**
(b) has been serving
(c) would serve
(d) will have served

Jerry는 현재 도시에서 가장 좋은 이탈리안 레스토랑인 Ciao Bella의 수석 주방장이다. 그는 지난주에 최고 직위로 승진하기 전에 2년 동안 그곳에서 부주방장으로 일해오고 있던 중이었다.

⟜○ 지텔프 치트키

'before + 과거 동사'가 있으면 과거완료진행 시제가 정답이다.

> 💡 과거완료진행과 자주 함께 쓰이는 시간 표현
> • before / when / since + 과거 동사 + (for + 기간 표현) ~하기 전에 / ~했을 때 / ~ 이래로 (~ 동안)
> • (for + 기간 표현) + (up) until + 과거 동사 (~ 동안) ~했을 때까지

해설 | 과거완료진행 시제와 함께 쓰이는 시간 표현 'for + 기간 표현'(for two years)과 'before + 과거 동사'(before ~ was promoted)가 있고, 문맥상 대과거(부주방장으로 일하기 시작한 시점)부터 과거(수석 주방장으로 승진한 시점)까지 2년 동안 부주방장으로 계속해서 일해오고 있던 중이었다는 의미가 되어야 자연스럽다. 따라서 과거완료진행 시제 (a) had been serving이 정답이다.

어휘 | head chef phr. 수석 주방장　sous-chef n. 부주방장

02 조동사　조동사 must　　　　　　　　　　　난이도 ●●○

Hawaii is one of the only US states that can grow coffee commercially because of the islands' tropical climate. For coffee trees to flourish, an area _____ have warm temperatures and plentiful rainfall all year round.

(a) will
(b) can
(c) may
(d) **must**

하와이는 섬의 열대성 기후 때문에 커피를 상업적으로 재배할 수 있는 유일한 미국의 주 중 한 곳이다. 커피나무가 잘 자라려면, 지역은 일 년 내내 따뜻한 기온과 풍부한 강우량을 유지해야 한다.

⟜○ 지텔프 치트키

'~해야 한다'라고 말할 때는 must를 쓴다.

해설 | 문맥상 커피나무가 잘 자라려면 지역은 일 년 내내 따뜻한 기온과 풍부한 강우량을 유지해야 한다는 의미가 되어야 자연스러우므로, '~해야 한다'를 뜻하면서 의무를 나타내는 조동사 (d) must가 정답이다. 참고로, must와 should 모두 '~해야 한다'를 뜻하지만, must는 should보다 강한 어조로 조언을 하거나 의무를 나타낼 때 쓴다.

어휘 | commercially adv. 상업적으로　tropical climate phr. 열대성 기후　flourish v. 잘 자라다, 무성하다　plentiful adj. 풍부한, 많은　rainfall n. 강우량, 강수량

The local cotton mill has been operating since long before Susan was born. By the end of this year, the company that employs both of her parents ＿＿＿＿＿ quality cotton fabric for five decades.

(a) will be producing
(b) produces
(c) had been producing
(d) will have been producing

○─── 지텔프 치트키

'by + 미래 시점'과 'for + 기간 표현'이 함께 오면 미래완료진행 시제가 정답이다.

☼ 미래완료진행과 자주 함께 쓰이는 시간 표현
　• by the time / when / if + 현재 동사 + (for + 기간 표현)　~할 무렵이면 / ~할 때 / 만약 ~한다면 (~ 동안)
　• by / in + 미래 시점 + (for + 기간 표현)　~ 즈음에는 / ~에 (~ 동안)

해설 | 미래완료진행 시제와 함께 쓰이는 표현 'by + 미래 시점'(By the end of this year)과 'for + 기간 표현'(for five decades)이 있고, 문맥상 미래 시점인 올해가 끝날 즈음에는 지역 면직 공장이 50년 동안 계속해서 질 좋은 면직물을 생산해 오고 있는 중일 것이라는 의미가 되어야 자연스럽다. 따라서 미래완료진행 시제 (d) will have been producing이 정답이다.

오답분석
(a) 미래진행 시제는 특정 미래 시점에 진행 중일 일을 나타내므로, 과거 또는 현재에 시작해서 특정 미래 시점까지 계속해서 진행되고 있을 일을 표현할 수 없어 오답이다.

어휘 | cotton mill phr. 면직 공장, 방적 공장　born v. 태어나다　employ v. 고용하다　cotton fabric phr. 면직물

지역 면직 공장은 Susan이 태어나기 훨씬 전부터 운영되어 오고 있는 중이다. 올해가 끝날 즈음에는, 그녀의 부모님을 모두 고용한 회사는 50년 동안 질 좋은 면직물을 생산해 오고 있는 중일 것이다.

Melanie expects to keep tossing and turning later because her neighbors are having another noisy party. If they were more considerate, Melanie ＿＿＿＿＿ soundly tonight, but it seems unlikely.

(a) will have slept
(b) will sleep
(c) would sleep
(d) would have slept

○─── 지텔프 치트키

'if + 과거 동사'가 있으면 'would/could + 동사원형'이 정답이다.

☼ 가정법 과거
　If + 주어 + 과거 동사, 주어 + would/could(조동사 과거형) + 동사원형

해설 | If절에 과거 동사(were)가 있으므로, 주절에는 이와 짝을 이루어 가정법 과거를 만드는 'would(조동사 과거형) + 동사원형'이 와야 한다. 따라서 (c) would sleep이 정답이다.

어휘 | toss and turn phr. (잠이 들지 못하고) 뒤척이다　neighbor n. 이웃, 주변 사람　considerate adj. 배려하는　soundly adv. 푹, 깊이, 충분히

그녀의 이웃들이 또 시끄러운 파티를 열 것이기 때문에 Melanie는 나중에 계속 뒤척일 것으로 예상한다. 만약 그들이 조금만 더 배려한다면, Melanie는 오늘 밤에 잠을 푹 잘 텐데, 그럴 가능성은 없어 보인다.

A woman just walked into Delia's Beauty Shop claiming that a lotion bottle was half empty when purchased. She wants the store _____ it, but she is unable to prove that she never opened the lotion.

(a) **to replace**
(b) replacing
(c) having replaced
(d) to have replaced

한 여성이 방금 Delia's Beauty Shop에 들어와 로션 병을 구매했을 때 절반 정도 비어있었다고 주장했다. 그녀는 매장에서 그것을 <u>교환해 줄 것을</u> 원하지만, 로션을 한 번도 개봉하지 않았다는 것을 증명할 수 없다.

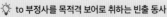

ㅡ○ 지텔프 치트키

want는 to 부정사를 목적격 보어로 취한다.

🔅 **to 부정사를 목적격 보어로 취하는 빈출 동사**
want 원하다　encourage 권장하다　require 요구하다　urge 강력히 촉구하다　allow 허락하다　ask 요청하다

해설 | 빈칸 앞 동사 want는 'want + 목적어 + 목적격 보어'의 형태로 쓰일 때 to 부정사를 목적격 보어로 취하여 '-에게 ~할 것을 원하다'라는 의미를 나타낸다. 따라서 to 부정사 (a) to replace가 정답이다.

오답분석

(d) to have replaced도 to 부정사이기는 하지만, 완료부정사(to have replaced)로 쓰일 경우 '원하는' 시점보다 '교환하는' 시점이 앞선다는 것을 나타내므로 문맥에 적합하지 않아 오답이다.

어휘 | claim v. 주장하다　prove v. 증명하다

At nearly seventy feet long, the megalodon was one of the largest fish to have existed. If this gigantic shark were still alive today, it _____ the whale shark, which is currently the largest living fish.

(a) **would dwarf**
(b) would have dwarfed
(c) will dwarf
(d) will have dwarfed

거의 70피트 길이에 이르는, 메갈로돈은 현존해 온 큰 물고기 중 하나였다. 만약 이 거대한 상어가 오늘날에도 여전히 살아 있다면, 고래상어를 <u>왜소해 보이게 만들 것</u>인데, 이것은 현재 살아있는 가장 큰 물고기이다.

ㅡ○ 지텔프 치트키

'if + 과거 동사'가 있으면 'would/could + 동사원형'이 정답이다.

해설 | If절에 과거 동사(were)가 있으므로, 주절에는 이와 짝을 이루어 가정법 과거를 만드는 'would(조동사 과거형) + 동사원형'이 와야 한다. 따라서 (a) would dwarf가 정답이다.

어휘 | megalodon n. 메갈로돈　gigantic adj. 거대한　whale shark phr. 고래상어　dwarf v. 왜소해 보이게 만들다

Michaela developed a fear of spiders because of a traumatic childhood experience. When she was eight, a large brown spider bit her knee while she _____ in the yard, causing it to swell and itch.

(a) has been playing
(b) was playing
(c) is playing
(d) had been playing

지텔프 치트키

'과거 동사 + while절'이 있으면 과거진행 시제가 정답이다.

해설 | 과거진행 시제와 함께 쓰이는 시간 표현 '과거 동사 + while절'(bit ~ while ~)이 있고, 문맥상 큰 갈색 거미가 Michaela를 물었던 과거 시점에 그녀가 마당에서 놀고 있던 도중이었다는 의미가 되어야 자연스럽다. 따라서 과거진행 시제 (b) was playing이 정답이다.

Michaela는 대단히 충격적인 어린 시절 경험 때문에 거미에 대한 두려움이 생겼다. 그녀가 8살이었을 때, 마당에서 놀고 있던 동안에 큰 갈색 거미가 그녀의 무릎을 물었고, 무릎이 붓고 가려워지게 했다.

어휘 | fear n. 두려움, 공포 traumatic adj. 대단히 충격적인 childhood n. 어린 시절, 어릴 적 bite v. (곤충·뱀 등이) 물다 knee n. 무릎 yard n. 마당 swell v. 붓다 itch v. 가렵다

Jack the Ripper, an infamous London serial killer, evaded justice and was never officially identified. _____, the Zodiac Killer from California was never caught after going on a brutal 1960s crime spree.

(a) Therefore
(b) Finally
(c) Similarly
(d) However

지텔프 치트키

'마찬가지로'라는 의미의 첨언을 나타낼 때는 Similarly를 쓴다.

해설 | 문맥상 Jack the Ripper는 처벌을 피해 갔고 결코 공식적으로 신원이 확인되지 않았으며, 마찬가지로 Zodiac Killer는 잔인한 범죄를 한바탕 저지른 후에도 절대 잡히지 않았다는 의미가 되어야 자연스럽다. 따라서 '마찬가지로'라는 의미의 첨언을 나타내는 접속부사 (c) Similarly가 정답이다.

악명 높은 런던 연쇄살인범 Jack the Ripper는 처벌을 피해 갔고 결코 공식적으로 신원이 확인되지 않았다. 마찬가지로, 캘리포니아 출신의 Zodiac Killer는 1960년대에 잔인한 범죄를 한바탕 저지른 후에도 절대 잡히지 않았다.

오답분석
(a) Therefore는 '그러므로', (b) Finally는 '마침내', (d) However는 '그러나'라는 의미로, 문맥에 적합하지 않아 오답이다.

어휘 | infamous adj. 악명 높은, 지독한 serial killer phr. 연쇄살인범 evade v. 피하다, 면하다 justice n. (범죄의) 처벌, 재판 officially adv. 공식적으로, 정식으로 identify v. 신원을 확인하다 brutal adj. 잔인한, 무자비한 crime n. 범죄, 범행 spree n. (범행을) 한바탕 저지르기

There has been a surge in the theft of packages delivered to our neighborhood. Just yesterday, a tall man, _____, was caught on a security camera stealing a box from our neighbor's porch.

우리 동네에 배송된 택배의 절도가 급증해 오고 있다. 바로 어제, 한 키 큰 남성은, 검은색 모자 달린 옷을 착용하고 있던 중이었는데, 이웃집 현관에서 상자를 훔치고 있는 것이 방범 카메라에 포착됐다.

(a) **who was wearing a black hoodie**
(b) what was wearing a black hoodie
(c) that was wearing a black hoodie
(d) which was wearing a black hoodie

⊶○ 지텔프 치트키

사람 선행사가 관계절 안에서 주어 역할을 하고, 빈칸 앞에 콤마(,)가 있으면 주격 관계대명사 who가 정답이다.

해설 | 사람 선행사 a tall man을 받으면서 콤마(,) 뒤에 올 수 있는 주격 관계대명사가 필요하므로, (a) who was wearing a black hoodie가 정답이다.

오답분석

(c) 관계대명사 that도 사람 선행사를 받을 수 있지만, 콤마 뒤에 올 수 없으므로 오답이다.

어휘 | surge n. 급증, 급등; v. 급증하다 theft n. 절도, 도둑질 neighborhood n. 동네, 인근 security camera phr. 방범 카메라 steal v. 훔치다, 빼앗다 porch n. 현관 hoodie n. 모자 달린 옷

Worried about the high cost of repairs, Eric tried fixing his broken phone himself, but the phone stopped working entirely. Had he hired a technician instead, his phone _____ before it sustained any further damage.

비싼 수리비가 걱정되어, Eric은 고장 난 휴대전화를 직접 고치려고 했지만, 휴대전화는 완전히 작동을 멈췄다. 그가 대신 기술자를 고용했다면, 그의 휴대전화는 더 큰 손상을 입기 전에 아마 고쳐졌을 것이다.

(a) would likely be fixed
(b) will likely be fixed
(c) **would likely have been fixed**
(d) will likely have been fixed

⊶○ 지텔프 치트키

Had p.p.가 있으면 'would/could + have p.p.'가 정답이다.

> 💡 **가정법 과거완료(도치)**
> • Had + 주어 + p.p., 주어 + would/could(조동사 과거형) + have p.p.

해설 | if가 생략되어 도치된 절에 'had p.p.' 형태의 Had ~ hired가 있으므로, 주절에는 이와 짝을 이루어 가정법 과거완료를 만드는 'would(조동사 과거형) + have p.p.'가 와야 한다. 따라서 (c) would likely have been fixed가 정답이다. 참고로, 'Had he hired ~'는 'If he had hired ~'로 바꿔 쓸 수 있다.

어휘 | repair n. 수리; v. 고치다 entirely adv. 완전히 technician n. 기술자, 수리공 sustain v. (피해 등을) 입다, 당하다 damage n. 손상, 훼손

11　준동사　to 부정사의 부사 역할　난이도 ●●●

Diamond Knoll School just installed a new digital public announcement system for better campus communication. The new PA system uses wireless technology and can be set _____ the whole school or just specific buildings and classrooms.

(a) addressing
(b) to have addressed
(c) having addressed
(d) to address

Diamond Knoll 학교는 더 나은 캠퍼스 커뮤니케이션을 위해 새로운 디지털 공공 안내 방송 시스템을 최근에 설치했다. 새로운 PA 시스템은 무선 기술을 사용하며 학교 전체 또는 특성 건물과 교실에만 ~설하기 위해 설정될 수 있다.

━○ 지텔프 치트키

'~하기 위해'라고 말할 때는 to 부정사를 쓴다.

해설 | 빈칸 앞에 주어(The new PA system), 동사(can be set)가 갖춰진 완전한 절이 있으므로, 빈칸 이하는 문장의 필수 성분이 아닌 수식어구이다. 따라서 목적을 나타내며 수식어구를 이끌 수 있는 to 부정사 (d) to address가 정답이다.

오답분석

(b) to have addressed도 to 부정사이기는 하지만, 완료부정사(to have addressed)로 쓰일 경우 '설정되는' 시점보다 '연설하는' 시점이 앞선다는 것을 나타내므로 문맥에 적합하지 않아 오답이다.

어휘 | install v. 설치하다　public adj. 공공의; n. 대중　wireless adj. 무선의

12　조동사　조동사 could　난이도 ●●●

Phrenology is the study of the cranial structure as it is related to mental function. Phrenologists once claimed they _____ determine someone's intelligence by the shape of their skull, but that theory lacked scientific support.

(a) might
(b) could
(c) would
(d) should

골상학은 그것이 뇌 기능과 관련이 있기 때문에 두개골 구조를 연구하는 학문이다. 골상학자들은 한때 두개골 모양으로 사람의 지능을 알아낼 수도 있다고 주장했지만, 그 이론은 과학적 근거가 부족했다.

━○ 지텔프 치트키

'~할 수도 있다'라고 말할 때는 could를 쓴다.

해설 | 문맥상 골상학자들은 한때 두개골 모양으로 사람의 지능을 알아낼 수도 있다고 주장했지만, 그 이론은 과학적 근거가 부족했다는 의미가 되어야 자연스럽다. 따라서 '~할 수도 있다'를 뜻하면서 추측을 나타내는 조동사 (b) could가 정답이다.

오답분석

(a) 빈칸에 약한 추측을 나타내는 might가 들어가면 '골상학자들은 한때 두개골 모양으로 사람의 지능을 알아낼지도 모른다고 주장했다'라는 의미가 될 수 있는데, 문맥상 골상학자들이 두개골 모양으로 사람의 지능을 알아낼지도 모른다는 불확실한 가능성을 주장했다는 것은 문맥에 적합하지 않으므로 오답이다.

(c) 빈칸에 소망/미래/예정/현재 사실의 반대 등을 나타내는 would가 들어가면 '골상학자들은 한때 두개골 모양으로 사람의 지능을 알아낼 수 있을 것이라고 주장했지만, 그 이론은 과학적 근거가 부족했다'라는 의미가 될 수 있는데, 문맥상 두개골 모양으로 사람의 지능을 알아낼 수도 있다는 것을 추측하는 내용이 되어야 더 자연스러우므로 문맥에 가장 적합하지는 않아 오답이다.

(d) should는 의무/당위성을 나타내어 문맥에 적합하지 않으므로 오답이다.

어휘 | phrenology n. 골상학 cranial structure phr. 두개골 구조 mental function phr. 뇌 기능 determine v. 알아내다, 밝히다
intelligence n. 지능 skull n. 두개골 theory n. 이론 support n. 근거, 증거; v. (사실임을) 뒷받침하다

---

13 가정법　　가정법 과거완료　　　　　　　　　　　　　　　　난이도 ●●○

When sales of Simple Scents perfume skyrocketed, the marketing team attributed the increase to their new celebrity spokesperson. If they had not made the deal with the superstar, sales _____ all last quarter.

(a) will have remained flat
(b) would have remained flat
(c) will remain flat
(d) would remain flat

Simple Scents 향수의 매출이 급상승하자, 마케팅팀은 매출 증가의 원인을 새로운 유명 인사 대표자 덕분으로 돌렸다. 만약 그들이 그 슈퍼스타와 계약을 맺지 않았었다면, 매출은 지난 분기 내내 저조했을 것이다.

─○ 지텔프 치트키

'if + had p.p.'가 있으면 'would/could + have p.p.'가 정답이다.

> 💡 **가정법 과거완료**
> If + 주어 + had p.p., 주어 + would/could(조동사 과거형) + have p.p.

해설 | If절에 'had p.p.' 형태의 had not made가 있으므로, 주절에는 이와 짝을 이루어 가정법 과거완료를 만드는 'would(조동사 과거형) + have p.p.'가 와야 한다. 따라서 (b) would have remained flat이 정답이다.

어휘 | skyrocket v. 급상승하다 attribute to phr. (~의 원인을) ~의 덕분으로 돌리다 celebrity n. 유명 인사 spokesperson n. 대표자, 대변인
deal n. 계약, 거래 flat adj. (매출 등이) 저조한

---

14 조동사　　조동사 should 생략　　　　　　　　　　　　　　　난이도 ●●○

Lawrence asked his mother if he could paint the doghouse she built. She agreed, but since it was Lawrence's very first painting project, she insisted that he _____ the floor with newspapers to avoid splatter marks.

(a) covered
(b) will cover
(c) was covering
(d) cover

Lawrence는 그의 어머니에게 그녀가 지은 개집을 페인트칠해도 되는지 물었다. 어머니는 동의했지만, 그것이 Lawrence의 첫 페인트칠 프로젝트였기 때문에, 어머니는 튄 자국을 피하기 위해 그에게 바닥을 신문지로 덮어야 한다고 주장했다.

─○ 지텔프 치트키

insist 다음에는 that절에 동사원형이 온다.

> 💡 **주장·요구·명령·제안을 나타내는 빈출 동사**
> insist 주장하다 recommend 권고하다 demand 요구하다 request 요청하다 suggest 제안하다 order 명령하다
> urge 강력히 촉구하다 ask 요청하다 propose 제안하다 advise 권고하다

해설 | 주절에 주장을 나타내는 동사 insist가 있으므로 that절에는 '(should +) 동사원형'이 와야 한다. 따라서 동사원형 (d) cover가 정답이다.

어휘 | doghouse n. 개집   floor n. 바닥   splatter n. 튀기기; v. (물·흙탕물 따위가) 튀기다   mark n. 자국, 흔적

15 시제   현재진행

난이도 ●○○

Rita saw a social media post that claimed her favorite granola bar contained dangerous traces of pesticides and could cause health problems when ingested. Now, she _____ the internet to see if the post is fake.

(a) is scouring
(b) has been scouring
(c) will be scouring
(d) would scour

Rita는 자기가 가장 좋아하는 그래놀라 바가 미량의 위험한 살충제를 포함하고 있어서 섭취 시 건강 문제를 일으킬 수 있다고 주장한 소셜 미디어 게시물을 보았다. 지금, 그녀는 이 게시물이 거짓인지 확인하기 위해 인터넷을 샅샅이 뒤지고 있는 중이다.

○ 지텔프 치트키

now가 있으면 현재진행 시제가 정답이다.

☼ 현재진행과 자주 함께 쓰이는 시간 표현
· right now / now / currently / at the moment 바로 지금 / 지금 / 현재 / 바로 지금
· these days / nowadays 요즘

해설 | 현재진행 시제와 함께 쓰이는 시간 표현 now가 있고, 문맥상 말하고 있는 현재 시점에 Rita가 게시물이 거짓인지 확인하기 위해 인터넷을 샅샅이 뒤지고 있는 중이라는 의미가 되어야 자연스럽다. 따라서 현재진행 시제 (a) is scouring이 정답이다.

어휘 | trace n. 미량   pesticide n. 살충제, 농약   ingest v. 섭취하다   fake adj. 거짓의, 가짜의   scour v. 샅샅이 뒤지다, 철저히 조사하다

16 관계사   주격 관계대명사 that

난이도 ●●○

One reason fingernails generally grow faster than toenails is that hands are exposed to more sunlight. This extra exposure allows the fingernails to produce a nutrient _____ for them to outpace toenails in terms of growth.

(a) where is necessary
(b) what is necessary
(c) that is necessary
(d) who is necessary

일반적으로 손톱이 발톱보다 빨리 자라는 한 가지 이유는 손이 더 많은 햇빛에 노출되기 때문이다. 이러한 추가적인 노출은 길이의 증가 면에서 손톱이 발톱보다 앞서는 데 필요한 영양분을 생산하게 해준다.

○ 지텔프 치트키

사물 선행사가 관계절 안에서 주어 역할을 하면 주격 관계대명사 that이 정답이다.

해설 | 사물 선행사 a nutrient를 받으면서 보기의 관계절 내에서 동사 is의 주어가 될 수 있는 주격 관계대명사가 필요하므로, (c) that is necessary가 정답이다.

어휘 | fingernail n. 손톱   toenail n. 발톱   sunlight n. 햇빛   exposure n. 노출   nutrient n. 영양분, 영양소   outpace v. 앞서다, 능가하다   in terms of phr. ~ 면에서   growth n. 길이의 증가

There are many beautiful places to visit in the Chicago area, but Matthew's favorite is the Brookfield Zoo. He _____ the zoo ever since he got to feed a giraffe there as a child.

(a) had been frequenting
(b) has been frequenting
(c) will frequent
(d) is frequenting

시카고 지역에는 가볼 만한 아름다운 장소들이 많이 있지만, Matthew가 가장 좋아하는 곳은 브룩필드 동물원이다. 그가 어렸을 때 그곳에서 기린에게 먹이를 준 이래로 줄곧 동물원에 <u>자주 다녀오고 있는 중이다.</u>

🔑 **지텔프 치트키**

'ever since + 과거 동사'가 있으면 현재완료진행 시제가 정답이다.

💡 **현재완료진행과 자주 함께 쓰이는 시간 표현**
  • (ever) since + 과거 시점 + (for + 기간 표현) ~한 이래로 (줄곧) (~ 동안)
  • lately / for + 기간 표현 + now 최근에 / 현재 ~ 동안

해설 | 현재완료진행 시제와 함께 쓰이는 시간 표현 'ever since + 과거 동사'(ever since ~ got to feed)가 있고, 문맥상 Matthew가 어렸을 때 기린에게 먹이를 준 과거 시점부터 현재까지 계속해서 동물원에 자주 다녀오고 있는 중이라는 의미가 되어야 자연스럽다. 따라서 현재완료진행 시제 (b) has been frequenting이 정답이다.

오답분석
(d) 현재진행 시제는 특정 현재 시점에 한창 진행 중인 일을 나타내므로, 과거에 시작해서 현재 시점까지 계속해서 진행되고 있는 일을 표현할 수 없어 오답이다.

어휘 | feed v. 먹이를 주다 giraffe n. 기린 frequent v. 자주 다니다

The Chupa Chups lollipop logo was designed by famous surrealist artist Salvador Dalí. He suggested that the logo _____ to the top of the wrapper instead of its original placement on the side.

(a) will be moved
(b) be moved
(c) would move
(d) has been moved

츄파춥스 막대사탕 로고는 유명한 초현실주의 예술가 Salvador Dalí에 의해 디자인되었다. 그는 로고가 옆면에 있는 원래 배치 대신에 포장지 상단으로 <u>옮겨져야 한다</u>고 제안했다.

🔑 **지텔프 치트키**

suggest 다음에는 that절에 동사원형이 온다.

해설 | 주절에 제안을 나타내는 동사 suggest가 있으므로 that절에는 '(should +) 동사원형'이 와야 한다. 따라서 동사원형 (b) be moved가 정답이다.

어휘 | lollipop n. 막대사탕 surrealist adj. 초현실주의의; n. 초현실주의 wrapper n. 포장지 placement n. 배치

19 준동사   동명사를 목적어로 취하는 동사

Daphne is tired of her quiet office job at the insurance company. When she is not busy, she daydreams about escaping and imagines _____ on a tropical beach with a cocktail in hand.

Daphne는 보험 회사에서의 단조로운 사무직에 싫증이 났다. 그녀는 바쁘지 않을 때, 탈출에 관한 공상에 잠기고 칵테일을 손에 들고 열대 해변에서 <u>휴식을 취하는 것</u>을 상상한다.

(a) having relaxed
(b) to relax
(c) relaxing
(d) to have relaxed

⟶◯ 지텔프 치트키

imagine은 동명사를 목적어로 취한다.

> ☼ **동명사를 목적어로 취하는 빈출 동사**
> imagine 상상하다   dread 두려워하다   avoid 피하다   mind 개의하다   keep 계속하다   consider 고려하다   prevent 방지하다
> enjoy 즐기다   recommend 권장하다   risk 위험을 무릅쓰다   involve 포함하다

해설 | 빈칸 앞 동사 imagine은 동명사를 목적어로 취하므로, 동명사 (c) relaxing이 정답이다.

> 오답분석
>
> (a) having relaxed도 동명사이기는 하지만, 완료동명사(having relaxed)로 쓰일 경우 '상상하는' 시점보다 '휴식을 취하는' 시점이 앞선다는 것을 나타내므로 문맥에 적합하지 않아 오답이다.

어휘 | be tired of phr. ~이 싫증 나다   quiet adj. 단조로운, 변화 없는   office job phr. 사무직   insurance company phr. 보험 회사
daydream v. 공상에 잠기다; n. 공상   tropical adj. 열대(지방)의

20 시제   미래진행

Joey has been excited ever since he was accepted into his school's two-month foreign exchange program. Later this afternoon, he _____ for his flight to Germany next week.

Joey는 학교의 두 달간의 외국 교류 프로그램에 합격한 이래로 줄곧 신이 나 있다. 오늘 오후 늦게, 그는 다음 주의 독일행 비행기를 위해 <u>짐을 싸고 있는 중일 것이다.</u>

(a) packs
(b) has packed
(c) will be packing
(d) will have been packing

⟶◯ 지텔프 치트키

'for + 기간 표현' 없이 특정 미래 시점을 나타내는 표현만 있으면 미래진행 시제가 정답이다.

> ☼ **미래진행과 자주 함께 쓰이는 시간 표현**
> • when / if + 현재 동사 ~할 때 / 만약 ~한다면   • until / by + 미래 시점 ~까지
> • next + 시간 표현 다음 ~에   • starting + 미래 시점 / tomorrow ~부터 / 내일

해설 | 미래진행 시제와 함께 자주 쓰이는 특정 미래 시점을 나타내는 시간 표현 later this afternoon이 있고, 문맥상 오늘 오후 늦게, Joey는 다음 주의 독일행 비행기를 위해 짐을 싸고 있는 중일 것이라는 의미가 되어야 자연스럽다. 따라서 미래진행 시제 (c) will be packing이 정답이다.

어휘 | foreign exchange program phr. 외국 교류 프로그램 **pack** v. 짐을 싸다; n. 묶음, 꾸러미

---

21 연결어　접속사　　　　　　　　　　　　　　　　　난이도 ●●○

The word *orange* was initially only used as the name of the citrus fruit. _____ it was used to describe the color in the 1500s, most people used *red* or *yellow* to describe the hue.

(a) Until
(b) Because
(c) Given that
(d) In case

*오렌지*라는 단어는 원래 감귤류 과일의 이름으로만 사용되었다. 1500년대에 그것이 그 색깔을 묘사하는 데 사용될 때까지, 대부분의 사람은 그 색깔을 묘사하는 데 <u>빨간색</u>이나 <u>노란색</u>을 사용했다.

◁─○ 지텔프 치트키

'~할 때까지'라는 의미의 시간을 나타낼 때는 until을 쓴다.

> ☀ 시간을 나타내는 빈출 접속사
> until ~할 때까지　whenever ~할 때마다　while ~하는 동안　after ~한 이후에　before ~하기 전에

해설 | 문맥상 *오렌지*라는 단어가 1500년대에 그 색깔을 묘사하는 데 사용될 때까지 대부분의 사람은 그 색깔을 묘사하는 데 *빨간색*이나 *노란색*을 사용했다는 의미가 되어야 자연스럽다. 따라서 '~할 때까지'라는 의미의 시간을 나타내는 부사절 접속사 (a) Until이 정답이다.

오답분석
(b) Because는 '~이기 때문에', (c) Given that은 '~을 고려했을 때', (d) In case는 '~할 경우에 대비하여'라는 의미로, 문맥에 적합하지 않아 오답이다.

어휘 | initially adv. 원래, 처음에　citrus fruit phr. 감귤류의 과일　describe v. 묘사하다, 서술하다　hue n. 색깔, 색조

---

22 준동사　동명사를 목적어로 취하는 동사　　　　　　　난이도 ●●●

Most of the bank's employees refused to transfer to a new branch in another city. However, Shane welcomed _____ at another branch just so he could enjoy a change of scenery and meet new people.

(a) having worked
(b) to work
(c) **working**
(d) to be working

그 은행의 직원 대부분은 다른 도시에 있는 새로운 지점으로 옮기는 것을 거부했다. 하지만, Shane은 기분 전환을 즐기고 새로운 사람들을 만날 수 있도록 다른 지점에서 <u>일하는 것</u>을 환영했다.

◁─○ 지텔프 치트키

welcome은 동명사를 목적어로 취한다.

해설 | 빈칸 앞 동사 welcome은 동명사를 목적어로 취하므로, 동명사 (c) working이 정답이다.

오답분석
(a) having worked도 동명사이기는 하지만, 완료동명사(having worked)로 쓰일 경우 '환영하는' 시점보다 '일하는' 시점이 앞선다는

것을 나타내므로 문맥에 적합하지 않아 오답이다.

어휘 | refuse v. 거부하다, 거절하다 transfer v. 옮기다, 전근 가다 branch n. 지점, 지사 change of scenery phr. 기분 전환

---

23 가정법   가정법 과거   난이도 ●●○

The sun is important for all life forms on Earth. Plants rely on sunlight for photosynthesis, while animals are dependent on plants for food. If the sun were to suddenly vanish, living things _____ very long.

(a) will not have survived
(b) will not survive
(c) would not survive
(d) would not have survived

태양은 지구상의 모든 생명체에게 중요하다. 동물이 식량을 위해 식물에 의존하는 반면, 식물은 광합성을 위해 햇빛에 의존한다. 만약 태양이 갑자기 사라진다면, 생명체들은 그리 오래 살아남지 못할 것이다.

○ 지텔프 치트키

'if + were to + 동사원형'이 있으면 'would/could + 동사원형'이 정답이다.

> 💡 **가정법 과거(were to)**
> If + 주어 + were to + 동사원형, 주어 + would/could(조동사 과거형) + 동사원형

해설 | If절에 과거 동사(were to ~ vanish)가 있으므로, 주절에는 이와 짝을 이루어 가정법 과거를 만드는 'would(조동사 과거형) + 동사원형'이 와야 한다. 따라서 (c) would not survive가 정답이다.

어휘 | photosynthesis n. 광합성 be dependent on phr. ~에 의존하다 vanish v. 사라지다, 없어지다 survive v. 살아남다, 생존하다

---

24 준동사   to 부정사의 형용사 역할   난이도 ●●○

The southern counterpart to the aurora borealis is called the aurora australis. The best time _____ both of these amazing displays of northern and southern lights is in the winter season.

(a) to witness
(b) having witnessed
(c) to have witnessed
(d) witnessing

북극광에 대해 남쪽에 상응하는 것은 남극광이라고 불린다. 이 놀리운 북극광과 남극광을 모두 볼 가장 좋은 시기는 겨울철이다.

○ 지텔프 치트키

'~(해야) 할', '~하는'이라고 말할 때는 to 부정사를 쓴다.

해설 | 빈칸 앞에 명사(time)가 있고 문맥상 '북극광과 남극광을 모두 볼 시기'라는 의미가 되어야 자연스러우므로, 빈칸은 명사를 수식하는 형용사의 자리이다. 따라서 명사를 꾸며주는 형용사적 수식어구를 이끌 수 있는 to 부정사 (a) to witness가 정답이다.

어휘 | counterpart n. ~에 상응하는 것, 대응물 aurora borealis phr. 북극광 aurora australis phr. 남극광 witness v. 보다

25 준동사   동명사를 목적어로 취하는 동사   난이도 ●●○

My sister tried a recipe that she saw in an online video: a potato chip omelet made inside the chips' bag. It took a while to cook, but she appreciated _____ an unusual new culinary technique.

(a) to learn
(b) having learned
(c) to have learned
(d) learning

나의 여동생은 온라인 영상에서 본 감자칩 봉지 안에서 만든 감자칩 오믈렛 요리법을 시도해 보았다. 요리하는 데 시간이 좀 걸렸지만, 그녀는 새로운 특이한 요리 기술을 배우는 것을 높이 평가했다.

⊶○ 지텔프 치트키

appreciate는 동명사를 목적어로 취한다.

해설 | 빈칸 앞 동사 appreciate는 동명사를 목적어로 취하므로, 동명사 (d) learning이 정답이다.

> **오답분석**
> (b) having learned도 동명사이기는 하지만, 완료동명사(having learned)로 쓰일 경우 '높이 평가하는' 시점보다 '배우는' 시점이 앞선다는 것을 나타내므로 문맥에 적합하지 않아 오답이다.

어휘 | appreciate v. 높이 평가하다, 감사하다   unusual adj. 특이한, 색다른   culinary adj. 요리의

---

26 가정법   가정법 과거완료   난이도 ●●○

After four years of development, the mumps vaccine was released in 1967. At the time, this was the fastest development of a vaccine. Had the vaccine taken longer to produce, more people _____ by the virus.

(a) will be infected
(b) would have been infected
(c) will have been infected
(d) would be infected

4년간의 개발 끝에, 1967년에 볼거리 백신이 나왔다. 당시에는, 이것이 가장 빠른 백신 개발이었다. 백신이 생산되는 데 시간이 더 오래 걸렸다면, 더 많은 사람이 바이러스에 감염됐을 것이다.

⊶○ 지텔프 치트키

Had p.p.가 있으면 'would/could + have p.p.'가 정답이다.

해설 | if가 생략되어 도치된 절에 'had p.p.' 형태의 Had ~ taken이 있으므로, 주절에는 이와 짝을 이루어 가정법 과거완료를 만드는 'would(조동사 과거형) + have p.p.'가 와야 한다. 따라서 (b) would have been infected가 정답이다. 참고로 'Had the vaccine taken longer ~'는 'If the vaccine had taken longer ~'로 바꿔 쓸 수 있다.

어휘 | mumps n. 볼거리, 유행성 이하선염   vaccine n. 백신   infect v. 감염시키다, 옮기다

LISTENING

PART 1 (27-33) 일상 대화   조류 보호구역 답사에 관한 두 친구의 대화

안부 인사

F: Wow, that was fun, Richard! [27]Thanks for bringing me to the Amaya Sanctuary for Rescued Birds.

M: You're very welcome, Lily. [27]I'm glad you're having a good birthday.

주제 제시: 조류 보호 구역 답사

F: I am! You know, when we first walked into the bird sanctuary, I felt like I was walking into a peaceful forest, with all the birds chirping in the trees.

M: Yeah, it was very relaxing to hear the birds singing while the leaves rustled in the breeze. [28]I felt my stress slipping away more and more the farther we walked.

F: [28]It's really perfect for people who want to take a break from city life. Plus, the place is so accessible from the city.

M: That's true. So, [29]what was your favorite part of the visit?

F: Hmm . . . [29]I loved the bird-feeding activity. Being inside the enclosure with all those birds was exciting! [29]I couldn't believe it when that bright green parrot flew over and ate the grains right out of my hand.

먹이 주기 체험

M: I got a few shots of you feeding the birds. Here—take a look!

F: Great pictures, Richard! You know, it was nice to see that the birds were not scared of people. Maybe it's because many of them were kept as pets before they came to the sanctuary.

M: Could be. Although, since some of the birds were rescued because they were injured or because they had owners who didn't treat them well, [30]I had expected the birds to be afraid of people.

F: [30]I guess they spend so much of their time here around visitors and the sanctuary volunteers who take care of them.

M: I think you're right, Lily. I'm glad the birds were rescued and given a safe and comfortable home.

센터의 설명

F: So, how about you? Which part did you like the most?

M: Well, [31]the Welcome Center really caught my attention. I liked learning more about how the sanctuary operates. For instance, they had information about some of the rescued birds that are up for adoption.

여: 와, 재미있었어, Richard! [27]구조된 새들을 위한 Amaya 보호구역으로 데려가 줘서 고마워.

남: 천만에, Lily. [27]네가 생일을 잘 보내고 있어서 다행이야.

여: 그래! 알다시피, 우리가 처음 조류 보호구역에 들어섰을 때, 나는 마치 나무에서 새들이 지저귀는 가운데 평화로운 숲속으로 걸어 들어가고 있는 것 같았어.

남: 응, 나뭇잎이 바람에 바스락거리면서 새들이 지저귀는 소리를 들으니 마음이 정말 편안했어. [28]우리가 멀리 걸어갈수록 스트레스가 점점 사라지는 것 같았어.

여: [28]이곳은 도시 생활에서 벗어나 휴식을 취하고 싶은 사람들에게 정말 완벽해. 게다가, 이곳은 도시에서 접근하기도 쉬워.

남: 맞아. 그래서, [29]방문 중에 가장 마음에 들었던 부분은 뭐였어?

여: 흠... [29]새 먹이 주기 체험이 정말 좋았어. 그 모든 새와 함께 울타리 안에 있는 건 신났어! [29]나는 그 밝은 녹색 앵무새가 날아와서 바로 내 손에서 곡물을 먹었을 때 믿을 수 없었어.

남: 네가 새들에게 먹이를 주는 사진을 몇 장 찍었어. 여기, 한 번 봐봐!

여: 멋진 사진들이야, Richard! 알다시피, 그 새들이 사람들을 두려워하지 않는 걸 볼 수 있어서 좋았어. 아마도 그것 중 많은 새가 보호구역에 오기 전에 반려동물로 길러졌기 때문일 거야.

남: 그럴 수도 있어. 하지만, 일부 새들은 다쳤거나 치료를 잘해주지 않은 주인들이 있어서 구조되었기 때문에, [30]나는 새들이 사람들을 무서워할 거라고 예상했어.

여: [30]새들이 방문객들과 그들을 돌보는 보호구역 자원봉사자들 주변에서 많은 시간을 보내는 것 같아.

남: 네 말이 맞는 것 같아, Lily. 나는 새들이 구조돼서 안전하고 편안한 보금자리를 얻게 되어 기뻐.

여: 그래서, 너는 어때? 어떤 부분이 제일 마음에 들었어?

남: 음. [31]Welcome 센터가 정말로 내 주의를 끌었어. 보호구역이 운영되는 방식에 관해 자세히 배우는 것이 좋았어. 예를 들어, 그들은 입양을 기다리고 있는 구조된 일부 새들에 대한 정보도 가지고 있었어.

| | F: | Yes, they even had a picture of each bird that people can adopt, along with a story about where it came from and what its personality is like. | | 여: | 응, 그들은 심지어 사람들이 입양할 수 있는 각각의 새의 사진과 함께, 그 새가 어디에서 왔는지, 성격이 어떤지에 대한 이야기도 있었어. |

자원봉사 프로그램

M: I might not be ready for bird ownership yet, but [32]I did snag a pamphlet about the sanctuary's volunteer program.

F: I'd like to look at that pamphlet later, Richard. Maybe we should consider signing up as volunteers.

M: That could be fun!

남: 나는 아직 새를 키울 준비가 안 됐을 수도 있지만, [32]보호구역의 자원봉사 프로그램에 대한 팸플릿을 가져왔어.

여: 나도 나중에 그 팸플릿을 보고 싶어, Richard. 우리가 자원봉사자로 등록하는 것도 고려해 봐야겠어.

남: 그거 재미있겠네!

기념품 가게

F: I thought the souvenir shop was great too. I bought this stuffed animal that looks just like my new friend, the green parrot!

M: And I got this key chain for my little sister.

F: Cute! It's nice to know that the profits from the souvenir shop are used to maintain the sanctuary.

여: 나는 기념품 가게도 멋지다고 생각했어. 내 새 친구인 녹색 앵무새랑 꼭 닮은 봉제 동물 인형을 샀어!

남: 그리고 내 여동생을 위해 열쇠고리를 샀어.

여: 귀여워! 기념품 가게의 수익금이 보호구역을 유지하는 데 쓰인다는 걸 알게 되어 정말 좋아.

마코앵무새 동상

M: Hey, [33]did you see the really big statue of the sanctuary's mascot, Petey the blue-and-gold macaw, near the entrance?

F: Oh, thanks for reminding me, Richard! [33]I'd love to get a picture of Petey and me.

M: Me too, Lily! [33]Maybe we can even find someone who'll take a picture of both of us.

남: 저기, [33]입구 근처에 있는 보호구역의 마스코트인 파란색과 금색 마코앵무새 Petey의 정말 큰 동상 봤어?

여: 오, 상기시켜 줘서 고마워, Richard! [33]Petey랑 같이 사진 찍고 싶어.

남: 나도 그래, Lily! [33]우리 둘 다 사진을 찍어줄 사람을 찾을 수 있을지도 몰라.

어휘 | sanctuary[sǽŋktʃuèri] 보호구역 chirp[tʃə:rp] 지저귀다, 울다 rustle[rʌsl] 바스락거리다, 살랑거리다 breeze[bri:z] 바람, 순풍 slip away 사라지다, 없어지다 enclosure[inklóuʒər] 울타리 parrot[pǽrət] 앵무새 grain[grein] 곡물, (곡식의) 낟알 shot[ʃat] 사진, 한 장면 rescue[réskju:] 구조하다 treat[tri:t] 치료하다 volunteer[vàləntíər] 자원봉사자; 자원하다 take care of ~을 돌보다 catch attention 주의를 끌다 operate[ápərèit] 운영하다, 작동하다 adoption[ədápʃən] 입양 adopt[ədápt] 입양하다 personality[pə̀:rsənǽləti] 성격 snag[snæg] (다른 사람보다 먼저) 잡아채다 souvenir shop 기념품 가게 stuffed animal 봉제 동물 인형 key chain 열쇠고리 profit[práfit] 수익, 이윤 statue[stǽtʃu:] 동상, 조각상 mascot[mǽskat] 마스코트 macaw[məkɔ́:] 마코앵무새 take a picture 사진을 찍다

---

27 특정세부사항   What   난이도 ●●○

What are Lily and Richard doing at the bird sanctuary?

(a) enjoying a peaceful picnic
(b) working on a school project
(c) celebrating a special occasion
(d) looking for a specific bird

Lily와 Richard는 조류 보호구역에서 무엇을 하고 있는가?

(a) 평화로운 소풍을 즐기는 것
(b) 학교 프로젝트를 작업하는 것
(c) 특별한 때를 축하하는 것
(d) 특정한 새를 찾는 것

─○ 정답 잡는 치트키

질문의 키워드 sanctuary가 그대로 언급된 주변 내용을 주의 깊게 듣는다.

해설 | 여자가 'Thanks for bringing me to the Amaya Sanctuary for Rescued Birds.'라며 구조된 새들을 위한 Amaya 보호구역으로 데려가 줘서 고맙다고 하자, 남자가 'I'm glad you're having a good birthday.'라며 여자가 생일을 잘 보내고 있어서 다행이라고 했다. 따라서 (c)가 정답이다.

⇄ **Paraphrasing**

birthday 생일 → a special occasion 특별한 때

어휘 | occasion[əkéiʒən] 특별한 때, 중요한 행사

---

28 추론   특정사실   난이도 ●●●

Why, most likely, is the sanctuary tour perfect for people who live in the city?

(a) It offers discounts for locals.
(b) It allows them to breathe clean air.
(c) It can lower their anxiety.
(d) It gives them a place to walk.

보호구역 투어는 왜 도시에 사는 사람들에게 완벽한 것 같은가?

(a) 주민들에게 할인 혜택을 제공한다.
(b) 깨끗한 공기를 마실 수 있게 해준다.
(c) 불안을 낮출 수 있다.
(d) 걸을 만한 장소를 제공한다.

─○ 정답 잡는 치트키

질문의 키워드 perfect for people who ~ city가 그대로 언급된 주변 내용을 주의 깊게 듣는다.

해설 | 남자가 'I felt my stress slipping away more and more the farther we walked.'라며 멀리 걸어갈수록 스트레스가 점점 사라지는 것 같았다고 하자, 여자가 'It's really perfect for people who want to take a break from city life.'라며 도시 생활에서 벗어나 휴식을 취하고 싶은 사람들에게 정말 완벽하다고 한 것을 통해, 보호구역 투어가 불안을 낮출 수 있어서 도시에 사는 사람들에게 완벽한 것임을 추론할 수 있다. 따라서 (c)가 정답이다.

⇄ **Paraphrasing**

stress 스트레스 → anxiety 불안

어휘 | local[lóukəl] 주민 breathe[briːð] (공기를) 마시다 anxiety[æŋzáiəti] 불안

---

29 특정세부사항   What   난이도 ●●○

What was Lily's favorite experience at the bird sanctuary?

(a) feeding the birds by hand
(b) touring the bird enclosures
(c) watching the birds fly around
(d) seeing an exciting bird show

Lily가 조류 보호구역에서 가장 좋아한 경험은 무엇이었는가?

(a) 새들에게 손으로 먹이를 주는 것
(b) 새 울타리를 둘러보는 것
(c) 새들이 날아다니는 것을 지켜보는 것
(d) 흥미진진한 새 쇼를 관람하는 것

─○ 정답 잡는 치트키

질문의 키워드 favorite가 그대로 언급된 주변 내용을 주의 깊게 듣는다.

해설 | 남자가 'what was your favorite part of the visit?'이라며 방문 중에 가장 마음에 들었던 부분이 무엇이었는지 묻자, 여자가 'I loved the bird-feeding activity.'라며 새 먹이 주기 체험이 정말 좋았다고 한 뒤, 'I couldn't believe it when that bright green parrot ~ ate the grains right out of my hand.'라며 그 밝은 녹색 앵무새가 바로 자기 손에서 곡물을 먹었을 때 믿을 수 없었다고 했다. 따라서 (a)가 정답이다.

어휘 | by hand 손으로

30 특정세부사항   Why   난이도 ●●○

Based on Lily's guess, why are the birds not afraid of the visitors?

(a) because they are trained by the volunteers
(b) because they were raised in a pet store
(c) because they are used to being around people
(d) because they were previously kept in a zoo

Lily의 추측에 따르면, 새들은 왜 방문객들을 두려워하지 않는가?

(a) 자원봉사자들에 의해 훈련을 받기 때문에
(b) 반려동물 가게에서 길러졌기 때문에
(c) 사람들 주변에 있는 것에 익숙해져 있기 때문에
(d) 이전에 동물원에서 길러졌기 때문에

━━○ 정답 잡는 치트키

질문의 키워드 afraid of the visitors가 afraid of people로 paraphrasing되어 언급된 주변 내용을 주의 깊게 듣는다.

해설 | 남자가 'I had expected the birds to be afraid of people'이라며 새들이 사람들을 무서워할 거라고 예상했다고 하자, 여자가 'I guess they spend so much of their time here around visitors and the sanctuary volunteers who take care of them.'이라며 새들이 방문객들과 그들을 돌보는 보호구역 자원봉사자들 주변에서 많은 시간을 보내는 것 같다고 했다. 따라서 (c)가 정답이다.

   ↻ **Paraphrasing**
visitors and ~ volunteers 방문객들과 자원봉사자들 → people 사람들

어휘 | previously [príːviəsli] 이전에, 과거에

---

31 특정세부사항   How   난이도 ●●○

How did Richard learn more about how the sanctuary operates?

(a) by reading a story about its history
(b) by talking with the rescue workers
(c) by seeing pictures in the bird museum
(d) by looking around the visitor center

Richard는 어떻게 보호구역이 운영되는 방식에 관해 자세히 알게 되었는가?

(a) 역사에 관한 이야기를 읽음으로써
(b) 구조대원들과 이야기 나눔으로써
(c) 조류 박물관에서 사진을 봄으로써
(d) 방문자 센터를 둘러봄으로써

━━○ 정답 잡는 치트키

질문의 키워드 how the sanctuary operates가 그대로 언급된 주변 내용을 주의 깊게 듣는다.

해설 | 남자가 'the Welcome Center really caught my attention. I liked learning more about how the sanctuary operates.'라며 Welcome 센터가 정말로 주의를 끌었는데, 보호구역이 운영되는 방식에 관해 자세히 배우는 것이 좋았다고 했다. 따라서 (d)가 정답이다.

어휘 | rescue worker 구조대원   look around 둘러보다

---

32 특정세부사항   What   난이도 ●●○

What is the pamphlet that Richard picked up about?

(a) the process for bird adoption
(b) how people can donate their time

Richard가 가져온 팸플릿은 무엇에 관한 것인가?

(a) 새의 입양 절차
(b) 사람들이 그들의 시간을 기부할 수 있는 방법

(c) the souvenir items for sale
(d) how the facility is maintained

(c) 판매 중인 기념품
(d) 시설이 유지되는 방법

━━○ 정답 잡는 치트키

질문의 키워드 pamphlet이 그대로 언급된 주변 내용을 주의 깊게 듣는다.

해설 | 남자가 'I did snag a pamphlet about the sanctuary's volunteer program'이라며 보호구역의 자원봉사 프로그램에 대한 팸플릿을 가져왔다고 했다. 따라서 (b)가 정답이다.

어휘 | for sale 판매 중인, 팔려고 내놓은

33 추론   다음에 할 일   난이노 ●●○

What will Richard and Lily probably do after the conversation?

(a) **take photos by the bird statue**
(b) look at the pictures they took
(c) shake hands with the mascot
(d) ask someone for directions

Richard와 Lily는 대화 이후에 무엇을 할 것 같은가?

(a) **새 동상 옆에서 사진을 찍는다**
(b) 그들이 찍은 사진을 본다
(c) 마스코트와 악수한다
(d) 누군가에게 길을 묻는다

━━○ 정답 잡는 치트키

다음에 할 일을 언급하는 후반을 주의 깊게 듣는다.

해설 | 남자가 'did you see the really big statue of the sanctuary's mascot, Petey the blue-and-gold macaw, ~?'라며 보호구역의 마스코트인 파란색과 금색 마코앵무새 Petey의 정말 큰 동상을 봤는지 묻자, 여자가 'I'd love to get a picture of Petey and me.'라며 Petey랑 같이 사진 찍고 싶다고 했고, 남자가 'Maybe we can even find someone who'll take a picture of both of us.'라며 둘 다 사진을 찍어줄 사람을 찾을 수 있을지도 모른다고 한 것을 통해, Richard와 Lily는 대화 이후에 보호구역의 마스코트인 마코앵무새 Petey의 동상 옆에서 사진을 찍을 것임을 추론할 수 있다. 따라서 (a)가 정답이다.

↻ **Paraphrasing**
picture 사진 → photos 사진

어휘 | shake hands with ~와 악수하다   direction [dirékʃən] 길, 방향

PART 2 [34~39] 발표 스마트 연기 감지 시스템 홍보

음성 바로 듣기

주제
제시:
스마트
연기
감지
시스템

Welcome to Green Lake County's annual Fire Prevention Seminar. Are you tired of covering your home smoke detector or fanning smoke away just so its alarm won't trigger while you're cooking? Concerned about potential fires when you're not home to call emergency services? [34]Say goodbye to these problems with the Fire-Zap smart smoke detection system!

그린 레이크 카운티의 연례 화재 예방 세미나에 오신 것을 환영합니다. 요리하는 동안 경보가 작동하지 않도록 가정용 연기 탐지기를 가리거나 연기를 부채질해서 내보내는 데 지치셨나요? 응급 서비스를 부르기에는 부재 중일 때 있을 수 있는 화재가 걱정되시나요? [34]Fire-Zap 스마트 연기 감지 시스템으로 이러한 문제에 작별을 고하세요!

Fire-Zap is the latest and most accurate in our line of smoke detection systems that use state-of-the-art technologies. [35]The finely tuned sensors can determine the severity of the fire, so there's no need to worry that firefighters will show up for false alarms. [35]If there's only a small amount of smoke that quickly goes away, you'll receive a gentle alert about a potential fire situation. On the other hand, if Fire-Zap detects a fast-burning fire, a loud alarm will go off, notifying you of immediate danger.

As for the product's other smart features, each Fire-Zap device is equipped with a high-definition camera that can produce 360-degree images of its surroundings. Several of these can be installed strategically around your home. [36]When the built-in sensor detects smoke, the camera takes a snapshot of the source. It then analyzes the picture by comparing it with thousands of cataloged images in our database and assesses whether the threat is real or not.

Now, what if you're not home when a fire starts? That beeping alarm won't be much use if nobody is around to hear it. With Fire-Zap, you can have simultaneous alerts sent to the contacts saved in its memory. Fire-Zap can store up to ten contacts including yourself, close family members, neighbors, and nearby fire stations. In case of an emergency, Fire-Zap will send them an alert via all available channels to ensure the best chances for a response. [37]You never know when a neighbor may be able to grab your precious pets or assist elderly loved ones before first responders arrive.

The message alert includes an image of the source of smoke and an analysis of the possible cause. The message also provides a GPS location that makes it easier for responders to locate your home. Fire-Zap works in partnership with emergency response teams, which allows users to receive periodic status updates about the responders' location and progress.

Fire-Zap is also equipped with voice alerts that tell you the exact location of the fire. If you have devices in multiple rooms, Fire-Zap will tell you which area of the house is affected so your family can avoid it and take the necessary steps toward safety. [38]When evacuating your home, these alerts are particularly helpful by providing spoken commands to guide you through the best escape route.

Fire-Zap은 최첨단 기술을 사용하는 연기 감지 시스템 제품군에서 가장 최신이고 가장 정확합니다. [35]미세하게 조정된 센서가 화재의 심각성을 판단할 수 있으므로, 소방관들이 거짓 경보로 인해 도착하는 것을 걱정할 필요가 없습니다. [35]금방 사라지는 소량의 연기만 있어도, 잠재적인 화재 상황에 대한 가벼운 경보를 받게 됩니다. 반면에, Fire-Zap이 빠르게 타오르는 화재를 감지하면, 큰 경보음이 울려, 즉각적인 위험을 알려줍니다.

제품의 다른 스마트 기능과 관련하여, 각 Fire-Zap 장치에는 주변 환경의 360도 이미지를 촬영할 수 있는 고화질 카메라를 갖추고 있습니다. 이 중 여러 대는 집 주변에 전략적으로 설치될 수 있습니다. [36]내장 센서가 연기를 감지하면, 카메라가 발화 지점의 스냅숏을 찍습니다. 그런 다음 데이터베이스에 분류된 수천 개의 이미지와 비교하여 사진을 분석하고 위협이 실제인지의 여부를 평가합니다.

이제, 화재가 시작됐을 때 집에 없으면 어떻게 될까요? 주변에 경보음을 들을 만한 사람이 아무도 없다면 경보음은 소용이 없을 것입니다. Fire-Zap을 사용하면, 메모리에 저장된 연락처에 동시에 경보가 전송되게 할 수 있습니다. Fire-Zap은 본인, 가까운 가족, 이웃, 인근 소방서를 포함하여 10개의 연락처까지 저장할 수 있습니다. 긴급 상황의 경우에는, Fire-Zap은 사용할 수 있는 모든 경로를 통해 경보를 전송하여 최상의 대응 기회를 보장합니다. [37]첫 번째 응급 처치 요원이 도착하기 전에 이웃이 소중한 반려동물을 붙잡거나 연로한 가족을 도울 수 있을지도 모릅니다.

메시지 알림은 연기 발생원 이미지와 가능한 원인에 대한 분석을 포함합니다. 또한 메시지는 응급 처치 요원들이 집의 위치를 쉽게 찾을 수 있도록 GPS 위치도 제공합니다. Fire-Zap은 긴급 구조대와 협력하여 작동하므로, 이는 사용자들이 응급 처치 요원들의 위치 및 진행 상황에 대한 주기적인 상태 업데이트를 받게 합니다.

Fire-Zap은 화재의 정확한 위치를 알려주는 음성 알림도 갖추고 있습니다. 장치가 여러 방에 있다면, Fire-Zap은 집의 어느 구역이 영향을 받는지 알려주므로 가족은 이를 피하고 안전을 위해 필요한 조치를 할 수 있습니다. [38]집을 비우고 떠날 때, 이러한 알림은 음성 명령을 제공하여 최적의 탈출로를 안내해 주므로 특히 유용합니다.

<table>
<tr><td>특징5:
앱
제공</td><td>You can access all of these features anytime and anywhere by downloading the Fire-Zap App. The app offers a quick and easy way to shut off the alarm once the problem has been resolved. The application will also allow you to view live camera feeds of any prospective dangers.</td><td>Fire-Zap 앱을 다운로드하여 언제 어디서나 이러한 모든 기능에 접근할 수 있습니다. 이 앱은 문제가 해결되면 경보를 빠르고 쉽게 끄는 방법을 제공합니다. 또한 이 애플리케이션은 잠재적인 위험에 대한 실시간 카메라 피드를 볼 수 있게 해줍니다.</td></tr>
<tr><td>문의 및
신청
안내</td><td>For more information on pricing and installation, please call 555-0122 or email us. The system is available nationwide, but free installation is available to the lucky residents of the Green Lake County area. That's right—³⁹if you're a local and you mention this seminar, we'll install the system at no charge!</td><td>가격 및 설치에 관한 자세한 정보는, 555-0122로 전화하거나 이메일을 보내주세요. 이 시스템은 전국에서 사용할 수 있지만, 그린 레이크 카운티 지역의 운 좋은 거주자들에게는 무료 설치가 가능합니다. ³⁹당신이 지역 주민이면서 이 세미나를 언급하시면, 무료로 이 시스템을 설치해 드리는 것이 맞습니다!</td></tr>
<tr><td>끝인사</td><td>Why wait? Be protected. Feel safe. Get access to help when and only when you need it.</td><td>왜 기다리시나요? 보호받으세요. 안전함을 느끼세요. 필요한 때에만 도움을 받으세요.</td></tr>
</table>

어휘 | smoke detector 연기 탐지기 fan[fæn] 부채질을 하다 alarm[əlɑ́ːrm] 경보, 알람; ~을 놀라게 하다 trigger[trígər] (장치를) 작동시키다 potential[pəténʃəl] 있을 수 있는, 잠재적인 state-of-the-art[stéitəvðiɑ̀ːrt] 최첨단의, 최신식의 finely[fáinli] 미세하게 tune[tjuːn] 조정하다 severity[səvérəti] 심각성 show up 도착하다, 나타나다 go away 사라지다, 가버리다 gentle[dʒéntl] 가벼운, 적당한 alert[ələ́ːrt] 경보, 경계 detect[ditékt] 감지하다, 발견하다 go off 울리다 be equipped with ~을 갖추고 있다 high-definition 고화질의 strategically[strətíːdʒikəli] 전략적으로, 체계적으로 built-in 내장된 analyze[ǽnəlàiz] 분석하다, 조사하다 cataloge[kǽtəlɔ̀g] 분류하다; 목록, 카탈로그 threat[θret] 위협 simultaneous[sàiməltéiniəs] 동시에 하는 neighbor[néibər] 이웃 fire station 소방서 channel[tʃǽnl] 경로 response[rispáns] 대응, 조치 grab[græb] 붙잡다, 움켜잡다 first responder 응급 처치 요원 locate[lóukeit] ~의 위치를 찾아내다 in partnership with ~과 협력하여 evacuate[ivǽkjuèit] (집 따위를) 비우고 떠나다 command[kəmǽnd] 명령; 명령하다 escape route 탈출로 shut off 끄다, 멈추다 resolve[rizɑ́lv] 해결하다 prospective[prəspéktiv] 잠재적인 installation[ìnstəléiʃən] 설치 nationwide[néiʃənwàid] 전국적인 at no charge 무료로

---

34 주제/목적   담화의 주제   난이도 ●●●

What is the talk all about?

(a) a guide for emergency preparation
(b) an interactive alarm system
(c) a system for detecting intrusion
(d) a device for preventing fires

담화의 주제는 무엇인가?

(a) 비상사태 대비 가이드
(b) 쌍방향 경보 시스템
(c) 침입 감지 시스템
(d) 화재 예방 장치

〰O 정답 잡는 치트키

담화의 주제를 언급하는 초반을 주의 깊게 듣고 전체 맥락을 파악한다.

해설 | 화자가 'Say goodbye to these problems with the Fire-Zap smart smoke detection system!'이라며 Fire-Zap 스마트 연기 감지 시스템으로 문제에 작별을 고하라고 한 뒤, 담화 전반에 걸쳐 쌍방향 화재 알림 경보 시스템인 Fire-Zap을 홍보하는 내용이 이어지고 있다. 따라서 (b)가 정답이다.

오답분석
(d) Fire-Zap은 연기 감지 시스템으로, 화재를 예방하는 장치는 아니므로 오답이다.

어휘 | interactive[ìntərǽktiv] 쌍방향의

How, most likely, can Fire-Zap users determine the severity of a house fire?	Fire-Zap 사용자들은 어떻게 주택 화재의 심각성을 판단할 수 있는 것 같은가?
(a) by listening for different sounds (b) by calling the tech company (c) by watching for flashing lights (d) by checking in with firefighters	**(a)** 다른 소리를 들음으로써 (b) 기술 회사에 전화함으로써 (c) 번쩍이는 불빛을 관찰함으로써 (d) 소방관들에게 확인함으로써

━○ 정답 잡는 치트키

질문의 키워드 determine the severity가 그대로 언급된 주변 내용을 주의 깊게 듣는다.

해설 ┃ 화자가 'The finely tuned sensors can determine the severity of the fire'라며 미세하게 조정된 센서가 화재의 심각성을 판단할 수 있다고 한 뒤, 'If there's only a small amount of smoke that quickly goes away, you'll receive a gentle alert ~. On the other hand, if Fire-Zap detects a fast-burning fire, a loud alarm will go off'라며 금방 사라지는 소량의 연기만 있어도 가벼운 경보를 받게 되지만, Fire-Zap이 빠르게 타오르는 화재를 감지하면 큰 경보음이 울린다고 한 것을 통해, Fire-Zap 사용자들은 화재의 규모에 따라 다르게 울리는 소리를 들음으로써 주택 화재의 심각성을 판단할 수 있음을 추론할 수 있다. 따라서 (a)가 정답이다.

어휘 ┃ flashing[flǽʃiŋ] 번쩍이는

Why does Fire-Zap take a picture of the area where smoke is detected?	Fire-Zap은 왜 연기가 감지되는 부분의 사진을 찍는가?
(a) to evaluate the threat level (b) to show to the insurance company (c) to add to a photo database (d) to keep a record for researchers	**(a)** 위협 수준을 평가하기 위해서 (b) 보험 회사에 보여주기 위해서 (c) 사진 데이터베이스에 추가하기 위해서 (d) 연구자들을 위해 기록해 두기 위해서

━○ 정답 잡는 치트키

질문의 키워드 take a picture가 takes a snapshot으로 paraphrasing되어 언급된 주변 내용을 주의 깊게 듣는다.

해설 ┃ 화자가 'When the built-in sensor detects smoke, the camera takes a snapshot of the source. It then analyzes the picture by comparing it with thousands of cataloged images in our database and assesses whether the threat is real or not.'이라며 내장 센서가 연기를 감지하면 카메라가 발화 지점의 스냅숏을 찍고, 그런 다음 데이터베이스에 분류된 수천 개의 이미지와 비교하여 사진을 분석하고 위협이 실제인지의 여부를 평가한다고 했다. 따라서 (a)가 정답이다.

⟳ **Paraphrasing**
assesses 평가하다 → evaluate 평가하다

어휘 ┃ insurance company 보험 회사   keep a record 기록해 두다

37

특정세부사항　　How　　　　　　　　　　　　　　　　　난이도 ●●○

Based on the talk, how can neighbors be of assistance during a fire emergency?

(a) They can call the fire department.
(b) They can check on anyone in the house.
(c) They can alert people in nearby houses.
(d) They can contact the homeowner.

담화에 따르면, 화재 응급상황 동안 이웃들이 어떻게 도움이 될 수 있는가?

(a) 소방서에 전화할 수 있다.
(b) 집 안에 있는 누군가를 확인할 수 있다.
(c) 근처의 집에 있는 사람들에게 주의를 줄 수 있다.
(d) 주택 소유자에게 연락할 수 있다.

◀─○ **정답 잡는 치트키**

질문의 키워드 neighbors가 그대로 언급된 주변 내용을 주의 깊게 듣는다.

해설 | 화자가 'You never know when a neighbor may be able to grab your precious pets or assist elderly loved ones before first responders arrive.'라며 첫 번째 응급 처치 요원이 도착하기 전에 이웃이 소중한 반려동물을 붙잡거나 연로한 가족을 도울 수 있을지도 모른다고 했다. 따라서 (b)가 정답이다.

어휘 | assistance[əsístəns] 도움, 지원　fire department 소방서　homeowner[hóumòunər] 주택 소유자

38

특정세부사항　　What　　　　　　　　　　　　　　　　　난이도 ●●○

According to the speaker, what is particularly helpful when one is trying to find the best evacuation route?

(a) having a prepared escape plan
(b) having the voice alert function
(c) seeing accurate visual maps
(d) wearing a protective mask

화자에 따르면, 최적의 대피 경로를 찾으려고 할 때 특히 도움이 되는 것은 무엇인가?

(a) 준비된 탈출 계획이 있는 것
(b) 음성 경보 기능이 있는 것
(c) 정확한 시각 지도를 보는 것
(d) 보호 마스크를 착용하는 것

◀─○ **정답 잡는 치트키**

질문의 키워드 best evacuation route가 best escape route로 paraphrasing되어 언급된 주변 내용을 주의 깊게 듣는다.

해설 | 화자가 'When evacuating your home, these alerts are particularly helpful by providing spoken commands to guide you through the best escape route.'라며 집을 비우고 떠날 때 이러한 알림은 음성 명령을 제공하여 최적의 탈출로를 안내해 주므로 특히 유용하다고 했다. 따라서 (b)가 정답이다.

⇄ **Paraphrasing**
spoken commands 음성 명령 → the voice alert function 음성 경보 기능

어휘 | evacuation route 대피 경로

39

특정세부사항　　How　　　　　　　　　　　　　　　　　난이도 ●●●

How can one get free installation of the system?

(a) by visiting a local branch
(b) by living in a certain area

시스템 무료 설치는 어떻게 받을 수 있는가?

(a) 지역 지사를 방문함으로써
(b) 일정한 지역에 거주함으로써

(c) by downloading an application
(d) by attending the talk

(c) 애플리케이션을 다운로드함으로써
(d) 협의에 참석함으로써

해설 | 화자가 'if you're a local and you mention this seminar, we'll install the system at no charge'라며 지역 주민이면서 이 세미나를 언급하면 무료로 이 시스템을 설치해 준다고 했다. 따라서 (d)가 정답이다.

⇄ **Paraphrasing**
seminar 세미나 → the talk 협의

오답분석
(b) 화자가 지역 주민이면서 이 세미나를 언급하면 무료로 시스템을 설치해 준다고 언급하기는 했지만, 세미나에 참석하지 않은 지역 주민에게도 무료로 시스템을 설치해 주는 것은 아니므로 오답이다.

PART 3 (40~45) 장단점 논의 **2단 침대와 개별 침대의 장단점 비교**

음성 바로 듣기

안부 인사	M: Good afternoon, April. ⁴⁰What brings you to the Riverside Furniture Emporium? F: Hi, Kevin! I didn't know you worked here. ⁴⁰Maybe you can help me out with something for the bedroom my sons are sharing. You know, moving into a new house is tough, **especially with two kids.** M: I can imagine. Are the boys adjusting well to their new home?
주제 제시: 장단점 비교	F: They're doing okay, but their room isn't prepared yet because I'm still deciding if I should get a bunk bed or two separate beds for them. M: I see . . . I can help you think about the advantages and disadvantages of both options.
2단 침대의 장점	F: That would be really helpful, Kevin. What's your opinion about bunk beds? M: Well, one advantage is that ⁴¹bunk beds can save floor space. Since they're basically two beds stacked on top of one another, they occupy the space of only one bed. F: ⁴¹I like that about bunk beds. The boys have a slightly bigger bedroom in the new house than they did before, but it could still be cramped with two whole beds. M: It's always nice to save some space for other things. F: Another advantage is that my sons are at the age when kids get really excited about bunk beds.

남: 안녕, April. ⁴⁰Riverside 가구 백화점에는 무슨 일로 왔어?
여: 안녕, Kevin! 네가 여기서 일하는지 몰랐어. ⁴⁰내 아들들이 같이 쓰는 침실에 들일 가구 관련해서 좀 도와줄 수 있어? 너도 알다시피, 새집으로 이사하는 건, 특히 애가 둘이면 힘들잖아.
남: 상상이 되네. 아들들은 새집에 잘 적응하고 있어?

여: 잘 지내고는 있는데, 2단 침대를 둬야 할지, 별도의 침대 두 개를 둬야 할지 여전히 정하는 중이라 방이 아직 준비가 안 됐어.
남: 그렇구나… 두 가지 옵션의 장단점에 대해 생각해 보도록 도와줄게.

여: 정말 도움이 될 거야, Kevin. 2단 침대에 대한 너의 의견은 어때?
남: 음, 한 가지 장점은 ⁴¹2단 침대가 바닥 면적을 절약하게 해 줄 수 있다는 거야. 기본적으로 두 개의 침대를 서로 위에 쌓은 것이기 때문에, 침대 한 개 정도의 공간만 차지해.
여: ⁴¹나는 2단 침대에 관해 그게 마음에 들어. 아들들은 새집에서 이전보다 약간 더 큰 침실을 갖게 되겠지만, 여전히 침대 두 개로는 비좁을 수 있어.
남: 다른 것들을 위해 공간을 절약하는 건 언제나 좋지.
여: 또 다른 장점으로는 내 아들들은 아이들이 2단 침대에 굉장히 흥분하는 나이라는 거야. 여섯 살과

2단 침대의 단점

They're six and seven years old, so they might enjoy switching between the upper and lower beds every once in a while.

M: Children do have a lot of fun with that.

F: However, one disadvantage of choosing a bunk bed is that the kids could outgrow it in just a few years.

M: You have a point, April. They might not want to be sharing a bunk bed once they're in high school—maybe even middle school. And another downside is that one boy's sleep could get disturbed when the other boy is climbing the ladder.

F: I'm not too worried about that since they're deep sleepers. But ⁴²climbing up and down could be a serious problem since my boys have a lot of energy and can be careless at times.

M: ⁴²That could lead to a dangerous situation. ⁴³Now, let's talk about the advantages of buying your sons individual beds.

개별 침대의 장점

F: Okay, Kevin. One is that ⁴³I would have a much easier time changing the sheets. I wouldn't have to climb a ladder or worry about bumping my head when arranging the clean bedding.

M: That's true. You can also easily tuck them in at bedtime that way. Another advantage of getting separate beds is that the boys can have their own space.

F: That's a good point! They'll have separate areas that they can decorate with toys or pictures of their favorite cartoon characters. But won't buying two beds be expensive?

개별 침대의 단점

M: Well, yes. After all, you'd be paying for two products with two separate markups.

F: Another problem is that ⁴⁴the boys might fight about who gets to sleep where. They're both convinced there's a monster hiding in their closet, ha-ha. Neither of them would want to sleep in the bed closest to the spooky door!

M: Ha-ha, that could cause some conflict!

여자의 결정

F: Right. Well, this conversation has really been helpful.

M: So, ⁴⁵have you come up with a decision?

F: I think I have. ⁴⁵I'd like to give each of my boys his own space since they have different interests. Thanks, Kevin.

M: You're welcome, April. Now let me show you our selection.

일곱 살이니까, 가끔 위층과 아래층 침대를 바꿔가며 사용하는 걸 좋아할 거야.

남: 아이들은 그것에 관해 정말 즐거워해.

여: 하지만, 2단 침대를 선택하는 것의 한 가지 단점은 아이들이 단 몇 년 만에 2단 침대보다 더 커질 수 있다는 점이야.

남: 일리가 있어, April. 그들이 고등학교, 심지어 중학교에만 들어가도 2단 침대를 함께 쓰고 싶지 않아 할 수도 있어. 그리고 또 다른 부정적인 면은 아들 한 명이 사다리를 올라갈 때 다른 아들의 수면이 방해받을 수 있다는 거야.

여: 깊게 잠을 자는 애들이라 그런 건 크게 걱정하지 않아. 하지만 ⁴²아들들이 에너지가 넘치고 때때로 부주의할 수도 있어서 오르내리는 것이 심각한 문제일 수 있어.

남: ⁴²위험한 상황으로 이어질 수 있겠네. ⁴³이제, 아들들에게 개별 침대를 사주는 것의 장점에 관해 얘기해보자.

여: 알겠어, Kevin. 하나는 ⁴³내가 시트를 바꾸는 것이 훨씬 수월할 거라는 거야. 깨끗한 침구류를 정리할 때 사다리를 오르거나 머리를 부딪칠 염려를 할 필요가 없어.

남: 맞아. 취침 시간에도 그렇게 하면 쉽게 그것들을 넣을 수 있어. 별도의 침대를 두는 것의 또 다른 장점은 아들들이 자기만의 공간을 가질 수 있다는 거야.

여: 좋은 지적이야! 그들은 장난감이나 그들이 좋아하는 만화 캐릭터의 사진으로 장식할 수 있는 별도의 공간을 갖게 될 거야. 하지만 침대 두 개를 사는 건 비싸지 않아?

남: 음, 맞아. 결국, 두 개 각각의 원가에 가산되는 금액이 포함된 두 제품에 대해 시불하게 되는 거야.

여: 또 다른 문제는 ⁴⁴아들들이 누가 어디서 자는지 싸울 수도 있다는 거야. 둘 다 옷장에 괴물이 숨어 있다고 확신하거든, 하하. 둘 다 무시무시한 문에서 가장 가까운 침대에서는 자고 싶지 않을 거야!

남: 하하, 그게 갈등을 일으킬 수도 있겠네!

여: 맞아. 음, 이 대화가 정말 도움이 됐어.

남: 그래서, ⁴⁵결정을 내렸어?

여: 그런 것 같아. ⁴⁵그들은 관심사가 다르기 때문에 내 아들들에게 각자의 공간을 주고 싶어. 고마워, Kevin.

남: 천만에, April. 이제 우리가 선택한 걸 보여줄게.

어휘 | emporium[impɔ́:riəm] 백화점, 큰 상점　tough[tʌf] 힘든, 어려운　adjust[ədʒʌ́st] 적응하다　bunk bed 2단 침대　floor space 바닥 면적
stack[stæk] 쌓다　on top of ~의 위에　occupy[ákjupài] 차지하다　cramped[kræmpt] 비좁은, 답답한　switch[switʃ] 바꾸다
once in a while 가끔, 때때로　outgrow[àutgróu] ~보다 더 커지다　downside[dáunsaid] 부정적인 면　disturb[distɔ́:rb] 방해하다
ladder[lǽdər] 사다리　careless[kérləs] 부주의한　bump[bʌmp] 부딪치다　bedding[bédiŋ] 침구류　tuck[tʌk] 넣다
bedtime[bédtaim] 취침 시간　decorate with ~으로 장식하다　cartoon[ka:rtú:n] 만화　markup[má:rkʌp] 원가에 가산되는 금액
convince[kənvíns] 확신시키다, 설득하다　spooky[spú:ki] 무시무시한　conflict[kənflíkt] 갈등, 분쟁　come up with (해답·돈 등을) 찾아내다

---

40 특정세부사항　Why

난이도 ●○○

Why do April's sons need some furniture from the store?

(a) because they want to reorganize their space
(b) because they have changed houses
(c) because they dislike sharing things
(d) because they have their own rooms

April의 아들들은 왜 가게에 있는 가구가 필요한가?

(a) 공간을 재구성하기를 원하기 때문에
(b) 집을 옮겼기 때문에
(c) 물건을 공유하는 것을 싫어하기 때문에
(d) 각자의 방이 있기 때문에

○ 정답 잡는 치트키

질문의 키워드 sons와 furniture가 그대로 언급된 주변 내용을 주의 깊게 듣는다.

해설 | 남자가 'What brings you to the Riverside Furniture Emporium?'이라며 Riverside 가구 백화점에는 무슨 일로 왔는지 묻자, 여자가 'Maybe you can help me out with something for the bedroom my sons are sharing. You know, moving into a new house is tough'라며 아들들이 같이 쓰는 침실에 들일 가구 관련해서 좀 도와줄 수 있는지 물으며, 새집으로 이사하는 건 힘들다고 했다. 따라서 (b)가 정답이다.

↻ **Paraphrasing**
moving into a new house 새집으로 이사하는 것 → have changed houses 집을 옮겼다

어휘 | reorganize[riɔ́rgənaiz] 재구성하다, 재조직하다

---

41 특정세부사항　Why

난이도 ●●○

Why does April like that a bunk bed will save floor space?

(a) She wants to have room for overnight guests.
(b) She wants to leave room for a study area.
(c) The room is not as big as before.
(d) The room is still not very spacious.

April은 왜 2단 침대가 바닥 면적을 절약해 줄 것이라고 좋아하는가?

(a) 하룻밤 묵는 손님들을 위한 공간을 갖고 싶어 한다.
(b) 공부 공간을 위한 자리를 남겨두고 싶어 한다.
(c) 방이 예전만큼 크지 않다.
(d) 방이 여전히 그다지 넓지 않다.

○ 정답 잡는 치트키

질문의 키워드 save floor space가 그대로 언급된 주변 내용을 주의 깊게 듣는다.

해설 | 남자가 'bunk beds can save floor space'라며 2단 침대가 바닥 면적을 절약하게 해 줄 수 있다고 하자, 여자가 'I like that about bunk beds. The boys have a slightly bigger bedroom in the new house than they did before, but it could still be cramped with two whole beds.'라며 2단 침대에 관해 그게 마음에 들고, 아들들은 새집에서 이전보다 약간 더 큰 침실을 갖게 되겠지만 여전히 침대 두 개로는 비좁을 수 있다고 했다. 따라서 (d)가 정답이다.

오답분석
(c) 여자가 새집의 침실이 이전보다 조금 더 커졌다고 했으므로 오답이다.

어휘 | overnight guest 하룻밤 묵는 손님 spacious[spéiʃəs] 넓은, 널찍한

42   추론   특정사실   난이도 ●●○

What, most likely, could be a serious problem for April's sons with a bunk bed?

(a) getting hurt while using the ladder
(b) having their sleep interrupted
(c) falling off in the middle of the night
(d) being afraid of heights

April의 아들들이 2단 침대를 사용하면 무엇이 심각한 문제가 될 수 있을 것 같은가?

(a) **사다리를 사용하는 동안 다치는 것**
(b) 수면이 방해받는 것
(c) 한밤중에 떨어지는 것
(d) 높은 곳을 무서워하는 것

정답 잡는 치트키

질문의 키워드 serious problem이 그대로 언급된 주변 내용을 주의 깊게 듣는다.

해설 | 여자가 'climbing up and down could be a serious problem since my boys have a lot of energy and can be careless at times'라며 아들들이 에너지가 넘치고 때때로 부주의할 수도 있어서 오르내리는 것이 심각한 문제일 수 있다고 하자, 남자가 'That could lead to a dangerous situation.'이라며 위험한 상황으로 이어질 수 있겠다고 한 것을 통해, April의 아들들이 2단 침대를 사용하면 사다리를 사용하는 동안 다치는 것이 심각한 문제가 될 수 있음을 추론할 수 있다. 따라서 (a)가 정답이다.

오답분석
(b) 남자가 아들 한 명이 사다리를 올라갈 때 다른 아들의 수면이 방해받을 수 있다고는 언급했지만, 여자가 아들들은 깊게 잠을 자는 애들이라 그런 건 크게 걱정하지 않는다고 했으므로 오답이다.

어휘 | interrupt[ìntərʌ́pt] 방해하다, 중단하다 fall off 떨어지다 in the middle of the night 한밤중에 height[hait] 높은 곳, 높이

43   특정세부사항   How   난이도 ●●○

How could April have an easier time with individual beds?

(a) She could have more storage space.
(b) She could get to the kids more quickly.
(c) She could do chores more comfortably.
(d) She could have more options for decorating.

April이 개별 침대에서 어떻게 더 편한 시간을 가질 수 있는가?

(a) 더 많은 수납공간을 가질 수 있다.
(b) 아이들에게 더 빨리 갈 수 있다.
(c) **집안일을 더 편하게 할 수 있다.**
(d) 장식할 수 있는 더 많은 선택권을 가질 수 있다.

정답 잡는 치트키

질문의 키워드 easier time과 individual beds가 그대로 언급된 주변 내용을 주의 깊게 듣는다.

해설 | 남자가 'Now, let's talk about the advantages of buying your sons individual beds.'라며 이제 아들들에게 개별 침대를 사주는 것의 장점에 관해 얘기해보자고 하자, 여자가 'I would have a much easier time changing the sheets'라며 시트를 바꾸는 것이 훨씬 수월할 거라고 했다. 따라서 (c)가 정답이다.

↻ **Paraphrasing**
changing the sheets 시트를 바꾸는 것 → chores 집안일

어휘 | storage space 수납공간, 저장 공간 chore[tʃɔːr] 집안일, 가사

According to April, why would her sons fight to sleep in a certain bed?

(a) to have a better window view
(b) to have more room to stretch out
(c) to be closest to the door
(d) **to avoid a scary spot**

April에 따르면, 아들들은 왜 특정 침대에서 자기 위해 싸울 것 같은가?

(a) 창밖 경치를 더 잘 보기 위해서
(b) 몸을 뻗고 누울 공간을 더 많이 갖기 위해서
(c) 문에서 가장 가까이 있기 위해서
(d) **무서운 곳을 피하기 위해서**

🔘 정답 잡는 치트키

질문의 키워드 fight가 그대로 언급된 주변 내용을 주의 깊게 듣는다.

해설 | 여자가 'the boys might fight about who gets to sleep where. They're both convinced there's a monster hiding in their closet, ~. Neither of them would want to sleep in the bed closest to the spooky door!'라며 아들들이 누가 어디서 자는지 싸울 수도 있는데, 둘 다 옷장에 괴물이 숨어 있다고 확신해서 무시무시한 문에서 가장 가까운 침대에서는 자고 싶지 않을 거라고 한 것을 통해, April의 아들들은 괴물이 숨어 있는 옷장 가까이에 있는 침대에서 자는 것을 피하기 위해 싸울 것임을 추론할 수 있다. 따라서 (d)가 정답이다.

🔁 **Paraphrasing**

spooky 무시무시한 → scary 무서운

어휘 | stretch out 몸을 뻗고 눕다

What will April probably do after the conversation?

(a) give her sons separate rooms
(b) get the least expensive bed
(c) **buy each of her sons a bed**
(d) let the boys choose their beds

April은 대화 이후에 무엇을 할 것 같은가?

(a) 아들들에게 별도의 방을 준다
(b) 가장 저렴한 침대를 구매한다
(c) **아들들 각자에게 침대를 사준다**
(d) 아들들이 자기 침대를 고르게 한다

🔘 정답 잡는 치트키

다음에 할 일을 언급하는 후반을 주의 깊게 듣는다.

해설 | 남자가 'have you come up with a decision?'이라며 결정을 내렸는지 묻자, 여자가 'I'd like to give each of my boys his own space since they have different interests.'라며 그들은 관심사가 다르기 때문에 아들들에게 각자의 공간을 주고 싶다고 한 것을 통해, April은 대화 이후에 아들들 각자에게 침대를 사줄 것임을 추론할 수 있다. 따라서 (c)가 정답이다.

오답분석

(a) 여자가 아들들에게 각자의 공간을 주고 싶다고는 언급했지만, 이것은 아들들이 같이 쓰는 침실에 들일 별도의 침대를 의미하므로 오답이다.

Welcome to *Get a Social Life*, the podcast where we explore the joys and pains of social media. From doing business to keeping in touch with loved ones, networking sites are a necessary part of life. But if we're not careful, it's easy to lose hours we'd rather spend doing something else. [46]Today, I'll tell you some ways to moderate your social media use.

The first tip is to reduce the number of people you follow. Minimize your use of social media by having fewer reasons for using it. You might be following accounts that don't add much value to your life. Checking out their posts can eat up your time without giving you any satisfaction in return. By "unfollowing" them, or disallowing their posts from appearing, you will avoid spending excessive time on social media. [47]Limit your follows to those whose posts make a positive impact on your life.

The second tip is to set a time limit on browsing social media. You can do this by using a timer. For example, set yourself a goal of visiting social media accounts for a total of one hour each day. The timer will remind you when you have reached the end of your allotted time. [48]There are certain timer applications you can download that will even lock you out of the sites when time's up.

The third tip is to manage the notifications that get sent to your phone. It can be hard to concentrate when your phone is buzzing every few minutes. These notifications are usually not urgent and may only serve to let you know about a new picture or video that someone has uploaded. Most networking sites let you manage what kind of notifications you receive. [49]I set my accounts to only notify me of direct messages from close friends and family members.

The fourth tip is to plan a "no social media day" once a week. To lessen your social media use, schedule one day a week when you will not visit any social networking sites for the whole day. [50]You can deactivate your accounts for the day and enable them again the following day. This will help you avoid the temptation to check your accounts throughout the day.

[51]The fifth tip is to find a new hobby. We don't always realize just how time-consuming social media can be. [51]I always assumed I didn't have enough time for the things I wanted to do. Then I started to replace some of

인사 + 주제 제시

조언1: 팔로우 줄이기

조언2: 타이머 설정

조언3: 알림 관리

조언4: 소셜 미디어 없는 날 정하기

조언5: 새로운 취미 가지기

소셜 미디어의 기쁨과 고통을 탐구하는 팟캐스트 *Get a Social Life*에 오신 것을 환영합니다. 비즈니스를 하는 것부터 사랑하는 사람들과 연락을 유지하는 것까지, 네트워킹 사이트는 삶의 필수적인 부분입니다. 하지만 우리가 조심하지 않는다면, 다른 일을 하는 데 쓸 수 있는 시간을 낭비하기 쉽습니다. [46]오늘, 소셜 미디어 사용을 조절하는 몇 가지 방법을 알려드리겠습니다.

첫 번째 조언은 팔로우하는 사람의 수를 줄이는 것입니다. 그것을 사용해야 할 이유를 줄임으로써 소셜 미디어 사용을 최소화하세요. 삶에 별다른 가치를 더해주지 않는 계정을 팔로우하고 있을 수도 있습니다. 이들의 게시물을 확인하는 것은 보답으로 아무런 만족도 주지 않으면서 시간만 잡아먹을 수 있습니다. 그것들을 "팔로우 취소"하거나, 게시물이 보이는 것을 허락하지 않음으로써, 소셜 미디어에 과도한 시간을 소비하는 것을 피할 것입니다. [47]삶에 긍정적인 영향을 주는 게시물을 올리는 사람들로만 팔로우를 제한하세요.

두 번째 조언은 소셜 미디어 검색하는 데 시간제한을 설정하는 것입니다. 이것은 타이머를 사용하여서 할 수 있습니다. 예를 들어, 매일 총 한 시간 동안 소셜 미디어 계정을 방문한다는 목표를 설정해 보세요. 타이머는 할당된 시간이 끝나면 알려줍니다. [48]시간이 다 되면 사이트에 들어가지 못하게 하는 특정 타이머 애플리케이션을 다운로드할 수도 있습니다.

세 번째 조언은 휴대전화로 전송되는 알림을 관리하는 것입니다. 휴대전화가 몇 분마다 윙윙거리면 집중하기 어려울 수 있습니다. 이러한 알림은 대개 긴급하지 않으며 다른 사람이 업로드한 새로운 사진이나 영상에 대해 알려주는 역할만 할 수 있습니다. 대부분의 네트워킹 사이트에서는 어떤 종류의 알림을 받을지 관리할 수 있게 합니다. [49]저는 친한 친구들과 가족들로부터의 직접 메시지만 알리도록 계정을 설정했습니다.

네 번째 조언은 일주일에 한 번 "소셜 미디어 없는 날"을 계획하는 것입니다. 소셜 미디어 사용을 줄이려면, 하루 종일 소셜 네트워킹 사이트를 방문하지 않는 때로 일주일에 하루를 정하세요. [50]그날은 계정을 비활성화했다가 다음 날 다시 활성화할 수 있습니다. 이렇게 하면 하루 종일 계정을 확인하고 싶은 유혹을 피하는 데 도움이 됩니다.

[51]다섯 번째 조언은 새로운 취미를 찾는 것입니다. 우리는 소셜 미디어가 얼마나 시간을 낭비할 수 있는지 항상 깨닫지 못합니다. [51]저는 항상 제가 하고 싶은 일을 할 시간이 충분하지 않다고 생각했습니다. 그러다가

the time I spent on networking sites with learning how to bake. **Now I love baking because it keeps my hands and my mind busy, so I don't even miss scrolling on my phone.**

조언6:
컴퓨터
이용
하기

[52]The final tip is to delete all social media apps from your phone. I'm not suggesting that you quit social media altogether! Here's a secret, though: [52]using networking sites on a computer is a very different experience from using them on your phone. The computer version has more settings that give you better control over what you see, like letting you filter out posts and topics that you're not interested in. Because the phone app settings are much simpler, you often get stuck with a cluttered feed.

끝인사

That concludes today's episode of *Get a Social Life*. By moderating your social media use, you'll be amazed at how much free time you get back.

네트워킹 사이트에서 보내는 시간 중 일부를 제빵을 배우는 것으로 대체하기 시작했습니다. 이제 저는 손과 마음을 바쁘게 하는 제빵을 좋아하기 때문에, 휴대전화를 스크롤 하는 것도 그리워하지 않습니다.

[52]마지막 조언은 휴대전화에서 모든 소셜 미디어 앱을 삭제하는 것입니다. 소셜 미디어를 완전히 끊으라고 제안하는 것은 아닙니다! 그러나, 여기 비밀이 있습니다: [52]컴퓨터에서 네트워킹 사이트를 이용하는 것은 휴대전화에서 그것들을 이용하는 것과 매우 다른 경험입니다. 컴퓨터 버전은 관심 없는 게시물과 주제를 걸러내도록 하는 것과 같이 여러분이 보는 것을 더 잘 제어할 수 있게 해주는 더 많은 설정이 있습니다. 휴대전화 앱 설정은 훨씬 더 간단하기 때문에, 종종 어수선한 피드에 꼼짝 못 하게 됩니다.

이것으로 오늘의 *Get a Social Life* 에피소드를 마칩니다. 소셜 미디어 사용을 조절함으로써, 얼마나 많은 자유 시간을 돌려받는지 놀라게 될 것입니다.

어휘 | keep in touch with ~와 연락을 유지하다   moderate[mádərət] 조절하다   minimize[mínəmàiz] 최소화하다, 축소하다   account[əkáunt] 계정   eat up ~을 잡아먹다   in return 보답으로, 대신에   disallow[dìsəláu] ~을 허락하지 않다   excessive[iksésiv] 과도한, 지나친   browse[brauz] 검색하다, 인터넷을 돌아다니다   allotted[əlátid] 할당된   notification[nòutəfikéiʃən] 알림   concentrate[kánsəntrèit] 집중시키다   buzzing[bʌziŋ] 윙윙거리는   urgent[ə́ːrdʒənt] 긴급한   deactivate[diːǽktəvèit] ~을 비활성화하다   temptation[temptéiʃən] 유혹   time-consuming 시간을 낭비하는, 많은 시간이 걸리는   replace[ripléis] 대체하다   scroll[skroul] 스크롤 하다(컴퓨터 화면의 텍스트를 두루마리 읽듯이 상하로 움직이다)   setting[sétiŋ] 설정, 환경   filter out ~을 걸러내다   get stuck 꼼짝 못 하게 되다   cluttered[klʌ́tərd] 어수선한, 어질러진

---

46 주제/목적   담화의 주제

난이도 ●○○

What is the speaker mainly discussing?

(a) learning to navigate social media
(b) managing social media anxiety
(c) choosing the best social media site
(d) limiting time on social media

화자가 주로 논하고 있는 것은 무엇인가?

(a) 소셜 미디어 돌아다니는 것을 배우는 것
(b) 소셜 미디어 불안을 관리하는 것
(c) 최고의 소셜 미디어 사이트를 고르는 것
(d) 소셜 미디어에 시간을 제한하는 것

━○ 정답 잡는 치트키

담화의 주제를 언급하는 초반을 주의 깊게 듣고 전체 맥락을 파악한다.

해설 | 화자가 'Today, I'll tell you some ways to moderate your social media use.'라며 오늘 소셜 미디어 사용을 조절하는 몇 가지 방법을 알려주겠다고 한 뒤, 담화 전반에 걸쳐 소셜 미디어에 사용하는 시간을 제한하는 방법에 관해 설명하는 내용이 이어지고 있다. 따라서 (d)가 정답이다.

어휘 | navigate[nǽvəgèit] (인터넷·웹사이트를) 돌아다니다

특정세부사항   What   난이도 ●●○

According to the speaker, what kinds of people should one follow on social media accounts?	화자에 따르면, 소셜 미디어 계정에서 어떤 부류의 사람들을 팔로우해야 하는가?
(a) those who provide meaningful content (b) those who value their appearance (c) those who are satisfied with their lives (d) those who make reasonable posts	**(a) 의미 있는 콘텐츠를 제공하는 사람들** (b) 외모를 중시하는 사람들 (c) 자기 생활에 만족하는 사람들 (d) 논리적인 게시물을 작성하는 사람들

━○ 정답 잡는 치트키

질문의 키워드 follow가 그대로 언급된 주변 내용을 주의 깊게 듣는다.

해설 | 화자가 'Limit your follows to those whose posts make a positive impact on your life.'라며 삶에 긍정적인 영향을 주는 게시물을 올리는 사람들로만 팔로우를 제한하라고 했다. 따라서 (a)가 정답이다.

어휘 | meaningful[míːniŋfəl] 의미 있는 appearance[əpíərəns] 외모 reasonable[ríːzənəbl] 논리적인, 합당한

---

48 **특정세부사항**   How   난이도 ●●○

How do certain timer applications help in minimizing social media use?	특정 타이머 애플리케이션이 소셜 미디어 사용을 최소화하는 데 어떻게 도움이 되는가?
(a) by filtering out the less important content (b) by reminding one to communicate quickly **(c) by removing one from the site after a while** (d) by setting a limit on social interaction	(a) 덜 중요한 내용을 걸러냄으로써 (b) 신속하게 의사소통하도록 상기시킴으로써 **(c) 얼마 후에 사이트로부터 내보냄으로써** (d) 사회적 상호작용에 대한 제한을 설정함으로써

━○ 정답 잡는 치트키

질문의 키워드 certain timer applications가 그대로 언급된 주변 내용을 주의 깊게 듣는다.

해설 | 화자가 'There are certain timer applications you can download that will even lock you out of the sites when time's up.'이라며 시간이 다 되면 사이트에 들어가지 못하게 하는 특정 타이머 애플리케이션을 다운로드할 수도 있다고 했다. 따라서 (c)가 정답이다.

⇄ **Paraphrasing**
lock ~ out of the sites 사이트에 들어가지 못하게 하다 → removing ~ from the site 사이트로부터 내보냄

어휘 | remove[rimúːv] 내보내다, 치우다 interaction[intərǽkʃən] 상호작용

---

49 **특정세부사항**   What   난이도 ●●○

What kind of social media notifications has the speaker chosen to receive?	화자는 어떤 종류의 소셜 미디어 알림을 받기로 결정했는가?
(a) alerts about new uploads (b) updates posted by friends **(c) messages from loved ones** (d) news about urgent situations	(a) 새로운 업로드에 관한 알림 (b) 친구들이 게시한 최신 정보 **(c) 사랑하는 사람들로부터의 메시지** (d) 긴급한 상황에 관한 뉴스

질문의 키워드 notifications가 notify로 paraphrasing되어 언급된 주변 내용을 주의 깊게 듣는다.

해설 | 화자가 'I set my accounts to only notify me of direct messages from close friends and family members.'라며 친한 친구들과 가족들로부터의 직접 메시지만 알리도록 계정을 설정했다고 했다. 따라서 (c)가 정답이다.

⇄ **Paraphrasing**
close friends and family members 친한 친구들과 가족들 → loved ones 사랑하는 사람들

50　특정세부사항　　How　　　　　　　　　　　　　　　　　　난이도 ●●○

According to the talk, how can one avoid the temptation to check one's social media accounts?

(a) by deleting one's web browsers
(b) by temporarily removing access
(c) by planning an all-day outing
(d) by turning off one's phone

담화에 따르면, 어떻게 소셜 미디어 계정을 확인하고 싶은 유혹을 피할 수 있는가?

(a) 웹 브라우저를 삭제함으로써
(b) 일시적으로 접근을 못 하게 함으로써
(c) 하루 종일 외출을 계획함으로써
(d) 휴대전화를 끔으로써

질문의 키워드 avoid the temptation이 그대로 언급된 주변 내용을 주의 깊게 듣는다.

해설 | 화자가 'You can deactivate your accounts for the day and enable them again the following day. This will help you avoid the temptation to check your accounts throughout the day.'라며 "소셜 미디어 없는 날"에는 계정을 비활성화했다가 다음 날 다시 활성화할 수 있는데, 이렇게 하면 하루 종일 계정을 확인하고 싶은 유혹을 피하는 데 도움이 된다고 했다. 따라서 (b)가 정답이다.

⇄ **Paraphrasing**
deactivate ~ accounts 계정을 비활성화하다 → removing access 접근을 못 하게 함

어휘 | turn off (등불·라디오·텔레비전을) 끄다

51　특정세부사항　　Why　　　　　　　　　　　　　　　　　　난이도 ●●○

Why did the speaker decide to find a new hobby?

(a) He no longer enjoyed social media.
(b) He was bored of other activities.
(c) He was looking for friends with common interests.
(d) He wanted to use his time more wisely.

화자는 왜 새로운 취미를 찾기로 결심했는가?

(a) 더 이상 소셜 미디어를 즐기지 않았다.
(b) 다른 활동에 싫증이 났다.
(c) 공통의 관심사를 가진 친구들을 찾고 있었다.
(d) 시간을 좀 더 현명하게 사용하고 싶었다.

질문의 키워드 find a new hobby가 그대로 언급된 주변 내용을 주의 깊게 듣는다.

해설 | 화자가 'The fifth tip is to find a new hobby.'라며 다섯 번째 조언은 새로운 취미를 찾는 것이라고 한 뒤, 'I always assumed I didn't have enough time for the things I wanted to do. Then I started to replace some of the time I spent on networking sites with learning how to bake.'라며 항상 하고 싶은 일을 할 시간이 충분하지 않다고 생각했는데, 그러다가 네트워킹 사이트에서 보내는 시간 중 일부를 제빵을 배우는 것으로 대체하기 시작했다고 했다. 따라서 (d)가 정답이다.

어휘 | common[kάmən] 공통의 wisely[wáizli] 현명하게

52 **추론** **특정사실**

Based on the final tip, what, most likely, is the speaker suggesting that listeners do?

(a) **check social media on a computer**
(b) use specialized phone settings
(c) delete all social media accounts
(d) stop posting from public spaces

마지막 조언에 따르면, 화자는 청자들에게 무엇을 하라고 제안하고 있는 것 같은가?

(a) **컴퓨터로 소셜 미디어를 확인한다**
(b) 전문화된 휴대전화 설정을 사용한다
(c) 모든 소셜 미디어 계정을 삭제한다
(d) 공공장소에서의 게시를 중단한다

정답 잡는 치트키

질문의 키워드 final tip이 그대로 언급된 주변 내용을 주의 깊게 듣는다.

해설 | 화자가 'The final tip is to delete all social media apps from your phone.'이라며 마지막 조언은 휴대전화에서 모든 소셜 미디어 앱을 삭제하는 것이라고 한 뒤, 'using networking sites on a computer is a very different experience from using them on your phone. The computer version has more settings that give you better control over what you see'라며 컴퓨터에서 네트워킹 사이트를 이용하는 것은 휴대전화에서 그것들을 이용하는 것과 매우 다른 경험이며, 컴퓨터 버전은 보는 것을 더 잘 제어할 수 있게 해주는 더 많은 설정이 있다고 한 것을 통해, 화자는 청자들에게 휴대전화 대신 컴퓨터로 소셜 미디어를 확인하라고 제안하고 있음을 추론할 수 있다. 따라서 (a)가 정답이다.

오답분석

(c) 화자가 휴대전화에서 모든 소셜 미디어 앱을 삭제하라고 언급하기는 했지만, 소셜 미디어를 완전히 끊으라고 제안하는 것은 아니라고 했으므로 오답이다.

어휘 | specialized[spéʃəlàizd] 전문화된

READING & VOCABULARY

PART 1 [53~59] 인물의 일대기 영화의 타이틀 시퀀스에 혁신을 일으킨 솔 바스

인물 이름	**SAUL BASS** / 솔 바스

SAUL BASS

인물 이름

소개 + 유명한 이유

Saul Bass was an American graphic designer and filmmaker. He produced some of the world's most recognizable brand logos and film posters. However, [53]Bass is most known for revolutionizing title sequences for films by using eye-catching graphics and animation.

어린 시절 + 업적 시작 계기

Saul Bass was born on May 8, 1920, in the Bronx, New York, to Jewish immigrant parents. Bass acquired an interest in visual arts as a boy and frequented the Metropolitan Museum of Art to study famous artworks. After high school, he went to a prominent art school, the Art Students League of New York, on a fellowship. He also worked as a freelance graphic artist to fund his studies.

예술적 표현에 영향을 준 요소

[54]Bass then went to Brooklyn College, where he was mentored by György Kepes, a well-known graphic designer and art theorist. [54]There, his artistic expression was further influenced by the Bauhaus art movement, which focused on minimalist yet functional designs.

주요 업적1: 영화 타이틀 시퀀스 제작 성공

In 1946, Bass moved to California and designed print advertisements for films, as well as magazine covers, [58]corporate logos, and other works. [55]Director Otto Preminger hired him to produce the poster for the film *Carmen Jones* in 1954. The work impressed Preminger so much that he also asked Bass to create the movie's title sequence—the introductory clip in which the title, cast members, and production credits appear before the film starts. His work was an iconic success.

주요 업적2: 움직 이는 텍스트 개발

[56]Traditional opening sequences were often stationary lists too plain to draw viewers' interest. Bass took an entirely different approach by adding movement and sound to an otherwise unremarkable introduction to a movie. This led to the development of kinetic typography, in which letters moved across the screen. Combined with striking color contrast and cut-out animation, Bass's title sequences served as a visual reflection of a film's story.

솔 바스

솔 바스는 미국의 그래픽 디자이너이자 영화 제작 자였다. 그는 세계에서 가장 쉽게 알아볼 수 있는 브 랜드 로고와 영화 포스터를 제작했다. 하지만, [53]바스 는 눈길을 끄는 그래픽과 애니메이션을 사용하여 영 화의 타이틀 시퀀스에 혁신을 일으킨 것으로 가장 잘 알려져 있다.

솔 바스는 1920년 5월 8일에 뉴욕주 브롱크스에서 유대인 이민자 부모 사이에서 태어났다. 바스는 소년 일 때 시각 예술에 대한 관심을 뒀고 유명한 예술작품 을 살펴보기 위해 메트로폴리탄 미술관에 자주 갔다. 고등학교 이후, 그는 연구 장학금을 받아 저명한 예술 학교인 Art Students League of New York에 진학했 다. 그는 또한 프리랜서 그래픽 아티스트로 일하며 학 비를 충당했다.

[54]바스는 그 후 브루클린 대학에 진학했고, 그곳에 서 유명한 그래픽 디자이너이자 예술 이론가인 기요 르기 케피쉬의 지도를 받았다. [54]그곳에서, 그의 예술 적 표현은 미니멀리스트이면서도 기능적인 디자인에 초점을 맞춘 바우하우스 예술 운동에 의해 더욱 영향 을 받았다.

1946년에, 바스는 캘리포니아로 이사를 했고 잡지 표지, [58]회사의 로고, 기타 작품뿐만 아니라 영화의 지 면 광고를 디자인했다. [55]1954년에 오토 프레밍거 감독 은 영화 *Carmen Jones*의 포스터를 제작하기 위해 그 를 고용했다. 이 작업은 프레밍거에게 깊은 인상을 남 겨서 바스에게 영화가 시작되기 전에 제목, 출연진, 제 작 크레딧이 등장하는 도입부 영상인 영화의 타이틀 시퀀스도 제작하도록 의뢰했다. 그의 작업은 상징적인 성공을 거두었다.

[56]전통적인 시작 장면들은 종종 변하지 않는 목록 이었기 때문에 관객들의 흥미를 끌기에는 너무 평범 했다. 바스는 달리 특별한 것 없는 영화 도입부에 움직 임과 소리를 추가함으로써 완전히 다른 접근법을 취했 다. 이것은 움직이는 텍스트의 개발로 이어졌는데, 글 자들이 화면을 가로질러 움직이는 것이었다. 눈에 띄 는 색상 대비와 컷아웃 애니메이션이 합쳐져, 바스의 타이틀 시퀀스는 영화 줄거리를 시각적으로 반영하는 역할을 했다.

영향력	Bass received commissions from the film industry's top directors, including Alfred Hitchcock, Stanley Kubrick, and Martin Scorsese. [57]Bass's innovative style was also adopted by other designers, making title sequences an important part of films. Among Bass's last title sequence credits were the Scorsese films *Goodfellas* and *Casino*.	바스는 알프레드 히치콕, 스탠리 큐브릭, 마틴 스코세이지를 포함하여, 영화 산업의 최고 감독들로부터 의뢰를 받았다. [57]바스의 혁신적인 스타일은 다른 디자이너들에 의해서도 채택되어, 타이틀 시퀀스를 영화에서 중요한 부분으로 만들었다. 바스의 마지막 타이틀 시퀀스 크레딧 중에는 스코세이지 영화인 *Goodfellas*와 *Casino*가 있었다.
죽음 + 후기 업적	Bass died in 1996, but his legacy lives on. His entire body of work, consisting of 2,700 items, is stored at the Academy Film Archive. [59]His designs are still featured as the logos of renowned companies such as AT&T and Kleenex.	바스는 1996년에 사망했지만, 그의 업적은 여전히 남아있다. 2,700여 점으로 구성된 그의 작품 전체가 아카데미 영화 아카이브에 보관되어 있다. [59]그의 디자인은 AT&T와 크리넥스 같은 유명한 회사들의 로고로 여전히 중요한 역할을 한다.

어휘 | recognizable adj. 쉽게 알아볼 수 있는 revolutionize v. 혁신을 일으키다 title sequence phr. 타이틀 시퀀스(영화의 제목이 나오는 장면)
eye-catching adj. 눈길을 끄는 immigrant adj. 이민자의; n. 이주민 acquire v. 갖다, 얻다 visual arts phr. 시각 예술
frequent v. ~에 자주 가다; adj. 자주 일어나는 prominent adj. 저명한 fellowship n. 연구 장학금
freelance adj. 프리랜서로 일하는; v. 자유 계약으로 일하다 mentor v. 지도하다; n. 멘토, 조언자 art theorist phr. 예술 이론가
artistic expression phr. 예술적 표현 minimalist n. 미니멀리스트(되도록 소수의 단순한 요소를 통해 최대 효과를 이루려는 사고방식을 지닌 예술가)
introductory clip phr. 도입부 영상 cast member phr. 출연진, 배역
production credit phr. 제작 크레딧(제작 담당자나 기타 영화제작에 도움을 준 사람들의 이름을 화면에 나타내는 자막) iconic adj. 상징적인
opening sequence phr. 시작 장면 stationary adj. 변하지 않는, 정지한 plain adj. 평범한, 보통의 approach n. 접근법
unremarkable adj. 특별한 것 없는, 평범한 kinetic typography phr. 움직이는 텍스트 striking adj. 눈에 띄는
color contrast phr. 색상 대비 cut-out animation phr. 컷아웃 애니메이션 visual adj. 시각적인, 시각의 reflection n. 반영
commission n. 의뢰 innovative adj. 혁신적인 adopt v. 채택하다 legacy n. 업적, 유산 renowned adj. 유명한

---

53 **특정세부사항** 유명한 이유   난이도 ●●○

What is Saul Bass best known for?	솔 바스는 무엇으로 가장 잘 알려져 있는가?
(a) directing award-winning movies	(a) 상을 받은 영화들을 연출한 것
(b) designing famous brand logos	(b) 유명 브랜드 로고를 디자인한 것
(c) inventing the film title sequence	(c) 영화 타이틀 시퀀스를 개발한 것
(d) creating appealing opening credits	**(d) 매력적인 오프닝 크레딧을 만든 것**

○— 정답 잡는 치트키

질문의 키워드 best known이 most known으로 paraphrasing되어 언급된 주변 내용을 주의 깊게 읽는다.

해설 | 1단락의 'Bass is most known for revolutionizing title sequences for films by using eye-catching graphics and animation'에서 바스가 눈길을 끄는 그래픽과 애니메이션을 사용하여 영화의 타이틀 시퀀스에 혁신을 일으킨 것으로 가장 잘 알려져 있다고 했다. 따라서 (d)가 정답이다.

⇄ Paraphrasing
title sequences 타이틀 시퀀스 → opening credits 오프닝 크레딧

오답분석
(b) 1단락에서 솔 바스가 세계에서 가장 쉽게 알아볼 수 있는 브랜드 로고를 제작했다고는 언급했지만, 유명 브랜드 로고를 디자인한 것으로 가장 잘 알려진 것은 아니므로 오답이다.
(c) 1단락에서 솔 바스가 영화의 타이틀 시퀀스에 혁신을 일으켰다고는 언급했지만, 영화 타이틀 시퀀스를 개발한 것은 아니므로 오답이다.

어휘 | award-winning adj. 상을 받은 appealing adj. 매력적인, 마음을 끄는
opening credit phr. 오프닝 크레딧(영화의 첫 부분에 표시하는 크레딧 타이틀)

What helped influence Bass's creative expression?

(a) the theories he formed with a famous designer
(b) the experiences he gained as a mentor
(c) an art class he attended in his childhood
(d) an artistic trend he learned about in college

바스의 창의적인 표현에 영향을 주도록 도운 것은 무엇이었는가?

(a) 유명한 디자이너와 형성했던 이론
(b) 멘토로서 얻었던 경험
(c) 어린 시절에 다녔던 미술 수업
(d) 대학에서 배웠던 예술 사조

━○ 정답 잡는 치트키

질문의 키워드 influence가 그대로 언급되고, creative expression이 artistic expression으로 paraphrasing되어 언급된 주변 내용을 주의 깊게 읽는다.

해설 | 3단락의 'Bass then went to Brooklyn College'에서 바스는 그 후 브루클린 대학에 진학했다고 한 뒤, 'There, his artistic expression was further influenced by the Bauhaus art movement'에서 그곳에서 그의 예술적 표현은 바우하우스 예술 운동에 의해 더욱 영향을 받았다고 했다. 따라서 (d)가 정답이다.

⇄ Paraphrasing
art movement 예술 운동 → an artistic trend 예술 사조

어휘 | gain v. 얻다, 획득하다　artistic trend phr. 예술 사조

---

55 **특정세부사항** Why　　　　　　　　　　　　　　　　　　　　　　　　　　　　　　난이도 ●●○

Why did Otto Preminger hire Bass to create the title sequence for *Carmen Jones*?

(a) because he needed someone on relatively short notice
(b) because he wanted his most trusted designer on board
(c) because he liked Bass's promotional art for the film
(d) because he admired Bass's work on previous credits

오토 프레밍거는 *Carmen Jones*의 타이틀 시퀀스를 제작하기 위해 왜 바스를 고용했는가?

(a) 비교적 짧은 시간 내에 누군가를 필요로 했기 때문에
(b) 가장 신뢰받고 있는 디자이너가 합류하기를 원했기 때문에
(c) 영화를 위한 바스의 홍보용 예술 작품을 좋아했기 때문에
(d) 이전의 크레딧에 대한 바스의 작업에 감탄했기 때문에

━○ 정답 잡는 치트키

질문의 키워드 Otto Preminger와 *Carmen Jones*가 그대로 언급된 주변 내용을 주의 깊게 읽는다.

해설 | 4단락의 'Director Otto Preminger hired him to produce the poster for the film *Carmen Jones* ~. The work impressed Preminger so much that he also asked Bass to create the movie's title sequence'에서 오토 프레밍거 감독은 영화 *Carmen Jones*의 포스터를 제작하기 위해 바스를 고용했는데, 이 작업은 프레밍거에게 깊은 인상을 남겨서 바스에게 영화의 타이틀 시퀀스도 제작하도록 의뢰했다고 했다. 따라서 (c)가 정답이다.

⇄ Paraphrasing
the poster for the film 영화 포스터 → promotional art for the film 영화를 위한 홍보용 예술 작품

오답분석
(d) 4단락에서 오토 프레밍거 감독이 바스가 제작한 영화 포스터에 깊은 인상을 받았다고는 언급했지만, 바스가 이전에 작업한 크레딧에 대해 감탄한 것은 아니므로 오답이다.

어휘 | relatively adv. 비교적, 상대적으로　trusted adj. 신뢰받고 있는　on board phr. 합류한　promotional adj. 홍보용의

56 특정세부사항   How   난이도 ●●○

How did Bass's opening sequences differ from traditional sequences?

(a) They appeared after the movie's first scene.
(b) They presented information in an unusual format.
(c) They offered mysterious clues to the film's plot.
(d) They showed a clip of the film in animated form.

바스의 오프닝 시퀀스는 전통적인 시퀀스와 어떻게 달랐는가?

(a) 영화의 첫 장면 이후에 등장했다.
(b) 특이한 형식으로 정보를 제시했다.
(c) 영화의 줄거리에 대한 불가사의한 단서를 제공했다.
(d) 영화의 한 장면을 애니메이션 형식으로 보여주었다.

───○ 정답 잡는 치트키

질문의 키워드 traditional sequences가 그대로 언급된 주변 내용을 주의 깊게 읽는다.

해설 | 5단락의 'Traditional opening sequences were ~ too plain to draw viewers' interest. Bass took an entirely different approach by adding movement and sound to an otherwise unremarkable introduction to a movie.'에서 전통적인 시작 징면들은 관객들의 흥미를 끌기에는 너무 평범했는데, 바스는 달리 특별한 것 없는 영화 도입부에 움직임과 소리를 추가함으로써 완전히 다른 접근법을 취했다고 했다. 따라서 (b)가 정답이다.

어휘 | scene n. 장면 unusual adj. 특이한, 독특한 format n. 형식, 구성 mysterious adj. 불가사의한 clue n. 단서, 실마리 plot n. 줄거리

57 추론   특정사실   난이도 ●●●

How, most likely, did Bass's contributions change the film industry?

(a) Title sequences are now produced in color.
(b) Audiences now pay more attention to title sequences.
(c) Audiences now arrive early to avoid missing title sequences.
(d) Title sequences have now become longer.

바스의 공헌이 영화 산업을 어떻게 변화시켰을 것 같은가?

(a) 타이틀 시퀀스는 이제 컬러로 제작된다.
(b) 관객들은 이제 타이틀 시퀀스에 더 많은 주의를 기울인다.
(c) 관객들은 이제 타이틀 시퀀스를 놓치지 않기 위해 일찍 도착한다.
(d) 타이틀 시퀀스는 이제 더 길어졌다.

───○ 정답 잡는 치트키

질문의 키워드 change the film industry와 관련된 주변 내용을 주의 깊게 읽는다.

해설 | 6단락의 'Bass's innovative style was also adopted by other designers, making title sequences an important part of films.'에서 바스의 혁신적인 스타일은 다른 디자이너들에 의해서도 채택되어, 타이틀 시퀀스를 영화에서 중요한 부분으로 만들었다고 한 것을 통해, 바스의 공헌으로 인해 타이틀 시퀀스가 영화에서 중요한 부분이 되었고, 관객들이 이제 이것에 더 많은 주의를 기울이게 되었음을 추론할 수 있다. 따라서 (b)가 정답이다.

어휘 | contribution n. 공헌, 기여 audience n. 관객, 청중 pay attention to phr. ~에 주의를 기울이다

58 어휘   유의어   난이도 ●○○

In the context of the passage, <u>corporate</u> means _____.

(a) business

지문의 문맥에서, 'corporate'는 -을 의미한다.

(a) 사업상의

(b) worker
(c) management
(d) financial

(b) 근로자의
(c) 경영의
(d) 재정적인

◀─○ 정답 잡는 치트키

밑줄 친 어휘의 유의어를 찾는 문제이므로, corporate가 포함된 구절을 읽고 문맥을 파악한다.

해설 | 4단락의 'corporate logos'는 회사의 로고라는 뜻이므로, corporate가 '회사의'라는 의미로 사용된 것을 알 수 있다. 따라서 '사업상의'라는 비슷한 의미의 (a) business가 정답이다.

59 어휘 유의어   난이도 ●●○

In the context of the passage, <u>featured</u> means _____.

(a) faced
(b) reported
(c) used
(d) recommended

지문의 문맥에서, 'featured'는 ~을 의미한다.

(a) 직면하는
(b) 발표되는
(c) 사용되는
(d) 권고되는

◀─○ 정답 잡는 치트키

밑줄 친 어휘의 유의어를 찾는 문제이므로, featured가 포함된 구절을 읽고 문맥을 파악한다.

해설 | 7단락의 'His designs are still featured as the logos'는 그의 디자인이 로고로 여전히 중요한 역할을 한다는 뜻이므로, featured가 '중요한 역할을 하는'이라는 의미로 사용된 것을 알 수 있다. 따라서 '사용되는'이라는 비슷한 의미의 (c) used가 정답이다.

PART 2 [60~66] 잡지 기사   "OK"라는 단어의 유래 및 확산

기사 제목	[60]**HOW THE WORD "OK" ORIGINATED**

[60]어떻게 "OK"라는 단어가 생겨났는가

정의

[60]The word "OK" is one of the most common abbreviations in the English language. Signifying agreement or acceptance, it is alternatively spelled as "okay." The word is often used as an interjection, as in "OK, I understand."

[60]"OK"라는 단어는 영어에서 가장 흔한 약어 중 하나이다. 동의 혹은 수락을 의미하여, 이것은 대신에 "okay"라고 철자를 쓰기도 한다. 이 단어는 "네, 이해했습니다."와 같이, 종종 감탄사로 사용된다.

유래에 관한 이론1

[60]There are several theories about the word's origins. These include the word being shorthand for a German phrase that means "no changes," or being derived from the Native American Choctaw language's word for "it is so." However, a story involving the *Boston Morning Post* is the most widely accepted.

[60]이 단어의 유래에 대한 여러 가지 이론이 있다. 이것들은 "변화가 없다"라는 뜻의 독일어 구절을 속기로 쓴 단어이거나, "그렇다"라는 뜻의 아메리카 원주민 촉토 언어의 단어에서 유래된 것을 포함한다. 그러나, *Boston Morning*지와 관련된 이야기가 가장 널리 받아들여진다.

유래에 관한 이론2

In the 1830s, young intellectuals in Boston would create language fads by coming up with abbreviations for

1830년대에, 보스턴의 젊은 지식인들은 의도적으로 철자가 틀린 단어의 약어를 생각해 냄으로써 일시

intentionally misspelled words. The practice resulted in such expressions as "KC" for "knuff ced," which is slang for "enough said," and "OW" for "oll wright," meaning "all right." Most of these acronyms faded over time, but one remained. [01/06]"OK" is believed to have first surfaced in 1839, when the *Boston Morning Post* editor ended an article with "OK," for "oll korrect." Indicating that the content was "all correct," the abbreviation was picked up by other newspapers and used often in publishing.

[62]"OK" further spread through the United States during the 1840 presidential elections. President Martin Van Buren, who hailed from Kinderhook, New York, used "Old Kinderhook," or "OK," as his 1840 re-election campaign nickname. He coined "Vote for OK" as his campaign slogan. Van Buren lost the presidential race, but "OK" endured and became part of Americans' everyday speech.

[63]The word later gained worldwide popularity with the invention of the telegraph. Telegram messages became more expensive to send when more letters were used. Thus, "OK" became the code used by telegraph operators to acknowledge receipt of a message. This was how "OK" traveled to Great Britain and, eventually, to the rest of the world.

"OK" has been adopted into most of the world's languages with variations in spelling and pronunciation. It is also expressed as a hand signal formed by touching the thumb and index finger to form a circle while holding the other fingers straight. [64]The word itself can serve as an adjective, adverb, noun, or verb, making it [66]highly versatile and useful in many situations.

적인 언어 유행을 만들곤 했다. 이 관행은 "충분히 말했다"의 은어인 "knuff ced"의 "KC"와, "괜찮다"라는 뜻의 "oll wright"의 "OW"와 같은 표현을 낳았다. 이러한 약어 대부분은 시간이 지나면서 사라졌지만, 한 가지는 남았다. [61/65]"OK"는 1839년에 *Boston Morning 지* 편집자가 "oll korrect"의 "OK"로 기사를 끝내면서 처음 나타난 것으로 추정된다. 내용이 "모두 정확하다"라는 것을 나타내는, 이 약어는 다른 신문사에서도 채택되어 출판에 자주 사용되었다.

[62]"OK"는 1840년 대통령 선거 기간에 미국 전역에 더욱 널리 퍼졌다. 뉴욕주 킨더후크 출신의 대통령 마틴 밴 뷰런은 1840년 재선 캠페인 별명으로 "올드 킨더후크" 또는 "OK"를 사용했다. 그는 자신의 선거 슬로건으로 "OK에 투표하세요"를 새로 만들었다. 밴 뷰런은 대통령 선거전에서 졌지만, "OK"는 지속되었고 미국인들의 일상어 일부가 되었다.

[63]이 단어는 이후 전신의 발명과 함께 세계적인 인기를 얻었다. 전보 메시지는 더 많은 문자가 사용되면 전송 비용이 더 비싸졌다. 따라서, "OK"는 전신 기사들이 메시지의 수신을 확인하는 데 사용되는 코드가 되었다. 이것이 "OK"가 영국으로, 그리고 결국에는, 기타 국가들로 퍼져나간 방식이었다.

"OK"는 철자와 발음의 변형으로 세계 대부분의 언어에 받아들여졌다. 또한 엄지손가락과 집게손가락을 맞대어 원을 만들고 다른 손가락들은 곧게 펴서 만드는 수신호로 표현되기도 한다. [64]단어 자체가 형용사, 부사, 명사, 동사의 역할을 할 수 있어서, 다양한 상황에서 [66]아주 다목적으로 쓰이고 유용하게 만든다.

어휘 | abbreviation n. 약어 signify v. 의미하다, 나타내다 agreement n. 동의, 합의 acceptance n. 수락 alternatively adv. 그 대신에 spell v. 철자를 쓰다 interjection n. 감탄사 origin n. 유래, 기원 shorthand adj. 속기로 쓴, 간단명료한 phrase n. 구절 derive from phr. ~에서 유래하다, 파생하다 intellectual n. 지식인; adj. 지적인 fad n. 일시적 유행 come up with phr. ~을 생각하다, 떠올리다 intentionally adv. 의도적으로 misspelled adj. 철자가 틀린 slang n. 은어, 속어 acronym n. 약어, 두문자어 fade v. 사라지다 presidential election phr. 대통령 선거 hail from phr. ~의 출신이다 nickname n. 별명, 명칭 coin v. 새로 만들다; n. 신조어 slogan n. (정당·단체·제품 등의) 슬로건, 표어 presidential race phr. 대통령 선거전 endure v. 지속되다, 견디다 everyday speech phr. 일상어 telegraph n. 전신 telegram message phr. 전보 메시지 letter n. 문자, 글자 telegraph operator phr. 전신 기사 acknowledge v. 확인하다 receipt n. 수령, 받기 variation n. 변형, 차이 pronunciation n. 발음 hand signal phr. 수신호 thumb n. 엄지손가락 index finger phr. 집게손가락

What is mainly being discussed in the article?

(a) the world's most common word
(b) the declining use of a word
(c) the benefits of abbreviated words
(d) the origin of a popular word

기사에서 주로 논의되고 있는 것은 무엇인가?

(a) 세계에서 가장 흔한 단어
(b) 단어 사용의 쇠퇴
(c) 축약된 단어의 이점
(d) 대중적인 단어의 유래

─○ 정답 잡는 치트키

제목과 지문의 초반을 주의 깊게 읽고 전체 맥락을 파악한다.

해설 | 기사의 제목 'How The Word "OK" Originated'에서 어떻게 "OK"라는 단어가 생겨났는가를 언급하였다. 그다음에, 1단락의 'The word "OK" is one of the most common abbreviations in the English language.'에서 "OK"라는 단어는 영어에서 가장 흔한 약어 중 하나라고 했고, 2단락의 'There are several theories about the word's origins.'에서 이 단어의 유래에 대한 여러 가지 이론이 있다고 한 뒤, 대중적인 단어인 "OK"의 유래에 관한 세부 내용이 이어지고 있다. 따라서 (d)가 정답이다.

⇄ Paraphrasing
the most common abbreviations 가장 흔한 약어 → a popular word 대중적인 단어

오답분석
(a) 1단락에서 "OK"라는 단어가 영어에서 가장 흔한 약어 중 하나라고는 언급했지만, 기사에서 주로 논의되고 있는 내용이 세계에서 가장 흔한 단어가 무엇인지에 대한 내용은 아니므로 오답이다.

How was the abbreviation "OK" used in the late 1830s?

(a) as a slang expression in spoken conversation
(b) as a short version of an editorial phrase
(c) as a printer's stamp indicating that newsprint was dry
(d) as a way to describe young intellectuals

1830년대 후반에 "OK"라는 약어는 어떻게 사용되었는가?

(a) 말로 하는 대화에서 은어 표현으로
(b) 편집상 어구의 축약 버전으로
(c) 신문 인쇄용지가 건조되었음을 나타내는 인쇄용 도장으로
(d) 젊은 지식인들을 묘사하는 방식으로

─○ 정답 잡는 치트키

질문의 키워드 late 1830s가 1839으로 paraphrasing되어 언급된 주변 내용을 주의 깊게 읽는다.

해설 | 3단락의 '"OK" is believed to have first surfaced in 1839, when the *Boston Morning Post* editor ended an article with "OK," for "oll korrect." Indicating that the content was "all correct," the abbreviation was picked up by other newspapers and used often in publishing.'에서 "OK"는 1839년에 *Boston Morning지* 편집자가 "oll korrect"의 "OK"로 기사를 끝내면서 처음 나타난 것으로 추정되며, 내용이 "모두 정확하다"라는 것을 나타내는 이 약어는 다른 신문사에서도 채택되어 출판에 자주 사용되었다고 했다. 따라서 (b)가 정답이다.

⇄ Paraphrasing
the abbreviation 약어 → a short version 축약 버전

어휘 | editorial adj. 편집상의, 편집자의 newsprint n. 신문 인쇄용지

62   특정세부사항   When   난이도 ●●●

When did "OK" become widely used in America?

(a) when the president made a nickname using his initials
(b) when it played a role in a presidential campaign
(c) when it became a symbol for the president's hometown
(d) when a re-elected president said it in his victory speech

"OK"는 언제 미국에서 널리 쓰이게 되었는가?

(a) 대통령이 자신의 이니셜을 사용하여 별명을 만들었을 때
(b) 대통령 선거 운동에서 역할을 했을 때
(c) 대통령의 고향에 대한 상징이 되었을 때
(d) 재당선된 대통령이 당선 연설에서 말했을 때

○ 정답 잡는 치트키

질문의 키워드 widely used in America가 spread through the United States로 paraphrasing되어 언급된 주변 내용을 주의 깊게 읽는다.

해설 | 4단락의 '"OK" further spread through the United States during the 1840 presidential elections. President Martin Van Buren, ~, used "Old Kinderhook," or "OK," as his 1840 re-election campaign nickname. He coined "Vote for OK" as his campaign slogan.'에서 "OK"는 1840년 대통령 선거 기간에 미국 전역에 더욱 널리 퍼졌는데, 대통령 마틴 밴 뷰런이 1840년 재선 캠페인 별명으로 "올드 킨더후크" 또는 "OK"를 사용했고, 자신의 선거 슬로건으로 "OK에 투표하세요"를 새로 만들었다고 했다. 따라서 (b)가 정답이다.

오답분석

(a) 4단락에서 대통령 마틴 밴 뷰런이 재선 캠페인 별명으로 "올드 킨더후크" 또는 "OK"를 사용했다고는 언급했지만, 이것이 대통령 이름의 이니셜을 사용한 별명은 아니므로 오답이다.

어휘 | play a role phr. 역할을 하다

63   추론   특정사실   난이도 ●●○

Why, most likely, did "OK" become popular when sending telegrams?

(a) It was easily understood by operators worldwide.
(b) It served as a positive way to end a message.
(c) It allowed operators to type a reply quickly.
(d) It cost less to use when sending confirmation.

전보를 보낼 때 왜 "OK"가 인기를 끌었을 것 같은가?

(a) 전 세계 기사들이 쉽게 이해할 수 있었다.
(b) 메시지를 끝내는 긍정적인 방식으로 기능했다.
(c) 기사들이 빠르게 답장을 입력하게 했다.
(d) 확인을 보낼 때 쓰는 비용이 적게 들었다.

○ 정답 잡는 치트키

질문의 키워드 telegrams가 그대로 언급되고, become popular가 gained ~ popularity로 paraphrasing되어 언급된 주변 내용을 주의 깊게 읽는다.

해설 | 5단락의 'The word later gained worldwide popularity with the invention of the telegraph. Telegram messages became more expensive to send when more letters were used. Thus, "OK" became the code used by telegraph operators to acknowledge receipt of a message.'에서 "OK" 단어는 이후 전신의 발명과 함께 세계적인 인기를 얻었는데, 전보 메시지는 더 많은 문자가 사용되면 전송 비용이 더 비싸졌기 때문에, "OK"는 전신 기사들이 메시지의 수신을 확인하는 데 사용되는 코드가 되었다고 한 것을 통해, 전신 기사들이 메시지의 수신 확인을 보낼 때 더 적은 문자를 보내야 비용이 더 적게 들었기 때문에 "OK"가 인기를 끌었음을 추론할 수 있다. 따라서 (d)가 정답이다.

어휘 | type v. 입력하다, 타자를 치다   confirmation n. 확인

How has "OK" further evolved in the present times? 　　　 "OK"는 어떻게 현재에 더 발전해 왔는가?

(a) by being useful in many language situations 　　　 **(a) 다양한 언어 상황에서 유용해짐으로써**

(b) by showing up mostly as a hand signal 　　　 (b) 대부분 수신호로 나타남으로써

(c) by taking the place of traditional words for agreement 　　　 (c) 동의를 뜻하는 전통적인 단어를 대신함으로써

(d) by being able to express any kind of meaning 　　　 (d) 모든 종류의 의미를 표현할 수 있게 됨으로써

➤─○ 정답 잡는 치트키

질문의 키워드 evolved in the present times와 관련된 주변 내용을 주의 깊게 읽는다.

해설 | 6단락의 'The word itself can serve as an adjective, adverb, noun, or verb, making it highly versatile and useful in many situations.'에서 단어 자체가 형용사, 부사, 명사, 동사의 역할을 할 수 있어서 다양한 상황에서 아주 다목적으로 쓰이고 유용하게 만든다고 했다. 따라서 (a)가 정답이다.

어휘 | evolve v. 발전하다, 변하다　 show up phr. 나타나다, 등장하다　 take the place of phr. ~을 대신하다

---

65 어휘 　　유의어 　　　　　　　　　　　　　　　　　　　　　　　　　　 난이도 ●●○

In the context of the passage, underline{surfaced} means _____. 　　　 지문의 문맥에서, 'surfaced'는 -을 의미한다.

(a) declared 　　　 (a) 선언한

(b) landed 　　　 (b) 착륙한

(c) appeared 　　　 **(c) 나타난**

(d) hidden 　　　 (d) 숨겨진

➤─○ 정답 잡는 치트키

밑줄 친 어휘의 유의어를 찾는 문제이므로, surfaced가 포함된 구절을 읽고 문맥을 파악한다.

해설 | 3단락의 '"OK" is believed to have first surfaced in 1839'은 "OK"가 1839년에 처음 나타난 것으로 추정된다는 뜻이므로, surfaced가 '나타난'이라는 의미로 사용된 것을 알 수 있다. 따라서 '나타난'이라는 같은 의미의 (c) appeared가 정답이다.

---

66 어휘 　　유의어 　　　　　　　　　　　　　　　　　　　　　　　　　　 난이도 ●●○

In the context of the passage, underline{versatile} means _____. 　　　 지문의 문맥에서, 'versatile'은 -을 의미한다.

(a) inventive 　　　 (a) 창의성이 풍부한

(b) skillful 　　　 (b) 솜씨 있는

(c) flexible 　　　 **(c) 적응성 있는**

(d) realistic 　　　 (d) 현실적인

➤─○ 정답 잡는 치트키

밑줄 친 어휘의 유의어를 찾는 문제이므로, versatile이 포함된 구절을 읽고 문맥을 파악한다.

해설 | 6단락의 'highly versatile and useful'은 아주 다목적으로 쓰이고 유용하다는 뜻이므로, versatile이 '다목적으로 쓰이는'이라는 의미로 사용된 것을 알 수 있다. 따라서 '적응성 있는'이라는 비슷한 의미의 (c) flexible이 정답이다.

표제어

ASIAN AROWANA

정의

The Asian arowana is a fish species found primarily in the fresh waters of Southeast Asia. It is one of the most sought-after and expensive ornamental fish in the world. The Asian arowana is highly prized for its beauty and cultural significance.

특징1:
외형
및
수염

[67(c)]With a long, narrow body that can grow up to three feet in the wild, the Asian arowana comes in many colors, but solid red, silver, and gold are the most common. [67(d)]Arowanas have whisker-like appendages called "barbels" that jut out of their chins and are used to detect prey. The fish are also covered in shiny, coin-like scales resembling those of mythical Asian dragons. [67(a)]The Asian arowana can live for over sixty years in captivity.

특징2:
먹이

In the wild, arowanas are carnivorous. [68]Classified as surface feeders, their diet includes insects, spiders, frogs, and lizards that sit on vegetation close to the water. Arowanas are also able to jump out of the water to catch their prey. They hunt their food discreetly, often hiding in the shade before jumping on their meal.

특징3:
부성
구내
보육

Reproduction for the Asian arowana involves a process called "paternal mouthbrooding." [69]The male arowana, whose mouth is wider than the female's, keeps the eggs in its mouth, protecting them until they hatch. Then, the hatchlings remain in the mouth for a few months before being released into the water.

특징4:
헤엄
치는
동작

Another trait of the Asian arowana is its graceful swimming motion. The movement is said to resemble that of a dragon as the fish glides through the water, earning it the "dragon fish" nickname. [70]Because dragons symbolize good luck in Chinese culture, the arowana [72]is particularly coveted as an aquarium pet because it is also believed to bring its owner money and good fortune.

보존
상태
및
현황

Due to its popularity as a pet and the destruction of its habitats, the Asian arowana has become critically endangered. [71]Import and trade of the fish is now banned in many countries, including the US. However, this protected status reinforces [73]the arowana's reputation as a rare and prized fish, raising its market value considerably. Reports say that a single fish was once bought for $300,000.

아시아 아로와나

아시아 아로와나는 동남아시아의 담수에서 주로 발견되는 어종이다. 그것은 세계에서 가장 수요가 많고 비싼 관상용 물고기 중 하나이다. 아시아 아로와나는 아름다움과 문화적인 중요성으로 인해 매우 귀중히 여겨진다.

[67(c)]야생에서 3피트까지 자랄 수 있는 길고 좁은 몸을 가진, 아시아 아로와나는 다양한 색상이 있지만, 완전한 빨간색, 은색, 금색이 가장 흔하다. [67(d)]아로와나는 턱 밖으로 튀어나온 "바벨"이라고 불리는 수염 같은 부속기관이 있는데 먹이를 감지하는 데 사용된다. 이 물고기는 또한 신화 속에 나오는 아시아 용의 비늘을 닮은 반짝이는 동전 같은 비늘로 덮여 있다. [67(a)]아시아 아로와나는 포획된 상태로 60년 넘게 살 수 있다.

야생에서, 아로와나는 육식성이다. [68]수면 먹이를 먹는 동물로 분류되는, 그들의 먹이는 물가에 있는 초목 위에 앉아 있는 곤충, 거미, 개구리, 도마뱀을 포함한다. 아로와나는 먹이를 잡기 위해 물 밖으로 뛰어오를 수도 있다. 그것들은 먹이에 뛰어들기 전에 종종 그늘에 숨어 있다가, 조심스럽게 먹이를 사냥한다.

아시아 아로와나의 번식은 "부성 구내보육"이라고 불리는 과정을 포함한다. [69]암컷보다 입이 더 넓은 수컷 아로와나는 입 속에 알을 넣어, 그것들이 부화할 때까지 보호한다. 그런 다음, 부화한 새끼들은 물속에 놓아지기 전에 몇 달 동안 입 안에 남아 있게 된다.

아시아 아로와나의 또 다른 특징은 우아한 헤엄치는 동작이다. 이 움직임은 물고기가 물속을 미끄러지듯 나아갈 때 용의 움직임과 닮았다고 해서, "용 물고기"라는 별명을 얻었다. [70]용은 중국 문화에서 행운을 상징하므로, 아로와나는 주인에게 돈과 행운을 가져다 준다고 믿어지기도 하기 때문에 [72]수조 반려동물로 특히 탐내어진다.

반려동물로의 인기와 서식지의 파괴로 인해, 아시아 아로와나는 심각한 멸종 위기에 처해 있다. [71]이 물고기의 수입과 거래는 미국을 포함한 많은 나라에서 현재 금지되어 있다. 그러나, 이러한 보호받는 지위는 [73]희귀하고 귀한 물고기라는 아로와나의 명성을 강화하여, 시장 가치를 상당히 높였다. 보도에 따르면 한 마리의 물고기가 한때 300,000달러에 구입되었다고 한다.

어휘 | **fresh water** phr. 담수 **sought-after** adj. 수요가 많은 **ornamental fish** phr. 관상용 물고기 **prize** v. 귀중히 여기다 **significance** n. 중요성, 의의 **solid** adj. (색깔이) 완전한, 다른 색깔이 섞이지 않은 **whisker** n. 수염 **appendage** n. 부속기관, 부속물

chin n. 턱 detect v. 감지하다, 찾아내다 prey n. 먹이 scale n. 비늘 resemble v. 닮다, 유사하다 mythical adj. 신화 속에 나오는
captivity n. 사로잡힘, 감금 carnivorous adj. 육식성의 surface feeder phr. 수면 먹이를 먹는 동물 vegetation n. 초목, 식물
hunt v. 사냥하다, 찾다; n. 사냥 discreetly adv. 조심스럽게, 신중히 shade n. 그늘 reproduction n. 번식
paternal adj. 부계의, 아버지의 mouthbrooding n. 구내보육 hatch v. 부화하다 hatchling n. 부화한지 얼마 안 되는 어린 물고기
trait n. 특징, 특성 graceful adj. 우아한, 기품 있는 glide v. 미끄러지듯 가다 symbolize v. 상징하다, 나타내다 good fortune phr. 행운
destruction n. 파괴 habitat n. 서식지 endangered adj. 멸종 위기의 import n. 수입; v. 수입하다 trade n. 거래; v. 거래하다
ban v. 금지하다 status n. 지위, 신분, 상태 reinforce v. 강화하다 market value phr. 시장 가치

67 Not/True Not 문제 난이도 ●●○

Which is NOT true of the Asian arowana?

(a) that it has a life expectancy of more than half a century
(b) that it has a body that can change colors over time
(c) that it has a long and slender body of about three feet
(d) that it has a facial feature that senses nearby prey

아시아 아로와나에 관해 사실이 아닌 것은 무엇인가?

(a) 기대 수명이 반세기가 넘는다는 것
**(b) 시간이 지남에 따라 색을 바꿀 수 있는 몸을 지닌
다는 것**
(c) 약 3피트의 길고 가느다란 몸을 가진다는 것
(d) 주변의 먹이를 감지하는 얼굴의 특징이 있다는 것

━○ 정답 잡는 치트키

질문의 키워드 Asian arowana가 그대로 언급된 주변 내용을 주의 깊게 읽고, 보기의 키워드와 지문 내용을 대조하며 언급되는 것을 하나씩 소
거한다.

해설 | (b)는 지문에 언급되지 않았으므로, (b)가 정답이다.

오답분석
(a) 보기의 키워드 more than half a century가 over sixty years로 paraphrasing되어 언급된 2단락에서 아시아 아로와나는 포획
된 상태로 60년 넘게 살 수 있다고 언급되었다.
(c) 보기의 키워드 long과 three feet이 그대로 언급되고, slender가 narrow로 paraphrasing되어 언급된 2단락에서 아시아 아로와
나가 야생에서 3피트까지 자랄 수 있는 길고 좁은 몸을 가지고 있다고 언급되었다.
(d) 보기의 키워드 senses ~ prey가 detect prey로 paraphrasing되어 언급된 2단락에서 아시아 아로와나는 턱 밖으로 튀어나온 "바
벨"이라고 불리는 수염 같은 부속기관이 있는데 이것은 먹이를 감지하는 데 사용된다고 언급되었다.

어휘 | life expectancy phr. 기대 수명 slender adj. 가느다란, 날씬한 facial adj. 얼굴의, 안면의 sense v. 감지하다; n. 감각

68 특정세부사항 How 난이도 ●●○

How does the Asian arowana get its food?

(a) by eating plants that grow at the water's edge
(b) by hunting only in the shaded parts of the water
(c) by jumping out of the water to hunt on land
(d) by pouncing on prey that lingers near the water

아시아 아로와나는 어떻게 먹이를 얻는가?

(a) 물가에서 자라는 식물을 먹음으로써
(b) 물의 그늘진 곳에서만 사냥함으로써
(c) 육지에서 사냥하기 위해 물 밖으로 뛰어오름으로써
(d) 물 근처에 계속 머물러 있는 먹이를 덮침으로써

━○ 정답 잡는 치트키

질문의 키워드 food가 diet로 paraphrasing되어 언급된 주변 내용을 주의 깊게 읽는다.

해설 | 3단락의 'Classified as surface feeders, their diet includes insects, spiders, frogs, and lizards that sit on vegetation
close to the water.'에서 수면 먹이를 먹는 동물로 분류되는 아시아 아로와나의 먹이는 물가에 있는 초목 위에 앉아 있는 곤충, 거미, 개구

리, 도마뱀을 포함한다고 했다. 따라서 (d)가 정답이다.

⇄ **Paraphrasing**
close to the water 물가에 있는 → near the water 물 근처에 있는

오답분석
(b) 3단락에서 아시아 아로나가 먹이에 뛰어들기 전에 종종 그늘에 숨어 있다가 사냥한다고는 언급했지만, 물의 그늘진 곳에서만 사냥하는 것은 아니므로 오답이다.
(c) 3단락에서 아시아 아로나가 물 밖으로 뛰어올라 먹이를 잡을 수 있다고는 언급했지만, 물 밖으로 뛰어올라 육지에서도 사냥할 수 있다고 한 것은 아니므로 오답이다.

어휘 | water's edge phr. 물가 pounce on phr. ~을 덮치다 linger v. 계속 머물다, 남아 있다

---

69 특정세부사항 ____ Why   난이도 ●○○

Why are young arowanas kept in the male arowana's mouth and not in the female's?

(a) The temperature of a male's mouth is warmer.
(b) The male's mouth has a larger capacity.
(c) The teeth in a male's mouth are not as sharp.
(d) The male's mouth has multiple compartments.

새끼 아로나는 왜 암컷의 입 속이 아닌 수컷 아로나의 입 속에 넣어지는가?

(a) 수컷의 입 온도가 더 따뜻하다.
(b) 수컷의 입이 더 큰 수용력을 가진다.
(c) 수컷의 입 안에 있는 이빨은 그렇게 날카롭지 않다.
(d) 수컷의 입에는 여러 구획이 있다.

정답 잡는 치트키
질문의 키워드 mouth가 그대로 언급된 주변 내용을 주의 깊게 읽는다.

해설 | 4단락의 'The male arowana, whose mouth is wider than the female's, keeps the eggs in its mouth, protecting them until they hatch.'에서 암컷보다 입이 더 넓은 수컷 아로나는 입 속에 알을 넣어, 그것들이 부화할 때까지 보호한다고 했다. 따라서 (b)가 정답이다.

⇄ **Paraphrasing**
is wider 더 넓다 → has a larger capacity 더 큰 수용력을 가지다

어휘 | capacity n. 수용력, 용량 compartment n. 구획, 칸

---

70 특정세부사항 ____ What   난이도 ●●○

What is the connection between dragons and the Asian arowana in Chinese culture?

(a) They are both popular in children's stories.
(b) They are both believed to bring good luck.
(c) They are both used in religious symbolism.
(d) They are both used in major celebrations.

중국 문화에서 용과 아시아 아로나의 연관성은 무엇인가?

(a) 둘 다 동화에서 인기가 있다.
(b) 둘 다 행운을 가져다준다고 믿어진다.
(c) 둘 다 종교적인 상징으로 사용된다.
(d) 둘 다 중요한 축하 행사에서 사용된다.

정답 잡는 치트키
질문의 키워드 dragons ~ in Chinese culture가 그대로 언급된 주변 내용을 주의 깊게 읽는다.

해설 | 5단락의 'Because dragons symbolize good luck in Chinese culture, the arowana ~ is also believed to bring its owner money and good fortune.'에서 용은 중국 문화에서 행운을 상징하므로, 아로와나는 주인에게 돈과 행운을 가져다준다고 믿어지기도 한다고 했다. 따라서 (b)가 정답이다.

어휘 | children's story phr. 동화 religious symbolism phr. 종교적인 상징

---

71 추론 특정사실   난이도 ●●○

Based on the article, what has probably contributed to the high price of Asian arowanas?

(a) the limitations on where it can be sold
(b) the laws against entering its habitats
(c) the absence of any populations in the wild
(d) the difficulty of breeding it in captivity

기사에 따르면, 아시아 아로와나의 높은 가격에 기여한 것은 무엇인 것 같은가?

(a) 판매될 수 있는 장소의 제한
(b) 서식지 침입을 금지하는 법
(c) 야생에 있는 개체수의 부족
(d) 포획된 상태에서 기르는 것의 어려움

🔑 정답 잡는 치트키

질문의 키워드 contributed to the high price가 raising its market value로 paraphrasing되어 언급된 주변 내용을 주의 깊게 읽는다.

해설 | 6단락의 'Import and trade of the fish is now banned in many countries, including the US. However, this protected status reinforces the arowana's reputation as a rare and prized fish, raising its market value considerably.'에서 아시아 아로와나의 수입과 거래는 미국을 포함한 많은 나라에서 현재 금지되어 있지만, 이러한 보호받는 지위는 희귀하고 귀한 물고기라는 아로와나의 명성을 강화하여 시장 가치를 상당히 높였다고 한 것을 통해, 아시아 아로와나가 미국 등 많은 나라에서 판매가 금지되어 있어서 판매 가격이 높아졌음을 추론할 수 있다. 따라서 (a)가 정답이다.

오답분석
(c) 6단락에서 아시아 아로와나가 심각한 멸종 위기에 처해 있다고는 언급했지만, 이것이 높은 가격에 기여한 직접적인 원인으로 언급된 것은 아니므로 오답이다.

어휘 | limitation n. 제한, 제약 absence n. 부족, 없음 population n. 개체수, 집단 breed v. 기르다, 사육하다

---

72 어휘 유의어   난이도 ●●●

In the context of the passage, coveted means _____.

(a) desired
(b) needed
(c) accepted
(d) envied

지문의 문맥에서, 'coveted'는 -을 의미한다.

(a) 원해진
(b) 필요해진
(c) 받아들여진
(d) 시기 되는

🔑 정답 잡는 치트키

밑줄 친 어휘의 유의어를 찾는 문제이므로, coveted가 포함된 구절을 읽고 문맥을 파악한다.

해설 | 5단락의 'is particularly coveted as an aquarium pet'은 수조 반려동물로 특히 탐내어진다는 뜻이므로, coveted가 '탐내어진'이라는 의미로 사용된 것을 알 수 있다. 따라서 '원해진'이라는 비슷한 의미의 (a) desired가 정답이다.

In the context of the passage, reputation means _____.

(a) knowledge
(b) journey
(c) link
(d) place

지문의 문맥에서, 'reputation'은 ~을 의미한다.

(a) 인지
(b) 여정
(c) 연관
(d) 지위

─○ 정답 잡는 치트키

밑줄 친 어휘의 유의어를 찾는 문제이므로, reputation이 포함된 구절을 읽고 문맥을 파악한다.

해설 | 6단락의 'the arowana's reputation as a rare and prized fish'는 희귀하고 귀한 물고기라는 아로와나의 명성이라는 뜻이므로, reputation이 '명성'이라는 의미로 사용된 것을 알 수 있다. 따라서 '지위'라는 비슷한 의미의 (d) place가 정답이다.

PART 4 (74~80) 비즈니스 편지 멘토가 되어준 것에 감사하는 편지

수신인 정보

Barbara West
Manager, White Plains Hotel
52 Hartland Ave.
Atlantic City, NJ

Dear Mrs. West,

편지의 목적: 감사 표시

⁷⁴I am writing this letter to express my gratitude to you for being my mentor for the past few years. **As you already know,** ⁷⁵I will be moving to a different branch of the hotel. The newly opened location on Mammoth Avenue needs staff, and I have been assigned to be its branch manager.

교훈1: 호텔 관리

I believe that working as your assistant manager here at the White Plains Hotel ⁷⁹has helped shape me for my new position. ⁷⁴I would therefore like to thank you for your training and guidance over the last three years. Through you, I learned how to effectively meet the many demands of hotel management. ^{76(a)/(b)/(d)}I became skilled at accommodating guests, hosting events, and ensuring the hotel's overall upkeep. **You also taught me how to successfully handle customer complaints.**

교훈2: 비상 시에 대처하는 방법

⁷⁷Another important lesson I learned from you is how to keep my presence of mind and stay focused in times of emergency. I admired how professionally you acted when the adjacent building caught fire last year. You managed to ⁸⁰reassure the guests who were panicking and guide them to a safer place. I was honored to have witnessed your dedication to serve and protect our clients that day.

Barbara West
White Plains 호텔 관리자
하틀랜드 가 52번지
뉴저지주 애틀랜틱시티

Mrs. West께,

⁷⁴지난 몇 년간 저의 멘토가 되어주신 귀하께 감사를 표하기 위해 이 편지를 씁니다. 이미 알고 계시다시피, ⁷⁵저는 호텔의 다른 지점으로 옮기게 되었습니다. 매머드 가에 새로 연 지점에 직원이 필요한데, 제가 그곳의 지점장을 맡게 되었습니다.

저는 이곳 White Plains 호텔에서 부관리자로 근무한 것이 ⁷⁹저의 새로운 직책을 위해 저를 발전시키는 것을 도왔다고 생각합니다. ⁷⁴따라서 지난 3년이 넘는 동안 귀하의 교육과 지도에 감사드리고 싶습니다. 귀하를 통해, 저는 호텔 관리의 많은 요구 사항을 효과적으로 충족시키는 방법을 배웠습니다. ^{76(a)/(b)/(d)}저는 고객의 편의를 도모하고, 행사를 주최하고, 호텔의 전반적인 유지를 보장하는 데 능숙해졌습니다. 귀하는 고객의 불만 사항을 성공적으로 처리하는 방법도 제게 가르쳐 주었습니다.

⁷⁷제가 귀하로부터 배운 또 다른 중요한 교훈은 비상시에 침착성을 지키고 집중력을 유지하는 방법입니다. 작년에 인접한 건물에 불이 붙었을 때 귀하가 얼마나 전문적으로 대처했는지에 감탄했습니다. ⁸⁰당황한 손님들을 안심시키고 더 안전한 곳으로 안내해 주셨죠. 그날 고객들에게 봉사하고 그들을 보호하려는 귀하의 헌신을 목격하게 되어 영광이었습니다.

예상 되는 효과	I am confident that the experience and knowledge I have gained while working with you will help me manage the Mammoth Avenue branch effectively. Moreover, I am certain that the person who will replace me as your assistant manager will be lucky to be working with you.	저는 귀하와 함께 일하면서 얻은 경험과 지식이 제가 매머드 가 지점을 효율적으로 운영하는 데 도움이 될 것이라고 확신합니다. 게다가, 저를 대신하여 부관리자로 일하게 될 분도 귀하와 함께 일하게 되어 행운일 것이라고 확신합니다.
끝인사	Thank you once again for everything. ⁷⁸I look forward to seeing you again at the managers' monthly strategy meeting.	다시 한번 모든 것에 감사드립니다. ⁷⁸월례 관리자 전략 회의에서 다시 뵙기를 기대하겠습니다.
발신인 정보	Sincerely, *Andy Johnson* Andy Johnson	Andy Johnson 드림

어휘 | assign v. (일·책임 등을) 맡기다, 배정하다 guidance n. 지도 accommodate v. (손님의) 편의를 도모하다 upkeep n. 유지
handle v. 처리하다, 다루다 keep one's presence of mind phr. 침착성을 유지하다 focused adj. 집중한 emergency n. 비상, 응급
admire v. 감탄하다 professionally adv. 전문적으로, 직업적으로 adjacent adj. 인접한, 근방의 catch fire phr. 불이 붙다
panic v. 당황하다; n. 당황 honor v. ~에게 영광을 주다 witness v. ~을 목격하다, 보다 dedication n. 헌신, 전념
serve v. 봉사하다, 제공하다 look forward to phr. ~을 기대하다, 고대하다 strategy meeting phr. 전략 회의

---

74 주제/목적   편지의 목적   난이도 ●●○

Why is Andy Johnson writing a letter to Barbara West?

(a) to show appreciation for her recent recommendation
(b) to thank her for aiding his professional development
(c) to express his gratitude for promoting him to manager
(d) to let her know that he is leaving for a different company

왜 Andy Johnson은 Barbara West에게 편지를 쓰고 있는가?

(a) 최근의 추천에 감사를 표하기 위해서
(b) 전문성 개발을 도와준 것에 감사하기 위해서
(c) 관리자로 승진시켜 준 것에 감사를 표하기 위해서
(d) 다른 회사로 떠나는 것을 알리기 위해서

━○ 정답 잡는 치트키

지문의 초반을 주의 깊게 읽고 전체 맥락을 파악한다.

해설 | 1단락의 'I am writing this letter to express my gratitude to you for being my mentor for the past few years.'에서 지난 몇 년간 멘토가 되어준 Barbara West에게 감사를 표하기 위해 이 편지를 쓴다고 했고, 2단락의 'I would therefore like to thank you for your training and guidance over the last three years.'에서 지난 3년이 넘는 동안의 교육과 지도에 감사하고 싶다고 한 뒤, 자기의 전문성 개발을 도와준 것에 대해 Barbara West에게 감사하는 내용이 이어지고 있다. 따라서 (b)가 정답이다.

어휘 | appreciation n. 감사

---

75 특정세부사항   Why   난이도 ●●○

Why did the hotel decide to transfer Andy to another branch?

(a) The manager of the branch has been dismissed.
(b) The branch has been recently launched in a new area.

호텔은 왜 Andy를 다른 지점으로 옮기기로 결정했는가?

(a) 지점장이 해고되었다.
(b) 지점은 최근에 새로운 지역에 진출했다.

(c) The branch has grown steadily for several years.

(d) The hotel is closing its current location.

(c) 지점은 몇 년 동안 꾸준히 성장해 왔다.

(d) 호텔은 현재 위치를 폐쇄하고 있다.

질문의 키워드 transfer ~ to another branch가 moving to a different branch로 paraphrasing되어 언급된 수련 내용을 수의 싶게 읽는다.

해설 | 1단락의 'I will be moving to a different branch of the hotel. The newly opened location on Mammoth Avenue needs staff, and I have been assigned to be its branch manager.'에서 호텔의 다른 지점으로 옮기게 되었는데, 매머드 가에 새로 연 지점에 직원이 필요해서 그곳의 지점장을 맡게 되었다고 했다. 따라서 (b)가 정답이다.

어휘 | transfer v. 옮기다 dismiss v. 해고하다 steadily adv. 꾸준히, 지속해서

76 Not/True   Not 문제
난이도 ●●○

According to the letter, what is NOT true about Andy's work experience with Barbara?

(a) She familiarized him with the hotel's maintenance needs.

(b) She showed him how to make customers a priority.

(c) She taught him how to deal with difficult employees.

(d) She gave him skills for managing hotel activities.

편지에 따르면, Andy가 Barbara와 함께 일한 경험에 관해 사실이 아닌 것은 무엇인가?

(a) 호텔의 유지 보수 필요 사항을 숙지시켰다.

(b) 고객들을 우선시하는 방법을 보여주었다.

(c) 어려운 직원들을 대하는 방법을 가르쳐 주었다.

(d) 호텔 활동을 관리하는 기술을 알려주었다.

질문의 키워드 work experience with Barbara와 관련된 주변 내용을 주의 깊게 읽고, 보기의 키워드와 지문 내용을 대조하며 언급되는 것을 하나씩 소거한다.

해설 | (c)는 지문에 언급되지 않았으므로, (c)가 정답이다.

오답분석
(a) 보기의 키워드 hotel's maintenance needs가 hotel's overall upkeep으로 paraphrasing되어 언급된 2단락에서 호텔의 전반적인 유지를 보장하는 데 능숙해졌다고 언급되었다.

(b) 보기의 키워드 customers가 guests로 paraphrasing되어 언급된 2단락에서 고객의 편의를 도모하는 것에 능숙해졌다고 언급되었다.

(d) 보기의 키워드 activities가 events로 paraphrasing되어 언급된 2단락에서 행사를 주최하는 것에 능숙해졌다고 언급되었다.

어휘 | priority n. 우선, 우선 사항 deal with phr. ~을 (상)대하다

77 특정세부사항   What
난이도 ●●○

What did Andy learn from Barbara's actions when a major mishap occurred at work?

(a) the value of staying calm in the face of a crisis

(b) the trick to distracting worried guests

(c) the importance of being ready for sudden disasters

(d) the best ways to handle minor injuries

Andy는 직장에서 큰 사고가 일어났을 때, Barbara의 행동으로부터 무엇을 배웠는가?

(a) 위기 직면 상황에서 침착함을 유지하는 것의 가치

(b) 걱정하는 고객들의 주의를 딴 데로 돌리는 요령

(c) 갑작스러운 사고에 대비하는 것의 중요성

(d) 경미한 부상을 다루는 가장 좋은 방법

질문의 키워드 when a major mishap occurred가 in times of emergency로 paraphrasing되어 언급된 주변 내용을 주의 깊게 읽는다.

해설 | 3단락의 'Another important lesson I learned from you is how to keep my presence of mind and stay focused in times of emergency.'에서 Andy가 Barbara로부터 배운 또 다른 중요한 교훈은 비상시에 침착성을 지키고 집중력을 유지하는 방법이라고 했다. 따라서 (a)가 정답이다.

⇄ **Paraphrasing**
keep ~ presence of mind 침착성을 지키다 → staying calm 침착함을 유지하는 것
in times of emergency 비상시에 → in the face of a crisis 위기 직면 상황에서

어휘 | mishap n. 사고, 재난 crisis n. 위기, 고비 distract v. 주의를 딴 데로 돌리다 sudden adj. 갑작스러운 disaster n. 사고, 재해

---

78 추론   특정사실   난이도 ●●○

How, most likely, will Andy be interacting with Barbara in the future?

(a) by collaborating together as managers
(b) by helping her train his replacement
(c) by interviewing people for staff positions
(d) by meeting at regular social occasions

Andy는 앞으로 Barbara와 어떻게 상호작용할 것 같은가?

(a) 관리자로서 함께 협력함으로써
(b) 후임자를 교육하는 것을 도움으로써
(c) 직원 일자리를 위해 사람들을 면접함으로써
(d) 정기적인 사교 행사에서 만남으로써

질문의 키워드 interacting ~ in the future와 관련된 주변 내용을 주의 깊게 읽는다.

해설 | 5단락의 'I look forward to seeing you again at the managers' monthly strategy meeting.'에서 월례 관리자 전략 회의에서 다시 보기를 기대한다고 한 것을 통해, 앞으로 Andy와 Barbara가 관리자로서 월례 관리자 전략 회의에서 함께 협력하며 상호작용하게 될 것임을 추론할 수 있다. 따라서 (a)가 정답이다.

어휘 | collaborate v. 협력하다 replacement n. 후임자 occasion n. 행사

---

79 어휘   유의어   난이도 ●●○

In the context of the passage, shape means _____.

(a) adjust
(b) consider
(c) pattern
(d) prepare

지문의 문맥에서, 'shape'는 -을 의미한다.

(a) 적응하다
(b) 고려하다
(c) 패턴을 형성시키다
(d) 준비시키다

밑줄 친 어휘의 유의어를 찾는 문제이므로, shape가 포함된 구절을 읽고 문맥을 파악한다.

해설 | 2단락의 'has helped shape me for my new position'은 새로운 직책을 위해 자신을 발전시키는 것을 도왔다는 뜻이므로, shape가 '발전시키다'라는 의미로 사용된 것을 알 수 있다. 따라서 '준비시키다'라는 비슷한 의미의 (d) prepare가 정답이다.

In the context of the passage, <u>reassure</u> means _____.

(a) satisfy
(b) silence
(c) question
(d) comfort

지문의 문맥에서, 'reassure'는 -을 의미한다.

(a) 충족시키다
(b) 조용하게 만들다
(c) 이의를 제기하다
(d) 안심시키다

─○ **정답 잡는 치트키**

밑줄 친 어휘의 유의어를 찾는 문제이므로, reassure가 포함된 구절을 읽고 문맥을 파악한다.

해설 | 3단락의 'reassure the guests who were panicking'은 당황한 손님들을 안심시킨다는 뜻이므로, reassure가 '안심시키다'라는 의미로 사용된 것을 알 수 있다. 따라서 '안심시키다'라는 같은 의미의 (d) comfort가 정답이다.

TEST 1
TEST 2
TEST 3
TEST 4
TEST 5
TEST 6
TEST 7

지텔프 공식 기출문제집 7회분 Level 2

공식기출
TEST 4
정답 · 스크립트 · 해석 · 해설

GRAMMAR

LISTENING

READING & VOCABULARY

GRAMMAR _____ / 26 (점수 : _____ 점)
LISTENING _____ / 26 (점수 : _____ 점)
READING & VOCABULARY _____ / 28 (점수 : _____ 점)

TOTAL _____ / 80 (평균 점수 : _____ 점)

*각 영역 점수: 맞은 개수 × 3.75
*평균 점수: 각 영역 점수 합계 ÷ 3

정답 및 취약 유형 분석표

자동 채점 및 성적 분석 서비스 ▶

GRAMMAR

번호	정답	유형
01	a	시제
02	a	가정법
03	c	관계사
04	d	준동사
05	d	조동사
06	a	조동사
07	a	시제
08	c	준동사
09	d	가정법
10	d	연결어
11	b	준동사
12	a	가정법
13	c	연결어
14	a	조동사
15	d	시제
16	c	가정법
17	b	준동사
18	b	관계사
19	a	조동사
20	d	시제
21	a	준동사
22	c	시제
23	c	시제
24	a	가정법
25	d	가정법
26	b	준동사

LISTENING

PART	번호	정답	유형
PART 1	27	c	특정세부사항
	28	c	특정세부사항
	29	a	특정세부사항
	30	d	특정세부사항
	31	a	추론
	32	b	특정세부사항
	33	b	추론
PART 2	34	a	주제/목적
	35	c	특정세부사항
	36	d	특정세부사항
	37	d	특정세부사항
	38	d	특정세부사항
	39	c	추론
PART 3	40	a	특정세부사항
	41	c	특정세부사항
	42	b	추론
	43	b	특정세부사항
	44	a	추론
	45	b	추론
PART 4	46	d	주제/목적
	47	a	특정세부사항
	48	c	추론
	49	c	특정세부사항
	50	a	추론
	51	d	특정세부사항
	52	a	특정세부사항

READING & VOCABULARY

PART	번호	정답	유형
PART 1	53	a	특정세부사항
	54	b	추론
	55	b	특정세부사항
	56	c	Not/True
	57	c	특정세부사항
	58	a	어휘
	59	b	어휘
PART 2	60	d	특정세부사항
	61	b	Not/True
	62	d	특정세부사항
	63	b	추론
	64	b	추론
	65	a	어휘
	66	c	어휘
PART 3	67	a	특정세부사항
	68	c	추론
	69	d	추론
	70	d	Not/True
	71	a	특정세부사항
	72	b	어휘
	73	d	어휘
PART 4	74	d	주제/목적
	75	b	특정세부사항
	76	a	특정세부사항
	77	a	추론
	78	b	특정세부사항
	79	c	어휘
	80	d	어휘

유형	맞힌 개수
시제	/ 6
가정법	/ 6
준동사	/ 6
조동사	/ 4
연결어	/ 2
관계사	/ 2
TOTAL	/ 26

유형	맞힌 개수
주제/목적	/ 2
특정세부사항	/ 16
Not/True	/ 0
추론	/ 8
TOTAL	/ 26

유형	맞힌 개수
주제/목적	/ 1
특정세부사항	/ 10
Not/True	/ 3
추론	/ 6
어휘	/ 8
TOTAL	/ 28

GRAMMAR

01 시제 현재진행

난이도 ●○○

Derrick has been hired to audit the finances of Landsdale Security Company. Right now, he _____ the company's invoices to their financial records to check for fraudulent spending and calculation errors.

(a) is comparing
(b) was comparing
(c) would compare
(d) has been comparing

Derrick은 Landsdale Security사의 재무를 감사하기 위해 고용되었다. 바로 지금, 그는 부정한 지출과 계산 착오를 확인하기 위해 회사의 청구서와 재무 기록을 <u>비교하고 있는 중이다</u>.

○ 지텔프 치트키

right now가 있으면 현재진행 시제가 정답이다.

> ☀ **현재진행과 자주 함께 쓰이는 시간 표현**
> • right now / now / currently / at the moment 바로 지금 / 지금 / 현재 / 바로 지금
> • these days / nowadays 요즘

해설 | 현재진행 시제와 함께 쓰이는 시간 표현 right now가 있고, 문맥상 말하고 있는 현재 시점에 Derrick이 회사의 청구서와 재무 기록을 비교하고 있는 중이라는 의미가 되어야 자연스럽다. 따라서 현재진행 시제 (a) is comparing이 정답이다.

어휘 | audit v. (회계를) 감사하다 **finance** n. 재무, 재정 **invoice** n. 청구서, 송장 **financial record** phr. 재무 기록
fraudulent adj. 부정한, 사기적인 **calculation error** phr. 계산 착오

02 가정법 가정법 과거

난이도 ●●○

Bees are an important part of the natural ecosystem, as they pollinate many plants. Ecologists believe that if bees were to suddenly disappear, entire ecosystems _____ immediately.

(a) would collapse
(b) will have collapsed
(c) would have collapsed
(d) will collapse

벌들은 많은 식물들을 수분시키기 때문에 자연 생태계의 중요한 부분이다. 생태학자들은 만약 벌들이 갑자기 사라진다면, 전체 생태계가 즉시 <u>붕괴할 것이라</u>고 믿는다.

○ 지텔프 치트키

'if + were to + 동사원형'이 있으면 'would/could + 동사원형'이 정답이다.

> ☀ **가정법 과거(were to)**
> If + 주어 + were to + 동사원형, 주어 + would/could(조동사 과거형) + 동사원형

해설 | if절에 과거 동사(were to ~ disappear)가 있으므로, 주절에는 이와 짝을 이루어 가정법 과거를 만드는 'would(조동사 과거형) + 동사원형'이 와야 한다. 따라서 (a) would collapse가 정답이다.

어휘 | natural ecosystem phr. 자연 생태계 pollinate v. 수분시키다 ecologist n. 생태학자, 환경 보호론자 collapse v. 붕괴하다, 무너지다

03 관계사   주격 관계대명사 who

Radio XCZR has a promo for the summer music festival. The first caller _____ the entire festival lineup will be given a free festival ticket and a meet-and-greet pass for an artist of their choice.

(a) what can recite
(b) when can recite
(c) who can recite
(d) which can recite

라디오 XCZR에서는 여름 음악 축제를 위한 프로그램 예고를 진행한다. 축제 라인업 전체를 죽 말할 수 있는 첫 번째 발신자에게는 무료 축제 입장권과 원하는 아티스트를 만나는 허가증이 주어질 것이다.

─○ 지텔프 치트키

사람 선행사가 관계절 안에서 주어 역할을 하면 주격 관계대명사 who가 정답이다.

해설 | 사람 선행사 The first caller를 받으면서 보기의 관계절 내에서 주어 역할을 할 수 있는 주격 관계대명사가 필요하므로, (c) who can recite가 정답이다.

어휘 | promo n. 프로그램 예고, 판촉 활동 caller n. 발신자, 전화를 건 사람 lineup n. 라인업, (방송 프로·행사 따위의) 예정표
meet-and-greet adj. (유명인을) 만나는, 팬 미팅을 위한 pass n. 허가증, 무료입장권 recite v. (열거하듯) 죽 말하다, 나열하다

04 준동사   to 부정사의 진주어 역할

Frequent hydration in hot weather is important because it keeps the body cool and replaces fluids lost through sweating. Therefore, it is advisable _____ a water bottle along when going outside on a hot day.

(a) bringing
(b) having brought
(c) to have brought
(d) to bring

더운 날씨에 빈번한 수분 공급은 몸을 시원하게 유지해 주고 땀을 흘리는 것으로 인해 손실된 체액을 대체하기 때문에 중요하다. 따라서, 더운 날 외출할 때는 물병을 챙겨가는 것이 바람직하다.

─○ 지텔프 치트키

가주어 it이 있으면 to 부정사가 정답이다.

해설 | 빈칸 문장의 주어 자리에 가주어 it이 있고 문맥상 '물병을 챙겨가는 것이 바람직하다'라는 의미가 되어야 자연스러우므로, 빈칸에는 동사 is의 진주어인 '챙겨가는 것'이 와야 한다. 따라서 진주어 자리에 올 수 있는 to 부정사 (d) to bring이 정답이다.

어휘 | frequent adj. 빈번한, 잦은 hydration n. 수분 공급 fluid n. 체액 sweat v. 땀을 흘리다 advisable adj. 바람직한, 권할 만한

Lisa wants to be a full-time college professor, for which she needs a PhD. Her adviser suggests that she _____ applying for doctoral programs as soon as the final year of her master's program begins.

(a) started
(b) has started
(c) will start
(d) start

Lisa는 대학 전임 교수가 되기를 원하는데, 이를 위해서는 박사학위가 필요하다. 그녀의 지도교수는 석사 과정의 마지막 해가 시작되자마자 박사과정에 지원하기 시작해야 한다고 제안한다.

◄─○ 지텔프 치트키

suggest 다음에는 that절에 동사원형이 온다.

> ☀ **주장·요구·명령·제안을 나타내는 빈출 동사**
> suggest 제안하다 insist 주장하다 recommend 권고하다 demand 요구하다 request 요청하다 order 명령하다
> urge 강력히 촉구하다 ask 요청하다 propose 제안하다 advise 권고하다

해설 | 주절에 제안을 나타내는 동사 suggest가 있으므로 that절에는 '(should +) 동사원형'이 와야 한다. 따라서 동사원형 (d) start가 정답이다.

어휘 | full-time professor phr. 전임 교수 PhD n. 박사학위 doctoral program phr. 박사과정 master's program phr. 석사과정

There are several things that need to be done regularly to keep a violin in optimal condition. For example, strings _____ be changed at least once per year so that the violin's sound does not deteriorate.

(a) must
(b) might
(c) can
(d) will

바이올린을 최상의 상태로 유지하기 위해 정기적으로 해야 할 몇 가지 일들이 있다. 예를 들어, 바이올린의 소리가 나빠지지 않도록 적어도 일 년에 한 번씩 현이 교체되어야 한다.

◄─○ 지텔프 치트키

'~해야 한다'라고 말할 때는 must를 쓴다.

해설 | 문맥상 바이올린의 소리가 나빠지지 않도록 적어도 일 년에 한 번씩 현이 교체되어야 한다는 의미가 되어야 자연스러우므로, '~해야 한다'를 뜻하면서 의무를 나타내는 조동사 (a) must가 정답이다. 참고로, must와 should 모두 '~해야 한다'를 뜻하지만, must는 should보다 강한 어조로 조언을 하거나 의무를 나타낼 때 쓴다.

어휘 | optimal adj. 최상의 string n. (악기의) 현 deteriorate v. 나쁘게 하다, 악화시키다

Miranda landed her first leading role on a sitcom when she was just nineteen. By the time she turns thirty next month, she _____ in a major TV show for over a decade.

(a) **will have been starring**
(b) will be starring
(c) has been starring
(d) would star

Miranda는 겨우 열아홉 살 때 시트콤에서 첫 주연을 얻었다. 다음 달에 그녀가 서른 살이 될 무렵이면, 10년이 넘는 기간 동안 주요 TV 쇼에서 주역을 맡아오고 있는 중일 것이다.

지텔프 치트키

'by the time + 현재 동사'와 'for + 기간 표현'이 함께 오면 미래완료진행 시제가 정답이다.

> 💡 **미래완료진행과 자주 함께 쓰이는 시간 표현**
> • by the time / when / if + 현재 동사 + (for + 기간 표현) ~할 무렵이면 / ~할 때 / 만약 ~한다면 (~ 동안)
> • by / in + 미래 시점 + (for + 기간 표현) ~ 즈음에는 / ~에 (~ 동안)

해설 | 현재 동사로 미래의 의미를 나타내는 시간의 부사절 'by the time + 현재 동사'(By the time ~ turns)가 사용되었고, 미래완료진행 시제와 함께 쓰이는 시간 표현 next month와 'for + 기간 표현'(for over a decade)이 있다. 또한, 문맥상 미래 시점인 다음 달에 Miranda가 서른 살이 될 무렵이면 그녀는 10년이 넘는 기간 동안 계속해서 주요 TV 쇼에서 주역을 맡아오고 있는 중일 것이라는 의미가 되어야 자연스럽다. 따라서 미래완료진행 시제 (a) will have been starring이 정답이다.

> 오답분석
>
> (b) 미래진행 시제는 특정 미래 시점에 한창 진행 중일 일을 나타내므로, 과거 또는 현재에 시작해서 특정 미래 시점까지 계속해서 진행되고 있을 일을 표현할 수 없어 오답이다.

어휘 | land v. 얻다, 차지하다 leading role phr. 주연 sitcom n. (텔레비전에 방영되는) 시트콤 star v. 주역을 맡다; n. 유명인

---

08 | **준동사** 분사를 목적격 보어로 취하는 동사 | 난이도 ●●●

During the 1920s Prohibition era, bars were forced to close because of government laws that prohibited the sale of alcohol. Whenever bar owners were caught _____ alcohol to the public, they were heavily fined.

(a) having sold
(b) to sell
(c) **selling**
(d) to have sold

1920년대 금주법 시행 시대 동안, 주류 판매를 금지하는 정부 법안으로 인해 술집이 문을 닫아야 했다. 술집 주인들이 대중에게 술을 팔고 있는 것이 적발될 때마다, 과하게 벌금이 부과되었다.

지텔프 치트키

catch는 분사를 목적격 보어로 취한다.

해설 | 빈칸 앞 동사 catch는 'catch + 목적어 + 목적격 보어'의 형태로 쓰일 때 분사를 목적격 보어로 취하여, '-이 ~하는 것을 적발하다'라는 의미로 사용된다. 참고로, 'bar owners were caught selling'은 'caught(동사) + bar owners(목적어) + selling(목적격 보어)'에서 변형된 수동태 구문으로, 수동태가 되어도 목적격 보어인 분사는 그대로 유지된다. 따라서 현재분사 (c) selling이 정답이다.

어휘 | Prohibition n. 금주법 시행 시대 era n. 시대 heavily adv. 과하게, 상당히 fine v. 벌금을 부과하다

09 가정법   가정법 과거

My cousin tends to make impulsive decisions that she often regrets afterward. When she asks me for advice, I say that if I were her, I _____ a pros and cons list before making major decisions.

(a) will write
(b) will have written
(c) would have written
(d) would write

나의 사촌은 종종 나중에 후회하는 충동적인 결정을 하는 경향이 있다. 그녀가 내게 조언을 구할 때, 만약 내가 그녀라면, 나는 중요한 결정을 하기 전에 장단점 목록을 작성할 것이라고 말한다.

🔗 지텔프 치트키

'if + 과거 동사'가 있으면 'would/could + 동사원형'이 정답이다.

> 💡 **가정법 과거**
> If + 주어 + 과거 동사, 주어 + would/could(조동사 과거형) + 동사원형

해설 | if절에 과거 동사(were)가 있으므로, 주절에는 이와 짝을 이루어 가정법 과거를 만드는 'would(조동사 과거형) + 동사원형'이 와야 한다. 따라서 (d) would write가 정답이다.

어휘 | impulsive adj. 충동적인, 즉흥적인   regret v. 후회하다   pros and cons phr. 장단점

10 연결어   접속부사

Many people believe that goldfish have a short memory span. _____, this assumption has been proven false, as studies show that goldfish can remember their owners' faces and even distinguish them from other people.

(a) Thus
(b) In other words
(c) In addition
(d) However

많은 사람은 금붕어가 기억력이 짧다고 생각한다. 그러나, 연구들에서 금붕어가 주인의 얼굴을 기억할 수 있고 심지어 다른 사람들과 구별할 수 있다는 것을 보여주기 때문에, 이 추측은 틀린 것이 증명되었다.

🔗 지텔프 치트키

'그러나'라는 의미의 대조를 나타낼 때는 However를 쓴다.

> 💡 **대조를 나타내는 빈출 접속부사**
> However 그러나   On the other hand 반면에   Otherwise 그렇지 않으면   In contrast 그에 반해

해설 | 빈칸 앞 문장은 많은 사람은 금붕어가 기억력이 짧다고 생각한다는 내용이고, 빈칸 뒤 문장은 이 추측은 틀린 것이 증명되었다는 대조적인 내용이다. 따라서 '그러나'라는 의미의 대조를 나타내는 접속부사 (d) However가 정답이다.

> **오답분석**
> (a) Thus는 '그러므로', (b) In other words는 '다시 말해서', (c) In addition은 '게다가'라는 의미로, 문맥에 적합하지 않아 오답이다.

어휘 | goldfish n. 금붕어   memory span phr. 기억력   assumption n. 추측, 가정   false adj. 틀린, 거짓의   distinguish v. 구별하다

TEST 1
TEST 2
TEST 3
TEST 4
TEST 5
TEST 6
TEST 7
지텔프 공식 기출문제집 7회분 Level 2

11 준동사 — to 부정사를 목적격 보어로 취하는 동사

난이도 ●●○

The sky was beautiful this morning, so Kyle decided to take the day off from work. He asked his friends _____ boating on the lake for a few hours so they could all relax together.

(a) going
(b) to go
(c) to have gone
(d) having gone

오늘 아침에 하늘이 아름다워서, Kyle은 일을 하루 쉬기로 결정했다. 그는 친구들에게 그들이 모두 함께 쉴 수 있도록 몇 시간 동안 호수에 보트를 타러 갈 것을 요정했다.

◆─○ 지텔프 치트키

ask는 to 부정사를 목적격 보어로 취한다.

💡 to 부정사를 목적격 보어로 취하는 빈출 동사
   ask 요청하다   want 원하다   encourage 권장하다   require 요구하다   urge 강력히 촉구하다   allow 허락하다

해설 | 빈칸 앞 동사 ask는 'ask + 목적어 + 목적격 보어'의 형태로 쓰일 때 to 부정사를 목적격 보어로 취하여, '-에게 ~할 것을 요청하다'라는 의미로 사용된다. 따라서 to 부정사 (b) to go가 정답이다.

오답분석

(c) to have gone도 to 부정사이기는 하지만, 완료부정사(to have gone)로 쓰일 경우 '요청하는' 시점보다 '(보트를 타러) 가는' 시점이 앞선다는 것을 나타내므로 문맥에 적합하지 않아 오답이다.

어휘 | boat v. (뱃놀이로) 보트를 타다; n. 보트

12 가정법 — 가정법 과거완료

난이도 ●●○

Matt and his girlfriend Katie were going to visit his hometown last Saturday, but their flight was canceled due to engine problems. If their plane hadn't broken down, Matt _____ Katie to his parents that night.

(a) would have introduced
(b) would introduce
(c) will introduce
(d) will have introduced

Matt과 그의 여자친구 Katie는 지난 토요일에 그의 고향을 방문하려 했지만, 엔진 문제로 인해 그들의 비행기가 결항하였다. 만약 비행기가 고장 나지 않았었다면, Matt은 그날 밤에 그의 부모님에게 Katie를 소개했을 것이다.

◆─○ 지텔프 치트키

'if + had p.p.'가 있으면 'would/could + have p.p.'가 정답이다.

💡 가정법 과거완료
   If + 주어 + had p.p., 주어 + would/could(조동사 과거형) + have p.p.

해설 | If절에 'had p.p.' 형태의 hadn't broken down이 있으므로, 주절에는 이와 짝을 이루어 가정법 과거완료를 만드는 'would(조동사 과거형) + have p.p.'가 와야 한다. 따라서 (a) would have introduced가 정답이다.

어휘 | hometown n. 고향

Black Swan is a 2010 psychological horror movie about rival ballerinas competing for the lead role in *Swan Lake*. _____, the competition is so intense that it slowly drives the main character insane.

(a) After all
(b) Nonetheless
(c) In fact
(d) Therefore

블랙 스완은 백조의 호수에서 주인공 역할을 두고 경쟁하는 라이벌 발레리나들에 관한 2010년 심리 공포 영화이다. 실제로, 이 경쟁은 너무 치열해서 주인공을 서서히 미치게 한다.

─○ 지텔프 치트키

'실제로'라는 의미의 강조를 나타낼 때는 In fact를 쓴다.

> ☆ **강조를 나타내는 빈출 접속부사**
> In fact 실제로 In truth 사실은 In other words 즉, 다시 말해서 Surprisingly 놀랍게도 Undoubtedly 의심할 여지 없이

해설 | 문맥상 블랙 스완은 백조의 호수에서 주인공 역할을 두고 경쟁하는 라이벌 발레리나들에 관한 영화라는 앞 문장의 내용을 강조하여 '실제로, 이 경쟁은 너무 치열해서 주인공을 서서히 미치게 한다'라는 의미가 되어야 자연스럽다. 따라서 '실제로'라는 의미의 강조를 나타내는 접속부사 (c) In fact가 정답이다.

> **오답분석**
> (a) After all은 '(예상과는 달리) 결국', (b) Nonetheless는 '그런데도', (d) Therefore는 '그러므로'라는 의미로 문맥에 적합하지 않아 오답이다.

어휘 | psychological adj. 심리의, 정신적인 lead role phr. 주인공 역할 intense adj. 치열한, 극심한 insane adj. 미친, 정신 이상의

To stay productive while working from home, one should minimize distractions. It is best that one _____ a workspace separate from one's other living areas so that keeping out distractions is easier.

(a) create
(b) will create
(c) has created
(d) created

재택근무를 하는 동안 생산적으로 유지하기 위해서는, 집중을 방해하는 것을 최소화해야 한다. 집중을 방해하는 것을 막는 것이 쉽도록 다른 생활 공간과 분리된 작업 공간을 만드는 것이 제일 좋다.

─○ 지텔프 치트키

best 다음에는 that절에 동사원형이 온다.

> ☆ **주장·요구·명령·제안을 나타내는 빈출 형용사**
> best 제일 좋은 essential 필수적인 important 중요한 necessary 필요한 mandatory 의무적인

해설 | 주절에 주장을 나타내는 형용사 best가 있으므로 that절에는 '(should +) 동사원형'이 와야 한다. 따라서 동사원형 (a) create가 정답이다.

어휘 | productive adj. 생산적인 minimize v. 최소화하다 distraction n. 집중을 방해하는 것 separate from phr. ~에서 분리된 keep out phr. ~을 막다

The Browns go on a family vacation together every summer. This year, the kids _____ summer camp around the same time that their family trip is usually scheduled, so their parents will probably just stay home.

(a) have been attending
(b) will have attended
(c) attended
(d) will be attending

Brown 가족은 매년 여름에 함께 가족 휴가를 간다. 올해, 아이들은 보통 가족 여행이 예정되는 것과 같은 시기에 여름 캠프에 <u>참가하고 있는 중일 것</u>이어서, 아마도 부모는 그냥 집에 머무를 것이다.

○ 지텔프 치트키

'for + 기간 표현' 없이 특정 미래 시점을 나타내는 표현만 있으면 미래진행 시제가 정답이다.

미래진행과 자주 함께 쓰이는 시간 표현
- when / if + 현재 동사 ~할 때 / 만약 ~한다면
- next + 시간 표현 다음 ~에
- until / by + 미래 시점 ~까지
- starting + 미래 시점 / tomorrow ~부터 / 내일

해설 | 미래진행 시제와 함께 자주 쓰이는 특정 미래 시점을 나타내는 시간 표현 This year가 있고, 문맥상 올해 아이들은 보통 가족 여행이 예정되는 것과 같은 시기에 여름 캠프에 참가하고 있는 중일 것이어서 부모는 그냥 집에 머무를 것이라는 의미가 되어야 자연스럽다. 따라서 미래진행 시제 (d) will be attending이 정답이다.

In 1775, the French helped the Americans win the Revolutionary War by supplying them with money and military forces. Had France refused to give its support, the US _____ its independence from Britain.

(a) will not win
(b) might not win
(c) might not have won
(d) will not have won

1775년에, 프랑스는 자금과 군대를 제공함으로써 미국이 독립전쟁에서 승리하도록 도왔다. 프랑스가 지원해 주는 것을 거부했다면, 미국은 영국으로부터 독립을 <u>얻지 못했을지도 모른다</u>.

○ 지텔프 치트키

Had p.p.가 있으면 'would/could/might + have p.p.'가 정답이다.

가정법 과거완료(도치)
Had + 주어 + p.p., 주어 + would/could/might(조동사 과거형) + have p.p.

해설 | if가 생략되어 도치된 절에 'had p.p.' 형태의 Had ~ refused가 있으므로, 주절에는 이와 짝을 이루어 가정법 과거완료를 만드는 'might(조동사 과거형) + have p.p.'가 와야 한다. 따라서 (c) might not have won이 정답이다. 참고로 'Had France refused to give ~'는 'If France had refused to give ~'로 바꿔 쓸 수 있다.

어휘 | Revolutionary War phr. 독립전쟁 supply v. 제공하다, 대주다 military force phr. 군대, 군사 independence n. 독립, 자립

When Elijah was accepted to an out-of-state university, he moved into a campus dorm. He was initially excited to be on his own but, after a few months, he realized that he missed _____ at home.

(a) to have lived
(b) living
(c) having lived
(d) to live

Elijah가 다른 주의 대학에 합격했을 때, 그는 캠퍼스 기숙사로 이사했다. 그는 처음에는 혼자 지내는 것이 신났지만, 몇 달 후에, 집에서 <u>사는 것</u>을 그리워한다는 것을 깨달았다.

──○ **지텔프 치트키**

miss는 동명사를 목적어로 취한다.

> ☆ **동명사를 목적어로 취하는 빈출 동사**
> miss 그리워하다 dread 두려워하다 avoid 피하다 imagine 상상하다 mind 개의하다 keep 계속하다 consider 고려하다
> prevent 방지하다 enjoy 즐기다 recommend 권장하다 risk 위험을 무릅쓰다 involve 포함하다

해설 | 빈칸 앞 동사 miss는 동명사를 목적어로 취하므로, 동명사 (b) living이 정답이다.

> 오답분석
> (c) having lived도 동명사이기는 하지만, 완료동명사(having lived)로 쓰일 경우 '그리워하는' 시점보다 '(집에서) 사는' 시점이 앞선다는 것을 나타내므로 문맥에 적합하지 않아 오답이다.

어휘 | out-of-state adj. 다른 주의 dorm n. 기숙사

Based on the 1982 movie of the same name, *E.T. the Extra-Terrestrial* is one of the worst-selling video games in history. In fact, the game, _____, did so poorly that it bankrupted its creators.

(a) that was released by Atari
(b) which was released by Atari
(c) who was released by Atari
(d) what was released by Atari

1982년의 동명의 영화를 원작으로 한, *E.T. the Extra-Terrestrial*은 역사상 가장 잘 팔리지 않은 비디오 게임 중 하나이다. 실제로, 그 게임은, <u>Atari에 의해 출시되었는데</u>, 성적이 너무 저조해서 제작자들을 파산시켰다.

──○ **지텔프 치트키**

사물 선행사가 관계절 안에서 주어 역할을 하고, 빈칸 앞에 콤마(,)가 있으면 주격 관계대명사 which가 정답이다.

해설 | 사물 선행사 the game을 받으면서 콤마(,) 뒤에 올 수 있는 주격 관계대명사가 필요하므로, (b) which was released by Atari가 정답이다.

> 오답분석
> (a) 관계대명사 that도 사물 선행사를 받을 수 있지만, 콤마 뒤에 올 수 없으므로 오답이다.

어휘 | bankrupt v. 파산시키다 creator n. 제작자, 창작자

In the 1800s, poor farmers were occasionally allowed to live on a nobleman's lands. In exchange, these sharecroppers were required to farm the land, and the nobleman _____ take some of their crops as payment.

(a) **would**
(b) can
(c) should
(d) might

─○ 지텔프 치트키

'~하곤 했다'라고 말할 때는 would를 쓴다.

1800년대에, 가난한 농부들은 때때로 귀족의 땅에서 사는 것이 허용되었다. 그 대신, 이 소작인들은 땅을 경작해야 했고, 귀족은 그들의 농작물의 일부를 보상으로 <u>가져가곤 했다</u>.

해설 | 문맥상 귀족은 자기 땅에 가난한 농부들을 살게 해주는 대신 소작인들이 수확한 농작물의 일부를 보상으로 가져가곤 했다는 의미가 되어야 자연스러우므로, '~하곤 했다'를 뜻하면서 과거의 불규칙한 습관을 나타내는 조동사 will의 과거형 (a) would가 정답이다.

어휘 | nobleman n. 귀족 in exchange phr. 그 대신, 답례로 sharecropper n. 소작인 farm v. (토지를) 경작하다; n. 농장 crop n. 농작물, 수확물 payment n. 보상

Mary went to the hospital because she fractured her left foot. When asked how it happened, she told the doctor that she _____ the floor when she suddenly became dizzy and slipped on the slick tiles.

(a) will have mopped
(b) mopped
(c) has been mopping
(d) **had been mopping**

─○ 지텔프 치트키

'when + 과거 동사'가 오면 과거완료진행 시제가 정답이다.

Mary는 왼쪽 발이 골절되어 병원에 갔다. 어떻게 된 일인지 질문을 받았을 때, 그녀는 갑자기 어지러워져서 미끄러운 타일 위에서 미끄러졌을 때 바닥을 <u>닦아오고 있던 중이었다</u>고 의사에게 말했다.

💡 **과거완료진행과 자주 함께 쓰이는 시간 표현**
 • before / when / since + 과거 동사 + (for + 기간 표현) ~하기 전에 / ~했을 때 / ~ 이래로 (~ 동안)
 • (for + 기간 표현) + (up) until + 과거 동사 (~ 동안) ~했을 때까지

해설 | 과거완료진행 시제와 함께 쓰이는 시간 표현 'when + 과거 동사'(When ~ became, slipped)가 있고, 문맥상 대과거(Mary가 바닥을 닦기 시작한 시점)부터 과거(갑자기 어지러워져서 타일 위에서 미끄러진 시점)까지 계속해서 바닥을 닦아오고 있던 중이었다는 의미가 되어야 자연스럽다. 따라서 과거완료진행 시제 (d) had been mopping이 정답이다.

어휘 | fracture v. ~을 골절시키다; n. 골절 dizzy adj. 어지러운, 현기증이 나는 slip v. 미끄러지다 slick adj. 미끄러운 mop v. (대걸레로) 닦다; n. 대걸레

Sitting in front of a computer all day can increase the risk of cardiovascular problems and other health concerns. If one wishes _____ this, one should stand up and walk around every thirty minutes.

(a) **to avoid**
(b) to have avoided
(c) having avoided
(d) avoiding

하루 종일 컴퓨터 앞에 앉아 있는 것은 심혈관 문제와 다른 건강 문제의 위험을 증가시킬 수 있다. 만약 누군가가 이것을 <u>예방하는 것을</u> 희망한다면, 30분마다 일어나서 걸어 다녀야 한다.

━━○ 지텔프 치트키

wish는 to 부정사를 목적어로 취한다.

> 🔆 **to 부정사를 목적어로 취하는 빈출 동사**
> wish 희망하다 promise 약속하다 expect 예상하다 vow 맹세하다 plan 계획하다 decide 결정하다 hope 바라다 agree 동의하다
> intend 계획하다 prepare 준비하다

해설 | 빈칸 앞 동사 wish는 to 부정사를 목적어로 취하므로, to 부정사 (a) to avoid가 정답이다.

> 오답분석
> (b) to have avoided도 to 부정사이기는 하지만, 완료부정사(to have avoided)로 쓰일 경우 '희망하는' 시점보다 '예방하는' 시점이 앞선다는 것을 나타내므로 문맥에 적합하지 않아 오답이다.

어휘 | cardiovascular adj. 심혈관의 avoid v. 예방하다, 막다

Christina found a lost puppy under her back porch three months ago. After making sure it didn't belong to anyone else, she decided to keep the dog and _____ of it ever since.

(a) takes care
(b) will have taken care
(c) **has been taking care**
(d) had been taking care

Christina는 3개월 전에 뒤쪽 현관 아래에서 길 잃은 강아지를 발견했다. 강아지가 다른 사람의 소유가 아닌지 확인한 후, 그녀는 그 강아지를 키우기로 결정했고 그 이래로 줄곧 <u>강아지를 돌봐오고 있는 중이다.</u>

━━○ 지텔프 치트키

'과거 동사 + ever since'가 있으면 현재완료진행 시제가 정답이다.

> 🔆 **현재완료진행과 자주 함께 쓰이는 시간 표현**
> • (ever) since + 과거 시점 + (for + 기간 표현) ~한 이래로 (줄곧) (~ 동안)
> • lately / for + 기간 표현 + now 최근에 / 현재 ~ 동안

해설 | 현재완료진행 시제와 함께 쓰이는 시간 표현 '과거 동사 + ever since'(decided to keep ~ ever since)가 있고, 문맥상 과거 시점인 강아지를 키우기로 결정한 시점부터 현재까지 계속해서 Christina가 강아지를 돌봐오고 있는 중이라는 의미가 되어야 자연스럽다. 따라서 현재완료진행 시제 (c) has been taking care가 정답이다.

어휘 | porch n. 현관, 문간 make sure phr. 확인하다 belong to phr. ~ 소유이다, ~에 속하다 take care of phr. ~을 돌보다

23 시제   과거진행   난이도 ●●○

Laminated glass is a type of glass that does not shatter. The inventor accidentally discovered this while he _____ a glass flask covered with chemicals. After dropping the flask by mistake, he found it surprisingly intact.

(a) would use
(b) has been using
(c) was using
(d) had used

합판 유리는 산산이 부서지지 않는 유리의 한 종류이다. 발명가는 화학물질로 덮인 유리 플라스크를 <u>사용하고 있던</u> 도중에 우연히 이것을 발견했다. 실수로 플라스크를 떨어뜨린 후, 그는 놀랍게도 그것이 손상되지 않은 것을 발견했다.

○ 지텔프 치트키

'과거 동사 + while절'이 있으면 과거진행 시제가 정답이다.

☼ **과거진행과 자주 함께 쓰이는 시간 표현**
  • when / while + 과거 동사 ~했을 때 / ~하던 도중에
  • last + 시간 표현 / yesterday 지난 ~에 / 어제

해설 | 과거진행 시제와 함께 쓰이는 시간 표현 '과거 동사 + while절'(discovered ~ while ~)이 있고, 문맥상 우연히 합판 유리를 발견한 과거 시점에 발명가는 화학물질로 덮인 유리 플라스크를 사용하고 있던 도중이었다는 의미가 되어야 자연스럽다. 따라서 과거진행 시제 (c) was using이 정답이다.

어휘 | laminated glass phr. 합판 유리 shatter v. 산산이 부서지다, 산산조각이 나다 flask n. (화학실험용) 플라스크 chemical n. 화학물질, 화합물 by mistake phr. 실수로, 잘못하여 intact adj. 손상되지 않은, 온전한

24 가정법   가정법 과거완료   난이도 ●●○

Mike put off writing his final research paper and lost points for turning it in two days past the deadline. If he had started his paper earlier, he _____ a better grade on the assignment.

(a) would have earned
(b) will earn
(c) will have earned
(d) would earn

Mike는 마지막 연구 논문 작성을 미루다가 마감일이 이틀이나 지나서야 제출하여 점수를 잃었다. 만약 그가 논문을 더 일찍 시작했었다면, 과제에 더 좋은 점수를 <u>얻었을 것이다</u>.

○ 지텔프 치트키

'if + had p.p.'가 있으면 'would/could + have p.p.'가 정답이다.

해설 | If절에 'had p.p.' 형태의 had started가 있으므로, 주절에는 이와 짝을 이루어 가정법 과거완료를 만드는 'would(조동사 과거형) + have p.p.'가 와야 한다. 따라서 (a) would have earned가 정답이다.

어휘 | put off phr. ~을 미루다, 연기하다 research paper phr. 연구 논문 assignment n. 과제, 숙제

25 가정법 　가정법 과거

My favorite restaurant changed management recently, and the new owners have announced that they will change the menu completely. If I were them, I _____ at least a few of the dishes from the old menu.

(a) would have kept
(b) will have kept
(c) will keep
(d) would keep

내가 좋아하는 식당이 최근에 경영자를 바꿨는데, 새로운 주인들이 메뉴를 완전히 바꾸겠다고 발표했다. 만약 내가 그들이라면, 예전 메뉴에서 적어도 몇 가지 메뉴는 유지할 것이다.

─○ 지텔프 치트키

'if + 과거 동사'가 있으면 'would/could + 동사원형'이 정답이다.

해설 | If절에 과거 동사(were)가 있으므로, 주절에는 이와 짝을 이루어 가정법 과거를 만드는 'would(조동사 과거형) + 동사원형'이 와야 한다. 따라서 (d) would keep이 정답이다.

어휘 | management n. 경영자, 관리자　completely adv. 완전히　at least phr. 적어도, 최소한

26 준동사 　동명사를 목적어로 취하는 동사

Leo has locked himself in his dorm room so he can focus on studying for finals. He refuses to check social media or even meet his friends at the cafeteria until he finishes _____ his notes.

(a) having reviewed
(b) reviewing
(c) to have reviewed
(d) to review

Leo는 기말시험 공부에 집중할 수 있도록 기숙사 방에 틀어박혀 있다. 그는 노트를 복습하는 것을 끝낼 때까지 소셜 미디어를 확인하거나 구내식당에서 친구들을 만나는 것조차 거부한다.

─○ 지텔프 치트키

finish는 동명사를 목적어로 취한다.

해설 | 빈칸 앞 동사 finish는 동명사를 목적어로 취하므로, 동명사 (b) reviewing이 정답이다.

> **오답분석**
> (a) having reviewed도 동명사이기는 하지만, 완료동명사(having reviewed)로 쓰일 경우 '끝내는' 시점보다 '복습하는' 시점이 앞선다는 것을 나타내므로 문맥에 적합하지 않다.

어휘 | lock oneself in phr. 틀어박히다　final n. 기말시험; adj. 마지막의

LISTENING

PART 1⁽²⁷~³³⁾ 일상 대화 아스텍 전시회에 관한 두 친구의 내화

안부 인사

M: ²⁷I'm so glad that we went to the museum today, Anna! The Aztec exhibit was really interesting.

주제 제시: 아스텍 전시회

F: Totally agree, Kevin. ²⁷I enjoyed learning about various Aztec tribes. What was your favorite part of the exhibit?

건축 양식에 관한 다큐멘터리

M: ²⁸My favorite part was the documentary on Aztec architecture. It featured such beautiful temples and palaces. Best of all, it showed us how the Aztecs built such incredible stone structures.

F: I enjoyed the documentary too. The Aztecs were masterful builders!

M: Yeah, and some of their structures are still standing today. So, what about you, Anna? What was your favorite part of the exhibit?

실물 크기의 밀랍 인형

F: Hmm. My favorite part was probably the life-size wax figures. ²⁹The Eagle and Jaguar Warriors were so cool. Their costumes were amazing! I mean, they resembled eagles and jaguars as much as they did human warriors.

M: They were cool, but scary. I mean, their swords were no joke. And they looked so real . . . at times, I almost thought the wax figures were going to come to life and start walking toward me.

F: ³⁰I did see you kind of shivering while looking at the figures. But I thought it was because it was cold in the museum, not because you were scared.

해골 전시

M: Well, I wouldn't say that I was actually *scared*. Just a little, I don't know . . . uneasy. Also, the skeleton display was rather unsettling.

F: Those weren't real skeletons though, Kevin. They were just replicas.

M: Oh. I thought they were real.

신들에 관한 전시회

F: Nope. Anyway, what'd you think about the exhibit on Aztec gods, like the Feathered Serpent?

M: ³¹The Feathered Serpent? Oh, right. Well . . . a lot of the artwork depicting the deity was really impressive. The painters were clearly very talented and put so much hard work and detail into their paintings of the massive dragon. But it didn't seem to be the most forgiving god! In many depictions, it was eating the

---

남: ²⁷오늘 우리가 박물관에 가서 정말 기뻐, Anna! 아스텍 전시회는 정말 흥미로웠어.

여: 전적으로 동의해, Kevin. ²⁷나는 다양한 아스텍 부족들에 관해 배우는 게 즐거웠어. 전시회에서 가장 마음에 들었던 부분은 뭐였어?

남: ²⁸내가 가장 좋아하는 부분은 아스텍 건축 양식에 관한 다큐멘터리였어. 정말 아름다운 사원들과 궁전들이 등장했어. 무엇보다도, 아스텍 사람들이 어떻게 그렇게 놀라운 석조 건축물들을 지었는지 보여줬어.

여: 나도 그 다큐멘터리를 재미있게 봤어. 아스텍 사람들은 훌륭한 건축가였어!

남: 응, 그리고 몇몇 구조물들은 오늘날에도 여전히 세워져 있어. 그래서, 너는 어때, Anna? 전시회에서 네가 가장 마음에 들었던 부분은 뭐였어?

여: 흠. 내가 가장 좋아하는 부분은 아마도 실물 크기의 밀랍 인형이었어. ²⁹독수리와 재규어 전사가 정말 멋졌어. 그들의 의상은 대단했어! 내 말은, 그들은 인간 전사들이 그랬던 만큼이나 독수리와 재규어를 닮았어.

남: 그들은 멋있었지만, 무섭기도 했어. 내 말은, 그들의 칼은 장난이 아니었어. 그리고 그것들은 정말 진짜 같아 보여서... 가끔은, 밀랍 인형들이 의식을 되찾아서 내 쪽으로 걸어오기 시작하는 것 같았어.

여: ³⁰네가 인형을 보면서 몸을 약간 떨고 있는 걸 봤어. 하지만 박물관이 추워서 그런 거지, 무서워서 그런 건 아니라고 생각했어.

남: 음, 실제로 *무서웠다*고 말하진 않을래. 그냥 조금, 나도 잘 모르겠는데... 꺼림칙했어. 그리고, 해골 전시가 다소 불안했어.

여: 하지만 그것들은 진짜 해골이 아니었어, Kevin. 그냥 복제품이었어.

남: 오. 난 진짜라고 생각했어.

여: 아니야. 어쨌든, 날개 달린 뱀 같은 아스텍 신들에 관한 전시회는 어땠어?

남: ³¹날개 달린 뱀? 오, 맞아. 음... 그 신을 묘사하는 많은 작품은 정말 인상적이었어. 그 화가들은 분명히 매우 재능이 있었고 그 거대한 용에 관한 그들의 그림에 너무나 큰 노력과 세부 양식을 담았어. 그러나 그것은 가장 관대한 신처럼 보이지는 않았어! 많은 묘사에서, 그것은 마을 사람들을 잡아먹고 있었어.

villagers.

F: Well, to me, the Feathered Serpent seems like such a wise and powerful god. Anyway, Kevin, you have to remember that the Aztecs were an ancient culture. They were pretty violent, sure. But the world was a more violent place back then.

장례 의식

M: Speaking of which, we still haven't talked about their death rituals . . .

F: Maybe we can skip that topic, Kevin. The death rituals were a bit disturbing, even for me!

다음에 있을 전시회

M: Well, [32]I grabbed a museum pamphlet before we left. It talks about upcoming exhibits. [33]There's one devoted to early Japanese pottery next month.

F: How "early" is this pottery we're talking about?

M: It says the Neolithic period. So, a really long time ago! Thousands of years.

F: The Neolithic period, huh? Well, [33]that sounds pretty interesting.

남녀가 다음에 할 일

M: Let me know if you want to go. I had a great time today, Anna, so [33]I'd love to visit the museum with you again next month.

F: Really? I thought the violent warriors and the angry gods and the shocking death rituals . . . well, Kevin, I thought it all might have been a bit too much for you.

M: Maybe so, Anna. But I think I can handle pottery.

여: 음, 내게는, 날개 달린 뱀이 정말 지혜롭고 강력한 신처럼 보여. 어쨌든, Kevin, 아스텍은 고대 문명이 었다는 것을 기억해야 해. 물론, 그들은 꽤 폭력적이었지. 하지만 그 당시에는 세상이 더 폭력적인 곳이었어.

남: 말이 나온 김에, 우리는 그들의 장례 의식에 관해 아직 얘기하지 않았어...

여: 어쩌면 그 주제는 생략해도 돼, Kevin. 장례 의식은 나에게도 약간 충격적이었어!

남: 음, [32]떠나기 전에 박물관 소책자를 들고 왔어. 다가 오는 전시회에 관해 설명되어 있어. [33]다음 달에 초기 일본 도자기를 다룬 전시회가 있어.

여: 우리가 이야기하고 있는 이 도자기는 얼마나 "초 기"인 걸까?

남: 신석기 시대라고 적혀있어. 그러니까, 아주 오래전 이네! 수천 년 전이야.

여: 신석기 시대구나, 그렇지? 음, [33]꽤 흥미롭게 들리 네.

남: 만약 가고 싶으면 알려줘. 오늘 정말 즐거워서, Anna, [33]다음 달에도 너랑 같이 다시 박물관에 가 고 싶어.

여: 정말? 난 폭력적인 전사들과 화난 신들, 충격적인 장례 의식들이... 음, Kevin, 그 모든 게 너한테는 너 무 과한 것 같았어.

남: 아마 그럴지도 몰라, Anna. 하지만 난 도자기는 감 당할 수 있을 것 같아.

어휘 | architecture[ɑ́rkitèktʃər] 건축 양식, 설계 temple[templ] 사원, 절 palace[pǽlis] 궁전, 왕실 incredible[inkrédəbl] 놀라운, 엄청난 masterful[mǽstərfəl] 훌륭한, 대가의 builder[bíldər] 건축가 life-size 실물 크기의 wax figure 밀랍 인형 warrior[wɔ́:riər] 전사, 병사 costume[kάstju:m] 의상, 복장 resemble[rizémbl] 닮다 come to life 의식을 되찾다, 정신이 들다 shiver[ʃívər] 떨다, 전율하다 skeleton[skélətn] 해골, 뼈 unsettling[ənsétəliŋ] 불안하게 하는 듯한, 동요시키는 replica[réplikə] 복제품, 모조품 serpent[sə́:rpənt] 뱀, 악마 depict[dipíkt] 묘사하다, 그리다 deity[díːəti] 신 talented[tǽləntid] 재능 있는, 뛰어난 forgiving[fərgíviŋ] 관대한, 너그러운 depiction[dipíkʃən] 묘사, 서술 villager[vílidʒər] 마을 사람, 주민 violent[vάiələnt] 폭력적인, 격렬한 death ritual 장례 의식 skip[skip] 생략하다, 거르다 disturbing[distə́:rbiŋ] 충격적인, 혼란을 주는 grab[græb] 거머쥐다 devoted[divóutid] ~을 다룬 pottery[pάtəri] 도자기 Neolithic period 신석기 시대 handle[hǽndl] 감당하다, 다루다

---

27 특정세부사항 What   난이도 ●●○

What were Anna and Kevin doing today?

(a) touring a modern art museum
(b) visiting a historic landmark
(c) exploring a culture of the past
(d) watching a tribal ceremony

Anna와 Kevin은 오늘 무엇을 하고 있었는가?

(a) 현대 미술관을 견학하는 것
(b) 역사적인 명소를 방문하는 것
(c) 과거의 문화를 탐구하는 것
(d) 부족의 의식을 관람하는 것

정답 잡는 치트키

질문의 키워드 today가 그대로 언급된 주변 내용을 주의 깊게 듣는다.

해설 | 남자가 'I'm so glad that we went to the museum today, Anna! The Aztec exhibit was really interesting.'이라며 오늘 박물관에 가서 정말 기쁘고 아스텍 전시회가 정말 흥미로웠다고 하자, 여자가 'I enjoyed learning about various Aztec tribes.'라며 다양한 아스텍 부족들에 관해 배우는 게 즐거웠다고 했다. 따라서 (c)가 정답이다.

어휘 | landmark[lǽndmɑ̀ːrk] 명소, 주요 지형지물 explore[iksplɔ́ːr] 탐구하다, 탐험하다 tribal[tráibl] 부족의, 종족의

---

28 | 특정세부사항 What   난이도 ●●○

What was Kevin's favorite part of the Aztec exhibit?

(a) the documentary on royal families
(b) the narration of major exhibits
(c) the film about building design
(d) the showcase of an artist's works

아스텍 전시회에서 Kevin이 가장 좋아하는 부분은 무엇이었는가?

(a) 왕실에 관한 다큐멘터리
(b) 주요 전시품에 관한 이야기
(c) 건물 디자인에 관한 영화
(d) 예술가의 작품에 관한 전시

━○ 정답 잡는 치트키

질문의 키워드 favorite part가 그대로 언급된 주변 내용을 주의 깊게 듣는다.

해설 | 남자가 'My favorite part was the documentary on Aztec architecture.'라며 가장 좋아하는 부분은 아스텍 건축 양식에 관한 다큐멘터리였다고 했다. 따라서 (c)가 정답이다.

⇄ **Paraphrasing**
the documentary on ~ architecture 건축 양식에 관한 다큐멘터리 → the film about building design 건물 디자인에 관한 영화

어휘 | royal family 왕실, 왕가 narration[næréiʃən] 이야기 showcase[ʃóukeis] 전시

---

29 | 특정세부사항 Why   난이도 ●●○

Why did Anna think that the Eagle and Jaguar Warriors were cool?

(a) because of their outfits
(b) because of their weapons
(c) because of their movement
(d) because of their size

Anna는 왜 독수리와 재규어 전사가 멋지다고 생각했는가?

(a) 의상 때문에
(b) 무기 때문에
(c) 움직임 때문에
(d) 크기 때문에

━○ 정답 잡는 치트키

질문의 키워드 Eagle and Jaguar Warriors were cool이 그대로 언급된 주변 내용을 주의 깊게 듣는다.

해설 | 여자가 'The Eagle and Jaguar Warriors were so cool. Their costumes were amazing!'이라며 독수리와 재규어 전사가 정말 멋졌고 그들의 의상이 대단했다고 했다. 따라서 (a)가 정답이다.

⇄ **Paraphrasing**
costumes 의상 → outfits 의상

어휘 | outfit[áutfit] 의상, 복장 weapon[wépən] 무기 movement[múːvmənt] 움직임, 운동

30 특정세부사항   What

What did Anna think was the reason for Kevin's shivering?

(a) He was nervous about getting lost.
(b) He was frightened of skeletons.
(c) He was afraid of the dark.
(d) He was in a cold place.

Anna는 Kevin이 떨었던 이유가 무엇이라고 생각했는가?

(a) 길을 잃을까 봐 긴장했다.
(b) 해골을 무서워했다.
(c) 어둠을 두려워했다.
(d) 추운 곳에 있었다.

━○ 정답 잡는 치트키

질문의 키워드 shivering이 그대로 언급된 주변 내용을 주의 깊게 듣는다.

해설 | 여자가 'I did see you kind of shivering while looking at the figures. But I thought it was because it was cold in the museum, not because you were scared.'라며 남자가 인형을 보면서 몸을 약간 떨고 있는 모습을 봤지만, 박물관이 추워서 그런 거지, 무서워서 그런 건 아니라고 생각했다고 했다. 따라서 (d)가 정답이다.

오답분석
(b) 남자가 해골 전시가 다소 불안했다고는 언급했지만, Anna가 이것 때문에 Kevin이 떨었다고 생각한 것은 아니므로 오답이다.

어휘 | be frightened of ~을 무서워하다 dark[dɑːrk] 어둠; 어두운

---

31 추론   특정사실

Why, most likely, was Kevin impressed with the paintings of the Feathered Serpent?

(a) because they were skillfully made
(b) because they looked realistic
(c) because they were massive
(d) because they seemed peaceful

Kevin이 날개 달린 뱀의 그림에 감명받은 이유는 무엇이었을 것 같은가?

(a) 능숙하게 제작되었기 때문에
(b) 사실적으로 보였기 때문에
(c) 거대했기 때문에
(d) 평화로워 보였기 때문에

━○ 정답 잡는 치트키

질문의 키워드 Feathered Serpent가 그대로 언급된 주변 내용을 주의 깊게 듣는다.

해설 | 남자가 'The Feathered Serpent? ~ a lot of the artwork depicting the deity was really impressive. The painters were clearly very talented and put so much hard work and detail into their paintings of the massive dragon.'이라며 날개 달린 뱀을 묘사하는 많은 작품이 정말 인상적이었는데, 그 화가들은 분명히 매우 재능이 있었고, 그 거대한 용에 관한 그들의 그림에 너무나 큰 노력과 세부 양식을 담았다고 한 것을 통해, Kevin은 날개 달린 뱀의 그림이 능숙하게 제작되었기 때문에 감명받았음을 추론할 수 있다. 따라서 (a)가 정답이다.

어휘 | skillfully[skílfəli] 능숙하게, 솜씨 있게 realistic[rìːəlístik] 사실적인, 현실적인

---

32 특정세부사항   How

How did Kevin find out about upcoming exhibits?

(a) by asking the staff directly

Kevin은 다가오는 전시회에 관해 어떻게 알았는가?

(a) 직원에게 직접 물어봄으로써

174 본 교재 인강·무료 지텔프 문법 총정리강의 HackersIngang.com

(b) by looking at a brochure
(c) by hearing an announcement
(d) by checking the message board

(b) 소책자를 봄으로써
(c) 안내 방송을 들음으로써
(d) 전자 게시판을 확인함으로써

질문의 키워드 upcoming exhibits가 그대로 언급된 주변 내용을 주의 깊게 듣는다.

해설 | 남자가 'I grabbed a museum pamphlet before we left. It talks about upcoming exhibits'라며 떠나기 전에 박물관 소책자를 들고 왔는데, 다가오는 전시회에 관해 설명되어 있다고 했다. 따라서 (b)가 정답이다.

⇄ **Paraphrasing**
pamphlet 소책자 → a brochure 소책자

어휘 | message board 전자 게시판

TEST 1 TEST 2 TEST 3 TEST 4 TEST 5 TEST 6 TEST 7

33 추론 다음에 할 일

난이도 ●●○

What will Anna and Kevin probably do next month?

(a) attend a museum opening
(b) **view a special exhibit**
(c) visit a new art gallery
(d) take a pottery class

Anna와 Kevin은 다음 달에 무엇을 할 것 같은가?

(a) 박물관 개관식에 참석한다
(b) **특별 전시회를 관람한다**
(c) 새로운 미술관을 방문한다
(d) 도예 수업을 듣는다

정답 잡는 치트키

다음에 할 일을 언급하는 후반을 주의 깊게 듣는다.

해설 | 남자가 'There's one devoted to early Japanese pottery next month.'라며 다음 달에 초기 일본 도자기를 다룬 전시회가 있다고 하자, 여자가 'that sounds pretty interesting'이라며 꽤 흥미롭게 들린다고 했고, 남자가 'I'd love to visit the museum with you again next month'라며 다음 달에도 여자와 같이 다시 박물관에 가고 싶다고 한 것을 통해, Anna와 Kevin은 다음 달에 초기 일본 도자기를 다룬 특별 전시회를 관람할 것임을 추론할 수 있다. 따라서 (b)가 정답이다.

PART 2 [34~39] 발표 엄격한 채식주의자 축제 홍보

음성 바로 듣기

주제
제시:
엄격한
채식
주의자
축제
홍보

Have you ever thought about going vegan? Or does it seem too restrictive to completely remove eggs, meat, and dairy from your diet? Well, vegans and non-vegans alike are welcome at our upcoming Vegan Festival, where you can discover a variety of vegan items and learn more about the vegan lifestyle. ³⁴We can show you the benefits of going vegan and the many delicious food options available with a vegan diet. Here are the activities you can look forward to.

엄격한 채식주의자가 되는 것에 대해 생각해 본 적이 있나요? 아니면 달걀, 육류, 유제품을 식단에서 완전히 배제하기에는 너무 제한적인 것 같나요? 음, 엄격한 채식주의자와 아닌 사람 모두 다양한 엄격한 채식주의자 제품을 발견하고 생활 방식에 대해 자세히 알아볼 수 있는 다가오는 엄격한 채식주의자 축제에 환영받습니다. ³⁴저희는 엄격한 채식주의자가 되는 것의 이점과 엄격한 채식주의자 식단으로 즐길 수 있는 다양한 맛있는 음식을 보여드릴 수 있습니다. 기대하실 수 있는 활동들은 다음과 같습니다.

지털프 공식 기출문제집 7회분 Level 2

TEST 4 LISTENING 175

활동1: 세미나	For all three days of the festival, we will be holding seminars about the benefits of veganism. ³⁵On the first day, the seminar will be about the health benefits of a vegan diet. Learn about how going vegan can improve your cholesterol levels and reduce the risk of heart disease. On the second day, world-renowned ecologist and activist Theodore T. Jones will give a talk about the environmental benefits of veganism. Finally, on the last day of the event, leading vegan personalities will be giving talks on ethical consumption.
활동2: 공예 섹션 부스	³⁶Throughout the festival, you can also browse the booths in the arts and crafts section. Local celebrity fashion designer Michelle Ashland will be unveiling her new line of vegan footwear at the festival. That's right! You'll be the first ones to get a glimpse of her upcoming fall collection. Her shoes are so elegant and durable— you'll never believe they're not made from genuine leather! ³⁶Michelle sold handmade bags at our very first Vegan Festival ten years ago, and we couldn't be prouder to have her back this year.
활동3: 푸드 코트	Feeling hungry? Just head over to the food court, where you can find various local and international offerings. ³⁷If you think vegan food might taste bland or unexciting, these food sellers will prove you wrong. Just try the veggie burger from Mighty Lentil Bistro. Many claim it's the tastiest burger they've ever had! Or maybe you're in the mood for a piece of Meatless Mario's lasagna, one of the most popular items at the festival. Be sure to get there early before the lasagna sells out!
활동4: 식재료 판매 부스	If you're feeling inspired to make your own vegan dishes at home, you can buy ingredients right at the festival. We'll have fruit and vegetable booths, as well as a wide range of sauces and vegan butters from local farms and grocers. Many booths will also be offering free samples. And if you don't see any samples, just ask for one! The vendors at the festival are always happy to share their creations with new customers.
활동5: 요리 대회	³⁸To cap off the event, we'll have a cooking competition on the final day of the festival. Show off your skills in the kitchen and make your favorite animal-free recipe. Each dish in the competition will be judged by three celebrity chefs. The winner of the cooking competition will take home 5,000 dollars and a brand-new stand mixer. ³⁸Simply sign up for the cooking competition on the day itself.

축제의 3일 내내, 채식주의자의 이점에 대한 세미나가 열립니다. ³⁵첫째 날에, 세미나는 엄격한 채식주의자 식단의 건강상 이점에 대한 것입니다. 엄격한 채식주의자가 되는 것이 어떻게 콜레스테롤 수치를 개선하고 심장병의 위험을 줄일 수 있는지 알아보세요. 둘째 날에는, 세계적으로 유명한 생태학자이자 활동가인 Theodore T. Jones가 채식주의자의 환경적 이점에 대해 강연할 것입니다. 마지막으로, 행사 마지막 날에는, 엄격한 채식주의자를 대표하는 유명 인사들이 윤리적 소비에 대해 강연할 것입니다.

³⁶축제 동안, 공예 섹션의 부스도 둘러볼 수 있습니다. 지역 유명 패션 디자이너 Michelle Ashland가 축제에서 새로운 엄격한 채식주의자 신발 라인을 발표할 것입니다. 맞습니다! 여러분이 처음으로 다가오는 가을 컬렉션을 얼핏 보게 될 것입니다. 그녀의 신발은 매우 우아하고 내구력이 있어서, 천연 가죽으로 만들어진 것이 아니라는 것을 절대 믿지 않을 것입니다! ³⁶Michelle은 10년 전 저희의 첫 번째 엄격한 채식주의자 축제에서 수제 가방을 팔았는데, 올해 그녀를 다시 모셔오는 것이 더 이상 자랑스러울 수가 없었습니다.

배가 고프신가요? 다양한 현지 및 세계 각국의 음식을 찾을 수 있는 푸드 코트로 가보세요. ³⁷엄격한 채식주의자 음식이 맛이 없거나 자극적이지 않을 거로 생각하신다면, 이 음식 판매자들은 여러분이 틀렸다는 것을 증명할 것입니다. Mighty Lentil Bistro의 엄격한 채식주의자 버거를 맛보세요. 많은 사람이 지금까지 먹어본 것 중 가장 맛있는 버거라고 말합니다! 아니면 축제에서 가장 인기 있는 메뉴 중 하나인 Meatless Mario의 라자냐 한 조각을 먹고 싶으실 수도 있습니다. 라자냐가 다 팔리기 전에 그곳에 꼭 일찍 가세요!

만약 집에서 엄격한 채식주의자 요리를 직접 만들어 보고 싶으시다면, 축제 현장에서 바로 재료를 구입하실 수 있습니다. 과일과 채소 부스뿐만 아니라, 현지 농장과 식료품점으로부터의 다양한 소스와 엄격한 채식주의자 버터도 있을 것입니다. 많은 부스에서 무료 샘플도 제공할 것입니다. 그리고 만약 샘플이 보이지 않는다면, 그냥 요청하세요! 축제의 행상인들은 항상 새로운 고객들과 자신의 제품을 기꺼이 공유합니다.

³⁸행사를 끝마치기 위해, 축제의 마지막 날에 요리 대회가 있을 것입니다. 주방에서 기술을 뽐내고 가장 좋아하는 동물질이 사용되지 않은 요리법을 만들어 보세요. 대회의 각 요리는 세 명의 유명 요리사들에 의해 심사될 것입니다. 요리 대회의 우승자는 5,000달러와 신제품 스탠드 믹서를 가지고 돌아갈 것입니다. ³⁸요리 대회는 당일에 신청하기만 하면 됩니다.

You can get your tickets to the Vegan Festival right after this talk. ³⁹Tickets cost fifteen dollars and come with two coupons for twenty percent off any dish ordered from the food court. This year we have a special promotion where all tickets purchased in advance come with one additional coupon. **The festival will run from November 13 to 15 at Oaken Park.** See you there!

이 연설 이후에 바로 엄격한 채식주의자 축제 티켓을 사실 수 있습니다. ³⁹티켓은 15달러이며 푸드 코트에서 주문하는 모든 요리에 대해 20% 할인받을 수 있는 쿠폰 두 장이 딸려 있습니다. 올해는 미리 구매한 모든 티켓에 쿠폰 한 장이 추가로 딸린 특별 판촉이 있습니다. 축제는 11월 13일부터 15일까지 오켄 파크에서 열립니다. 거기서 뵙겠습니다!

어휘 | vegan[víːgən] 엄격한 채식주의자 restrictive[ristríktiv] 제한적인, 한정적인 dairy[déri] 유제품; 유제품의 lifestyle[láifstail] 생활 방식 cholesterol level 콜레스테롤 수치 heart disease 심장병 world-renowned 세계적으로 유명한 ecologist[ikálədʒist] 생태학자 activist[ǽktəvist] 활동가, 운동가 personality[pə̀ːrsənǽləti] 유명 인사 ethical consumption 윤리적 소비 browse[brauz] 둘러보다, 훑어보다 arts and crafts 공예 unveil[ʌ̀nvéil] 발표하다, 선보이다 footwear[fútwer] 신발 get a glimpse of ~을 얼핏 보다 elegant[éligənt] 우아한, 훌륭한 durable[dúrəbl] 내구력이 있는 genuine leather 천연 가죽 bland[blænd] 맛이 없는, 담백한 veggie[védʒi] 채식주의자의 lasagna[ləzáːnjə] 라자냐(파스타·치즈·고기·토마토 소스 등으로 만드는 이탈리아 요리) ingredient[ingríːdiənt] 재료, 성분 vendor[véndər] 행상인, 판매자 cap off 끝마치다, 완료하다 show off ~을 뽐내다, 자랑하다 judge[dʒʌdʒ] 심사하다, 판단하다 brand-new 신제품인 come with ~이 딸려 있다

34 주제/목적   담화의 목적   난이도 ●●○

What is the purpose of the talk?

(a) **to share information about healthy eating**
(b) to promote a gardening festival
(c) to provide tips for successful dieting
(d) to support local farming projects

담화의 목적은 무엇인가?

(a) **건강한 음식에 관한 정보를 공유하기 위해서**
(b) 원예 축제를 홍보하기 위해서
(c) 성공적인 다이어트를 위한 조언을 주기 위해서
(d) 지역 농업 프로젝트를 지원하기 위해서

정답 잡는 치트키

담화의 목적을 언급하는 초반을 주의 깊게 듣고 전체 맥락을 파악한다.

해설 | 화자가 'We can show you the benefits of going vegan and the many delicious food options available with a vegan diet.'이라며 엄격한 채식주의자가 되는 것의 이점과 엄격한 채식주의자 식단으로 즐길 수 있는 다양한 맛있는 음식을 보여줄 수 있다고 한 뒤, 담화 전반에 걸쳐 건강한 음식인 엄격한 채식주의사 식난에 관한 성보를 공유하기 위한 죽제를 홍보하는 내용이 이어지고 있다. 따라서 (a)가 정답이다.

어휘 | gardening[gáːrdniŋ] 원예, 정원 가꾸기 support[səpóːrt] 지원하다, 지지하다

35 특정세부사항   What   난이도 ●●○

What will one learn about at the seminar on the first day?

(a) how to adopt an active lifestyle
(b) how to lose weight quickly
(c) **how to better one's physical health**
(d) how to protect the environment

첫날 세미나에서 무엇에 관해 배울 것인가?

(a) 활동적인 생활 방식을 취하는 방법
(b) 빨리 체중을 감량하는 방법
(c) **신체 건강을 개선하는 방법**
(d) 환경을 보호하는 방법

질문의 키워드 seminar와 on the first day가 그대로 언급된 주변 내용을 주의 깊게 듣는다.

해설 | 화자가 'On the first day, the seminar will be about the health benefits of a vegan diet. Learn about how going vegan can improve your cholesterol levels and reduce the risk of heart disease.'라며 첫째 날에 세미나는 엄격한 채식주의자 식단의 건강상 이점에 대한 것이며, 엄격한 채식주의자가 되는 것이 어떻게 콜레스테롤 수치를 개선하고 심장병의 위험을 줄일 수 있는지 알아보라고 했다. 따라서 (c)가 정답이다.

어휘 | adopt[ədápt] (특정한 방식이나 자세를) 취하다, 채택하다 active[ǽktiv] 활동적인, 적극적인 lose weight 체중을 감량하다, 살을 빼다
better[bétər] ~을 개선하다; 보다 좋은 physical health 신체 건강

---

36 특정세부사항 What

난이도 ●●●

What will attendees in the arts and crafts section be able to experience?

(a) an opportunity to watch artists work
(b) an opportunity to order custom footwear
(c) a chance to make a leather bag
(d) a chance to buy handcrafted shoes

공예 섹션의 참가자들은 무엇을 경험할 수 있을 것인가?

(a) 예술가들이 작업하는 것을 볼 기회
(b) 맞춤 신발을 주문할 기회
(c) 가죽 가방을 만들 기회
(d) 수제 신발을 살 기회

질문의 키워드 arts and crafts section이 그대로 언급된 주변 내용을 주의 깊게 듣는다.

해설 | 화자가 'Throughout the festival, you can also browse the booths in the arts and crafts section. Local celebrity fashion designer Michelle Ashland will be unveiling her new line of vegan footwear at the festival.'이라며 축제 동안 공예 섹션의 부스도 둘러볼 수 있는데, 지역 유명 패션 디자이너 Michelle Ashland가 축제에서 새로운 엄격한 채식주의자 신발 라인을 발표할 것이라고 한 뒤, 'Michelle sold handmade bags at our very first Vegan Festival ten years ago, and we couldn't be prouder to have her back this year.'라며 Michelle이 10년 전 첫 번째 엄격한 채식주의자 축제에서 수제 가방을 팔았는데, 올해 그녀를 다시 데려오는 것이 더 이상 자랑스러울 수가 없었다고 한 것을 통해, Michelle Ashland가 10년 전에 수제 가방을 팔았던 것처럼 이번에는 수제 신발을 팔 것이고, 공예 섹션의 참가자들은 이를 구매할 기회를 가질 수 있을 것임을 알 수 있다. 따라서 (d)가 정답이다.

⇄ **Paraphrasing**
footwear 신발 → shoes 신발

오답분석
(b) 화자가 공예 섹션의 부스에서 채식주의자 신발 라인을 볼 수 있다고는 언급했지만, 맞춤 신발을 주문할 수 있다고 한 것은 아니므로 오답이다.

어휘 | custom[kΛstəm] 맞춤의, 주문품의 leather[léðər] 가죽의; 가죽 handcrafted[hǽndkrǽftid] 수제의

---

37 특정세부사항 How

난이도 ●○○

How will the food court prove people wrong about vegan food?

(a) by highlighting its versatility

푸드 코트는 어떻게 엄격한 채식주의자 음식에 관해 사람들이 틀렸다는 것을 증명할 것인가?

(a) 다양성을 강조함으로써

(b) by highlighting its affordability
(c) by showing that it is easy to cook
(d) by showing that it is tasty

(b) 감당할 수 있는 비용을 강조함으로써
(c) 요리하기 쉽다는 것을 보여줌으로써
(d) 맛있다는 것을 보여줌으로써

🔑 **정답 잡는 치트키**

질문의 키워드 prove ~ wrong이 그대로 언급된 주변 내용을 주의 깊게 듣는다.

해설 | 화자가 'If you think vegan food might taste bland or unexciting, these food sellers will prove you wrong. Just try the veggie burger ~. Many claim it's the tastiest burger they've ever had!'라며 엄격한 채식주의자 음식이 맛이 없거나 자극적이지 않을 거로 생각한다면 이 음식 판매자들은 사람들이 틀렸다는 것을 증명할 것이며, 엄격한 채식주의자 버거는 많은 사람이 지금까지 먹어본 것 중 가장 맛있는 버거라고 말한다고 했다. 따라서 (d)가 정답이다.

어휘 | highlight[háilait] ~을 강조하다 versatility[və̀:rsətíləti] 다양성 affordability[əfɔ̀rdəbíləti] 감당할 수 있는 비용

---

38 **특정세부사항**   How   난이도 ●○○

How can attendees enjoy the final day of the festival?

(a) They can sign up for a free giveaway.
(b) They can apply to be an event judge.
(c) They can take part in eating competitions.
(d) They can participate in a cooking contest.

참석자들은 축제의 마지막 날을 어떻게 즐길 수 있는가?

(a) 무료 경품에 응모할 수 있다.
(b) 행사 심사위원이 되기 위해 지원할 수 있다.
(c) 먹기 대회에 참가할 수 있다.
(d) 요리 대회에 참가할 수 있다.

🔑 **정답 잡는 치트키**

질문의 키워드 final day of the festival이 그대로 언급된 주변 내용을 주의 깊게 듣는다.

해설 | 화자가 'To cap off the event, we'll have a cooking competition on the final day of the festival.'이라며 행사를 끝마치기 위해 축제의 마지막 날에 요리 대회가 있을 것이라고 한 뒤, 'Simply sign up for the cooking competition on the day itself.'라며 요리 대회는 당일에 신청하기만 하면 된다고 했다. 따라서 (d)가 정답이다.

🔁 **Paraphrasing**
a cooking competition 요리 대회 → a cooking contest 요리 대회

어휘 | sign up 등록하다, 신청하다 giveaway[gívəwei] 경품, 증정품 take part in ~에 참가하다

---

39 **추론**   특정사실   난이도 ●●○

Why, most likely, would one purchase tickets in advance?

(a) to be entered into a contest
(b) to receive an event T-shirt
(c) to access additional discounts
(d) to get them before they sell out

왜 미리 티켓을 구매할 것 같은가?

(a) 대회에 참가하기 위해서
(b) 행사 티셔츠를 받기 위해서
(c) 추가적인 할인을 이용하기 위해서
(d) 다 팔리기 전에 구입하기 위해서

🔑 **정답 잡는 치트키**

질문의 키워드 tickets in advance가 그대로 언급된 주변 내용을 주의 깊게 듣는다.

해설 | 화자가 'Tickets cost fifteen dollars and come with two coupons for twenty percent off any dish ordered from the food court. This year we have a special promotion where all tickets purchased in advance come with one additional coupon.'이라며 티켓은 15달러이며 푸드 코트에서 주문하는 모든 요리에 대해 20% 할인받을 수 있는 쿠폰 두 장이 딸려 있고, 올해는 미리 구매한 모든 티켓에 쿠폰 한 장이 추가로 딸린 특별 판촉이 있다고 한 것을 통해, 할인 쿠폰 한 장이 추가로 딸린 판촉을 이용하기 위해서 미리 티켓을 구매할 것임을 추론할 수 있다. 따라서 (c)가 정답이다.

어휘 | access[ǽkses] ~을 이용하다; 이용, 접근 sell out 다 팔리다, 매진되다

음성 바로 듣기

PART 3 [40~45] 장단점 논의 자비 출판과 전통적인 출판의 장단점 비교

안부 인사	**F:** Hey, Marcus! [40]I just read your magazine article about the state of the publishing industry in the US. **M:** I'm glad you read my article, Samantha!
주제 제시: 장단점 비교	**F:** It was interesting to me because I'm actually writing a book right now. [40]Since your article was so well researched, I thought I'd ask your advice on whether it's better to self-publish or publish my work traditionally. **M:** I'm more than happy to talk about it, Samantha. Shall we discuss the pros and cons of both options?
자비 출판의 장점	**F:** All right! First, what do you consider the biggest advantages of self-publishing? **M:** Well, [41]with self-publishing, you'll have full creative control of your book. You don't have to satisfy anyone's writing preferences but your own. **F:** Hmm. [41]I appreciate having that sort of creative freedom since I like experimenting with different genres. The book I'm working on now is a crime thriller that takes place in outer space. **M:** Sounds original! Well, another advantage of self-publishing is that you won't have strict deadlines. **F:** Oh, because I'll be the one deciding when my book is released?
자비 출판의 단점	**M:** Exactly. Now, can you recall the disadvantages of self-publishing I mentioned in my article? **F:** Sure. You said [42]one disadvantage is that self-publishing can be expensive. In most cases, you have to pay up front to print the books. **M:** Yes, [42]those fees can get expensive depending on how many copies you need printed. **F:** And another disadvantage you mentioned is that marketing the book will be hard. **M:** Right. You'll have to promote it on your own, which is

여: 안녕, Marcus! [40]방금 미국의 출판 산업 현황에 관한 너의 잡지 기사를 읽었어.
남: 네가 내 기사를 읽다니 기뻐, Samantha!

여: 나도 실제로 지금 책을 쓰고 있어서 흥미로웠어. [40]너의 기사가 매우 잘 조사되어 있어서, 내 작품을 자비 출판하는 게 더 나을지, 아니면 전통적인 방식으로 출판하는 게 더 나을지에 관해 조언을 구해야겠다고 생각했어.
남: 내가 기꺼이 그것에 관해 이야기해 줄게, Samantha. 두 가지 옵션의 장단점을 논의해 볼까?

여: 좋아! 먼저, 자비 출판의 가장 큰 장점은 뭐라고 생각해?
남: 음, [41]자비 출판하면, 너의 책에 대한 완전한 창의적인 통제권을 갖게 될 거야. 다른 사람의 글쓰기 선호도를 만족시켜야 할 필요 없이 자신의 선호도만 만족시키면 돼.
여: 흠. [41]나는 다양한 장르를 시도하는 것을 좋아하기 때문에 그런 창의적인 자유를 가지는 걸 좋아해. 내가 지금 작업하고 있는 책은 우주 공간에서 벌어지는 범죄 스릴러야.
남: 독창적인 것 같네! 음, 자비 출판의 또 다른 장점은 엄격한 마감 기한이 없을 거란 것이야.
여: 오, 내 책이 언제 나올지 내가 결정할 거니까?

남: 맞아. 자, 내가 기사에서 언급했던 자비 출판의 단점을 기억해 낼 수 있겠어?
여: 물론이지. [42]한 가지 단점은 자비 출판이 비용이 많이 들 수도 있다고 했잖아. [42]대부분은, 책을 인쇄하려면 선불로 비용을 내야 해.
남: 응, [42]인쇄해야 하는 부수에 따라 비용이 많이 들 수 있어.
여: 그리고 네가 언급한 또 다른 단점은 책을 광고하는 게 어려울 거라는 거야.
남: 맞아. 혼자서 책을 홍보해야 할 텐데, 인맥 없이는

difficult to do without connections.

F: I see. I don't have many connections with reviewers or booksellers, and I don't spend much time on social media. So promoting my book would be hard. What about the advantages of traditional publishing, then?

M: Well, if you're working with a publisher, you'll get an in-house editor assigned to you.

F: That's definitely an advantage. [43]A professional editor would be able to look over my book and give me tips on improving it.

M: Right—[43]a good editor can mean the difference between a mediocre book and a great one. Another advantage is that a publisher will be able to easily distribute your book.

F: Ah, I remember that from your article. You wrote about how big publishing houses have contracts with bookstores around the world.

M: Exactly. However, there are still disadvantages with traditional publishing.

F: Yeah, I've heard that the publishing world moves slowly. It can take a really long time before your work is accepted for publication.

M: Yup. [44]You'll probably end up getting rejected a few times, or a few hundred times.

F: [44]I know that rejection is something I have to get used to as a writer, but it would still be the most frustrating part for me. You also said in your article that many writers have to sign away their publishing rights. What does that mean?

M: Well, when you sign a contract with a publishing house, they will often ask you for exclusive publishing rights. So if you want to change publishers later, you may no longer have that option.

F: Oh, I see. Once you sign the contract, you're stuck. Thanks, Marcus. This conversation was really helpful.

M: [45]Have you decided how you will publish your book, Samantha?

F: Yep. [45]I don't mind using my own money for publishing expenses as long as I still have creative control of my writing.

하기가 어려워.

여: 그렇구나. 나는 평론가들이나 서점 관계자들과 인맥이 많지 않고, 소셜 미디어에 많은 시간을 할애하지 않아. 그래서 내 책을 홍보하는 게 어려울 것 같아. 그렇다면, 전통적인 출판의 장점은 뭐야?

남: 음, 출판사와 일하면, 사내 편집자가 너에게 배정될 거야.

여: 그건 확실히 장점이야. [43]전문 편집자가 내 책을 검토하고 개선할 만한 조언을 줄 수 있을 거야.

남: 맞아, [43]좋은 편집자란 평범한 책과 훌륭한 책의 차이를 의미할 수 있어. 또 다른 장점은 출판사에서 책을 쉽게 유통할 수 있을 거라는 거야.

여: 아, 네 기사에서 그 부분이 기억나. 대형 출판사가 전 세계 서점들과 계약을 맺는 방식에 관해 썼었지.

남: 맞아. 하지만, 전통적인 출판에는 여전히 단점이 있어.

여: 응, 출판계가 천천히 움직인다고 들었어. 작품은 출판이 받아들여지기까지 정말 오랜 시간이 걸릴 수도 있어.

남: 응. [44]아마 너는 몇 번, 아니 수백 번 거절당하게 될 거야.

여: [44]거절은 작가로서 익숙해져야 하는 부분이라는 것은 알지만, 그래도 내게는 여전히 가장 좌절하게 하는 부분일 거야. 너는 기사에서 많은 작가들이 출판권을 양도해야 한다고도 썼더라. 그게 무슨 뜻이야?

남: 음, 출판사와 계약을 하면, 그들이 종종 독점적 출판권을 요구할 거야. 그래서 나중에 출판사를 바꾸고 싶다면, 더 이상 그 선택권이 없을 수도 있어.

여: 오, 그렇구나. 일단 계약서에 서명하면, 꼼짝 못 하게 되는구나. 고마워, Marcus. 이 대화가 정말 도움이 되었어.

남: [45]네 책을 어떻게 출판할 건지 결정했어, Samantha?

여: 응. [45]나는 내 글에 대한 창의적인 통제권이 여전히 있는 한 출판 비용은 내 돈으로 충당해도 상관없어.

어휘 | state[steit] 형세, 형편 self-publish 자비 출판하다(출판사를 거치지 않고 자비를 들여 스스로 책을 출판하다) control[kəntróul] 통제(력)
preference[préfərəns] 선호(도) freedom[fríːdəm] 자유 crime thriller 범죄 스릴러 outer space 우주 공간
original[ərídʒənl] 독창적인 recall[rikɔ́ːl] 기억하다, 상기하다 up front 선불로 market[máːrkit] 광고하다; 시장
connections[kənékʃəns] 인맥, 연줄 reviewer[rivjúːər] 평론가, 비평가 in-house 사내의, 조직 내의 editor[édətər] 편집자
assign[əsáin] 배정하다, 할당하나 look over 검토하다 mediocre[mìːdióukər] 평범한, 그저 그런 distribute[distríbjuːt] 유통하다, 배포하다
contract[kɑ́ntrækt] 계약 end up ~하게 되다, 결국 ~되다 reject[ridʒékt] 거절하다, 거부하다 rejection[ridʒékʃən] 거절, 거부

전통적인 출판의 장점

전통적인 출판의 단점

여자의 결정

지털고 영어 기출구제집 7개녀 Level 2

get used to 익숙해지다, 적응하다 sign away (서명하여) 양도하다 publishing rights 출판권 exclusive [iksklúːsiv] 독점적인, 유일한
stuck [stʌk] 꼼짝 못 하는, 갇힌

40 특정세부사항 Why
난이도 ●●○

Why did Samantha decide to ask Marcus for help?

(a) **He has researched publishing.**
(b) He is a well-known publisher.
(c) He is working for a publisher.
(d) He has published books before.

Samantha는 왜 Marcus에게 도움을 요청하기로 결
정했는가?

(a) **출판을 조사했다.**
(b) 유명한 출판인이다.
(c) 출판사에서 일하고 있다.
(d) 이전에 책을 출판한 적이 있다.

━○ 정답 잡는 치트키

질문의 키워드 ask ~ for help가 ask ~ advice로 paraphrasing되어 언급된 주변 내용을 주의 깊게 듣는다.

해설 | 여자가 'I just read your magazine article about the state of the publishing industry in the US.'라며 방금 미국의 출판 산
업 현황에 관한 남자의 잡지 기사를 읽었다고 한 뒤, 'Since your article was so well researched, I thought I'd ask your advice
on whether it's better to self-publish or publish my work traditionally.'라며 남자의 기사가 매우 잘 조사되어 있어서, 작품을 자
비 출판하는 게 더 나을지, 아니면 전통적인 방식으로 출판하는 게 더 나을지에 관해 조언을 구해야겠다고 생각했다고 했다. 따라서 (a)가 정
답이다.

어휘 | well-known 유명한, 잘 알려진

41 특정세부사항 How
난이도 ●●○

According to Samantha, how can she benefit from having
full creative control?

(a) She can experiment with narration.
(b) She can create her own language.
(c) **She can try out various genres.**
(d) She can focus on darker themes.

Samantha에 따르면, 완전한 창의적인 통제권을 가짐
으로써 어떻게 이익을 얻을 수 있는가?

(a) 이야기를 서술하는 방식을 시험할 수 있다.
(b) 자신만의 문체를 만들 수 있다.
(c) **다양한 장르를 시도할 수 있다.**
(d) 좀 더 어두운 주제에 집중할 수 있다.

━○ 정답 잡는 치트키

질문의 키워드 full creative control이 그대로 언급된 주변 내용을 주의 깊게 듣는다.

해설 | 남자가 'with self-publishing, you'll have full creative control of your book'이라며 자비 출판을 하면 책에 대한 완전한 창의적
인 통제권을 갖게 될 거라고 하자, 여자가 'I appreciate having that sort of creative freedom since I like experimenting with
different genres.'라며 다양한 장르를 시도하는 것을 좋아하기 때문에 그런 창의적인 자유를 가지는 것을 좋아한다고 했다. 따라서 (c)가
정답이다.

⇄ Paraphrasing
experimenting with different genres 다양한 장르를 시도하는 것 → try out various genres 다양한 장르를 시도하다

어휘 | narration [næréiʃən] 이야기를 서술하기, 화법 try out 시도하다

Why would self-publishing be expensive for Samantha?	Samantha에게 왜 자비 출판이 큰 비용이 들 것 같은가?
(a) because of the marketing expenses	(a) 마케팅 비용 때문에
(b) because of the printing costs	**(b) 인쇄 비용 때문에**
(c) because of the equipment costs	(c) 장비 비용 때문에
(d) because of the illustrator expenses	(d) 삽화가 비용 때문에

─○ 정답 잡는 치트키

질문의 키워드 self-publishing be expensive가 그대로 언급된 주변 내용을 주의 깊게 듣는다.

해설 | 여자가 'one disadvantage is that self-publishing can be expensive. In most cases, you have to pay up front to print the books.'라며 한 가지 단점은 자비 출판이 비용이 많이 들 수 있고, 대부분은 책을 인쇄하려면 선불로 비용을 내야 한다고 하자, 남자가 'those fees can get expensive depending on how many copies you need printed'라며 인쇄해야 하는 부수에 따라 비용이 많이 들 수 있다고 한 것을 통해, 인쇄에 드는 비용 때문에 Samantha에게 자비 출판이 큰 비용이 들 것임을 추론할 수 있다. 따라서 (b)가 정답이다.

⇄ **Paraphrasing**
fees 비용 → costs 비용

오답분석
(a) 여자가 인맥이 없어서 책을 홍보하기 어렵겠다고는 언급했지만, 마케팅 비용 때문에 자비 출판이 큰 비용이 들 것이라고 한 것은 아니므로 오답이다.

어휘 | marketing[má:rkitiŋ] 마케팅(제조 계획에서 최종 판매까지의 전 과정)   illustrator[íləstrèitər] 삽화가

43 **특정세부사항** How   난이도 ●●○

According to the conversation, how can Samantha avoid publishing a mediocre book?	대화에 따르면, Samantha는 어떻게 평범한 책을 출판하는 것을 피할 수 있는가?
(a) by outlining her ideas first	(a) 그녀의 생각에 관하여 먼저 간추려 말함으로써
(b) by having a good editor	**(b) 좋은 편집자를 고용함으로써**
(c) by getting tips from other writers	(c) 다른 작가들로부터 조언을 얻음으로써
(d) by writing multiple drafts	(d) 여러 차례 초고를 작성함으로써

─○ 정답 잡는 치트키

질문의 키워드 mediocre book이 그대로 언급된 주변 내용을 주의 깊게 듣는다.

해설 | 여자가 'A professional editor would be able to look over my book and give me tips on improving it.'이라며 전문 편집자가 책을 검토하고 개선할 만한 조언을 줄 수 있을 거라고 하자, 남자가 'a good editor can mean the difference between a mediocre book and a great one'이라며 좋은 편집자란 평범한 책과 훌륭한 책의 차이를 의미할 수 있다고 했다. 따라서 (b)가 정답이다.

어휘 | outline[áutlain] ~에 관하여 간추려 말하다   draft[dræft] 초고, 초안

What would frustrate Samantha the most about traditional publishing?

(a) **getting repeatedly turned down**
(b) being misled by publishers
(c) having to wait for feedback
(d) losing her publishing rights

전통적인 출판에 관해 Samantha를 가장 좌절하게 하는 것은 무엇인 것 같은가?

(a) **반복적으로 거절당하는 것**
(b) 출판사들에 의해 잘못된 방향으로 이끌어지는 것
(c) 피드백을 기다려야 하는 것
(d) 출판권을 잃는 것

─○ 정답 잡는 치트키

질문의 키워드 frustrate ~ the most가 be the most frustrating으로 paraphrasing되어 언급된 주변 내용을 주의 깊게 듣는다.

해설 | 남자가 'You'll probably end up getting rejected a few times, or a few hundred times.'라며 아마 몇 번, 아니 수백 번 거절당하게 될 것이라고 하자, 여자가 'I know that rejection is something I have to get used to as a writer, but it would still be the most frustrating part for me.'라며 거절은 작가로서 익숙해져야 하는 부분이라는 것은 알지만, 그래도 여전히 가장 좌절하게 하는 부분일 거라고 한 것을 통해, 전통적인 출판에 관해 Samantha를 가장 좌절하게 하는 것은 반복적으로 거절당하는 것임을 추론할 수 있다. 따라서 (a)가 정답이다.

↪ **Paraphrasing**
getting rejected 거절당하는 것 → getting ~ turned down 거절당하는 것

오답분석
(d) 여자가 출판사에서 종종 독점적 출판권을 요구하는 것에 관해 일단 계약서에 서명하면 꼼짝 못 하게 되겠다고는 언급했지만, 이것이 Samantha를 가장 좌절하게 하는 부분은 아니므로 오답이다.

어휘 | repeatedly [ripíːtidli] 반복적으로, 여러 차례 turn down 거절하다, 거부하다 mislead [mislíd] 잘못된 방향으로 이끌다

What has Samantha probably decided to do?

(a) hire a professional agent
(b) **launch her book on her own**
(c) seek funds for self-publication
(d) pitch her book to publishers

Samantha는 무엇을 하기로 결정한 것 같은가?

(a) 전문 대리인을 고용한다
(b) **혼자서 책을 출간한다**
(c) 자비 출판을 위한 자금을 구한다
(d) 책을 출판사들에 투고한다

─○ 정답 잡는 치트키

다음에 할 일을 언급하는 후반을 주의 깊게 듣는다.

해설 | 남자가 'Have you decided how you will publish your book, Samantha?'라며 책을 어떻게 출판할 건지 결정했는지 묻자, 여자가 'I don't mind using my own money for publishing expenses as long as I still have creative control of my writing.'이라며 글에 대한 창의적인 통제권이 여전히 있는 한 출판 비용은 자기 돈으로 충당해도 상관없다고 한 것을 통해, Samantha가 출판 비용은 직접 부담하지만, 창의적인 통제권을 가질 수 있는 자비 출판을 할 것임을 추론할 수 있다. 따라서 (b)가 정답이다.

어휘 | agent [éidʒənt] 대리인 launch [lɔːntʃ] 출간하다, 발표하다 on one's own 혼자서, 단독으로 pitch [pitʃ] 권유하려 하다, 설득하려 하다

PART 4 (46~52) 설명 비행에 대한 두려움을 관리하기 위한 6가지 조언

인사 + 주제 제시

Welcome to *The Travelour*, a podcast for all your travel needs! Today we will talk about some ways to make flying a more comfortable experience. Although air travel is quite common these days, ⁴⁶many people are still understandably nervous about getting on a plane. Here are six tips for managing your fear of flying.

조언1: 두려움 원인 파악

The first tip is to identify which part of flying makes you the most uncomfortable. Once you understand the source of your fear, you can make a plan of action to deal with it. ⁴⁷Personally, I'm afraid of heights, so I always make sure to reserve a seat away from the windows. Others may be bothered by people walking up and down the aisles, but I appreciate the extra leg room.

조언2: 지식 쌓기

⁴⁸The second tip is to educate yourself about airplanes. Knowledge really is power! It's common for fliers to experience some anxiety whenever the plane goes through a rough patch of air. ⁴⁸Learning about how the airplane works and how it's designed to fly safely through turbulence might give you some reassurance. I often find it helpful to remind myself that flying is significantly safer than driving a car.

조언3: 소음 제거 헤드폰 사용

The third tip is to bring noise-canceling headphones. ⁴⁹Many people dread flying because of the loud noises produced by the plane's engines. By using noise-canceling headphones during the flight, you can tune out noises that make you feel uneasy. You can also listen to calming music, such as classical or other instrumental music, especially during turbulence.

조언4: 좋아하는일 계획 하기

The fourth tip is to plan on doing something you enjoy during the flight. You won't have access to your normal distractions, like work or social media, so take the opportunity to do something special. Some passengers like catching up on podcasts or having a movie marathon. ⁵⁰For me, it's a chance to read a good book. Not only does reading take my mind off my worries, but it also gives me positive associations with flying.

조언5: 카페인 섭취 피하기

⁵¹The fifth tip is to avoid caffeinated drinks before and during your flight. Caffeine increases brain activity, which could make you imagine worst-case scenarios and make your upcoming flight seem even scarier. Drinking caffeinated beverages during your flight will also speed up your heart rate and breathing, which can cause you to feel ill and add to your discomfort. Instead of coffee or soda, drink something like chamomile tea, which is a

여행에 필요한 모든 것을 위한 팟캐스트, *Travelour* 에 오신 것을 환영합니다! 오늘 우리는 비행을 더 편안한 경험으로 만들기 위한 몇 가지 방법들에 관해 이야기할 것입니다. 비록 요즘은 항공 여행이 꽤 보편화되었지만, ⁴⁶많은 사람이 비행기를 타는 것에 대해 여전히 긴장하는 것은 당연합니다. 여기에 비행에 대한 두려움을 관리하기 위한 여섯 가지 조언이 있습니다.

첫 번째 조언은 비행의 어떤 부분이 여러분을 가장 불편하게 만드는지를 파악하는 것입니다. 일단 여러분이 두려움의 원인을 깨닫게 되면, 그것에 대처하기 위한 대처 방안을 세울 수 있습니다. ⁴⁷개인적으로, 저는 높은 곳을 두려워하기 때문에, 항상 창문에서 멀리 떨어진 좌석을 예약합니다. 다른 사람들은 통로를 왔다 갔다 하는 사람들 때문에 신경 쓰일지 모르지만, 저는 다리를 뻗을 수 있는 여분의 공간이 좋습니다.

⁴⁸두 번째 조언은 비행기에 대한 지식을 쌓는 것입니다. 아는 것은 정말 힘입니다! 비행기가 거친 기류 부분을 통과할 때마다 승객들이 불안감을 느끼는 것은 일반적입니다. ⁴⁸비행기가 어떻게 작동하고 어떻게 난기류를 안전하게 통과하도록 설계되었는지 아는 것은 안도감을 줄 수 있습니다. 저는 비행기를 타는 것이 자동차를 운전하는 것보다 훨씬 더 안전하다고 스스로 상기시켜 주는 것이 종종 도움이 된다고 생각합니다.

세 번째 조언은 소음 제거 헤드폰을 가지고 가는 것입니다. ⁴⁹많은 사람은 비행기 엔진에서 발생하는 시끄러운 소리 때문에 비행을 두려워합니다. 비행 중에 소음 제거 헤드폰을 사용함으로써, 여러분을 불안하게 만드는 소음을 듣지 않을 수 있습니다. 특히 난기류 동안에는, 클래식이나 다른 기악곡과 같은 진정시키는 음악을 들을 수도 있습니다.

네 번째 조언은 비행 중에 좋아하는 일 하는 것을 계획하는 것입니다. 업무나 소셜 미디어와 같이 집중을 방해하는 일상적인 것에 접근할 수 없으므로, 기회를 이용하여 특별한 무언가를 하세요. 일부 승객들은 팟캐스트 방송을 따라잡거나 영화를 몰아 보는 것을 좋아하기도 합니다. ⁵⁰저에게는, 좋은 책을 읽을 기회입니다. 독서는 걱정을 잊게 할 뿐만 아니라, 비행에 대해 긍정적인 연상도 하게 해줍니다.

⁵¹다섯 번째 조언은 비행 전과 비행 중에 카페인이 든 음료를 피하는 것입니다. 카페인은 두뇌 활동을 증가시키는데, 이것은 최악의 시나리오를 상상하게 하고 다가오는 비행을 더욱 무섭게 보이게 만들 수 있습니다. 비행 중에 카페인이 든 음료를 마시는 것은 심박수와 호흡 또한 빨라지게 할 것인데, 이것은 몸을 아프게 하고 불안을 가중할 수 있습니다. 커피나 탄산음료 대신, 일반적인 수면 보조물이자 긴장을 완화하는

common sleep aid and has been found to have relaxing effects.

⁵²The sixth and final tip is to tell your flight attendant about your fears. Experienced flight attendants have picked up a few tricks for making sure nervous fliers like you feel as safe as possible during the flight, whether that means checking on you every once in a while or talking you through your anxieties. ⁵²There is no shame in seeking support from people whose job is to help you. Rest assured that the cabin crew will be glad to assist you in any way they can.

There you have it—six tips on managing your fears while flying. Remember, it may be difficult to completely overcome your fear, but you can at least manage it until you arrive at your destination. Thanks for tuning in!

효과가 있는 것으로 밝혀진 카밀러 차 같은 것을 마셔보세요.

⁵²여섯 번째이자 마지막 조언은 두려움에 대해 승무원에게 말하는 것입니다. 숙련된 승무원들은 가끔 여러분의 상태를 확인하거나 불안에 관해 여러분과 이야기 나누는 등 여러분과 같은 긴장한 승객들이 비행 중 가능한 한 안전하다고 느낄 수 있도록 만드는 몇 가지 요령을 터득했습니다. ⁵²여러분을 돕는 것이 직업인 사람들에게 도움을 요청하는 것은 부끄러운 일이 아닙니다. 승무원은 그들이 할 수 있는 어떤 방법으로든 여러분을 기꺼이 도울 것이니 안심하세요.

지금까지 비행 중 두려움을 관리하는 여섯 가지 조언을 알려드렸습니다. 기억하세요, 두려움을 완전히 극복하기는 어렵겠지만, 적어도 목적지에 도착할 때까지는 관리할 수 있습니다. 청취해 주셔서 감사합니다!

조언6: 승무원 에게 도움 요청

끝인사

어휘 | understandably [ʌndərstǽndəbli] 당연히, 이해할 수 있게 manage [mǽnidʒ] 관리하다 fear [fiər] 두려움, 공포 source [sɔːrs] 원인, 원천 deal with 대처하다, 다루다 reserve [rizə́ːrv] 예약하다 bother [báðər] 신경 쓰이게 하다, 성가시게 하다 leg room 다리를 뻗을 수 있는 공간 knowledge [nálidʒ] 아는 것, 지식 flier [fláiər] 비행기 승객 rough [rʌf] 거친, 힘든 patch [pætʃ] 부분, 지역 turbulence [tə́ːrbjuləns] 난기류 reassurance [rìəʃúrəns] 안도감 dread [dred] 두려워하다 tune out 듣지 않다, 무시하다 uneasy [ʌníːzi] 불안한 instrumental music 기악곡 distraction [distrǽkʃən] 집중을 방해하는 것, 기분 전환 catch up on ~을 따라잡다 take one's mind off ~을 잊다 association [əsòusiéiʃən] 연상, 연관 caffeinated [kǽfənèitid] 카페인이 들어간 brain activity 두뇌 활동 heart rate 심박수 discomfort [diskʌ́mfərt] 불안, 불편 aid [eid] 보조물 pick up 요령을 터득하다, 익히게 되다 trick [trik] 요령 rest assured that ~에 안심하다 cabin crew 승무원 overcome [òuvərkʌ́m] 극복하다 destination [dèstənéiʃən] 목적지

---

46 주제/목적   담화의 주제

난이도 ●●○

What is the talk all about?

(a) managing stress on a long trip
(b) overcoming a fear of small spaces
(c) entertaining oneself on a plane
(d) handling anxiety about flying

담화는 무엇에 관한 것인가?

(a) 장거리 여행에서 스트레스를 관리하는 것
(b) 좁은 공간에 대한 두려움을 극복하는 것
(c) 비행기에서 즐겁게 지내는 것
(d) 비행에 대한 불안을 다스리는 것

⊸○ 정답 잡는 치트키

담화의 주제를 언급하는 초반을 주의 깊게 듣고 전체 맥락을 파악한다.

해설 | 화자가 'many people are still understandably nervous about getting on a plane. Here are six tips for managing your fear of flying.'이라며 많은 사람이 비행기를 타는 것에 대해 여전히 긴장하는 것은 당연하며, 비행에 대한 두려움을 관리하기 위한 여섯 가지 조언이 있다고 한 뒤, 비행에 대한 불안을 다스리는 것에 관한 내용이 이어지고 있다. 따라서 (d)가 정답이다.

⇄ Paraphrasing
managing ~ fear of flying 비행에 대한 두려움을 관리하는 것 → handling anxiety about flying 비행에 대한 불안을 다스리는 것

어휘 | entertain [èntərtéin] 즐겁게 하다

47 특정세부사항   How

How does the speaker take action to manage his fear of heights on a plane?

(a) by choosing an aisle seat
(b) by talking to others during takeoff
(c) by lowering the window shade
(d) by watching a film as a distraction

화자는 비행기에서 고소공포증을 관리하기 위해 어떻게 조치하는가?

(a) 통로 쪽 좌석을 선택함으로써
(b) 이륙 중에 다른 사람들과 이야기함으로써
(c) 창문 가리개를 내림으로써
(d) 기분 전환으로 영화를 시청함으로써

━○ 정답 잡는 치트키

질문의 키워드 fear of heights가 afraid of heights로 paraphrasing되어 언급된 주변 내용을 주의 깊게 듣는다.

해설 | 화자가 'Personally, I'm afraid of heights, so I always make sure to reserve a seat away from the windows.'라며 개인적으로, 높은 곳을 두려워하기 때문에 항상 창문에서 멀리 떨어진 좌석을 예약한다고 했다. 따라서 (a)가 정답이다.

⇄ Paraphrasing
a seat away from the windows 창문에서 멀리 떨어진 좌석 → an aisle seat 통로 쪽 좌석

어휘 | fear of heights 고소공포증 takeoff[téikɔ̀:f] 이륙 shade[ʃeid] 빛 가리개, 차양

48 추론   특정사실

According to the speaker, why, most likely, should passengers educate themselves about airplanes?

(a) to remind themselves that pilots are experts
(b) to know what to do during turbulence
(c) to understand that planes are reliable
(d) to learn about emergency procedures

화자에 따르면, 승객들은 왜 비행기에 관해 지식을 쌓아야 하는 것 같은가?

(a) 조종사들이 전문가라는 것을 스스로 상기시키기 위해서
(b) 난기류 동안 무엇을 해야 할지 알기 위해서
(c) 비행기가 믿을 만하다는 것을 깨닫기 위해서
(d) 비상조치에 관해 배우기 위해서

━○ 정답 잡는 치트키

질문의 키워드 educate ~ about airplanes가 그대로 언급된 주변 내용을 주의 깊게 듣는다.

해설 | 화자가 'The second tip is to educate yourself about airplanes.'라며 두 번째 조언은 비행기에 대한 지식을 쌓는 것이라고 한 뒤, 'Learning about how the airplane works and how it's designed to fly safely through turbulence might give you some reassurance.'라며 비행기가 어떻게 작동하고 어떻게 난기류를 안전하게 통과하도록 설계되었는지 아는 것은 안도감을 줄 수 있다고 한 것을 통해, 승객들은 비행기가 믿을 만하다는 것을 깨닫고 안도감을 얻기 위해 비행기에 관해 지식을 쌓아야 함을 추론할 수 있다. 따라서 (c)가 정답이다.

어휘 | pilot[páilət] 조종사, 비행사 expert[ékspə:rt] 전문가, 권위자 reliable[riláiəbl] 믿을 만한, 신뢰할 만한 emergency procedure 비상조치

49 특정세부사항   What

According to the speaker, what can passengers use their headphones for on a flight?

화자에 따르면, 승객들은 비행기에서 어떤 용도로 헤드폰을 사용할 수 있는가?

(a) to protect their ears from engine noises
(b) to tune out loud conversations
(c) to block worrisome mechanical sounds
(d) to listen to guided meditations

(a) 엔진 소음으로부터 귀를 보호하기 위해서
(b) 시끄러운 대화를 듣지 않기 위해서
(c) 걱정스럽게 만드는 기계 소리를 차단하기 위해서
(d) 가이드가 안내하는 명상을 듣기 위해서

━━○ **정답 잡는 치트키**

질문의 키워드 headphones가 그대로 언급된 주변 내용을 주의 깊게 듣는다.

해설 | 화자가 'Many people dread flying because of the loud noises produced by the plane's engines. By using noise-canceling headphones during the flight, you can tune out noises that make you feel uneasy.'라며 많은 사람이 비행기 엔진에서 발생하는 시끄러운 소리 때문에 비행을 두려워하는데, 비행 중에 소음 제거 헤드폰을 사용함으로써 불안하게 만드는 소음을 듣지 않을 수 있다고 했다. 따라서 (c)가 정답이다.

⇄ **Paraphrasing**
tune out noises 소음을 듣지 않다 → block ~ sounds 소리를 차단하다
make ~ feel uneasy 불안하게 만들다 → worrisome 걱정스럽게 만드는

어휘 | conversation[kànvərséiʃən] 대화 worrisome[wə́:risəm] 걱정스럽게 만드는, 걱정스러운 meditation[mèdətéiʃən] 명상

---

50 추론   특정사실   난이도 ●●○

Why probably does the speaker enjoy reading on a plane?

(a) It eases his anxiety.
(b) It keeps him from being bothered.
(c) It takes his mind off work.
(d) It helps him stay off social media.

화자는 왜 비행기에서 독서를 즐기는 것 같은가?

(a) 불안감을 덜어준다.
(b) 귀찮게 하지 않는다.
(c) 일을 잊도록 한다.
(d) 소셜 미디어를 멀리하도록 도와준다.

━━○ **정답 잡는 치트키**

질문의 키워드 reading이 그대로 언급된 주변 내용을 주의 깊게 듣는다.

해설 | 화자가 'For me, it's a chance to read a good book. Not only does reading take my mind off my worries, but it also gives me positive associations with flying.'이라며 자기에게는 좋은 책을 읽을 기회이며, 독서는 걱정을 잊게 할 뿐만 아니라, 비행에 대해 긍정적인 연상도 하게 해준다고 한 것을 통해, 화자는 독서가 비행에 대한 불안감을 덜어주므로 비행기에서 독서를 즐긴다는 것을 추론할 수 있다. 따라서 (a)가 정답이다.

⇄ **Paraphrasing**
take mind off ~ worries 걱정을 잊게 하다 → eases ~ anxiety 불안감을 덜어주다

어휘 | ease[i:z] 덜어주다, 완화하다 stay off 멀리하다, 삼가다

---

51 특정세부사항   What   난이도 ●●○

What does the speaker say that passengers should do before their flights?

(a) do some breathing exercises

화자는 승객들이 비행 전에 무엇을 해야 한다고 말하는가?

(a) 호흡 운동을 한다

(b) avoid consuming too much food

(c) take motion sickness medicine

(d) refrain from drinking caffeine

(b) 음식을 너무 많이 먹지 않는다

(c) 멀미약을 복용한다

(d) 카페인 섭취를 삼간다

TEST 1 TEST 2 TEST 3 TEST 4 TEST 5 TEST 6 TEST 7

○ 정답 잡는 치트키

질문의 키워드 before ~ flights가 그대로 언급된 주변 내용을 주의 깊게 듣는다.

해설 | 화자가 'The fifth tip is to avoid caffeinated drinks before and during your flight.'라며 다섯 번째 조언은 비행 전과 비행 중에 카페인이 든 음료를 피하는 것이라고 했다. 따라서 (d)가 정답이다.

⇄ **Paraphrasing**
avoid caffeinated drinks 카페인이 든 음료를 피하다 → refrain from drinking caffeine 카페인 섭취를 삼가다

어휘 | breathing exercise 호흡 운동   consume[kənsúːm] 먹다, 마시다   motion sickness 멀미   refrain from ~을 삼가다

---

52   특정세부사항   What   난이도 ●●○

What is the final tip in the talk?

(a) ask the flight staff for help

(b) thank the pilot personally

(c) be patient with the attendants

(d) bring gifts for the cabin crew

담화의 마지막 조언은 무엇인가?

(a) 승무원에게 도움을 요청한다

(b) 조종사에게 직접 감사를 표한다

(c) 승무원에게 인내심을 가진다

(d) 승무원을 위한 선물을 가져간다

○ 정답 잡는 치트키

질문의 키워드 final tip이 그대로 언급된 주변 내용을 주의 깊게 듣는다.

해설 | 화자가 'The sixth and final tip is to tell your flight attendant about your fears.'라며 여섯 번째이자 마지막 조언은 두려움에 대해 승무원에게 말하는 것이라고 한 뒤, 'There is no shame in seeking support from people whose job is to help you.'라며 돕는 것이 직업인 사람들에게 도움을 요청하는 것은 부끄러운 일이 아니라고 했다. 따라서 (a)가 정답이다.

⇄ **Paraphrasing**
seeking support 도움을 요청하는 것 → ask ~ for help 도움을 요청하다
flight attendant 승무원 → the flight staff 승무원

어휘 | patient[péiʃənt] (남에게) 인내심이 있는

READING & VOCABULARY

PART 1 (53~59) 인물의 일대기 공상 과학 소설 작가 테리 프래쳇

인물 이름	### TERRY PRATCHETT	테리 프래쳇

인물
이름

소개
+
유명한
이유

[53]Terry Pratchett was a critically acclaimed English author most famous for his humorous take on popular fantasy and science fiction plot lines. He was the United Kingdom's bestselling author of the '90s, and his best-known work is the science fiction series Discworld.

어린
시절

Terence David John Pratchett was born on April 28, 1948, in Buckinghamshire, England. At a young age, he was already a fan of science fiction and would often attend sci-fi fan conventions. [54]He was also an avid writer, publishing many articles for his school newspaper. At thirteen, Pratchett published his first science fiction short story, "The Hades Business," in a school magazine.

업적
시작
계기

[54]After high school, Pratchett decided to work as a journalist for his local newspaper. [55]There he met a publisher named Colin Smythe, who was intrigued when Pratchett mentioned that he was writing a science fiction novel. After reading the draft, Smythe praised the unique concept and agreed to publish it. *The Carpet People* was released in 1971 and was well received, [58]marking the beginning of Pratchett's career as a novelist. He published two more novels shortly afterward, both of which received mostly positive reviews.

초기
업적

In 1983, Pratchett released the first book of the Discworld series, *The Colour of Magic*. [56(a)/(c)]Set on a disc-like planet being carried through space by four elephants and a giant turtle, the novel is an absurd fantasy comedy that made fun of common science fiction plot lines. [56(b)]Pratchett's humorous tone received considerable praise and became a trademark of the Discworld series. [56(d)]*The Colour of Magic* was later adapted into a television show, a video game, and a graphic novel.

주요
업적

Pratchett continued to write the Discworld series for the next three decades, with most of the books landing on the UK bestseller list. He also wrote several sci-fi novels for children. [57]In 2007, he was diagnosed with Alzheimer's disease, which somewhat affected his reading and writing abilities. Nevertheless, he continued to write books and even accepted a teaching position at

[53]테리 프래쳇은 일반적인 판타지와 공상 과학 소설의 줄거리를 유머러스하게 풀어내는 것으로 가장 유명한, 비평가들의 극찬을 받은 영국 작가였다. 그는 90년대 영국의 인기도서 작가였으며, 그의 가장 유명한 작품은 공상 과학 소설 시리즈인 Discworld이다.

테런스 데이비드 존 프래쳇은 1948년 4월 28일에 영국 버킹엄셔에서 태어났다. 어린 나이에, 이미 공상 과학 소설의 팬이었으며 공상 과학 팬 컨벤션에 자주 참석하곤 했다. [54]또한 열렬한 작가였는데, 학교 신문에 많은 기사를 게재했다. 열세 살 때, 프래쳇은 학교 잡지에 첫 공상 과학 단편소설인 "The Hades Business"를 게재했다.

[54]고등학교 이후, 프래쳇은 지역 신문사에서 기자로 일하기로 결심했다. [55]그곳에서 콜린 스미더라는 이름의 출판업자를 만났는데, 그는 프래쳇이 공상 과학 소설을 쓴다고 언급했을 때 아주 흥미로워했다. 초고를 읽은 후, 스미더는 독특한 발상을 칭찬하며 출판하는 데 동의했다. *The Carpet People*은 1971년에 출간되었고 [58]작가로서 프래쳇의 경력의 시작을 나타내며 호평을 받았다. 곧 두 편의 소설을 더 출간했는데, 두 작품 모두 대부분 긍정적인 평가를 받았다.

1983년에, 프래쳇은 Discworld 시리즈의 첫 번째 책인 *The Colour of Magic*을 출간했다. [56(a)/(c)]네 마리의 코끼리와 거대한 거북이에 의해 우주로 운반되는 디스크 모양의 행성을 배경으로 한, 이 소설은 일반적인 공상 과학 소설의 줄거리를 비웃는 우스꽝스러운 판타지 코미디이다. [56(b)]프래쳇의 유머러스한 어투는 상당한 찬사를 받았고 Discworld 시리즈의 트레이드마크가 되었다. [56(d)]*The Colour of Magic*은 이후에 텔레비전 쇼, 비디오 게임, 그래픽 소설로 각색되었다.

프래쳇은 이후 30년 동안 Discworld 시리즈를 계속 집필했고, 대부분 책은 영국 베스트셀러 목록에 올랐다. 그는 또한 어린이를 위한 여러 편의 공상 과학 소설도 썼다. [57]2007년에, 그는 알츠하이머병을 진단받았고, 이것은 그의 읽기와 쓰기 능력에 어느 정도 영향을 미쳤다. 그럼에도 불구하고, 그는 책을 계속 썼고 심지어 대학에서 교수직을 수락했다. 2년 후, 그는 영문

a university. Two years later, he was knighted by Queen Elizabeth II for his contributions to English literature.

Pratchett died on March 12, 2015, and his last Discworld novel was published later that year. [59]Comprising forty-one novels, the series has sold more than 80 million copies worldwide. His works remain among the most popular fantasy novels.

죽음
+
후기
업적

학에 대한 기여로 엘리자베스 2세 여왕으로부터 나이트 작위를 받았다.

프래쳇은 2015년 3월 12일에 사망했으며, 그의 마지막 Discworld 소설은 그 해 말에 출판되었다. [59]41편의 소설을 포함한, 이 시리즈는 전 세계적으로 8천만 부 넘게 팔렸다. 그의 작품은 가장 인기 있는 판타지 소설 중 하나로 남아 있다.

어휘 | critically acclaimed phr. 비평가들의 극찬을 받은 humorous adj. 유머러스한, 재미있는 plot line phr. 줄거리 avid adj. 열렬한, 열광적인 journalist n. 기자, 언론인 publisher n. 출판업자, 출판사 intrigued adj. 아주 흥미로워하는 draft n. 초고, 초안 unique adj. 독특한, 특유의 concept n. 발상, 구상 be well received phr. 호평을 받다 novelist n. 작가, 소설가 shortly afterward phr. 곧 planet n. 행성 giant adj. 거대한 absurd adj. 우스꽝스러운, 황당한 make fun of phr. ~을 비웃다, 조롱하다 trademark n. 트레이드마크(어떤 사람의 특징이 되는 행위·복장 등) be adapted into phr. ~으로 각색되다 be diagnosed with phr. ~으로 진단받다 knight v. ~에게 나이트 작위를 수여하다; n. (중세의) 기사 contribution n. 기여, 이바지

---

53 특정세부사항   유명한 이유   난이도 ●●○

What is Pratchett best known for?

(a) his comedic approach to common fictional storyline
(b) his status as the bestselling fantasy author of all time
(c) his literary contributions as a popular nonfiction novelist
(d) his direction of a groundbreaking sci-fi film series

프래쳇은 무엇으로 가장 잘 알려져 있는가?

(a) 일반적인 소설 줄거리에 대한 희극적 접근법
(b) 역사상 가장 많이 팔린 판타지 작가의 지위
(c) 인기 있는 논픽션 작가로서의 문학적 기여
(d) 획기적인 공상 과학 영화 시리즈에 대한 연출

─○ 정답 잡는 치트키

질문의 키워드 best known이 most famous로 paraphrasing되어 언급된 주변 내용을 주의 깊게 읽는다.

해설 | 1단락의 'Terry Pratchett was a critically acclaimed English author most famous for his humorous take on popular fantasy and science fiction plot lines.'에서 테리 프래쳇은 일반적인 판타지와 공상 과학 소설의 줄거리를 유머러스하게 풀어내는 것으로 가장 유명한, 비평가들의 극찬을 받은 영국 작가였다고 했다. 따라서 (a)가 정답이다.

어휘 | comedic adj. 희극적인, 희극풍의 approach n. 접근법 fictional adj. 소설의, 허구의 storyline n. 줄거리 status n. 지위, 상태 literary adj. 문학적인, 문학의 direction n. (영화 등의) 연출, 감독 groundbreaking adj. 획기적인

---

54 추론   특정사실   난이도 ●●○

Why, most likely, did Pratchett decide against continuing his education after high school?

(a) because his school grades were below average
(b) because he wanted to gain professional experience
(c) because he got a job offer from a national newspaper
(d) because his family was unable to support him financially

프래쳇은 왜 고등학교 이후에 학업을 계속하지 않기로 결심했을 것 같은가?

(a) 성적이 평균 이하였기 때문에
(b) 전문적인 경험을 얻고 싶어 했기 때문에
(c) 국내 신문사로부터 일자리 제안을 받았기 때문에
(d) 가족이 재정적으로 지원해 줄 수 없었기 때문에

지텔프 공식 기출문제집 7회분 Level 2

질문의 키워드 after high school이 그대로 언급된 주변 내용을 주의 깊게 읽는다.

해설 | 2단락의 'He was also an avid writer, publishing many articles for his school newspaper.'에서 프래쳇은 열렬한 작가였는데, 학교 신문에 많은 기사를 게재했다고 한 뒤, 3단락의 'After high school, Pratchett decided to work as a journalist for his local newspaper.'에서 고등학교 이후, 지역 신문사에서 기자로 일하기로 결심했다고 한 것을 통해, 프래쳇이 고등학교 이후에 작가로서의 전문적인 경험을 얻기 위해 학업을 계속하지 않고 지역 신문사에서 기자로 일하기로 결심했음을 추론할 수 있다. 따라서 (b)가 정답이다.

어휘 | school grades phr. 성적 below average phr. 평균 이하인 gain v. 얻다 national adj. 국내의 support v. 지원하다, 뒷받침하다 financially adv. 재정적으로, 경제적으로

---

55 특정세부사항 Why

난이도 ●●○

Why did Smythe agree to release Pratchett's first book?

(a) because Pratchett asked him to do so as a personal favor
(b) because he thought Pratchett's ideas were original
(c) because he and Pratchett had worked together as journalists
(d) because Pratchett agreed to add more novels to the series

스미더는 왜 프래쳇의 첫 번째 책을 출간하는 데 동의했는가?

(a) 프래쳇이 개인적인 호의로 그렇게 해달라고 부탁했기 때문에
(b) 프래쳇의 아이디어가 독창적이라고 생각했기 때문에
(c) 그와 프래쳇은 기자로 함께 일했기 때문에
(d) 프래쳇이 시리즈에 더 많은 소설을 추가하는 데 동의했기 때문에

🔑 정답 잡는 치트키

질문의 키워드 Smythe agree to release가 Smythe ~ agreed to publish로 paraphrasing되어 언급된 주변 내용을 주의 깊게 읽는다.

해설 | 3단락의 'There he met a publisher named Colin Smythe, ~. After reading the draft, Smythe praised the unique concept and agreed to publish it.'에서 그곳에서 콜린 스미더라는 이름의 출판업자를 만났는데, 초고를 읽은 후에 스미더는 독특한 발상을 칭찬하며 출판하는 데 동의했다고 했다. 따라서 (b)가 정답이다.

⇄ **Paraphrasing**
unique 독특한 → original 독창적인

어휘 | personal favor phr. 개인적인 호의 original adj. 독창적인

---

56 Not/True Not 문제

난이도 ●●●

Which of the following is NOT true about *The Colour of Magic*?

(a) that it features animals in the story
(b) that it established the series' tone
(c) that it is set in a fictional city on planet Earth
(d) that it inspired other forms of media

다음 중 *The Colour of Magic*에 관해 사실이 아닌 것은 무엇인가?

(a) 이야기에 동물들을 특별히 포함하는 것
(b) 시리즈의 분위기를 확립했던 것
(c) 지구상에 있는 허구의 도시를 배경으로 하는 것
(d) 다른 형태의 미디어에 영감을 주었던 것

🔑 정답 잡는 치트키

질문의 키워드 *The Colour of Magic*이 그대로 언급된 주변 내용을 주의 깊게 읽고, 보기의 키워드와 지문 내용을 대조하며 언급되는 것을 하나

씩 소거한다.

해설 | 4단락의 'Set on a disc-like planet being carried through space by four elephants and a giant turtle'에서 네 마리의 코끼리와 거대한 거북이에 의해 우주로 운반되는 디스크 모양의 행성을 배경으로 한다고 언급되었으므로, *The Colour of Magic*이 지구상에 있는 허구의 도시를 배경으로 한다는 것은 지문의 내용과 일치하지 않는다. 따라서 (c)가 정답이다.

　　오답분석

(a) 보기의 키워드 animals가 four elephants and a ~ turtle로 paraphrasing되어 언급된 4단락에서 네 마리의 코끼리와 거대한 거북이에 의해 우주로 운반되는 디스크 모양의 행성을 배경으로 한다고 언급되었다.

(b) 보기의 키워드 series' tone이 trademark of the ~ series로 paraphrasing되어 언급된 4단락에서 프래쳇의 유머러스한 어투는 상당한 찬사를 받았고 시리즈의 트레이드마크가 되었다고 언급되었다.

(d) 보기의 키워드 other forms of media가 a television show, a video game, and a graphic novel로 paraphrasing되어 언급된 4단락에서 *The Colour of Magic*은 이후에 텔레비전 쇼, 비디오 게임, 그래픽 소설로 각색되었다고 언급되었다.

어휘 | feature v. 특별히 포함하다, 특징으로 삼다　inspire v. 영감을 주다, 고무하다

57　특정세부사항　What
난이도 ●●○

What was Pratchett's career like after his Alzheimer's diagnosis?

(a) He quit writing to become a university professor.
(b) He started writing books geared toward children.
(c) He was able to keep working on new projects.
(d) He accepted a position working for Queen Elizabeth II.

알츠하이머 진단 후에 프래쳇의 경력은 어땠는가?

(a) 대학 교수가 되기 위해 집필을 그만뒀다.
(b) 어린이를 대상으로 한 책을 쓰기 시작했다.
(c) 계속해서 새로운 프로젝트를 할 수 있었다.
(d) 엘리자베스 2세 여왕을 위해 일하는 직책을 수락했다.

　　정답 잡는 치트키

질문의 키워드 Alzheimer가 그대로 언급된 주변 내용을 주의 깊게 읽는다.

해설 | 5단락의 'In 2007, he was diagnosed with Alzheimer's disease, ~. Nevertheless, he continued to write books and even accepted a teaching position at a university.'에서 2007년에, 프래쳇은 알츠하이머병을 진단받았는데, 그럼에도 불구하고, 책을 계속 썼고 심지어 대학에서 교수직을 수락했다고 했다. 따라서 (c)가 정답이다.

　　오답분석

(a) 5단락에서 대학 교수직을 수락했다고 언급했지만, 대학 교수가 되기 위해 집필을 그만둔 것은 아니므로 오답이다.

어휘 | diagnosis n. 진단　quit v. 그만두다, 포기하다　geared adj. (~에 맞도록) 설계된

58　어휘　유의어
난이도 ●●○

In the context of the passage, marking means _____.

(a) indicating
(b) recording
(c) accepting
(d) grading

지문의 문맥에서, 'marking'은 -을 의미한다.

(a) 나타내며
(b) 기록하며
(c) 받아들이며
(d) 등급을 매기며

밑줄 친 어휘의 유의어를 찾는 문제이므로, marking이 포함된 구절을 읽고 문맥을 파악한다.

해설 | 3단락의 'marking the beginning of Pratchett's career as a novelist'는 작가로서 프래쳇의 경력의 시작을 나타낸다는 뜻이므로, marking이 '나타내며'라는 의미로 사용된 것을 알 수 있다. 따라서 '나타내며'라는 같은 의미의 (a) indicating이 정답이다.

59 어휘   유의어   난이도 ●●○

In the context of the passage, <u>comprising</u> means _____.

(a) taking in
(b) including
(c) extending
(d) setting up

지문의 문맥에서, 'comprising'은 -을 의미한다.

(a) 받아들인
(b) 포함한
(c) 확장한
(d) 설립한

밑줄 친 어휘의 유의어를 찾는 문제이므로, comprising이 포함된 구절을 읽고 문맥을 파악한다.

해설 | 6단락의 'Comprising forty-one novels'는 41편의 소설을 포함한다는 뜻이므로, comprising이 '포함한'이라는 의미로 사용된 것을 알 수 있다. 따라서 '포함한'이라는 같은 의미의 (b) including이 정답이다.

PART 2 (60~66)   잡지 기사   극도로 높은 실내 온도와 인지 능력의 연관성

연구 결과

EXTREME INDOOR HEAT CAN REDUCE COGNITIVE PERFORMANCE

극도의 실내 열기는 인지 수행을 저하할 수 있다

연구 소개

Heat waves—periods of extremely high temperatures during the summer season—are proven to have many harmful physical effects, such as heatstroke and dehydration. However, not much is known about the effects of high indoor temperatures on cognition. [60]To find out more about how extreme heat can affect cognitive ability, researchers from the Harvard T.H. Chan School of Public Health tested a group of university students.

여름철 동안 극도로 높은 기온이 지속되는 기간인 폭염은 열사병과 탈수증과 같이 여러 가지 해로운 신체적 영향을 미치는 것으로 밝혀졌다. 그러나, 높은 실내 온도가 인지에 미치는 영향에 대해서는 알려진 것이 많지 않다. [60]극도의 열기가 인지 능력에 어떻게 영향을 미칠 수 있는지 자세히 알아보기 위해, 하버드 T.H. Chan 공중보건 대학 연구진은 대학생 그룹을 대상으로 실험을 진행했다.

연구 배경

Cognitive abilities are skills required for completing mental tasks. The sharper one's cognitive abilities, the faster one can solve problems. [61(a)/(c)]For this study, the researchers tested the cognitive skills of twenty-four students who lived in a dormitory with central air conditioning and another twenty who lived in a dormitory without air conditioning. [61(b)]The study took place over twelve days, during which time the researchers placed

인지 능력은 정신적인 과제를 완수하는 데 필요한 기술이다. 인지 능력이 예리할수록, 문제를 더 빨리 해결할 수 있다. [61(a)/(c)]이 연구를 위해, 연구진은 중앙 에어컨이 설치된 기숙사에 거주하는 24명의 학생과 에어컨이 없는 기숙사에 거주하는 또 다른 20명의 인지 기술을 시험했다. [61(b)]연구는 12일에 걸쳐 이루어졌으며,

devices in the students' rooms to record daily indoor temperatures.

For the first five days of the study, indoor temperatures in each building were average for the season. Then, a five-day heat wave occurred, followed by two days where the weather gradually cooled. For each day, the participants were required to take two cognitive tests on their smartphone, right after waking up. For the first test, [62]the participants had to quickly and correctly identify the color of the displayed words to test their cognitive speed. The second test consisted of basic arithmetic problems to assess the students' working memory.

[61(d)/63/65]The researchers observed that during the heat wave, students who lived in the building without air conditioning performed about thirteen percent worse than their peers living in the air-conditioned building. [63]The most significant difference came during the two-day period after the heat wave. In the air-conditioned building, temperatures somewhat decreased, but in the non-air-conditioned building, temperatures stayed relatively high. Even when the heat wave had passed, its effects could still be experienced indoors.

In their discussion of the study's findings, [64/66]researchers stressed the importance of designing buildings with proper safeguards against extreme temperatures so that occupants can stay healthy and productive, even in hot weather.

그 기간 연구진은 학생들의 방에 장치를 설치하여 매일 실내 온도를 기록했다.

연구의 첫 5일 동안, 각 건물의 실내 온도는 계절에 맞는 평균 수준이었다. 그리고 나서, 5일 동안 폭염이 발생했고, 이후 이틀 동안 날씨가 서서히 선선해졌다. 매일, 참가자들은 기상 직후에 스마트폰으로 두 번의 인지 테스트를 받도록 요구되었다. 첫 번째 테스트에서는, [62]참가자들은 그들의 인지 속도를 시험하기 위해 표시된 단어의 색을 빠르고 정확하게 파악해야 했다. 두 번째 테스트는 학생들의 작동 기억을 평가하기 위한 기본적인 산수 문제로 구성되었다.

[61(d)/63/65]연구진은 폭염 동안 에어컨이 없는 건물에 사는 학생들이 에어컨이 있는 건물에 사는 또래들보다 약 13% 더 나쁜 성적을 거둔 것을 깨달았다. [63]가장 큰 차이는 폭염 이후 이틀 동안 나타났다. 에어컨이 설치된 건물에서는 온도가 다소 낮아졌지만, 에어컨이 설치되지 않은 건물에서는 온도가 상대적으로 높게 유지됐다. 폭염이 지나간 후에도, 실내에서는 여전히 폭염의 영향을 경험할 수 있었다.

연구 결과에 대한 토론에서, [64/66]연구진은 거주자들이 더운 날씨에도 건강하고 생산적으로 지낼 수 있도록 극도의 온도에 대한 적절한 보호 수단을 갖춘 건물 설계의 중요성을 강조했다.

실험 방식

실험 결과

시사점

어휘 | extreme adj. 극도의, 극한의 cognitive performance phr. 인지 수행 heat wave phr. 폭염 harmful adj. 해로운 physical adj. 신체의, 육체의 heatstroke n. 열사병 dehydration n. 탈수증 cognition n. 인지, 인식 cognitive ability phr. 인지 능력 mental adj. 정신적인, 정신의 cognitive skill phr. 인지 기술 dormitory n. 기숙사, 숙소 average adj. 평균의, 보통의 gradually adv. 서서히, 점진적으로 correctly adv. 정확하게, 제대로 cognitive speed phr. 인지 속도 arithmetic adj. 산수의, 산술의 assess v. 평가하다, 판단하다 working memory phr. 작동 기억 peer n. 또래, 동료 somewhat adv. 다소, 어느 정도 relatively adv. 상대적으로, 비교적으로 proper adj. 적절한, 올바른 safeguard n. 보호 수단; v. 보호하다 occupant n. 거주자, 임차인 productive adj. 생산적인, 생산력이 있는

60 특정세부사항   Why   난이도 ●●○

Why did researchers perform the study?

(a) to find out how heat affects students' moods
(b) to establish a link between temperature and mental health

연구진은 왜 연구를 수행했는가?

(a) 열기가 학생들의 기분에 어떻게 영향을 미치는지 알아내기 위해서
(b) 온도와 정신 건강 사이의 관련성을 밝히기 위해서

(c) to explore a correlation between heat waves and motivation

(d) to test the impact of extreme heat on brain function

(c) 폭염과 동기부여 사이의 상관관계를 조사하기 위해서

(d) 극도의 열기가 뇌 기능에 미치는 영향을 시험하기 위해서

질문의 키워드 researchers perform the study가 researchers ~ tested로 paraphrasing되어 언급된 주변 내용을 주의 깊게 읽는다.

해설 | 1단락의 'To find out more about how extreme heat can affect cognitive ability, researchers ~ tested a group of university students.'에서 극도의 열기가 인지 능력에 어떻게 영향을 미칠 수 있는지 자세히 알아보기 위해, 연구진은 대학생 그룹을 대상으로 실험을 진행했다고 했다. 따라서 (d)가 정답이다.

⇄ **Paraphrasing**
cognitive ability 인지 능력 → brain function 뇌 기능

어휘 | mood n. 기분, 분위기 link n. 관련성, 관계 correlation n. 상관관계 motivation n. 동기부여 impact n. 영향
brain function phr. 뇌 기능

61 Not/True   True 문제   난이도 ●●●

What is true about the participants in the study?

(a) They lived on the same floor of a dormitory.
(b) They completed tasks for almost two weeks.
(c) They were equally divided into two groups.
(d) They came from many different age groups.

연구 참가자들에 관해 사실인 것은 무엇인가?

(a) 기숙사의 같은 층에 살았다.
(b) 거의 2주 동안 과제를 완료했다.
(c) 두 그룹으로 똑같이 나누어졌다.
(d) 다양한 연령대에서 왔다.

질문의 키워드 participants가 students로 paraphrasing되어 언급된 주변 내용을 주의 깊게 읽고, 보기의 키워드와 지문 내용을 대조하며 읽는다.

해설 | (b)의 키워드인 almost two weeks가 twelve days로 paraphrasing되어 언급된 2단락의 'The study took place over twelve days, during which time the researchers placed devices in the students' rooms'에서 연구가 12일에 걸쳐 이루어졌으며, 그 기간 연구진은 학생들의 방에 장치를 설치했다고 했으므로 지문의 내용과 일치한다. 따라서 (b)가 정답이다.

오답분석
(a) 보기의 키워드 dormitory가 그대로 언급된 2단락에서 연구진은 중앙 에어컨이 설치된 기숙사에 거주하는 학생들과 에어컨이 없는 기숙사에 거주하는 학생들의 인지 기술을 시험했다고는 했지만, 연구 참가자들이 기숙사의 같은 층에 살았는지는 언급되지 않았다.
(c) 2단락에서 연구진은 중앙 에어컨이 설치된 기숙사에 거주하는 24명의 학생과 에어컨이 없는 기숙사에 거주하는 또 다른 20명의 인지 기술을 시험했다고 했으므로 지문의 내용과 일치하지 않는다.
(d) 보기의 키워드 age groups가 peers로 언급된 4단락에서 연구진은 폭염 동안 에어컨이 없는 건물에 사는 학생들이 에어컨이 있는 건물에 사는 또래보다 약 13% 더 나쁜 성적을 거둔 것을 깨달았다고 했으므로 지문의 내용과 일치하지 않는다.

어휘 | be divided into phr. ~으로 나누어지다 age group phr. 연령대

62 특정세부사항 What

난이도 ●●○

What were participants tested on to measure their cognitive speed?

(a) their skill at identifying a word's meaning
(b) their skill at spelling color names correctly
(c) their ability to quickly solve basic math problems
(d) their ability to rapidly choose the correct color of a word

참가자들은 인지 속도를 측정하기 위해 무엇을 시험 받았는가?

(a) 단어의 뜻을 파악하는 기술
(b) 색이름의 철자를 정확히 말하는 기술
(c) 기본적인 수학 문제를 빨리 푸는 능력
(d) 단어의 정확한 색을 신속하게 선택하는 능력

─○ 정답 잡는 치트키

질문의 키워드 cognitive speed가 그대로 언급된 주변 내용을 주의 깊게 읽는다.

해설 | 3단락의 'the participants had to quickly and correctly identify the color of the displayed words to test their cognitive speed'에서 참가자들은 그들의 인지 속도를 시험하기 위해 표시된 단어의 색을 빠르고 정확하게 파악해야 했다고 했다. 따라서 (d)가 정답이다.

⇄ **Paraphrasing**
quickly 빠르게 → rapidly 신속하게

오답분석
(c) 3단락에서 두 번째 테스트가 기본적인 산수 문제로 구성되었다고는 언급했지만, 이것은 학생들의 작동 기억을 평가하기 위한 테스트였으므로 오답이다.

어휘 | measure v. 측정하다, 평가하다 spell v. 철자를 말하다 rapidly adv. 신속하게

63 추론 특정사실

난이도 ●●○

What probably happened to the students' cognitive performance right after the heat wave subsided?

(a) Both groups showed signs of improvement.
(b) Students without air conditioning still did worse.
(c) Students with air conditioning fell behind slightly.
(d) Neither group showed any significant change.

폭염이 진정된 직후에 학생들의 인지 수행에 무슨 일이 일어났을 것 같은가?

(a) 두 그룹 모두 개선의 조짐을 보였다.
(b) 에어컨이 없는 학생들은 여전히 더 나빴다.
(c) 에어컨이 있는 학생들은 약간 뒤처졌다.
(d) 두 그룹 모두 아주 큰 변화를 보이지 않았다.

─○ 정답 잡는 치트키

질문의 키워드 after the heat wave가 그대로 언급된 주변 내용을 주의 깊게 읽는다.

해설 | 4단락의 'The researchers observed that during the heat wave, students who lived in the building without air conditioning performed about thirteen percent worse than their peers living in the air-conditioned building. The most significant difference came during the two-day period after the heat wave.'에서 연구진은 폭염 동안 에어컨이 없는 건물에 사는 학생들이 에어컨이 있는 건물에 사는 또래들보다 약 13% 더 나쁜 성적을 거둔 것을 깨달았는데, 가장 큰 차이는 폭염 이후 이틀 동안 나타났다고 한 것을 통해, 폭염이 진정된 직후에 에어컨이 없는 기숙사에 사는 학생들의 인지 수행이 에어컨이 있는 건물에 사는 또래들에 비해 여전히 더 나빴음을 추론할 수 있다. 따라서 (b)가 정답이다.

어휘 | subside v. 진정되다, 가라앉다 sign n. 조짐, 징후 improvement n. 개선, 향상 fall behind phr. 뒤처지다 slightly adv. 약간 significant adj. 아주 큰, 의미 있는

지텔프 양식 기출문제집 7회분 Level 2

64 추론 특정사실 난이도 ●●○

Based on the final paragraph, how might building designers contribute to improving health and productivity?

(a) by engineering a new cooling device
(b) by paying special attention to temperature control
(c) by checking in regularly with residents
(d) by evaluating recent weather patterns

마지막 단락에 따르면, 건축 설계자들은 건강과 생산성 향상에 어떻게 기여할 것 같은가?

(a) 새로운 냉방 장치를 설계함으로써
(b) 온도조절에 각별한 주의를 기울임으로써
(c) 거주자들을 정기적으로 확인함으로써
(d) 최근의 기후 패턴을 검토함으로써

──○ 정답 잡는 치트키

질문의 키워드 improving health and productivity가 stay healthy and productive로 paraphrasing되어 언급된 주변 내용을 주의 깊게 읽는다.

해설 | 5단락의 'researchers stressed the importance of designing buildings with proper safeguards against extreme temperatures so that occupants can stay healthy and productive, even in hot weather'에서 연구진은 거주자들이 더운 날씨에도 건강하고 생산적으로 지낼 수 있도록 극도의 온도에 대한 적절한 보호 수단을 갖춘 건물 설계의 중요성을 강조했다고 한 것을 통해, 건축 설계자들은 극도의 온도를 조절할 수 있도록 각별한 주의를 기울임으로써 거주자들의 건강과 생산성 향상에 기여할 수 있음을 추론할 수 있다. 따라서 (b)가 정답이다.

어휘 | productivity n. 생산성, 생산력 cooling device phr. 냉방 장치 pay attention to phr. ~에 주의를 기울이다
temperature control phr. 온도조절 resident n. 거주자, 주민 evaluate v. 검토하다, 평가하다 weather pattern phr. 기후 패턴

65 어휘 유의어 난이도 ●●○

In the context of the passage, observed means _____.

(a) noticed
(b) guaranteed
(c) repeated
(d) confessed

지문의 문맥에서, 'observed'는 -을 의미한다.

(a) 깨달았다
(b) 보장했다
(c) 따라 했다
(d) 시인했다

──○ 정답 잡는 치트키

밑줄 친 어휘의 유의어를 찾는 문제이므로, observed가 포함된 구절을 읽고 문맥을 파악한다.

해설 | 4단락의 'The researchers observed'는 연구진이 깨달았다는 뜻이므로, observed가 '깨달았다'라는 의미로 사용된 것을 알 수 있다. 따라서 '깨달았다'라는 같은 의미의 (a) noticed가 정답이다.

66 어휘 유의어 난이도 ●○○

In the context of the passage, stressed means _____.

(a) featured
(b) listed
(c) emphasized
(d) enlarged

지문의 문맥에서, 'stressed'는 -을 의미한다.

(a) 특별히 포함했다
(b) 목록을 작성했다
(c) 강조했다
(d) 확장했다

밑줄 친 어휘의 유의어를 찾는 문제이므로, stressed가 포함된 구절을 읽고 문맥을 파악한다.

해설 | 5단락의 'researchers stressed the importance of designing buildings'는 연구진이 건물 설계의 중요성을 강조했다는 뜻이므로, stressed가 '강조했다'라는 의미로 사용된 것을 알 수 있다. 따라서 '강조했다'라는 같은 의미의 (c) emphasized가 정답이다.

PART 3 [67~73] 지식 백과 보로부두르 사원의 특징과 역할

<table>
<tr><td>표제어</td><td colspan="2">BOROBUDUR TEMPLE</td></tr>
</table>

표제어	**BOROBUDUR TEMPLE**	보로부두르 사원
정의	The Borobudur Temple is located in central Java, Indonesia. [67]It is known as the largest Buddhist temple in the world, covering an area of 27,125 square feet and reaching nearly 115 feet in height.	보로부두르 사원은 인도네시아 중앙 자바에 자리 잡고 있다. [67]이곳은 27,125제곱피트에 이르는 면적과 거의 115피트에 달하는 높이로, 세계에서 가장 큰 불교 사원으로 알려져 있다.
건축된 시기	There are no precise records of Borobudur's construction, but most historians estimate that it occurred sometime during the eighth or ninth century. [68]The temple was initially a site for Buddhist pilgrimage and rituals, but it was abandoned for nearly 400 years, beginning around the time Islam became the dominant religion in Indonesia. In 1814, the temple was rediscovered by British explorers. However, it was almost completely hidden by ash from a nearby volcano and needed major rebuilding.	보로부두르의 건축에 대한 정확한 기록은 없지만, 대부분의 역사가는 8세기 또는 9세기 중 어느 시점에 건축된 것으로 추정한다. [68]이 사원은 처음에 불교 순례와 의식을 위한 장소였지만, 이슬람교가 인도네시아에서 지배적인 종교가 될 무렵부터, 거의 400년 동안 버려져 있었다. 1814년에, 이 사원은 영국 탐험가들에 의해 재발견되었다. 그러나, 이곳은 인근 화산의 화산재에 의해 거의 완전히 가려져 대대적인 재건이 필요했다.
복원 프로젝트	[69]In 1907, a team began restoring the temple but ran into several costly architectural problems and had to contend with artifacts being frequently stolen from the site. [69/72]The project was <u>suspended</u>, and it was only in 1983 that a second restoration project was completed, with the help of monetary donations from five other countries.	[69]1907년에, 한 팀이 그 사원을 복원하기 시작했지만 몇몇 큰 비용이 드는 건축 문제를 겪었고 그 장소에서 공예품들이 자주 도난당하는 것과 씨름해야 했다. [69/72]이 프로젝트는 중단되었고, 1983년에야 다른 다섯 개국의 금전적 기부금에 힘입어, 두 번째 복원 프로젝트가 완료되었다.
구조	The temple was rebuilt with many of its original stones. It is shaped like a pyramid and contains several levels: a square base with five square terraces and three circular platforms, all stacked on top of each other. [70(c)]There is a large, dome-shaped structure at the top called a "stupa," a Buddhist place of burial that typically contains religious objects.	이 사원은 원래의 많은 돌로 재건되었다. 이곳은 피라미드처럼 생겼고 정사각형 바닥에 다섯 개의 정사각형 테라스와 세 개의 원형 연단이 서로 포개어진 여러 층으로 이루어져 있다. [70(c)]꼭대기에는 "스투파"라고 불리는 커다란 돔 모양의 구조물이 있는데, 일반적으로 종교적인 물건을 포함하는 불교의 매장 장소이다.
층별 특징	Each level of the temple represents a step on the journey to enlightenment. [70(a)]The lowest level features carved depictions of human desires, while [70(b)]the next few levels show the life of Buddha and Buddhist writings. Farther up, the circular platforms have several smaller	사원의 각 층은 깨달음을 향한 여정의 단계를 나타낸다. [70(a)]가장 낮은 층은 인간 욕망의 조각품을 특징으로 하지만, [70(b)]다음 몇 개의 층은 부처의 생애와 법문을 보여준다. 더 위로, 원형 연단에는 여러 개의 작은

stupas, many with a hidden Buddha statue still inside. The lack of decoration in the upper levels signifies detachment from the material world.

탑이 있는데, 많은 곳에서 그 안에 여전히 숨겨진 불상이 있다. 위층에 장식이 없는 것은 물질세계로부터의 분리를 의미한다.

[71]Visitors can go through each of the nine levels, starting at the bottom and gradually walking clockwise around the monument to the last stupa at the highest level, which represents enlightenment. Today, the Borobudur Temple is once again a popular site of pilgrimage. It [73]holds cultural and religious significance and is recognized by UNESCO as a World Heritage Site.

[71]방문객들은 아래쪽부터 시작하여 기념물의 주변을 시계 방향으로 서서히 걸어가면서, 깨달음을 상징하는 가장 높은 층의 마지막 탑까지 아홉 개의 각 층을 통과할 수 있다. 오늘날, 보로부두르 사원은 다시 한 번 인기 있는 순례지이다. 그것은 [73]문화적이면서 종교적인 중요성을 지니며 유네스코에 의해 세계 문화유산으로 인정되었다.

역할 및 중요성

어휘 | temple n. 사원, 절 Buddhist adj. 불교의, 부처의 construction n. 건축, 건설 historian n. 역사가 estimate v. 추정하다 pilgrimage n. 순례; v. 순례하다 ritual n. 의식, 제사 abandon v. 버리다, 포기하다 dominant adj. 지배적인, 우세한 religion n. 종교, 신앙 ash n. 화산재, 재 rebuild v. 재건하다, 다시 짓다 restore v. 복원하다 run into phr. (곤경 등을) 겪다 costly adj. 큰 비용이 드는 contend with phr. (곤란한 문제나 상황과) 씨름하다 artifact n. 공예품 monetary adj. 금전(상)의 donation n. 기부(금) level n. 층 circular adj. 원형의 platform n. 연단, 강단 stack v. 포개다, 쌓다 burial n. 매장 typically adv. 일반적으로 religious adj. 종교적인, 종교의 journey n. 여정 enlightenment n. 깨달음 carve v. 조각하다 depiction n. 묘사 desire n. 욕망 Buddhist writings phr. 법문 statue n. (동)상 signify v. 의미하다, 나타내다 detachment n. 분리 material world phr. 물질세계 clockwise adv. 시계 방향으로 monument n. 기념물, 기념비 significance n. 중요성 recognize v. 인정하다 World Heritage Site phr. 세계 문화유산

---

67 특정세부사항 What

난이도 ●●○

What is most significant about the Borobudur Temple?

보로부두르 사원에 관한 가장 중요한 점은 무엇인가?

(a) its status as a sizeable religious monument
(b) its standing as the oldest temple in the world
(c) its history of mysterious construction
(d) its ranking as the world's most beautiful temple

(a) 상당한 크기의 종교적 기념물의 지위
(b) 세계에서 가장 오래된 사원의 지위
(c) 불가사의한 건축의 역사
(d) 세계에서 가장 아름다운 사원으로서의 순위

━○ 정답 잡는 치트키

질문의 키워드 most significant와 관련된 주변 내용을 주의 깊게 읽는다.

해설 | 1단락의 'It is known as the largest Buddhist temple in the world, covering an area of 27,125 square feet and reaching nearly 115 feet in height.'에서 이곳은 27,125제곱피트에 이르는 면적과 거의 115피트에 달하는 높이로, 세계에서 가장 큰 불교 사원으로 알려져 있다고 했다. 따라서 (a)가 정답이다.

⮂ Paraphrasing
the largest Buddhist temple 가장 큰 불교 사원 → a sizeable religious monument 상당한 크기의 종교적 기념물

어휘 | status n. 지위, 중요도 sizeable adj. 상당한 크기의, 꽤 큰 standing n. 지위 mysterious adj. 불가사의한 ranking n. 순위, 위치

---

68 추론 특정사실

난이도 ●●○

Why, most likely, was the Borobudur Temple abandoned?

보로부두르 사원은 왜 버려졌을 것 같은가?

(a) because its primary caregiver passed away
(b) because religious practices became forbidden
(c) because its visitors converted to a different faith
(d) because a volcanic eruption led to evacuations

(a) 주 관리인이 사망했기 때문에
(b) 종교적 관습이 금지되었기 때문에
(c) 방문객들이 다른 신앙으로 개종했기 때문에
(d) 화산 폭발로 인해 대피가 이루어졌기 때문에

─○ 정답 잡는 치트키

질문의 키워드 abandoned가 그대로 언급된 주변 내용을 주의 깊게 읽는다.

해설 | 2단락의 'The temple was initially a site for Buddhist pilgrimage and rituals, but it was abandoned for nearly 400 years, beginning around the time Islam became the dominant religion in Indonesia.'에서 이 사원은 처음에 불교 순례와 의식을 위한 장소였지만, 이슬람교가 인도네시아에서 지배적인 종교가 될 무렵부터 거의 400년 동안 버려져 있었다고 한 것을 통해, 이슬람교가 인도네시아에서 지배적인 종교가 되자 보로부두르 사원의 방문객들이 불교에서 이슬람교로 개종하면서 사원이 버려져 있었음을 추론할 수 있다. 따라서 (c)가 정답이다.

> **오답분석**
> (b) 2단락에서 이슬람교가 인도네시아에서 지배적인 종교가 되었다고는 언급했지만, 이에 따라 종교적 관습이 금지되었는지는 언급되지 않았으므로 오답이다.

어휘 | primary adj. 주된, 주요한 caregiver n. 돌보는 사람 pass away phr. 사망하다 practice n. 관습 forbidden adj. 금지된 convert to phr. ~으로 개종하다 faith n. 신앙 volcanic eruption phr. 화산 폭발 evacuation n. 대피, 피난

---

69 추론 특정사실
난이도 ●●○

Why, most likely, was the initial restoration project discontinued?

(a) It made the construction team vulnerable to injury.
(b) It made the site vulnerable to severe weather.
(c) The damage was too severe to fix.
(d) The damage was too costly to fix.

초기 복원 프로젝트는 왜 중단되었을 것 같은가?

(a) 건설팀을 부상에 취약하게 만들었다.
(b) 현장을 험한 날씨에 취약하게 만들었다.
(c) 손상은 수리하기에 너무 심각했다.
(d) 손상은 수리하기에 비용이 너무 많이 들었다.

─○ 정답 잡는 치트키

질문의 키워드 restoration project가 restoring the temple로, discontinued가 suspended로 paraphrasing되어 언급된 주변 내용을 주의 깊게 읽는다.

해설 | 3단락의 'In 1907, a team began restoring the temple but ran into several costly architectural problems'에서 1907년에 한 팀이 그 사원을 복원하기 시작했지만 몇몇 큰 비용이 드는 건축 문제를 겪었다고 한 뒤, 'The project was suspended, and it was only in 1983 that a second restoration project was completed, with the help of monetary donations from five other countries.'에서 이 프로젝트는 중단되었고, 1983년에야 다른 다섯 개국의 금전적 기부금에 힘입어 두 번째 복원 프로젝트가 완료되었다고 한 것을 통해, 초기 복원 프로젝트는 손상을 수리하는 데 비용이 너무 많이 들어서 중단되었음을 추론할 수 있다. 따라서 (d)가 정답이다.

어휘 | discontinue v. 중단하다 vulnerable to phr. ~에 취약한, 피해를 보기 쉬운 severe weather phr. 험한 날씨

70 Not/True 　　Not 문제

What CANNOT be found at the temple?

(a) carvings illustrating human desires
(b) images representing religious scenes
(c) figures inside domed structures
(d) **texts praising benefits of the physical world**

사원에서 찾을 수 없는 것은 무엇인가?

(a) 인간의 욕망을 묘사한 조각품
(b) 종교적 장면을 나타내는 이미지
(c) 돔형 구조물 내의 형체
(d) **물질계의 혜택을 찬양하는 글**

━○ 정답 잡는 치트키

질문의 키워드 found at the temple과 관련된 주변 내용을 주의 깊게 읽고, 보기의 키워드와 지문 내용을 대조하며 언급되는 것을 하나씩 소거한다.

해설 | (d)는 지문에 언급되지 않았으므로, (d)가 정답이다.

　　오답분석

(a) 보기의 키워드 human desires가 그대로 언급된 5단락에서 가장 낮은 층은 인간 욕망의 조각품을 특징으로 한다고 언급되었다.
(b) 보기의 키워드 religious scenes가 life of Buddha and Buddhist writings로 paraphrasing되어 언급된 5단락에서 다음 몇 개의 층은 부처의 생애와 법문을 보여준다고 언급되었다.
(c) 보기의 키워드 domed structures가 dome-shaped structure로 paraphrasing되어 언급된 4단락에서 꼭대기에는 "스투파"라고 불리는 커다란 돔 모양의 구조물이 있는데, 일반적으로 종교적인 물건을 포함하는 불교의 매장 장소라고 언급되었다.

어휘 | carving n. 조각품　scene n. 장면, 상황　figures n. 형체, 형상　physical world phr. 물질계

71 특정세부사항 　　How

How does the temple embody the Buddhist concept of movement toward spiritual insight?

(a) **by having visitors progress upward**
(b) by welcoming visitors with a message of inclusion
(c) by guiding visitors in a circular path
(d) by leading visitors deeper into the monument

사원은 어떻게 영적 통찰을 향한 움직임이라는 불교의 개념을 구체화하는가?

(a) **방문객들을 위로 나아가도록 함으로써**
(b) 방문객들을 포용의 메시지로 맞이함으로써
(c) 방문객들을 원형 경로로 안내함으로써
(d) 방문객들을 기념물 안으로 더 깊숙이 안내함으로써

━○ 정답 잡는 치트키

질문의 키워드 spiritual insight가 enlightenment로 paraphrasing되어 언급된 주변 내용을 주의 깊게 읽는다.

해설 | 6단락의 'Visitors can go through each of the nine levels, starting at the bottom and gradually walking clockwise around the monument to the last stupa at the highest level, which represents enlightenment.'에서 방문객들은 아래쪽부터 시작하여 기념물의 주변을 시계 방향으로 서서히 걸어가면서 깨달음을 상징하는 가장 높은 층의 마지막 탑까지 아홉 개의 각 층을 통과할 수 있다고 했다. 따라서 (a)가 정답이다.

　　오답분석

(c) 6단락에서 방문객들이 아래쪽부터 시작하여 시계 방향으로 걸어가면서 깨달음을 상징하는 가장 높은 층의 마지막 탑까지 오르는 것을 언급하기는 했지만, 방문객들을 원형 경로로 안내하는 것만으로 영적 통찰을 구체화할 수 있는 것은 아니므로 오답이다.

어휘 | embody v. 구체화하다, 구현하다　spiritual adj. 영적인, 정신의　insight n. 통찰, 식견　progress v. 나아가다, 이동하다
inclusion n. 포용, 통합　path n. 경로, 방향

72 어휘 유의어

In the context of the passage, <u>suspended</u> means _____.

(a) hung
(b) paused
(c) punished
(d) born

지문의 문맥에서, 'suspended'는 -을 의미한다.

(a) 정체된
(h) 중단된
(c) 처벌된
(d) 생긴

◆○ 정답 잡는 치트키

밑줄 친 어휘의 유의어를 찾는 문제이므로, suspended가 포함된 구절을 읽고 문맥을 파악한다.

해설 | 3단락의 'The project was suspended'는 이 프로젝트가 중단되었다는 뜻이므로, suspended가 '중단된'이라는 의미로 사용된 것을 알 수 있다. 따라서 '중단된'이라는 같은 의미의 (b) paused가 정답이다.

73 어휘 유의어
난이도 ●○○

In the context of the passage, <u>holds</u> means _____.

(a) conducts
(b) finds
(c) takes
(d) carries

지문의 문맥에서, 'holds'는 -을 의미한다.

(a) 실시한다
(b) 찾는다
(c) 가지고 간다
(d) 지닌다

◆○ 정답 잡는 치트키

밑줄 친 어휘의 유의어를 찾는 문제이므로, holds가 포함된 구절을 읽고 문맥을 파악한다.

해설 | 6단락의 'holds cultural and religious significance'는 문화적이면서 종교적인 중요성을 지닌다는 뜻이므로, holds가 '지닌다'라는 의미로 사용된 것을 알 수 있다. 따라서 '지닌다'라는 같은 의미의 (d) carries가 정답이다.

PART 4 [74~80] 비즈니스 편지 연구 보조금을 신청하는 편지

수신인 정보	Leia Summerhold Funding Manager American Literary Research Society 728 Oak Lawn Cook County, IL Dear Ms. Summerhold:	Leia Summerhold 자금 관리자 미국 문학 연구 협회 오크 론 728번지 일리노이주 쿡 카운티 Ms. Summerhold께:
편지의 목적: 연구 보조금 신청	I am an American Studies PhD student specializing in American literature, art, and culture at Longmore University. [74]I am writing this letter to apply for a one-time research grant of $5,000 for my dissertation.	저는 Longmore 대학교에서 미국 문학, 예술, 문화를 전공하는 미국학 박사과정 학생입니다. [74]저는 논문을 위해 5,000달러의 일회성 연구 보조금을 신청하기 위

TEST 4 READING & VOCABULARY **203**

	My research is titled "Working-Class Narratives in American Music."	해 이 편지를 씁니다. 저의 연구 제목은 "미국 음악에서 노동자 계층 묘사"입니다.
논문 내용	[75]My research is about how the American working class influences certain pieces of music. From rhythmic folk songs to more radical modern anthems, music has historically been a valuable reflection of workers' lives. [75]My dissertation aims to examine how certain songs can be used to [79]trace the experiences of the working class to as far back as the late 1800s.	[75]제 연구는 미국 노동자 계층이 특정 음악에 어떤 영향을 미치는지에 관한 것입니다. 율동적인 민속 음악부터 더욱 급진적인 현대 노래에 이르기까지, 음악은 역사적으로 노동자의 삶을 반영하는 중요한 것이었습니다. [75]제 논문은 1800년대 후반까지 거슬러 올라가 [79]노동자 계층의 경험을 추적하는 데 특정 노래가 어떻게 사용될 수 있는지 조사하는 것을 목표로 합니다.
예상 되는 긍정적 효과	[76]I believe my dissertation is in line with your institution's mission to document and expand understanding of different American literary movements. Throughout history, music has been closely linked to poetry, in particular. Given that [80]strong connection between literature and music, my dissertation will allow for greater understanding of the role of the working class in the evolution of both types of art over the years.	[76]저의 논문은 미국의 다양한 문학 운동을 기록하고 이해를 넓히려는 귀 기관의 사명과 비슷하다고 생각합니다. 역사를 통틀어, 음악은 특히 시와 밀접하게 관련되어 왔습니다. [80]문학과 음악 사이의 밀접한 연관성을 고려할 때, 저의 논문은 수년에 걸쳐 두 유형의 예술이 진화하는 과정에서 노동자 계층의 역할을 더 잘 이해할 수 있게 해 줄 것입니다.
회신 요청 + 끝인사	[77]Many of the resources related to my research are unavailable through online databases and require paid access. With the help of your grant, I would be able to research the history of music in working-class communities more thoroughly. [78]I have attached my complete research proposal to this letter, which includes details about the methods I will use and the resources I would like to access. I hope that you will consider my application, and I eagerly await your response.	[77]제 연구와 관련 있는 많은 자료는 온라인 데이터베이스를 통해서는 이용할 수 없고 유료 접근이 필요합니다. 지원금이 있다면, 노동자 계층 공동체의 음악사를 더욱 철저히 연구할 수 있을 것입니다. [78]이 편지에 제가 사용할 방법과 접근하고자 하는 자료들에 대한 세부 정보를 포함한 연구 계획서 전체를 첨부했습니다. 제 지원서를 검토해 주시길 바라며, 회신을 간절히 기다리겠습니다.
발신인 정보	Sincerely, *Mike Graves* Mike Graves	Mike Graves 드림

어휘 | specialize in phr. ~을 전공하다 research grant phr. 연구 보조금 dissertation n. 논문 working-class adj. 노동자 계층의 narrative n. 묘사, 이야기 rhythmic adj. 율동적인 folk n. 민속 음악, 민요 radical adj. 급진적인 anthem n. (국가·단체 등에 중요한 의미가 있는) 노래 reflection n. 반영한 것 aim to phr. ~을 목표로 하다 examine v. 조사하다, 검토하다 in line with phr. ~과 비슷한 mission n. 사명, 임무 document v. 기록하다; n. 기록, 문서 literary movement phr. 문학 운동 linked to phr. ~과 관련된 role n. 역할 evolution n. 진화, 변화 related to phr. ~과 관련 있는 access n. 접근 thoroughly adv. 철저하게, 완벽하게 research proposal phr. 연구 계획서 method n. 방법 resource n. 자료, 자원 eagerly adv. 간절히, 고대하여 response n. 회신, 대답

74 주제/목적 편지의 목적   난이도 ●●○

Why is Mike Graves writing a letter to Leia Summerhold?	왜 Mike Graves는 Leia Summerhold에게 편지를 쓰고 있는가?
(a) to apply for admission to a doctoral program (b) to submit his dissertation for approval	(a) 박사 과정에 입학 원서를 제출하기 위해서 (b) 승인을 위해 논문을 제출하기 위해서

(c) to ask for necessary research materials
(d) to request financial support for a project

(c) 필요한 연구 자료를 요청하기 위해서
(d) 프로젝트에 재정적 지원을 요청하기 위해서

해설 | 1단락의 'I am writing this letter to apply for a one-time research grant of $5,000 for my dissertation.'에서 논문을 위해 5,000달러의 일회성 연구 보조금을 신청하기 위해 이 편지를 쓴다고 한 뒤, 논문의 주제 및 예상되는 긍정적 효과에 관해 설명하는 내용이 이어지고 있다. 따라서 (d)가 정답이다.

⇄ **Paraphrasing**
apply for a ~ research grant 연구 보조금을 신청하다 → request financial support 재정적 지원을 요청하다

어휘 | doctoral program phr. 박사 과정 approval n. 승인, 허가

---

75 특정세부사항   What   난이도 ●●●

What is the aim of Mike's research?

(a) to compare different American music genres
(b) to explore the way music is affected by society
(c) to investigate the effects of playing music while working
(d) to trace the origins of American folk music

Mike의 연구 목적은 무엇인가?

(a) 다른 미국 음악 장르를 비교하는 것
(b) 음악이 사회에 의해 영향을 받은 방식을 연구하는 것
(c) 일하는 동안 음악을 듣는 것의 효과를 조사하는 것
(d) 미국 민속 음악의 유래를 추적하는 것

해설 | 2단락의 'My research is about how the American working class influences certain pieces of music.'에서 연구는 미국 노동자 계층이 특정 음악에 어떤 영향을 미치는지에 관한 것이라고 한 뒤, 'My dissertation aims to examine how certain songs can be used to trace the experiences of the working class to as far back as the late 1800s.'에서 논문이 1800년대 후반까지 거슬러 올라가 노동자 계층의 경험을 추적하는 데 특정 노래가 어떻게 사용될 수 있는지 조사하는 것을 목표로 한다고 한 것을 통해, Mike의 연구는 노동지 계층의 경험과 같은 사회적 상횡이 특정 음악에 어떤 영향을 미지는지를 연구하는 것을 목료로 함을 알 수 있다. 따라서 (b)가 정답이다.

어휘 | compare v. 비교하다 investigate v. 조사하다, 살피다 origin n. 유래, 기원

---

76 특정세부사항   How   난이도 ●●●

How is Mike's research objective related to the American Literary Research Society's goal?

(a) Both encourage better understanding of an art form.
(b) Both emphasize the impact of literature on music.

Mike의 연구 목표는 어떻게 미국 문학 연구 협회의 목표와 관련이 있는가?

(a) 둘 다 예술 형식에 대한 더 나은 이해를 장려한다.
(b) 둘 다 문학이 음악에 미치는 영향을 강조한다.

(c) Both honor the contributions of workers to the performing arts.
(d) Both focus on analyzing modern music.

(c) 둘 다 공연 예술에 대한 노동자들의 공헌을 기린다.
(d) 둘 다 현대 음악을 분석하는 데 초점을 맞춘다.

━○ 정답 잡는 치트키

질문의 키워드 related to가 in line with로 paraphrasing되어 언급된 주변 내용을 주의 깊게 읽는다.

해설 | 3단락의 'I believe my dissertation is in line with your institution's mission to ~ expand understanding of different American literary movements.'에서 자신의 논문은 미국의 다양한 문학 운동의 이해를 넓히려는 미국 문학 연구 협회의 사명과 비슷하다고 생각한다고 한 뒤, 'Throughout history, music has been closely linked to poetry, in particular. Given that strong connection ~, my dissertation will allow for greater understanding of the role of the working class in the evolution of both types of art over the years.'에서 역사를 통틀어 음악은 특히 시와 밀접하게 관련되어 왔고, 밀접한 연관성을 고려할 때 자신의 논문은 수년에 걸쳐 두 유형의 예술이 진화하는 과정에서 노동자 계층의 역할을 더 잘 이해할 수 있게 해 줄 것이라고 했다. 이를 통해, Mike의 연구와 미국 문학 연구 협회는 각각 음악과 시라는 두 유형의 예술에 관해 사람들에게 더 나은 이해를 장려하는 것을 목표로 함을 알 수 있다. 따라서 (a)가 정답이다.

어휘 | emphasize v. 강조하다 honor v. ~을 기리다, 존경하다 focus on phr. ~에 초점을 맞추다 analyze v. 분석하다

77 추론 특정사실
난이도 ●●○

According to the letter, why, most likely, does Mike need funding?

(a) so he can view some important resources
(b) so he can visit working-class communities
(c) so he can afford to hire a research assistant
(d) so he can publish his findings independently

편지에 따르면, Mike는 왜 자금이 필요한 것 같은가?

(a) 중요한 자료를 볼 수 있도록
(b) 노동자 계층 공동체를 방문할 수 있도록
(c) 연구 조교를 고용할 여유가 있도록
(d) 연구 결과를 독립적으로 발표할 수 있도록

━○ 정답 잡는 치트키

질문의 키워드 funding이 grant로 paraphrasing되어 언급된 주변 내용을 주의 깊게 읽는다.

해설 | 4단락의 'Many of the resources related to my research are unavailable through online databases and require paid access. With the help of your grant, I would be able to research the history of music in working-class communities more thoroughly.'에서 자신의 연구와 관련 있는 많은 자료는 온라인 데이터베이스를 통해서는 이용할 수 없고 유료 접근이 필요하므로, 지원금이 있다면 노동자 계층 공동체의 음악사를 더욱 철저히 연구할 수 있을 것이라고 한 것을 통해, Mike는 연구를 위한 중요한 자료를 보기 위해 자금이 필요함을 추론할 수 있다. 따라서 (a)가 정답이다.

어휘 | view v. 보다 research assistant phr. 연구 조교 publish v. 발표하다 finding n. (조사·연구 등의) 결과 independently adv. 독립적으로, 남에게 의존하지 않고

78 특정세부사항 What
난이도 ●●○

What did Mike attach to the letter?

(a) a proposal for a second research study
(b) a detailed overview of his research plan

Mike는 편지에 무엇을 첨부했는가?

(a) 두 번째 조사 연구를 위한 제안서
(b) 연구 계획에 대한 상세한 개요

(c) a copy of his completed dissertation
(d) a list of resources he has already consulted

(c) 완성된 논문의 사본
(d) 이미 참고한 자료 목록

●━○ 정답 잡는 치트키

질문의 키워드 attach가 그대로 언급된 주변 내용을 주의 깊게 읽는다.

해설 | 4단락의 'I have attached my complete research proposal to this letter, which includes details about ~ the resources I would like to access.'에서 이 편지에 접근하고자 하는 자료들에 대한 세부 정보를 포함한 연구 계획서 전체를 첨부했다고 했다. 따라서 (b)가 정답이다.

⇄ **Paraphrasing**
research proposal 연구 계획서 → a detailed overview of ~ research plan 연구 계획에 대한 상세한 개요

어휘 | overview n. 개요 consult v. (사전·서적 등을) 참고하다

---

79 어휘   유의어

난이도 ●●○

In the context of the passage, <u>trace</u> means _____.

지문의 문맥에서, 'trace'는 -을 의미한다.

(a) find
(b) chase
(c) follow
(d) draw

(a) 찾다
(b) 쫓아가다
(c) 추적하다
(d) 끌어당기다

●━○ 정답 잡는 치트키

밑줄 친 어휘의 유의어를 찾는 문제이므로, trace가 포함된 구절을 읽고 문맥을 파악한다.

해설 | 2단락의 'trace the experiences of the working class'는 노동자 계층의 경험을 추적한다는 뜻이므로, trace가 '추적하다'라는 의미로 사용된 것을 알 수 있다. 따라서 '추적하다'라는 같은 의미의 (c) follow가 정답이다.

오답분석
(b) '쫓아가다'라는 의미의 chase는 주로 사람·동물을 뒤쫓고 추적할 때 사용하므로, 문맥에 어울리지 않아 오답이다.

---

80 어휘   유의어

난이도 ●○○

In the context of the passage, <u>connection</u> means _____.

지문의 문맥에서, 'connection'은 -을 의미한다.

(a) limit
(b) balance
(c) agreement
(d) relationship

(a) 한계
(b) 균형
(c) 조화
(d) 연관성

●━○ 정답 잡는 치트키

밑줄 친 어휘의 유의어를 찾는 문제이므로, connection이 포함된 구절을 읽고 문맥을 파악한다.

해설 | 3단락의 'strong connection between literature and music'은 문학과 음악 사이의 밀접한 연관성이라는 뜻이므로, connection이 '연관성'이라는 의미로 사용된 것을 알 수 있다. 따라서 '연관성'이라는 같은 의미의 (d) relationship이 정답이다.

공식기출

TEST 5

정답 · 스크립트 · 해석 · 해설

GRAMMAR

LISTENING

READING & VOCABULARY

GRAMMAR _____ / 26 (점수 : _____ 점)
LISTENING _____ / 26 (점수 : _____ 점)
READING & VOCABULARY _____ / 28 (점수 : _____ 점)

TOTAL _____ / 80 (평균 점수 : _____ 점)

*각 영역 점수: 맞은 개수 × 3.75
*평균 점수: 각 영역 점수 합계 ÷ 3

정답 및 취약 유형 분석표

자동 채점 및 성적 분석 서비스 ▶

GRAMMAR

번호	정답	유형
01	b	관계사
02	b	준동사
03	a	조동사
04	d	준동사
05	c	가정법
06	d	시제
07	d	시제
08	c	가정법
09	c	조동사
10	a	연결어
11	b	준동사
12	d	준동사
13	c	시제
14	a	가정법
15	c	연결어
16	b	관계사
17	a	시제
18	a	가정법
19	b	시제
20	b	준동사
21	b	가정법
22	d	조동사
23	d	조동사
24	a	준동사
25	c	시제
26	d	가정법

LISTENING

PART	번호	정답	유형
PART 1	27	c	특정세부사항
	28	c	특정세부사항
	29	a	특정세부사항
	30	d	특정세부사항
	31	b	특정세부사항
	32	b	특정세부사항
	33	c	추론
PART 2	34	a	주제/목적
	35	a	특정세부사항
	36	c	추론
	37	d	특정세부사항
	38	d	특정세부사항
	39	d	특정세부사항
PART 3	40	a	특정세부사항
	41	c	특정세부사항
	42	b	특정세부사항
	43	b	추론
	44	c	특정세부사항
	45	c	추론
PART 4	46	a	주제/목적
	47	b	특정세부사항
	48	d	특정세부사항
	49	a	특정세부사항
	50	c	추론
	51	d	특정세부사항
	52	b	특정세부사항

READING & VOCABULARY

PART	번호	정답	유형
PART 1	53	c	특정세부사항
	54	a	특정세부사항
	55	c	특정세부사항
	56	a	추론
	57	d	특정세부사항
	58	d	어휘
	59	b	어휘
PART 2	60	a	주제/목적
	61	c	특정세부사항
	62	b	Not/True
	63	b	추론
	64	a	추론
	65	d	어휘
	66	c	어휘
PART 3	67	a	특정세부사항
	68	a	Not/True
	69	c	추론
	70	b	특정세부사항
	71	d	특정세부사항
	72	d	어휘
	73	b	어휘
PART 4	74	d	주제/목적
	75	b	특정세부사항
	76	a	추론
	77	d	추론
	78	b	특정세부사항
	79	a	어휘
	80	d	어휘

유형	맞힌 개수
시제	/ 6
가정법	/ 6
준동사	/ 6
조동사	/ 4
연결어	/ 2
관계사	/ 2
TOTAL	/ 26

유형	맞힌 개수
주제/목적	/ 2
특정세부사항	/ 19
Not/True	/ 0
추론	/ 5
TOTAL	/ 26

유형	맞힌 개수
주제/목적	/ 2
특정세부사항	/ 10
Not/True	/ 2
추론	/ 6
어휘	/ 8
TOTAL	/ 28

GRAMMAR

01 관계사   주격 관계대명사 which   난이도 ●●○

Power outages can result from calamities such as thunderstorms and even car crashes. But amusingly, squirrels, _____, are behind many outages in the US, even outnumbering those caused by storms.

(a) who are fond of climbing electric posts
(b) which are fond of climbing electric posts
(c) what are fond of climbing electric posts
(d) that are fond of climbing electric posts

정전은 뇌우와 심지어 자동차 충돌과 같은 재난으로부터 발생할 수 있다. 그러나 재미있게도, 다람쥐는, 전봇대를 오르는 것을 좋아하는데, 미국에서 많은 정전의 배후에 있으며, 심지어 폭풍에 의해 야기된 정전보다 빈도가 더 높다.

지텔프 치트키

동물 선행사가 관계절 안에서 주어 역할을 하고, 빈칸 앞에 콤마(,)가 있으면 주격 관계대명사 which가 정답이다.

해설 | 동물 선행사 squirrels를 받으면서 콤마(,) 뒤에 올 수 있는 주격 관계대명사가 필요하므로, (b) which are fond of climbing electric posts가 정답이다.

오답분석

(d) 관계대명사 that도 동물 선행사를 받을 수 있지만, 콤마 뒤에 올 수 없으므로 오답이다.

어휘 | power outage phr. 정전   calamity n. 재난, 불행   thunderstorm n. 뇌우, 폭풍우   crash n. (자동차·열차 등의) 충돌; v. 충돌하다 amusingly adv. 재미있게, 즐겁게   outnumber v. ~보다 수가 더 많다   be fond of phr. ~을 좋아하다   electric post phr. 전봇대

02 준동사   to 부정사의 진주어 역할   난이도 ●●○

Harriet's dentist says that wisdom tooth extraction can cause pain and soreness for several days after the procedure. He says that it will be best _____ only soft foods after the minor surgery.

(a) having consumed
(b) to consume
(c) consuming
(d) to have consumed

Harriet의 치과 의사는 사랑니 발치가 수술 후 며칠 동안 통증과 아픔을 유발할 수 있다고 말한다. 그는 경미한 수술 후에는 부드러운 음식만 먹는 것이 가장 좋을 것이라고 말한다.

지텔프 치트키

가주어 it이 있으면 to 부정사가 정답이다.

해설 | 빈칸 문장에 있는 that절의 주어 자리에 가주어 it이 있고 문맥상 '부드러운 음식만 먹는 것이 가장 좋을 것이다'라는 의미가 되어야 자연스러우므로, 빈칸에는 동사 will의 진주어인 '먹는 것'이 와야 한다. 따라서 진주어 자리에 올 수 있는 to 부정사 (b) to consume이 정답이다.

어휘 | dentist n. 치과 의사   wisdom tooth phr. 사랑니   extraction n. 발치, 이를 뽑음   soreness n. 아픔   procedure n. 수술 surgery n. 수술   consume v. 먹다

Professor Wiley saw Chelsea texting six times during his lecture. He became so frustrated when he caught her for the seventh time that he demanded she _____ her phone on his desk until class ended.

(a) **leave**
(b) will leave
(c) left
(d) had left

Wiley 교수는 Chelsea가 그의 강의 중에 여섯 번이나 문자를 보내고 있는 것을 보았다. 그는 그녀를 일곱 번째로 발견했을 때 매우 실망해서 그녀에게 수업이 끝날 때까지 그녀의 휴대전화를 그의 책상 위에 <u>둬야 한</u>다고 요구했다.

⟜○ 지텔프 치트키

demand 다음에는 that절에 동사원형이 온다.

☀ **주장·요구·명령·제안을 나타내는 빈출 동사**
demand 요구하다 request 요청하다 recommend 권고하다 suggest 제안하다 order 명령하다 urge 강력히 촉구하다 ask 요청하다
propose 제안하다 insist 주장하다 advise 권고하다

해설 | 빈칸 앞에 요구를 나타내는 동사 demand가 있으므로 빈칸 문장에 있는 that절에는 '(should +) 동사원형'이 와야 한다. 따라서 동사원형 (a) leave가 정답이다.

어휘 | frustrated adj. 실망한, 좌절한

Contrary to popular belief, the color red doesn't make the bulls used in bullfighting angry; bulls are actually colorblind. Rather, they can't resist _____ the matador's cape because of its waving motion.

(a) having attacked
(b) to have attacked
(c) to attack
(d) **attacking**

일반적인 믿음과는 반대로, 빨간색은 투우에 사용되는 황소들을 화나게 하는 것이 아닌데, 황소들은 사실 색맹이다. 오히려, 그들은 그것의 흔들리는 동작 때문에 투우사의 망토를 <u>공격하는 것을</u> 참을 수가 없다.

⟜○ 지텔프 치트키

resist는 동명사를 목적어로 취한다.

☀ **동명사를 목적어로 취하는 빈출 동사**
resist 참다 discuss 논의하다 avoid 피하다 imagine 상상하다 mind 개의하다 keep 계속하다 consider 고려하다
prevent 방지하다 enjoy 즐기다 recommend 권장하다 risk 위험을 무릅쓰다 involve 포함하다

해설 | 빈칸 앞 동사 resist는 동명사를 목적어로 취하므로, 동명사 (d) attacking이 정답이다.

오답분석
(a) having attacked도 동명사이기는 하지만, 완료동명사(having attacked)로 쓰일 경우 '참을 수가 없는' 시점보다 '공격하는' 시점이 앞선다는 것을 나타내므로 문맥에 적합하지 않다.

어휘 | belief n. 믿음, 신념 bull n. 황소 bullfighting n. 투우 colorblind adj. 색맹의 matador n. 투우사 cape n. 망토

When Carl goes on vacation next week, he will be traveling by boat rather than by plane, even though boats are much slower. If he were not afraid of heights, Carl _____ by plane instead.

Carl이 다음 주에 휴가를 갈 때, 비록 배가 훨씬 느리지만, 비행기보다는 배를 타고 여행할 것이다. 만약 그가 높은 곳을 두려워하지 않는다면, Carl은 대신 비행기를 타고 <u>여행할 것이다</u>.

(a) would have traveled
(b) will travel
(c) would travel
(d) will have traveled

⟿○ 지텔프 치트키

'if + 과거 동사'가 있으면 'would/could + 동사원형'이 정답이다.

> 💡 **가정법 과거**
> If + 주어 + 과거 동사, 주어 + would/could(조동사 과거형) + 동사원형

해설 | If절에 과거 동사(were)가 있으므로, 주절에는 이와 짝을 이루어 가정법 과거를 만드는 'would(조동사 과거형) + 동사원형'이 와야 한다. 따라서 (c) would travel이 정답이다.

어휘 | rather than phr. ~보다   heights n. 높은 곳, 고지

---

06 **시제** 과거진행   난이도 ●●○

Jennifer fell asleep on the couch in the middle of the afternoon. She _____ when a moderately strong earthquake started, and she woke up to find that all the books on her shelves were shaking.

Jennifer는 대낮에 소파에서 잠이 들었다. 그녀는 꽤 강한 지진이 시작되었을 때 <u>낮잠을 자고 있던 중이었</u>고, 잠에서 깨서 선반에 있는 모든 책이 흔들리고 있던 중인 것을 발견했다.

(a) would nap
(b) had napped
(c) has been napping
(d) was napping

⟿○ 지텔프 치트키

'for + 기간 표현' 없이 'when + 과거 동사'만 있으면 과거진행 시제가 정답이다.

> 💡 **과거진행과 자주 함께 쓰이는 시간 표현**
> • when / while + 과거 동사 ~했을 때 / ~하던 도중에
> • last + 시간 표현 / yesterday 지난 ~에 / 어제

해설 | 과거진행 시제와 함께 쓰이는 시간 표현 'when + 과거 동사'(when ~ started)가 있고, 꽤 강한 지진이 시작된 과거 시점에 Jennifer는 낮잠을 자고 있던 중이었다는 의미가 되어야 자연스럽다. 따라서 과거진행 시제 (d) was napping이 정답이다.

어휘 | couch n. 소파   moderately adv. 꽤, 적당히   nap v. 낮잠을 자다; n. 낮잠

07 시제 현재완료진행

난이도 ●●○

Poaching has grown so severe in Africa that elephants may be adapting to the situation. Some researchers believe that African elephants _____ to be tuskless since the 1990s to give themselves a better chance of survival.

(a) will have evolved
(b) are evolving
(c) had been evolving
(d) have been evolving

밀렵이 아프리카에서 너무 심해져서 코끼리들이 그 상황에 적응하고 있는 중일지도 모른다. 일부 학자들은 아프리카코끼리들이 1990년대 이래로 자기들에게 더 나은 생존 기회를 주기 위해 엄니가 없는 상태로 진화해 오고 있는 중이라고 믿는다.

━○ 지텔프 치트키

'since + 과거 시점'이 있으면 현재완료진행 시제가 정답이다.

> 💡 현재완료진행과 자주 함께 쓰이는 시간 표현
> • (ever) since + 과거 시점 + (for + 기간 표현) ~한 이래로 (줄곧) (~ 동안)
> • lately / for + 기간 표현 + now 최근에 / 현재 ~ 동안

해설 | 현재완료진행 시제와 함께 쓰이는 시간 표현 'since + 과거 시점'(since the 1990s)이 있고, 문맥상 과거 시점인 1990년대부터 현재까지 계속해서 아프리카코끼리들이 엄니가 없는 상태로 진화해 오고 있는 중이라는 의미가 되어야 자연스럽다. 따라서 현재완료진행 시제 (d) have been evolving이 정답이다.

어휘 | poaching n. 밀렵, 포획 adapt v. 적응하다 tuskless adj. 엄니가 없는 survival n. 생존 evolve v. 진화하다, 변하다

08 가정법 가정법 과거완료

난이도 ●●○

While Gary was swimming, he developed a muscle cramp in his thigh and began sinking into the pool. Fortunately, a lifeguard noticed and rescued him. If it had not been for that lifeguard, Gary _____.

(a) will drown
(b) could drown
(c) could have drowned
(d) will have drowned

Gary가 수영하고 있던 중인 동안, 그는 허벅지에 근육 경련이 생겼고 수영장으로 가라앉기 시작했다. 다행히도, 인명구조 요원이 그를 알아차렸고 구조했다. 만약 그 인명구조 요원이 없었다면, Gary는 익사할 수도 있었을 것이다.

━○ 지텔프 치트키

'if + had p.p.'가 있으면 'would/could + have p.p.'가 정답이다.

> 💡 가정법 과거완료
> If + 주어 + had p.p., 주어 + would/could(조동사 과거형) + have p.p.

해설 | If절에 'had p.p.' 형태의 had not been이 있으므로, 주절에는 이와 짝을 이루어 가정법 과거완료를 만드는 'could(조동사 과거형) + have p.p.'가 와야 한다. 따라서 (c) could have drowned가 정답이다.

어휘 | cramp n. (근육에 생기는) 경련 thigh n. 허벅지 sink into phr. ~으로 가라앉다 lifeguard n. 인명구조 요원 rescue v. 구조하다 drown v. 익사하다

The blue whale is the largest animal ever to have lived. There are reports of individuals up to thirty-three meters in length, and the blue whale's tongue _____ weigh as much as an elephant.

(a) should
(b) must
(c) can
(d) will

대왕고래는 지금까지 살았던 것 중 가장 큰 동물이다. 길이가 33미터에 이르는 개체들에 관한 보고가 있고, 대왕고래의 혀는 코끼리 한 마리만큼 무게가 나갈 <u>수 있다</u>.

◎─○ 지텔프 치트키

'~할 수 있다'라고 말할 때는 can을 쓴다.

해설ㅣ 문맥상 대왕고래는 길이가 33미터에 이르기도 하고, 그들의 혀는 코끼리 한 마리만큼 무게가 나갈 수 있다는 의미가 되어야 자연스러우므로, '~할 수 있다'를 뜻하면서 가능성을 나타내는 조동사 (c) can이 정답이다.

어휘ㅣ blue whale phr. 대왕고래   tongue n. 혀

The oldest computer virus, called Creeper, was created as an experiment to prove that it was possible to make self-replicating applications. _____ modern computer viruses are harmful, Creeper never actually damaged any computers.

(a) Although
(b) Because
(c) In case
(d) Unless

가장 오래된 컴퓨터 바이러스인 Creeper는 자기복제 응용프로그램을 만드는 것이 가능하다는 것을 증명하기 위한 실험으로 만들어졌다. 현대의 컴퓨터 바이러스는 해로움에도 불구하고, Creeper는 실제로 어떤 컴퓨터도 손상시키지 않았다.

◎─○ 지텔프 치트키

'~에도 불구하고'라는 의미의 양보를 나타낼 때는 although를 쓴다.

> 💡 **양보를 나타내는 빈출 접속사**
> although ~에도 불구하고   even though ~에도 불구하고   while ~이긴 하지만

해설ㅣ 문맥상 현대의 컴퓨터 바이러스는 해로움에도 불구하고, Creeper는 실제로 어떤 컴퓨터도 손상시키지 않았다는 의미가 되어야 자연스럽다. 따라서 '~에도 불구하고'라는 의미의 양보를 나타내는 부사절 접속사 (a) Although가 정답이다.

> 오답분석
> (b) Because는 '~ 때문에', (c) In case는 '~할 경우에 대비하여', (d) Unless는 '~하지 않는 한'이라는 의미로, 문맥에 적합하지 않아 오답이다.

어휘ㅣ self-replicating adj. 자기복제의   harmful adj. 해로운, 유해한   damage v. 손상하다

준동사   to 부정사의 부사 역할   난이도 ●●○

In Longyearbyen, Norway, the climate is so cold that conditions are impractical for burial. That's why locals who pass away are sent _____ in cemeteries on the mainland.

(a) having been buried
(b) to be buried
(c) to have been buried
(d) being buried

노르웨이 롱위에아르뷔엔에서는 날씨가 너무 추워서 조건이 매장하기에는 비현실적이다. 그것이 죽은 현지인들이 본토의 묘지에 <u>매장되기 위해</u> 보내지는 이유이다.

━○ **지텔프 치트키**

'~하기 위해'라고 말할 때는 to 부정사를 쓴다.

해설 | 빈칸 앞에 주어(locals)와 동사(are sent)가 갖춰진 완전한 절이 있으므로, 빈칸 이하는 문장의 필수 성분이 아닌 수식어구이다. 따라서 목적을 나타내며 수식어구를 이끌 수 있는 to 부정사 (b) to be buried가 정답이다.

어휘 | impractical adj. 비현실적인   burial n. 매장   local n. 현지인, 주민; adj. 현지의   pass away phr. 죽다   cemetery n. 묘지, 무덤   mainland n. 본토, 대륙   bury v. 매장하다

---

12 **준동사**   동명사를 목적어로 취하는 동사   난이도 ●●○

In addition to being a rich source of potassium, bananas provide much of the vitamin B6 and fiber we need in our diets. So, people who enjoy _____ bananas receive many health benefits.

(a) to have eaten
(b) to eat
(c) having eaten
(d) eating

칼륨의 풍부한 공급원이 될 뿐만 아니라, 바나나는 우리의 식단에 필요한 비타민 B6와 섬유질을 많이 제공한다. 그래서, 바나나 <u>먹는 것을</u> 즐기는 사람들은 많은 건강상의 이익을 누린다.

━○ **지텔프 치트키**

enjoy는 동명사를 목적어로 취한다.

해설 | 빈칸 앞 동사 enjoy는 동명사를 목적어로 취하므로, 동명사 (d) eating이 정답이다.

오답분석

(c) having eaten도 동명사이기는 하지만, 완료동사(having eaten)로 쓰일 경우 '즐기는' 시점보다 '먹는' 시점이 앞선다는 것을 나타내므로 문맥에 적합하지 않다.

어휘 | potassium n. 칼륨   fiber n. 섬유질   diet n. 식단, 음식

13 시제 미래진행

After months of hesitation, Eugene finally asked his officemate Sherry out for dinner. He finishes before her today, but he _____ for her by the building's entrance when her work shift ends at 7:30 p.m.

(a) waits
(b) would wait
(c) will be waiting
(d) was waiting

몇 달간의 망설임 끝에, Eugene은 마침내 사무실 동료인 Sherry에게 저녁 식사를 같이하자고 했다. 그는 오늘 그녀보다 먼저 마치지만, 오후 7시 30분에 그녀의 근무 시간이 끝날 때 건물 입구에서 그녀를 기다리고 있는 중일 것이다.

━━○ 지텔프 치트키

'for + 기간 표현' 없이 'when + 현재 동사'만 있으면 미래진행 시제가 정답이다.

> 💡 **미래진행과 자주 함께 쓰이는 시간 표현**
> • when / if + 현재 동사 ~할 때 / 만약 ~한다면
> • next + 시간 표현 다음 ~에
> • until / by + 미래 시점 ~까지
> • starting + 미래 시점 / tomorrow ~부터 / 내일

해설 | 현재 동사로 미래의 의미를 나타내는 시간의 부사절 'when + 현재 동사'(when ~ ends)가 있고, 문맥상 미래 시점인 오후 7시 30분에 Eugene은 Sherry의 근무 시간이 끝날 때 건물 입구에서 그녀를 기다리고 있는 중일 것이라는 의미가 되어야 자연스럽다. 따라서 미래진행 시제 (c) will be waiting이 정답이다.

어휘 | hesitation n. 망설임, 주저

---

14 가정법 가정법 과거

The theme of nature reclaiming Earth's cities is prevalent in apocalyptic science fiction. According to the book *The World Without Us*, if humans were to disappear, vegetation _____ manmade structures as plants re-establish their dominance.

(a) would replace
(b) will replace
(c) will have replaced
(d) would have replaced

자연이 지구의 도시들을 되찾는다는 주제는 종말론적인 공상 과학 소설에서 일반적이다. 책 *The World Without Us*에 따르면, 만약 인간이 사라진다면, 초목이 그들의 지배를 회복함에 따라 초목은 인공적인 구조물들을 대체할 것이다.

━━○ 지텔프 치트키

'if + were to + 동사원형'이 있으면 'would/could + 동사원형'이 정답이다.

> 💡 **가정법 과거(were to)**
> If + 주어 + were to + 동사원형, 주어 + would/could(조동사 과거형) + 동사원형

해설 | if절에 과거 동사(were to disappear)가 있으므로, 주절에는 이와 짝을 이루어 가정법 과거를 만드는 'would(조동사 과거형) + 동사원형'이 와야 한다. 따라서 (a) would replace가 정답이다.

어휘 | reclaim v. 되찾다 prevalent adj. 일반적인, 널리 퍼진 apocalyptic adj. 종말론적인 science fiction phr. 공상 과학 소설 vegetation n. 초목, 식물 manmade adj. 인공의, 사람이 만든 re-establish v. ~을 회복하다, 재건하다 dominance n. 지배

The commercially successful cellphone game *Flappy Bird* was once criticized for some of its unoriginal features. _____, the game was rumored to have been taken down because of plagiarism. That accusation was later proven false.

(a) Meanwhile
(b) However
(c) In fact
(d) In other words

상업적으로 성공한 휴대전화 게임 *Flappy Bird*는 그것의 독창적이지 않은 기능 중 일부로 한때 비판을 받았다. 실제로, 그 게임은 표절 때문에 중단되었다는 소문이 있었냐. 그 비난는 나중에 거짓으로 판명되었다.

해설 | 문맥상 *Flappy Bird*는 그것의 독창적이지 않은 기능 중 일부로 한때 비판을 받았다는 앞 문장의 내용을 강조하여 '실제로, 그 게임은 표절 때문에 중단되었다는 소문이 있었다'라는 의미가 되어야 자연스럽다. 따라서 '실제로'라는 의미의 강조를 나타내는 접속부사 (c) In fact가 정답이다.

오답분석
(a) Meanwhile은 '그동안에', (b) However는 '그러나', (d) In other words는 '다시 말해서'라는 의미로, 문맥에 적합하지 않아 오답이다.

어휘 | commercially adv. 상업적으로　criticize v. 비판하다, 비난하다　unoriginal adj. 독창적이 아닌, 본래의 것이 아닌　feature n. 기능, 특징; v. ~의 특징을 이루다　rumor v. 소문내다; n. 소문　take down phr. 중단하다, 제거하다　plagiarism n. 표절　accusation n. 비난　false adj. 거짓의, 틀린

Samantha fully understands the responsibilities outlined in her new contract. The only detail _____ is how many weeks of paid vacation she will be entitled to each year.

(a) where is still unclear
(b) that is still unclear
(c) who is still unclear
(d) what is still unclear

Samantha는 새 계약서에 약술된 채무들을 완전히 이해한다. 아직도 명확하지 않은 유일한 항목은 그녀가 매년 몇 주의 유급 휴가를 받을 자격이 있을 것인지이다.

해설 | 사물 선행사 detail을 받으면서 보기의 관계절 내에서 동사 is의 주어가 될 수 있는 주격 관계대명사가 필요하므로, (b) that is still unclear가 정답이다.

어휘 | responsibility n. 채무, 책임　outline v. ~을 약술하다, ~의 요점을 말하다　contract n. 계약(서)　paid vacation phr. 유급 휴가　be entitled to phr. ~을 받을 자격이 있다

When Steve Irwin died from a stingray attack in 2006, shock could be felt around the globe. The seemingly fearless zookeeper, known as "The Crocodile Hunter," _____ exotic animals since 1992.

(a) **had been documenting**
(b) documented
(c) has been documenting
(d) would document

Steve Irwin이 2006년에 노랑가오리의 공격으로 죽었을 때, 전 세계적으로 충격이 느껴질 수 있었다. "악어 사냥꾼"으로 알려진, 겉보기에 겁 없는 이 사육사는 1992년 이래로 이국적인 동물들을 <u>기록해 오고 있던 중이었다</u>.

━━○ 지텔프 치트키

'since + 과거 동사/시점'이 있으면 과거완료진행 시제가 정답이다.

> 💡 **과거완료진행과 자주 함께 쓰이는 시간 표현**
> • before / when / since + 과거 동사 + (for + 기간 표현) ~하기 전에 / ~했을 때 / ~ 이래로 (~ 동안)
> • (for + 기간 표현) + (up) until + 과거 동사 (~ 동안) ~했을 때까지

해설 | 과거완료진행 시제와 함께 쓰이는 시간 표현 'since + 과거 동사/시점'(since 1992)이 있고, 문맥상 대과거(1992년)부터 과거(2006년에 죽기 전)까지 Steve Irwin이 이국적인 동물들을 기록해 오고 있던 중이었다는 의미가 되어야 자연스럽다. 따라서 과거완료진행 시제 (a) had been documenting이 정답이다.

> **오답분석**
> (c) has been documenting은 'since + 과거 시점'이 있으면 현재완료진행 시제가 정답인 경우가 많기는 하지만, 문맥상 Steve Irwin이 이국적인 동물들을 기록해 오고 있는 것이 현재까지 계속해서 일어나고 있는 일이 아니므로 오답이다.

어휘 | stingray n. 노랑가오리   seemingly adv. 겉보기에는   fearless adj. 겁 없는, 무서워하지 않는   zookeeper n. 사육사
exotic adj. 이국적인, 외국의   document v. (상세한 내용을) 기록하다; n. 서류, 문서

---

18 **가정법** 가정법 과거   난이도 ●●○

Wallace's Alehouse burned down last night. Wallace's girlfriend, who just returned from a trip, is coming to stay with him. If it weren't for her support, he _____ difficulty handling his grief in the days ahead.

(a) **would have**
(b) will have
(c) will have had
(d) would have had

어젯밤 Wallace의 선술집이 불에 타버렸다. Wallace의 여자 친구는, 여행에서 막 돌아와서, 그와 함께 지낼 것이다. 만약 그녀의 도움이 아니었다면, 그는 앞으로 며칠 동안 자기의 슬픔을 다스리는 데 어려움을 <u>겪을 것이다</u>.

━━○ 지텔프 치트키

'if + 과거 동사'가 있으면 'would/could + 동사원형'이 정답이다.

해설 | If절에 과거 동사(weren't)가 있으므로, 주절에는 이와 짝을 이루어 가정법 과거를 만드는 'would(조동사 과거형) + 동사원형'이 와야 한다. 따라서 (a) would have가 정답이다.

어휘 | alehouse n. 선술집, 맥줏집   burn down phr. (건물 등을) 태우다   handle v. (감정을) 다스리다, 다루다   grief n. 슬픔, 고뇌
ahead adv. 앞으로

Due to insomnia, Nathaniel hasn't been able to sleep since going to bed around 11 p.m. If he remains awake for thirty more minutes, he _____ unsuccessfully to sleep for almost three hours.

불면증 때문에, Nathaniel은 밤 11시쯤 잠자리에 든 이래로 잠을 이루지 못했다. 만약 그가 30분만 더 깨어 있다면, 그는 거의 세 시간 동안 잠을 자려고 헛되이 노력해 오고 있는 중일 것이다.

(a) had tried
(b) will have been trying
(c) has been trying
(d) will be trying

━○ 지텔프 치트키

'if + 현재 동사'와 'for + 기간 표현'이 함께 오면 미래완료진행 시제가 정답이다.

> 💡 미래완료진행과 자주 함께 쓰이는 시간 표현
> • by the time / when / if + 현재 동사 + (for + 기간 표현) ~할 무렵이면 / ~할 때 / 만약 ~한다면 (~ 동안)
> • by / in + 미래 시점 + (for + 기간 표현) ~ 즈음에는 / ~에 (~ 동안)

해설 | 현재 동사로 미래의 의미를 나타내는 조건의 부사절 'if + 현재 동사'(If ~ remains)와 지속을 나타내는 'for + 기간 표현'(for almost three hours)이 있고, Nathaniel이 30분 더 깨어 있는 미래 시점에 그는 거의 세 시간 동안 잠을 자려고 헛되이 노력해 오고 있는 중일 것이라는 의미가 되어야 자연스럽다. 따라서 미래완료진행 시제 (b) will have been trying이 정답이다. 참고로, if는 미래진행 시제나 미래완료진행 시제 문제에서 간혹 조건의 부사절을 이끄는 접속사로 사용되기도 한다.

어휘 | insomnia n. 불면증 unsuccessfully adv. 헛되이, 성공적이지 못하게

In 2007, PepsiCo showed responsibility in practicing "corporate citizenship." When an ex-employee of Coca-Cola offered _____ confidential documents to PepsiCo, they notified their rival company, which led to an FBI investigation and the suspect's arrest.

2007년에, PepsiCo는 "기업 시민의식"을 실천하는 데 책임감을 보였다. Coca-Cola의 전 직원이 PepsiCo에 기밀문서를 판매하는 것을 제안했을 때, 그들은 경쟁사에 통보했고, 이것은 FBI 수사와 용의자 체포를 이끌었다.

(a) having sold
(b) to sell
(c) selling
(d) to have sold

━○ 지텔프 치트키

offer는 to 부정사를 목적어로 취한다.

> 💡 to 부정사를 목적어로 취하는 빈출 동사
> offer 제안하다 decide 결정하다 promise 약속하다 expect 예상하다 vow 맹세하다 wish 희망하다 plan 계획하다 hope 바라다
> agree 동의하다 intend 계획하다 prepare 준비하다

해설 | 빈칸 앞 동사 offer는 to 부정사를 목적어로 취하므로, to 부정사 (b) to sell이 정답이다.

오답분석

(d) to have sold도 to 부정사이기는 하지만, 완료부정사(to have sold)로 쓰일 경우 '제안하는' 시점보다 '판매하는' 시점이 앞선다는 것을 나타내므로 문맥에 적합하지 않아 오답이다.

어휘 | **corporate citizenship** phr. 기업 시민의식 **confidential** adj. 기밀의, 비밀의 **rival company** phr. 경쟁사 **investigation** n. 수사, 조사 **suspect** n. 용의자; v. 의심하다 **arrest** n. 체포; v. 체포하다

21 가정법   가정법 과거   난이도 ●●○

Margaret has been allergic to peanut butter since she was a baby. If she were to try eating it today as an adult, the same rash _____ again. This time, it might even be worse.

(a) will probably have occurred
(b) would probably occur
(c) will probably occur
(d) would probably have occurred

Margaret은 아기였을 때부터 땅콩버터에 대해 알레르기 반응이 있어왔다. 만약 그녀가 오늘날 성인이 되어서 그것을 먹는 것을 시도해 본다면, 같은 발진이 <u>아마도</u> 다시 <u>발생할 것이다</u>. 이번에는, 더 심할 수도 있다.

━○ 지텔프 치트키

'if + were to + 동사원형'이 있으면 'would/could + 동사원형'이 정답이다.

해설 | If절에 과거 동사(were to try)가 있으므로, 주절에는 이와 짝을 이루어 가정법 과거를 만드는 'would(조동사 과거형) + 동사원형'이 와야 한다. 따라서 (b) would probably occur가 정답이다.

어휘 | **allergic to** phr. ~에 대해 알레르기 반응이 있는 **rash** n. 발진

22 조동사   조동사 may   난이도 ●○○

When having guests over, Mrs. Rogers's priority is to make the visitors feel at home. She lets her guests know that they _____ help themselves to any of the snacks they find in her kitchen.

(a) shall
(b) will
(c) must
(d) may

손님들을 초대할 때, Mrs. Rogers의 우선 사항은 손님들이 집에 있는 것처럼 편안하게 느끼도록 하는 것이다. 그녀는 손님들에게 주방에서 찾은 간식 중 어떤 것이든 마음껏 먹어도 <u>된다</u>고 알려준다.

━○ 지텔프 치트키

'~해도 된다'라고 말할 때는 may를 쓴다.

해설 | 문맥상 Mrs. Rogers가 손님들에게 주방에서 찾은 간식 중 어떤 것이든 마음껏 먹어도 된다고 알려준다는 의미가 되어야 자연스러우므로, '~해도 된다'를 뜻하면서 허락을 나타내는 조동사 (d) may가 정답이다.

어휘 | **priority** n. 우선 사항

23 조동사   조동사 should 생략

Eleanor has just come out of a five-year relationship and has been feeling down lately. Her best friend advises that she _____ a new hobby so she can keep her mind off the breakup.

Eleanor는 이제 막 5년간의 연애를 끝냈고 최근에 마음이 울적했다. 그녀의 가장 친한 친구는 그녀가 이별을 잊을 수 있기 위해 새로운 취미를 찾아야 한다고 조언한다.

(a) will find
(b) found
(c) has found
(d) find

━○ 지텔프 치트키

advise 다음에는 that절에 동사원형이 온다.

해설 | 주절에 제안을 나타내는 동사 advise가 있으므로 that절에는 '(should +) 동사원형'이 와야 한다. 따라서 동사원형 (d) find가 정답이다.

어휘 | come out of phr. ~에서 나오다   relationship n. 연애   feel down phr. 마음이 울적하다   breakup n. 이별, 불화

24 준동사   동명사를 목적어로 취하는 동사

The earliest record players, called phonographs, did not need electricity in order to play music. Operation of the machine involved _____ a crank until the motor had enough power to keep the turntable spinning.

축음기라고 불리는 초기의 전축들은 곡을 재생하기 위해 전기가 필요하지 않았다. 이 기계의 작동은 모터가 충분한 동력을 얻어 턴테이블을 계속 회전시킬 때까지 L자형 핸들을 돌리는 것을 필요로 했다.

(a) turning
(b) to turn
(c) having turned
(d) to have turned

━○ 지텔프 치트키

involve는 동명사를 목적어로 취한다.

해설 | 빈칸 앞 동사 involve는 동명사를 목적어로 취하므로, 동명사 (a) turning이 정답이다.

오답분석
(c) having turned도 동명사이기는 하지만, 완료동명사(having turned)로 쓰일 경우 '필요로 하는' 시점보다 '돌리는' 시점이 앞선다는 것을 나타내므로 문맥에 적합하지 않아 오답이다.

어휘 | record player phr. 전축   phonograph n. 축음기   operation n. (기계·시스템의) 작동, 운용   crank n. L자형 핸들   turntable n. (음반을 돌리는) 턴테이블   spin v. 회전하다, 돌리다

Tess will be late for her friend's wedding procession because the car broke down on the way to the church. Her husband _____ their car, and they'll try to catch up before the exchange of vows.

(a) now fixed
(b) was now fixing
(c) is now fixing
(d) would now fix

Tess는 교회로 가는 길에 차가 고장 나서 친구의 결혼 행진에 늦을 것이다. 그녀의 남편은 차를 <u>지금 고치고 있는</u> 중이고, 그들은 서약 교환 전에 따라잡기 위해 노력할 것이다.

○— 지텔프 치트키

보기에 now가 있으면 현재진행 시제가 정답이다.

> ☼ **현재진행과 자주 함께 쓰이는 시간 표현**
> · right now / now / currently / at the moment 바로 지금 / 지금 / 현재 / 바로 지금
> · these days / nowadays 요즘

해설 | 보기에 현재진행 시제와 함께 쓰이는 시간 표현 now가 있고, 문맥상 말하고 있는 현재 시점에 차를 고치고 있는 중이라는 의미가 되어야 자연스럽다. 따라서 현재진행 시제 (c) is now fixing이 정답이다.

Political writer Jose Rizal was instrumental in hastening the Philippines' independence from Spanish rule. If it hadn't been for Rizal's patriotic writings, the Filipinos _____ against their colonizers in the 1890s.

(a) would not revolt
(b) will not revolt
(c) will not have revolted
(d) would not have revolted

정치 작가 Jose Rizal은 스페인의 지배로부터 필리핀의 독립을 앞당기는 데 중요한 역할을 했다. 만약 Rizal의 애국적인 글들이 없었다면, 필리핀 사람들은 1890년대에 식민지 개척자들에게 대항하여 <u>반란을 일으키지 않았을 것이다</u>.

○— 지텔프 치트키

'if + had p.p.'가 있으면 'would/could + have p.p.'가 정답이다.

해설 | If절에 'had p.p.' 형태의 hadn't been이 있으므로, 주절에는 이와 짝을 이루어 가정법 과거완료를 만드는 'would(조동사 과거형) + have p.p.'가 와야 한다. 따라서 (d) would not have revolted가 정답이다.

어휘 | instrumental adj. 중요한 hasten v. ~의 (속도·진행 등을) 앞당기다 independence n. 독립, 자립 patriotic adj. 애국적인 colonizer n. 식민지 개척자 revolt v. 반란을 일으키다

TEST 1
TEST 2
TEST 3
TEST 4
TEST 5
TEST 6
TEST 7

PART 1 (27~33) 일상 대화 대학 동창의 결혼 소식에 관한 두 친구의 대화

안부 인사

F: Hi, Jesse. ²⁷Thanks for inviting me to lunch. I really needed a break from work.

M: You're welcome, Abby. ²⁷It's great that our companies are so close together and we can meet up like this. I was ready to get away from all the paperwork.

주제 제시: 대학 친구의 안부

F: Things were simpler when we were in college. Can you believe it's already been a year since we graduated from South Point University?

M: I know, right? Speaking of college life, ²⁸have you talked to our friend Harold since he started working at the insurance company?

F: ²⁸It's been a few months since we caught up, but he seemed to really like his job, and he said his relationship with his girlfriend was going well!

친구의 결혼 소식

M: If it's been a while then I guess you didn't hear that he and his girlfriend are getting married this November!

F: Oh, really? Wow—that's amazing! Tell Harold congratulations the next time you see him.

M: ²⁹Actually, you can tell him yourself because he wants you to come to the wedding. That's part of why I asked you to lunch today. Harold asked me to deliver the invitation—here, I brought it with me.

친구와 여자 친구의 첫만남

F: Thanks, Jesse. I'm so happy for him. Remember how Harold and his girlfriend first met?

M: Of course I do, Abby. ³⁰That was the night the three of us met, at that big party for freshmen.

F: Yes, ³⁰I remember you were wearing a *Battle for the Galaxy* T-shirt, and since Harold and I were obsessed with that TV show, we both went over to talk to you.

M: ³⁰I almost forgot about our shared love of *Battle for the Galaxy*. We really bonded that night. And then Harold saw this girl on the other side of the room and he thought she looked . . . different. Remember? He couldn't really explain it. But he felt there was just something special about her . . .

F: Right, and you kept urging him to go and talk to her, but he was too shy.

여: 안녕, Jesse. ²⁷점심 식사에 초대해 줘서 고마워. 업무로부터 휴식이 정말 필요했어.

남: 천만에, Abby. ²⁷우리 회사가 서로 가까워서 이렇게 만날 수 있어서 정말 좋아. 나는 모든 서류 작업에서 벗어날 준비가 되었어.

여: 우리가 대학에 다닐 때는 일이 더 간단했어. 우리가 South Point 대학교를 졸업한 지 벌써 1년이 되었다는 게 믿어져?

남: 알아, 그렇지? 대학 생활에 관해서 말하자면, ²⁸우리 친구 Harold가 보험 회사에서 일하기 시작한 이후로 얘기해 본 적 있어?

여: ²⁸대화한 지 몇 달이 지났지만, 그는 자기 일을 정말 좋아하는 것 같았고, 여자 친구와의 관계도 잘되고 있다고 했어!

남: 오랜만이라면 그와 여자친구가 올해 11월에 결혼한다는 소식을 못 들었나 봐!

여: 오, 진짜? 와, 정말 대단하다! 다음에 만나면 Harold에게 축하한다고 전해줘.

남: ²⁹사실, Harold는 네가 결혼식에 오길 원하니 직접 얘기해 줘도 돼. 그게 오늘 점심을 먹자고 한 이유의 일부야. Harold가 청첩장을 전달해 달라고 부탁해서, 여기, 내가 가져왔어.

여: 고마워, Jesse. 난 정말 기뻐. Harold와 여자친구가 어떻게 처음 만났는지 기억나?

남: 물론 기억하지, Abby. ³⁰그건 신입생들을 위한 그 큰 파티에서 우리 셋이 만났던 날 밤이었잖아.

여: 응, ³⁰네가 *Battle for the Galaxy* 티셔츠를 입고 있었던 게 기억나는데, Harold와 내가 그 TV쇼에 열중해 있었기 때문에, 우리는 둘 다 너와 이야기를 나누러 갔지.

남: ³⁰*Battle for the Galaxy*에 대한 우리의 공통된 애정을 거의 잊을 뻔했어. 그날 밤 우리는 정말 유대감을 형성했어. 그리고 Harold는 방 반대편에 있는 여자애를 보았고 그녀가... 달라 보인다고 생각했어. 기억나? 그는 그것을 정말로 설명할 수 없었어. 하지만 그는 그녀에게 뭔가 특별한 게 있다고 느꼈지...

여: 맞아, 그리고 네가 계속 Harold에게 그녀에게 가서 얘기해 보라고 설득했는데, 그가 너무 부끄러워했어.

지텔프 공식 기출문제집 7회분 Level 2

여자의 도움	M: ³¹So then you made Harold write down his phone number and you marched over to the girl and gave it to her, saying that your friend was interested in going out for coffee. I couldn't believe how bold you were, ha-ha. F: Ha-ha, that's me! But ³²Harold was so embarrassed. He thought for sure the girl would never call him. M: She did, though! She called him a few days later and said she'd love to meet him. So your bold gesture really paid off. F: And now they're getting married.	남: ³¹그래서 네가 Harold에게 휴대전화 번호를 적으라고 한 다음에 그 여자에게 걸어가서 그걸 주면서, 친구가 커피를 마시러 가고 싶어 한다고 말했어. 네가 얼마나 대담했는지 믿을 수가 없었어, 하하. 여: 하하, 그게 나야! 그런데 ³²Harold가 너무 당황했어. 그는 그 여자가 자기에게 절대 전화하지 않을 거라고 확실히 생각했지. 남: 그런데 그녀는 전화했어! 그녀가 그에게 며칠 후에 전화해서 꼭 만나고 싶다고 했어. 그래서 너의 대담한 행위가 정말 성공했던 거지. 여: 그리고 이제 그들은 결혼할 거야.
친구의 결혼식 초대	M: Yup. Harold really hopes you'll come to the wedding since it's all thanks to you. F: I wouldn't miss it for the world. M: The invitation says you can bring one guest, but if you don't have anyone else in mind, how about you and I attend the wedding together? F: That's a great idea. The wedding will be like a little college reunion.	남: 응. Harold는 이 모든 것이 네 덕분이니까 네가 결혼식에 오길 정말 바라. 여: 무슨 일이 있어도 절대 빠지지 않을 거야. 남: 초대장에는 하객 한 명을 데려올 수 있다고 되어 있는데, 다른 사람이 없다면, 우리 둘이 함께 결혼식에 참석하는 건 어때? 여: 좋은 생각이야. 결혼식은 작은 대학 동창회 같을 거야.
남녀가 다음에 할 일	M: Perfect! Well, Abby, ³³lunchtime's almost over. I guess we need to go back to work. I can't wait for the wedding. F: I can't either, Jesse! See you there!	남: 완벽해! 음, Abby, ³³점심시간이 거의 끝나가. 우린 다시 일하러 가야겠어. 결혼식이 너무 기다려져. 여: 나도 기다려져, Jesse! 거기서 봐!

어휘 | get away from ~에서 벗어나다 graduate[grǽdʒuət] 졸업하다 insurance company 보험 회사 catch up 대화하다
relationship[riléiʃənʃip] 관계 deliver[dilívər] 전달하다, 전하다 invitation[ìnvitéiʃən] 청첩장, 초대장 freshman[fréʃmən] 신입생
be obsessed with ~에 열중하다 bond[band] 유대감을 형성하다 urge to ~하도록 설득하다 write down 적어두다, 기록하다
march[ma:rtʃ] 걸어가다 bold[bould] 대담한, 용감한 gesture[dʒéstʃər] 행위 pay off 성공하다, 성과를 올리다
reunion[rijú:niən] 동창회, 모임

---

27 특정세부사항   Why
난이도 ●●○

Why is Jesse able to meet Abby during their lunch break?

(a) because they both work for the same company
(b) because their work schedules are flexible
(c) because their workplaces are near each other
(d) because they are clients of the same company

Jesse는 왜 점심시간 동안 Abby를 만날 수 있는가?

(a) 둘 다 같은 회사에서 일하기 때문에
(b) 그들의 근무 일정이 유연하기 때문에
(c) 그들의 직장이 서로 가깝기 때문에
(d) 같은 회사의 고객들이기 때문에

┍━○ 정답 잡는 치트키

질문의 키워드 lunch가 그대로 언급된 주변 내용을 주의 깊게 듣는다.

해설 | 여자가 'Thanks for inviting me to lunch.'라며 점심 식사에 초대해 줘서 고맙다고 하자, 남자가 'It's great that our companies are so close together and we can meet up like this.'라며 회사가 서로 가까워서 이렇게 만날 수 있어서 정말 좋다고 했다. 따라서 (c)가 정답이다.

지텔프 유식 기출문제집 7회분 Level 2

⇄ **Paraphrasing**

companies are so close together 회사가 서로 가깝다 → workplaces are near each other 직장이 서로 가깝다

어휘 | flexible[fléksəbl] 유연한, 탄력적인   workplace[wə́rkpleis] 직장

---

28 특정세부사항   What   난이도 ●●○

What did Abby hear about Harold the last time she talked to him?	Abby가 Harold와 마지막으로 대화를 나눴을 때 그에 관해 들은 것은 무엇이었는가?
(a) that he was returning to college (b) that he just ended a relationship **(c) that he was enjoying his work** (d) that he found his girlfriend a job	(a) 대학에 복학했다는 것 (b) 막 연인 관계를 끝냈다는 것 **(c) 자기의 일을 즐기고 있었다는 것** (d) 여자친구에게 직장을 찾아줬다는 것

⟜○ 정답 잡는 치트키

질문의 키워드 talked to him이 talked to ~ Harold로 paraphrasing되어 언급된 주변 내용을 주의 깊게 듣는다.

해설 | 남자가 'have you talked to ~ Harold since he started working at the insurance company?'라며 Harold가 보험 회사에서 일하기 시작한 이후로 얘기해 본 적 있는지 묻자, 여자가 'It's been a few months since we caught up, but he seemed to really like his job'이라며 대화한 지 몇 달이 지났지만 Harold가 자기 일을 정말 좋아하는 것 같았다고 했다. 따라서 (c)가 정답이다.

⇄ **Paraphrasing**

seemed to really like ~ job 일을 정말 좋아하는 것 같았다 → was enjoying ~ work 일을 즐기고 있었다

---

29 특정세부사항   Why   난이도 ●●○

Why did Jesse want to have lunch with Abby today?	Jesse는 왜 오늘 Abby와 점심을 먹고 싶어 했는가?
(a) to tell her about a friend's special occasion (b) to congratulate her for getting engaged (c) to ask her advice about wedding decorations (d) to invite her to a party he is planning	**(a) 친구의 특별한 행사에 관해 그녀에게 말해주기 위해서** (b) 그녀가 약혼한 것을 축하해 주기 위해서 (c) 결혼식 장식에 관한 그녀의 조언을 구하기 위해서 (d) 그가 계획하고 있는 파티에 그녀를 초대하기 위해서

⟜○ 정답 잡는 치트키

질문의 키워드 want to have lunch가 asked ~ to lunch로 paraphrasing되어 언급된 주변 내용을 주의 깊게 듣는다.

해설 | 남자가 'Actually, ~ he wants you to come to the wedding. That's part of why I asked you to lunch today. Harold asked me to deliver the invitation'이라며 사실 Harold는 여자가 결혼식에 오길 원해서 그게 남자가 여자에게 오늘 점심을 먹자고 한 이유의 일부이고, Harold가 청첩장을 전달해 달라고 부탁했다고 했다. 따라서 (a)가 정답이다.

⇄ **Paraphrasing**

the wedding 결혼식 → special occasion 특별한 행사

어휘 | occasion[əkéiʒən] 행사, (특정한) 때   get engaged 약혼하다

What did Abby find that she and Jesse shared in common on the first night they met?

(a) that they owned the same T-shirt
(b) that they had the same friends
(c) that they loved the same movie
(d) that they liked the same series

Abby는 그녀와 Jesse가 만난 첫날 밤에 무슨 공통점을 발견했는가?

(a) 같은 티셔츠를 소유하고 있었다는 것
(b) 같은 친구들이 있었다는 것
(c) 같은 영화를 좋아했다는 것
(d) 같은 텔레비전 시리즈를 좋아했다는 것

○ 정답 잡는 치트키

질문의 키워드 shared와 night ~ met이 그대로 언급된 주변 내용을 주의 깊게 듣는다.

해설 | 남자가 'That was the night the three of us met, at that big party for freshmen.'이라며 그건 신입생들을 위한 그 큰 파티에서 셋이 만났던 날 밤이었다고 했고, 여자가 'I remember you were wearing a *Battle for the Galaxy* T-shirt, and since ~ I were obsessed with that TV show'라며 남자가 *Battle for the Galaxy* 티셔츠를 입고 있었던 게 기억나는데 자기가 그 TV쇼에 열중해 있었기 때문이라고 하자, 남자가 'I almost forgot about our shared love of *Battle for the Galaxy*.'라며 *Battle for the Galaxy*에 대한 공통된 애정을 거의 잊을 뻔했다고 했다. 따라서 (d)가 정답이다.

어휘 | own[oun] ~을 소유하다; 자신의

How did Harold meet the woman he would eventually marry?

(a) by dancing with her at a party
(b) by accepting the help of his friend
(c) by serving her at his coffee shop
(d) by running into her at the park

Harold는 결국 결혼할 여자를 어떻게 만났는가?

(a) 파티에서 그녀와 춤을 춤으로써
(b) 친구의 도움을 받아들임으로써
(c) 그의 커피숍에서 그녀에게 대접함으로써
(d) 공원에서 그녀와 우연히 마주침으로써

○ 정답 잡는 치트키

질문의 키워드 woman이 girl로 paraphrasing되어 언급된 주변 내용을 주의 깊게 듣는다.

해설 | 남자가 'So then you made Harold write down his phone number and you marched over to the girl and gave it to her, saying that your friend was interested in going out for coffee.'라며 여자가 Harold에게 휴대전화 번호를 적으라고 한 다음에 그 여자에게 걸어가서 그걸 주면서 친구가 커피를 마시러 가고 싶어 한다고 말했다고 했다. 따라서 (b)가 정답이다.

어휘 | accept[æksépt] ~을 받아들이다, 응하다 run into 우연히 마주치다

What was Harold's response to Abby's action at the party?

(a) He seemed confused.
(b) He felt uncomfortable.
(c) He started laughing.
(d) He became furious.

파티에서 Abby의 행동에 대한 Harold의 반응은 어땠는가?

(a) 혼란스러워 보였다.
(b) 곤란함을 느꼈다.
(c) 웃기 시작했다.
(d) 몹시 화를 냈다.

질문의 키워드 Harold's response와 관련된 주변 내용을 주의 깊게 듣는다.

해설 | 여자가 'Harold was so embarrassed'라며 Harold가 너무 당황했다고 했다. 따라서 (b)가 정답이다.

어휘 | **furious**[fjúəriəs] 몹시 화를 낸, 격노한

33 추론 다음에 할 일 난이도 ●●○

What will Jesse most likely do next?

(a) order some food for lunch
(b) go to a college reunion
(c) **return to his workplace**
(d) attend his friend's wedding

Jesse는 다음에 무엇을 할 것 같은가?

(a) 점심으로 음식을 주문한다
(b) 대학 동창회에 간다
(c) **직장에 복귀한다**
(d) 친구의 결혼식에 간다

정답 잡는 치트키
다음에 할 일을 언급하는 후반을 주의 깊게 듣는다.

해설 | 남자가 'lunchtime's almost over. I guess we need to go back to work.'라며 점심시간이 거의 끝나가서 다시 일하러 가야겠다고 한 것을 통해, Jesse가 다음에 직장에 복귀할 것임을 추론할 수 있다. 따라서 (c)가 정답이다.

⇄ **Paraphrasing**
go back to work 다시 일하러 가다 → return to ~ workplace 직장에 복귀하다

오답분석
(d) 친구 Harold의 결혼식에 참석할 것이라고 언급했지만, 다음에 할 일은 아니므로 오답이다.

PART 2 [34-39] 발표 새로운 자전거 액세서리 홍보

음성 바로 듣기

주제 제시: 제품 홍보

Good morning, everyone. I want to thank you all for attending this year's Cycler's Expo. [34]I'm the representative for Inno-Cycle, a company that aims to ease the life of cyclists by manufacturing innovative bicycle accessories. Today, I would like to introduce to you our latest product that will hit the market soon: the Inno-Cycle Co-Pilot.

필요성 제기

The Co-Pilot has most of the functions you need for cycling all combined into a single smart gadget. With the Co-Pilot, you won't need much else for your bicycle. All you'll have to do is mount the device on your bike's handlebar, download the smart device's app onto your phone, and you're all set to experience the wonders of the Co-Pilot. So, here are its features.

안녕하세요, 여러분. 올해 Cycler's Expo에 참석해 주신 모든 분께 감사드리고 싶습니다. [34]저는 혁신적인 자전거 액세서리를 제조하여 사이클리스트의 삶을 편하게 하는 것을 목표로 하는 회사인 Inno-Cycle사의 대표입니다. 오늘은, 곧 출시할 저희의 최신 제품인 Inno-Cycle Co-Pilot을 소개하고자 합니다.

Co-Pilot은 사이클링에 필요한 대부분의 기능을 하나의 스마트 기기에 모두 통합했습니다. Co-Pilot을 사용하면, 자전거에 더 많은 것이 필요하지 않을 것입니다. 여러분이 해야 할 것은 자전거 핸들에 기기를 고정하고, 스마트 기기의 앱을 휴대전화에 다운로드하고, Co-Pilot의 경이를 경험할 준비를 하는 것입니다. 자, 여기 이것의 특징이 있습니다.

장점1:
음성
안내
GPS
내비
게이션
시스템

[35]The Co-Pilot uses a voice-guided GPS navigation system. Today, getting to one's destination has been made easy by all the navigating apps available for vehicles. The Co-Pilot adds exactly that feature to your bicycle. By setting your destination using the app on your phone, the Co-Pilot will find the shortest possible route to the location so you can get there quickly. The device will then announce the directions as you ride towards your destination, which you can clearly hear through wireless earphones.

장점2:
도난
방지
알람

Another useful feature of the Co-Pilot is its anti-theft alarm. Every time you leave your bicycle, the smart device will go into "lock mode." The Co-Pilot will then detect your bicycle's movements. [36]If the device detects that you are far from your bicycle and the bike suspiciously gets moved, it will sound a loud alarm and send notifications to your phone. However, when the device detects that you're near or on the bike, it will turn off the alarm so it doesn't accidentally sound off as you ride.

장점3:
위치
탐지기
기능

In the event your bicycle does get stolen, the Co-Pilot's Locator feature will be of help. [37]Just open the Locator tab in the app, and it will show where your bicycle is on the app's map. You can then seek assistance from the authorities to retrieve your bicycle. [37]This feature is also useful if you forget where you parked your bicycle.

장점4:
건강
추적기

[38]The Co-Pilot can even assist with your health goals with its Fitness Tracker. Input your height and weight into the phone app, and then, as you ride your bicycle, [38]the device will automatically record the distance and speed of your travels. It then uses this data to calculate how many calories you've burned. This information is sent to your phone, so [38]you can have an idea of how much exercise you've done.

장점5:
전방
조명
기능

Lastly, the Co-Pilot has the Front Light feature that can help you find your way through the dark. The device has a sensor that automatically detects the lighting in your surroundings. Depending on how dark it is, the Co-Pilot will produce enough light to shine on your path so you can see where you are going. This is especially useful if you often ride your bicycle at night.

할인
정보

The Inno-Cycle Co-Pilot will be available starting July 24 for only $79. [39]All email subscribers to our website will receive a ten percent discount. If you're not a subscriber yet, visit the Inno-Cycle website and subscribe to our newsletter.

---

[35]Co-Pilot은 음성 안내 GPS 내비게이션 시스템을 사용합니다. 오늘날, 목적지까지 가는 것은 차량에서 사용할 수 있는 모든 내비게이션 앱에 의해 쉬워졌습니다. Co-Pilot은 바로 그 기능을 자전거에 추가합니다. 휴대전화의 앱을 사용하여 목적지를 설정함으로써, Co-Pilot은 해당 위치로 가는 가능한 최단 경로를 찾아 빠르게 도착할 수 있습니다. 그러면 목적지를 향해 자전거를 타고 갈 때 기기가 길 안내를 알려줄 것이고, 이것은 무선 이어폰을 통해 선명하게 들을 수 있습니다.

Co-Pilot의 또 다른 유용한 특징은 도난 방지 알람입니다. 자전거를 떠날 때마다, 스마트 장치가 "잠금 모드"로 전환됩니다. 그러면 Co-Pilot은 자전거의 움직임을 감지합니다. [36]만약 여러분이 자전거에서 멀리 떨어져 있고 자전거가 의심스럽게 움직이는 것을 장치가 감지한다면, 큰 알람이 울리고 휴대전화로 알림을 보냅니다. 그러나, 여러분이 자전거 근처에 있거나 자전거를 타고 있다는 것을 장치가 감지하면, 여러분이 자전거를 타는 동안 뜻하지 않게 울리지 않도록 알람을 끌 것입니다.

자전거를 도난당했을 경우, Co-Pilot의 위치탐지기 기능이 도움이 될 것입니다. [37]앱에서 위치탐지기 탭을 열기만 하면, 자전거가 어디에 있는지 앱 지도에 표시됩니다. 그런 다음 당국에 도움을 요청하여 자전거를 되찾을 수 있습니다. [37]이 기능은 자전거를 어디에 주차했는지 잊어버리는 경우에도 유용합니다.

[38]Co-Pilot은 건강 추적기로 건강 목표에도 도움을 줄 수 있습니다. 휴대전화 앱에 키와 몸무게를 입력한 다음, 자전거를 타면, [38]기기가 자동으로 이동 거리와 속도를 기록합니다. 그리고 나서 이 데이터를 사용하여 소모한 열량을 계산합니다. 이 정보는 휴대전화로 전송되므로, [38]얼마나 많은 운동을 했는지 알 수 있습니다.

마지막으로, Co-Pilot은 어둠 속에서 길을 찾도록 도와줄 수 있는 전방 조명 기능이 있습니다. 이 장치는 주변의 빛을 자동으로 감지하는 센서가 있습니다. 얼마나 어두운지에 따라, 어디로 가고 있는지 확인할 수 있도록 Co-Pilot이 경로를 비추는 충분한 빛을 만들 것입니다. 특히 밤에 자전거를 자주 탄다면 유용합니다.

Inno-Cycle Co-Pilot은 7월 24일부터 단돈 79달러에 구매할 수 있습니다. [39]당사 웹사이트의 모든 이메일 구독자들은 10% 할인을 받을 것입니다. 아직 구독자가 아니라면, Inno-Cycle사 웹사이트를 방문하여 소식지를 구독하세요.

어휘 | **aim to** ~하는 것을 목표로 하다 **ease**[i:z] ~을 편하게 하다; 편함, 안락함 **cyclist**[sáiklist] 사이클리스트(자전거 타는 사람)
hit the market 출시하다 **gadget**[gǽdʒit] 기기, 장치 **mount**[maunt] 고정시키다, 탑재하다
handlebar[hǽndəlbar] (자전거·오토바이 등의) 핸들 **wonder**[wʌ́ndər] 경이(로운 것) **route**[ru:t] 경로, 길 **wireless**[wáiərlis] 무선의
feature[fí:tʃər] 특징, 기능; ~의 특징을 이루다 **detect**[ditékt] 감지하다, 발견하다 **suspiciously**[səspíʃəsli] 의심스럽게
notification[nòutəfikéiʃən] 알림, 통보 **turn off** 끄다 **accidentally**[æksədéntəli] 뜻하지 않게, 우연히 **get stolen** 도난당하다, 도둑 맞다
authority[əθɔ́:rəti] 당국 **retrieve**[ritrí:v] 되찾다 **input**[ínput] 입력하다, 입력 **automatically**[ɔ̀:təmǽtikəli] 자동으로
distance[dístəns] 거리, 간격 **calculate**[kǽlkjulèit] 계산하다 **burn**[bə:rn] (에너지 등을) 소비하다 **shine**[ʃain] 빛을 비추다
subscriber[səbskráibər] 구독자, 가입자

34 주제/목적   담화의 주제

난이도 ●○○

What is the talk mainly about?

(a) **introducing a device for cycling**
(b) promoting a smart bicycle
(c) announcing a bicycle race
(d) launching a company for cyclists

담화는 주로 무엇에 관한 것인가?

(a) **사이클링을 위한 장치 소개하기**
(b) 스마트 자전거 홍보하기
(c) 자전거 경주 발표하기
(d) 사이클리스트들을 위한 회사 설립하기

○ 정답 잡는 치트키

담화의 주제를 언급하는 초반을 주의 깊게 듣고 전체 맥락을 파악한다.

해설 | 화자가 'I'm the representative for Inno-Cycle, a company that aims to ease the life of cyclists by manufacturing innovative bicycle accessories. Today, I would like to introduce to you our latest product that will hit the market soon: the Inno-Cycle Co-Pilot.'이라며 혁신적인 자전거 액세서리를 제조하여 사이클리스트의 삶을 편하게 하는 것을 목표로 하는 회사인 Inno-Cycle사의 대표이며, 오늘은 곧 출시할 최신 제품인 Inno-Cycle Co-Pilot을 소개하고자 한다고 한 뒤, 담화 전반에 걸쳐 사이클링을 위한 장치인 Co-Pilot을 소개하는 내용이 이어지고 있다. 따라서 (a)가 정답이다.

⇄ **Paraphrasing**
bicycle accessories 자전거 액세서리 → a device for cycling 사이클링을 위한 장치

어휘 | **promote**[prəmóut] 홍보하다

35 특정세부사항   How

난이도 ●●●

How does the Inno-Cycle Co-Pilot help cyclists get to their destination?

(a) **by giving them voice prompts**
(b) by suggesting multiple routes
(c) by showing the turns on a map
(d) by finding the most scenic route

Inno-Cycle Co-Pilot은 어떻게 사이클리스트들이 목적지에 도착하도록 돕는가?

(a) **음성 조언을 제공함으로써**
(b) 여러 경로를 제시함으로써
(c) 지도에 방향 전환을 표시함으로써
(d) 가장 경치가 좋은 길을 찾음으로써

○ 정답 잡는 치트키

질문의 키워드 get to ~ destination이 그대로 언급된 주변 내용을 주의 깊게 듣는다.

해설 | 화자가 'The Co-Pilot uses a voice-guided GPS navigation system. Today, getting to one's destination has been made easy by all the navigating apps available for vehicles. The Co-Pilot adds exactly that feature to your bicycle.'

이라며 Co-Pilot은 음성 안내 GPS 내비게이션 시스템을 사용하는데, 오늘날 목적지까지 가는 것은 차량에서 사용할 수 있는 모든 내비게이션 앱에 의해 쉬워졌고, Co-Pilot은 바로 그 기능을 자전거에 추가한다고 했다. 따라서 (a)가 정답이다.

어휘 | prompt[prɑːmpt] 조언, 주의; 즉각적인　turn[təːrn] 방향 전환(하기), 회전; ~을 회전시키다　scenic[síːnik] 경치가 좋은

36　추론　특정사실　　　　　　　　　　　　　난이도 ●●○

When does the device probably detect that the bicycle has been stolen?	장치는 자전거가 도난당한 것을 언제 감지하는 것 같은가?
(a) when someone tries to remove the lock	(a) 누군가가 자물쇠를 제거하려고 할 때
(b) when the owner walks away too quickly	(b) 주인이 너무 빨리 떠날 때
(c) when the owner is far from the moving bike	**(c) 주인이 움직이는 자전거에서 멀리 떨어져 있을 때**
(d) when someone gets too close to the bike	(d) 누군가가 자전거에 너무 가까이 다가갈 때

━○ 정답 잡는 치트키

질문의 키워드 detect가 그대로 언급된 주변 내용을 주의 깊게 듣는다.

해설 | 화자가 'If the device detects that you are far from your bicycle and the bike suspiciously gets moved, it will sound a loud alarm and send notifications to your phone.'이라며 만약 자전거에서 멀리 떨어져 있고 자전거가 의심스럽게 움직이는 것을 장치가 감지한다면 큰 알람이 울리고 휴대전화로 알림을 보낸다고 한 것을 통해, 주인이 움직이는 자전거에서 멀리 떨어져 있을 때 장치는 자전거가 도난당한 것을 감지함을 추론할 수 있다. 따라서 (c)가 정답이다.

어휘 | remove[rimúːv] 제거하다, 없애다　owner[óunər] 주인, 소유자

37　특정세부사항　　What　　　　　　　　　　난이도 ●●○

According to the talk, what can bike owners do if they forget where the bike is parked?	담화에 따르면, 자전거가 어디에 주차되어 있는지 잊어버린다면 자전거 주인들은 무엇을 할 수 있는가?
(a) ask for help from the authorities	(a) 당국에 도움을 요청한다
(b) download a special locator app	(b) 특별 위치탐지기 앱을 다운로드한다
(c) activate an alarm on the phone	(c) 휴대전화에서 알림을 활성화한다
(d) use the map in the application	**(d) 애플리케이션에서 지도를 사용한다**

━○ 정답 잡는 치트키

질문의 키워드 forget where ~ parked가 그대로 언급된 주변 내용을 주의 깊게 듣는다.

해설 | 화자가 'Just open the Locator tab in the app, and it will show where your bicycle is on the app's map.'이라며 앱에서 위치탐지기 탭을 열기만 하면 자전거가 어디에 있는지 앱 지도에 표시된다고 한 뒤, 'This feature is also useful if you forget where you parked your bicycle.'이라며 이 기능은 자전거를 어디에 주차했는지 잊어버리는 경우에도 유용하다고 했다. 따라서 (d)가 정답이다.

오답분석

(a) 화자가 당국에 도움을 요청하는 것을 언급했지만, 도난당했을 경우에 앱에서 위치탐지기 탭을 열어서 자전거의 위치를 지도에서 확인한 후 당국에 도움을 요청하라고 했으므로 오답이다.

어휘 | activate[金ktəvèit] 활성화하다

38 특정세부사항 How

난이도 ●●○

How does the product's Fitness Tracker feature help improve a biker's health?

(a) It suggests ways to burn more calories.
(b) It sends the rider reminders to exercise.
(c) It records the rider's weight changes.
(d) It measures the rider's activity levels.

제품의 건강 추적기 기능은 어떻게 자전거를 타는 사람의 건강을 개선하는 데 도움이 되는가?

(a) 더 많은 열량을 소모할 방법을 제시한다.
(b) 자전거를 타는 사람에게 운동하라는 신호를 보낸다.
(c) 자전거를 타는 사람의 체중 변화를 기록한다.
(d) 자전거를 타는 사람의 활동 수준을 측정한다.

━○ 정답 잡는 치트키

질문의 키워드 Fitness Tracker가 그대로 언급된 주변 내용을 주의 깊게 듣는다.

해설 | 화자가 'The Co-Pilot can even assist with your health goals with its Fitness Tracker.'라며 Co-Pilot은 건강 추적기로 건강 목표에도 도움을 줄 수 있다고 한 뒤, 'the device will automatically record the distance and speed of your travels', 'you can have an idea of how much exercise you've done'이라며 기기가 자동으로 이동 거리와 속도를 기록하고 얼마나 많은 운동을 했는지 알 수 있다고 했다. 따라서 (d)가 정답이다.

어휘 | rider[ráidər] (자전거·오토바이를) 타는 사람 reminder[rimáindər] 신호, 생각나게 하는 것 measure[méʒər] 측정하다

39 특정세부사항 What

난이도 ●●○

What can a customer do to get a discount?

(a) purchase a lighting accessory
(b) subscribe to paid content
(c) visit a nearby store location
(d) agree to receive news updates

고객은 할인받기 위해 무엇을 할 수 있는가?

(a) 조명 액세서리를 구입하다
(b) 유료 콘텐츠를 구독하다
(c) 가까운 매장을 방문하다
(d) 뉴스 업데이트를 수신하는 것에 동의한다

━○ 정답 잡는 치트키

질문의 키워드 get a discount가 receive a ~ discount로 paraphrasing되어 언급된 주변 내용을 주의 깊게 듣는다.

해설 | 화자가 'All email subscribers to our website will receive a ten percent discount.'라며 당사 웹사이트의 모든 이메일 구독자들은 10% 할인을 받을 것이라고 했다. 따라서 (d)가 정답이다.

어휘 | paid[peid] 유료인

음성 바로 듣기

PART 3 (40~45) 장단점 논의 새끼 고양이 입양과 나이 든 고양이 입양의 장단점 비교

안부 인사	M: Hi, ⁴⁰Alyssa! You have a cat, right? F: Hello, James. ⁴⁰Actually, I have two. Why?	남: 안녕, ⁴⁰Alyssa! 너 고양이 키우지, 맞지? 여: 안녕, James. ⁴⁰실은, 두 마리를 키워. 왜?
주제 제시: 장단점 비교	M: Well, my wife wants to adopt a cat from the animal shelter. But we don't know whether to adopt a kitten or an older cat. F: I see. Well, they both have their pros and cons. ⁴⁰I've	남: 음, 내 아내가 동물 보호소에서 고양이를 입양하고 싶어 해. 그런데 우리는 새끼 고양이를 입양할지, 나이 든 고양이를 입양할지 모르겠어. 여: 그렇구나. 음, 둘 다 장단점이 있어. ⁴⁰나는 몇 년 동

had my cats for years, so maybe I can help you make a decision.

M: Great. First of all, [41]I just love how cute kittens are! They're so tiny and fuzzy and have such sweet little faces.

F: Who doesn't find kittens adorable? Ha-ha. You remember seeing pictures of my cat Peanut when I first got him, right? He was so small that he fit in the palm of my hand.

M: Playing with a cute kitten every day would put me in a good mood.

F: Another advantage is that you'll enjoy their company longer. Since kittens are young, you'll get to spend more time with them as they grow older.

M: Right. I heard that housecats can live more than twenty years.

F: Well, that's pretty rare. But it does happen.

M: What about the disadvantages of getting a kitten, Alyssa?

F: Well, kittens need a lot of attention. They're always curious and tend to play with things they're not supposed to, which can be destructive or even dangerous. When Peanut was a kitten, he chewed up two of my phone chargers.

M: Oh no! My wife loves her houseplants, so I'd worry about the kitten tearing up the leaves.

F: Yeah, [42]you really need to watch over young kittens to prevent them from destroying things. Another disadvantage is that you should really adopt two kittens instead of one . . . Are you willing to do that?

M: Two? Why is that?

F: Well, it's not good for a kitten to be home alone if you're working all day. Vets recommend getting two kittens at the same time so they can keep each other company.

M: I don't know if I'm ready for that. So, what about the advantages of adopting an older cat?

F: One good thing about older cats is that you know exactly what their personality is like when you adopt them. You can tell if they're going to be calm, or friendly, or shy.

M: Yeah, that makes sense—they won't change much because they've already grown up.

F: Exactly. Also, it feels good to adopt an older cat. [43]Many families want kittens, but older cats in the shelter often get overlooked.

안 고양이를 키웠으니, 결정하는 걸 도와줄 수 있을 것 같아.

남: 좋아. 우선, [41]난 그냥 새끼 고양이들이 아주 귀여워서 좋아! 그것들은 정말 작고 솜털이 보송보송하고 사랑스러운 작은 얼굴을 가지고 있어.

여: 누가 새끼 고양이들을 사랑스럽게 생각하지 않겠어? 하하. 내 고양이 Peanut을 처음 키웠을 때 그것의 사진을 봤던 거 기억해? 내 손바닥에 들어갈 정도로 작았어.

남: 귀여운 새끼 고양이와 매일 노는 건 기분이 좋을 거야.

여: 또 다른 장점은 네가 고양이와 더 오래 함께할 수 있다는 거야. 새끼 고양이들은 어리기 때문에, 너는 새끼 고양이들이 나이가 들수록 더 많은 시간을 함께 보내게 될 거야.

남: 맞아. 집고양이는 20년 넘게 살 수 있다고 들었어.

여: 음, 그건 꽤 드문 일이야. 하지만 그런 일이 일어나기도 해.

남: 새끼 고양이를 키우는 것의 단점은 뭐야, Alyssa?

여: 음, 새끼 고양이들은 많은 관심이 필요해. 그들은 항상 호기심이 많고 해롭거나 심지어 위험할 수 있는, 그렇게 해서는 안 되는 것들을 가지고 노는 경향이 있어. Peanut이 새끼 고양이였을 때, 그는 내 휴대전화 충전기 두 개를 물어뜯었어.

남: 안 돼! 아내가 화초를 좋아해서, 새끼 고양이가 잎을 갈기갈기 찢을까 봐서 걱정이야.

여: 응, [42]새끼 고양이들이 물건을 손상시키는 걸 막기 위해서는 그것들을 지켜보는 게 정말로 필요해. 또 다른 단점은 한 마리 대신에 실제로 두 마리의 새끼 고양이를 입양해야 한다는 거야... 기꺼이 그렇게 할 거야?

남: 두 마리? 왜 그래야 해?

여: 음, 네가 하루 종일 일을 한다면 새끼 고양이가 집에 혼자 있는 것은 좋지 않아. 수의사들은 서로 친구가 되어줄 수 있도록 두 마리의 새끼 고양이를 동시에 키우는 것을 추천해.

남: 내가 그럴 준비가 되어있는지 모르겠어. 그러면, 나이 든 고양이를 입양하는 것의 장점은 뭐야?

여: 나이 든 고양이들의 한 가지 좋은 점은 입양할 때 고양이들의 성격이 어떤지 정확하게 안다는 거야. 고양이들이 침착할지, 다정할지, 수줍어할지 판단할 수 있어.

남: 응, 그들은 이미 자랐기 때문에 별로 변하지 않을 거니까 일리가 있네.

여: 맞아. 또한, 나이 든 고양이를 입양하는 건 기분이 좋아. [43]많은 가족이 새끼 고양이들을 원하지만, 보호소에 있는 나이 든 고양이들은 종종 간과돼.

M: I didn't think about that. It would be nice knowing that we're providing a loving home to a cat that really needs it.

F: Absolutely. I adopted my other cat, Caramel, when he was older, and he's a great companion.

M: And what about the disadvantages of older cats?

F: The sad truth is that, depending on how old the cat is when you adopt it, you might only have a few short years together.

M: I've thought about that.

F: ⁴⁴I had an older cat in the past that only lived for three years after I adopted him, and it was so hard to let go. I wish I'd had more time with him.

M: That does sound really tough.

F: So, ⁴⁵James, have you come to a decision?

M: I think I have, Alyssa. ⁴⁵All things considered, I think I'd rather keep my wife's precious plants in one piece!

남: 그런 생각은 못 했어. 정말 집이 필요한 고양이에게 사랑이 깃든 보금자리를 제공하게 될 거라는 걸 알면 기분이 좋겠네.

여: 물론이지. 나는 다른 고양이 Caramel이 더 컸을 때 입양했는데, Caramel은 정말 좋은 친구야.

남: 그러면 나이 든 고양이들의 단점은 뭐야?

여: 슬픈 사실은, 고양이를 입양할 때 고양이의 나이에 따라, 몇 년밖에 함께하지 못할 수도 있다는 거야.

남: 나도 그런 생각을 해봤어.

여: ⁴⁴예전에 입양한 후에 3년만 살았던 나이 든 고양이가 있었는데, 떠나보내기가 너무 힘들었어. 더 많은 시간을 고양이와 함께했으면 좋았을 텐데.

남: 정말 힘들었겠다.

여: 그래서, ⁴⁵James, 결정을 내렸어?

남: 그런 것 같아, Alyssa. ⁴⁵모든 것을 고려하면, 아내의 소중한 식물을 온전하게 지켜주는 게 나을 것 같아!

나이 든 고양이 입양의 단점

남자의 결정

어휘ㅣ adopt[ədápt] 입양하다 shelter[ʃéltər] 보호소, 대피소 kitten[kitn] 새끼 고양이 tiny[táini] 작은 fuzzy[fʌ́zi] 솜털이 보송보송한 adorable[ədɔ́:rəbl] 사랑스러운, 귀여운 palm[pa:m] 손바닥 attention[əténʃən] 관심, 주의 curious[kjúriəs] 호기심이 많은, 궁금한 destructive[distrʌ́ktiv] 해로운, 파괴적인 chew up 물어뜯다, 물다 charger[tʃá:rdʒər] 충전기 houseplant[háusplænt] 화초 tear up 갈기갈기 찢다, 뿌리째 뽑다 keep company 친구가 되어 주다, ~의 곁에 있어 주다 personality[pə̀:rsənǽləti] 성격 calm[ka:m] 침착한, 차분한 overlook[òuvərlúk] 간과하다, 눈감아주다 companion[kəmpǽniən] 친구, 동반자 tough[tʌf] 힘든, 어려운 precious[préʃəs] 소중한, 귀중한

---

40 **특정세부사항** **Why** 난이도 ●●○

Why is James asking for Alyssa's advice about cats?

(a) because she takes care of cats
(b) because she is working at a cat shelter
(c) because she recently adopted a cat
(d) because she is considering getting cats

James는 왜 고양이에 관해 Alyssa의 조언을 구하고 있는가?

(a) 그녀가 고양이들을 돌보기 때문에
(b) 그녀가 고양이 보호소에서 일하고 있기 때문에
(c) 그녀가 최근에 고양이를 입양했기 때문에
(d) 그녀가 고양이들을 키우는 것을 고려하고 있기 때문에

⌁─○ 정답 잡는 치트키

질문의 키워드 Alyssa's advice about cats와 관련된 주변 내용을 주의 깊게 듣는다.

해설ㅣ 남자가 'Alyssa! You have a cat, right?'이라며 Alyssa에게 고양이를 키우는지 묻자, 여자가 'Actually, I have two.'라며 실은 두 마리를 키운다고 했고, 'I've had my cats for years, so maybe I can help you make a decision.'이라며 몇 년 동안 고양이를 키웠으니 결정하는 걸 도와줄 수 있을 것 같다고 했다. 따라서 (a)가 정답이다.

⇄ Paraphrasing

have a cat 고양이를 키우다 → takes care of cats 고양이들을 돌보다

어휘ㅣ take care of ~을 돌보나

TEST 5 LISTENING 233

What does James love about kittens?

(a) the way they sleep
(b) the way they fit in one hand
(c) the way they look
(d) the way they play together

James가 새끼 고양이들에 관해 좋아하는 것은 무엇인가?

(a) 잠자는 방식
(b) 한 손에 들어오는 방식
(c) 생긴 방식
(d) 함께 노는 방식

━━○ 정답 잡는 치트키

질문의 키워드 love ~ kittens가 그대로 언급된 주변 내용을 주의 깊게 듣는다.

해설 | 남자가 'I just love how cute kittens are! They're so tiny and fuzzy and have such sweet little faces.'라며 그냥 새끼 고양이들이 아주 귀여워서 좋고, 그것들은 정말 작고 솜털이 보송보송하고 사랑스러운 작은 얼굴을 가지고 있다고 했다. 따라서 (c)가 정답이다.

---

42 특정세부사항   How   난이도 ●●○

Based on the conversation, how can James prevent a kitten from destroying his wife's houseplants?

(a) by hiding plants away from it
(b) by keeping a close eye on it
(c) by getting fake plants for it
(d) by spraying a scent on the plants

대화에 따르면, James는 새끼 고양이가 아내의 화초를 손상시키는 것을 어떻게 막을 수 있는가?

(a) 식물을 고양이에게 숨김으로써
(b) 고양이를 주의 깊게 봄으로써
(c) 고양이를 위해 가짜 식물을 놓음으로써
(d) 식물에 향을 뿌림으로써

━━○ 정답 잡는 치트키

질문의 키워드 prevent ~ from destroying이 그대로 언급된 주변 내용을 주의 깊게 듣는다.

해설 | 여자가 'you really need to watch over young kittens to prevent them from destroying things'라며 새끼 고양이들이 물건을 손상시키는 걸 막기 위해서는 그것들을 지켜보는 게 정말로 필요하다고 했다. 따라서 (b)가 정답이다.

    ⤵ **Paraphrasing**
watch 지켜보다 → keeping a close eye 주의 깊게 봄

어휘 | hide away ~을 숨기다, 감추다   keep a close eye on ~을 주의 깊게 보다, 감시하다   fake [feik] 가짜의, 위조의   spray [sprei] 뿌리다, 분사하다   scent [sent] 향기, 향수

---

43 추론   특정사실   난이도 ●●○

Why, probably, are adult cats at animal shelters often overlooked for adoption?

(a) They tend to be overly aggressive.
(b) They are less popular than kittens.
(c) They are less friendly than kittens.
(d) They tend to hide from strangers.

동물 보호소에 있는 다 자란 고양이들은 왜 입양에 종종 간과되는 것 같은가?

(a) 지나치게 공격적인 경향이 있다.
(b) 새끼 고양이들보다 덜 인기가 있다.
(c) 새끼 고양이들보다 덜 친근하다.
(d) 낯선 사람들로부터 숨는 경향이 있다.

질문의 키워드 adult cats ~ overlooked가 older cats ~ overlooked로 paraphrasing되어 언급된 주변 내용을 주의 깊게 듣는다.

해설 | 여자가 'Many families want kittens, but older cats in the shelter often get overlooked.'라며 많은 가족이 새끼 고양이들을 원하지만 보호소에 있는 나이 든 고양이들은 종종 간과된다고 한 것을 통해, 동물 보호소에 있는 다 자란 고양이들은 새끼 고양이들보다 덜 인기가 있으므로 입양에 종종 간과됨을 추론할 수 있다. 따라서 (b)가 정답이다.

어휘 | overly[óuvərli] 지나치게, 과도하게 aggressive[əgrésiv] 공격적인, 적극적인 stranger[stréindʒər] 낯선 사람, 이방인

---

44 특정세부사항   What   난이도 ●●○

What was hard for Alyssa in the past about having an older cat?

(a) spending extra money on its care
(b) teaching it to break bad habits
(c) having it for such a short time
(d) trying to keep it more active

Alyssa는 예전에 나이 든 고양이를 키우는 것에 관해 무엇이 힘들었는가?

(a) 고양이 돌봄에 추가 비용을 지출하는 것
(b) 나쁜 버릇을 고치도록 가르치는 것
(c) 너무 짧은 시간 동안 키우는 것
(d) 좀 더 활동적으로 키우려고 노력하는 것

질문의 키워드 in the past와 older cat이 그대로 언급된 주변 내용을 주의 깊게 듣는다.

해설 | 여자가 'I had an older cat in the past that only lived for three years after I adopted him, and it was so hard to let go.' 라며 예전에 입양한 후에 3년만 살았던 나이 든 고양이가 있었는데 떠나보내기가 너무 힘들었다고 했다. 따라서 (c)가 정답이다.

어휘 | care[ker] 돌봄, 보호 break[breik] ~의 나쁜 버릇을 고치다, 그만두다 active[éktiv] 활동적인, 적극적인

---

45 추론   다음에 할 일   난이도 ●●○

What has James most likely decided to do?

(a) choose a kitten as a pet
(b) purchase some new houseplants
(c) adopt a more mature cat
(d) convince his wife to get a dog

James는 무엇을 하기로 결정한 것 같은가?

(a) 새끼 고양이를 반려동물로 선택한다
(b) 새로운 화초를 구입한다
(c) 더욱 완전히 자란 고양이를 입양한다
(d) 아내에게 개를 키우도록 설득한다

다음에 할 일을 언급하는 후반을 주의 깊게 듣는다.

해설 | 여자가 'James, have you come to a decision?'이라며 결정을 내렸는지 묻자, 남자가 'All things considered, I think I'd rather keep my wife's precious plants in one piece!'라며 모든 것을 고려하면 아내의 소중한 식물을 온전하게 지켜주는 게 나을 것 같다고 한 것을 통해, James는 더욱 완전히 자란 고양이를 입양할 것임을 추론할 수 있다. 따라서 (c)가 정답이다.

어휘 | mature[mətjúər] 완전히 자란 convince[kənvíns] 설득하다

지텔프 공식 기출문제집 7회분 Level 2

인사
+
주제
제시

Good morning, students of Northern Colorado University. Thanks for attending today's seminar entitled "The Working Student." As a means of funding tuition and other expenses, many NCU students have chosen to get a part-time job while studying. However, [46]balancing work and studies can be challenging. So, whether you already have a job or are planning to apply for one, here are a few tips on how to manage your time as a working student.

조언1:
일정
투명
하게
관리

Tip number one: be transparent about your schedule. Give management a copy of your class schedule so that they'll know how to handle your work shifts. Many workplaces are glad to arrange a student's work schedule to make it more convenient to work while studying. And remember that [47]here at NCU, every campus employer is required to schedule student workers around their classes.

조언2:
휴식
시간
활용

Tip number two: [48]capitalize on break times at work. During lunch hours and coffee breaks, you may find yourself having a few minutes to spare before going back to work. If you have nothing urgent to do, [48]use this extra time to review your notes and textbooks instead of texting or browsing social media websites. You'll be surprised how fifteen to thirty minutes of reading can help you recall what you've studied in class.

조언3:
고정된
공부
시간
확보

Tip number three: [49]set aside fixed times for studying. Allocating time to study makes sure that work doesn't get in the way of education. If your work and class schedules both get tight, assign a regular time to study outside your work and class hours. Depending on your schedule, this can be an hour every day, two hours every other day, or every weekend. Be sure to eliminate distractions during those times so you can focus on studying.

조언4:
충분한
수면

Tip number four: get enough sleep. Working while attending school can be physically and mentally exhausting. [50]Get the right amount of sleep every night so your body can keep up with the demands of your activities. You may have to cut back on some lower priority hobbies, such as watching TV or playing computer games late into the night. Remember that NCU students can grab quick naps during the day at the library's new Rest Center when they find themselves running low on sleep.

안녕하세요, Northern Colorado 대학교 학생 여러분. 오늘 "The Working Student"라는 제목의 세미나에 참석해 주셔서 감사합니다. 학비와 기타 비용 충당의 수단으로, 많은 NCU 학생이 공부하면서 아르바이트하는 것을 택하고 있습니다. 하지만, [46]일과 학업의 균형을 맞추는 것은 힘들 수 있습니다. 그래서, 여러분이 이미 일자리를 구했든지, 아니면 구할 계획이 있든지, 일하는 학생으로서 시간을 관리하는 방법에 관한 몇 가지 조언이 여기 있습니다.

첫 번째 조언: 일정에 관해 투명하게 해주세요. 관리자가 근무 교대를 어떻게 처리할지 알 수 있도록 수업 일정 사본을 제공하세요. 많은 직장에서 공부하는 동안 더 편리하게 일할 수 있도록 학생의 근무 일정을 기꺼이 조정해 줍니다. 그리고 [47]여기 NCU에서는, 모든 캠퍼스 고용주가 학생 근로자들의 일정을 수업 시간에 맞춰야 한다는 점을 기억하세요.

두 번째 조언: [48]직장에서의 휴식 시간을 활용하세요. 점심시간과 커피 휴식 시간 동안, 업무에 복귀하기 전에 할애할 몇 분이 있는 것을 발견할 수도 있습니다. 해야 할 긴급한 일이 없다면, 문자 메시지를 보내거나 소셜 미디어 웹사이트를 훑어보는 대신에 [48]이 여유 시간을 노트와 교재를 복습하는 데 사용하세요. 15분에서 30분 정도 읽는 것이 수업 시간에 공부했던 것을 기억하는 데 얼마나 도움이 될 수 있는지에 놀랄 것입니다.

세 번째 조언: [49]공부를 위해 고정된 시간을 확보하세요. 공부할 시간을 할당하는 것은 일이 교육에 방해가 되지 않도록 보장합니다. 일과 수업 일정이 모두 빡빡하다면, 일과 수업 시간 외에 공부할 수 있는 정기적인 시간을 할당하세요. 일정에 따라, 이것은 매일 한 시간, 이틀에 두 시간, 또는 매 주말이 될 수 있습니다. 공부에 집중할 수 있도록 그 시간 동안 집중을 방해하는 것을 반드시 없애세요.

네 번째 조언: 충분히 자세요. 학교에 다니면서 일하는 것은 신체적으로나 정신적으로 지칠 수 있습니다. [50]매일 밤 적절한 양의 잠을 자 신체가 활동의 요구를 따라갈 수 있도록 하세요. 여러분은 TV 시청이나 밤늦게 컴퓨터 게임을 하는 것과 같은 우선순위가 낮은 일부 취미들을 줄여야 할지도 모릅니다. NCU 학생들은 잠이 부족할 때 도서관에 새로 생긴 휴식 센터에서 낮에 잠깐의 낮잠을 잘 수 있다는 것을 기억하세요.

Tip number five: schedule time to do things you enjoy. Without leisure, you won't be able to release the stress that has built up from all the working and studying. Find an appropriate time each week to kick back and take it easy. [51]For many at NCU, this is "Fab Friday," when the local bars and clubs offer discounts to NCU students. But whether you're out dancing on Fab Friday, or simply playing cards with your friends in the dorm, [51]make sure to schedule some time every week to relax and let off some steam.

주어5;
여가
시간
고려

다섯 번째 조언: 좋아하는 일을 할 시간을 일정에 넣으세요. 여가가 없다면, 여러분은 일과 공부 모두로부터 쌓인 스트레스를 풀 수 없을 것입니다. 매주 적절한 시간을 찾아서 휴식을 취하고 여유를 가지세요. [51]NCU의 많은 사람에게, "굉장한 금요일"이 있는데, 이것은 지역 술집과 클럽이 NCU 학생들에게 할인을 제공하는 날입니다. 하지만 여러분이 굉장한 금요일에 밖에 나가 춤을 추든, 기숙사에서 친구들과 단순히 카드놀이를 하든, [51]휴식을 취하고 울분을 발산하기 위해 매주 일부 시간을 반드시 일정에 넣으세요.

Tip number six: remember that your education comes first. Ideally, you should maintain a balance between work and school. But [52]if it comes to a point where your work comes into conflict with your studies, always prioritize your studies. If you are forced to resign from your job to have more time to study, don't fret because you can always find another job. Remember: getting a good education is the best way to get the job you really want.

조언6:
학업에
우선
순위
두기

여섯 번째 조언: 교육이 최우선임을 기억하세요. 이상적으로는, 일과 학교의 균형을 유지해야 합니다. 하지만 [52]일이 학업과 충돌하는 상황이 발생하면, 항상 학업을 우선시하세요. 공부에 더 많은 시간을 할애하기 위해 부득이하게 직장을 그만두게 된다면, 언제나 다른 직장을 찾을 수 있으니 고민하지 마세요. 좋은 교육을 받는 것이 진정으로 원하는 직장을 얻을 수 있는 가장 좋은 방법이라는 것을 기억하세요.

어휘 | entitle[intáitl] 제목을 붙이다 means[miːnz] 수단, 방법 tuition[tjuːíʃən] 학비, 등록금 balance[bǽləns] ~의 균형을 맞추다; 균형, 조화 challenging[tʃǽlindʒiŋ] 힘든, 도전적인 transparent[trænspǽərənt] 투명한, 솔직한 work shift 근무 교대 employer[implɔ́iər] 고용주 capitalize on ~을 활용하다 spare[sper] 할애하다 urgent[ə́ːrdʒənt] 긴급한, 급박한 browse[brauz] 훑어보다 recall[rikɔ́ːl] 기억하다, 상기하다 set aside 확보하다 fixed[fikst] 고정된 get in the way 방해가 되다 assign[əsáin] 할당하다, 정하다 eliminate[ilímənèit] 없애다, 제거하다 distraction[distrǽkʃən] 집중을 방해하는 것 exhausting[igzɔ́ːstiŋ] (심신을) 지쳐버리게 하는 keep up with ~을 따르다 cut back 줄이다, 삭감하다 priority[praiɔ́ːrəti] 우선하는; 우선순위 nap[næp] 낮잠 leisure[líːʒər] 여가 kick back 휴식을 취하다 take it easy 여유롭다 fab[fæb] 굉장한, 놀라운 dorm[dɔːrm] 기숙사 let off steam 울분을 발산하다 prioritize[praiɔ́ːrətàiz] 우선시하다, 먼저 처리하다 resign[rizáin] 그만두다 fret[fret] 고민하다, 애타다

46 주제/목적   담화의 주제
난이도 ●●○

What is the topic of the presentation?

(a) **how to balance work and school**
(b) how to prevent exam stress
(c) how to study effectively in college
(d) how to find a job on campus

발표의 주제는 무엇인가?

(a) **일과 학업의 균형을 맞추는 방법**
(b) 시험 스트레스를 예방하는 방법
(c) 대학에서 효과적으로 공부하는 방법
(d) 캠퍼스에서 일자리를 구하는 방법

━○ 정답 잡는 치트키

담화의 주제를 언급하는 초반을 주의 깊게 듣고 전체 맥락을 파악한다.

해설 | 화자가 'balancing work and studies can be challenging. So, whether you already have a job or are planning to apply for one, here are a few tips on how to manage your time as a working student.'라며 일과 학업의 균형을 맞추는 것은 힘들 수 있으므로 이미 일자리를 구했든지, 아니면 구할 계획이 있든지, 일하는 학생으로서 시간을 관리하는 방법에 관한 몇 가지 조언이 여기 있다고 한 뒤, 담화 전반에 걸쳐 일과 학업의 균형을 맞추는 방법을 설명하는 내용이 이어지고 있다. 따라서 (a)가 정답이다.

어휘 | effectively[iféktivli] 효과적으로, 효율적으로

How should an NCU employer handle the schedules of
working students?

(a) by hiring students with the fewest courses
(b) by working around student availability
(c) by advising students about their class schedules
(d) by letting students study during work hours

NCU 고용주는 어떻게 일하는 학생들의 일정을 처리
해야 하는가?

(a) 가장 적은 과목을 듣는 학생들을 고용함으로써
(b) 학생을 가능한 시간에 일하게 함으로써
(c) 학생들에게 그들의 수업 일정에 관해 조언함으로써
(d) 학생들이 근무 시간 동안 공부하도록 허용함으로
써

── 정답 잡는 치트키

질문의 키워드 employer가 그대로 언급된 주변 내용을 주의 깊게 듣는다.

해설 | 화자가 'here at NCU, every campus employer is required to schedule student workers around their classes'라며 여
기 NCU에서는 모든 캠퍼스 고용주가 학생 근로자들의 일정을 수업 시간에 맞춰야 한다고 했다. 따라서 (b)가 정답이다.

어휘 | advise[ædváiz] 조언하다, 권하다

What does the speaker recommend that students do with
their break times at work?

(a) catch up on social media
(b) relax and text with friends
(c) take care of personal errands
(d) go over class materials

화자는 학생들이 직장에서의 휴식 시간에 무엇을 할
것을 권하는가?

(a) 소셜 미디어를 따라잡는다
(b) 긴장을 풀고 친구들과 문자를 한다
(c) 개인적인 용무를 처리한다
(d) 수업 자료를 복습한다

── 정답 잡는 치트키

질문의 키워드 break times at work가 그대로 언급된 주변 내용을 주의 깊게 듣는다.

해설 | 화자가 'capitalize on break times at work'라며 직장에서의 휴식 시간을 활용하라고 한 뒤, 'use this extra time to review your
notes and textbooks'라며 이 여유 시간을 노트와 교재를 복습하는 데 사용하라고 했다. 따라서 (d)가 정답이다.

↻ Paraphrasing
review ~ notes and textbooks 노트와 교재를 복습하다 → go over class materials 수업 자료를 복습하다

어휘 | catch up 따라잡다, 밀린 일을 하다　take care of ~을 처리하다　errand[érənd] 용무, 볼일　go over 복습하다, 검토하다

Why should students set aside fixed study times outside of
work and class hours?

(a) so their work does not interfere with their studies
(b) so they can do their job without distractions

학생들은 왜 일과 수업 시간 외에 고정된 공부 시간을
확보해야 하는가?

(a) 일이 학업을 방해하지 않게 하기 위해서
(b) 집중을 방해하는 것 없이 자기 일을 할 수 있기 위
해서

(c) so their study time is always on weekends

(d) so they can avoid working overtime

(c) 그들의 공부 시간이 항상 주말이 되도록 하게 하기 위해서

(d) 야근하는 것을 피할 수 있기 위해서

정답 잡는 치트키

질문의 키워드 set aside fixed ~ times가 그대로 언급된 주변 내용을 주의 깊게 듣는다.

해설 | 화자가 'set aside fixed times for studying. Allocating time to study makes sure that work doesn't get in the way of education'이라며 공부를 위해 고정된 시간을 확보해야 하며, 공부할 시간을 할당하는 것은 일이 교육에 방해가 되지 않도록 보장한다고 했다. 따라서 (a)가 정답이다.

⇄ **Paraphrasing**

get in the way of education 교육에 방해가 되다 → interfere with ~ studies 학업을 방해하다

어휘 | interfere with ~을 방해하다, 지장을 주다 work overtime 야근하다

---

50 추론   특정사실   난이도 ●●○

Based on the talk, why, most likely, should students cut back on some of their hobbies?

(a) to work more hours

(b) to socialize more often

(c) to get more sleep

(d) to do more reading

담화에 따르면, 학생들은 왜 그들의 취미 중 일부를 줄여야 하는 것 같은가?

(a) 더 많은 시간을 일하기 위해서

(b) 더 자주 사람들과 어울리기 위해서

(c) 잠을 더 자기 위해서

(d) 독서를 더 많이 하기 위해서

정답 잡는 치트키

질문의 키워드 cut back on some ~ hobbies가 그대로 언급된 주변 내용을 주의 깊게 듣는다.

해설 | 화자가 'Get the right amount of sleep every night ~. You may have to cut back on some lower priority hobbies'라며 매일 밤 적절한 양의 잠을 자야 하며, 우선순위가 낮은 일부 취미들을 줄여야 할지도 모른다고 한 것을 통해, 학생들은 잠을 더 자기 위해 그들의 취미 중 우선순위가 낮은 일부를 줄여야 함을 추론할 수 있다. 따라서 (c)가 정답이다.

어휘 | socialize [sóuʃəlàiz] 사람들과 어울리다

---

51 특정세부사항   How   난이도 ●●○

According to the talk, how can Fab Friday benefit working students?

(a) It introduces them to support groups.

(b) It provides them with job opportunities.

(c) It forces them to get out more.

(d) It helps them release stress.

담화에 따르면, 굉장한 금요일은 어떻게 일하는 학생들에게 혜택을 줄 수 있는가?

(a) 단체들을 지원하도록 소개한다.

(b) 취업 기회를 제공한다.

(c) 밖으로 더 나가도록 한다.

(d) 스트레스를 해소하는 데 도움을 준다.

정답 잡는 치트키

질문의 키워드 Fab Friday가 그대로 언급된 주변 내용을 주의 깊게 듣는다.

해설 | 화자가 'For many at NCU, this is "Fab Friday," when the local bars and clubs offer discounts to NCU students.'라며 NCU의 많은 사람에게 "굉장한 금요일"이 있는데, 이것은 지역 술집과 클럽이 NCU 학생들에게 할인을 제공하는 날이라고 한 뒤, 'make sure to schedule some time every week to relax and let off some steam'이라며 휴식을 취하고 울분을 발산하기 위해 매주 일부 시간을 반드시 일정에 넣으라고 했다. 따라서 (d)가 정답이다.

⇄ **Paraphrasing**
let off some steam 울분을 발산하다 → release stress 스트레스를 해소하다

어휘 | support[səpɔ́:rt] 지원하다

---

52 특정세부사항 What   난이도 ●●○

According to the talk, what should one do when work gets into conflict with schooling?	담화에 따르면, 일이 수업과 충돌할 때 무엇을 해야 하는가?
(a) talk to management	(a) 관리자에게 이야기한다
(b) give up the job	**(b) 일을 그만둔다**
(c) take fewer classes	(c) 수업을 적게 듣는다
(d) speak with professors	(d) 교수님들과 이야기한다

─○ 정답 잡는 치트키

질문의 키워드 work gets into conflict with schooling이 work comes into conflict with ~ studies로 paraphrasing되어 언급된 주변 내용을 주의 깊게 듣는다.

해설 | 화자가 'if it comes to a point where your work comes into conflict with your studies, always prioritize your studies. If you are forced to resign from your job ~, don't fret because you can always find another job.'이라며 일이 학업과 충돌하는 상황이 발생하면 항상 학업을 우선시해야 하며, 부득이하게 직장을 그만두게 된다면 언제나 다른 직장을 찾을 수 있으니 고민하지 말라고 했다. 따라서 (b)가 정답이다.

어휘 | schooling[skú:liŋ] 수업, 학교 교육 give up 그만두다

공식기출 TEST 5

READING & VOCABULARY

PART 1 (53~59) 인물의 일대기　최초의 아프리카계 미국인 여성 비행사인 베시 콜먼

인물 이름	**BESSIE COLEMAN**	**베시 콜먼**

[소개 + 유명한 이유]

[53]Bessie Coleman was an aviator best known for being the first African American woman to hold a pilot's license. Having succeeded to do so in the 1920s, Coleman inspired other women, as well as African Americans in general, to pursue careers in aviation, despite the limited opportunities for minorities at the time.

[53]베시 콜먼은 조종사 면허를 가진 최초의 아프리카계 미국인 여성으로 가장 잘 알려진 비행사였다. 1920년대에 그렇게 하는 데 성공한, 콜먼은 그 당시 소수 집단에게 제한된 기회에도 불구하고, 일반적인 아프리카계 미국인들뿐만 아니라 다른 여성들도 항공 분야에서 계속 경력을 추구하도록 영감을 주었다.

[어린 시절]

Bessie Coleman was born on January 26, 1892, in Atlanta, Texas. Her mother was a housekeeper, and her father was a poor tenant farmer. As a child, Coleman helped her mother [58]harvest cotton in the fields and do laundry to save money for college. Coleman was able to study at a "colored" university but, due to financial difficulties, did not complete her education.

베시 콜먼은 1892년 1월 26일에 텍사스주 애틀랜타에서 태어났다. 어머니는 가정부였고, 아버지는 가난한 소작농이었다. 어린 시절에, 콜먼은 어머니가 대학을 위한 돈을 모으기 위해 들판에서 [58]목화를 수확하고 빨래하는 것을 도왔다. 콜먼은 "유색인" 대학교에서 공부할 수 있었지만, 재정적인 어려움 때문에, 교육을 마치지 못했다.

[업적 시작 계기]

In 1915, Coleman was working in Chicago as a beautician when she heard stories of French women serving as aircraft pilots during the First World War. [54]Her brother teased her about French women being able to do something that she could not, and Coleman, who had always been ambitious, took the joke as a challenge. She developed an interest in flying and attempted to enroll at aviation schools. However, no school would accept her because at the time, working in American aviation was only open to white men.

1915년에, 제1차 세계대전 중에 프랑스 여성들이 항공기 조종사로 복무하고 있었다는 이야기를 들었을 때 콜먼은 시카고에서 미용사로 일하고 있었다. [54]그녀의 오빠는 프랑스 여성들이 그녀가 할 수 없는 것을 할 수 있다는 것에 대해 그녀를 놀렸고, 항상 야심에 차 있던 콜먼은 그 농담을 도전으로 받아들였다. 그녀는 비행에 관해 흥미가 생겼고 항공 학교에 입학하려고 시도했다. 그러나, 그 당시에 미국 항공 업계에서 일하는 것은 백인 남성에게만 열려 있었기 때문에 어떤 학교도 그녀를 받아들이지 않았다.

[초기 업적]

Coleman's friend Robert Abbott, a newspaper publisher, advised her to go to France, where aviation schools were more integrated. [55]After studying French, she moved to France in 1920 and was accepted at the Caudron Brothers' School of Aviation in Le Crotoy. She received her pilot's license in 1921. Coleman's achievements attracted worldwide interest, and her return to the US was met by a great deal of press coverage.

콜먼의 친구이자 신문 발행인인 로버트 애보트는 그녀에게 프랑스로 가라고 조언했는데, 그곳은 항공 학교가 인종 차별을 더욱 하지 않는 곳이었다. [55]프랑스어를 공부한 후, 1920년에 프랑스로 건너가 르 크로토이에 있는 꼬드롱 브라더스 항공 학교에 입학했다. 그녀는 1921년에 조종사 면허를 취득했다. 콜먼의 성취는 세계적인 관심을 끌었고, 그녀의 미국 복귀는 많은 언론 보도를 받았다.

[주요 업적]

[56]Coleman performed remarkable feats in air shows and became a celebrity in early aviation exhibitions, earning the nickname "Brave Bess." She wanted to make enough money to open an aviation school for women and African Americans. Having worked so hard to overcome discrimination, she refused to appear in shows that [59]reinforced racist beliefs, such as barring black audiences from using the same entrance white people used.

[56]콜먼은 항공 쇼에서 놀라운 묘기를 보였고, 초기 항공 전시회에서 "용감한 베스"라는 별명을 얻으며 유명 인사가 되었다. 그녀는 여성과 아프리카계 미국인들을 위한 항공 학교를 열기에 충분한 돈을 벌고 싶어 했다. 차별을 극복하기 위해 매우 열심히 노력했던, 그녀는 흑인 관객들이 백인들이 사용했던 것과 같은 출입구를 사용하는 것을 금지하는 것과 같은 [59]인종차별적 신념을 강화했던 쇼에 출연하는 것을 거부했다.

During a test flight for an air show in 1926, [57]Coleman was killed when her plane spun out of control due to a mechanical failure. [57]Her dream of building an aviation school was realized, however, when her fellow pilots founded the Bessie Coleman Aero Club in 1929. Her many accolades include being inducted into the National Aviation Hall of Fame.

1926년에 항공 쇼를 위한 시험 비행 중에, 기계 고장으로 인해 비행기가 통제 불능 상태가 되면서 [57]콜먼은 사망했다. 그러나 항공 학교를 짓고자 했던 그녀의 꿈은 1929년 동료 조종사들이 베시 콜먼 에어로 클럽을 설립하면서 실현되었다. 그녀의 많은 영예는 국립 항공 명예의 전당에 임명된 것을 포함한다.

어휘 | aviator n. 비행사, 조종사   pilot n. 조종사   license n. 면허   pursue v. 계속 추구하다   aviation n. 항공(술), 항공기 산업   minority n. 소수 집단   housekeeper n. 가정부, 주부   tenant farmer phr. 소작농   cotton n. 목화   do laundry phr. 빨래하다   beautician n. 미용사   tease about phr. ~에 대해 놀리다   ambitious adj. 야심에 찬   challenge n. 도전; v. ~에 도전하다   aviation school phr. 항공 학교   integrated adj. (학교 등에서) 인종 차별을 하지 않는   achievement n. 성취, 달성   press coverage phr. 언론 보도   feat n. 묘기, 위업   air show phr. 항공 쇼   overcome v. 극복하다   discrimination n. 차별, 편견   refuse v. 거부하다, 거절하다   racist adj. 인종차별의; n. 인종차별주의자   spin out of control phr. 통제 불능 상태가 되다   mechanical failure phr. 기계 고장   fellow adj. 동료의; n. 동료   accolade n. 영예   be inducted into phr. ~에 임명되다

---

53   특정세부사항   유명한 이유   난이도 ●●●

What is Bessie Coleman most known for?

(a) being the first African American aviator
(b) being the first woman to earn a pilot's license
(c) being the first female African American pilot
(d) being the first advocate for racial equality

베시 콜먼은 무엇으로 가장 잘 알려져 있는가?

(a) 최초의 아프리카계 미국인 비행사인 것
(b) 조종사 면허를 취득한 최초의 여성인 것
(c) 최초의 여성인 아프리카계 미국인 비행사인 것
(d) 인종적 평등에 대한 최초의 지지자인 점

⊸○ 정답 잡는 치트키

질문의 키워드 most known이 best known으로 paraphrasing되어 언급된 주변 내용을 주의 깊게 읽는다.

해설 | 1단락의 'Bessie Coleman was an aviator best known for being the first African American woman to hold a pilot's license.'에서 베시 콜먼은 조종사 면허를 가진 최초의 아프리카계 미국인 여성으로 가장 잘 알려진 비행사였다고 했다. 따라서 (c)가 정답이다.

⇄ Paraphrasing
woman 여성 → female 여성인
aviator 비행사 → pilot 비행사

어휘 | advocate n. 지지자, 옹호자; v. 지지하다, 옹호하다   racial equality phr. 인종적 평등

---

54   특정세부사항   Why   난이도 ●●○

Why did Coleman decide to start applying to flight schools?

(a) to prove that her brother was wrong
(b) to be like the French women she admired
(c) to get away from her hometown of Chicago
(d) to overcome her lifelong fear of heights

콜먼은 왜 비행 학교에 지원하는 것을 시작하기로 결심했는가?

(a) 오빠가 틀렸다는 것을 증명하기 위해서
(b) 존경했던 프랑스 여성들과 같아지기 위해서
(c) 고향인 시카고를 떠나기 위해서
(d) 평생의 고소 공포증을 극복하기 위해서

해설 | 3단락의 'Her brother teased her about French women being able to do something that she could not, and Coleman, ~, took the joke as a challenge. She ~ attempted to enroll at aviation schools.'에서 콜먼의 오빠는 프랑스 여성들이 콜먼이 할 수 없는 것을 할 수 있다는 것에 대해 그녀를 놀렸고, 콜먼은 그 농담을 도전으로 받아들였고, 항공 학교에 입학하려고 시도했다고 했다. 따라서 (a)가 정답이다.

어휘 | flight school phr. 비행 학교   admire v. 존경하다, 감탄하다   lifelong adj. 평생의, 일생의   fear of heights phr. 고소 공포증

---

55 특정세부사항   How   난이도 ●●○

How was Coleman able to obtain her pilot's license?

(a) by writing to the aviation board
(b) by asking a friend to train her
(c) by studying in a different country
(d) by taking a special examination

콜먼은 어떻게 조종사 면허를 딸 수 있었는가?

(a) 항공 위원회에 편지를 씀으로써
(b) 친구에게 가르쳐달라고 부탁함으로써
(c) 다른 나라에서 공부함으로써
(d) 특별 시험을 치름으로써

해설 | 4단락의 'After studying French, she moved to France in 1920 and was accepted at the Caudron Brothers' School of Aviation in Le Crotoy. She received her pilot's license in 1921.'에서 콜먼이 프랑스어를 공부한 후 1920년에 프랑스로 건너가 르 크로토이에 있는 꼬드롱 브라더스 항공 학교에 입학했고, 1921년에 조종사 면허를 취득했다고 했다. 따라서 (c)가 정답이다.

어휘 | board n. 위원회   examination n. 시험

---

56 추론   특정사실   난이도 ●●○

Why, most likely, did Coleman earn the nickname "Brave Bess"?

(a) because she performed dangerous stunts
(b) because she fought against discrimination
(c) because she refused to work without equal pay
(d) because she fought hard to open a school

콜먼은 왜 "용감한 베스"라는 별명을 얻었을 것 같은가?

(a) 위험한 묘기를 보였기 때문에
(b) 차별에 맞서 싸웠기 때문에
(c) 동등한 임금을 받지 않고 일하기를 거부했기 때문에
(d) 학교를 열기 위해 열심히 싸웠기 때문에

해설 | 5단락의 'Coleman performed remarkable feats in air shows and became a celebrity ~, earning the nickname "Brave Bess."'에서 콜먼은 항공 쇼에서 놀라운 묘기를 보였고, "용감한 베스"라는 별명을 얻으며 유명 인사가 되었다고 한 것을 통해, 콜먼이 항공 쇼에서 위험한 묘기를 보였기 때문에 "용감한 베스"라는 별명을 얻었음을 추론할 수 있다. 따라서 (a)가 정답이다.

↻ **Paraphrasing**
remarkable feats 놀라운 묘기 → dangerous stunts 위험한 묘기

(b) 5단락에서 콜먼이 차별을 극복하기 위해 매우 열심히 노력했다고는 언급했지만, 이것이 "용감한 베스"라는 별명을 얻은 이유는 아니므로 오답이다.

어휘 | stunt n. 묘기

---

57 특정세부사항   What   난이도 ●●○

What role did the Aero Club play in Coleman's story?	콜먼의 이야기에서 에어로 클럽은 어떤 역할을 했는가?
(a) It donated a plane while hers was being repaired.	(a) 그녀의 비행기가 수리하는 동안 비행기를 기증했다.
(b) It provided training for her fellow pilots.	(b) 그녀의 동료 조종사들에게 훈련을 제공했다.
(c) It funded a scholarship in her name.	(c) 그녀의 이름으로 장학금을 지원했다.
(d) It was established by friends after her death.	**(d) 그녀의 사망 후 친구들에 의해 설립되었다.**

─○ 정답 잡는 치트키

질문의 키워드 Aero Club이 그대로 언급된 주변 내용을 주의 깊게 읽는다.

해설 | 6단락의 'Coleman was killed'에서 콜먼이 사망했다고 한 뒤, 'Her dream of building an aviation school was realized, ~, when her fellow pilots founded the Bessie Coleman Aero Club in 1929.'에서 항공 학교를 짓고자 했던 콜먼의 꿈은 1929년 동료 조종사들이 베시 콜먼 에어로 클럽을 설립하면서 실현되었다고 했다. 따라서 (d)가 정답이다.

⇄ Paraphrasing

fellow pilots founded 동료 조종사들이 설립했다 → was established by friends 친구들에 의해 설립되었다
was killed 사망했다 → death 사망

어휘 | donate v. 기증하다, 기부하다   scholarship n. 장학금   death n. 사망

---

58 어휘   유의어   난이도 ●○○

In the context of the passage, <u>harvest</u> means _____.	지문의 문맥에서, 'harvest'는 -을 의미한다.
(a) save	(a) 구하다
(b) make	(b) 만들다
(c) lose	(c) 잃어버리다
(d) pick	**(d) 따다**

─○ 정답 잡는 치트키

밑줄 친 어휘의 유의어를 찾는 문제이므로, harvest가 포함된 구절을 읽고 문맥을 파악한다.

해설 | 2단락의 'harvest cotton'은 목화를 수확한다는 뜻이므로, harvest가 '수확하다'라는 의미로 사용된 것을 알 수 있다. 따라서 '따다'라는 비슷한 의미의 (d) pick이 정답이다.

In the context of the passage, <u>reinforced</u> means _____.

(a) managed
(b) supported
(c) stretched
(d) guarded

지문의 문맥에서, 'reinforced'는 -을 의미한다.

(a) 다뤘다
(b) 지지했다
(c) 이어졌다
(d) 지켰다

➤○ 정답 잡는 치트키

밑줄 친 어휘의 유의어를 찾는 문제이므로, reinforced가 포함된 구절을 읽고 문맥을 파악한다.

해설 | 5단락의 'reinforced racist beliefs'는 인종차별적 신념을 강화했다는 뜻이므로, reinforced가 '강화했다'라는 의미로 사용된 것을 알 수 있다. 따라서 '지지했다'라는 비슷한 의미의 (b) supported가 정답이다.

PART 2^(60~66) 잡지 기사 인터넷 장난인 릭롤링

기사
제목

"RICKROLLING": THE INTERNET JOKE THAT BECAME A CULTURAL PHENOMENON

"릭롤링": 문화 현상이 된 인터넷 장난

정의

[60]"Rickrolling" is an Internet meme that involves tricking someone into watching a video of the 1987 hit song "Never Gonna Give You Up" by Rick Astley. The trend started as an Internet prank in which people were tricked into clicking the video's link, which was disguised as an interesting—but different—hyperlink.

[60]"릭롤링"은 릭 애슬리의 1987년 히트곡 "Never Gonna Give You Up"의 영상을 보도록 누군가를 속이는 것을 포함하는 인터넷 밈이다. 이 유행은 사람들이 흥미롭지만 다른 하이퍼링크로 위장한 영상의 링크를 클릭하도록 속이는 인터넷 장난에서 시작되었다.

유래

[61]The first well-known appearance of the prank came in 2007 when a user from the forum website 4chan posted a link of what was claimed to be a trailer for *Grand Theft Auto IV*, a much-anticipated video game. When clicked, however, the link brought people to a music video of "Never Gonna Give You Up" instead. While some people were dismayed, most took the joke lightheartedly. The prank was given the name "rickrolling," with "rick" taken from Rick Astley's name. It then became trendy among the site users to rickroll more people, and the practice spread throughout the US.

[61]이 장난의 잘 알려진 첫 등장은 2007년에 포럼 웹사이트인 4chan의 한 이용자가 매우 기대되던 비디오 게임인 *Grand Theft Auto IV*의 예고편이라고 주장되는 링크를 올렸을 때였다. 그러나, 클릭하면, 그 링크는 대신 사람들을 "Never Gonna Give You Up"의 뮤직비디오로 이끌었다. 일부 사람들은 당황했지만, 대부분 사람은 이 장난을 쾌활하게 받아들였다. 이 장난은 릭 애슬리의 이름에서 "릭"을 따서, "릭롤링"이라는 이름이 붙여졌다. 그 후 사이트 이용자들 사이에서 더 많은 사람에게 릭롤을 하도록 유행이 되었고, 이 관행은 미국 전역으로 퍼져나갔다.

인터넷
밖으
로의
확산

Outside the Internet, people sought other ways to rickroll: stadiums suddenly played the song during sports events, [62(a)]a flash mob sang the song at a train station, and [62(c)]students rickrolled during class presentations. Rickrolling even made its way into politics. [62(d)]During an Oregon House of Representatives session, members snuck snippets of the song's lyrics into their speeches. While the lawmakers secretly had a little fun, their joke

인터넷 밖에서, 사람들은 릭롤을 하는 다른 방법을 찾았는데, 스포츠 경기 중에 갑자기 그 노래를 틀었고, [62(a)]플래시몹이 기차역에서 그 노래를 불렀고, [62(c)]학생들이 수업 발표 중에 릭롤을 했다. 릭롤링은 심지어 정계에 진출했다. [62(d)]오리건주 하원 회의 중에, 구성원들은 그 노래 가사의 토막을 그들의 연설에 슬쩍 집어넣었다. 의원들은 비밀스럽게 즐겼지만, 그들의 장

did not affect legislation, and [65]their proposed laws were ultimately <u>passed</u>. An edited video of the speeches was later released for April Fools' Day.

현황

[63]The most frequently used Internet upload of the music video has been removed twice for terms-of-use violations: once in 2010 and again in 2014. It has since been unblocked and has gained over one billion views. [64]Rickrolling continues to be relevant today, mostly appearing on social media and at gatherings. [64]The catchy lyrics and classic '80s vibe of the song used, as well as its retro music video make it ideal for pranks.

원곡
가수의
반응

When Astley himself was asked about his thoughts regarding rickrolling, he replied that he found it hilarious and [66]<u>recognized</u> it as a harmless way for people to have fun. Astley even thanked 4chan's founder for the rickrolling phenomenon.

난은 입법에 영향을 미치지 않았고, [65]제안된 법은 결국 승인되었다. 그 연설의 편집된 영상은 이후 만우절에 공개되었다.

[63]가장 자주 사용되는 이 뮤직비디오의 인터넷 업로드는 이용약관 위반으로 2010년과 2014년에 한 번씩 삭제되었다. 이후 차단이 해제되어 10억 회가 넘는 조회수를 얻었다. [64]릭롤링은 주로 소셜 미디어와 모임에서 등장하며, 오늘날에도 계속해서 사람들의 삶에 유의미하다. 복고풍 뮤직비디오뿐만 아니라 사용된 노래의 기억하기 쉬운 가사와 고전적인 80년대 분위기는 장난을 치기에 이상적으로 만든다.

애슬리는 릭롤링에 대한 그의 생각에 관해 질문받았을 때, 그는 그것이 유쾌했고 [66]사람들이 재미있게 즐기는 무해한 방식으로 인식했다고 대답했다. 애슬리는 심지어 릭롤링 현상에 대해 4chan의 설립자에게 감사를 표했다.

어휘 | phenomenon n. 현상 meme n. 밈(재현·모방을 되풀이하며 이어지는 사회 관습) trick into phr. 속여서 ~하게 하다 prank n. 장난, 가짜
disguise v. 위장시키다, 감추다 appearance n. 등장, 출연 trailer n. 예고편 anticipate v. 기대하다, 예상하다 dismay v. 당황하게 하다
lightheartedly adv. 쾌활하게, 근심 없게 trendy adj. 유행의, 멋진 practice n. 관행, 습관
flash mob phr. 플래시몹(미리 정한 장소에 모여 아주 짧은 시간 동안 약속한 행동을 한 후, 바로 흩어지는 불특정 다수의 군중 행위) politics n. 정계
House of Representatives phr. 하원 sneak v. ~을 슬쩍 집어넣다 snippet n. (대화·음악 등의) 한 토막 lyric n. 가사
lawmaker n. 의원, 입법자 legislation n. 입법 ultimately adv. 결국, 마침내 April Fools' Day phr. 만우절
terms-of-use n. 이용약관 violation n. 위반, 침해 relevant adj. (사람들의 삶 등에) 유의미한, 관련이 있는 gathering n. 모임
catchy adj. 기억하기 쉬운 vibe n. 분위기, 느낌 retro adj. 복고풍의; n. 재유행 hilarious adj. 유쾌한, 즐거운
harmless adj. 무해한, 악의 없는

60 주제/목적 　기사의 주제

난이도 ●○○

What is mainly being discussed in the article?

(a) how an online practical joke became widespread
(b) how a popular country song was revived
(c) how using memes can bring people together
(d) how harmless pranks influence people's lives

기사에서 주로 논의되고 있는 것은 무엇인가?

(a) 온라인 장난이 어떻게 널리 퍼지게 되었는지
(b) 인기 있는 컨트리 노래가 어떻게 재유행되었는지
(c) 밈을 이용하는 것이 어떻게 사람들을 하나로 모을 수 있는지
(d) 무해한 장난이 사람들의 삶에 어떻게 영향을 미치는지

🔑 정답 잡는 치트키

지문의 초반을 주의 깊게 읽고 전체 맥락을 파악한다.

해설 | 1단락의 '"Rickrolling" is an Internet meme that involves tricking someone into watching a video of the 1987 hit song ~ by Rick Astley.'에서 "릭롤링"은 릭 애슬리의 1987년 히트곡의 영상을 보도록 누군가를 속이는 것을 포함하는 인터넷 밈이라고 한 뒤, 온라인 장난인 릭롤링의 유래 및 확산에 관해 설명하는 내용이 이어지고 있다. 따라서 (a)가 정답이다.

어휘 | practical joke phr. 장난 revive v. 재유행하다, 소생하다

How did the first rickrollers entice people to click the link to Rick Astley's music video?

(a) by claiming it would show them a car ad
(b) by suggesting it would lead to a movie trailer
(c) by saying it was about a popular game
(d) by insisting it was an important message

최초의 릭롤러들은 어떻게 사람들이 릭 애슬리의 뮤직비디오 링크를 클릭하도록 유인했는가?

(a) 그들에게 자동차 광고를 보여줄 것이라고 주장함으로써
(b) 영화 예고편으로 이어질 것이라고 암시함으로써
(c) 인기 있는 게임에 관한 것이라고 언급함으로써
(d) 중요한 메시지라고 주장함으로써

⊷○ 정답 잡는 치트키

질문의 키워드 click ~ music video가 그대로 언급된 주변 내용을 주의 깊게 읽는다.

해설 | 2단락의 'The first well-known appearance of the prank came in 2007 when a user ~ posted a link of what was claimed to be a trailer for ~ a much-anticipated video game. When clicked, however, the link brought people to a music video ~ instead.'에서 이 장난의 잘 알려진 첫 등장은 2007년에 한 이용자가 매우 기대되던 비디오 게임의 예고편이라고 주장되는 링크를 올렸을 때였고, 클릭하면 그 링크는 대신 사람들을 뮤직비디오로 이끌었다고 했다. 따라서 (c)가 정답이다.

⇄ Paraphrasing
a much-anticipated video game 매우 기대되던 비디오 게임 → a popular game 인기 있는 게임

어휘 | entice v. 유인하다　insist v. 주장하다

62　Not/True　　　Not 문제　　　　　　　　　　　　　　난이도 ●●○

Which of the following is NOT an example of how rickrolling was done outside the Internet?

(a) people performing the song in a train station
(b) politicians using the song in their campaign ads
(c) students playing the song while presenting in school
(d) lawmakers using the song's words in their address

다음 중 릭롤링이 인터넷 밖에서 어떻게 이루어졌는지에 관한 예시가 아닌 것은 무엇인가?

(a) 기차역에서 그 노래를 부르는 사람들
(b) 캠페인 광고에 그 노래를 사용하는 정치인들
(c) 학교에서 발표하면서 그 노래를 부르는 학생들
(d) 연설에 그 노래의 가사를 사용하는 의원들

⊷○ 정답 잡는 치트키

질문의 키워드 outside the Internet이 그대로 언급된 주변 내용을 주의 깊게 읽고, 보기의 키워드와 지문 내용을 대조하며 언급되는 것을 하나씩 소거한다.

해설 | (b)는 지문에 언급되지 않았으므로, (b)가 정답이다.

오답분석
(a) 보기의 키워드 train station이 그대로 언급된 3단락에서 플래시몹이 기차역에서 그 노래를 불렀다고 언급되었다.
(c) 보기의 키워드 presenting in school이 class presentations로 paraphrasing되어 언급된 3단락에서 학생들이 수업 발표 중에 릭롤을 했다고 언급되었다.
(d) 보기의 키워드 lawmakers가 House of Representatives로 paraphrasing되어 언급된 3단락에서 오리건주 하원 회의 중에 구성원들은 그 노래 가사의 토막을 그들의 연설에 슬쩍 집어넣었다고 언급되었다.

어휘 | politician n. 정치인　word n. 가사

Why, most likely, was the original Astley video taken down? | 애슬리의 영상 원본은 왜 내려졌을 것 같은가?

(a) because the prank offended many people

(b) because the video had been used without permission

(c) because the entertainment company had closed

(d) because the singer claimed copyright violations

(a) 장난이 많은 사람들을 불쾌하게 했기 때문에

(b) 영상이 허가 없이 사용되었기 때문에

(c) 엔터테인먼트 회사가 문을 닫았기 때문에

(d) 가수가 저작권 침해를 주장했기 때문에

━━○ 정답 잡는 치트키

질문의 키워드 video taken down이 music video has been removed로 paraphrasing되어 언급된 주변 내용을 주의 깊게 읽는다.

해설 | 4단락의 'The most frequently used Internet upload of the music video has been removed twice for terms-of-use violations'에서 가장 자주 사용되는 뮤직비디오인 애슬리의 뮤직비디오 인터넷 업로드가 이용약관 위반으로 삭제되었다고 한 것을 통해, 애슬리의 영상 원본은 영상이 허가 없이 사용되었기 때문에 내려졌음을 추론할 수 있다. 따라서 (b)가 정답이다.

어휘 | take down phr. 내리다, 치우다　offend v. 불쾌하게 하다　permission n. 허가, 허락　copyright violation phr. 저작권 침해

Why might audiences still feel drawn to the song "Never Gonna Give You Up"? | 팬들은 왜 "Never Gonna Give You Up"이라는 노래에 여전히 마음이 끌린다고 느끼는 것 같은가?

(a) People think the song is charmingly outdated.

(b) The music video shows people getting pranked.

(c) People think it carries a positive message.

(d) The original artist still performs it regularly.

(a) 사람들은 그 노래가 매력적으로 시대에 뒤진다고 생각한다.

(b) 뮤직비디오는 사람들이 장난치는 것을 보여준다.

(c) 사람들은 그것이 긍정적인 메시지를 전달한다고 생각한다.

(d) 원작자는 여전히 그것을 정기적으로 공연한다.

━━○ 정답 잡는 치트키

질문의 키워드 still feel drawn이 continues to be relevant today로 paraphrasing되어 언급된 주변 내용을 주의 깊게 읽는다.

해설 | 4단락의 'Rickrolling continues to be relevant today'에서 릭롤링은 오늘날에도 계속해서 사람들의 삶에 유의미하다고 한 뒤, 'The catchy lyrics and classic '80s vibe of the song used, as well as its retro music video make it ideal for pranks.'에서 복고풍 뮤직비디오뿐만 아니라 사용된 노래의 기억하기 쉬운 가사와 고전적인 80년대 분위기는 장난을 치기에 이상적으로 만든다고 한 것을 통해, 팬들은 "Never Gonna Give You Up"이라는 노래가 매력적으로 시대에 뒤진다고 생각하기 때문에 그 노래에 여전히 마음이 끌린다고 느끼는 것임을 추론할 수 있다. 따라서 (a)가 정답이다.

어휘 | audience n. (예술(가) 등의) 팬, 지지자　feel drawn to phr. ~에 마음이 끌리다　charmingly adv. 매력적으로　outdated adj. 시대에 뒤진, 구식인

In the context of the passage, <u>passed</u> means _____. | 지문의 문맥에서, 'passed'는 -을 의미한다.

(a) saved

(a) 보호된

(b) offered
(c) ignored
(d) approved

(b) 제안된
(c) 무시된
(d) 승인된

정답 잡는 치트키

밑줄 친 어휘의 유의어를 찾는 문제이므로, passed가 포함된 구절을 읽고 문맥을 파악한다.

해설 | 3단락의 'their proposed laws were ultimately passed'는 제안된 법이 결국 승인되었다는 뜻이므로, passed가 '승인된'이라는 의미로 사용된 것을 알 수 있다. 따라서 '승인된'이라는 같은 의미의 (d) approved가 정답이다.

---

66 어휘　유의어　　　　난이도 ●●○

In the context of the passage, <u>recognized</u> means _____.

(a) tolerated
(b) noticed
(c) accepted
(d) signaled

지문의 문맥에서, 'recognized'는 -을 의미한다.

(a) 견뎠다
(b) 알아차렸다
(c) 인정했다
(d) 신호를 보냈다

정답 잡는 치트키

밑줄 친 어휘의 유의어를 찾는 문제이므로, recognized가 포함된 구절을 읽고 문맥을 파악한다.

해설 | 5단락의 'recognized it as a harmless way for people to have fun'은 사람들이 재미있게 즐기는 무해한 방식으로 인식했다는 뜻이므로, recognized가 '인식했다'라는 의미로 사용된 것을 알 수 있다. 따라서 '인정했다'라는 비슷한 의미의 (c) accepted가 정답이다.

PART 3 [67~73]　지식 백과　나그네비둘기의 멸종

표제어	**PASSENGER PIGEON**	**나그네비둘기**

정의 + 소개

The passenger pigeon is an extinct species of pigeon native to and once abundant in North America. Because of the birds' extremely dense population, they had been reported to blacken the skies when they flew in flocks. The pigeons went extinct in 1914.

나그네비둘기는 북아메리카 토종의 멸종된 비둘기 종으로 한때 북아메리카에 많았다. 그 새들의 극도로 밀집한 개체수 때문에, 그것들은 무리를 이뤄 날 때 하늘을 검게 하는 것으로 보고되었다. 그 비둘기들은 1914년에 멸종했다.

외형적 특징

Passenger pigeons were medium-sized birds, measuring about 15 to 16 inches in length and weighing about 9 to 12 ounces. The male had blue-gray feathers on its body and red on its breast, while the female had a brownish body, gray breast, and white belly. [67]The bird was notable for being compact and streamlined for prolonged flight.

나그네비둘기들은 길이가 약 15에서 16인치이고 무게가 약 9에서 12온스인 중간 크기의 새였다. 수컷은 몸에 청회색 깃털이 있고 가슴이 빨간색이지만, 암컷은 갈색을 띤 몸과, 회색 가슴, 하얀 배를 가지고 있었다. [67]이 새는 장기간의 비행을 위해 작고 유선형인 것이 주목할 만했다.

A unique trait of passenger pigeons was the way they congregated in order to breed. [68(b)]A colony of birds could cover hundreds of thousands of acres and have hundreds of nests per tree. One nesting site in Wisconsin was estimated to have about 136 million birds. [68(c)]Passenger pigeons may have numbered up to five billion at the height of their population. When searching for food, [68(d)]the pigeons were observed to fly by the millions, blotting out the sky and darkening it.

나그네비둘기의 독특한 특징은 번식하기 위해 모여드는 방식이었다. [68(b)]새들의 무리는 수십만 에이커의 면적을 차지하며 나무 한 그루당 수백 개의 둥지를 가질 수 있었다. 위스콘신의 한 둥지 터에는 약 1억 3,600만 마리의 새들이 있는 것으로 추정되었다. [68(c)]나그네비둘기들은 그들의 개체수가 최고조일 때 50억 마리까지 달했을 것이다. 먹이를 찾을 때, [68(d)]비둘기들은 수백만 마리씩 날아다니며, 하늘을 완전히 가려서 어둡게 만드는 것이 관찰되었다.

While many animals preyed on the pigeons, [72]humans were the main culprit of the birds' extinction. Forests were cut down for farmlands, an act that destroyed the pigeons' home and primary food source. Mass hunting of the birds began in the 1800s. [69]Farmers considered the birds to be pests and gunned them down to protect the grain fields. Pigeon meat was also sold for a cheap price.

많은 동물이 비둘기들을 잡아먹었지만, [72]사람들이 이 새의 멸종의 주요 원인이었다. 농지를 위해 숲이 벌목되었는데, 이것은 비둘기들의 보금자리와 주요 식량원을 파괴했던 행위였다. 이 새들에 대한 대규모 사냥은 1800년대에 시작되었다. [69]농부들은 이 새들을 유해 동물로 간주했고 곡물 밭을 보호하기 위해 총으로 쏘아 죽였다. 비둘기 고기도 싼 가격에 팔렸다.

The passenger pigeons' numbers were noticeably decreasing by the 1860s. [70]When a bill was finally introduced in the Michigan legislature for a ten-year halt to hunting, it was too late to save the pigeons. The once-plentiful birds were now mostly living as individual survivors in the wild or in captivity. [70]The remaining pigeons were not enough to repopulate the species.

나그네비둘기의 개체 수는 1860년대에 눈에 띄게 줄어들고 있었다. [70]마침내 사냥하기를 10년간 중단하는 법안이 미시간주 입법부에 제출되었을 때는, 비둘기들을 구하기에 너무 늦었다. 한때 많았던 새들은 이제 대부분 야생이나 사육 상태에서 개별적인 생존 개체로 살고 있었다. [70]남아 있던 비둘기들은 그 종을 다시 번식시키기에는 충분하지 않았다.

On September 1, 1914, the last living passenger pigeon, Martha, died in the Cincinnati Zoo, [73]stirring public concern for the conservation of animals. Since 2012, attempts have been made to revive the species. [71]A wildlife conservation group called Revive and Restore hopes to use genetic cloning to return the passenger pigeon to the forests and fields of North America.

1914년 9월 1일에, 마지막으로 살아있던 나그네비둘기인 마사가 동물 보호에 대한 [73]대중의 관심을 일으키며, 신시내티 동물원에서 죽었다. 2012년부터, 이 종을 되살리기 위해 시도가 있어왔다. [71]Revive and Restore라고 불리는 야생동물 보호 단체는 유전자 복제를 사용하여 이 나그네비둘기를 북아메리카의 숲과 들판으로 돌려보내기를 희망한다.

어휘 | passenger pigeon phr. 나그네비둘기 extinct adj. 멸종된 native to phr. 토종의 abundant adj. 많은, 풍부한 dense adj. 밀집한 population n. 개체수, 집단 blacken v. ~을 검게 하다 in flock phr. 무리를 이뤄 breast n. 가슴 belly n. 배, 복부 compact adj. 작은, 다부진 streamlined adj. 유선형의, 날씬한 prolonged adj. 장기간의 trait n. 특징, 특성 congregate v. 모이다, 집합하다 breed v. 번식하다, 기르다 estimate v. 추정하다, 예상하다 number v. ~수에 달하다; n. 수, 숫자 blot out phr. ~을 완전히 가리다 darken v. ~을 어둡게 하다 prey v. 잡아먹다; n. 먹이 farmland n. 농지 food source phr. 식량원 mass adj. 대규모의, 대량의 pest n. 유해 동물, 해충 gun down phr. ~을 총으로 쏘아 죽이다 grain field phr. 곡물 밭 bill n. 법안 introduce v. (법안을) 제출하다 legislature n. 입법부 halt v. 중단시키다, 멈추다 survivor n. 생존자 in captivity phr. 사육 상태에 repopulate v. 다시 번식시키다, 다시 ~에 살게 하다 public concern phr. 대중의 관심 conservation n. 보호, 보존 revive v. 되살리다, 소생시키다 genetic cloning phr. 유전자 복제

67 특정세부사항 What

난이도 ●●○

According to the text, what was noteworthy about passenger pigeons?

(a) their ability to travel for extended periods
(b) their unusual flock shape when flying
(c) their tendency to migrate away from populated areas
(d) their ability to fly at record-breaking speeds

본문에 따르면, 나그네비둘기에 관해 주목할 만한 점은 무엇이었는가?

(a) 장기간 동안 이동하는 능력
(b) 날 때 특이한 무리 모양
(c) 개체수가 많은 지역을 떠나 이주하려는 경향
(d) 기록적인 속도로 나는 능력

━○ 정답 잡는 치트키

질문의 키워드 noteworthy가 notable로 paraphrasing되어 언급된 주변 내용을 주의 깊게 읽는다.

해설 | 2단락의 'The bird was notable for being compact and streamlined for prolonged flight.'에서 나그네비둘기는 장기간의 비행을 위해 작고 유선형인 것이 주목할 만했다고 했다. 따라서 (a)가 정답이다.

⇄ **Paraphrasing**
prolonged 장기간의 → for extended periods 장기간 동안

어휘 | noteworthy adj. 주목할 만한 unusual adj. 특이한, 드문 tendency n. 경향 migrate v. 이주하다, 이동하다
record-breaking adj. 기록적인, 기록을 깨는

68 Not/True Not 문제

난이도 ●●●

Which of the following was NOT true about passenger pigeons before their population declined?

(a) Their females formed small groups for breeding.
(b) Their habitat was spread across wide areas.
(c) Their population peaked at billions of birds.
(d) Their flocks blocked sunlight when flying.

다음 중 개체수가 감소하기 전의 나그네비둘기에 관해 사실이 아닌 것은?

(a) 암컷들은 번식을 위해 작은 무리를 이뤘다.
(b) 서식지는 넓은 지역에 퍼져있었다.
(c) 개체수는 수십억 마리에 이르렀다.
(d) 무리는 날 때 햇빛을 막았다.

━○ 정답 잡는 치트키

질문의 키워드 before their population declined와 관련된 주변 내용을 주의 깊게 읽고, 보기의 키워드와 지문 내용을 대조하며 언급되는 것을 하나씩 소거한다.

해설 | (a)는 지문에 언급되지 않았으므로, (a)가 정답이다.

오답분석
(b) 보기의 키워드 wide areas가 hundreds of thousands of acres로 paraphrasing되어 언급된 3단락에서 새들의 무리는 수십만 에이커의 면적을 차지할 수 있었다고 언급되었다.
(c) 보기의 키워드 population이 그대로 언급된 3단락에서 나그네비둘기들은 그들의 개체수가 최고조일 때 50억 마리까지 달했을 것이라고 언급되었다.
(d) 보기의 키워드 blocked가 blotting out으로 paraphrasing되어 언급된 3단락에서 비둘기들은 수백만 마리씩 날아다니며 하늘을 완전히 가려서 어둡게 하는 것이 관찰되었다고 언급되었다.

어휘 | habitat n. 서식지 peak v. 절정에 이르다 block v. 막다

Why, most likely, did the pigeons become hunted?	비둘기들은 왜 사냥당하게 되었을 것 같은가?
(a) because they were taking over the forests (b) because they were the main source of income for farmers **(c) because they were feeding on valuable crops** (d) because they attracted many other pests	(a) 숲을 장악하고 있었기 때문에 (b) 농부들의 주된 수입원이었기 때문에 **(c) 소중한 농작물을 먹고 살았기 때문에** (d) 다른 많은 해충을 끌어들였기 때문에

←○ 정답 잡는 치트키

질문의 키워드 hunted가 gunned ~ down으로 paraphrasing되어 언급된 주변 내용을 주의 깊게 읽는다.

해설 | 4단락의 'Farmers ~ gunned them down to protect the grain fields.'에서 농부들이 곡물 밭을 보호하기 위해 비둘기들을 총으로 쏘아 죽였다고 한 것을 통해, 비둘기들이 곡물 밭에서 소중한 농작물을 먹고 살았기 때문에 농부들이 비둘기들을 사냥했음을 추론할 수 있다. 따라서 (c)가 정답이다.

어휘 | hunt v. 사냥하다; n. 사냥, 수렵 take over phr. 장악하다 source of income phr. 수입원, 소득원천 feed on phr. ~을 먹고 살다 crop n. 농작물 attract v. 끌어들이다

70 특정세부사항 Why 난이도 ●●○

Why was the law that outlawed pigeon hunting unable to save the species?	비둘기 사냥을 금지한 법이 왜 그 종을 구할 수 없었는가?
(a) The period it covered was too short. **(b) The birds were already too few in number.** (c) The last of their kind had already been captured. (d) The majority of hunters refused to cooperate.	(a) 적용된 기간은 너무 짧았다. **(b) 새들은 이미 수가 너무 적었다.** (c) 그 종의 마지막 개체는 이미 포획되어 있었다. (d) 대부분 사냥꾼은 협조하기를 거부했다.

←○ 정답 잡는 치트키

질문의 키워드 law가 bill로 paraphrasing되어 언급된 주변 내용을 주의 깊게 읽는다.

해설 | 5단락의 'When a bill was finally introduced ~ for a ten-year halt to hunting, it was too late to save the pigeons.'에서 마침내 사냥하기를 10년간 중단하는 법안이 제출되었을 때는 비둘기들을 구하기에 너무 늦었다고 한 뒤, 'The remaining pigeons were not enough to repopulate the species.'에서 남아 있던 비둘기들은 그 종을 다시 번식시키기에는 충분하지 않았다고 했다. 따라서 (b)가 정답이다.

⇄ Paraphrasing
not enough 충분하지 않은 → too few in number 수가 너무 적은

어휘 | outlaw v. 금지하다, 불법화하다 capture v. ~을 포획하다, 붙잡다 majority n. 대부분 cooperate v. 협조하다, 협력하다

71 특정세부사항 How 난이도 ●●○

How have conservation groups been trying to bring back the species?	환경보호 단체들은 어떻게 이 종을 되찾으려고 노력해 오고 있는가?

(a) by rebuilding the pigeons' former habitat
(b) by offering a reward for remaining specimens
(c) by trying to breed the last two remaining birds
(d) by carrying out experimental procedures

(a) 비둘기의 이전 서식지를 재건함으로써
(b) 남은 표본에 대하여 보상을 제공함으로써
(c) 마지막으로 남은 두 마리의 새들을 번식시키려고 시도함으로써
(d) 실험 절차를 수행함으로써

← 정답 잡는 치트키

질문의 키워드 conservation groups가 그대로 언급된 주변 내용을 주의 깊게 읽는다.

해설 | 6단락의 'A wildlife conservation group ~ hopes to use genetic cloning to return the passenger pigeon to the forests and fields of North America.'에서 야생동물 보호 단체는 유전자 복제를 사용하여 이 나그네비둘기를 북아메리카의 숲과 들판으로 돌려보내기를 희망한다고 했다. 따라서 (d)가 정답이다.

⇄ **Paraphrasing**
genetic cloning 유전자 복제 → experimental procedures 실험 절차

어휘 | bring back phr. ~을 되찾다 rebuild v. 재건하다 reward n. 보상, 보답; v. 상을 주다 specimen n. 표본, 견본 carry out phr. 수행하다
procedure n. 절차, 과정

---

72 어휘 유의어   난이도 ●●○

In the context of the passage, <u>culprit</u> means _____.

(a) excuse
(b) proof
(c) solution
(d) cause

지문의 문맥에서, 'culprit'은 -을 의미한다.

(a) 변명
(b) 근거
(c) 해결책
(d) 원인

← 정답 잡는 치트키

밑줄 친 어휘의 유의어를 찾는 문제이므로, culprit이 포함된 구절을 읽고 문맥을 파악한다.

해설 | 4단락의 'humans were the main culprit'은 사람들이 주요 원인이었다는 뜻이므로, culprit이 '원인'이라는 의미로 사용된 것을 알 수 있다. 따라서 '원인'이라는 같은 의미의 (d) cause가 정답이다.

---

73 어휘 유의어   난이도 ●●○

In the context of the passage, <u>stirring</u> means _____.

(a) touching
(b) raising
(c) beating
(d) mixing

지문의 문맥에서, 'stirring'은 -을 의미한다.

(a) 감동하게 하며
(b) 일으키며
(c) 물리치며
(d) 결합하며

← 정답 잡는 치트키

밑줄 친 어휘의 유의어를 찾는 문제이므로, stirring이 포함된 구절을 읽고 문맥을 파악한다.

해설 | 6단락의 'stirring public concern'은 대중의 관심을 일으켰다는 뜻이므로, stirring이 '일으키며'라는 의미로 사용된 것을 알 수 있다. 따라서 '일으키며'라는 같은 의미의 (b) raising이 정답이다.

수신인 정보	Jessica Florence HR Representative Justice Resource, Inc. 45 Oak Street New York City, NY Dear Ms. Florence,

Jessica Florence
인사 담당자
Justice Resource사
오크가 45번지
뉴욕주, 뉴욕시

Ms. Florence께,

편지의 목적: 면접 불참 사과

⁷⁴I was scheduled for a job interview last Monday but was unable to attend due to ⁷⁹an unforeseen event. I have already spoken with you about this matter, and ⁷⁴I am now writing this letter to formally apologize and explain the situation behind my absence.

⁷⁴저는 지난 월요일에 면접이 예정되어 있었는데 ⁷⁹예기치 않은 일로 참석할 수 없었습니다. 이 문제에 관해 이미 귀하와 이야기를 나눴으며, ⁷⁴정식으로 사과하고 저의 불참 이면의 상황을 설명하기 위해 이 편지를 씁니다.

면접 불참 이유

On the day of our interview, I received a call from my son's elementary school informing me that he was sick and had been admitted to the school's clinic. ⁷⁵He needed to be fetched urgently, and since my wife is currently out of the country, I had no choice but to cancel our interview.

면접 당일에, 제 아들의 초등학교에서 아들이 아파서 학교 진찰실에 입원했다는 것을 알리는 전화를 받았습니다. ⁷⁵아들을 급히 데려와야 했는데, 제 아내가 현재 국외에 있어서, 면접을 취소할 수밖에 없었습니다.

회사에 바라는 사항

⁷⁶We went to see a doctor, who said my son was suffering from food poisoning. (I suspect the cause to be the school's drinking fountain, as my son asserted that the water "tasted funny.") In any case, my son's health is much better now. He knows that I missed my interview and feels guilty, and he even offered to somehow "fix" the situation, but I explained to him that ⁷⁷family comes first. He will always be my top priority, and ⁷⁷I hope that any potential employer can understand and perhaps even respect that sense of duty as a sign of good character.

⁷⁶저희는 진찰받으러 갔는데, 의사는 아들이 식중독을 앓고 있다고 했습니다.(아들이 물에서 "이상한 맛이 났다"라고 주장한 것으로 보아, 저는 학교의 식수대가 원인일 거로 생각합니다.) 어쨌든, 제 아들의 건강은 지금 훨씬 좋아졌습니다. 아들은 제가 면접을 놓친 것을 알고 죄책감을 느끼며, 심지어 이 상황을 어떻게든 "해결하겠다"고 제안하기도 했지만, 저는 그에게 ⁷⁷가족이 최우선이라고 설명했습니다. 그는 항상 저의 최우선 순위가 될 것이며, ⁷⁷저는 잠재적인 고용주라면 누구나 이해하고 어쩌면 이러한 책임감을 좋은 인격의 표시로 존중해 줄 수 있기를 바랍니다.

포부 + 요청 사항

⁷⁸/⁸⁰I want to assure you that I take work-related responsibilities seriously, and I would never break a professional commitment without a pressing reason. I apologize for missing the interview. ⁷⁸I would like to request another chance to prove my value to your team at Justice Resource, Inc.

⁷⁸/⁸⁰저는 업무와 관련된 책임을 진지하게 받아들이고 있으며, 긴급한 이유 없이는 절대로 직업적 의무를 어기지 않을 것임을 장담하고 싶습니다. 면접에 불참한 것에 대해 사과드립니다. ⁷⁸저는 저의 가치를 Justice Resource사에 있는 귀하의 팀에 증명할 기회를 한 번 더 요청하고 싶습니다.

끝인사

Attached to this letter is a record of my son's medical visit. Thank you for your understanding.

이 편지에 제 아들의 병원 방문 기록이 첨부되어 있습니다. 양해해 주셔서 감사합니다.

발신인 정보

Sincerely,

Brandon Smith
Brandon Smith

Brandon Smith 드림

어휘 | formally adv. 정식으로, 공식적으로   apologize v. 사과하다   absence n. 불참, 부재   admit v. 입원시키다   clinic n. 진찰실, 진료소   fetch v. ~을 데리고 오다   urgently adv. 급히, 긴급하게   out of the country phr. 국외로   have no choice but to phr. ~할 수밖에 없다   see a doctor phr. 진찰을 받다   suffer from phr. (병을) 앓다   food poisoning phr. 식중독   drinking fountain phr. 식수대, 음수대   assert v. 주장하다   funny adj. 이상한, 수상한   guilty adj. 죄책감이 드는, 유죄의   come first phr. 최우선이다   priority n. 우선 순위   potential adj. 잠재적인   sense of duty phr. 책임감, 의무감   sign n. 표시, 징조   responsibility n. 책임, 의무   seriously adv. 진지하게, 심각하게   commitment n. 의무, 책임   pressing adj. 긴급한, 시급한   value n. 가치

74 주제/목적   편지의 목적

난이도 ●●○

What is the purpose of Brandon Smith's letter?

(a) to request feedback on his job interview
(b) to apologize for his absence at a client meeting
(c) to establish why he cannot attend employee training
(d) **to explain why he missed an appointment**

Brandon Smith의 편지의 목적은 무엇인가?

(a) 면접에 관한 피드백을 요청하기 위해서
(b) 고객 미팅에 불참한 것을 사과하기 위해서
(c) 직원 교육에 왜 참석할 수 없는지를 분명히 하기 위해서
(d) **약속을 왜 어겼는지를 설명하기 위해서**

🔑 정답 잡는 치트키

지문의 초반을 주의 깊게 읽고 전체 맥락을 파악한다.

해설 ┃ 1단락의 'I was scheduled for a job interview last Monday but was unable to attend due to an unforeseen event.'에서 지난 월요일에 면접이 예정되어 있었는데 예기치 않은 일로 참석할 수 없었다고 했고, 'I am now writing this letter to formally apologize and explain the situation behind my absence'에서 정식으로 사과하고 불참 이면의 상황을 설명하기 위해 이 편지를 쓴다고 한 뒤, 면접에 불참한 이유를 설명하는 내용이 이어지고 있다. 따라서 (d)가 정답이다.

⇄ Paraphrasing

a job interview 면접 → an appointment 약속

75 특정세부사항   Why

난이도 ●●○

Why did Brandon have to cancel his plans?

(a) His international flight was delayed.
(b) **He was the only one able to handle the emergency.**
(c) He needed to take care of his wife who was ill.
(d) His son's school needed to close suddenly.

Brandon은 왜 그의 계획을 취소해야 했는가?

(a) 그의 국제선 비행기가 연착되었다.
(b) **그는 비상사태를 처리할 수 있는 유일한 사람이었다.**
(c) 그는 아픈 아내를 돌봐야 했다.
(d) 그의 아들의 학교는 갑자기 문을 닫아야 했다.

🔑 정답 잡는 치트키

질문의 키워드 cancel ~ plans가 cancel ~ interview로 paraphrasing되어 언급된 주변 내용을 주의 깊게 읽는다.

해설 ┃ 2단락의 'He needed to be fetched urgently, and since my wife is currently out of the country, I had no choice but to cancel our interview.'에서 아들을 급히 데려와야 했는데 아내가 현재 국외에 있어서 면접을 취소할 수밖에 없었다고 했다. 따라서 (b)가 정답이다.

어휘 ┃ emergency n. 비상사태 take care of phr. ~을 돌보다, 신경 쓰다 suddenly adv. 갑자기

76 추론   특정사실

난이도 ●●○

How did Brandon's son probably get sick?

(a) **from problems with the school's water supply**
(b) from someone in his class who was running a fever
(c) from outdated food served in the school's lunchroom
(d) from an allergy to an item packed in his lunch

Brandon의 아들은 어떻게 병에 걸렸을 것 같은가?

(a) **학교 급수 시설의 문제로부터**
(b) 그의 반에서 열이 나고 있던 누군가로부터
(c) 학교 구내식당에서 제공되는 기한이 지난 음식으로부터
(d) 점심 도시락에 포장된 품목에 대한 알레르기로부터

질문의 키워드 get sick이 was suffering으로 paraphrasing되어 언급된 주변 내용을 주의 깊게 읽는다.

해설 | 3단락의 'We went to see a doctor, who said my son was suffering from food poisoning. (I suspect the cause to be the school's drinking fountain ~)'에서 진찰을 받으러 갔는데 의사는 아들이 식중독을 앓고 있다고 했고, 학교의 식수대가 원인이라고 생각한다고 한 것을 통해, Brandon의 아들은 학교 급수 시설인 식수대의 문제로부터 식중독에 걸렸음을 추론할 수 있다. 따라서 (a)가 정답이다.

  ⇄ **Paraphrasing**
drinking fountain 식수대 → water supply 급수 시설

어휘 | water supply phr. 급수 시설　run a fever phr. 열이 나다　outdated adj. 기한이 지난　lunchroom n. 구내식당

77　추론　　특정사실　　　　　　　　　　　　　난이도 ●●●

Why, most likely, does Brandon explain to Jessica that family is the most important thing in his life?

(a) so she can see that he maintains a happy household
(b) so she understands that he can only work limited hours
(c) so she will assign him fewer duties as an employee
(d) so she will admire his loyalty as a potential worker

Brandon은 왜 Jessica에게 가족이 그의 인생에서 가장 중요한 것이라고 설명하는 것 같은가?

(a) 그가 행복한 가정을 유지하고 있다는 것을 그녀가 알 수 있도록 하기 위해서
(b) 그가 제한된 시간만 일할 수 있다는 것을 그녀가 이해하도록 하기 위해서
(c) 그녀가 직원으로서 더 적은 업무를 그에게 맡기도록 하기 위해서
(d) 잠재적인 직원으로서 그의 충성심을 그녀가 높이 평가하도록 하기 위해서

질문의 키워드 family is the most important thing이 family comes first로 paraphrasing되어 언급된 주변 내용을 주의 깊게 읽는다.

해설 | 3단락의 'family comes first'에서 가족이 최우선이라고 한 뒤, 'I hope that any potential employer can ~ perhaps even respect that sense of duty as a sign of good character'에서 잠재적인 고용주라면 누구나 어쩌면 이러한 책임감을 좋은 인격의 표시로 존중해 줄 수 있기를 바란다고 한 것을 통해, Brandon은 잠재적인 직원으로서 그의 충성심을 Jessica가 높이 평가하도록 하기 위해 가족이 그의 인생에서 가장 중요한 것이라고 설명하고 있음을 추론할 수 있다. 따라서 (d)가 정답이다.

  ⇄ **Paraphrasing**
respect 존중하다 → admire 높이 평가하다
sense of duty 책임감 → loyalty 충성심

어휘 | household n. 가정, 가구　duty n. 업무, 임무　admire v. 높이 평가하다, 감탄하다　loyalty n. 충성심

78　특정세부사항　　Why　　　　　　　　　　　난이도 ●●●

Why does Brandon think he deserves another chance for an interview?

(a) because he openly admitted his mistake
(b) because he is ordinarily more reliable

Brandon은 왜 인터뷰할 기회를 한 번 더 가질 자격이 있다고 생각하는가?

(a) 자기의 실수를 솔직히 시인했기 때문에
(b) 보통은 더 신뢰할 만하기 때문에

(c) because he demonstrated his value to the company
(d) because he has never missed an interview before

(c) 회사에 자기의 가치를 보여줬기 때문에
(d) 이전에는 면접을 불참한 적이 없기 때문에

─○ 정답 잡는 치트키

질문의 키워드 another chance가 그대로 언급된 주변 내용을 수의 깊게 읽는다.

해설 | 4단락의 'I want to assure you that I take work-related responsibilities seriously, and I would never break a professional commitment without a pressing reason.'에서 업무와 관련된 책임을 진지하게 받아들이고 있으며 긴급한 이유 없이는 절대로 직업적 의무를 어기지 않을 것임을 장담하고 싶다고 한 뒤, 'I would like to request another chance to prove my value to your team'에서 자기의 가치를 팀에 증명할 기회를 한 번 더 요청하고 싶다고 했다. 따라서 (b)가 정답이다.

어휘 | deserve v. ~할 자격이 있다　openly adv. 솔직하게, 터놓고　admit v. 시인하다, 인정하다　ordinarily adv. 보통　reliable adj. 신뢰할 만한

79　어휘　유의어
난이도 ●○○

In the context of the passage, <u>unforeseen</u> means _____.

(a) unexpected
(b) unlikely
(c) unpopular
(d) unsafe

지문의 문맥에서, 'unforeseen'은 -을 의미한다.

(a) 예기치 않은
(b) 가망이 없는
(c) 평판이 좋지 않은
(d) 위험한

─○ 정답 잡는 치트키

밑줄 친 어휘의 유의어를 찾는 문제이므로, unforeseen이 포함된 구절을 읽고 문맥을 파악한다.

해설 | 1단락의 'an unforeseen event'는 예기치 않은 일이라는 뜻이므로, unforeseen은 '예기치 않은'이라는 의미로 사용된 것을 알 수 있다. 따라서 '예기치 않은'이라는 같은 의미의 (a) unexpected 가 정답이다.

80　어휘　유의어
난이도 ●●○

In the context of the passage, <u>assure</u> means _____.

(a) teach
(b) concern
(c) ask
(d) promise

지문의 문맥에서, 'assure'는 -을 의미한다.

(a) 가르치다
(b) 관련시키다
(c) 요청하다
(d) 약속하다

─○ 정답 잡는 치트키

밑줄 친 어휘의 유의어를 찾는 문제이므로, assure가 포함된 구절을 읽고 문맥을 파악한다.

해설 | 4단락의 'I want to assure you'는 장담하고 싶다는 뜻이므로, assure가 '장담하다'라는 의미로 사용된 것을 알 수 있다. 따라서 '약속하다'라는 비슷한 의미의 (d) promise가 정답이다.

공식기출
TEST 6
정답 · 스크립트 · 해석 · 해설

GRAMMAR

LISTENING

READING & VOCABULARY

GRAMMAR	_____ / 26	(점수 : _____ 점)
LISTENING	_____ / 26	(점수 : _____ 점)
READING & VOCABULARY	_____ / 28	(점수 : _____ 점)

TOTAL _____ / 80 **(평균 점수 : _____ 점)**

*각 영역 점수: 맞은 개수 × 3.75

*평균 점수: 각 영역 점수 합계 ÷ 3

정답 및 취약 유형 분석표

자동 채점 및 성적 분석 서비스 ▶

GRAMMAR

번호	정답	유형
01	a	준동사
02	c	시제
03	b	관계사
04	d	가정법
05	a	연결어
06	b	시제
07	c	준동사
08	c	가정법
09	d	관계사
10	a	조동사
11	a	시제
12	d	준동사
13	d	시제
14	c	조동사
15	a	조동사
16	b	준동사
17	c	가정법
18	a	연결어
19	a	가정법
20	b	시제
21	b	준동사
22	c	가정법
23	b	시제
24	d	조동사
25	d	가정법
26	c	준동사

LISTENING

PART	번호	정답	유형
PART 1	27	a	특정세부사항
	28	b	특정세부사항
	29	a	특정세부사항
	30	d	특정세부사항
	31	d	추론
	32	c	특정세부사항
PART 2	33	c	추론
	34	d	주제/목적
	35	a	특정세부사항
	36	d	특정세부사항
	37	b	특정세부사항
	38	b	추론
	39	d	추론
PART 3	40	c	특정세부사항
	41	a	특정세부사항
	42	b	추론
	43	b	특정세부사항
	44	c	특정세부사항
	45	a	추론
	46	d	주제/목적
PART 4	47	d	특정세부사항
	48	b	특정세부사항
	49	a	추론
	50	c	특정세부사항
	51	d	특정세부사항
	52	b	추론

READING & VOCABULARY

PART	번호	정답	유형
PART 1	53	a	특정세부사항
	54	a	특정세부사항
	55	c	추론
	56	b	특정세부사항
	57	c	특정세부사항
	58	d	어휘
	59	d	어휘
PART 2	60	a	주제/목적
	61	a	Not/True
	62	c	특정세부사항
	63	b	추론
	64	b	추론
	65	a	어휘
	66	d	어휘
PART 3	67	d	특정세부사항
	68	c	Not/True
	69	d	추론
	70	a	특정세부사항
	71	b	추론
	72	c	어휘
	73	a	어휘
PART 4	74	c	특정세부사항
	75	d	추론
	76	b	특정세부사항
	77	a	추론
	78	c	특정세부사항
	79	d	어휘
	80	b	어휘

유형	맞힌 개수
시제	/ 6
가정법	/ 6
준동사	/ 6
조동사	/ 4
연결어	/ 2
관계사	/ 2
TOTAL	/ 26

유형	맞힌 개수
주제/목적	/ 2
특정세부사항	/ 16
Not/True	/ 0
추론	/ 8
TOTAL	/ 26

유형	맞힌 개수
주제/목적	/ 1
특정세부사항	/ 10
Not/True	/ 2
추론	/ 7
어휘	/ 8
TOTAL	/ 28

GRAMMAR

01 준동사   동명사를 목적어로 취하는 동사   난이도 ●●○

Research shows that many adults are still afraid of the dark. Among those who admit to having the fear, however, nearly 70% said they dislike _____ the issue to others.

(a) mentioning
(b) to mention
(c) having mentioned
(d) to have mentioned

연구는 많은 어른들이 여전히 어둠을 두려워한다는 것을 보여준다. 그러나 두려움을 가지고 있음을 인정하는 사람 중에, 거의 70%가 다른 사람들에게 그 문제를 <u>언급하는 것</u>을 싫어한다고 말했다.

━━○ 지텔프 치트키

dislike는 동명사를 목적어로 취한다.

> ☀ **동명사를 목적어로 취하는 빈출 동사**
> dislike 싫어하다   avoid 피하다   imagine 상상하다   mind 개의하다   keep 계속하다   consider 고려하다   prevent 방지하다
> enjoy 즐기다   recommend 권장하다   risk 위험을 무릅쓰다   involve 포함하다

해설 | 빈칸 앞 동사 dislike는 동명사를 목적어로 취하므로, 동명사 (a) mentioning이 정답이다.

> 오답분석
> (c) having mentioned도 동명사이기는 하지만, 완료동명사(having mentioned)로 쓰일 경우 '싫어하는' 시점보다 '언급하는' 시점이 앞선다는 것을 나타내므로 문맥에 적합하지 않아 오답이다.

어휘 | be afraid of phr. ~을 두려워하다   admit v. 인정하다, 시인하다   fear n. 두려움, 공포

02 시제   미래진행   난이도 ●●○

After a grueling admissions process, Lea was finally accepted into a prestigious arts school in the United Kingdom. Starting this semester, she _____ in London with a relative while she goes to school.

(a) stayed
(b) has been staying
(c) will be staying
(d) will have stayed

기진맥진하게 하는 입학 과정 후에, Lea는 마침내 영국에 있는 명망 있는 예술 학교에 받아들여졌다. 이번 학기부터, 그녀는 학교에 다니는 동안 친척과 함께 런던에 <u>머무르고 있는 중일 것</u>이다.

━━○ 지텔프 치트키

'for + 기간 표현' 없이 'starting + 미래 시점'만 있으면 미래진행 시제가 정답이다.

> ☀ **미래진행과 자주 함께 쓰이는 시간 표현**
> • when / if + 현재 동사 ~할 때 / 만약 ~한다면   • until / by + 미래 시점 ~까지
> • next + 시간 표현 다음 ~에   • starting + 미래 시점 / tomorrow ~부터 / 내일

해설 | 미래진행 시제와 함께 쓰이는 시간 표현 'starting + 미래 시점'(Starting this semester)이 있고, 문맥상 Lea는 마침내 영국에 있는 명망 있는 예술 학교에 받아들여져서 미래 시점인 이번 학기부터 런던에 머무르고 있는 중일 것이라는 의미가 되어야 자연스럽다. 따라서 미래진행 시제 (c) will be staying이 정답이다.

어휘 | grueling adj. 기진맥진하게 하는 prestigious adj. 명망 있는, 일류의 semester n. 학기 relative n. 친척; adj. 관계가 있는

---

03 관계사　주격 관계대명사 which　난이도 ●●○

My brothers are arguing with each other over who should retrieve the ball that got kicked into the yard of the abandoned house next door. The house, _____, is believed by local kids to be haunted.

(a) that has been vacant for years
(b) which has been vacant for years
(c) who has been vacant for years
(d) what has been vacant for years

나의 형들이 버려진 옆집 마당에 찬 공을 누가 되찾아 와야 하는지를 두고 서로 말다툼하고 있는 중이다. 그 집은, 수년째 비어 있는데, 동네 아이들은 유령이 출몰할 것으로 믿는다.

○ 지텔프 치트키

사물 선행사가 관계절 안에서 주어 역할을 하고, 빈칸 앞에 콤마(,)가 있으면 주격 관계대명사 which가 정답이다.

해설 | 사물 선행사 The house를 받으면서 콤마(,) 뒤에 올 수 있는 주격 관계대명사가 필요하므로, (b) which has been vacant for years 가 정답이다.

오답분석
(a) 관계대명사 that도 사물 선행사를 받을 수 있지만, 콤마 뒤에 올 수 없으므로 오답이다.

어휘 | argue v. 말다툼하다, 논쟁하다 retrieve v. 되찾다, 회수하다 kick v. (걷어)차다 yard n. 마당 abandoned adj. 버려진, 유기된 haunt v. (유령 등이) 출몰하다, 자주 나오다 vacant adj. 비어 있는, 텅 빈

---

04 가정법　가정법 과거완료　난이도 ●●○

The hiring manager rejected a job candidate this morning saying, "He had impressive qualifications, but he couldn't recall anything about our mission. If he had researched our company, he _____ the job on the spot."

(a) would get
(b) will have gotten
(c) will get
(d) would have gotten

채용 담당자는 오늘 아침 한 입사 지원자를, "그는 인상적인 자질을 가지고 있었지만, 우리의 임무에 관해 아무것도 기억하지 못했습니다. 만약 그가 우리 회사를 조사했었다면, 그 직위에 일자리를 얻었을 것입니다."라며 거절했다.

○ 지텔프 치트키

'if + had p.p.'가 있으면 'would/could + have p.p.'가 정답이다.

☼ 가정법 과거완료
If + 주어 + had p.p., 주어 + would/could(조동사 과거형) + have p.p.

해설 | If절에 'had p.p.' 형태의 had researched가 있으므로, 주절에는 이와 짝을 이루어 가정법 과거완료를 만드는 'would(조동사 과거형) + have p.p.'가 와야 한다. 따라서 (d) would have gotten이 정답이다.

어휘 | reject v. 거절하다 job candidate phr. 입사 지원자 qualification n. 자질 recall v. 기억하다, 상기하다 mission n. 임무, 사명
spot n. 직위, 직

---

05 연결어   접속부사   난이도 ●●○

Movie previews are called "trailers" because they were originally shown after the movie, not before. _____, this proved rather ineffective, as the audience did not stay around after the film to watch them.

(a) **However**
(b) In particular
(c) In addition
(d) Meanwhile

영화 시사회는 원래 영화 이전이 아닌 이후에 상영되었기 때문에 "트레일러"라고 불린다. 그러나, 관객은 영화 이후에 그것들을 보기 위해 머무르지 않았기 때문에, 이것은 그다지 효과적이지 못한 것으로 드러났다.

해설 | 빈칸 앞 문장은 영화 시사회는 원래 영화 이전이 아닌 이후에 상영되었다는 내용이고, 빈칸 뒤 문장은 이것이 그다지 효과적이지 못한 것으로 드러났다는 대조적인 내용이다. 따라서 '그러나'라는 의미의 대조를 나타내는 접속부사 (a) However가 정답이나.

오답분석
(b) In particular는 '특히', (c) In addition은 '게다가', (d) Meanwhile은 '그동안에'라는 의미로, 문맥에 적합하지 않아 오답이다.

어휘 | preview n. 시사회 trailer n. 트레일러, (영화의) 예고편 ineffective adj. 효과적이지 못한 audience n. 관객, 관중

---

06 시제   미래완료진행   난이도 ●●○

Patrick is not even halfway through his flight, yet he has been in the air since his 6 a.m. departure from Chicago. By the time he reaches Melbourne tomorrow, he _____ for sixteen hours!

(a) would fly
(b) **will have been flying**
(c) will be flying
(d) has been flying

Patrick은 비행의 절반도 지나지 않았지만, 시카고에서의 오전 6시 출발 이래로 공중에 떠 있다. 그가 내일 멜버른에 도착할 무렵이면, 그는 16시간 동안 비행해오고 있는 중일 것이다!

> 💡 미래완료진행과 자주 함께 쓰이는 시간 표현
> • by the time / when / if + 현재 동사 + (for + 기간 표현) ~할 무렵이면 / ~할 때 / 만약 ~한다면 (~ 동안)
> • by / in + 미래 시점 + (for + 기간 표현) ~ 즈음에는 / ~에 (~ 동안)

해설 | 현재 동사로 미래의 의미를 나타내는 시간의 부사절 'by the time + 현재 동사'(By the time ~ reaches)와 지속을 나타내는 'for + 기간 표현'(for sixteen hours)이 있고, 문맥상 미래 시점인 내일 Patrick이 멜버른에 도착할 무렵이면 그는 16시간 동안 계속해서 비행해 오고 있는 중일 것이라는 의미가 되어야 자연스럽다. 따라서 미래완료진행 시제 (b) will have been flying이 정답이다.

오답분석

(c) 미래진행 시제는 특정 미래 시점에 한창 진행 중일 일을 나타내므로, 과거 또는 현재에 시작해서 특정 미래 시점까지 계속해서 진행되고 있을 일을 표현할 수 없어 오답이다.

어휘 | in the air phr. 공중에

---

07 준동사   to 부정사를 목적격 보어로 취하는 동사   난이도 ●●○

Clyde is organizing the company's annual talent competition, which is set for three months from now. To ensure smooth planning for the event, he is encouraging interested performers _____ their applications on time.

(a) to have submitted
(b) submitting
(c) to submit
(d) having submitted

Clyde는 회사의 연례 장기 자랑을 조직하고 있는 중인데, 이것은 지금으로부터 석 달 후로 예정되어 있다. 행사의 원활한 계획을 보장하기 위해, 그는 관심 있는 출연자들에게 제때 지원서를 제출할 것을 장려하고 있는 중이다.

🔑 지텔프 치트키

encourage는 to 부정사를 목적격 보어로 취한다.

> 💡 to 부정사를 목적격 보어로 취하는 빈출 동사
> encourage 장려하다   urge 강력히 촉구하다   require 요구하다   allow 허락하다   ask 요청하다

해설 | 빈칸 앞 동사 encourage는 'encourage+ 목적어 + 목적격 보어'의 형태로 쓰일 때 to 부정사를 목적격 보어로 취하여, '-에게 ~할 것을 장려하다'라는 의미로 사용된다. 따라서 to 부정사 (c) to submit이 정답이다.

오답분석

(a) to have submitted도 to 부정사이기는 하지만, 완료부정사(to have submitted)로 쓰일 경우 '장려하는' 시점보다 '제출하는' 시점이 앞선다는 것을 나타내므로 문맥에 적합하지 않아 오답이다.

어휘 | talent competition phr. 장기 자랑   smooth adj. 원활한, 매끄러운   on time phr. 제때

---

08 가정법   가정법 과거   난이도 ●●○

Despite being a highly paid software developer at a multinational company, Sheila still dreams of quitting her job someday. In fact, if money were no longer a factor, she _____ a full-time illustrator of children's books.

다국적 기업에서 높은 급료를 받는 소프트웨어 개발자임에도 불구하고, Sheila는 언젠가 직장을 그만두는 것을 여전히 꿈꾼다. 사실, 만약 돈이 더 이상 요인이 아니라면, 그녀는 아동 도서의 전업 삽화가가 될 것이다.

(a) will have become
(b) will become
(c) would become
(d) would have become

해설 | if절에 과거 동사(were)가 있으므로, 주절에는 이와 짝을 이루어 가정법 과거를 만드는 'would(조동사 과거형) + 동사원형'이 와야 한다. 따라서 (c) would become이 정답이다.

어휘 | highly paid phr. 높은 급료를 받는 multinational adj. 다국적의; n. 다국적 기업 dream v. (바라는 일을) 꿈꾸다 quit v. 그만두다

---

09 관계사   주격 관계대명사 who   난이도 ●●○

While visiting the set of *Game of Thrones*, Queen Elizabeth II declined to sit on the Iron Throne. The queen, _____ to not sit on a foreign throne, refused to even sit on a fictional one.

(a) that may have been following a royal rule
(b) which may have been following a royal rule
(c) what may have been following a royal rule
(d) who may have been following a royal rule

왕좌의 게임 세트장을 방문하는 동안, Elizabeth 2세 여왕은 철 왕좌에 앉기를 거절했다. 그 여왕은, 외국 왕좌에 앉지 않는 왕실의 규칙을 따라오고 있는 중일 지도 모르는데, 허구적인 왕좌에 앉는 것조차 거부했다.

해설 | 사람 선행사 The queen을 받으면서 콤마(,) 뒤에 올 수 있는 주격 관계대명사가 필요하므로, (d) who may have been following a royal rule이 정답이다.

오답분석
(a) 관계대명사 that도 사람 선행사를 받을 수 있지만, 콤마 뒤에 올 수 없으므로 오답이다.

어휘 | throne n. 왕좌, 왕위 decline v. 거절하다 refuse v. 거부하다, 거절하다 fictional adj. 허구적인, 지어낸 royal adj. 왕실의

---

10 조동사   조동사 must   난이도 ●○○

Globally, there is a growing initiative to plant more trees. Some countries even put tree planting into their legislation. In the Philippines, for instance, all students _____ plant at least ten trees before they can graduate.

전 세계적으로, 더 많은 나무를 심으려는 계획이 증가하고 있는 중이다. 일부 국가들은 심지어 나무 심기를 그들의 제정법에 포함했다. 예를 들어, 필리핀에서는, 모든 학생이 졸업하기 전에 적어도 열 그루의 나무를 <u>심어야 한다</u>.

(a) **must**
(b) would
(c) might
(d) can

해설 | 문맥상 일부 국가들은 나무 심기를 그들의 제정법에 포함했는데, 예를 들어, 필리핀에서는 모든 학생이 졸업하기 전에 적어도 열 그루의 나무를 심어야 한다는 의미가 되어야 자연스러우므로, '~해야 한다'를 뜻하면서 의무를 나타내는 조동사 (a) must가 정답이다. 참고로, must와 should 모두 '~해야 한다'를 뜻하지만, must는 should보다 강한 어조로 조언을 하거나 의무를 나타낼 때 쓴다.

어휘 | initiative n. 계획 legislation n. 제정법, 법률

---

11 시제   과거진행

난이도 ●●○

Richard's prized collection of vintage baseball cards was stolen from his house last night. According to him, nobody was home, as he _____ when the robbery took place.

(a) **was grocery shopping**
(b) grocery shopped
(c) is grocery shopping
(d) has grocery shopped

Richard의 고전적인 야구 카드의 중요한 수집품이 어젯밤 그의 집에서 도난당했다. 그에 따르면, 강도 사건이 일어났을 때 그는 장을 보고 있던 중이었기 때문에, 아무도 집에 없었다.

해설 | 과거진행 시제와 함께 쓰이는 시간 표현 'when + 과거 동사'(when ~ took place)가 있고, 문맥상 강도 사건이 일어났던 과거 시점에 Richard는 장을 보고 있던 중이었다는 의미가 되어야 자연스럽다. 따라서 과거진행 시제 (a) was grocery shopping이 정답이다.

오답분석
(b) 특정 과거 시점에 한창 진행 중이었던 행동을 표현하기에는 과거 시제보다 과거진행 시제가 더 적절하므로, 과거 시제는 오답이다.

어휘 | prized adj. 중요한, 가치 있는 collection n. 수집품 vintage adj. 고전적인, 유서 있는 be stolen phr. 도난당하다 robbery n. 강도 사건

---

12 준동사   동명사를 목적어로 취하는 동사

난이도 ●●○

During the Great Plague, people had little understanding of how the disease spread. Even so, business owners who did not want to risk _____ the plague asked customers to clean coins in vinegar before paying.

대역병 동안, 사람들은 어떻게 그 병이 퍼지는지에 대해 거의 이해하지 못했다. 그렇다고 해도, 역병에 걸릴 위험을 무릅쓰고 싶지 않았던 사업주들은 고객들에게 돈을 지불하기 전에 식초로 동전을 닦으라고 요청했다.

(a) having contracted
(b) to contract
(c) to have contracted
(d) contracting

risk는 동명사를 목적어로 취한다.

해설 | 빈칸 앞 동사 risk는 동명사를 목적어로 취하므로, 동명사 (d) contracting이 정답이다.

오답분석
(a) having contracted도 동명사이기는 하지만, 완료동명사(having contracted)로 쓰일 경우 '위험을 무릅쓰는' 시점보다 '(역병에) 걸리는' 시점이 앞선다는 것을 나타내므로 문맥에 적합하지 않아 오답이다.

어휘 | Great Plague phr. 대역병(1664-1665년 런던에서 발생한 페스트) spread v. 퍼지다, 확산되다 plague n. 역병, 페스트 vinegar n. 식초 contract v. (병에) 걸리다

---

13 시제 현재완료진행 난이도 ●●●

The Great Red Spot is the most noticeable feature on the planet Jupiter. The reddish dot is actually a giant storm that _____ on Jupiter's surface for at least 150 years.

(a) had been raging
(b) raged
(c) Is raging
(d) has been raging

대적점은 행성 목성에서 가장 눈에 띄는 특징이다. 이 붉은 점은 실제로는 목성의 표면에서 적어도 150년 동안 맹위를 떨쳐오고 있는 중인 거대한 폭풍이다.

'for + 기간 표현'과 현재 동사가 함께 오면 현재완료진행 시제가 정답이다.

해설 | 빈칸 문장에 현재 동사가 사용되었고, 지속을 나타내는 시간 표현 'for + 기간 표현'(for at least 150 years)이 있다. 또한, 문맥상 대적점이 목성의 표면에서 과거(대적점이 맹위를 떨치기 시작했던 시점)부터 현재까지 적어도 150년 동안 맹위를 떨쳐오고 있는 중이라는 의미가 되어야 자연스럽다. 따라서 현재완료진행 시제 (d) has been raging이 정답이다.

오답분석
(c) 현재진행 시제는 특정 현재 시점에 한창 진행 중인 일을 나타내므로, 과거에 시작해서 현재 시점까지 계속해서 진행되고 있는 일을 표현할 수 없어 오답이다.

어휘 | Great Red Spot phr. (목성의) 대적점 noticeable adj. 눈에 띄는, 두드러진 Jupiter n. 목성 giant adj. 거대한 storm n. 폭풍 rage v. 맹위를 떨치다

---

14 조동사 조동사 can 난이도 ●○○

Carla is finding it easy to get back into her exercise routine, even after a two-week break. Before that, she somewhat struggled to hold a two-minute plank. Now, surprisingly, she

Carla는 2주간의 휴식 후에도 그녀의 운동 루틴으로 돌아가는 것이 쉽다는 것을 발견하고 있는 중이다. 이전에는, 그녀는 2분간 플랭크를 유지하려고 어느 정

_____ do it with relative ease.

(a) should
(b) would
(c) can
(d) might

해설 | 문맥상 지금 Carla가 비교적 쉽게 2분간 플랭크를 유지할 수 있다는 내용이 되어야 자연스럽다. 따라서 '~할 수 있다'를 뜻하면서 능력을 나타내는 조동사 (c) can이 정답이다.

어휘 | routine n. 루틴(정해진 순서) somewhat adv. 어느 정도, 다소 struggle v. ~하려고 버둥거리다
plank n. 플랭크(바닥에 팔과 발을 대고 복부를 단련시키는 등척성 수축 운동) with ease phr. 쉽게, 용이하게

15 조동사   조동사 should 생략   난이도 ●●○

During Daryl's birthday dinner, two of his friends started arguing loudly in the restaurant. It got so bad that the manager demanded that the friends _____ the restaurant immediately.

(a) leave
(b) were leaving
(c) will leave
(d) left

Daryl의 생일 저녁 식사 중에, 그의 친구 두 명이 식당에서 크게 말다툼하기 시작했다. 상황이 너무 안 좋아져서 관리자는 그 친구들에게 즉시 식당을 나가야 한다고 요구했다.

해설 | 빈칸 앞에 요구를 나타내는 동사 demand가 있으므로 빈칸 문장에 있는 that절에는 '(should +) 동사원형'이 와야 한다. 따라서 동사원형 (a) leave가 정답이다.

16 준동사   동명사를 목적어로 취하는 동사   난이도 ●●○

My brother was under some stress at work, so I suggested watercolor painting as a way to help him relax. He had anticipated _____ the hobby, but he was surprised by how soothing it actually was.

(a) to have enjoyed

내 동생이 직장에서 스트레스를 받고 있어서, 나는 그가 편안하도록 도울 방법으로 수채화를 제안했다. 그는 그 취미를 즐기는 것을 예상했지만, 실제로 그것이 얼마나 진정시켜 주는지에 놀랐다.

TEST 1
TEST 2
TEST 3
TEST 4
TEST 5
TEST 6
TEST 7

지텔프 공식 기출문제집 7회분 Level 2

(b) **enjoying**
(c) to enjoy
(d) having enjoyed

anticipate는 동명사를 목적어로 취한다.

해설 | 빈칸 앞 동사 anticipate는 동명사를 목적어로 취하므로, 동명사 (b) enjoying이 정답이다.

> 오답분석
> (d) having enjoyed도 동명사이기는 하지만, 완료동명사(having enjoyed)로 쓰일 경우 '예상하는' 시점보다 '즐기는' 시점이 앞선다는 것을 나타내므로 문맥에 적합하지 않아 오답이다.

어휘 | under stress phr. 스트레스를 받는 watercolor painting phr. 수채화 anticipate v. 예상하다, 기대하다 soothing adj. 진정시키는, 달래는

---

17 가정법   가정법 과거완료   난이도 ●●○

In 1979, Elvita Adams jumped from the 86th floor of the Empire State Building and survived. If she had not been blown by a gust of wind, she _____ instead of landing on the 85th floor.

(a) will likely have perished
(b) would likely perish
(c) would likely have perished
(d) will likely perish

1979년에, Elvita Adams는 Empire State 건물의 86층에서 뛰어내렸고 살아남았다. 만약 그녀가 광풍에 의해 날아가지 않았었다면, 85층에 착륙하는 대신에 아마 죽었을 것이다.

'if + had p.p.'가 있으면 'would/could + have p.p.'가 정답이다.

해설 | If절에 'had p.p.' 형태의 had not been blown이 있으므로, 주절에는 이와 짝을 이루어 가정법 과거완료를 만드는 'would(조동사 과거형) + have p.p.'가 와야 한다. 따라서 (c) would likely have perished가 정답이다.

어휘 | survive v. 살아남다, 생존하다 gust of wind phr. 광풍, 돌풍 perish v. 죽다, 사라지다

---

18 연결어   접속부사   난이도 ●●○

Last week, a designer outlet store announced that it was having a big sale the next day. _____, hundreds of eager shoppers lined up outside the store before it opened. The lines stretched for two blocks!

(a) As a result
(b) On the contrary
(c) In other words
(d) For example

지난주에, 한 디자이너 아웃렛 매장이 다음날 대규모 할인할 것이라고 발표했다. 그 결과, 수백 명의 열광적인 쇼핑객들은 문이 열리기 전에 매장 밖에 줄을 섰다. 줄은 두 블록이나 뻗어 있었다!

━○ **지텔프 치트키**

'그 결과'라는 의미의 결과를 나타낼 때는 As a result를 쓴다.

해설ㅣ 문맥상 한 디자이너 아웃렛 매장이 할인할 것이라고 발표한 것이 원인이 되어, 그 결과로 수백 명의 열광적인 쇼핑객들은 문이 열리기 전에 매장 밖에 줄을 섰다는 의미가 되어야 자연스럽다. 따라서 '그 결과'라는 의미의 결과를 나타내는 접속부사 (a) As a result가 정답이다.

오답분석

(b) On the contrary는 '반면', (c) In other words는 '다시 말해서', (d) For example은 '예를 들어서'라는 의미로, 문맥에 적합하지 않아 오답이다.

어휘ㅣ eager adj. 열광적인, 열심인   stretch v. (어떤 지역에 걸쳐) 뻗어 있다, 이어지다

---

19 **가정법**   가정법 과거완료   난이도 ●●○

In 1928, Alexander Fleming noticed *Penicillium* mold on a half-finished experiment when he returned from vacation. Had it not been for the petri dish that he left lying around, he _____ penicillin.

(a) **would probably not have discovered**
(b) would probably not discover
(c) will probably not discover
(d) will probably not have discovered

1928년에, Alexander Fleming은 휴가에서 돌아왔을 때 반쯤 완성된 실험에서 *페니실륨* 곰팡이를 발견했다. 그가 놓고 간 페트리 접시가 없었다면, 그는 페니실린을 아마 발견하지 못했을 것이다.

━○ **지텔프 치트키**

Had p.p.가 있으면 'would/could + have p.p.'가 정답이다.

☼ **가정법 과거완료(도치)**
Had + 주어 + p.p., 주어 + would/could(조동사 과거형) + have p.p.

해설ㅣ if가 생략되어 도치된 절에 'had p.p.' 형태의 Had ~ been이 있으므로, 주절에는 이와 짝을 이루어 가정법 과거완료를 만드는 'would(조동사 과거형) + have p.p.'가 와야 한다. 따라서 (a) would probably not have discovered가 정답이다. 참고로, 'Had it not been ~'은 'If it had not been ~'으로 바꿔 쓸 수 있다.

어휘ㅣ Penicillium n. 페니실륨(페니실린의 원료)   mold n. 곰팡이   petri dish phr. 페트리 접시(세균 배양 따위에 쓰이는 둥글넓적한 작은 접시)

---

20 **시제**   과거완료진행   난이도 ●●●

Jenna recently moved to Buffalo and was warmly welcomed by her new housemates. Before the move, she _____ in Albany alone, so having companions was a refreshing change from her solitary living situation.

(a) is living
(b) **had been living**
(c) will live
(d) has been living

Jenna는 최근에 버팔로로 이사를 했고 새로운 동거인들로부터 따뜻하게 환영받았다. 이사 전에, 그녀는 올버니에서 혼자 살아오고 있던 중이었기 때문에, 친구들을 사귀는 것은 그녀의 고독한 생활 환경으로부터의 신선한 변화였다.

'before + 과거 시점/과거에 일어난 일'이 있으면 과거완료진행 시제가 정답이다.

해설 | 과거완료진행 시제와 함께 쓰이는 시간 표현 'before + 과거 시점/과거에 일어난 일'(Before the move)이 있고, 문맥상 대과거(올버니에서 살기 시작한 시점)부터 과거(버팔로로 이사한 시점)까지 Jenna는 올버니에서 혼자 살아오고 있던 중이었다는 의미가 되어야 자연스럽다. 따라서 과거완료진행 시제 (b) had been living이 정답이다.

어휘 | housemate n. 동거인 companion n. 친구, 동반자 refreshing adj. 신선한 solitary adj. 고독한, 고립된

---

21 준동사 to 부정사의 진주어 역할   난이도 ●●○

St. Jerome earned a place in religious history with the Vulgate, the first official Latin translation of the Bible from the original Hebrew and Greek. It took St. Jerome twenty-two years _____ the translation.

(a) to have completed
(b) to complete
(c) completing
(d) having completed

St. Jerome은 히브리어와 그리스어 원본으로부터 성경의 첫 번째 공식적인 라틴어 번역인 불가타 성서로 종교사에서 자리매김했다. St. Jerome이 번역을 <u>완성하는 것은</u> 22년이 걸렸다.

🔑 지텔프 치트키

가주어 it이 있으면 to 부정사가 정답이다.

해설 | 빈칸 문장의 주어 자리에 가주어 it이 있고 문맥상 'St. Jerome이 번역을 완성하는 것은 22년이 걸렸다'라는 의미가 되어야 자연스러우므로, 빈칸에는 동사 took의 진주어인 '완성하는 것'이 와야 한다. 따라서 진주어 자리에 올 수 있는 to 부정사 (b) to complete가 정답이다. 참고로, 'it takes + A + 시간 + to 부정사'는 'A가 ~하는 데 ~만큼 걸리다'라는 의미로 쓰인다.

어휘 | religious history phr. 종교사 Vulgate n. 불가타 성서(St. Jerome이 4세기 말에 번역한 라틴어역 성서) translation n. 번역, 해석 Bible n. 성경 Hebrew n. 히브리어; adj. 히브리인의 Greek n. 그리스어; adj. 그리스인의

---

22 가정법 가정법 과거   난이도 ●●○

Jake will be given an "Employee of the Month" certificate at next week's meeting for being such a talented salesperson. If I were his manager, I _____ him with a raise or an all-expense-paid vacation instead.

(a) will have rewarded
(b) will reward
(c) would reward
(d) would have rewarded

Jake는 매우 유능한 영업사원인 것에 대해 다음 주의 회의에서 "월간 우수 직원" 상장을 받을 것이다. 만약 내가 그의 관리자라면, 나는 그 대신 그에게 임금 인상이나 모든 비용을 지급하는 휴가를 <u>상으로 줄 것이다.</u>

🔑 지텔프 치트키

'if + 과거 동사'가 있으면 'would/could + 동사원형'이 정답이다.

---

23 시제   현재진행

난이도 ●○○

From a startup of just three employees, ARB, Inc. has scaled up to over 200 employees in five years. Currently, the company executives _____ for a new office, as their building is already packed to capacity.

(a) look
(b) are looking
(c) will look
(d) have been looking

ARB, Inc.는 단 세 명의 직원이 있는 신생기업에서, 5년 동안 200명이 넘는 직원들로 규모를 확대했다. 현재, 회사 임원들은 건물이 이미 수용 인원까지 빽빽이 차 있기 때문에 새로운 사무실을 찾고 있는 중이다.

→○ 지텔프 치트키

currently가 있으면 현재진행 시제가 정답이다.

해설 | 현재진행 시제와 함께 쓰이는 시간 표현 currently가 있고, 문맥상 말하고 있는 현재 시점에 새로운 사무실을 찾고 있는 중이라는 의미가 되어야 자연스럽다. 따라서 현재진행 시제 (b) are looking이 정답이다.

어휘 | scale up phr. ~의 규모를 확대하다 pack v. 빽빽이 채우다 capacity n. (건물 따위의) 수용 인원, 정원

24 조동사   조동사 should 생략

난이도 ●●○

The government has been alerting the public to an ongoing flu outbreak. They advise that everyone _____ the strict health and sanitation guidelines put in place to stop the spread of the disease.

(a) has followed
(b) is following
(c) will follow
(d) follow

정부는 계속되는 독감 발생을 대중에게 경고해 오고 있는 중이다. 그들은 모든 사람이 그 병의 확산을 막기 위해 시행된 엄격한 보건 및 위생 지침을 따라야 한다고 충고한다.

→○ 지텔프 치트키

advise 다음에는 that절에 동사원형이 온다.

해설 | 주절에 제안을 나타내는 동사 advise가 있으므로 that절에는 '(should +) 동사원형'이 와야 한다. 따라서 동사원형 (d) follow가 정답이다.

어휘 | alert v. 경고하다 outbreak n. 발생, 발발 sanitation n. 위생 spread n. 확산; v. 확산시키다

Fred has been an editor with YJ Communications for only six months, but he is already job hunting. He works long hours for unfair pay. Even if he were to be offered a promotion, he _____ it.

(a) would not have taken
(b) will not take
(c) will not have taken
(d) would not take

Fred는 YJ Communications사에서 단 6개월 동안 편집자로 일해왔지만, 이미 구직하고 있는 중이다. 그는 부당한 급여를 받고 장시간 일을 한다. 설령 그가 승진을 제의받는다 해도, 그는 그것을 받아들이지 않을 것이다.

─○ 지텔프 치트키

'if + were to + 동사원형'이 있으면 'would/could + 동사원형'이 정답이다.

> 💡 **가정법 과거(were to)**
> If + 주어 + were to + 동사원형, 주어 + would/could(조동사 과거형) + 동사원형

해설 | if절에 과거 동사(were to be offered)가 있으므로, 주절에는 이와 짝을 이루어 가정법 과거를 만드는 'would(조동사 과거형) + 동사원형'이 와야 한다. 따라서 (d) would not take가 정답이다.

어휘 | job hunting phr. 구직하다   unfair adj. 부당한, 불공정한   promotion n. 승진

---

26 준동사   to 부정사의 의미상 주어   난이도 ●●●

Mr. and Mrs. Simmons were filled with joy when they found out that their son was going to graduate *summa cum laude*. All they ever wanted was for him _____ college, but he exceeded their expectations.

(a) finishing
(b) to be finishing
(c) to finish
(d) having finished

Simmons 부부는 아들이 최우등으로 졸업할 것임을 알았을 때 기쁨으로 충만했다. 그들이 그동안 원했던 것은 그가 대학을 마치는 것이었지만, 그는 그들의 기대를 능가했다.

─○ 지텔프 치트키

'for + 대명사의 목적격'이 있으면 to 부정사가 정답이다.

해설 | 빈칸 앞의 for him은 'for + 대명사의 목적격'으로, to 부정사의 행위의 주체를 나타내는 의미상 주어 역할을 하고 있으므로 to 부정사 (c) to finish가 정답이다. 참고로, 문장의 주어와 to 부정사의 행위의 주체가 달라서 to 부정사의 의미상 주어가 필요할 경우, 'for + 명사/대명사의 목적격 + to 부정사'의 형태로 쓴다.

> **오답분석**
> (b) to be finishing도 to 부정사이기는 하지만, 문맥상 진행의 의미가 없으므로 오답이다.

어휘 | summa cum laude phr. 최우등으로   exceed v. 능가하다, 넘어서다   expectation n. 기대, 예상

LISTENING

PART I [27~33] 일상 대화 개기 일식에 관한 두 친구의 대화

안부 인사

F: Hey, Cousin Frank. ²⁷Did you see the solar eclipse yesterday? It was amazing!

M: Hi, Cousin Hailey! Were you able to see the eclipse in person? I watched it online.

주제 제시: 일식 관측

F: Yeah. ²⁷My parents and I went to Clayton's Hill for an eclipse watch party, and we saw it from there. The party was organized by a local astronomy club whose members were on site, explaining what was going to happen during the eclipse.

M: That's similar to what the host did in the live stream that I watched, but he was showing the eclipse from his home in Russia.

F: Russia? I didn't know you could speak Russian.

M: Oh, he was speaking English most of the time! ²⁸It was a virtual watch party, and there were viewers from all over the world, chatting together and sharing information about the eclipse.

F: ²⁸That's so cool, Frank! I had a good time, too. Watching the eclipse in person was a truly unique experience, and ²⁹I'm so glad I could witness it with the astronomy club. The members of the club taught me so much! Plus, we had barbecue and snacks while we waited and even listened to some music.

개기 일식 통과선

M: Sounds fun! Hey, your town was on the eclipse's path of totality, wasn't it? You know, that area where you can see the moon completely blocking the sun?

F: Path of totality? Oh, right. I remember the guide talking about that. Yeah, ³⁰apparently, the path where the total solar eclipse is visible is very narrow—only seventy miles wide. But we're lucky enough to live along it!

M: ³¹Here, we only got a partial eclipse, which just isn't the same. The live stream host said that you need to witness a total solar eclipse firsthand to fully appreciate it.

F: It was amazing, Frank. I never understood the hype about total eclipses until I saw one with my own eyes.

개기 일식 과정

M: It looked pretty good on the live stream, but I bet it was even more impressive in person. Some things just can't be fully captured by a camera. Tell me more about it!

여: 안녕, 사촌 Frank. ²⁷어제 일식 봤어? 정말 멋졌어!

남: 안녕, 사촌 Hailey! 일식을 직접 볼 수 있었어? 난 온라인으로 봤어.

여: 응. ²⁷부모님과 나는 일식 관측 파티를 위해 Clayton's Hill에 갔는데, 거기서 일식을 봤어. 파티는 회원들이 현장에 나와 있는 지역 천문학 동아리에 의해 주최되었는데, 일식 동안 무슨 일이 일어날지 설명해 줬어.

남: 내가 본 실시간 방송에서 진행자가 했던 거랑 비슷한데, 진행자가 러시아에 있는 자택에서 일식을 보여주고 있었어.

여: 러시아? 네가 러시아어를 할 수 있는 줄은 몰랐어.

남: 오, 그는 대부분 영어로 말하고 있었어! ²⁸가상 시청 파티였고, 전 세계의 시청자와 함께 이야기를 나누며 일식에 관한 정보를 공유했어.

여: ²⁸정말 멋지다, Frank! 나도 좋은 시간을 보냈어. 일식을 직접 보는 건 정말 독특한 경험이었고, ²⁹천문학 동아리와 함께 볼 수 있어서 정말 기뻐. 동아리 회원들이 나에게 아주 많이 가르쳐줬어! 게다가, 우리는 기다리는 동안 바비큐와 간식을 먹으며 음악도 들었어.

남: 재미있겠다! 저기, 너희 마을은 개기 일식 통과선에 있었잖아, 그렇지 않았어? 너도 알다시피, 달이 태양을 완전히 가리는 것을 볼 수 있는 그 지역이지?

여: 개기 일식 통과선? 오, 맞아. 가이드가 그것에 관해 얘기한 게 기억나. 응, ³⁰듣자 하니, 개기 일식이 보이는 통과선은 폭이 70마일에 불과할 정도로 매우 좁다고 하더라. 하지만 우리는 그것을 따라 살 정도로 운이 좋아!

남: ³¹여기에서, 우리는 부분 일식만 봤는데, 똑같지 않아. 실시간 방송 진행자가 개기 일식을 제대로 감상하려면 직접 봐야 한다고 했어.

여: 정말 대단했어, Frank. 개기 일식을 내 눈으로 직접 보기 전까지는 그것에 관한 과장 보도를 이해하지 못했어.

남: 실시간 방송에서도 꽤 멋져 보였는데, 직접 보면 훨씬 더 인상적이었을 것 같아. 어떤 것들은 카메라로 완전히 담을 수 없잖아. 그것에 관해 더 자세히 말해줘!

F: Well, right when the moon was about to hide the sun, I put on the eclipse glasses we'd been given.

M: That's good, because the live stream host said that looking directly at the sun during an eclipse without protection can damage the eyes.

F: Right. So, ³²slowly, the moon covered the sun. From one side, a wall of dark shadow rushed toward us and covered us all. It suddenly felt colder, and ³²the crowd became totally silent. You couldn't hear a single sound as everyone just stared at the sky.

M: Sounds intense!

F: Then, after a few minutes, the first rays of the sun escaped the moon's shadow, and slowly, daylight returned.

M: Incredible. I wish I could have been there with you!

남자가 다음에 할 일

F: Well, Frank, ³³my little sister did record a video of it. I know that watching a video is not the same as being there, so you're probably not interested, but . . .

M: ³³You better send me that video, Hailey! I'll watch it as soon as we get off the phone.

여: 음, 달이 태양을 가리려고 했던 바로 그때, 나는 우리가 받았던 일식 안경을 꼈어.

남: 다행이네, 실시간 방송 진행자가 일식 중에 보호 장비 없이 태양을 직접 보는 건 눈을 손상시킬 수 있다고 했거든.

여: 맞아. 그러니까, ³²천천히, 달이 태양을 가렸어. 한 쪽에서, 어두운 그림자 장벽이 우리 쪽으로 몰려와 우리 모두를 가렸어. 갑자기 더 추워졌고, ³²군중은 완전히 침묵했어. 모두가 하늘만 쳐다보고 있었기 때문에 어떤 소리도 들을 수 없었어.

남: 강렬할 것 같아!

여: 그리고 나서, 몇 분 후에, 첫 태양 광선이 달의 그림자를 벗어났고, 천천히 햇빛이 돌아왔어.

남: 엄청나네. 나도 너랑 같이 거기에 있었으면 좋았을 텐데!

여: 음, Frank, ³³내 여동생이 그걸 영상으로 찍었어. 영상을 보는 것이 그곳에 있는 것과 같지 않다는 걸 알기 때문에, 너는 아마 흥미가 없겠지만…

남: ³³그 영상 내게 보내줘, Hailey! 전화 끊는 대로 바로 볼게.

어휘 | solar eclipse 일식 in person 직접 astronomy[əstrάnəmi] 천문학 on site 현장에서, 현지의 virtual[vɔ́ːrtʃuəl] 가상의, 인터넷의 witness[wítnis] 보다, 목격하다 path of totality 개기 일식 통과선 apparently[əpǽrəntli] 듣자 하니 total solar eclipse 개기 일식 visible[vízəbl] 보이는 partial eclipse 부분 일식 firsthand[fə́rsthǽnd] 직접 hype[haip] 과장 보도, 과대광고 capture[kǽptʃər] 담다, 포착하다 directly[diréktli] 직접(적)으로, 똑바로 damage[dǽmidʒ] ~을 손상하다, 해치다 shadow[ʃǽdou] 그림자, 그늘 rush[rʌʃ] 몰려오다, 서두르다 silent[sáilənt] 침묵의, 말 없는 stare[stɛr] 쳐다보다, 응시하다 intense[inténs] 강렬한 rays of the sun 태양 광선 daylight[déilait] 햇빛 incredible[inkrédəbl] 엄청난, 놀라운

---

27   특정세부사항   What   난이도 ●●○

What was Hailey doing yesterday?

(a) attending a viewing of a rare phenomenon
(b) watching a live stream about astronomy
(c) organizing a total eclipse watch party
(d) going to her parents' place to stargaze

Hailey는 어제 무엇을 하고 있었는가?

(a) 희귀한 현상 구경에 참석하는 것
(b) 천문학에 관한 실시간 방송을 시청하는 것
(c) 일식 관측 파티를 주최하는 것
(d) 별을 관측하러 부모님 집에 가는 것

━○ 정답 잡는 치트키

질문의 키워드 yesterday가 그대로 언급된 주변 내용을 주의 깊게 듣는다.

해설 | 여자가 'Did you see the solar eclipse yesterday?'라며 어제 일식을 봤는지 물은 뒤, 'My parents and I went to ~ an eclipse watch party, and we saw it from there.'라며 부모님과 일식 관측 파티에 갔는데, 거기서 일식을 봤다고 했다. 따라서 (a)가 정답이다.

⇄ Paraphrasing
an eclipse watch party 일식 관측 파티 → a viewing of a rare phenomenon 희귀한 현상 구경

오답분석
(c) 여자가 일식 관측 파티에 갔다고 언급하기는 했지만, 일식 관측 파티는 지역 천문학 동아리에 의해 주최되었으므로 오답이다.

어휘 | rare[rer] 희귀한, 드문 phenomenon[fənɑ́:minən] 현상 stargaze[stɑ:rgéiz] 별을 관측하다

28 특정세부사항   What

난이도 ●●○

According to Hailey, what was cool about how Frank watched the eclipse?

(a) that he was actually in Russia
(b) that he watched with a global audience
(c) that he live streamed it for his viewers
(d) that he saw it from his home

Hailey에 따르면, Frank가 일식을 관측한 방법은 무엇이 멋졌는가?

(a) 실제로 러시아에 있었던 것
(b) 전 세계 시청자와 함께 시청했던 것
(c) 그의 시청자들을 위해 실시간 방송을 했던 것
(d) 그의 집에서 그걸 봤던 것

─○ 정답 잡는 치트키

질문의 키워드 cool이 그대로 언급된 주변 내용을 주의 깊게 듣는다.

해설 | 남자가 'It was a virtual watch party, and there were viewers from all over the world, chatting together and sharing information about the eclipse.'라며 가상 시청 파티였고 전 세계의 시청자와 함께 이야기를 나누며 일식에 관한 정보를 공유했다고 하자, 여자가 'That's so cool'이라며 정말 멋지다고 했다. 따라서 (b)가 정답이다.

⇄ Paraphrasing
viewers from all over the world 전 세계의 시청자 → a global audience 전 세계 시청자

어휘 | audience[ɔ́:diəns] 시청자, 관객

29 특정세부사항   Why

난이도 ●●○

Why was Hailey glad that she watched the eclipse with the astronomy club?

(a) She learned a lot from them.
(b) They brought delicious food.
(c) She made many new friends.
(d) They played enjoyable music.

Hailey는 왜 천문학 동아리와 함께 일식을 관측한 것이 기뻤는가?

(a) 그녀는 그들로부터 많이 배웠다.
(b) 그들이 맛있는 음식을 가져왔다.
(c) 그녀는 많은 새로운 친구들을 사귀었다.
(d) 그들이 즐거운 곡을 연주했다.

─○ 정답 잡는 치트키

질문의 키워드 glad와 astronomy club이 그대로 언급된 주변 내용을 주의 깊게 듣는다.

해설 | 여자가 'I'm so glad I could witness it with the astronomy club. The members of the club taught me so much!'라며 천문학 동아리와 함께 볼 수 있어서 정말 기쁘고 동아리 회원들이 아주 많이 가르쳐줬다고 했다. 따라서 (a)가 정답이다.

오답분석
(b) 여자가 기다리는 동안 바비큐와 간식을 먹었다고 언급하기는 했지만, 천문학 동아리 회원들이 음식을 가져왔는지는 언급되지 않았으므로 오답이다.

어휘 | enjoyable[indʒɔ́iəbl] 즐거운, 재미있는

지텔프 유식 기출문제집 7회분 Level 2

How was Hailey able to experience a total solar eclipse?

(a) by benefiting from clear weather
(b) by getting advice from a teacher
(c) by hiking to the top of a mountain
(d) by living within the right area

Hailey는 어떻게 개기 일식을 경험할 수 있었는가?

(a) 맑은 날씨의 혜택을 입음으로써
(b) 선생님으로부터 조언을 얻음으로써
(c) 산 정상까지 하이킹함으로써
(d) 적절한 지역 내에 거주함으로써

──○ **정답 잡는 치트키**

　　질문의 키워드 total solar eclipse가 그대로 언급된 주변 내용을 주의 깊게 듣는다.

해설 | 여자가 'apparently, the path where the total solar eclipse is visible is very narrow—only seventy miles wide. But we're lucky enough to live along it!'이라며 듣자 하니 개기 일식이 보이는 통과선은 폭이 70마일에 불과할 정도로 매우 좁은데, 그것을 따라 살 정도로 운이 좋다고 했다. 따라서 (d)가 정답이다.

어휘 | benefit from ~으로부터 혜택을 입다

Why, most likely, could Frank not fully appreciate the eclipse?

(a) He did not have protective glasses.
(b) He tuned into the event late.
(c) He was busy adjusting his camera.
(d) He could not attend in person.

Frank는 왜 일식을 제대로 보지 못했을 것 같은가?

(a) 보호안경을 가지고 있지 않았다.
(b) 행사에 늦게 채널을 맞췄다.
(c) 카메라를 조정하느라 바빴다.
(d) 직접 참석할 수 없었다.

──○ **정답 잡는 치트키**

　　질문의 키워드 fully appreciate가 그대로 언급된 주변 내용을 주의 깊게 듣는다.

해설 | 남자가 'Here, we only got a partial eclipse ~. The live stream host said that you need to witness a total solar eclipse firsthand to fully appreciate it.'이라며 여기에서 부분 일식만 봤는데, 실시간 방송 진행자가 개기 일식을 제대로 감상하려면 직접 봐야 한다고 했다고 한 것을 통해, Frank는 개기 일식을 보러 직접 참석할 수 없어서 일식을 제대로 보지 못했음을 추론할 수 있다. 따라서 (d)가 정답이다.

↻ **Paraphrasing**
firsthand 직접 → in person 직접

어휘 | protective glasses 보호안경　tune into ~으로 채널을 맞추다

What was the crowd at Clayton's Hill doing as the moon completely covered the sun?

(a) covering up against the cold
(b) taking pictures of the sky

달이 태양을 완전히 가렸을 때 Clayton's Hill의 군중은 무엇을 하고 있었는가?

(a) 추위를 피해 몸을 가리는 것
(b) 하늘 사진을 찍는 것

(c) watching the event quietly
(d) rushing to get a better view

(c) 조용히 일어난 일을 지켜보는 것
(d) 더 좋은 경치를 보기 위해 서두르는 것

해설 | 여자가 'slowly, the moon covered the sun'이라며 천천히 달이 태양을 가렸다고 한 뒤, 'the crowd became totally silent. You couldn't hear a single sound as everyone just stared at the sky.'라며 군중은 완전히 침묵했고 모두가 하늘만 쳐다보고 있었기 때문에 어떤 소리도 들을 수 없었다고 했다. 따라서 (c)가 정답이다.

어휘 | quietly[kwáiətli] 조용히, 고요히

---

33 추론 다음에 할 일
난이도 ●○○

What will Frank probably do after the phone conversation?

(a) look at photos of the event online
(b) make plans to visit his cousin
(c) view a recording of the event
(d) join a local stargazing club

Frank는 전화 통화 후에 무엇을 할 것 같은가?

(a) 온라인에서 행사 사진을 본다
(b) 사촌을 방문할 계획을 세운다
(c) 일어난 일의 녹화 영상을 본다
(d) 지역의 별 관측 동아리에 가입한다

해설 | 여자가 'my little sister did record a video of it'이라며 자기 여동생이 개기 일식을 영상으로 찍었다고 하자, 남자가 'You better send me that video, Hailey! I'll watch it as soon as we get off the phone.'이라며 그 영상을 보내달라고 하면서 전화 끊는 대로 바로 보겠다고 한 것을 통해, Frank가 전화 통화 후에 개기 일식이 촬영된 녹화 영상을 볼 것임을 추론할 수 있다. 따라서 (c)가 정답이다.

⇄ **Paraphrasing**
watch 보다 → view 보다
a video 영상 → a recording 녹화 영상

어휘 | recording[rikɔ́ːrdiŋ] 녹화한 영상, 녹음한 음성

PART 2 [34~39] 발표 병원 관리자의 은퇴 파티

음성 바로 듣기

주제
제시:
병원
관리자
은퇴

Thank you for coming to our meeting. As you might have heard, ³⁴our beloved hospital administrator, Dr. Sean Garrick, is retiring. Although we are saddened by his retirement, we're sure he is happy to finally have more time for his family after his many years of service here at Glad Tidings Hospital.

은퇴
파티
개최

We're going to miss his iconic red-and-white-striped bow tie and his frequent words of encouragement.

회의에 참석해 주셔서 감사합니다. 들으셨겠지만, ³⁴우리의 사랑하는 병원 관리자인 Sean Garrick 박사가 은퇴할 것입니다. 그의 은퇴는 슬프지만, 우리는 그가 이곳 Glad Tidings 병원에서 수년간의 근무 끝에 마침내 가족을 위해 더 많은 시간을 가지게 되어 기쁘다고 확신합니다.

그의 상징적인 빨간색과 흰색 줄무늬 나비 넥타이와 잦은 격려의 말이 그리울 것입니다. ³⁴그를 떠나보

[34]Before we let him go, we are throwing him a special "Not-So-Surprise Retirement Party!" The event will be held on July 1 from 7 to 11 p.m. at the Glad Tidings Hospital Auditorium. All employees are invited to come.

To celebrate Dr. Garrick, [35]you are encouraged to come in your best Dr. Garrick costume. He himself will judge who does the best impersonation of him. You will be judged on your overall appearance, and on how well you can deliver the doctor's favorite phrase: "Laughter is the best medicine." Get your costumes soon, as the local shops are sure to run out of suspenders and bow ties! Ha-ha.

The venue will open at 6:30 p.m., at which time you can start visiting the various activity booths prepared by the organizers. [36]One of the booths is the Glad Tidings Survivors' Fund. Dr. Garrick founded the charity over ten years ago, and it has been helping patients who are battling cancer or other terminal illnesses ever since. While donations are welcome, the main goal of the booth is not to solicit funding. Instead, [36]our intention is to honor the doctor who made such great work possible when he established the organization. Be sure to visit the message wall where you can write well-wishes for Dr. Garrick.

The program will start at exactly 7 p.m. with a performance by the Glad Tidings Choir, a singing group of our very own staff. Their performance will feature a number of Dr. Garrick's favorite songs, including "Only You" and "The Great Pretender."

Dinner will be a buffet prepared by Dr. Garrick's best friend and famous restaurateur, Chef Luca de Castille. As we feast on the delicious spread, we will be holding a "Dr. Garrick Quiz Night." [37]How well do you know our hospital administrator? Better brush up on his thirty-year career at the hospital if you want to win exciting prizes.

After dinner, we will hear from Dr. Garrick himself. Do stick around to hear his heartfelt farewell speech. We will also ask some of you to say a few kind words to Dr. Garrick. If you wish to say something at the event, let us know and we will include your name on the list. However, please keep in mind that we may have to limit the number of speakers due to time constraints.

Finally, [38]it'll be time for what is sure to be the highlight of the evening! Rumor has it that Dr. Garrick recently learned the "Pop & Chop" dance, and he's ready to

내기 전에, 특별한 "그다지 깜짝은 아닌 은퇴 파티"를 개최할 것입니다! 이 행사는 7월 1일 오후 7시부터 11시까지 Glad Tidings 병원 강당에서 열릴 것입니다. 모든 직원이 초대됩니다.

Garrick 박사를 축하하기 위해, [35]최고의 Garrick 박사 의상을 입고 오는 것이 권장됩니다. 누가 그를 가장 잘 흉내 내는지 Garrick 박사가 직접 평가할 것입니다. 전체적인 외모와, 박사가 가장 좋아하는 구절인 "웃음이 최고의 약이다."를 얼마나 잘 전달할 수 있는지에 따라 평가될 것입니다. 현지 상점에 바지 멜빵과 나비 넥타이가 동이 날 것이 분명하니 서둘러 의상을 준비하세요! 하하.

행사장은 오후 6시 30분에 열며, 이때부터 주최 측에서 준비한 다양한 활동 부스를 방문하실 수 있습니다. [36]부스 중 하나는 Glad Tidings Survivors' Fund 입니다. Garrick 박사는 10년도 더 전에 이 자선 단체를 설립했으며, 그 이후로 암이나 기타 불치병과 싸우고 있는 환자들을 돕고 있습니다. 기부는 환영하지만, 부스의 주요 목표는 기금을 요청하는 것이 아닙니다. 대신, [36]우리의 의도는 단체를 설립했을 때 그러한 훌륭한 일을 가능하게 했던 의사를 기리는 것입니다. Garrick 박사를 위해 덕담을 적을 수 있는 메시지 벽을 꼭 방문하세요.

프로그램은 정확히 오후 7시에 우리의 직원들로 구성된 합창단인 Glad Tidings 합창단의 공연으로 시작할 것입니다. 그들의 공연은 "Only You"와 "The Great Pretender"를 포함하여, Garrick 박사가 가장 좋아하는 여러 곡을 선보일 것입니다.

저녁 식사는 Garrick 박사의 가장 친한 친구이자 유명한 식당 경영자인 요리사 Luca de Castille에 의해 준비된 뷔페일 것입니다. 맛있는 음식을 맘껏 먹으면서, "Garrick 박사 퀴즈의 밤"을 열 것입니다. [37]여러분은 우리 병원의 관리자를 얼마나 잘 알고 있나요? 흥미로운 상을 타고 싶다면 병원에서의 그의 30년 경력을 다시 공부하는 것이 좋습니다.

저녁 식사 후에는, Garrick 박사로부터 직접 이야기를 들을 것입니다. 그의 진심 어린 고별사를 듣기 위해 머물러주세요. 또한 여러분들 중 몇 분에게는 Garrick 박사에게 친절한 말을 몇 마디 해 달라고 부탁할 것입니다. 행사에서 하고 싶은 말이 있으시다면, 저희에게 알려주시면 명단에 이름을 포함해 드릴 것입니다. 하지만, 시간 제약으로 인해 발표자들의 수를 제한해야 할 수도 있다는 점을 명심하시기를 바랍니다.

마지막으로, [38]저녁의 하이라이트가 될 게 분명한 시간입니다! Garrick 박사가 최근에 "Pop & Chop" 춤을 배웠으며, 그가 자기 루틴을 무대에서 선보일 준비

debut his routine on the dance floor. **As most of you know, Dr. Garrick's great love—apart from medicine, of course—is dancing! If we're lucky, he may even teach us some of his groovy moves.**

끝인사 We hope you can join us in one last hurrah for Dr. Garrick. ³⁹Please email Samantha Moore by Monday about whether you plan to attend so we can give the final count to the caterer.

가 되었다는 소문이 있습니다 여러분 중 대부분이 아시다시피, Garrick 박사의 큰 취미는 물론 의학을 제외하고는 춤을 추는 것입니다! 우리가 운이 좋다면, 그는 우리에게 그의 멋진 동작 중 일부를 가르쳐 줄 수도 있을 것입니다.

Garrick 박사를 위한 마지막 만세를 함께 불러주시길 바랍니다. ³⁹음식 공급업체에 최종 총수를 전달할 수 있도록 참석할 계획인지를 월요일까지 Samantha Moore에게 이메일로 보내주시기를 바랍니다.

어휘 | beloved[bilʌ́vd] 사랑하는, 소중한 sadden[sædn] ~을 슬프게 하다 iconic[aikánik] ~의 상징이 되는 encouragement[inkɔ́ːridʒmənt] 격려, 장려 auditorium[ɔ̀ːditɔ́ːriəm] 강당 costume[kástjuːm] 의상 judge[dʒʌdʒ] 평가하다, 판단하다 impersonation[impə̀ːrsənéiʃən] 흉내 phrase[freiz] 구절, 문구 run out of ~이 동나다, 다 써버리다 suspender[səspéndər] 바지의 멜빵 charity[tʃǽrəti] 자선 단체, 시설 battle[bǽtl] 싸우다; 전쟁 terminal illness 불치병 donation[dounéiʃən] 기부, 기증 solicit[səlísit] 요청하다 well-wish[wélwìʃ] 덕담, 호의 choir[kwaiər] 힙창단 restaurateur[rèstərətə́ːr] 식당 경영지 feast[fiːst] 맘껏 먹다; 축세 spread[spred] 맛있는 음식; 확산되다, 퍼지다 brush up 다시 공부하다 stick around 미무르다, 대기하다 heartfelt[hártfelt] 진심 어린, 마음에서 우러난 farewell speech 고별사 keep in mind 명심하다 constraint[kənstréint] 제약, 제한 highlight[háilait] 하이라이트, 절정 rumor[rúːmər] 소문, 루머 debut[deibjúː] 선보이다; 데뷔, 출시 routine[ruːtíːn] 루틴(정해진 순서); 일상적인 groovy[grúːvi] 멋진 hurrah[həráː] 만세 count[kaunt] 총수, 총계

---

34 주제/목적 담화의 목적

난이도 ●●○

What is the purpose of the presentation?

(a) to inform people about a surprise party
(b) to invite people to a charity event
(c) to celebrate a coworker's birthday
(d) to announce an event in honor of a colleague

발표의 목적은 무엇인가?

(a) 사람들에게 깜짝 파티에 관해 알리기 위해서
(b) 자선 행사에 사람들을 초대하기 위해서
(c) 동료의 생일을 축하하기 위해서
(d) 동료를 축하하여 행사를 공지하기 위해서

━○ 정답 잡는 치트키

담화의 목적을 언급하는 초반을 주의 깊게 듣고 전체 맥락을 파악한다.

해설 | 화자가 'our beloved hospital administrator, Dr. Sean Garrick, is retiring'이라며 사랑하는 병원 관리자인 Sean Garrick 박사가 은퇴할 것이라고 하며, 'Before we let him go, we are throwing him a special "Not-So-Surprise Retirement Party!"'라며 그를 떠나보내기 전에 특별한 "그다지 깜짝은 아닌 은퇴 파티"를 개최할 것이라고 한 뒤, 담화 전반에 걸쳐 은퇴하는 동료인 Garrick 박사를 축하하여 은퇴 파티 행사를 공지하고 있다. 따라서 (d)가 정답이다.

오답분석
(a) 화자가 은퇴 파티를 알리고 있지만, "그다지 깜짝은 아닌 은퇴 파티"를 개최할 것이라고 했으므로 오답이다.

어휘 | in honor of ~을 축하하여

---

35 특정세부사항 Why

난이도 ●●○

Why are attendees encouraged to dress like Dr. Garrick?

참석자들은 왜 Garrick 박사처럼 옷을 입도록 권장되는가?

(a) to participate in a fun contest

(b) to appear more professional

(c) to surprise him with a prank

(d) to be more comfortable

(a) 재미있는 대회에 참가하기 위해서

(b) 더 전문적으로 보이기 위해서

(c) 장난으로 그를 놀라게 하기 위해서

(d) 더 편안해 보이기 위해서

⊶○ 정답 잡는 치트키

질문의 키워드 encouraged to dress가 encouraged to come in ~ costume으로 paraphrasing되어 언급된 주변 내용을 주의 깊게 듣는다.

해설 | 화자가 'you are encouraged to come in your best Dr. Garrick costume. He himself will judge who does the best impersonation of him.'이라며 최고의 Garrick 박사 의상을 입고 오는 것이 권장되며, 누가 그를 가장 잘 흉내 내는지 Garrick 박사가 직접 평가할 것이라고 했다. 따라서 (a)가 정답이다.

어휘 | prank[præŋk] 장난, 농담

---

36 특정세부사항   What   난이도 ●○○

What is Dr. Garrick's contribution to the Glad Tidings Survivors' Fund?

(a) He developed new treatments.

(b) He made a major donation.

(c) He kept it from closing down.

(d) He set up the organization.

Glad Tidings Survivors' Fund에 대한 Garrick 박사의 기여는 무엇인가?

(a) 새로운 치료법을 개발했다.

(b) 큰 기부를 했다.

(c) 폐쇄되지 않도록 했다.

(d) 단체를 설립했다.

⊶○ 정답 잡는 치트키

질문의 키워드 Glad Tidings Survivors' Fund가 그대로 언급된 주변 내용을 주의 깊게 듣는다.

해설 | 화자가 'One of the booths is the Glad Tidings Survivors' Fund. Dr. Garrick founded the charity over ten years ago'라며 부스 중 하나는 Glad Tidings Survivors' Fund인데, Garrick 박사가 10년도 더 전에 이 자선 단체를 설립했다고 한 뒤, 'our intention is to honor the doctor who made such great work possible when he established the organization'이라며 의도는 단체를 설립했을 때 그러한 훌륭한 일을 가능하게 했던 의사를 기리는 것이라고 했다. 따라서 (d)가 정답이다.

⇄ Paraphrasing

founded the charity 자선 단체를 설립했다 → set up the organization 단체를 설립했다

어휘 | treatment[tríːtmənt] 치료(법)   organization[ɔ̀rgənizéiʃən] 단체, 조직

---

37 특정세부사항   How   난이도 ●●○

How can attendees win exciting prizes during the event?

(a) by guessing the ingredients in the special dessert

(b) by knowing facts about the guest of honor's life

(c) by remembering the words to popular songs

(d) by answering questions about the hospital correctly

참석자들은 행사 동안 어떻게 흥미로운 상을 탈 수 있는가?

(a) 특별 후식의 재료를 추측함으로써

(b) 귀빈의 생활에 관한 사실을 알고 있음으로써

(c) 대중가요의 가사를 기억함으로써

(d) 병원에 관한 질문에 정확하게 대답함으로써

질문의 키워드 win exciting prizes가 그대로 언급된 주변 내용을 주의 깊게 듣는다.

해설 | 화자가 'How well do you know our hospital administrator? Better brush up on his thirty-year career at the hospital if you want to win exciting prizes.'라며 병원의 관리자를 얼마나 잘 알고 있는지 물으며, 흥미로운 상을 타고 싶다면 병원에서의 그의 30년 경력을 다시 공부하는 것이 좋다고 했다. 따라서 (b)가 정답이다.

어휘 | ingredient [ingríːdiənt] 재료, 성분 guest of honor 귀빈, 주빈

---

38 추론 특정사실   난이도 ●●○

What does the speaker think will probably be the highlight of the evening?

(a) a dance competition
(b) a special performance
(c) a farewell speech
(d) a gift presentation

화자는 저녁의 하이라이트가 무엇이 될 거로 생각하는 것 같은가?

(a) 댄스 경연 대회
(b) 특별 공연
(c) 고별사
(d) 선물 증정

질문의 키워드 highlight of the evening이 그대로 언급된 주변 내용을 주의 깊게 듣는다.

해설 | 화자가 'it'll be time for what is sure to be the highlight of the evening! Rumor has it that Dr. Garrick recently learned the ~ dance, and he's ready to debut his routine on the dance floor.'라며 저녁의 하이라이트가 될 것이 분명한 시간이라며, Garrick 박사가 최근에 춤을 배웠고, 자기 루틴을 무대에서 선보일 준비가 되었다는 소문이 있다고 한 것을 통해, Garrick 박사가 춤을 선보이는 특별 공연이 저녁의 하이라이트가 될 것임을 추론할 수 있다. 따라서 (b)가 정답이다.

어휘 | farewell speech 고별사

---

39 추론 특정사실   난이도 ●●○

Why, most likely, is everyone asked to email about their plans to attend?

(a) to receive directions to the event
(b) to figure out seating arrangements
(c) to find the right-sized venue
(d) to make sure there is enough food

모든 사람이 왜 참석할 계획에 관해 이메일을 보내도록 요청받는 것 같은가?

(a) 행사장까지의 길 안내를 받기 위해서
(b) 좌석 배치를 파악하기 위해서
(c) 적당한 크기의 장소를 찾기 위해서
(d) 음식이 충분한지 확인하기 위해서

질문의 키워드 email이 그대로 언급된 주변 내용을 주의 깊게 듣는다.

해설 | 화자가 'Please email ~ about whether you plan to attend so we can give the final count to the caterer.'라며 음식 공급업체에 최종 총수를 전달할 수 있도록 참석할 계획인지를 이메일로 보내달라고 한 것을 통해, 음식 공급업체에 음식이 충분한지 확인할 수 있도록 모든 사람이 참석할 계획에 관해 이메일을 보내도록 요청받는 것임을 추론할 수 있다. 따라서 (d)가 정답이다.

어휘 | figure out 파악하다, 이해하다 make sure 확인하다

음성 바로 듣기

안부 인사	F: Hey, Carl. I can't thank you enough for helping me move. M: No problem, Megan. I'm happy to help. So, how do you like sunny Fresno so far?	여: 안녕, Carl. 이사를 도와줘서 정말 고마워. 남: 문제없어, Megan. 기꺼이 도와줄게. 그래서, 지금까지 화창한 프레즈노는 어때?
주제 제시: 장단점 비교	F: I like it, but ⁴⁰I'm still getting used to the drier California air. Also, I have a front yard now! And I was surprised to see quite a few houses here in Fresno with artificial lawns. So, I was wondering if I should grow a natural lawn or install artificial grass instead. M: Well, they're both good options, but each has its pros and cons.	여: 마음에 들지만, ⁴⁰캘리포니아의 건조한 공기에 여전히 적응하는 중이야. 또, 이제 앞마당이 생겼어! 그리고 이곳 프레즈노에 인조 잔디가 있는 집들을 꽤 많이 보게 되어서 놀랐어. 그래서, 나는 천연 잔디를 키워야 할지 아니면 대신에 인조 잔디를 설치해야 할지 고민 중이었어. 남: 음, 둘 다 좋은 선택이긴 하지만, 각각 장단점이 있어.
천연 잔디의 장점	F: Okay. Let's talk about the advantages of having a natural lawn first. M: Sure. First, a natural lawn improves air quality because grass is a natural air filter that traps air pollutants. F: Right. Grass also absorbs carbon dioxide and releases breathable oxygen in return. M: Another advantage of a real lawn is that looking at natural landscapes has psychological benefits. Seeing healthy green plants is good for your well-being! F: Definitely. Plus, ⁴¹I love the smell of fresh cut grass because it reminds me of being a kid. I always had fun helping my big brother with yard work when I was little. Although, maintaining our lawn was a lot of work.	여: 응. 우선 천연 잔디를 갖는 것의 장점에 관해 이야기해보자. 남: 물론이지. 첫 번째로, 잔디는 대기 오염 물질을 빨아들이는 천연 공기 필터이기 때문에 천연 잔디는 대기질을 개선해. 여: 맞아. 잔디는 또한 이산화탄소를 흡수하고 대신에 호흡하기에 적당한 산소를 방출해. 남: 실제 잔디밭의 또 다른 장점은 자연 풍경을 바라보는 것이 심리적인 이로움을 가진다는 거야. 건강한 녹색 식물을 보는 것은 행복에 도움이 돼! 여: 당연하지. 게다가, ⁴¹나는 갓 깎은 잔디 냄새가 어릴 적을 생각나게 해서 좋아. 나는 어렸을 때 오빠를 도와 정원 손질하는 게 항상 즐거웠어. 하지만, 잔디밭을 관리하는 건 정말 힘들었어.
천연 잔디의 단점	M: That's one disadvantage of natural lawns. You'd need to do maintenance work like mowing and fertilizing. Then there's also weedkillers and insecticides and figuring out how much to use. F: Sounds like a lot of work! Also, ⁴²real grass can't handle much heavy foot traffic. I love hosting backyard parties, but I'm afraid the grass will get worn down from guests walking on it. M: That's true, Megan. Too much activity will damage the grass and the upper roots, leading to bare patches on your lawn. So, if you're planning to hold frequent barbecues, then a natural lawn might not be the best choice.	남: 그건 천연 잔디의 한 가지 단점이야. 잔디 깎기와 비료 주기 같은 유지관리 작업을 해야 해. 그러고 나서 제초제와 살충제도 있고 얼마나 사용할지 알아내야 하는 것도 있어. 여: 손이 많이 가는 것 같아! 또한, ⁴²실제 잔디는 많은 사람들의 왕래를 감당하지 못해. 나는 뒤뜰에서 파티를 여는 것을 좋아하지만, 잔디 위를 걷는 손님들로 인해 잔디가 닳을까 봐서 걱정이야. 남: 그건 맞아, Megan. 너무 많은 활동은 잔디와 위 뿌리에 손상을 입혀서, 잔디밭에 노출된 부분이 생길 수 있어. 그래서, 잦은 바비큐 파티를 열 계획이라면, 그러면 천연 잔디는 최선의 선택이 아닐 수도 있어.
인조 잔디의 장점	F: Right, Carl. What about artificial lawns? What do they have to offer? M: For starters, an artificial lawn is easy to install. Just call the professionals to lay the artificial grass, and presto! You'll have a beautiful lawn within hours.	여: 맞아, Carl. 인조 잔디는 어때? 어떤 걸 해야 해? 남: 우선, 인조 잔디는 설치하기 쉬워. 전문가들을 불러 인조 잔디를 깔게 하면, 짠! 몇 시간 안에 아름다운 잔디밭을 가지게 될 거야.

F: Hmm. And since it's not real grass, I won't need to water it, right?

M: That's correct. ⁴³It requires no watering, which is helpful for saving water—especially in drought-prone areas like here in California. Convenient, right?

F: Very convenient. How about the disadvantages?

M: Well, an artificial lawn doesn't come cheap. With your lawn area, you'd probably spend more up front to get artificial grass. But the cost to maintain it is much lower than the cost of keeping a real lawn healthy and well-groomed.

F: My budget is limited right now, so the higher up-front cost is something for me to consider.

M: Another disadvantage is that synthetic grass absorbs heat in the sunlight. In some extreme situations, the plastic grass can even melt! But since you don't have a dog or any kids that would be running around outside, it might be okay.

F: Hmmm . . . ⁴⁴I'm not sure I like the idea of hot grass, though. I usually love feeling the grass under my feet, so it's a bit of a problem if I can't go outside barefoot.

M: That's true. So, ⁴⁵Megan, have you decided?

F: Yes, Carl. ⁴⁵I think, after years of being surrounded by concrete, I want to feel closer to nature. Besides, I can offset the water usage by using recycled water instead.

여: 흠. 그리고 실제 잔디가 아니니까, 나는 물을 줄 필요가 없겠네, 맞지?

남: 맞아. ⁴³물을 줄 필요가 없으니, 특히 여기 캘리포니아처럼 가뭄이 들기 쉬운 지역에서는 물 절약에 도움이 돼. 편리해, 그렇지?

여: 아주 편리하네. 단점은 어때?

남: 음, 인조 잔디는 저렴하지 않아. 네 잔디밭 면적에는, 아마 인조 잔디를 까는 데 더 많은 초기 비용이 들 거야. 하지만 유지 관리 비용은 실제 잔디를 건강하고 깔끔하게 유지하는 데 드는 비용보다 훨씬 저렴해.

여: 지금 내 예산이 한정되어 있어서, 초기 비용이 더 많이 드는 건 고려해야 할 사항이야.

남: 또 다른 단점은 인조 잔디가 햇빛에 있는 열을 흡수한다는 거야. 극단적인 상황에서는, 플라스틱 잔디가 녹을 수도 있어! 하지만 밖에서 뛰어노는 개나 아이들이 없으니까, 괜찮을 수도 있어.

여: 흠... ⁴⁴그래도 뜨거운 잔디가 마음에 들지 모르겠어. 나는 평소 발밑의 잔디를 느끼는 것을 좋아해서, 맨발로 밖에 나갈 수 없다면 그건 좀 문제야.

남: 그건 그래. 그래서, ⁴⁵Megan, 결정했어?

여: 응, Carl. ⁴⁵내 생각에는, 몇 년 동안 콘크리트에 둘러싸여 지내다 보니, 자연과 더 가까워지고 싶어. 게다가, 재사용된 물을 대신 사용함으로써 물 사용량을 상쇄할 수 있어.

어휘 | get used to ~에 적응하다, 익숙해지다 artificial[ɑ̀ːrtəfíʃəl] 인조의, 인공의 trap[træp] 빨아들이다, 가두다 pollutant[pəlúːtənt] 오염 물질 absorb[æbsɔ́ːrb] 흡수하다 carbon dioxide 이산화탄소 breathable[bríːðəbl] 호흡하기에 적당한 oxygen[ɑ́ksidʒen] 산소 landscape[lǽndskèip] 풍경, 경관 psychological[sàikəlɑ́dʒikəl] 심리적인 well-being 행복, 복지 remind of ~을 생각나게 하다 yard work 정원 손질 mowing[móuiŋ] 잔디 깎기 fertilize[fə́ːrtəlàiz] 비료를 주다 weedkiller[wíːdkilər] 제초제 insecticide[inséktəsàid] 살충제 traffic[trǽfik] 왕래, 통행 wear down 닳다, 마모시키다 root[ruːt] 뿌리 bare[bɛər] 노출된, 드러난 patch[pætʃ] 부분, 조각 presto[préstou] 짠(무슨 일을 마술처럼 쉽고 빨리 해냈을 때 내는 소리) prone[proun] ~하기 쉬운 up front 처음부터, 선불로 well-groomed 깔끔한, 손질이 잘 된 synthetic[sinθétik] 인조의, 합성의 melt[melt] 녹다 barefoot[bɛ́rfut] 맨발로 offset[ɔ́ːfsèt] ~을 상쇄하다

---

40 특정세부사항   What

난이도 ●○○

What is Megan still getting used to after moving to a new town?

(a) living in a spacious home
(b) seeing houses with big yards
(c) having a different climate
(d) living in a coastal region

Megan은 새로운 마을로 이사를 간 후에도 여전히 무엇에 적응하고 있는가?

(a) 넓은 집에 사는 것
(b) 마당이 넓은 집을 보는 것
(c) 기후가 다른 것
(d) 해안 지역에 사는 것

질문의 키워드 still getting used to가 그대로 언급된 주변 내용을 주의 깊게 듣는다.

해설 | 여자가 'I'm still getting used to the drier California air'라며 캘리포니아의 건조한 공기에 여전히 적응하는 중이라고 했다. 따라서 (c)가 정답이다.

어휘 | spacious[spéiʃəs] 넓은 climate[kláimit] 기후, 날씨 coastal[kóustəl] 해안의

---

41 특정세부사항   What   난이도 ●●○

What does Megan love about freshly cut grass?

(a) that it brings back good memories of her childhood
(b) that it gives her a feeling of well-being
(c) that it reminds her of her father's love for nature
(d) that it gives her a sense of pride in her hard work

Megan은 갓 깎은 잔디에 관해 무엇을 좋아하는가?

(a) 어린 시절의 좋은 추억을 떠올리게 하는 것
(b) 그녀에게 행복감을 주는 것
(c) 자연에 대한 아버지의 사랑을 생각나게 하는 것
(d) 그녀의 노력에 대한 자부심을 느끼게 해주는 것

━○ 정답 잡는 치트키

질문의 키워드 freshly cut grass가 fresh cut grass로 paraphrasing되어 언급된 주변 내용을 주의 깊게 듣는다.

해설 | 여자가 'I love the smell of fresh cut grass because it reminds me of being a kid. I always had fun helping my big brother with yard work when I was little.'이라며 갓 깎은 잔디 냄새가 어릴 적을 생각나게 해서 좋으며, 어렸을 때 오빠를 도와 정원 손질하는 게 항상 즐거웠다고 했다. 따라서 (a)가 정답이다.

⇄ Paraphrasing
reminds ~ of being a kid 어릴 적을 생각나게 하다 › brings back ~ memories of ~ childhood 어린 시절의 추억을 떠올리게 하나

어휘 | childhood[tʃáildhùd] 어린 시절 hard work 노력

---

42 추론   특정사실   난이도 ●●○

Why, most likely, is a natural lawn not good for holding regular outdoor parties?

(a) because it grows too slowly
(b) because it damages easily
(c) because it attracts insects
(d) because it has too many weeds

천연 잔디는 왜 정기적인 야외 파티를 열기에 좋지 않은 것 같은가?

(a) 너무 느리게 자라기 때문에
(b) 쉽게 손상되기 때문에
(c) 곤충을 끌어들이기 때문에
(d) 잡초가 너무 많기 때문에

━○ 정답 잡는 치트키

질문의 키워드 outdoor parties가 backyard parties로 paraphrasing되어 언급된 주변 내용을 주의 깊게 듣는다.

해설 | 여자가 'real grass can't handle much heavy foot traffic. I love hosting backyard parties, but I'm afraid the grass will get worn down from guests walking on it.'이라며 실제 잔디는 많은 사람들의 왕래를 감당하지 못하며, 뒤뜰에서 파티를 여는 것을 좋아하지만 잔디 위를 걷는 손님들로 인해 잔디가 닳을까 봐 걱정이라고 한 것을 통해, 천연 잔디는 쉽게 손상되기 때문에 정기적인 야외 파티를 열기에 좋지 않음을 추론할 수 있다. 따라서 (b)가 정답이다.

⇄ Paraphrasing

get worn down 닳다 → damages 손상되다

어휘 | attract[ətrǽkt] 끌어들이다, 유인하다 weed[wiːd] 잡초

---

43 특정세부사항   How

난이도 ●●●

According to Carl, how will an artificial lawn be convenient for Megan?

(a) by being easy for her to install
(b) by not needing to be watered
(c) by being easy for her to repair
(d) by not needing to be cleaned

Carl에 따르면, 인조 잔디가 어떻게 Megan에게 편리할 것인가?

(a) 그녀가 설치하기 쉽게 함으로써
(b) 물을 줄 필요가 없게 함으로써
(c) 그녀가 수리하기 쉽게 함으로써
(d) 청소할 필요가 없게 함으로써

←─○ 정답 잡는 치트키

질문의 키워드 convenient가 그대로 언급된 주변 내용을 주의 깊게 듣는다.

해설 | 남자가 'It requires no watering, which is helpful for saving water ~. Convenient, right?'라며 물을 줄 필요가 없으니 물 절약에 도움이 되며 편리하다고 했다. 따라서 (b)가 정답이다.

⇄ Paraphrasing

requires no watering 물을 줄 필요가 없다 → not needing to be watered 물을 줄 필요가 없음

오답분석

(a) 남자가 인조 잔디는 설치하기 쉽다고 언급했으나, Megan이 설치하는 것이 아니라, 전문가들을 불러 설치하면 쉽다는 의미이므로 오답이다.

---

44 특정세부사항   Why

난이도 ●○○

Why could it be a problem for Megan to have hot grass?

(a) She would dislike the smell.
(b) Her kids like to play in the yard.
(c) She enjoys being without shoes.
(d) Her dog likes to run outside.

Megan에게 왜 뜨거운 잔디가 있는 것이 문제가 될 수 있는가?

(a) 그녀는 냄새를 싫어할 것이다.
(b) 그녀의 아이들이 마당에서 노는 것을 좋아한다.
(c) 그녀는 신발 없이 있는 것을 즐긴다.
(d) 그녀의 개는 밖에서 뛰는 것을 좋아한다.

←─○ 정답 잡는 치트키

질문의 키워드 hot grass가 그대로 언급된 주변 내용을 주의 깊게 듣는다.

해설 | 여자가 'I'm not sure I like the idea of hot grass, though. I usually love feeling the grass under my feet, so it's a bit of a problem if I can't go outside barefoot.'이라며 뜨거운 잔디가 마음에 들지 모르겠다며, 평소 발밑의 잔디를 느끼는 것을 좋아해서 맨발로 밖에 나갈 수 없다면 그건 좀 문제라고 했다. 따라서 (c)가 정답이다.

⇄ Paraphrasing

barefoot 맨발로 → without shoes 신발 없이

45 추론 다음에 할 일

Based on the conversation, what will Megan most likely do after the conversation?

(a) allow a natural lawn to grow
(b) hire professional landscapers
(c) plant trees and flowers outside
(d) settle for an artificial backyard

대화에 따르면, Megan은 대화 이후에 무엇을 할 것 같은가?

(a) 천연 잔디를 기른다
(b) 전문 정원사들을 고용한다
(c) 밖에 나무와 꽃을 심는다
(d) 인조 뒷마당에 만족한다

○ 정답 잡는 치트키

다음에 할 일을 언급하는 후반을 주의 깊게 듣는다.

해설 | 남자가 'Megan, have you decided?'라며 결정했는지 묻자, 여자가 'I think, after years of being surrounded by concrete, I want to feel closer to nature. Besides, I can offset the water usage by using recycled water instead.'라며 몇 년 동안 콘크리트에 둘러싸여 지내다 보니 자연과 더 가까워지고 싶고, 재사용된 물을 대신 사용함으로써 물 사용량을 상쇄할 수 있다고 한 것을 통해, Megan은 앞마당에 천연 잔디를 기를 것임을 추론할 수 있다. 따라서 (a)가 정답이다.

어휘 | landscaper[lǽndskèipə] 정원사 settle for ~으로 만족하다

PART 4 [46~52] 설명 온라인 수업에서 지켜야 하는 네티켓을 위한 6가지 조언

음성 바로 듣기

인사 + 주제 제시	Welcome to the latest episode of *Freshman Cheer*, a podcast about adjusting to college life. We know that more and more students are taking online classes these days, in addition to traditional face-to-face classes.	대학 생활 적응에 관한 팟캐스트 *Freshman Cheer* 의 최신 에피소드에 오신 것을 환영합니다. 우리는 요즘 전통적인 대면 수업 외에도 온라인 수업을 듣는 학생들이 점점 늘어나고 있다는 것을 알고 있습니다.
네티켓 의 정의	[46]If you're going to be taking online classes for the first time, please take a listen to our netiquette guide. "Netiquette," or Internet etiquette, refers to the rules for good online behavior. As you might have guessed, the virtual classroom is different from a real classroom. To make sure that you conduct yourself properly in your online classes, it's important that you follow these netiquette tips.	[46]만약 여러분이 처음으로 온라인 수업을 듣게 된다면, 네티켓 가이드를 들어보세요. "네티켓", 즉 인터넷 에티켓은 좋은 온라인 행동을 위한 규칙을 말합니다. 여러분이 짐작했을 수도 있듯이, 가상 교실은 실제 교실과는 다릅니다. 여러분이 온라인 수업에서 제대로 행동하는지 확실히 하기 위해서, 이러한 네티켓 조언을 따르는 것이 중요합니다.
조언1: 개별 수업 규칙 숙지	First, familiarize yourself with the rules of your individual classes. [47]While there are some common rules for virtual classes, like muting your microphone when you're not talking, not all online classes have similar rules. Some teachers may require you to dress appropriately, as you would for regular school, while others won't care if you're in pajamas and a hoodie. Know the class rules and follow them as best you can.	먼저, 개별 수업의 규칙을 숙지하세요. [47]가상 수업에서 발언하지 않을 때 마이크 소리를 작게 하는 것과 같은 몇 가지 일반적인 규칙이 있지만, 모든 온라인 수업이 유사한 규칙을 가지는 것은 아닙니다. 어떤 선생님들은 여러분이 일반 학교에서처럼 옷을 적절하게 입도록 요구할 수도 있지만, 다른 선생님들은 여러분이 잠옷과 모자 달린 옷을 입어도 신경 쓰지 않을 것입니다. 수업 규칙을 알고 여러분이 할 수 있는 최선을 다해 그것들을 따르세요.
조언2: 예의 바른 행동	Second, [48]you should be respectful. The barrier of the screen should not be an excuse to say disrespectful or hurtful things to others. The lack of nonverbal cues	두 번째로, [48]예의 바르게 행동해야 합니다. 화면의 장벽이 다른 사람들에게 무례하거나 상처를 입히는 말을 하는 핑계가 되어서는 안 됩니다. 눈 맞춤과 같은 비

286 본 교재 인강·무료 지텔프 문법 총정리강의 HackersIngang.com

like eye contact can make some people forget that they're still interacting with real people. Remember that your teacher and classmates have feelings and may be affected by what you say and write online. So if you wouldn't say something in an actual classroom, don't say it in a virtual class either.

조언3: 유머 조심 하기

Third, [49]be careful with humor. This is not to say that online classes should be dull and lifeless. It's only a reminder that humor and sarcasm are difficult to convey virtually because people cannot see your body language or, in the case of audio classes, even your facial expressions. It gets even worse if you're communicating through writing because others will not hear the tone of your voice. So, [49]more often than not, your attempt at being funny might be misinterpreted as being rude. When in doubt, keep the humor light to avoid causing offense.

조언4: 문법에 맞는 커뮤 케이션

Fourth, [50]keep your communications formal to create an atmosphere of excellence. You are still advised to communicate professionally in your online classes— even though cyberspace is the birthplace of acronyms and slang shortcuts. Always use proper grammar when conversing with your teacher and classmates, both in speech and in text. This has the added benefit of keeping your conversations clear.

조언5: 마감일 준수

Fifth, respect deadlines. Many new members of an online classroom expect the experience to be less formal and view deadlines as mere suggestions. Even though an online class can be more flexible than a traditional class, you will still be expected to accomplish tasks and deliver work on time. [51]While some teachers do give extensions if you have valid reasons, you should still inform your teacher in advance if you won't be able to meet the deadline.

조언6: 타인의 사생활 존중

Finally, respect other people's privacy by not carelessly disclosing their information. [52]Always seek permission before taking a screenshot, recording a lecture, forwarding messages, or posting photos of someone else. Remember that sharing information online may compromise not just your security but also the security of others. Even if you don't intend to, your sharing of details can lead to hackers and other people with malicious intent getting hold of sensitive information.

끝인사

That's all for this week's *Freshman Cheer*! Thanks for listening.

언어적 신호의 부재는 일부 사람들에게는 자기가 여전히 실제 사람들과 상호작용하고 있다는 것을 잊게 만들 수 있습니다. 선생님과 같은 반 친구들도 감정을 가지고 있으며 온라인에서 여러분이 말하고 쓰는 것에 영향을 받을 수 있다는 점을 기억하세요. 그러므로 여러분이 실제 교실에서 무언가를 말하지 않을 것이라면, 가상 수업에서도 말하지 마세요.

세 번째로, [49]유머를 조심해야 합니다. 온라인 수업이 단조롭고 활력이 없어야 한다는 말은 아닙니다. 유머와 빈정거림은 사람들이 당신의 몸짓을 볼 수 없기 때문에, 또는 오디오 수업의 경우, 당신의 표정까지 볼 수 없기 때문에 가상으로 전달하기 어렵다는 것을 상기시켜 주는 것뿐입니다. 당신이 글을 통해 의사소통하고 있다면 다른 사람들이 당신의 목소리 톤을 듣지 않을 것이기 때문에 더욱 악화됩니다. 그래서, [49]종종, 우기려는 시도가 무례한 것으로 오해받을 수 있습니다. 의심스러울 때는, 불쾌감을 주지 않도록 유머를 가볍게 유지하세요.

네 번째로, [50]우수한 분위기를 조성하기 위해 커뮤니케이션은 문법에 맞게 하세요. 사이버 공간은 약어와 속어의 발생지이지만 온라인 수업에서는 여전히 전문적으로 소통하도록 권장됩니다. 선생님과 반 친구들과 대화할 때는 말과 글 모두 항상 올바른 문법을 사용하세요. 이렇게 하면 대화를 명료하게 하는 추가적인 이점이 있습니다.

다섯 번째로, 마감일을 준수하세요. 온라인 수업에 처음 참여하는 많은 학생은 경험이 덜 형식적일 것으로 기대하며 마감일을 단순한 제안으로 여깁니다. 온라인 수업은 전통적인 수업보다 더 유연할 수 있지만, 여전히 제시간에 과제를 완료하고 작업물을 제출하도록 기대될 것입니다. [51]일부 선생님들은 정당한 사유가 있는 경우 기한을 연장해 주기도 하지만, 마감일을 지키지 못할 거라면 미리 선생님에게 알려야 합니다.

마지막으로, 타인의 정보를 부주의하게 공개하지 않음으로써 타인의 사생활을 존중하세요. [52]스크린숏을 찍거나, 강의를 녹화하거나, 메시지를 전달하거나, 다른 사람의 사진을 게시하기 전에 항상 허락을 구하세요. 온라인에서 정보를 공유하는 것은 본인의 보안뿐만 아니라 다른 사람들의 보안도 위태롭게 할 수 있음을 기억하세요. 의도하지 않았더라도, 세부 정보를 공유하는 것은 해커나 악의적인 의도를 가진 다른 사람들이 민감한 정보를 손에 넣을 수 있게 할 수 있습니다.

이상으로 이번 주 *Freshman Cheer*를 마칩니다! 청취해 주셔서 감사합니다.

지텔프 공식 기출문제집 7회분 Level 2

어휘 | traditional[trədíʃənl] 전통적인 virtual[vɔ́:rtʃuəl] 가상의, 인터넷의 familiarize[fəmíliəràiz] 숙지시키다, 익숙해지게 하다
individual[ìndəvídʒuəl] 개별의, 개개인의 mute[mju:t] 소리를 작게 하다; 소리 없는 hoodie[húdi] 모자 달린 옷
respectful[rispéktfəl] 예의 바른 barrier[bǽriər] 장벽, 장애(물) excuse[ikskjú:z] 핑계, 변명 disrespectful[dìsrispéktfl] 무례한
hurtful[hə́:rtfəl] 상처를 입히는, 감정을 상하게 하는 lack[læk] 부재, 결핍 nonverbal[nànvə́rbəl] 비언어적인 cue[kju:] 신호, 단서
interact with ~과 상호작용하다 dull[dʌl] 단조로운, 지루한 lifeless[láiflis] 활력이 없는 sarcasm[sɑ́:rkæzm] 빈정거림, 비아냥
convey[kənvéi] 전달하다 virtually[vɔ́:rtʃuəli] 가상으로 facial expression 표정 attempt[ətémpt] 시도, 노력; 시도하다
misinterpret[mìsintə́rprət] ~을 오해하다 rude[ru:d] 무례한 offense[əféns] 불쾌, 모욕 formal[fɔ́:rml] (말·어법이) 문법에 맞는, 형식적인
atmosphere[ǽtməsfìər] 분위기 birthplace[bə́rθpleis] 발생지, 탄생지 acronym[ǽkrənim] 약어, 머리글자어 slang[slæŋ] 속어, 은어
converse with ~와 대화하다 mere[miər] 단순한 flexible[fléksəbl] 유연한, 탄력적인 extension[iksténʃən] 연장, 연기
valid[vǽlid] 정당한, 타당한 in advance 미리, 사전에 disclose[disklóuz] 공개하다, 밝히다 permission[pərmíʃən] 허락, 허가
forward[fɔ́:rwərd] 전달하다, 전송하다 compromise[kɑ́mprəmaiz] 위태롭게 하다, 손상시키다 malicious[məlíʃəs] 악의적인
sensitive[sénsətiv] 민감한

---

46 주제/목적 담화의 주제

난이도 ●●○

What is the talk all about?

(a) how to teach an online class
(b) how to choose the right course
(c) how to get good grades
(d) how to behave in a virtual class

담화는 무엇에 관한 것인가?

(a) 온라인 수업을 가르치는 방법
(b) 올바른 진로를 선택하는 방법
(c) 좋은 성적을 받는 방법
(d) 가상 수업에서 행동하는 방법

━○ 정답 잡는 치트키

담화의 주제를 언급하는 초반을 주의 깊게 듣고 전체 맥락을 파악한다.

해설 | 화자가 'If you're going to be taking online classes for the first time, please take a listen to our netiquette guide. "Netiquette," ~ refers to the rules for good online behavior.'라며 만약 처음으로 온라인 수업을 듣게 된다면 네티켓 가이드를 들어보라며, "네티켓"은 좋은 온라인 행동을 위한 규칙을 말한다고 한 뒤, 담화 전반에 걸쳐 가상 수업에서 행동하는 데 지켜야 할 네티켓을 설명하는 내용이 이어지고 있다. 따라서 (d)가 정답이다.

⇄ Paraphrasing
online classes 온라인 수업 → a virtual class 가상 수업

어휘 | behave[bihéiv] 행동하다, 처신하다

---

47 특정세부사항 What

난이도 ●●○

What does the speaker say about online class rules?

(a) that they are hard to follow
(b) that they depend on the group size
(c) that they apply to all classrooms
(d) that they vary between classes

화자는 온라인 수업 규칙에 관해 무엇을 말하는가?

(a) 따라가기 어렵다는 것
(b) 그룹 규모에 의해 결정된다는 것
(c) 모든 교실에 적용된다는 것
(d) 학급마다 다양하다는 것

━○ 정답 잡는 치트키

질문의 키워드 rules가 그대로 언급된 주변 내용을 주의 깊게 듣는다.

해설 | 화자는 'While there are some common rules for virtual classes, ~, not all online classes have similar rules.'라며 가상

수업에서 몇 가지 일반적인 규칙이 있지만 모든 온라인 수업이 유사한 규칙을 가지는 것은 아니라고 했다. 따라서 (d)가 정답이다.

어휘 | depend on ~에 의해 결정되다 apply to ~에 적용되다 vary[véri] 다양하다, 다르다

---

48 특정세부사항   How   난이도 ●●○

How can one be respectful to others online?

(a) by maintaining eye contact
(b) by using careful language
(c) by helping to answer questions
(d) by refraining from talking too much

온라인에서 다른 사람들에게 예의 바르려면 어떻게 할 수 있는가?

(a) 눈맞춤을 유지함으로써
(b) 신중한 언어를 사용함으로써
(c) 질문에 답하는 것을 도움으로써
(d) 너무 많이 말하는 것을 자제함으로써

⊶○ 정답 잡는 치트키

질문의 키워드 respectful이 그대로 언급된 주변 내용을 주의 깊게 듣는다.

해설 | 화자가 'you should be respectful. The barrier of the screen should not be an excuse to say disrespectful or hurtful things to others.'라며 예의 바르게 행동해야 하며, 화면의 장벽이 다른 사람들에게 무례하거나 상처를 입히는 말을 하는 핑계가 되어서는 안 된다고 했다. 따라서 (b)가 정답이다.

어휘 | refrain[rifréin] 자제하다, 삼가다

---

49 추론   특정사실   난이도 ●●○

Why, most likely, should students be careful with using humor during online classes?

(a) to avoid coming off as impolite
(b) to avoid facing penalties
(c) to keep from disrupting class
(d) to appear more professional

온라인 수업 중에 학생들은 왜 유머를 사용하는 것을 주의해야 하는 것 같은가?

(a) 무례하게 보이는 것을 피하기 위해서
(b) 처벌을 받는 것을 피하기 위해서
(c) 수업을 방해하지 않기 위해서
(d) 더 전문적으로 보이기 위해서

⊶○ 정답 잡는 치트키

질문의 키워드 careful with ~ humor가 그대로 언급된 주변 내용을 주의 깊게 듣는다.

해설 | 화자가 'be careful with humor'라며 유머를 조심해야 한다고 한 뒤, 'more often than not, your attempt at being funny might be misinterpreted as being rude'라며 종종 웃기려는 시도가 무례한 것으로 오해받을 수 있다고 한 것을 통해, 학생들은 온라인 수업 중에 무례하기 보이는 것을 피하기 위해서 유머를 사용하는 것을 주의해야 함을 추론할 수 있다. 따라서 (a)가 정답이다.

⇄ Paraphrasing
rude 무례한 → impolite 무례한

어휘 | penalty[pénəlti] 처벌, 불이익 disrupt[disrÁpt] 방해하다, 피해를 주다

How can students create an atmosphere of excellence in their online classes?

(a) They can correct others' grammar.
(b) They can make formal speeches.
(c) They can use a professional tone.
(d) They can keep conversations short.

학생들은 온라인 수업에서 어떻게 우수한 분위기를 조성할 수 있는가?

(a) 다른 사람들의 문법을 교정할 수 있다.
(b) 공식적인 연설을 할 수 있다.
(c) 전문적인 말투를 사용할 수 있다.
(d) 대화를 짧게 할 수 있다.

━○ 정답 잡는 치트키

질문의 키워드 create an atmosphere of excellence가 그대로 언급된 주변 내용을 주의 깊게 듣는다.

해설 | 화자가 'keep your communications formal to create an atmosphere of excellence. You are still advised to communicate professionally in your online classes'라며 우수한 분위기를 조성하기 위해 커뮤니케이션은 문법에 맞게 해야 하고, 온라인 수업에서는 여전히 전문적으로 소통하도록 권장된다고 했다. 따라서 (c)가 정답이다.

⇄ Paraphrasing
communicate professionally 전문적으로 소통하다 → use a professional tone 전문적인 말투를 사용하다

어휘 | correct[kɔ́rekt] 교정하다, 고치다

According to the talk, what should students do when they cannot meet a deadline?

(a) ask for extra credit
(b) offer a good excuse
(c) submit an incomplete assignment
(d) let the teacher know ahead of time

담화에 따르면, 학생들은 마감일을 지킬 수 없을 때 무엇을 해야 하는가?

(a) 추가 학점을 요청한다
(b) 그럴듯한 변명을 한다
(c) 미완성한 과제를 제출한다
(d) 선생님에게 미리 알린다

━○ 정답 잡는 치트키

질문의 키워드 cannot meet a deadline이 won't be able to meet the deadline으로 paraphrasing되어 언급된 주변 내용을 주의 깊게 듣는다.

해설 | 화자가 'While some teachers do give extensions if you have valid reasons, you should still inform your teacher in advance if you won't be able to meet the deadline.'이라며 일부 선생님들은 정당한 사유가 있는 경우 기한을 연장해 주기도 하지만 마감일을 지키지 못할 거라면 미리 선생님에게 알려야 한다고 했다. 따라서 (d)가 정답이다.

⇄ Paraphrasing
inform ~ teacher 선생님에게 알리다 → let the teacher know 선생님에게 알리다
in advance 미리 → ahead of time 미리

어휘 | credit[krédit] 학점   excuse[ikskjúːs] 변명, 이유   incomplete[ìnkəmplíːt] 미완성의   ahead of time 미리

How might students compromise the security of an online class?

(a) by asking an outsider to join class discussions
(b) by posting information without permission
(c) by sending a private message to the entire group
(d) by making their student profiles public

학생들은 어떻게 온라인 수업의 보안을 위태롭게 할 수 있는 것 같은가?

(a) 외부인에게 수업 토론에 참여하도록 요청함으로써
(b) 허락 없이 정보를 게시함으로써
(c) 전체 그룹에 사적인 메시지를 보냄으로써
(d) 학생 프로필을 공개함으로써

○ 정답 잡는 치트키

질문의 키워드 compromise ~ security가 그대로 언급된 주변 내용을 주의 깊게 듣는다.

해설 | 화자가 'Always seek permission before taking a screenshot, recording a lecture, forwarding messages, or posting photos of someone else. Remember that sharing information online may compromise not just your security but also the security of others.'라며 스크린숏을 찍거나, 강의를 녹화하거나, 메시지를 전달하거나, 다른 사람의 사진을 게시하기 전에 항상 허락을 구해야 하고, 온라인에서 정보를 공유하는 것은 본인의 보안뿐만 아니라 다른 사람들의 보안도 위태롭게 할 수 있음을 기억하라고 한 것을 통해, 학생들은 허락 없이 정보를 게시함으로써 온라인 수업의 보안을 위태롭게 할 수 있음을 추론할 수 있다. 따라서 (b)가 정답이다.

어휘 | outsider[àutsáidər] 외부인

READING & VOCABULARY

PART 1 ^[53~59] 인물의 일대기 유명한 인상주의 화가인 클로드 모네

인물 이름	**CLAUDE MONET**

CLAUDE MONET

소개 + 유명한 이유	⁵³Claude Monet was a French painter best known for developing Impressionism, a nineteenth-century art movement that aimed to capture the artist's "impression" or experience of a moment rather than an accurate depiction. Monet was one of the movement's founders, along with several other French painters.
작품에 영향을 미친 요인1: 외젠 부댕	Oscar-Claude Monet was born on November 14, 1840, in Paris, France, but the family moved to Normandy when he was five. As a child, Monet loved to draw and wanted to become an artist. With his mother's support, fifteen-year-old Monet enrolled in Le Havre secondary school of the arts. His talent in charcoal drawing was acknowledged by his neighbors, who often bought his works. However, ⁵⁴it was the landscape painter Eugène Boudin who urged him to try painting. Monet soon joined Boudin in painting outdoors, ⁵⁸a <u>practice</u> that would eventually become the foundation of Monet's work.
작품에 영향을 미친 요인2: 동료 예술가	At the age of nineteen, Monet moved back to Paris to study art. ⁵⁵He was disappointed with the traditional art methods being taught there, but he met fellow artists who shared his new approach to art by painting pictures that were not exact representations of real life. Instead, they were interpretations of what the painter sees. Often working outdoors, ⁵⁵Monet and his fellow artists used small brushstrokes that emphasized fleeting moments in time—particularly the changing light and colors—rather than the subject matter's details.
주요 작품1: 인상, 해돋이	⁵⁶In 1872, Monet painted *Impression, Sunrise*, which portrayed the port in his hometown during a morning fog. ⁵⁶It was exhibited in Paris, where art critics used the title of his work to ⁵⁹<u>discredit</u> him and his fellow artists by calling them "impressionists" because their paintings looked more like sketches than finished works. The name stuck, and the exhibition later became known as the First Impressionist Exhibition.
주요 작품2: 수련	Monet gained critical and financial success during the 1890s with his series of paintings on a single subject. The most notable of these was *Water Lilies*. The series consisted of approximately 250 large-scale water lily

클로드 모네

⁵³클로드 모네는 정확한 묘사보다는 그 예술가의 "인상" 혹은 순간의 경험을 포착하는 것을 목표로 했던 19세기 예술 운동인 인상주의를 발전시킨 것으로 가장 잘 알려진 프랑스 화가였다. 모네는 여러 다른 프랑스 화가들과 함께, 그 운동의 창시자 중 한 명이었다.

오스카 클로드 모네는 1840년 11월 14일에 프랑스 파리에서 태어났지만, 그가 다섯 살이었을 때 가족은 노르망디로 이사했다. 어린 시절, 모네는 그림 그리는 것을 좋아했고 예술가가 되기를 원했다. 그의 어머니의 지원으로, 15살의 모네는 르 아브르 미술 중학교에 입학했다. 목탄화에 대한 그의 재능은 이웃들에게 인정받았는데, 그들은 종종 그의 작품을 구입하기도 했다. 하지만, ⁵⁴그에게 그림을 그리도록 권유했던 사람은 풍경화 화가 외젠 부댕이었다. 모네는 곧 부댕과 함께 야외에서 그림을 그렸고, ⁵⁸이 습관은 결국 모네 작품의 기초가 되었다.

19세의 나이에, 모네는 예술을 공부하기 위해 파리로 돌아갔다. ⁵⁵그는 그곳에서 가르치는 전통적인 예술 방식에 실망했지만, 실물을 정확하게 표현하지 않은 그림들을 그리며 예술에 대한 그의 새로운 접근법을 공유하는 동료 예술가들을 만났다. 대신, 그것들은 화가가 보는 것에 대한 해석이었다. 종종 야외에서 작업을 했던, ⁵⁵모네와 그의 동료 예술가들은 주제의 세부 사항보다는 시간의 잠깐의 순간, 특히 변화하는 빛과 색상을 강조하는 작은 붓 놀림을 사용했다.

⁵⁶1872년에, 모네는 *인상, 해돋이*를 그렸는데, 이것은 아침 안개가 낀 고향에 있는 항구를 묘사했다. ⁵⁶이것은 파리에서 전시되었는데, 그곳에서 예술 비평가들은 그들의 그림이 완성된 작품이라기보다는 스케치에 더 가까워 보였기 때문에 ^{56/59}그와 그의 동료 예술가들의 평판을 나쁘게 하기 위해 그들을 "인상파"라고 부르면서 그의 작품명을 사용했다. 이 명칭은 굳어졌고, 전시회는 나중에 최초의 인상파 전시회로 알려지게 되었다.

모네는 단 하나의 주제에 관한 일련의 그림들로 1890년대에 비평적, 재정적인 성공을 얻었다. 이것 중 가장 주목할 만한 것은 *수련*이었다. 이 시리즈는 지베르니에 있는 그의 집의 꽃 정원을 묘사한 약 250개

paintings that depicted the flower garden at his home in Giverny, where he spent the last thirty years of his life.

Monet died on December 5, 1926. [57]Considered the greatest Impressionist painter, he continues to influence modern art styles, including abstract art, through his work. His paintings are displayed in museums worldwide, and a single painting can sell for tens of millions of dollars.

죽음 + 영향력

의 큰 규모의 수련 그림들로 구성되었는데, 지베르니는 그가 생의 마지막 30년을 보낸 곳이었다.

모네는 1926년 12월 5일에 사망했다. [57]가장 위대한 인상주의 화가로 여겨지는, 그는 자기 작품을 통해 추상 미술을 포함하여, 현대 미술 양식에 계속해서 영향을 미치고 있다. 그의 그림들은 전 세계 박물관에 전시되어 있고, 하나의 그림은 수천만 달러에 팔릴 수 있다.

어휘 | Impressionism n. 인상주의(19세기 후반 프랑스에서 발달한 화풍) capture v. 포착하다, 담아내다 accurate adj. 정확한 depiction n. 묘사, 서술 founder n. 창시자 enroll v. 입학하다, 등록하다 secondary school phr. 중등학교 charcoal drawing phr. 목탄화 urge v. 권유하다 fellow adj. 동료의; n. 동료 approach n. 접근법; v. 접촉하다 representation n. 표현, 묘사 interpretation n. 해석 brushstroke n. 붓 놀림 emphasize v. 강조하다 fleeting adj. 잠깐의, 순간의 portray v. 묘사하다 port n. 항구 hometown n. 고향 fog n. 안개 notable adj. 주목할 만한 water lily phr. 수련 consist of phr. ~으로 구성되다 depict v. 묘사하다, 그리다 abstract art phr. 추상 미술

53 특정세부사항 유명한 이유 난이도 ●●○

What is Claude Monet best known for?

(a) helping to introduce a new style of art
(b) producing more work than any other painter
(c) founding a school for promising artists
(d) creating highly realistic landscape paintings

클로드 모네는 무엇으로 가장 잘 알려져 있는가?

(a) 새로운 예술 양식을 소개하는 것을 도운 것
(b) 다른 어떤 화가보다 더 많은 작품을 제작한 것
(c) 유망한 예술가들을 위한 학교를 설립한 것
(d) 매우 사실적인 풍경화를 제작한 것

○ 정답 잡는 치트키

질문의 키워드 best known이 그대로 언급된 주변 내용을 주의 깊게 읽는다.

해설 | 1단락의 'Claude Monet was a French painter best known for developing Impressionism, a nineteenth-century art movement'에서 클로드 모네는 19세기 예술 운동인 인상주의를 발전시킨 것으로 가장 잘 알려진 프랑스 화가였다고 했다. 따라서 (a)가 정답이다.

어휘 | promising adj. 유망한, 장래성 있는 realistic adj. 사실적인, 현실적인

54 특정세부사항 Why 난이도 ●●○

Why did Monet start to take an interest in painting?

(a) because he was encouraged by another artist
(b) because he became bored with charcoal drawing
(c) because he was urged by his teachers
(d) because he was influenced by his mother

모네는 왜 그림 그리는 것에 관심을 가지기 시작했는가?

(a) 다른 예술가에게 권유를 받았기 때문에
(b) 목탄화에 싫증이 났기 때문에
(c) 선생님들의 권유를 받았기 때문에
(d) 어머니의 영향을 받았기 때문에

○ 정답 잡는 치트키

질문의 키워드 painting이 그대로 언급된 주변 내용을 주의 깊게 읽는다.

해설 | 2단락의 'it was the landscape painter Eugène Boudin who urged him to try painting. Monet soon joined Boudin in painting outdoors'에서 모네에게 그림을 그리도록 권유했던 사람은 풍경화 화가 외젠 부댕이었고, 모네는 곧 부댕과 함께 야외에서 그림을 그렸다고 했다. 따라서 (a)가 정답이다.

⇄ **Paraphrasing**

urged 권유했다 → encouraged 권유했다

---

55 추론 특정사실 난이도 ●●○

What probably distinguished Monet's artwork from the typical style at the time?

(a) a focus on capturing objects while they were completely still

(b) an emphasis on particular color schemes to create a modern look

(c) a focus on the way the scene changed while he was painting

(d) an emphasis on the finest details of the subject matter

모네의 작품이 당시의 전형적인 스타일과 구별되는 점은 무엇이었을 것 같은가?

(a) 사물들이 완전히 정지해 있을 때 그것들을 포착하는 것에 대한 초점

(b) 현대적인 느낌을 주기 위해 특정 색채 배합에 대한 강조

(c) 그림을 그리는 동안 장면이 변화하는 방식에 대한 초점

(d) 주제의 가장 세세한 사항들에 대한 강조

◄─○ 정답 잡는 치트키

질문의 키워드 typical이 traditional로 paraphrasing되어 언급된 주변 내용을 주의 깊게 읽는다.

해설 | 3단락의 'He was disappointed with the traditional art methods ~, but he met fellow artists who shared his new approach to art'에서 모네는 전통적인 예술 방식에 실망했지만, 예술에 대한 그의 새로운 접근법을 공유하는 동료 예술가들을 만났다고 한 뒤, 'Monet ~ used small brushstrokes that emphasized fleeting moments in time—particularly the changing light and colors—rather than the subject matter's details'에서 모네는 주제의 세부 사항보다는 시간의 잠깐의 순간, 특히 변화하는 빛과 색상을 강조하는 작은 붓 놀림을 사용했다고 한 것을 통해, 모네의 작품이 그림을 그리는 동안 장면이 변화하는 방식에 초점을 두어, 당시의 전형적인 스타일과 구별되었음을 추론할 수 있다. 따라서 (c)가 정답이다.

어휘 | typical adj. 전형적인, 일반적인 still adj. 정지해 있는, 움직이지 않는 color scheme phr. 색채의 배합 modern adj. 현대적인 scene n. 장면

---

56 특정세부사항 What 난이도 ●●○

What is the significance of Monet's *Impression, Sunrise*?

(a) It was his most well-received creation.

(b) It inspired the name for an entire movement.

(c) It captured the scene in his own backyard.

(d) It was the first painting to be sold at auction.

모네의 *인상, 해돋이*의 중요성은 무엇인가?

(a) 그의 가장 호평을 받은 작품이었다.

(b) 전체 운동의 이름에 영감을 주었다.

(c) 그의 뒷마당에서 그 장면을 포착했다.

(d) 경매에서 낙찰된 최초의 그림이었다.

◄─○ 정답 잡는 치트키

질문의 키워드 *Impression, Sunrise*가 그대로 언급된 주변 내용을 주의 깊게 읽는다.

해설 | 4단락의 'In 1872, Monet painted *Impression, Sunrise*'에서 1872년에 모네가 *인상, 해돋이*를 그렸다고 한 뒤, 'It was exhibited in Paris, where art critics used the title of his work to discredit him and his fellow artists by calling them "impressionists"'

에서 이것은 파리에서 전시되었는데, 그곳에서 예술 비평가들이 모네와 동료 예술가들의 평판을 나쁘게 하기 위해 그들을 "인상파"라고 부르면서 그의 작품명을 사용했다고 했다. 따라서 (b)가 정답이다.

어휘| significance n. 중요성 well-received adj. 호평을 받은 auction n. 경매

---

57 특정세부사항   How

How does Monet continue to impact the world of art?

(a) by altering the direction of all art forms
(b) by making painting profitable for artists
(c) by providing inspiration for other art styles
(d) by calling attention to the struggles of aspiring artists

모네는 어떻게 예술계에 계속 영향을 주는가?

(a) 모든 예술 형식의 방향을 바꾸어 놓음으로써
(b) 예술가들을 위해 그림 그리는 것을 수익성 있게 함으로써
(c) 다른 예술 스타일에 영감을 줌으로써
(d) 장차 예술가가 되려는 사람들의 분투에 주의를 환기함으로써

➜○ 정답 잡는 치트키

질문의 키워드 impact가 influence로 paraphrasing되어 언급된 주변 내용을 주의 깊게 읽는다.

해설| 6단락의 'Considered the greatest Impressionist painter, he continues to influence modern art styles, including abstract art, through his work.'에서 가장 위대한 인상주의 화가로 여겨지는 모네는 그의 작품을 통해 추상 미술을 포함하여, 현대 미술 양식에 계속해서 영향을 미치고 있다고 했다. 따라서 (c)가 정답이다.

어휘| alter v. 바꾸다, 변경하다 profitable adj. 수익성 있는 inspiration n. 영감 call attention phr. 주의를 환기하다 struggle n. 분투 aspiring adj. 장차 ~가 되려는

---

58 어휘   유의어

In the context of the passage, practice means _____.

(a) field
(b) rehearsal
(c) business
(d) habit

지문의 문맥에서, 'practice'는 –을 의미한다.

(a) 분야
(b) 예행연습
(c) 사업
(d) 습관

➜○ 정답 잡는 치트키

밑줄 친 어휘의 유의어를 찾는 문제이므로, practice가 포함된 구절을 읽고 문맥을 파악한다.

해설| 2단락의 'a practice that would eventually become the foundation'은 이 습관이 결국 기초가 되었다는 뜻이므로, practice가 '습관'이라는 의미로 사용된 것을 알 수 있다. 따라서 '습관'이라는 같은 의미의 (d) habit이 정답이다.

59 어휘　유의어

In the context of the passage, <u>discredit</u> means _____. (a) examine (b) imitate (c) fool **(d) insult**	지문의 문맥에서, 'discredit'은 -을 의미한다. (a) 조사하다 (b) 모방하다 (c) 속이다 **(d) 모욕하다**

⊶○ 정답 잡는 치트키

밑줄 친 어휘의 유의어를 찾는 문제이므로, discredit이 포함된 구절을 읽고 문맥을 파악한다.

해설 | 4단락의 'discredit him and his fellow artists'는 그와 그의 동료 예술가들의 평판을 나쁘게 한다는 뜻이므로, discredit이 '평판을 나쁘게 하다'라는 의미로 사용된 것을 알 수 있다. 따라서 '모욕하다'라는 비슷한 의미의 (d) insult가 정답이다.

PART 2 (60~66)　잡지 기사　소름이 돋는 이유

[기사 제목]

[60]WHY WE GET GOOSEBUMPS

[정의]

[60]Do you ever wonder why the hairs at the back of your neck stand up when you are cold, listening to a scary story, or feeling intense emotions? This sensation, where the base of the hair involuntarily springs up and causes tiny, raised bumps to appear on the skin, is called goosebumps.

[유래]

The term "goosebumps" derives its name from how [61(d)]the raised skin resembles the skin of a goose after its feathers have been plucked. Although [61(a)]hair rises all over the body when goosebumps occur, [61(c)]the bumps are most visible in places where hair is thinner, such as the arms and back of one's neck.

[소름의 초기 역할1: 체온 유지]

[61(b)]Goosebumps have no clear practical use for modern humans. Rather, they appear as an indication that someone is scared or wowed by something beautiful, like a song. However, [62]scientists think that goosebumps were useful to early humans. First, back when humans were still covered in thick hair, goosebumps provided added insulation from the cold. That is, when the hair stood up, it fluffed up. [65]This action <u>trapped</u> air close to the skin, which allowed early humans to retain body heat.

[소름의 초기 역할2: 위험에 대응]

Second, goosebumps are a by-product of the human "fight or flight" response, the involuntary reaction to a perceived danger or threat that prepares one to either fight or withdraw from a dangerous situation. Sensing

[60]왜 우리는 소름이 돋는가

[60]추울 때, 무서운 이야기를 들을 때, 혹은 강렬한 감정을 느낄 때, 왜 목뒤의 털이 서는지 궁금한 적이 있는가? 이 감각은 털의 밑부분이 무의식중에 갑자기 나타나서 피부에 작고 튀어나온 돌기들을 일으키는데, 이를 소름이라고 한다.

"소름"이라는 용어는 [61(d)]솟아오른 피부가 깃털이 뽑힌 후 거위의 피부와 닮았다는 데서 이름이 유래한다. [61(a)]소름이 생기면 온몸의 털이 서지만, [61(c)]팔이나 목뒤와 같이 털이 더 얇은 곳에서 가장 잘 보인다.

[61(b)]소름은 현대 인류에게 뚜렷한 실용성이 없다. 오히려, 그것들은 누군가가 겁을 먹거나 노래와 같은 아름다운 것에 열광하는 징후로 나타난다. 그러나, [62]과학자들은 소름이 초기 인류에게 유용했다고 생각한다. 첫 번째로, 인간이 여전히 두꺼운 털로 덮여 있을 때, 소름은 추위로부터 추가적인 단열을 제공했다. 즉, 털이 섰을 때, 그것은 부풀어 올랐다. [65]이 작용은 공기를 피부 가까이 가뒀고, 초기 인류가 체온을 유지할 수 있게 했다.

두 번째로, 소름은 인간의 "투쟁 혹은 도피" 반응의 부산물로, 누군가가 싸우거나 위험한 상황에서 물러설 준비를 하게 하는 인지된 위험 또는 위협에 대한 무의식적인 반응이다. 위험을 감지하는 것은 자동으로 반

danger automatically triggers the reflexes, which contract the small muscles at the base of the hairs, causing the hairs to stand up. [63]With their hair puffed up, early humans appeared bigger, which would have caused their enemy—perhaps a bear or a snake—to back off.

Although humans stopped growing fur a long time ago, goosebumps remain as a leftover survival instinct. When people hear a scary story, [66]their brains register the situation as life-threatening and react accordingly. [64]The same can be said about a reaction to something aesthetically pleasing, like good music. Unexpectedly strong emotional input can trigger the sympathetic nervous system, causing tiny muscles to contract and the hairs to stand up in response.

사신경을 일으키고, 이것은 털 아래쪽의 작은 근육을 수축시켜, 털이 설 수 있게 한다. [63]털이 부풀어 오르면서, 초기 인류는 더 크게 보였는데, 이것은 그들의 적인, 곰이나 뱀일지도 모르는 것을 물러나게 했을 것이다.

비록 인간은 오래전에 털이 자라는 것이 멈췄지만, 소름은 남아있는 생존 본능으로 잔존한다. 사람들이 무서운 이야기를 들을 때, [66]그들의 뇌는 그 상황을 생명을 위협하는 것으로 인식하고 그에 따라 반응한다. [64]좋은 음악과 같이 미적으로 즐거운 것에 대한 반응도 마찬가지이다. 예상치 못하게 강한 감정적인 자극은 교감 신경계를 자극할 수 있고, 이것이 작은 근육이 수축하고 털이 반응하여 서는 것을 야기한다.

어휘 | goosebumps n. 소름 intense adj. 강렬한 sensation n. 감각, 느낌 involuntarily adv. 무의식중에, 무심결에 spring up phr. 갑자기 나타나다 bump n. 돌기 derive from phr. ~에서 유래하다 resemble v. 닮다, 유사하다 feather n. 깃털 pluck v. (머리카락·눈썹 등을) 뽑다 visible adj. 보이는 indication n. 징후, 표시 wow v. 열광시키다 insulation n. 단열 fluff up phr. 부풀리다 retain v. 유지하다 by-product n. 부산물 withdraw v. 물러서다, 철수하다 sense v. 감지하다; n. 감각 trigger v. 일으키다 reflexes n. 반사신경 contract v. 수축하다 enemy n. 적, 원수 back off phr. 물러나다 fur n. 털 leftover adj. 남아있는 instinct n. 본능 accordingly adv. 그에 따라, 따라서 aesthetically adv. 미적으로 sympathetic nervous system phr. 교감 신경계 in response phr. 반응하여

---

60 주제/목적   기사의 주제

난이도 ●●○

What is the article all about?

(a) a human's automatic response to external stimulation

(b) an emotional response that occurs when humans receive bad news

(c) a human's controlled response to changes in the weather

(d) a natural response no longer experienced by humans

기사는 무엇에 관한 것인가?

(a) 외부 자극에 대한 인간의 무의식적인 반응

(b) 인간이 나쁜 소식을 접했을 때 발생하는 감정적 반응

(c) 날씨 변화에 대한 인간의 억제된 반응

(d) 인간이 더 이상 경험하지 않는 자연스러운 반응

⟶○ 정답 잡는 치트키

제목과 지문의 초반을 주의 깊게 읽고 전체 맥락을 파악한다.

해설 | 기사의 제목 'Why we get goosebumps'에서 왜 우리는 소름이 돋는지를 물었고, 1단락의 'Do you ever wonder why the hairs at the back of your neck stand up when you are cold, listening to a scary story, or feeling intense emotions? This sensation, where the base of the hair involuntarily springs up and causes tiny, raised bumps to appear on the skin, is called goosebumps.'에서 추울 때, 무서운 이야기를 들을 때, 혹은 강렬한 감정을 느낄 때, 왜 목뒤의 털이 서는지 궁금한 적이 있는지 물으며, 털의 밑부분이 무의식중에 갑자기 나타나서 피부에 작고 튀어나온 돌기들을 일으키는 것을 소름이라고 한다고 한 뒤, 소름에 관한 세부 내용이 이어지고 있다. 따라서 (a)가 정답이다.

어휘 | automatic adj. 무의식적인, 자동의 external adj. 외부의 stimulation n. 자극, 흥분 controlled adj. 억제된, 통제당한

Which of the following is NOT true about goosebumps?

(a) They only occur in areas of the body that have thick hair.
(b) They have little practical use to humans nowadays.
(c) They are most noticeable in areas of the body with thin hair.
(d) Their appearance mimics the look of real goose skin.

다음 중 소름에 관해 사실이 아닌 것은 무엇인가?

(a) 두꺼운 털이 있는 신체 부위에서만 발생한다.
(b) 오늘날 인간에게 실용성이 거의 없다.
(c) 얇은 털이 있는 신체 부위에서 가장 잘 보인다.
(d) 외형은 실제 거위 피부의 외관처럼 보인다.

━○ 정답 잡는 치트키

질문의 키워드 goosebumps가 그대로 언급된 주변 내용을 주의 깊게 읽고, 보기의 키워드와 지문 내용을 대조하며 언급되는 것을 하나씩 소거한다.

해설 | (a)는 화자가 'hair rises all over the body when goosebumps occur'에서 소름이 생기면 온몸의 털이 선다고 했으므로 지문의 내용과 일치하지 않는다. 따라서 (a)가 정답이다.

오답분석
(b) 보기의 키워드 practical use가 그대로 언급된 3단락에서 소름은 현대 인류에게 뚜렷한 실용성이 없다고 언급되었다.
(c) 보기의 키워드 most noticeable이 most visible로 paraphrasing되어 언급된 2단락에서 팔이나 목뒤와 같이 털이 더 얇은 곳에서 가장 잘 보인다고 언급되었다.
(d) 보기의 키워드 goose skin이 skin of a goose로 paraphrasing되어 언급된 2단락에서 솟아오른 피부가 깃털이 뽑힌 후 거위의 피부와 닮았다고 언급되었다.

어휘 | mimic v. ~처럼 보이다, ~을 모방하다

According to the article, how did having goosebumps help early humans survive harsh environments?

(a) by preventing the skin from absorbing moisture
(b) by keeping them cool in the summer months
(c) by protecting them in low temperatures
(d) by alerting them to upcoming storms

기사에 따르면, 소름이 돋는 것은 어떻게 초기 인류가 혹독한 환경에서 살아남는 것을 도왔는가?

(a) 피부가 수분을 흡수하는 것을 막음으로써
(b) 여름철에 그들을 시원하게 유지해 줌으로써
(c) 저온에서 그들을 보호해 줌으로써
(d) 다가오는 폭풍을 그들에게 경고함으로써

━○ 정답 잡는 치트키

질문의 키워드 early humans가 그대로 언급되고, harsh environments가 cold로 paraphrasing되어 언급된 주변 내용을 주의 깊게 읽는다.

해설 | 3단락의 'scientists think that goosebumps were useful to early humans. First, back when humans were still covered in thick hair, goosebumps provided added insulation from the cold.'에서 과학자들은 소름이 초기 인류에게 유용했다고 생각하는데, 인간이 여전히 두꺼운 털로 덮여 있었을 때, 소름은 추위로부터 추가적인 단열을 제공했다고 했다. 따라서 (c)가 정답이다.

↪ Paraphrasing
the cold 추위 → low temperatures 저온

어휘 | harsh adj. 혹독한, 가혹한 absorb v. 흡수하다 alert v. 경고하다, 알리다

63 추론 특정사실

Why was it probably helpful for early humans to have goosebumps around predators?

(a) because it helped them blend in with their environment
(b) because it made their bodies look more intimidating
(c) because it strengthened their skin's resistance to injury
(d) because it signaled a need for lightning-fast reflexes

초기 인류가 포식자 주변에서 소름이 돋는 것은 왜 도움이 되었을 것 같은가?

(a) 그들이 환경에 섞여 드는 것을 도와주었기 때문에
(b) 그들의 몸을 더 위협적으로 보이게 만들었기 때문에
(c) 상처에 대한 그들의 피부 저항력을 강화했기 때문에
(d) 번개처럼 빠른 반사신경의 필요성을 신호로 알렸기 때문에

─○ 정답 잡는 치트키

질문의 키워드 early humans가 그대로 언급되고, predators가 enemy로 paraphrasing되어 언급된 주변 내용을 주의 깊게 읽는다.

해설 | 4단락의 'With their hair puffed up, early humans appeared bigger, which would have caused their enemy—perhaps a bear or a snake—to back off.'에서 털이 부풀어 오르면서 초기 인류는 더 크게 보였는데, 이것은 그들의 적인, 곰이나 뱀일지도 모르는 것을 물러나게 했을 것이라고 한 것을 통해, 초기 인류가 포식자 주변에서 소름이 돋는 것은 그들의 몸을 더 크게, 위협적으로 보이게 만들었기 때문에 도움이 되었음을 추론할 수 있다. 따라서 (b)가 정답이다.

⇄ **Paraphrasing**

appeared 보였다 → made ~ look 보이게 만들었다

어휘 | blend in (with) phr. (주위 환경에) 섞여 들다, 조화를 이루다   intimidating adj. 위협적인, 겁을 주는   strengthen v. 강화시키다
resistance n. 저항(력)   injury n. 상처   signal v. 신호로 알리다

64 추론 특정사실

Why, most likely, do people have goosebumps when they experience something good?

(a) because they want other people to share in their excitement
(b) because they are surprised by the effect of certain input
(c) because they are preparing themselves to be let down
(d) because they want to show their appreciation for positive input

사람들은 왜 좋은 것을 경험할 때 소름이 돋는 것 같은가?

(a) 다른 사람들과 흥분을 공유하기를 원하기 때문에
(b) 특정한 자극의 영향에 놀랐기 때문에
(c) 실망할 준비를 하고 있기 때문에
(d) 긍정적인 자극에 대한 감사를 나타내고 싶기 때문에

─○ 정답 잡는 치트키

질문의 키워드 something good이 something ~ pleasing으로 paraphrasing되어 언급된 주변 내용을 주의 깊게 읽는다.

해설 | 5단락의 'The same can be said about a reaction to something aesthetically pleasing, like good music. Unexpectedly strong emotional input can trigger the sympathetic nervous system, causing tiny muscles to contract and the hairs to stand up in response.'에서 좋은 음악과 같이 미적으로 즐거운 것에 대한 반응도 마찬가지인데, 예상치 못하게 강한 감정적인 자극은 교감 신경계를 자극할 수 있고, 이것은 작은 근육이 수축하고 털이 반응하여 서는 것을 야기한다고 한 것을 통해, 사람들이 좋은 것을 경험할 때 특정한 자극의 영향에 놀랐기 때문에 소름이 돋는 것임을 추론할 수 있다. 따라서 (b)가 정답이다.

어휘 | let down phr. 실망시키다   appreciation n. 감사

65 어휘 유의어   난이도 ●●○

In the context of the passage, <u>trapped</u> means _____.

(a) **held**
(b) produced
(c) imprisoned
(d) packed

지문의 문맥에서, 'trapped'는 -을 의미한다.

(a) **가뒀다**
(b) 생산했다
(c) 감금했다
(d) (상자 등에) 넣었다

정답 잡는 치트키

밑줄 친 어휘의 유의어를 찾는 문제이므로, trapped가 포함된 구절을 읽고 문맥을 파악한다.

해설 | 3단락의 'This action trapped air'는 이 작용이 공기를 가뒀다는 뜻이므로, trapped가 '가뒀다'라는 의미로 사용된 것을 알 수 있다. 따라서 '가뒀다'라는 같은 의미의 (a) held가 정답이다.

---

66 어휘 유의어   난이도 ●●○

In the context of the passage, <u>register</u> means _____.

(a) enroll
(b) express
(c) include
(d) **recognize**

지문의 문맥에서, 'register'는 -을 의미한다.

(a) 등록한다
(b) 표현한다
(c) 포함한다
(d) **인식한다**

정답 잡는 치트키

밑줄 친 어휘의 유의어를 찾는 문제이므로, register가 포함된 구절을 읽고 문맥을 파악한다.

해설 | 5단락의 'their brains register the situation'은 그들의 뇌가 그 상황을 인식한다는 뜻이므로, register가 '인식한다'라는 의미로 사용된 것을 알 수 있다. 따라서 '인식한다'라는 같은 의미의 (d) recognize가 정답이다.

오답분석
(a) '등록하다'라는 의미의 enroll도 register의 사전적 유의어 중 하나이지만, 문맥상 사람들이 무서운 이야기를 들을 때, 뇌가 그 상황을 생명을 위협하는 것으로 인식한다는 의미가 되어야 적절하므로 문맥에 어울리지 않아 오답이다.

PART 3 [67~73] 지식 백과   무선 호출기의 유래 및 용도

표제어	**PAGERS**	**무선 호출기**
정의 + 소개	Pagers are portable telecommunication devices that receive and display alphanumeric messages. Also known as beepers, pagers either vibrate or make a beeping sound to ⁷²<u>notify</u> the user that a message has been received. Pagers are usually worn hanging from a belt loop or clipped to one's pocket.	무선 호출기는 영숫자 메시지를 수신하고 표시하는 휴대용 전기 통신 장치이다. 삐삐라고도 알려진, 무선 호출기는 진동하거나 삐 소리를 내어 메시지가 수신되었음을 ⁷²<u>사용자에게 알린다</u>. 무선 호출기는 보통 벨트 고리에 걸거나 주머니에 끼워 착용한다.

Devices similar to pagers were in use by some US police stations as early as 1921, but it was only in 1949 that [73]a patent for the telephone pager was secured. World War II veteran, Al Gross, had modified the technology used in radio-controlled bomb detonators to send signals to pagers instead. [67]Originally intended to aid communication among hospital doctors during emergencies, the pager was demonstrated at a medical convention that same year. A year later, it was being used in US hospitals.

The technology is simple. One uses a telephone or email to send a message, which is then forwarded to the pager of the intended recipient. The incoming message is then displayed on the pager's screen. [68(c)]The simplest pagers can only receive and display numbers, which function like a code, while some pagers show a combination of numbers and text.

Pagers became widely used in the 1980s and [69]reached their cultural heyday in the mid-1990s, with over 60 million users. Wearing a pager on one's belt became a status symbol that meant one was essential enough to need to be reachable at a moment's notice.

[70]Paging networks have more broadcast power than cellular networks. Paging signals can penetrate walls of almost any material and are thus more reliable. However, pagers also have disadvantages. One of their main downsides is the difficulty of replying. When a pager receives a message, the user needs to either send the reply on a network's website or find a phone and contact the sender.

Toward the late 1990s, [71]cell phones, which use two-way communication, became widely affordable. The pager was unable to compete with the cell phone's multiple features and ease of replying, so the number of pager subscribers soon dropped.

Nevertheless, many doctors, police officers, and other emergency responders still use paging systems today due to the devices' broadcast power and reliability in emergencies.

1921년 초부터 일부 미국 경찰서에서 무선 호출기와 유사한 장치가 사용되었지만, [73]전화 무선 호출기에 대한 특허가 확보된 것은 1949년이 되어서였다. 제2차 세계 대전 참전 용사인 Al Gross는 무선 제어 폭탄 기폭장치에 사용되는 기술을 대신 무선 호출기에 신호를 보내도록 개조했다. [67]원래 응급 상황에서 병원 의사 간의 의사소통을 돕기 위해 고안된, 이 무선 호출기는 같은 해 의학 학술대회에서 시연되었다. 1년 후, 그것은 미국 병원들에서 사용되고 있었다.

그 기술은 간단하다. 어떤 사람은 메시지를 보내기 위해 전화나 이메일을 사용하고, 그런 다음 의도된 수신자의 무선 호출기로 전달된다. 그다음에는 들어오는 메시지가 무선 호출기의 화면에 표시된다. [68(c)]가장 간단한 무선 호출기들은 코드처럼 기능하는 숫자만을 수신하고 표시할 수 있지만, 일부 무선 호출기들은 숫자와 문자의 조합을 보여준다.

무선 호출기는 1980년대에 널리 사용되어 [69]1990년대 중반에 6천만 명이 넘는 사용자를 보유하며 문화적 전성기에 이르렀다. 무선 호출기를 벨트에 차는 것은 즉시 연락할 수 있어야 할 정도로 필수적임을 의미하는 높은 지위를 부여하는 상징이 되었다.

[70]페이징 네트워크는 셀룰러 네트워크보다 전파력이 더 강하다. 페이징 신호는 거의 모든 재질의 벽을 통과할 수 있으므로 더 신뢰할 수 있다. 하지만, 무선 호출기에는 단점도 있다. 가장 큰 부정적인 면 중 하나는 응답의 어려움이다. 무선 호출기가 메시지를 수신하면, 사용자는 네트워크 웹사이트에서 답장을 보내거나 전화를 찾아 발신자에게 연락해야 한다.

1990년대 후반에 이르러, [71]양방향 통신을 사용하는 휴대전화가 매우 저렴해졌다. 무선 호출기는 휴대전화의 다양한 기능과 회신의 용이함을 따라갈 수 없었기 때문에, 무선 호출기 사용자 수는 곧 감소했다.

그럼에도 불구하고, 많은 의사, 경찰관, 응급 구조원은 장치의 전파력과 긴급 상황에서의 신뢰성 때문에 오늘날에도 여전히 페이징 시스템을 사용한다.

어휘 | pager n. 무선 호출기 portable adj. 휴대용의 telecommunication n. 전기 통신 alphanumeric adj. 영숫자의, 문자와 숫자를 포함하는 beeper n. 삐삐 vibrate v. 진동하다, 울리다 beeping sound phr. 삐 소리 loop n. 고리 clip v. 끼우다, 고정하다 patent n. 특허 veteran n. 참전 용사 detonator n. 기폭장치 demonstrate v. 시연하다 forward v. 전달하다, 보내다 recipient n. 수취인, 수령인 combination n. 조합, 결합 heyday n. 전성기, 절정 status adj. 높은 지위를 부여하는 reachable adj. 닿을 수 있는, 도달할 수 있는 at a moment's notice phr. 즉시, 당장 penetrate v. ~을 통과하다, 관통하다 reliable adj. 신뢰할 수 있는 downside n. 부정적인 면 affordable adj. 저렴한, (가격 능이) 알맞은 compete with phr. ~을 따라가다, 필적하다 ease n. 용이함, 쉬움 subscriber n. 사용자, 가입자 emergency responder phr. 응급 구조원 reliability n. 신뢰성

지텔프 유사 기출문제집 7회분 Level 2

What was the initial purpose of the telephone pager?

(a) to be a radio system for soldiers in times of war
(b) to be a bomb detonation device for the military
(c) to be a warning device for police officers
(d) **to be a communication device for medical professionals**

전화 무선 호출기의 원래 목적은 무엇이었는가?

(a) 전쟁 때 군인들을 위한 무선 시스템이 되는 것
(b) 군대의 폭탄 기폭장치가 되는 것
(c) 경찰관들을 위한 경보 장치가 되는 것
(d) **의료 전문가들을 위한 통신 장치가 되는 것**

정답 잡는 치트키

질문의 키워드 initial purpose가 Originally intended로 paraphrasing되어 언급된 주변 내용을 주의 깊게 읽는다.

해설 | 2단락의 'Originally intended to aid communication among hospital doctors during emergencies, the pager'에서 무선 호출기가 원래 응급 상황에서 병원 의사 간의 의사소통을 돕기 위해 고안되었다고 했다. 따라서 (d)가 정답이다.

⇄ **Paraphrasing**
hospital doctors 병원 의사들 → medical professionals 의료 전문가들

어휘 | initial adj. 원래의, 초기의   soldier n. 군인, 병사   military n. 군대, 군인   warning device phr. 경보 장치

According to the third paragraph, which of the following is true about the most basic type of pagers?

(a) They can only receive local messages.
(b) They can only display special characters.
(c) **They can only receive numeric characters.**
(d) They can only display short messages.

세 번째 단락에 따르면, 다음 중 가장 기본적인 무선 호출기 유형에 관해 사실인 것은 무엇인가?

(a) 특성한 장소의 메시지만 수신할 수 있다.
(b) 특수 문자만 보여줄 수 있다.
(c) **숫자 문자만 수신할 수 있다.**
(d) 짧은 메시지만 보여줄 수 있다.

정답 잡는 치트키

질문의 키워드 the most basic ~ pagers가 The simplest pagers로 paraphrasing되어 언급된 주변 내용을 주의 깊게 읽고, 보기의 키워드와 지문 내용을 대조하며 읽는다.

해설 | (c)의 키워드인 numeric characters가 numbers로 paraphrasing되어 언급된 3단락의 'The simplest pagers can only receive and display numbers, which function like a code'에서 가장 간단한 무선 호출기들은 코드처럼 기능하는 숫자만을 수신하고 표시할 수 있다고 했으므로 지문의 내용과 일치한다. 따라서 (c)가 정답이다.

오답분석
(a) 특정한 장소의 메시지만 수신할 수 있다는 내용은 언급되지 않았다.
(b) 특수 문자만 보여줄 수 있다는 내용은 언급되지 않았다.
(d) 짧은 메시지만 보여줄 수 있다는 내용은 언급되지 않았다.

어휘 | local adj. 특정한 장소의, 공간의   special character phr. 특수 문자   numeric adj. 숫자의, 수와 관련된

추론 　특정사실　　　　　　　　　　　　　　　　　　　　　　난이도 ●●●

Based on the text, why, most likely, did many people wear pagers during the '90s?

(a) so they could show off their ability to afford the device
(b) so they could communicate with friends more easily
(c) so they could feel a sense of belonging
(d) so they could appear important to others

본문에 따르면, 많은 사람이 왜 90년대에 무선 호출기를 착용했을 것 같은가?

(a) 그 장치를 구입할 수 있는 능력을 과시할 수 있기 위해서
(b) 친구들과 더 쉽게 의사소통할 수 있기 위해서
(c) 소속감을 느낄 수 있기 위해서
(d) 다른 사람들에게 중요하게 보일 수 있기 위해서

○ 정답 잡는 치트키

질문의 키워드 90s가 그대로 언급된 주변 내용을 주의 깊게 읽는다.

해설 | 4단락의 'reached their cultural heyday in the mid-1990s, ~. Wearing a pager on one's belt became a status symbol that meant one was essential enough to need to be reachable at a moment's notice.'에서 1990년대 중반에 문화적 전성기에 이르렀으며, 무선 호출기를 벨트에 차는 것은 즉시 연락할 수 있어야 할 정도로 필수적임을 의미하는 높은 지위를 부여하는 상징이 되었다고 한 것을 통해, 많은 사람이 90년대에 다른 사람들에게 중요하게 보일 수 있기 위해서 무선 호출기를 착용했음을 추론할 수 있다. 따라서 (d)가 정답이다.

어휘 | show off phr. 과시하다 　sense of belonging phr. 소속감

---

70 특정세부사항 　How　　　　　　　　　　　　　　　　　　　　　　난이도 ●●○

According to the fifth paragraph, how are pagers better than cell phones?

(a) They have more dependable signals.
(b) They are more reliable for tracking location.
(c) They are made of more durable materials.
(d) They can broadcast across more networks.

다섯 번째 단락에 따르면, 무선 호출기는 휴대전화보다 어떻게 더 나은가?

(a) 더 신뢰할 수 있는 신호를 가진다.
(b) 위치 추적을 위해 더 신뢰할 수 있다.
(c) 더 내구력이 있는 재료로 만들어졌다.
(d) 더 많은 네트워크를 통해 수신자에게 보내질 수 있다.

○ 정답 잡는 치트키

질문의 키워드 better와 관련된 주변 내용을 주의 깊게 읽는다.

해설 | 5단락의 'Paging networks have more broadcast power than cellular networks. Paging signals can penetrate walls of almost any material and are thus more reliable.'에서 페이징 네트워크는 셀룰러 네트워크보다 전파력이 더 강하고, 페이징 신호는 거의 모든 재질의 벽을 통과할 수 있으므로 더 신뢰할 수 있다고 한 것을 통해, 무선 호출기의 페이징 네트워크가 휴대전화의 셀룰러 네트워크보다 더 신뢰할 수 있는 신호를 가진다는 것을 알 수 있다. 따라서 (a)가 정답이다.

⇄ **Paraphrasing**
reliable 신뢰할 수 있는 → dependable 신뢰할 수 있는

어휘 | dependable adj. 신뢰할 수 있는, 신뢰할 만한 　durable adj. 내구력이 있는 　broadcast v. (같은 메시지)를 복수의 수신자에게 보내다

When, most likely, did pagers start to decline in popularity?

(a) when responding to pagers became more difficult
(b) **when a more versatile form of communication appeared**
(c) when certain features were updated
(d) when hospitals banned use of the devices

무선 호출기는 언제 인기가 떨어지기 시작했을 것 같은가?

(a) 무선 호출기에 응답하는 것이 더 어려워졌을 때
(b) **더 다기능인 형태의 통신이 등장했을 때**
(c) 특정 기능이 업데이트되었을 때
(d) 병원에서 기기의 사용을 금지했을 때

◁──○ 정답 잡는 치트키

질문의 키워드 decline이 dropped로 paraphrasing되어 언급된 주변 내용을 주의 깊게 읽는다.

해설 | 6단락의 'cell phones, which use two-way communication, became widely affordable. The pager was unable to compete with the cell phone's multiple features and ease of replying, so the number of pager subscribers soon dropped.'에서 양방향 통신을 사용하는 휴대전화가 매우 저렴해졌고, 무선 호출기는 휴대전화의 다양한 기능과 회신의 용이함을 따라갈 수 없었기 때문에 무선 호출기 사용자 수는 곧 감소했다고 한 것을 통해, 더 다기능인 형태의 통신인 휴대전화의 등장으로 인해 무선 호출기의 인기가 떨어지기 시작했음을 추론할 수 있다. 따라서 (b)가 정답이다.

어휘 | decline v. 떨어지다, 쇠퇴하다　respond v. 응답하다, 대응하다　versatile adj. 다기능의, 다양한　ban v. 금지하다

In the context of the passage, <u>notify</u> means _____.

(a) warn
(b) guide
(c) **inform**
(d) identify

지문의 문맥에서, 'notify'는 -을 의미한다.

(a) 경고하다
(b) 안내하다
(c) **알리다**
(d) 확인하다

◁──○ 정답 잡는 치트키

밑줄 친 어휘의 유의어를 찾는 문제이므로, notify가 포함된 구절을 읽고 문맥을 파악한다.

해설 | 1단락의 'notify the user'는 사용자에게 알린다는 뜻이므로, notify가 '알리다'라는 의미로 사용된 것을 알 수 있다. 따라서 '알리다'라는 같은 의미의 (c) inform이 정답이다.

In the context of the passage, <u>secured</u> means _____.

(a) **obtained**
(b) taken
(c) withheld
(d) known

지문의 문맥에서, 'secured'는 -을 의미한다.

(a) **획득된**
(b) (방도·방침 등이) 취해진
(c) 보류된
(d) 알려진

밑줄 친 어휘의 유의어를 찾는 문제이므로, secured가 포함된 구절을 읽고 문맥을 파악한다.

해설 | 2단락의 'a patent for the telephone pager was secured'는 전화 무선 호출기에 대한 특허가 확보되었다는 뜻이므로, secured가 '확보된'이라는 의미로 사용된 것을 알 수 있다. 따라서 '획득된'이라는 비슷한 의미의 (a) obtained가 정답이다.

오답분석

(b) '(방도·방침 등을) 취하다'라는 의미의 take가 답이 되기 위해서는 take out a patent(특허를 얻다)가 되어야 하므로 오답이다.

PART 4 (74~80) 비즈니스 편지   간행물에 에세이를 기고하고 싶다는 편지

수신인 정보

Evelyn Harding
Editor-in-Chief
The Traveling Post
8788 Main St.
Pikesville, MD

Dear Ms. Harding:

편지의 목적: 에세이 제출

I have been a long-time reader of your literary magazine, and some of my past professors are regular contributors. ⁷⁴Recently, I saw a call for articles on your website **on the topic of "home," and I am pleased to submit my essay entitled "The Heart of the Metro" for your publication.**

자기 소개

⁷⁵I know that you ⁷⁹mainly <u>feature</u> published authors in your magazine. I am pleased to share that my creative nonfiction has appeared in the *Observer Chronicles*, *Pinnacle Magazine*, and *The Daily Illustrated*. I teach creative nonfiction writing at Glengarry University. When I'm not writing or teaching, I volunteer for an organization that promotes adolescent literacy.

에세이 내용

⁷⁶In a nutshell, my essay talks about moving from my hometown of Burton, Ohio, to New York City. Growing up in a small town, I was equally frightened and amazed by NYC, with its skyscrapers, crowds, and busy streets. I was used to ⁸⁰the laid-back <u>atmosphere</u> of my hometown, **where everyone was relaxed, and time seemed to pass slowly.** ⁷⁶I was unsure if I would ever adapt to my new environment.

바라는 점

Five years later, I have grown to love NYC, with its diverse cultures and opportunities for adventure. ⁷⁷Through my essay, I hope to inspire newcomers who want to thrive wherever they decide to live. Likewise, I wish to encourage other people who might be anxious

---

Evelyn Harding
편집장
The Traveling Post
메인가 8788번지
메릴랜드주 파이크스빌

Ms. Harding께:

저는 귀사 문학잡지의 오랜 독자이고, 과거의 제 교수님 중 일부가 정기 기고자이기도 합니다. ⁷⁴최근에, 저는 귀사의 웹사이트에서 "집"이라는 주제에 관한 글 요청을 보았고, "The Heart of the Metro"라는 제목의 제 에세이를 귀사의 간행물을 위해 제출하게 되어 기쁩니다.

⁷⁵저는 귀사가 ⁷⁹주로 출간한 작가들을 잡지에 특별히 포함한다는 것을 알고 있습니다. 저의 창작 논픽션 작품이 *Observer Chronicles*, *Pinnacle Magazine*, *The Daily Illustrated*에 실렸다는 것을 공유하게 되어 기쁩니다. 저는 Glengarry 대학교에서 창작 논픽션 글쓰기를 가르칩니다. 제가 글을 쓰거나 가르치고 있지 않을 때는, 청년 문해력을 증진하는 단체에서 봉사합니다

⁷⁶아주 간단히 말하면, 제 에세이는 고향인 오하이오주 버튼에서 뉴욕시로 이사한 것에 관해 이야기합니다. 작은 마을에서 자라, 저는 고층 건물, 인파, 번잡한 거리가 있는 뉴욕시에 두려움을 느끼는 동시에 놀랐습니다. 저는 모두가 여유롭고 시간이 느리게 흘러가는 것 같은 ⁸⁰고향의 느긋한 분위기에 익숙했습니다. ⁷⁶저는 새로운 환경에 적응할 수 있을지 확신이 없었습니다.

5년 후에, 저는 다양한 문화와 모험의 기회가 있는 뉴욕시를 사랑하게 되었습니다. ⁷⁷저의 에세이를 통해, 살기로 결정한 곳이 어디든 성공하기를 원하는 새로 온 사람들을 격려하고 싶습니다. 마찬가지로, 고향을 떠나는 것에 대해 불안해할 수 있는 다른 사람들이 새로운

about leaving their hometown to not be afraid of new opportunities.

끝인사 [78] I have attached the full essay here for your reference. Thank you for considering my submission.

발신인 정보
Sincerely yours,
Lewis Bell
New York City, NY

기회를 두려워하지 않도록 격려하고 싶습니다.

[78] 참조를 위해 제 에세이 전문을 편지에 첨부하였습니다. 제출물을 검토해 주셔서 감사합니다.

Lewis Bell 드림
뉴욕주 뉴욕시

어휘 | contributor n. 기고자, 투고자 call n. 요청 entitled adj. ~라는 제목의 publication n. 간행물, 출판(물), 발행
volunteer v. 봉사하다, 자원하다 promote v. 증진시키다 adolescent adj. 청년의; n. 청소년 literacy n. 읽고 쓰는 능력
in a nutshell phr. 아주 간단히 말하면 hometown n. 고향 equally adv. 동시에 frightened adj. 두려움을 느끼는
skyscraper n. 고층 건물 crowd n. 인파, 군중 laid-back adj. 느긋한, 마음 편한 adapt v. 적응하다 adventure n. 모험
inspire v. 격려하다, 고무하다 newcomer n. 새로 온 사람, 이민자 thrive v. 성공하다, 번영하다 reference n. 참조, 참고

---

74 특정세부사항   How   난이도 ●○○

How did Lewis Bell know about the magazine's call for submissions?

(a) He read about it in the newspaper.
(b) He heard about it from a former professor.
(c) He saw a post on their webpage.
(d) He regularly contributes to the publication.

Lewis Bell은 잡지사의 제출 요청을 어떻게 알았는가?

(a) 신문에서 그것에 관해 읽었다.
(b) 그것에 관해 이전의 교수로부터 들었다.
(c) 웹페이지에서 게시물을 봤다.
(d) 정기적으로 간행물에 기고하고 있다.

○━━○ **정답 잡는 치트키**

질문의 키워드 call for submissions가 call for articles로 paraphrasing되어 언급된 주변 내용을 주의 깊게 읽는다.

해설 | 1단락의 'Recently, I saw a call for articles on your website'에서 최근에 잡지사의 웹사이트에서 글 요청을 보았다고 했다. 따라서 (c)가 정답이다.

⇄ **Paraphrasing**
website 웹사이트 → webpage 웹페이지

어휘 | contribute v. 기고하다, 투고하다

---

75 추론   특정사실   난이도 ●●●

Why, most likely, did Bell mention several publications to Evelyn Harding?

(a) to demonstrate to her that he understands many topics
(b) to prove to her that he has a diverse writing portfolio
(c) to encourage her to read his recently published work
(d) to show her that he is already an established author

Bell은 왜 Evelyn Harding에게 여러 출판물을 언급했을 것 같은가?

(a) 많은 주제를 이해하고 있음을 보여주기 위해서
(b) 다양한 글쓰기 포트폴리오를 가지고 있음을 증명하기 위해서
(c) 최근에 출간된 그의 작품을 읽으라고 권하기 위해서
(d) 이미 인정받는 작가임을 보여주기 위해서

질문의 키워드 publications가 magazine으로 paraphrasing되어 언급된 주변 내용을 주의 깊게 읽는다.

해설 | 2단락의 'I know that you mainly feature published authors in your magazine. I am pleased to share that my creative nonfiction has appeared in the *Observer Chronicles*, *Pinnacle Magazine*, and *The Daily Illustrated*.'에서 출판사가 주로 출간한 작가들을 잡지에 특별히 포함한다는 것을 알고 있고, 자기의 창작 논픽션 작품이 여러 출판물에 실렸다는 것을 공유하게 되어 기쁘다고 한 것을 통해, Bell은 자기가 이미 인정받는 작가임을 보여주기 위해서 Evelyn Harding에게 여러 출판물을 언급했음을 추론할 수 있다. 따라서 (d)가 정답이다.

어휘 | established adj. 인정받는, 저명한

76 특정세부사항 What
난이도 ●●○

What is Lewis Bell's essay mainly about?

(a) his fear of crowded places
(b) his experience as a newcomer
(c) his decision to move back home
(d) his search for new opportunities

Lewis Bell의 에세이는 주로 무엇에 관한 것인가?

(a) 사람이 많은 곳에 대한 공포
(b) 새로 온 사람으로서의 경험
(c) 고향으로 돌아가려는 결심
(d) 새로운 기회에 관한 추구

질문의 키워드 essay mainly about이 essay talks about으로 paraphrasing되어 언급된 주변 내용을 주의 깊게 읽는다.

해설 | 3단락의 'In a nutshell, my essay talks about moving from my hometown of Burton, Ohio, to New York City.'에서 아주 간단히 말하면 에세이는 고향인 오하이오주 버튼에서 뉴욕시로 이사한 것에 관해 이야기한다고 한 뒤, 'I was unsure if I would ever adapt to my new environment.'에서 새로운 환경에 적응할 수 있을지 확신이 없었다고 했다. 따라서 (b)가 정답이다.

어휘 | search n. 추구, 탐색

77 추론 특성사실
난이도 ●●○

Based on the letter, what does Bell probably want his essay to do?

(a) encourage others who are adjusting to a new home
(b) inspire city dwellers to write about their experiences
(c) encourage people in rural areas to move to a city
(d) inspire new writers who wish to get published

편지에 따르면, Bell은 자기의 에세이가 무엇을 하기를 바라는 것 같은가?

(a) 새 거주지에 적응하고 있는 다른 사람들을 격려한다
(b) 도시 거주자들이 자기의 경험에 관해 글을 쓰도록 격려한다
(c) 시골 지역에 있는 사람들에게 도시로 이주할 것을 권장한다
(d) 출판하기를 희망하는 신인 작가들에게 영감을 준다

질문의 키워드 want ~ essay to do가 Through ~ essay, ~ hope로 paraphrasing되어 언급된 주변 내용을 주의 깊게 읽는다.

해설 | 4단락의 'Through my essay, I hope to inspire newcomers who want to thrive wherever they decide to live.'에서 에세

이를 통해, 살기로 결정한 곳이 어디든 성공하기를 원하는 새로 온 사람들을 격려하고 싶다고 한 것을 통해, Bell은 자기의 에세이가 새 거주지에 적응하고 있는 다른 사람들을 격려하기를 바라고 있음을 추론할 수 있다. 따라서 (a)가 정답이다.

⇄ **Paraphrasing**

inspire 격려하다 → encourage 격려하다

어휘 ┃ dweller n. 거주자 rural area phr. 시골 지역

---

78 특정세부사항 What   난이도 ●●○

Aside from the letter, what else did Bell include in his correspondence with Harding?	편지 외에, Bell이 Harding과의 편지에 포함한 것은 무엇인가?
(a) a published piece of writing	(a) 출판된 글
(b) a recommendation letter	(b) 추천서
(c) a copy of his submission	**(c) 제출물의 사본**
(d) a list of character references	(d) 인물 참조 목록

━○ 정답 잡는 치트키

질문의 키워드 include가 attached로 paraphrasing되어 언급된 주변 내용을 주의 깊게 읽는다.

해설 ┃ 5단락의 'I have attached the full essay here for your reference. Thank you for considering my submission.'에서 참조를 위해 에세이 전문을 편지에 첨부했고, 제출물을 검토해 줘서 고맙다고 했다. 따라서 (c)가 정답이다.

어휘 ┃ recommendation letter phr. 추천서

---

79 어휘 유의어   난이도 ●●○

In the context of the passage, <u>feature</u> means _____.	지문의 문맥에서, 'feature'는 -을 의미한다.
(a) announce	(a) 발표한다
(b) contain	(b) 함유한다
(c) imagine	(c) 상상한다
(d) present	**(d) 등장시킨다**

━○ 정답 잡는 치트키

밑줄 친 어휘의 유의어를 찾는 문제이므로, feature가 포함된 구절을 읽고 문맥을 파악한다.

해설 ┃ 2단락의 'mainly feature published authors'는 주로 출간한 작가들을 특별히 포함한다는 뜻이므로, feature가 '특별히 포함한다'라는 의미로 사용된 것을 알 수 있다. 따라서 '등장시킨다'라는 비슷한 의미의 (d) present가 정답이다.

In the context of the passage, <u>atmosphere</u> means _____.

(a) approach
(b) feeling
(c) movement
(d) surface

지문의 문맥에서, 'atmosphere'는 -을 의미한다.

(a) 방법
(b) 분위기
(c) 움직임
(d) 겉보기

◀─○ 정답 잡는 치트키

밑줄 친 어휘의 유의어를 찾는 문제이므로, atmosphere가 포함된 구절을 읽고 문맥을 파악한다.

해설 | 3단락의 'the laid-back atmosphere of my hometown'은 고향의 느긋한 분위기라는 뜻이므로, atmosphere가 '분위기'라는 의미로 사용된 것을 알 수 있다. 따라서 '분위기'라는 같은 의미의 (b) feeling이 정답이다.

공식기출
TEST 7
정답·스크립트·해석·해설

GRAMMAR

LISTENING

READING & VOCABULARY

GRAMMAR _____ / 26 (점수 : _____ 점)
LISTENING _____ / 26 (점수 : _____ 점)
READING & VOCABULARY _____ / 28 (점수 : _____ 점)

TOTAL _____ / 80 (평균 점수 : _____ 점)

*각 영역 점수: 맞은 개수 × 3.75
*평균 점수: 각 영역 점수 합계 ÷ 3

정답 및 취약 유형 분석표

GRAMMAR

번호	정답	유형
01	c	준동사
02	a	조동사
03	d	가정법
04	d	시제
05	b	시제
06	c	가정법
07	d	조동사
08	c	시제
09	d	연결어
10	d	준동사
11	b	조동사
12	a	가정법
13	b	연결어
14	a	준동사
15	b	관계사
16	c	가정법
17	c	준동사
18	b	시제
19	a	관계사
20	b	시제
21	a	조동사
22	c	가정법
23	a	준동사
24	d	조동사
25	d	가정법
26	a	시제

LISTENING

PART	번호	정답	유형
PART 1	27	c	특정세부사항
	28	a	특정세부사항
	29	c	특정세부사항
	30	a	특정세부사항
	31	c	특정세부사항
	32	c	특정세부사항
	33	d	추론
PART 2	34	b	주제/목적
	35	c	특정세부사항
	36	b	특정세부사항
	37	a	추론
	38	d	특정세부사항
	39	b	특정세부사항
PART 3	40	a	특정세부사항
	41	a	특정세부사항
	42	b	추론
	43	d	특정세부사항
	44	c	추론
	45	a	추론
PART 4	46	a	주제/목적
	47	d	추론
	48	d	추론
	49	b	추론
	50	c	특정세부사항
	51	d	특정세부사항
	52	b	특정세부사항

READING & VOCABULARY

PART	번호	정답	유형
PART 1	53	b	특정세부사항
	54	a	추론
	55	c	특정세부사항
	56	a	특정세부사항
	57	d	특정세부사항
	58	b	어휘
	59	d	어휘
PART 2	60	c	특정세부사항
	61	d	추론
	62	b	특정세부사항
	63	d	특정세부사항
	64	c	추론
	65	d	어휘
	66	b	어휘
PART 3	67	a	특정세부사항
	68	a	특정세부사항
	69	c	특정세부사항
	70	d	특정세부사항
	71	c	특정세부사항
	72	a	어휘
	73	c	어휘
PART 4	74	d	주제/목적
	75	b	특정세부사항
	76	b	특정세부사항
	77	c	특정세부사항
	78	a	추론
	79	a	어휘
	80	b	어휘

유형	맞힌 개수
시제	/ 6
가정법	/ 6
준동사	/ 5
조동사	/ 5
연결어	/ 2
관계사	/ 2
TOTAL	/ 26

유형	맞힌 개수
주제/목적	/ 2
특정세부사항	/ 16
Not/True	/ 0
추론	/ 8
TOTAL	/ 26

유형	맞힌 개수
주제/목적	/ 1
특정세부사항	/ 15
Not/True	/ 0
추론	/ 4
어휘	/ 8
TOTAL	/ 28

GRAMMAR

---

01 준동사　　동명사와 to 부정사 모두를 목적어로 취하는 동사　　난이도 ●●○

Kenneth misplaced his reading glasses somewhere in the house and is trying to find them by retracing his steps. The last place he remembers _____ them is the kitchen, where he read the morning paper.

(a) to use
(b) to have used
(c) using
(d) having been using

Kenneth는 집 어딘가에 독서용 안경을 잘못 두었고 되돌아가서 그것들을 찾으려고 하고 있는 중이다. 그가 안경을 <u>사용한 것</u>을 기억하는 마지막 장소는 부엌인데, 그는 그곳에서 조간신문을 읽었다.

━○ 지텔프 치트키

remember 다음에는 동명사나 to 부정사가 오므로, 문맥에 맞는 것을 고른다.

> 💡 **동명사가 목적어일 때와 to 부정사가 목적어일 때 문장의 의미 변화가 있는 빈출 동사**
> remember -ing ~한 것을 기억하다 / remember to ~할 것을 기억하다
> forget -ing ~한 것을 잊다 / forget to ~할 것을 잊다
> regret -ing ~한 것을 후회하다 / regret to ~하게 되어 유감스럽다

해설 | 빈칸 앞 동사 remember는 동명사와 to 부정사 모두를 목적어로 취하므로, 문맥을 파악하여 정답을 선택해야 한다. 문맥상 그가 안경을 사용한 것을 기억한다는 의미가 되어야 자연스러우므로, 동사 remember와 함께 쓰일 때 '~한 것을 기억하다'라는 의미를 나타내는 동명사 (c) using이 정답이다.

> **오답분석**
> (a) to use는 동사 remember와 함께 쓰일 때 '~할 것을 기억하다'라는 의미를 나타내어, 문맥에서 안경을 사용할 것을 기억한다는 어색한 의미가 되므로 오답이다.

어휘 | misplace v. 잘못 두다, 둔 곳을 잊다　retrace one's steps phr. 되돌아가다

---

02 조동사　　조동사 can　　난이도 ●●○

Young artists should try out different creative exercises to develop their drawing skills. For example, they _____ turn a photograph upside down and draw the lines they see instead of thinking about the whole picture.

(a) can
(b) would
(c) shall
(d) will

젊은 예술가들은 그림 그리는 기술을 발전시키기 위해 다양한 창의적인 연습을 시험 삼아 해봐야 한다. 예를 들어, 그들은 전체 그림에 관해 생각하는 대신 사진을 거꾸로 <u>할 수 있고</u> 그들이 보는 선을 묘사할 <u>수도 있다</u>.

━○ 지텔프 치트키

'~할 수 있다'라고 말할 때는 can을 쓴다.

해설 | 문맥상 젊은 예술가들은 그림 그리는 기술을 발전시키기 위해 다양한 창의적인 연습을 시험 삼아 해봐야 하며, 예를 들어 전체 그림에 관해 생각하는 대신 사진을 거꾸로 할 수 있고 그들이 보는 선을 묘사할 수도 있다는 의미가 되어야 자연스럽다. 따라서 '~할 수 있다'를 뜻하면서 능력을 나타내는 조동사 (a) can이 정답이다.

어휘 | try out phr. 시험 삼아 해보다 turn upside down phr. ~을 거꾸로 하다 photograph n. 사진 whole adj. 전체의

---

03 가정법   가정법 과거완료

난이도 ●●○

Last week, my train was delayed for several hours, so it was late at night when I finally arrived home. If I had not been so exhausted, I _____ my brother's barbecue the next day.

(a) would attend
(b) will have attended
(c) will attend
(d) would have attended

지난주에, 기차가 몇 시간 동안 지연되어서, 마침내 내가 집에 도착했을 때는 늦은 밤이었다. 만약 내가 그렇게 지치지 않았었다면, 나는 그다음날 형의 바비큐 파티에 <u>참석했을 것이다</u>.

🔾 지텔프 치트키

'if + had p.p.'가 있으면 'would/could + have p.p.'가 정답이다.

> 💡 가정법 과거완료
> If + 주어 + had p.p., 주어 + would/could(조동사 과거형) + have p.p.

해설 | If절에 'had p.p.' 형태의 had not been이 있으므로, 주절에는 이와 짝을 이루어 가정법 과거완료를 만드는 'would(조동사 과거형) + have p.p.'가 와야 한다. 따라서 (d) would have attended가 정답이다.

어휘 | delay v. 지연시키다, 지체하게 하다 exhausted adj. 지친, 기진맥진한 barbecue n. 바비큐 파티

---

04 시제   현재완료진행

난이도 ●●○

James's daughter wants to start taking the bus to school soon. He _____ her to school every morning since she started kindergarten, so he will miss their routine.

(a) had been driving
(b) will drive
(c) was driving
(d) has been driving

James의 딸은 곧 학교에 버스를 타고 다니기 시작하기를 원한다. 그는 딸이 유치원에 다니기 시작한 이래로 매일 아침에 그녀를 학교에 <u>운전해서 데려다주고 있는 중이어서</u>, 그의 일상을 그리워할 것이다.

🔾 지텔프 치트키

'since + 과거 동사'가 있으면 현재완료진행 시제가 정답이다.

> 💡 현재완료진행과 자주 함께 쓰이는 시간 표현
> • (ever) since + 과거 시점 + (for + 기간 표현) ~한 이래로 (줄곧) (~ 동안)
> • lately / for + 기간 표현 + now 최근에 / 현재 ~ 동안

해설 | 현재완료진행 시제와 함께 쓰이는 시간 표현 'since + 과거 동사'(since ~ started)가 있고, 문맥상 James의 딸이 유치원에 다니기 시작한 과거 시점부터 현재까지 계속해서 매일 아침에 James가 딸을 학교에 운전해서 데려다주고 있는 중이라는 의미가 되어야 자연스럽다. 따라서 현재완료진행 시제 (d) has been driving이 정답이다.

어휘 | daughter n. 딸 kindergarten n. 유치원 routine n. 일상, 일과

---

05 시제   미래진행   난이도 ●●●

Andrew is flying to Chicago for the first time to attend a physics conference. He is usually bad with directions, so he is relieved that a driver _____ for him when he arrives at the airport.

(a) waits
(b) will be waiting
(c) was waiting
(d) has waited

Andrew는 물리학 학회에 참석하기 위해 처음으로 비행기를 타고 시카고에 가고 있는 중이다. 그는 보통 길눈이 어두워서, 공항에 도착할 때 그를 위해 운전기사가 <u>기다리고 있는 중일 것</u>이라서 안심이 된다.

⌐○ 지텔프 치트키

'for + 기간 표현' 없이 'when + 현재 동사'와 특정 미래 시점을 나타내는 표현만 있으면 미래진행 시제가 정답이다.

> ☼ 미래진행과 자주 함께 쓰이는 시간 표현
> • when / if + 현재 동사 ~할 때 / 만약 ~한다면   • until / by + 미래 시점 ~까지
> • next + 시간 표현 다음 ~에   • starting + 미래 시점 / tomorrow ~부터 / 내일

해설 | 현재 동사로 미래의 의미를 나타내는 시간의 부사절 'when + 현재 동사'(when ~ arrives)가 있고, 문맥상 미래 시점인 공항에 노착할 때 운전기사가 Andrew를 기다리고 있는 중일 것이라는 의미가 되어야 자연스럽다. 따라서 미래진행 시제 (b) will be waiting이 정답이다.

어휘 | physics n. 물리학 be bad with directions phr. 길눈이 어둡다 relieve v. 안심시키다, 안도하게 하다

---

06 가정법   가정법 과거   난이도 ●●○

About 800 people attempt to climb Mount Everest every year. If expeditions up the mountain were made easier, more people _____ to do it, just to say they climbed the tallest mountain in the world.

(a) will have probably tried
(b) will probably try
(c) would probably try
(d) would have probably tried

약 800명의 사람이 매년 에베레스트산을 오르려고 시도한다. 만약 산을 오르는 탐험이 더 쉬워진다면, <u>아마도</u> 더 많은 사람이 세계에서 가장 높은 산을 올랐다고 말하기 위해, 그렇게 하려고 <u>시도할 것이다</u>.

⌐○ 지텔프 치트키

'if + 과거 동사'가 있으면 'would/could + 동사원형'이 정답이다.

> ☼ 가정법 과거
> If + 주어 + 과거 동사, 주어 + would/could(조동사 과거형) + 동사원형

해설 | If절에 과거 동사(were made)가 있으므로, 주절에는 이와 짝을 이루어 가정법 과거를 만드는 'would(조동사 과거형) + 동사원형'이 와야 한다. 따라서 (c) would probably try가 정답이다.

어휘 | attempt to phr. ~하려고 시도하다   expedition n. 탐험, 원정

For tonight's dessert, Harriet has chosen to make a famously difficult dish: the soufflé. Her chef sister advises that she _____ the recipe exactly, or her soufflé will collapse.

(a) followed
(b) will follow
(c) has followed
(d) follow

오늘 밤의 후식으로, Harriet은 어렵기로 유명한 요리인 수플레를 만들기로 선택했다. 그녀의 요리사 언니는 그녀에게 요리법을 정확하게 <u>따라야 하고</u>, 그렇지 않으면 수플레가 무너질 것이라고 조언한다.

─○ 지텔프 치트키

advise 다음에는 that절에 동사원형이 온다.

> 💡 **주장·요구·명령·제안을 나타내는 빈출 동사**
> advise 조언하다   request 요청하다   recommend 권고하다   demand 요구하다   suggest 제안하다   order 명령하다
> urge 강력히 촉구하다   ask 요청하다   propose 제안하다   insist 주장하다

해설 | 주절에 제안을 나타내는 동사 advise가 있으므로 that절에는 '(should +) 동사원형'이 와야 한다. 따라서 동사원형 (d) follow가 정답이다.

어휘 | famously adv. 유명하게, 잘 알려져   soufflé n. 수플레(달걀 흰자위, 우유, 밀가루를 섞어 거품을 낸 것에 치즈·과일 등을 넣고 구운 것)
exactly adv. 정확하게, 엄밀히   collapse v. 무너지다, 붕괴하다

| 08 | 시제 | 미래완료진행 | 난이도 ●●● |

The Lowells are excited to become foster parents, but the licensing process has been intense. By the time they earn their license, they _____ rigorous background checks, first-aid training, and home assessments for almost six months.

(a) are undergoing
(b) will undergo
(c) will have been undergoing
(d) had been undergoing

Lowell 부부는 양부모가 되는 것에 신이 나지만, 인허가 절차는 매우 치열했다. 그들이 허가를 <u>얻을 무렵이면</u>, 그들은 거의 6개월 동안 철저한 신원 조사, 응급 처치 훈련, 가정 평가를 <u>받아오고 있는 중일 것이다</u>.

─○ 지텔프 치트키

'by the time + 현재 동사'와 'for + 기간 표현'이 함께 오면 미래완료진행 시제가 정답이다.

> 💡 **미래완료진행과 자주 함께 쓰이는 시간 표현**
> • by the time / when / if + 현재 동사 + (for + 기간 표현) ~할 무렵이면 / ~할 때 / 만약 ~한다면 (~ 동안)
> • by / in + 미래 시점 + (for + 기간 표현) ~ 즈음에는 / ~에 (~ 동안)

해설 | 현재 동사로 미래의 의미를 나타내는 시간의 부사절 'by the time + 현재 동사'(By the time ~ earn)와 지속을 나타내는 'for + 기간 표현'(for almost six months)이 있고, 문맥상 미래 시점에 Lowell 부부가 허가를 얻을 무렵이면 거의 6개월 동안 계속해서 철저한 신원 조사, 응급 처치 훈련, 가정 평가를 받아오고 있는 중일 것이라는 의미가 되어야 자연스럽다. 따라서 미래완료진행 시제 (c) will have been undergoing이 정답이다.

어휘 | foster parents phr. 양부모 licensing process phr. 인허가 절차 intense adj. 치열한, 극심한 rigorous adj. 철저한, 엄격한 first-aid adj. 응급 처치의; n. 응급 처치 assessment n. 평가 undergo v. 받다, 겪다

---

09 연결어 접속부사   난이도 ●●○

No one is certain what caused the dancing plague of 1518, in which roughly 400 people danced uncontrollably for days. _____, several theories have emerged to explain the phenomenon, including food poisoning and mass hysteria.

(a) Similarly
(b) Likewise
(c) Instead
(d) However

무엇이 1518년의 춤의 역병을 발생하게 했는지는 아무도 확실히 알지 못하며, 대략 400명의 사람이 며칠 동안 걷잡을 수 없이 춤을 췄다. 그러나, 이 현상을 설명하기 위해 식중독과 집단 히스테리를 포함하여 여러 가지 가설이 나타났다.

⊸ 지텔프 치트키

'그러나'라는 의미의 대조를 나타낼 때는 However를 쓴다.

> 💡 **대조를 나타내는 빈출 접속부사**
> However 그러나 On the other hand 반면에 Otherwise 그렇지 않으면 In contrast 그에 반해

해설 | 빈칸 앞 문장은 무엇이 춤의 역병을 발생하게 했는지는 아무도 확실히 알지 못한다는 내용이고, 빈칸 뒤 문장은 이 현상을 설명하기 위해 식중독과 집단 히스테리를 포함하여 여러 가지 가설이 나타났다는 대조적인 내용이다. 따라서 '그러나'라는 의미의 대조를 나타내는 접속부사 (d) However가 정답이다.

오답분석
(a) Similarly는 '비슷하게', (b) Likewise는 '마찬가지로', (c) Instead는 '대신에'라는 의미로, 문맥에 적합하지 않아 오답이다.

어휘 | plague n. 역병, 전염병 uncontrollably adv. 걷잡을 수 없이 theory n. 가설, 이론 emerge v. 나타나다 phenomenon n. 현상 food poisoning phr. 식중독 mass hysteria phr. 집단 히스테리

---

10 준동사 to 부정사의 형용사 역할   난이도 ●●●

Gail has been knitting for a month and is ready to try some more advanced techniques. So, she is taking the time _____ a few different types of stitches, including her mother's favorite: the herringbone stitch.

(a) to have learned
(b) having learned
(c) learning
(d) to learn

Gail은 한 달 동안 뜨개질을 해오고 있는 중이고 더 발전된 기술을 시도해 볼 준비가 되어 있다. 그래서, 그녀는 어머니가 가장 좋아하는 헤링본 무늬의 깁는 법을 포함하여 몇 가지 다른 종류의 깁는 법을 배우는 시간을 보내고 있는 중이다.

'~(해야) 할', '~하는'이라고 말할 때는 to 부정사를 쓴다.

해설 | 빈칸 앞에 명사(the time)가 있고 문맥상 '몇 가지 다른 종류의 깁는 법을 배우는 시간'이라는 의미가 되어야 자연스러우므로, 빈칸은 명사를 수식하는 형용사의 자리이다. 따라서 명사를 꾸며주는 형용사적 수식어구를 이끌 수 있는 to 부정사 (d) to learn이 정답이다.

어휘 | knit v. 뜨개질을 하다   stitch n. 깁는 법, 스티치   herringbone adj. 헤링본 무늬(V자형이 이루는 줄무늬가 계속 연결된 형태)의; n. 헤링본

---

11 조동사   조동사 should 생략   난이도 ●●○

Painting one's nails can be a complex process requiring several steps. For the first step, beauty experts recommend that a base coat _____ to prevent darker-colored nail polish from staining the nails.

(a) is being applied
(b) be applied
(c) has been applied
(d) will be applied

손톱에 칠을 하는 것은 여러 단계를 필요로 하는 복잡한 과정일 수 있다. 첫 번째 단계로, 미용 전문가들은 더 어두운색의 매니큐어가 손톱을 얼룩지게 하는 것을 막기 위해 베이스 코트가 <u>칠해져야 한다</u>고 권장한다.

recommend 다음에는 that절에 동사원형이 온다.

해설 | 주절에 제안을 나타내는 동사 recommend가 있으므로 that절에는 '(should +) 동사원형'이 와야 한다. 따라서 동사원형 (b) be applied가 정답이다.

어휘 | complex adj. 복잡한   expert n. 전문가   base coat phr. 베이스 코트(매니큐어를 바르기 전 손톱에 바르는 단계)
nail polish phr. (손톱에 바르는) 매니큐어   stain v. ~을 얼룩지게 하다   apply v. 칠하다, 바르다

---

12 가정법   가정법 과거   난이도 ●●○

Katherine has finally arrived in Paris and can't wait to tour all the famous sites. However, she has acrophobia, or fear of heights. If she weren't acrophobic, she _____ the Eiffel Tower right away.

(a) would climb
(b) will have climbed
(c) would have climbed
(d) will climb

Katherine은 마침내 파리에 도착했고 모든 유명한 장소를 빨리 관광하고 싶어 한다. 하지만, 그녀는 고소공포증이 있다. 만약 그녀가 고소 공포증이 아니라면, 그녀는 곧바로 에펠탑을 올라갈 것이다.

'if + 과거 동사'가 있으면 'would/could + 동사원형'이 정답이다.

해설 | If절에 과거 동사(weren't)가 있으므로, 주절에는 이와 짝을 이루어 가정법 과거를 만드는 'would(조동사 과거형) + 동사원형'이 와야 한다. 따라서 (a) would climb이 정답이다.

13 연결어 접속사

난이도 ●●●

Roger was not going to let a broken toe stop him from attending the yearly arts and crafts fair. He stayed at the fair all day, _____ his foot was causing him extreme pain.

(a) unless
(b) even though
(c) whereas
(d) in case

Roger는 부러진 발가락이 그를 연례 공예품 박람회에 참가하는 것을 막도록 내버려 두지 않을 작정이었다. 그의 발이 극심한 고통을 가져오고 있던 중이었음에도 불구하고, 그는 하루 종일 박람회장에 있었다.

☞○ 지텔프 치트키

'~에도 불구하고'라는 의미의 양보를 나타낼 때는 even though를 쓴다.

> 💡 **양보를 나타내는 빈출 접속사**
> even though ~에도 불구하고 although ~에도 불구하고 while ~이긴 하지만

해설 | 문맥상 Roger의 발이 극심한 고통을 가져오고 있던 중이었음에도 불구하고 그는 하루 종일 박람회장에 있었다는 의미가 되어야 자연스럽다. 따라서 '~에도 불구하고'라는 의미의 양보를 나타내는 부사절 접속사 (b) even though가 정답이다.

오답분석
(a) unless는 '~하지 않는 한'이라는 의미로 조건을 나타내므로 오답이다.
(c) whereas는 '~인 반면'이라는 의미로 양보를 나타내고, 상반된 내용을 설명할 때 쓰이므로 오답이다.
(d) in case는 '~할 경우에 대비하여'라는 의미로, 분맥에 적합하지 않아 오답이다.

어휘 | toe n. 발가락 yearly adj. 연례의, 연간의 fair n. 박람회, 전시회 extreme adj. 극심한

14 준동사 동명사를 목적어로 취하는 동사

난이도 ●○○

Rebecca moved away from home three years ago, and she often craves her mother's chocolate chip cookies. She is considering _____ an oven just so she can make the recipe for herself.

(a) buying
(b) to have bought
(c) having bought
(d) to buy

Rebecca는 3년 전에 집에서 이사 갔고, 종종 어머니의 초콜릿 칩 쿠키를 몹시 원한다. 그녀는 스스로 요리법을 만들 수 있도록 오븐을 구입하는 것을 고려하고 있는 중이다.

☞○ 지텔프 치트키

consider는 동명사를 목적어로 취한다.

> 💡 **동명사를 목적어로 취하는 빈출 동사**
> consider 고려하다 dread 두려워하다 avoid 피하다 imagine 상상하다 mind 꺼리다 keep 계속하다 prevent 방지하다
> enjoy 즐기다 recommend 권장하다 risk 위험을 무릅쓰다 involve 포함하다

해설 | 빈칸 앞 동사 consider는 동명사를 목적어 취하므로, 동명사 (a) buying이 정답이다.

오답분석
(c) having bought도 동명사이기는 하지만, 완료동명사(having bought)로 쓰일 경우 '고려하는' 시점보다 '구입하는' 시점이 앞선다는 것을 나타내므로 문맥에 적합하지 않아 오답이다.

어휘 | move away from phr. ~에서 이사 가다 crave v. ~을 몹시 원하다, 갈망하다

---

15 관계사   주격 관계대명사 who
난이도 ●●○

Margaret Atwood is a prolific Canadian author and environmental activist. She grew up spending time in the woods with her father, _____. Those experiences sparked her interest in environmental issues at a young age.

Margaret Atwood는 다작한 캐나다 작가이자 환경 운동가이다. 그녀는 그녀의 아버지와 숲에서 시간을 보내며 자랐고, 그는 삼림 곤충을 연구했다. 그러한 경험들은 어린 나이에 환경 문제에 관한 그녀의 관심을 촉발했다.

(a) that studied forest insects
(b) who studied forest insects
(c) which studied forest insects
(d) what studied forest insects

⟶○ 지텔프 치트키
사람 선행사가 관계절 안에서 주어 역할을 하고, 빈칸 앞에 콤마(,)가 있으면 주격 관계대명사 who가 정답이다.

해설 | 사람 선행사 her father를 받으면서 콤마(,) 뒤에 올 수 있는 주격 관계대명사가 필요하므로, (b) who studied forest insects가 정답이다.

오답분석
(a) 관계대명사 that도 사람 선행사를 받을 수 있지만, 콤마 뒤에 올 수 없으므로 오답이다.

어휘 | prolific adj. 다작의, 많은 activist n. 운동가, 활동가 spark v. 촉발하다, 야기하다 forest insect phr. 삼림 곤충

---

16 가정법   가정법 과거완료
난이도 ●●○

Watching previews is Matthew's favorite part of going to the movie theater, which is why he was annoyed when he arrived twenty minutes late. If he had not gotten stuck in traffic, he _____ the previews.

시사회 관람은 Matthew가 영화관 가는 것의 가장 좋아하는 부분인데, 그것은 그가 20분 늦게 도착했을 때 짜증이 났던 이유이다. 만약 그가 교통체증에 갇히지 않았더라면, 그는 시사회를 놓치지 않았을 것이다.

(a) would not miss
(b) will not miss
(c) would not have missed
(d) will not have missed

⟶○ 지텔프 치트키
'if + had p.p.'가 있으면 'would/could + have p.p.'가 정답이다.

해설 | If절에 'had p.p.' 형태의 had not gotten이 있으므로, 주절에는 이와 짝을 이루어 가정법 과거완료를 만드는 'would(조동사 과거형) + have p.p.'가 와야 한다. 따라서 (c) would not have missed가 정답이다.

17 준동사 to 부정사를 목적격 보어로 취하는 동사   난이도 ●●○

My father and I rarely have dinner together because of our different meal schedules. He is determined _____ right when he gets home from work at 5 p.m., while I usually wait until at least 7.

(a) having eaten
(b) eating
(c) to eat
(d) to have eaten

나의 아버지와 나는 서로 다른 식사 일정 때문에 저녁을 거의 함께 먹지 않는다. 그는 오후 5시에 퇴근해서 집에 오면 바로 <u>먹을 것</u>을 결심하는 반면, 나는 보통 적어도 7시까지는 기다린다.

🔾 지텔프 치트키

determine은 to 부정사를 목적격 보어로 취한다.

> 💡 to 부정사를 목적격 보어로 취하는 빈출 동사
> determine 결심하다 expect 예상하다 encourage 권장하다 require 요구하다 urge 강력히 촉구하다 allow 허락하다 ask 요청하다
> want 원하다

해설 | 빈칸 앞 동사 determine은 'determine + 목적어 + 목적격 보어'의 형태로 쓰일 때 to 부정사를 목적격 보어로 취하여, '-이 ~하는 것을 결심하다'라는 의미로 사용된다. 참고로, 'He is determined to eat'은 'determine(동사) + him(목적어) + to eat(목적격 보어)'에서 변형된 수동태 구문으로, 수동태가 되어도 목적격 보어인 to 부정사는 그대로 유지된다. 따라서 to 부정사 (c) to eat이 정답이다.

오답분석
(d) to have eaten도 to 부정사이기는 하지만, 완료부정사(to have eaten)로 쓰일 경우 '결심하는' 시점보다 '먹는' 시점이 앞선다는 것을 나타내므로 문맥에 적합하지 않아 오답이다.

어휘 | rarely adv. 거의 ~하지 않는, 드물게

18 시제 과거진행   난이도 ●●○

A beluga whale named Noc learned to mimic human speech while in captivity. A diver _____ Noc's tank when he heard someone say "out," realizing later that Noc was the one who had said it.

(a) will check
(b) was checking
(c) is checking
(d) has checked

Noc이라는 이름의 벨루가 고래는 감금되었던 동안 인간의 말을 흉내 내는 것을 배웠다. 잠수부가 누군가가 "밖으로"라고 말하는 것을 들었을 때 그는 Noc의 탱크를 확인하고 있던 중이었고, 나중에 Noc이 그것을 말했던 누군가였음을 깨달았다.

🔾 지텔프 치트키

'for + 기간 표현' 없이 'when + 과거 동사'만 있으면 과거진행 시제가 정답이다.

해설 | 과거진행 시제와 함께 쓰이는 시간 표현 'when + 과거 동사'(when ~ heard)가 있고, 문맥상 잠수부가 누군가가 "밖으로"라고 말하는 것

을 들었던 과거 시점에 Noc의 탱크를 확인하고 있던 중이었다는 의미가 되어야 자연스럽다. 따라서 과거진행 시제 (b) was checking이 정답이다.

어휘 | mimic v. 흉내 내다 in captivity phr. 감금되어, 사육상태에 realize v. 깨닫다, 알다

---

19 관계사 주격 관계대명사 which

난이도 ●●○

The bootlace worm, a creature that lives along the coast of Great Britain, excretes a toxic substance that is fatal to crabs and roaches. The worm, _____, can grow up to 200 feet long.

(a) **which spends most of its time tangled**
(b) what spends most of its time tangled
(c) that spends most of its time tangled
(d) who spends most of its time tangled

영국의 해안가에 사는 생물인 흑갈색을 띤 리본 모양의 벌레는 게와 바퀴벌레에게 치명적인 독성이 있는 물질을 분비한다. 이 벌레는, 대부분의 시간을 뒤얽혀 보내는데, 200피트 길이까지 자랄 수 있다.

━━○ 지텔프 치트키

동물 선행사가 관계절 안에서 주어 역할을 하고, 빈칸 앞에 콤마(,)가 있으면 주격 관계대명사 which가 정답이다.

해설 | 동물 선행사 The worm을 받으면서 콤마(,) 뒤에 올 수 있는 주격 관계대명사가 필요하므로, (a) which spends most of its time tangled가 정답이다.

오답분석
(c) 관계대명사 that도 동물 선행사를 받을 수 있지만, 콤마 뒤에 올 수 없으므로 오답이다.

어휘 | bootlace worm phr. 흑갈색을 띤 리본 모양의 벌레 excrete v. 분비하다, 방출하다 toxic adj. 독성이 있는, 유독한 fatal adj. 치명적인 roach n. 바퀴벌레 tangled adj. 뒤얽힌

---

20 시제 과거완료진행

난이도 ●●○

Kristen used to be very knowledgeable about her city's rock music scene. She _____ music reviews for the local paper until she got so busy with work that she could no longer go to live concerts.

(a) is writing
(b) **had been writing**
(c) has been writing
(d) will have written

Kristen은 도시의 록 음악계에 관해 아주 잘 알고 있곤 했다. 그녀는 일이 바빠져서 더 이상 라이브 콘서트에 갈 수 없었을 때까지 지역 신문에 음악 평론을 써오고 있던 중이었다.

━━○ 지텔프 치트키

'until + 과거 동사'가 오면 과거완료진행 시제가 정답이다.

☼ **과거완료진행과 자주 함께 쓰이는 시간 표현**
  · before / when / since + 과거 동사 + (for + 기간 표현) ~하기 전에 / ~했을 때 / ~ 이래로 (~ 동안)
  · (for + 기간 표현) + (up) until + 과거 동사 (~ 동안) ~했을 때까지

TEST 1 TEST 2 TEST 3 TEST 4 TEST 5 TEST 6 TEST 7

지텔프 공식 기출문제집 7회분 Level 2

해설 | 과거완료진행 시제와 함께 쓰이는 시간 표현 'until + 과거 동사'(until ~ got, could)가 있고, 문맥상 과거(일이 바빠져서 더 이상 라이브 콘 서트에 갈 수 없었던 시점)까지 지역 신문에 음악 평론을 써오고 있던 중이었다는 의미가 되어야 자연스럽다. 따라서 과거완료진행 시제 (b) had been writing이 정답이다.

어휘 | used to phr. ~하곤 했다 music scene phr. 음악계 review n. 평론, 논평 no longer phr. 더 이상 ~이 아닌

---

21 조동사   조동사 should 생략   난이도 ●●○

Chris wants to start a business selling kitchen utensils, but he isn't sure how to navigate the legal issues. His friends are suggesting that he _____ a lawyer to make sure his business follows all regulations.

(a) **hire**
(b) will hire
(c) has hired
(d) is hiring

Chris는 주방용품을 파는 사업을 시작하고 싶어 하지 만, 법적인 문제들을 어떻게 처리할지 잘 모른다. 그 의 친구들은 그의 사업이 모든 규정을 준수하는지 확 실히 하기 위해 변호사를 고용해야 한다고 제안하고 있는 중이다.

─○ 지텔프 치트키

suggest 다음에는 that절에 동사원형이 온다.

해설 | 주절에 제안을 나타내는 동사 suggest가 있으므로 that절에는 '(should +) 동사원형'이 와야 한다. 따라서 동사원형 (a) hire가 정답이다.

어휘 | utensil n. 용품, 기구 navigate v. (힘들거나 복잡한 상황을) 처리하다 legal adj. 법적인, 법률상의 regulation n. 규정, 법규

---

22 가정법   가정법 과거완료   난이도 ●●○

After retirement, Gina took up woodworking. She hoped that it would be a satisfying hobby, but she soon gave up. Had she known how complex and expensive woodworking would be, she _____ in the first place.

(a) will never start
(b) will never have started
(c) **would never have started**
(d) would never start

은퇴 후, Gina는 목공을 시작했다. 그녀는 이것이 만족 스러운 취미가 되길 바랐지만, 곧 포기했다. 그녀는 목 공이 얼마나 복잡하고 비용이 많이 드는지 알았었다 면, 애당초에 시작하지 않았을 것이다.

─○ 지텔프 치트키

Had p.p.가 있으면 'would/could + have p.p.'가 정답이다.

> 💡 **가정법 과거완료(도치)**
> Had + 주어 + p.p., 주어 + would/could(조동사 과거형) + have p.p.

해설 | if가 생략되어 도치된 절에 'had p.p.' 형태의 Had ~ known이 있으므로, 주절에는 이와 짝을 이루어 가정법 과거완료를 만드는 'would (조동사 과거형) + have p.p.'가 와야 한다. 따라서 (c) would never have started가 정답이다. 참고로, 'Had she known ~'은 'If she had known ~'으로 바꿔 쓸 수 있다.

어휘 | retirement n. 은퇴, 퇴직 woodworking n. 목공, 나무 세공; adj. 목공의 in the first place phr. 애당초에

23 준동사   동명사를 목적어로 취하는 동사

In Roald Dahl's "The Wonderful Story of Henry Sugar," a man becomes rich after he gains the ability to see through playing cards. He wears disguises to avoid _____ by casino authorities.

(a) **being detected**
(b) to have been detected
(c) to be detected
(d) having been detected

Roald Dahl의 "The Wonderful Story of Henry Sugar"에서, 한 남자는 카드놀이를 꿰뚫어 보는 능력을 얻은 후 부자가 된다. 그는 카지노 당국으로부터 감시받는 것을 피하기 위해 변장을 한다.

━○ 지텔프 치트키

avoid는 동명사를 목적어로 취한다.

> 💡 **동명사를 목적어로 취하는 빈출 동사**
> avoid 피하다 imagine 상상하다 mind 개의하다 keep 계속하다 consider 고려하다 prevent 방지하다 enjoy 즐기다
> recommend 권장하다 risk 위험을 무릅쓰다 involve 포함하다

해설 | 빈칸 앞 동사 avoid는 동명사를 목적어로 취하므로, 동명사 (a) being detected가 정답이다.

> 오답분석
> (d) having been detected도 동명사이기는 하지만, 완료동사(having been detected)로 쓰일 경우 '피하는' 시점보다 '감시받는' 시점이 앞선다는 것을 나타내므로 문맥에 적합하지 않아 오답이다.

어휘 | see through phr. 꿰뚫어 보다, 간파하다 disguise n. 변장; v. 변장하다 authority n. 당국

24 조동사   조동사 may

In spite of her piercing eyes and stern demeanor, students should not be afraid of Mrs. Hawke. She _____ look intimidating, but she is actually the kindest teacher at the school.

(a) must
(b) should
(c) will
(d) **may**

날카로운 눈과 엄격한 태도에도 불구하고, 학생들은 Mrs. Hawke를 두려워해서는 안 된다. 그녀는 위협적으로 보일지도 모르지만, 실제로 학교에서 가장 친절한 선생님이다.

━○ 지텔프 치트키

'~할지도 모른다'라고 말할 때는 may를 쓴다.

해설 | 문맥상 Mrs. Hawke는 위협적으로 보일지도 모르지만 실제로 학교에서 가장 친절한 선생님이라는 의미가 되어야 자연스러우므로, '~할지도 모른다'를 뜻하면서 약한 추측을 나타내는 조동사 (d) may가 정답이다. 참고로, may와 might 모두 '~할지도 모른다'를 뜻하지만, may는 might보다 일어날 가능성이 조금 더 큰 경우에 쓴다.

25 가정법　　가정법 과거

난이도 ●●○

Deep sea fish don't typically have air bladders, which help other fish float or sink. If deep sea fish had these air sacs, the enormous water pressure at the bottom of the ocean _____ them immediately.

(a) will have crushed
(b) would have crushed
(c) will crush
(d) would crush

심해어는 일반적으로 부레를 가지고 있지 않는데, 이것은 다른 물고기들이 떠다니거나 가라앉는 것을 도와주는 것이다. 만약 심해어가 이러한 공기주머니를 가지고 있다면, 바다 바닥에 있는 엄청난 수압이 그것들을 즉시 눌러 부술 것이다.

⟜◯ 지텔프 치트키

'if + 과거 동사'가 있으면 'would/could + 동사원형'이 정답이다.

해설 | If절에 과거 동사(had)가 있으므로, 주절에는 이와 짝을 이루어 가정법 과거를 만드는 'would(조동사 과거형) + 동사원형'이 와야 한다. 따라서 (d) would crush가 정답이다.

어휘 | deep sea fish phr. 심해어 air bladder phr. 부레 float v. 떠다니다 sink v. 가라앉다, 침몰하다 air sac phr. 공기주머니 water pressure phr. 수압 crush v. 눌러 부수다, 뭉개다

26 시제　　현재진행

난이도 ●○○

Max has drawn up detailed plans showing how he wants his bathroom to look after remodeling. Now he _____ all of the supplies he will need when he begins the project next month.

(a) is ordering
(b) has been ordering
(c) had ordered
(d) will have ordered

Max는 그의 욕실이 리모델링 후에 어떻게 보이기를 원하는지 나타내는 상세 계획서를 작성했다. 지금 그는 다음 달에 프로젝트를 시작할 때 필요할 모든 물품을 주문하고 있는 중이다.

⟜◯ 지텔프 치트키

now가 있으면 현재진행 시제가 정답이다.

> 🔆 **현재진행과 자주 함께 쓰이는 시간 표현**
> • (right) now / currently / at the moment (바로) 지금 / 현재 / 바로 지금
> • these days / nowadays 요즘

해설 | 현재진행 시제와 함께 쓰이는 시간 표현 now가 있고, 문맥상 말하고 있는 현재 시점에 Max가 모든 물품을 주문하고 있는 중이라는 의미가 되어야 자연스럽다. 따라서 현재진행 시제 (a) is ordering이 정답이다.

어휘 | supplies n. 물품

LISTENING

PART 1 [27~33] 일상 대화 마을 기념 축하 행사에 관한 두 친구의 대화

음성 바로 듣기

안부 인사	M: Hey, Gwen! It's nice to see you here at the park. How have you been? F: Hi, Troy! I'm doing well. [27]I've been busy organizing the town's anniversary celebration for next month.
주제 제시: 행사 준비	M: Oh yeah, you told me you volunteered for that. How's it going? F: Well, [27]we decided to hold the anniversary event at the park! I'm actually here to plan the layout.
활동1: 파이 만들기 대회	M: Wow, that's exciting. What activities do you have lined up for the event? F: Well, first, there will be a pie-making contest in the morning. We're inviting everyone in town to compete. M: So can I enter the competition too? F: Yes, of course, Troy. Do you like to bake? M: I love to bake! [28]I want to try making my grandma's special pecan pie for the contest. I'll call and ask her for the recipe.
활동2: 콘서트	F: I bet it's delicious. I can't wait to try some! After the contest, [29]there will be an afternoon concert featuring local musicians. M: Oh, which ones? F: Ha-ha, I can't tell you! It's going to be a surprise, but I can assure you they're all really good. You might be familiar with some of them. M: I guess I'll find out when I go to the concert, huh? Did you invite any famous bands or singers? F: Well, most of them are pretty well known locally. [29]They're all from our town, mainly because the idea for the event is to showcase local talent. In fact, [30]we still have openings on the schedule for other talented people if you know anyone who might be interested in getting involved.
활동 제안: 워크숍	M: Actually, I do have an idea, Gwen. [30]What about inviting local artists to hold workshops or classes at the event? F: Sure, that's a great idea. Do you have some artists in mind? M: Well, I'm part of a club for local artists. [30]During weekends, we often get together for art workshops. We also teach painting classes, though mostly to kids.

남: 안녕, Gwen! 여기 공원에서 너를 만나게 돼서 반가워. 어떻게 지냈어?

여: 안녕, Troy! 나는 잘 지내고 있어. [27]다음 달에 있을 마을 기념 축하 행사를 준비하느라 바빴어.

남: 오, 맞아, 네가 거기 자원했다고 했잖아. 어떻게 되어가고 있어?

여: 음, [27]기념행사를 공원에서 열기로 했어. 나는 사실 배치를 계획하러 여기 있어.

남: 와, 흥미진진하네. 행사에는 어떤 활동들이 준비되어 있어?

여: 음, 우선, 오전에 파이 만들기 대회가 있을 거야. 우리는 마을에 있는 모든 사람을 참가하도록 초대할 거야.

남: 그러면 나도 대회에 참가할 수 있어?

여: 응, 물론이지, Troy. 빵 굽는 거 좋아해?

남: 나는 빵 굽는 거 좋아해! [28]대회에서 할머니의 특별한 피칸 파이를 만들어 보고 싶어. 내가 할머니에게 전화해서 요리법을 물어봐야겠다.

여: 분명 맛있을 거야. 얼른 먹어보고 싶어! 대회 후에는, [28]지역 음악가들이 출연하는 오후 콘서트가 있을 거야.

남: 오, 어느 음악가야?

여: 하하, 나는 너에게 말해줄 수 없어! 깜짝 놀랄 일이겠지만, 내가 장담하건대 그들은 모두 정말 훌륭해. 너는 그들 중 몇몇을 잘 알고 있을 거야.

남: 콘서트에 가면 알게 되겠네, 그렇지? 유명한 밴드나 가수를 초청했어?

여: 음, 그들 대부분은 지역에서 꽤 잘 알려져 있어. [29]그들은 모두 우리 마을 출신인데, 주로 행사의 취지가 지역의 재능 있는 사람을 소개하기 위한 것이기 때문이야. 사실, 만약 네가 참여하는 데 관심이 있을 수도 있는 사람을 알고 있다면, [30]우린 재능 있는 다른 사람들을 위해 아직 일정에 빈자리가 있어.

남: 사실, 나도 생각이 있어, Gwen. [30]지역 예술가들을 초청해서 행사에서 워크숍이나 수업을 여는 건 어때?

여: 물론이지, 좋은 생각이네. 염두에 두고 있는 예술가들이 좀 있어?

남: 음, 나는 지역 예술가들을 위한 동아리에 소속해 있어. [30]주말 동안에, 우리는 종종 미술 워크숍을 위해 모여. 우리는 주로 아이들을 대상으로 하지만, 그림 수업도 가르쳐.

활동이 미칠 영향	F:	Well, it'd be nice if the artists are interested in participating. It would help promote your club too.	여:	음, 예술가들이 참여하는 데 관심을 두면 좋을 것 같아. 너희 동아리를 홍보하는 데도 도움이 될 거야.
	M:	Yeah, ³¹we've been looking for new members lately. Volunteering at the event will definitely help put our name out there and let more people know about our club.	남:	응, ³¹우리는 요즘 새로운 회원들을 찾고 있어. 행사에 자원봉사 하는 건 확실히 거기에서 우리 이름을 알리고 더 많은 사람이 우리 동아리를 알게 하는 데 도움이 될 거야.
	F:	Perfect! So, you'll get in touch with the club members?	여:	완벽해! 그럼, 동아리 회원들과 연락해 볼 거야?
예술품 판매를 위한 부스 신청	M:	Sure! Oh, and ³²Gwen, would it be possible for us to sell artwork at the event too?	남:	물론이지! 오, 그리고 ³²Gwen, 우리도 행사에서 예술품을 판매할 수 있을까?
	F:	Yes, of course! But ³²first you have to apply for a pop-up booth. There's an application form online, on the town's website.	여:	응, 당연하지! 하지만 ³²우선 팝업 부스를 신청해야 해. 마을 웹사이트에 온라인으로 신청서 양식이 있어.
	M:	I see.	남:	알겠어.
	F:	There's also a fee to set up the booth, but I can waive the fee for you guys if you really plan on holding workshops at the event.	여:	부스를 설치하는 데는 수수료도 있지만, 행사에서 워크숍을 실제로 열 예정이라면 내가 너희들을 위해 수수료를 면제해 줄 수 있어.
	M:	Thanks so much, Gwen. I'll let the other club members know. I'm sure they'll be grateful for the fee waiver!	남:	정말 고마워, Gwen. 다른 동아리 회원들에게 알려줄게. 그들은 분명 수수료 면제에 대해 고마워할 거야!
여자가 다음에 할 일	F:	No worries, Troy. ³³I have to go back to work on this booth layout. Just let me know soon what you and your club decide on for the event!	여:	걱정하지 마, Troy. ³³나는 부스 배치를 작업하러 다시 가봐야 해. 너와 너희 동아리가 행사에 관해 결정한 걸 곧 내게 알려줘!
	M:	Okay, I'll call you soon, Gwen.	남:	좋아, 내가 곧 전화할게, Gwen.

어휘 | organize[ɔ́ːrɡənàiz] 준비하다, 조직하다 anniversary celebration 기념 축하 행사
volunteer[vàləntíər] 자원하다, 자원봉사로 하다; 자원봉사자 layout[léiaut] 배치 line up 준비하다 compete[kəmpíːt] (경기에) 참가하다
competition[kàmpətíʃən] 대회, 경쟁 recipe[résəpi] 요리법 feature[fíːtʃər] 출연시키다 assure[əʃúər] 장담하다, 확인하다
idea[aidíːə] 취지, 목적, 생각 showcase[ʃóukeis] 소개하다 talent[tǽlənt] 재능이 있는 사람, 연예인 talented[tǽləntid] 재능 있는, 뛰어난
promote[prəmóut] 홍보하다, 촉진하다 get in touch with ~와 연락을 취하다 artwork[áːrtwə̀rk] 예술품
waive[weiv] (규칙 등을) 적용하지 않다, 생략하다 waiver[wéivər] (지불 의무 등의) 면제

---

27 | 특정세부사항　Why

난이도 ●●○

Why is Gwen at the park?	Gwen은 왜 공원에 있는가?
(a) to organize her anniversary party	(a) 그녀의 기념일 파티를 준비하기 위해서
(b) to find a location for a town meeting	(b) 마을 회의 장소를 찾기 위해서
(c) to plan for an upcoming local event	**(c) 곧 있을 지역 행사를 계획하기 위해서**
(d) to sign up as a community volunteer	(d) 지역사회 자원봉사자로 등록하기 위해서

━◯ 정답 잡는 치트키

질문의 키워드 park가 그대로 언급된 주변 내용을 주의 깊게 듣는다.

해설 | 여자가 'I've been busy organizing the town's anniversary celebration for next month.'라며 다음 달에 있을 마을 기념 축하 행사를 준비하느라 바빴다고 한 뒤, 'we decided to hold the anniversary event at the park! I'm actually here to plan the layout.'이라며 기념행사를 공원에서 열기로 해서 사실 배치를 계획하러 여기 왔다고 했다. 따라서 (c)가 정답이다.

⇄ Paraphrasing

the town's anniversary celebration for next month 다음 달에 있을 마을 기념 축하 행사 → an upcoming local event 곧 있을 지역 행사

오답분석

(a) 여자가 마을 기념 축하 행사를 준비하느라 바빴다고는 언급했지만, 기념일 파티는 언급되지 않았으므로 오답이다.

어휘 | upcoming [ʎpkʎmiŋ] 곧 있을, 다가오는 sign up 등록하다, 신청하다

---

28 특정세부사항   What   난이도 ●○○

What is Troy planning to call his grandmother about? | Troy는 무엇에 관해 그의 할머니에게 전화할 계획인가?

(a) **her special recipe** | (a) 특제 요리법
(b) her invitation to the event | (b) 행사 초대
(c) her favorite foods | (c) 좋아하는 음식
(d) her invitation to enter a contest | (d) 대회 참가 초대장

━○ 정답 잡는 치트키

질문의 키워드 call이 그대로 언급되고, grandmother가 grandma로 paraphrasing되어 언급된 주변 내용을 주의 깊게 듣는다.

해설 | 남자가 'I want to try making my grandma's special pecan pie for the contest. I'll call and ask her for the recipe.'라며 대회에서 할머니의 특별한 피칸 파이를 만들어 보고 싶다며, 전화해서 요리법을 물어봐야겠다고 했다. 따라서 (a)가 정답이다.

어휘 | favorite [féivərit] 좋아하는

---

29 특정세부사항   Why   난이도 ●●●

Why did Gwen invite only local musicians to the concert? | Gwen은 왜 지역 음악가들만 콘서트에 초대했는가?

(a) The goal is to surprise the audience with familiar faces. | (a) 목표는 익숙한 얼굴로 관객을 놀라게 하는 것이다.
(b) The organizers found famous singers too costly. | (b) 주최 측들은 유명한 가수들이 너무 많은 비용이 든다고 생각했다.
(c) **The goal is to highlight community members.** | (c) **목표는 지역사회 구성원들을 돋보이게 하는 것이다.**
(d) The organizers failed to secure talent in advance. | (d) 주최 측들은 사전에 재능 있는 사람을 확보하지 못했다.

━○ 정답 잡는 치트키

질문의 키워드 local musicians가 그대로 언급된 주변 내용을 주의 깊게 듣는다.

해설 | 여자가 'there will be an afternoon concert featuring local musicians'라며 지역 음악가들이 출연하는 오후 콘서트가 있을 것이라고 한 뒤, 'They're all from our town, mainly because the idea for the event is to showcase local talent.'라며 그들은 모두 마을 출신인데, 주로 행사의 취지가 지역의 재능 있는 사람을 소개하기 위한 것이기 때문이라고 했다. 따라서 (c)가 정답이다.

⇄ Paraphrasing

the idea 취지 → The goal 목표
local talent 지역의 재능 있는 사람 → community members 지역사회 구성원들

어휘 | audience [ɔ́:diəns] 관객, 관중 costly [kɔ́:stli] 많은 비용이 드는 highlight [háiláit] 돋보이게 하다, 강조하다 secure [sikjúər] 확보하다
in advance 사전에, 미리

지텔프 응시 기출문제집 7회분 Level 2

What does Troy suggest for filling up other openings in the schedule?

(a) **hosting group art lessons**
(b) involving a local dance club
(c) holding writing workshops
(d) having someone draw portraits

Troy가 일정의 다른 빈자리를 채우기 위해 제안한 것은 무엇인가?

(a) **그룹 미술 수업을 주최하는 것**
(b) 지역 댄스 동아리를 참여시키는 것
(c) 글쓰기 워크숍을 개최하는 것
(d) 누군가에게 초상화를 그리게 하는 것

─○ 정답 잡는 치트키

질문의 키워드 openings가 그대로 언급된 주변 내용을 주의 깊게 듣는다.

해설 | 여자가 'we still have openings on the schedule for other talented people'이라며 재능 있는 다른 사람들을 위해 아직 일정에 빈자리가 있다고 하자, 남자가 'What about inviting local artists to hold workshops or classes at the event?'라며 지역 예술가들을 행사에 초청해서 워크숍이나 수업을 여는 것을 제안했고, 'During weekends, we often get together for art workshops.'라며 주말 동안에 동아리는 종종 미술 워크숍을 위해 모인다고 했다. 따라서 (a)가 정답이다.

⇄ Paraphrasing
hold (행사 등을) 열다 → hosting (행사 등을) 주최하는 것
art workshops 미술 워크숍 → art lessons 미술 수업

어휘 | portrait[pɔ́:rtrət] 초상화, 인물화

How would volunteering at the event help Troy?

(a) He could gain recognition as an artist.
(b) He could advertise his painting business.
(c) **He could recruit new club members.**
(d) He could find sponsors for his upcoming show.

행사에서 자원봉사를 하는 것이 Troy에게 어떻게 도움이 되는가?

(a) 예술가로서 인정받을 수 있다.
(b) 그의 그림 사업을 광고할 수 있다.
(c) **새로운 동아리 회원들을 모집할 수 있다.**
(d) 곧 있을 전시회의 후원자들을 찾을 수 있다.

─○ 정답 잡는 치트키

질문의 키워드 volunteering ~ help가 그대로 언급된 주변 내용을 주의 깊게 듣는다.

해설 | 남자가 'we've been looking for new members lately. Volunteering at the event will definitely help put our name out there and let more people know about our club.'이라며 동아리는 요즘 새로운 회원들을 찾고 있는데, 행사에 자원봉사 하는 건 확실히 거기에서 이름을 알리고 더 많은 사람이 동아리를 알게 하는 데 도움이 될 것이라고 했다. 따라서 (c)가 정답이다.

⇄ Paraphrasing
been looking for new members 새로운 회원들을 찾고 있다 → recruit new club members 새로운 동아리 회원들을 모집하다

어휘 | recognition[rèkəgníʃən] 인정, 평가   recruit[rikrú:t] 모집하다, 채용하다   sponsor[spánsər] 후원자; 후원하다

32 특정세부사항   How   난이도 ●●○

According to Gwen, how can Troy sell artwork at the event?

(a) by uploading photos to the website
(b) by showing them in the town hall
(c) by applying for an available booth
(d) by displaying them at a restaurant

Gwen에 따르면, Troy는 어떻게 행사에서 예술품을 판매할 수 있는가?

(a) 웹사이트에 사진을 올림으로써
(b) 시청에 예술품을 보여줌으로써
(c) 사용할 수 있는 부스를 신청함으로써
(d) 식당에 예술품을 전시함으로써

정답 잡는 치트키

질문의 키워드 sell artwork at the event가 그대로 언급된 주변 내용을 주의 깊게 듣는다.

해설 | 남자가 'Gwen, would it be possible for us to sell artwork at the event too?'라며 Gwen에게 행사에서 예술품을 판매할 수 있을지 묻자, 여자가 'first you have to apply for a pop-up booth'라며 우선 팝업 부스를 신청해야 한다고 했다. 따라서 (c)가 정답이다.

어휘 | town hall 시청, 읍사무소   display [displéi] 전시하다, 진열하다

---

33 추론   다음에 할 일   난이도 ●●○

What will Gwen probably do right after the conversation?

(a) meet one of Troy's club members
(b) help Troy with an application form
(c) head home to get some more rest
(d) work on setup plans for the event

Gwen은 대화 직후에 무엇을 할 것 같은가?

(a) Troy의 동아리 회원 중 한 명을 만난다
(b) Troy의 지원서 작성을 돕는다
(c) 집에 가서 좀 더 휴식을 취한다
(d) 행사의 배치도를 작업한다

정답 잡는 치트키

다음에 할 일을 언급하는 후반을 주의 깊게 듣는다.

해설 | 여자가 'I have to go back to work on this booth layout.'이라며 부스 배치를 작업하러 다시 가봐야 한다고 한 것을 통해, Gwen은 마을 기념 축하 행사의 배치도를 작업할 것임을 추론할 수 있다. 따라서 (d)가 정답이다.

어휘 | head [hed] (특정 방향으로) 가다, 향하다   setup [sétəp] 배치   plan [plæn] 배치도

PART 2 [34~39]   발표   선술집 홍보

음성 바로 듣기

주제 제시: 선술집 소개	Ever wanted to travel back in time to the Middle Ages? Have you ever wondered what it would be like to dine like medieval royalty? Well, ³⁴come on down to the Basilisk Tavern for a unique dining experience that will surely bring you all the way back to Europe in the thirteenth and fourteenth centuries.
건물의 특징	To really make you feel like you've gone back in time, we've designed our restaurant like an actual medieval

중세 시대로 시간 여행을 떠나고 싶었던 적이 있었나요? 중세 왕족처럼 식사하는 것이 어떤지 궁금한 적이 있나요? 음, ³⁴13세기와 14세기의 유럽으로 되돌아가도록 당신을 확실히 데려다줄 독특한 식사 경험을 하러 Basilisk 선술집으로 오세요.

여러분이 과거로 돌아간 것처럼 실제로 느끼게 하도록, 실제 중세 선술집처럼 레스토랑을 꾸몄습니다.

주요
메뉴

오락
프로
그램1:
연극

오락
프로
그램2:
퀴즈

오락
프로
그램3:
음악
공연

tavern. The Basilisk Tavern has a stone exterior, while the inside is cozily lit with candles and an old fireplace. There is no electric lighting anywhere in the building, just like in medieval times! This will help give you a fully immersive dining experience. Don't forget to bring one of our gas lamps with you when you're headed to the bathroom! And turn on your camera flash when you're taking pictures with our Basilisk Tavern staff, who are dressed like medieval barkeeps.

Besides our interior and exterior design, we have also recreated recipes from the Middle Ages that will make you feel like you're eating at a royal feast. Our specialty is the King's Roast, which is a spiced rack of lamb. It is best eaten with the Queen's Dessert, a sweet pastry filled with strawberries. [35]Browse through our medieval menu and enjoy the food that kings and queens used to eat!

For entertainment, the Basilisk Tavern presents different programs several times a week. On Wednesday and Saturday nights, the Basilisk Acting Troupe enacts medieval tales such as "Camelot" and "The Knights of the Round Table" for the tavern's guests. Sit back and enjoy your meal as our actors bring to life stories of dashing knights and old kingdoms. [36]You can even participate in our plays as an extra! Just write your name on the sign-up sheet before the play, and we'll get you a costume right away. You'll play minor roles, so you don't need to memorize much dialogue. Just pull out your best improvisation skills and have fun!

If you want to showcase your knowledge of the medieval era, then our Friday trivia nights are for you. Bring your friends and family and battle it out with other Basilisk Tavern patrons as we quiz you on all things medieval. The winning group will get a free meal that night! And [37]at the end of the year, the highest-scoring teams will be entered into the Medieval Trivia Champion Cup. These teams compete not for money, but for possession of the Hero's Goblet and immortal fame upon the tavern's Wall of Legends.

We also have amazing musicians who play at the Basilisk Tavern all week. They play songs on musical instruments that were used more often in medieval times, such as harps and wooden flutes. [38]Be transported back in time as you listen to them sing of past kings, warriors, and their heroic deeds, just like medieval singers would do in the royal courts.

Basilisk 선술집은 석조 외관이지만, 내부는 촛불과 오래된 벽난로로 아늑하게 밝혀져 있습니다. 중세 시대처럼 건물 어디에도 전기 조명이 없습니다! 이것이 완전히 몰입할 수 있는 식사 경험을 제공하는 데 도움을 줄 것입니다. 화장실에 갈 때는 가스램프 중 하나를 가져가는 것을 잊지 마세요! 그리고 중세 바텐더 복장을 한 Basilisk 선술집 직원과 사진을 찍을 때는 카메라 플래시를 켜세요.

내부 및 외부 디자인 외에도, 마치 호화로운 잔치에서 먹는 것 같은 느낌을 주는 중세 시대의 요리법도 재현했습니다. 저희의 전문 요리는 King's Roast로, 매운 양 갈비구이입니다. 딸기가 가득한 달콤한 페이스트리인 Queen's Dessert와 함께 먹는 것이 가장 좋습니다. [35]중세 메뉴를 훑어보고 왕과 여왕이 먹곤 했던 음식을 즐겨보세요!

오락으로는, Basilisk 선술집은 일주일에 몇 번씩 다양한 프로그램을 선보입니다. 수요일과 토요일 밤마다, Basilisk 극단은 선술집 손님들을 위해 "캐머롯"과 "원탁의 기사"와 같은 중세 시대 이야기를 상연합니다. 배우들이 늠름한 기사와 옛 왕국의 이야기를 생생하게 재현하는 동안 편안히 앉아 식사를 즐기세요. [36]여러분은 연극에 엑스트라로 참여할 수도 있습니다! 연극 전에 참가 신청 용지에 이름을 적어만 주시면, 바로 의상을 제공해 드립니다. 단역을 맡게 되므로, 많은 대사를 외울 필요가 없습니다. 그저 즉흥적 공연 실력을 마음껏 발휘하고 즐기세요!

중세 시대에 관한 지식을 보이고 싶다면, 금요일 퀴즈 게임의 밤이 제격입니다. 친구들과 가족을 데리고 와서 우리가 중세 시대의 모든 것에 관해 퀴즈를 내면 다른 Basilisk 선술집 고객들과 필사적으로 싸우세요. 우승한 그룹에는 그날 밤 무료 식사가 제공됩니다! 그리고 [37]연말에는, 가장 높은 점수를 받은 팀들이 중세 퀴즈 게임 챔피언 컵에 참가하게 됩니다. 이 팀들은 상금을 위해서가 아니라, 영웅의 잔 소유와 선술집의 전설의 벽에 있는 불멸의 명성을 위해 경쟁합니다.

일주일 내내 Basilisk 선술집에서 연주하는 멋진 음악가들도 있습니다. 이들은 하프와 나무 피리 같이 중세 시대에 더 자주 사용되었던 악기로 노래를 연주합니다. [38]중세 가수들이 왕실에서 하곤 했던 것처럼 그들이 과거의 왕, 전사, 영웅의 위업을 노래하는 것을 들으면서 시간을 거슬러 올라가 보세요.

| 끝인사 | [39]Planning on having your birthday at the Basilisk Tavern? Just show the staff some form of ID to receive our discounted rate for anyone celebrating this special day at the restaurant. But whether you are celebrating a birthday or not, we hope to see you soon. And as they said in the Middle Ages, "Fare thee well!" | [39]Basilisk 선술집에서 생일을 맞이하실 계획인가요? 레스토랑에서 이 특별한 날을 축하하는 분을 위한 할인된 요금을 적용받기 위해서는 신분증을 직원에게 보여주시기만 하면 됩니다. 하지만 생일을 축하하든 축하하지 않든, 곧 뵙기를 바랍니다. 그리고 중세 시대에 그들이 말했듯이, "잘 가세요!" |

어휘 | medieval[mìːdíːvəl] 중세의 royalty[rɔ́iəlti] 왕족 tavern[tǽvərn] 선술집 surely[ʃúərli] 확실히, 분명히 exterior[ikstíriər] 외관 cozily[kóuzili] 아늑하게 light[lait] 밝게 하다 fireplace[fáiərpleis] 벽난로 immersive[imə́ːrsiv] 몰입형의 barkeep[báːrkìːp] 바텐더 royal feast 호화로운 잔치 specialty[spéʃəlti] 전문 요리 spiced[spaist] 매운 rack[ræk] (오븐에 구운 양·돼지) 갈비구이 pastry[péistri] 페이스트리(페이스트리 반죽으로 만든 작은 케이크) browse through ~을 훑어보다 troupe[truːp] (배우 등의) 일행 enact[inǽkt] 상연하다, 공연하다 tale[teil] 이야기 dashing[dǽʃiŋ] 늠름한 knight[nait] 기사 kingdom[kíŋdəm] 왕국, 왕조 costume[kástjuːm] 의상 memorize[méməràiz] 외우다, 암기하다 dialogue[dáiəlɔ̀ːg] 대사 improvisation[impràvəzéiʃən] 즉흥적 공연 trivia[tríviə] 퀴즈 게임, 일반상식 battle it out 필사적으로 싸우다 patron[péitrən] 고객 possession[pəzéʃən] 소유, 소지 immortal[imɔ́ːrtl] 불멸의, 불사의 fame[feim] 명성 warrior[wɔ́ːriər] 전사, 병사 deed[diːd] 위업, 공적, 행위 royal court 왕실, 궁중

---

34 주제/목적   담화의 주제   난이도 ●●○

What is the talk all about?

(a) a luxury outdoor restaurant
(b) a place to eat with a special theme
(c) a place to stay with medieval decor
(d) a restaurant with a modern menu

담화의 주제는 무엇인가?

(a) 고급 야외 식당
(b) 특별한 테마가 있는 식사 장소
(c) 중세풍의 장식이 된 숙박 장소
(d) 현대식 메뉴가 있는 식당

━○ 정답 잡는 치트키

담화의 주제를 언급하는 초반을 주의 깊게 듣고 전체 맥락을 파악한다.

해설 | 화자가 'come on down to the Basilisk Tavern for a unique dining experience that will surely bring you all the way back to Europe in the thirteenth and fourteenth centuries'라며 13세기와 14세기의 유럽으로 되돌아가도록 확실히 데려다줄 독특한 식사 경험을 하러 Basilisk 선술집으로 오라고 한 뒤, 담화 전반에 걸쳐 중세 유럽이라는 특별한 테마가 있는 식사 장소인 Basilisk 선술집에 관해 설명하는 내용이 이어지고 있다. 따라서 (b)가 정답이다.

어휘 | theme[θiːm] 테마, 주제 decor[deikɔ́ːr] 장식

---

35 특정세부사항   What   난이도 ●●○

What kind of food is on the tavern's menu?

(a) the kind that was typically served to travelers
(b) the kind that was commonly eaten by knights
(c) the kind that was often served to royalty
(d) the kind that was normally eaten by farmers

선술집의 메뉴에는 어떤 종류의 음식이 있는가?

(a) 여행자들에게 일반적으로 제공되었던 종류
(b) 기사들이 흔히 먹었던 종류
(c) 왕족에게 자주 제공되었던 종류
(d) 농부들이 일반적으로 먹었던 종류

━○ 정답 잡는 치트키

질문의 키워드 food와 menu가 그대로 언급된 주변 내용을 주의 깊게 듣는다.

해설 | 화자가 'Browse through our medieval menu and enjoy the food that kings and queens used to eat!'이라며 중세 메뉴를 훑어보고 왕과 여왕이 먹곤 했던 음식을 즐겨보라고 했다. 따라서 (c)가 정답이다.

⇄ **Paraphrasing**
kings and queens 왕과 여왕 → royalty 왕족

어휘 | typically [típikəli] 일반적으로, 전형적으로   normally [nɔ́ːrməli] 일반적으로, 보통

---

36 특정세부사항   What   난이도 ●●○

What should one do to participate in the tavern's stage plays? (a) attend a special audition (b) **sign up on a special list** (c) show up wearing a costume (d) email the director	선술집의 무대극에 참여하려면 무엇을 해야 하는가? (a) 특별 오디션에 참가한다 (b) **특별 명단에 등록한다** (c) 의상을 입고 나타난다 (d) 감독에게 이메일을 보낸다

⊸○ 정답 잡는 치트키

질문의 키워드 participate ~ plays가 그대로 언급된 주변 내용을 주의 깊게 듣는다.

해설 | 화자가 'You can even participate in our plays as an extra! Just write your name on the sign-up sheet before the play'라며 연극에 엑스트라로 참여할 수도 있으며, 연극 전에 참가 신청 용지에 이름을 적어만 주면 된다고 했다. 따라서 (b)가 정답이다.

⇄ **Paraphrasing**
write ~ name on the sign-up sheet 참가 신청 용지에 이름을 적다 → sign up on a special list 특별 명단에 등록하다

오답분석
(c) 화자가 의상을 제공해 준다고는 했지만, 연극 전에 참가 신청 용지에 이름을 적어주면 의상을 제공해 주겠다고 했으므로 오답이다.

어휘 | stage play 무대극   director [diréktər] 감독

---

37 추론   특정사실   난이도 ●●○

How, most likely, can one compete in the trivia championship? (a) **One must outscore other players.** (b) One must participate every week. (c) One must secure a sponsor. (d) One must pay an entry fee.	퀴즈 게임 결승전에 출전하려면 어떻게 해야 할 것 같은가? (a) **다른 선수들보다 많이 득점해야 한다.** (b) 매주 참가해야 한다. (c) 후원자를 확보해야 한다. (d) 참가비를 지불해야 한다.

⊸○ 정답 잡는 치트키

질문의 키워드 trivia championship이 Trivia Champion Cup으로 paraphrasing되어 언급된 주변 내용을 주의 깊게 듣는다.

해설 | 화자가 'at the end of the year, the highest-scoring teams will be entered into the Medieval Trivia Champion Cup'이라며 연말에는 가장 높은 점수를 받은 팀들이 중세 퀴즈 게임 챔피언 컵에 참가하게 된다고 한 것을 통해, 다른 선수들보다 많이 득점해야 퀴즈 게임 결승전에 출전할 수 있다는 것을 추론할 수 있다. 따라서 (a)가 정답이다.

⇄ **Paraphrasing**

the highest-scoring 가장 높은 점수를 받은 → outscore 많이 득점하다

어휘 | outscore[àutskɔ́:r] 많이 득점하다   entry fee 참가비

---

38   특정세부사항   Why

난이도 ●●○

Why do musicians at the tavern sing about kings and knights?

(a) to encourage people to dance
(b) to appeal to young guests
(c) to create a festive atmosphere
(d) to accurately reflect history

선술집에 있는 음악가들은 왜 왕들과 기사들에 관해 노래하는가?

(a) 사람들이 춤을 추도록 장려하기 위해서
(b) 젊은 손님들의 관심을 끌기 위해서
(c) 축제 분위기를 조성하기 위해서
(d) 역사를 정확하게 반영하기 위해서

━○ 정답 잡는 치트키

질문의 키워드 sing about kings and knights가 sing of past kings, warriors로 paraphrasing되어 언급된 주변 내용을 주의 깊게 듣는다.

해설 | 화자가 'Be transported back in time as you listen to them sing of past kings, warriors, and their heroic deeds, just like medieval singers would do in the royal courts.'라며 중세 가수들이 왕실에서 하곤 했던 것처럼 그들이 과거의 왕, 전사, 영웅의 위업을 노래하는 것을 들으면서 시간을 거슬러 올라가 보라고 했다. 따라서 (d)가 정답이다.

---

39   특정세부사항   How

난이도 ●○○

How can one who plans to have a birthday at the tavern get a discount?

(a) by bringing a family member
(b) by showing identification
(c) by ordering a special dinner
(d) by dressing in medieval clothing

선술집에서 생일을 맞이할 계획인 사람은 어떻게 할인받을 수 있는가?

(a) 가족을 동반함으로써
(b) 신분증을 보여줌으로써
(c) 특별한 저녁 식사를 주문함으로써
(d) 중세 시대의 옷을 입음으로써

━○ 정답 잡는 치트키

질문의 키워드 birthday가 그대로 언급되고, get a discount가 receive ~ discounted rate로 paraphrasing되어 언급된 주변 내용을 주의 깊게 듣는다.

해설 | 화자가 'Planning on having your birthday at the Basilisk Tavern? Just show the staff some form of ID to receive our discounted rate for anyone celebrating this special day at the restaurant.'라며 Basilisk 선술집에서 생일을 맞이할 계획이라면 레스토랑에서 이 특별한 날을 축하하는 사람을 위한 할인된 요금을 적용받기 위해서는 신분증을 직원에게 보여주기만 하면 된다고 했다. 따라서 (b)가 정답이다.

어휘 | identification[aidèntifəkéiʃən] 신분증   dress[dres] 옷을 입다; 원피스

안부
인사

M: Hey, Annie! I didn't expect to see you at a wedding convention.

F: Hi, Mike. Well, I got engaged recently, so I'm here looking for some ideas for my wedding.

M: Wow, congratulations!

주제
제시:
장단점
비교

F: Thanks. Hey, aren't you a wedding planner, Mike?

M: I am! I'm actually at this convention to promote my business. 40Maybe I can help you out? Weddings are my area of expertise, after all.

F: That'd be a huge help. We already know that we're holding the wedding ceremony at our church, but 40I'm still deciding on a venue for the wedding reception.

M: What are your choices for venues?

F: I've narrowed it down to either the Ember Grand Ballroom or Starlake Garden.

M: Hmm, I'm familiar with both venues.

연회장
의 장점

F: 41I've already visited the Ember Grand Ballroom, and it's really spacious! It can accommodate 300 people, and there's a big dance floor.

M: Yes, 41that venue is great for wedding parties with a lot of guests. Another advantage of the ballroom is that it's connected to a hotel.

F: Oh, that's right, it's connected to the Ember Grand Hotel.

M: If you're inviting people from out of town, they can stay there since it's right in the venue.

연회장
의 단점

F: That's definitely a plus! However, a disadvantage of the Ember Grand Ballroom is that renting it even for one day is expensive.

M: That, and 42booking the place can be very hard. I have former clients who had to postpone their wedding because the ballroom wasn't available on the dates they wanted.

F: Oh, that might be a problem because I would prefer my wedding to be set this spring. What about Starlake Garden then, Mike?

정원의
장점

M: One advantage of holding your reception at Starlake Garden is that it doesn't need a lot of decorating. It already looks beautiful with all the flowers and trees there.

F: Yeah, I wouldn't need many decorations. I can just let the natural setting speak for itself.

M: Exactly.

남: 안녕, Annie! 웨딩 컨벤션에서 너를 보게 될 줄은 몰랐어.

여: 안녕, Mike. 음, 내가 최근에 약혼해서, 결혼식에 관한 아이디어를 얻으려고 여기 왔어.

남: 와, 축하해!

여: 고마워. 저기, 너 웨딩 플래너 아니야, Mike?

남: 맞아! 사실 나는 사업을 홍보하기 위해 이 컨벤션에 왔어. 40내가 도와줄까? 어쨌든, 결혼식은 내 전문 지식 분야거든.

여: 그러면 큰 도움이 될 거야. 우리는 이미 교회에서 결혼식을 올리는 거로 알고 있지만, 40결혼 피로연 장소를 아직 정하는 중이야.

남: 장소에 관한 너의 선택은 뭐야?

여: Ember Grand 연회장이나 Starlake 정원 중 한 곳으로 좁혔어.

남: 흠, 난 두 장소 다 잘 알고 있어.

여: 41Ember Grand 연회장은 이미 가본 적이 있는데, 정말 넓어! 300명을 수용할 수 있고, 큰 댄스 플로어도 있어.

남: 응, 41그 장소는 하객이 많은 결혼식 파티에 적합해. 그 연회장의 또 다른 장점은 호텔과 연결되어 있다는 점이야.

여: 오, 맞아, 그곳은 Ember Grand 호텔과 연결되어 있어.

남: 만약 네가 다른 지역의 사람들을 초대한다면, 호텔이 그 장소 바로 옆에 있으니 거기에 묵을 수 있어.

여: 그건 확실히 이익이네! 하지만, Ember Grand 연회장의 단점은 하루만 빌려도 비용이 많이 든다는 점이야.

남: 그 점과, 42장소 예약이 매우 어려울 수 있어. 원하는 날짜에 연회장을 사용할 수 없어서 결혼식을 연기해야 했던 이전의 고객들도 있었어.

여: 오, 나는 이번 봄에 결혼식을 올리고 싶어서 그게 문제가 될지도 몰라. 그러면 Starlake 정원은 어때, Mike?

남: Starlake 정원에서 피로연을 여는 것의 한 가지 장점은 많은 장식이 필요하지 않다는 거야. 그곳은 꽃들과 나무로 이미 아름답게 보이거든.

여: 응, 많은 장식이 필요하지 않을 거야. 자연이 주는 분위기에 맡기면 되니까.

남: 맞아.

F: ⁴³Another advantage is that Starlake Garden is close to the church, so after the wedding ceremony is finished, we don't have to drive very far to get to the reception.

M: Yes, that's definitely an advantage. There's less of a chance you'll get caught in traffic. However, ⁴⁴since it's an outdoor venue, Annie, you might have some trouble with insects.

F: Oh, I hadn't thought of that. I might find myself battling insects instead of enjoying my own wedding reception!

M: Yeah, insects are the worst kind of wedding crasher. I wouldn't like having so many unwanted guests at my wedding either!

F: Ha-ha! Well, another disadvantage is that since the venue is outdoors, there's no protection from the weather.

M: That is definitely a problem. If it rains, the entire reception will be affected.

F: The ground would get all muddy. It might even flood! That's a bit scary.

M: So, what do you think, Annie? ⁴⁵Which venue are you going to pick for your wedding reception?

F: ⁴⁵I'm going to go with a more spacious venue. I can already picture that first dance with my future husband on that wonderful dance floor.

M: I'm glad I could help.

F: As a wedding planner, how much is your commission for something like this?

M: Oh, you don't have to pay me, Annie. I'm happy to just help out a friend.

F: Well, thank you, Mike. You'll be receiving a wedding invitation soon!

정원의 단점

여자의 결정

여: ⁴³또 다른 장점은 Starlake 정원이 교회와 가까워서, 결혼식이 끝난 후에, 피로연에 가기 위해 멀리 운전할 필요가 없다는 거야.

남: 응, 그건 확실히 장점이야. 교통 체증에 갇힐 확률도 낮잖아. 하지만, ⁴⁴야외 장소이기 때문에, Annie, 넌 벌레들로 인해 어려움을 겪을 수도 있어.

여: 오, 그건 생각 못 했어. 내 결혼 피로연을 즐기는 대신 벌레들과 싸워야 할지도 모르겠네!

남: 응, 곤충은 최악의 결혼식 불청객 유형이야. 나도 내 결혼식에 원치 않는 하객들이 너무 많이 오는 건 싫어!

여: 하하! 음, 또 다른 단점은 장소가 야외에 있기 때문에, 날씨로부터의 보호가 없다는 점이야.

남: 그건 확실히 문제야. 만약 비가 오면, 피로연 전체가 영향을 받을 거야.

여: 바닥이 온통 진흙투성이가 될 거야. 심지어 홍수가 날 수도 있어! 그건 좀 무섭네.

남: 그래서, 어떻게 생각해, Annie? ⁴⁵결혼 피로연을 위해 어느 장소를 고를 거야?

여: ⁴⁵나는 좀 더 넓은 장소를 고를 거야. 저 멋진 댄스 플로어에서 미래의 남편과의 첫 춤이 벌써 그려져.

남: 내가 도울 수 있어서 기뻐.

여: 웨딩 플래너로서, 이런 건 수수료가 얼마야?

남: 오, 돈은 안 줘도 돼, Annie. 친구를 도와주는 것만으로도 기뻐.

여: 음, 고마워, Mike. 너는 곧 청첩장을 받게 될 거야!

어휘 | get engaged 약혼하다 **expertise**[èkspərtíːz] 전문지식, 전문 기술 **after all** 어쨌든, 결국 **wedding ceremony** 결혼식
venue[vénjuː] 장소 **wedding reception** 결혼 피로연 **narrow down** 좁히다, 줄이다 **ballroom**[bɔ́ːlruːm] 연회장, 무도회장
spacious[spéiʃəs] 넓은 **dance floor** 댄스 플로어, 무도장 **definitely**[défənitli] 확실히, 분명히 **plus**[plʌs] 이익; ~을 더하여
postpone[poustpóun] 연기하다 **decorating**[dékərèitiŋ] 장식 **decoration**[dèkəréiʃən] 장식(물) **outdoor**[áutdɔr] 야외의, 실외의
battle[bætl] 싸우다, 격투하다 **crasher**[kræʃər] 불청객 **unwanted**[ʌnwántid] 원치 않는, 반갑지 않은 **muddy**[mʌ́di] 진흙투성이의, 진흙의
flood[flʌd] 홍수, 범람, 쇄도 **commission**[kəmíʃən] 수수료

---

40 특정세부사항   What   난이도 ●●○

What does Annie need help with?   Annie는 무엇에 도움이 필요한가?

(a) picking a location for her wedding   **(a) 결혼식 장소를 고르는 것**

(b) choosing a planner for her wedding

(c) selecting a theme for her wedding

(d) deciding on guests for her wedding

(b) 결혼식을 위한 플래너를 고르는 것

(c) 결혼식 테마를 선택하는 것

(d) 결혼식 하객들을 결정하는 것

━━○ 정답 잡는 치트키

질문의 키워드 help가 그대로 언급된 주변 내용을 주의 깊게 듣는다.

해설 | 남자가 'Maybe I can help you out?'이라며 자기가 도와줄지 묻자, 여자가 'I'm still deciding on a venue for the wedding reception'이라며 결혼 피로연 장소를 아직 정하는 중이라고 했다. 따라서 (a)가 정답이다.

⇄ **Paraphrasing**
a venue 장소 → a location 장소

---

41 특정세부사항   장·단점   난이도 ●●○

According to Mike, why is the Ember Grand Ballroom great for weddings?

(a) because it can handle large groups

(b) because it is connected to a chapel

(c) because it offers a dinner package

(d) because it includes a dance DJ

Mike에 따르면, Ember Grand 연회장은 왜 결혼식에 적합한가?

(a) 큰 단체를 감당할 수 있기 때문에

(b) 예배당과 연결되어 있기 때문에

(c) 저녁 식사 패키지를 제공하기 때문에

(d) 댄스 DJ를 포함하기 때문에

━━○ 정답 잡는 치트키

질문의 기워드 Ember Grand Ballroom과 관련된 긍정적인 흐름을 파악한다.

해설 | 여자가 'I've already visited the Ember Grand Ballroom, and it's really spacious! It can accommodate 300 people' 이라며 Ember Grand 연회장은 이미 가본 적이 있는데 정말 넓고 300명을 수용할 수 있다고 하자, 남자가 'that venue is great for wedding parties with a lot of guests'라며 그 장소는 하객이 많은 결혼식 파티에 적합하다고 했다. 따라서 (a)가 정답이다.

⇄ **Paraphrasing**
accommodate 300 people 300명을 수용하다 → handle large groups 큰 단체를 감당하다

어휘 | handle [hǽndl] ~을 감당하다, 통제하다   chapel [tʃǽpəl] 예배당

---

42 추론   특정사실   난이도 ●●●

Why might Annie have a difficult time booking the Ember Grand Ballroom?

(a) It is only open on weekdays.

(b) It is a popular location.

(c) It is out of her budget.

(d) It is often closed in the spring.

Annie는 왜 Ember Grand 연회장을 예약하는 데 어려움을 겪을 것 같은가?

(a) 평일에만 운영한다.

(b) 인기 있는 장소이다.

(c) 예산에서 벗어난다.

(d) 봄에는 종종 문을 닫는다.

━○ 정답 잡는 치트키

질문의 키워드 have a difficult time booking이 booking ~ can be very hard로 paraphrasing되어 언급된 주변 내용을 주의 깊게 듣는다.

해설 | 남자가 'booking the place can be very hard. I have former clients who had to postpone their wedding because the ballroom wasn't available on the dates they wanted.'라며 Ember Grand 연회장은 장소 예약이 매우 어려울 수 있는데, 원하는 날짜에 연회장을 사용할 수 없어서 결혼식을 연기해야 했던 이전의 고객들도 있었다고 한 것을 통해, Annie는 Ember Grand 연회장이 인기 있는 장소라서 예약하는 데 어려움을 겪을 것임을 추론할 수 있다. 따라서 (b)가 정답이다.

오답분석
(c) 여자가 Ember Grand 연회장의 단점은 하루만 빌려도 비용이 많이 든다는 점이라고는 언급했지만, 예산에서 벗어나는지는 알 수 없으므로 오답이다.

어휘 | budget[bʌ́dʒit] 예산

---

43 특정세부사항   장·단점   난이도 ●●●

How is Starlake Garden's location an advantage?

(a) There is free parking for guests nearby.
(b) There is very little traffic in the area.
(c) It is ideal for taking wedding photos.
(d) It is close to the ceremony location.

Starlake 정원의 위치는 어떤 이점이 있는가?

(a) 근처에 하객들을 위한 무료 주차장이 있다.
(b) 그 지역에는 교통량이 거의 없다.
(c) 결혼사진을 찍기에 이상적이다.
(d) 예식 장소와 가깝다.

━○ 정답 잡는 치트키

질문의 키워드 Starlake Garden's location과 관련된 긍정적인 흐름을 파악한다.

해설 | 여자가 'Another advantage is that Starlake Garden is close to the church, so after the wedding ceremony is finished, we don't have to drive very far to get to the reception.'이라며 또 다른 장점은 Starlake 정원이 교회와 가까워서 결혼식이 끝난 후에 피로연에 가기 위해 멀리 운전할 필요가 없다는 것이라고 했다. 따라서 (d)가 정답이다.

어휘 | ideal[aidí:əl] 이상적인

---

44 추론   특정사실   난이도 ●○○

According to the conversation, what would Annie have trouble with at Starlake Garden?

(a) the size of the rain shelter
(b) a flood of uninvited guests
(c) the presence of annoying bugs
(d) a lack of proper security

대화에 따르면, Annie는 Starlake 정원에서 무슨 어려움을 겪을 것 같은가?

(a) 비 대피처의 규모
(b) 불청객들의 쇄도
(c) 성가신 벌레들의 존재
(d) 적절한 보안의 결여

━○ 정답 잡는 치트키

질문의 키워드 have trouble with가 그대로 언급된 주변 내용을 주의 깊게 듣는다.

해설 | 남자가 'since it's an outdoor venue, Annie, you might have some trouble with insects'라며 야외 장소이기 때문에, 벌레들

로 인해 어려움을 겪을 수도 있다고 말한 것을 통해, Annie가 성가신 벌레들의 존재로 인해 Starlake 정원에서 어려움을 겪을 것임을 추론할 수 있다. 따라서 (c)가 정답이다.

⇄ **Paraphrasing**
insects 벌레들 → bugs 벌레들

어휘 | rain shelter 비 대피처 uninvited guest 불청객 presence[prezns] 존재 security[sikjúərəti] 보안

---

45 추론   다음에 할 일   난이도 ●●○

What will Annie most likely do after the conversation?

(a) reserve the ballroom space
(b) find a wedding consultant
(c) call her fiancé for advice
(d) book the garden venue

Annie는 대화 이후에 무엇을 할 것 같은가?

(a) 연회장 공간을 예약한다
(b) 웨딩 컨설턴트를 찾는다
(c) 약혼자에게 전화하여 조언을 구한다
(d) 정원 장소를 예약한다

⟲ 정답 잡는 치트키

다음에 할 일을 언급하는 후반을 주의 깊게 듣는다.

해설 | 남자가 'Which venue are you going to pick for your wedding reception?'이라며 결혼 피로연을 위해 어느 장소를 고를 것인지 묻자, 여자가 'I'm going to go with a more spacious venue.'라며 좀 더 넓은 장소를 고를 거라고 한 것을 통해, Annie는 피로연 장소로 좀 더 넓은 장소인 Ember Grand 연회장을 예약할 것임을 추론할 수 있다. 따라서 (a)가 정답이다.

어휘 | fiancé[fi:a:nséi] 약혼자

PART 4 [46~52]   설명   해외여행 갈 때 적합한 호텔을 선택하기 위한 6가지 조언

음성 바로 듣기

인사 + 주제 제시	Welcome to our new episode of *Drop By*, the podcast that's all about travel! [46]Today, we will be talking about choosing the right hotel when going on an overseas trip. If you're planning a long vacation, you will most likely need to book a hotel room at your destination. Choosing the right hotel is important because it's essentially your home away from home. It needs to be a safe and comfortable space for you to return to at the end of each day, just like your actual home.
조언1: 여행 계획 파악	My first tip for you is to know your travel plans. Are you planning to go out every day while you're on vacation? Or are you planning to spend most of your time relaxing in the hotel? Reviewing your trip plans allows you to know what kind of hotel you want to stay in. [47]If you're not really interested in exploring the area on your vacation, then a hotel with extra amenities like a pool or a spa will probably suit you more.

여행에 관한 모든 것인 팟캐스트 *Drop By*의 새로운 에피소드에 오신 것을 환영합니다! [46]오늘은, 해외여행을 갈 때 적합한 호텔을 선택하는 것에 관해 이야기할 것입니다. 긴 휴가를 계획하고 있다면, 목적지에서 호텔 객실을 예약해야 할 가능성이 높을 것입니다. 호텔은 본질적으로 집 밖의 다른 집이기 때문에 적합한 호텔을 선택하는 것이 중요합니다. 실제 집처럼, 하루의 끝에 돌아가는 안전하고 편안한 공간이어야 합니다.

여러분을 위한 첫 번째 조언은 여행 계획을 파악하는 것입니다. 휴가 동안 매일 외출할 계획인가요? 아니면 대부분의 시간을 호텔에서 편안하게 보낼 계획인가요? 여행 계획을 검토하는 것은 여러분이 머물고 싶은 호텔이 어떤 유형인지 알 수 있게 합니다. [47]만약 휴가 동안 그 지역을 답사하는 데 그다지 관심이 없다면, 수영장이나 스파 같은 추가적인 편의시설이 있는 호텔이 아마도 더 적합할 것입니다.

쪼인2.
위치
고려

My second tip is to make sure the hotel's location meets your needs. Your stay at the hotel may only be for a few days, but [48]you still want to be as safe as possible while you're there, right? Some hotels may be located in isolated areas that don't have many people around, which you may want to avoid if you tend to return to your hotel late at night. Another thing to consider is that some hotels are located in the center of the city or near tourist attractions. If you're looking for peace and quiet, then those hotels might not be suitable for you.

조언3:
대중
교통
수단
확인

The third tip is to take note of what types of public transportation are nearby. Choosing a hotel that is near public transportation, such as taxi stands, bus stops, or subway stations, will allow you to move around more freely. [49]You'd be surprised at how much exploring you can do when your hotel is accessible to a lot of public transportation! If there is no public transportation close by, you might have to compensate by walking or renting a car, which takes more time, money, and effort.

조언4:
호텔
주변
확인

My fourth tip is to [50]check what is in the general area of the hotel. Look at an online map and take note of pharmacies, convenience stores, and banks in the area. Knowing what is nearby will help you plan ahead. For example, if you think you'll need to withdraw cash frequently, you might want to choose a hotel with an ATM nearby.

조언5:
예산
고려

The fifth tip is to, of course, narrow down your choices based on your budget. You know what kinds of hotels to look for now, so check which ones are within your price range. [51]While some hotels might fit your standards, they may not fit your budget. It will be up to you to decide whether you'll adjust your budget for hotel expenses or adjust your standards for your preferred hotel.

조언6:
후기
읽기

The sixth and [52]final tip is to read hotel reviews. Travel websites often have pages for hotels where guests can leave reviews. Reading those reviews will make you aware of possible problems and will help you decide if the image of the hotel matches the reality.

끝인사

And that's it for this episode! Safe travels, and tune in again next week.

두 번째 조언은 호텔의 위치가 여러분의 요구를 충족시키는지 확인하는 것입니다. 호텔 체류는 며칠에 불과할 수도 있지만, [48]그곳에 머무는 동안 최대한 안전하기를 원할 것입니다, 그렇죠? 일부 호텔들은 주변에 사람이 많지 않은 외딴 지역에 위치할 수 있는데, 늦은 밤에 호텔에 돌아오는 경향이 있다면 피하고 싶을 수도 있습니다. 고려할 또 다른 사항은 일부 호텔들이 시내 중심가나 관광 명소 근처에 자리 잡고 있다는 점입니다. 만약 여러분이 평화와 고요를 찾고 있다면, 이러한 호텔들은 여러분에게 적합하지 않을 수 있습니다.

세 번째 조언은 근처에 어떤 유형의 대중교통 수단이 있는지 알아두는 것입니다. 택시 승강장, 버스 정류장, 지하철역과 같은 대중교통과 가까운 호텔을 선택하는 것은 여러분이 더 자유롭게 이동하도록 해줄 것입니다. [49]호텔에서 다양한 대중교통에 접근할 수 있다면 여러분은 얼마나 많은 곳을 답사할 수 있는지 놀랄 것입니다! 근처에 대중교통이 없다면, 걷거나 차를 빌려서 보완해야 할 수도 있는데, 이것은 더 많은 시간, 돈, 노력이 듭니다.

네 번째 조언은 [50]호텔의 주변에 무엇이 있는지 확인하는 것입니다. 온라인 지도를 보며 그 지역의 약국, 편의점, 은행에 주목하세요. 근처에 무엇이 있는지 아는 것은 미리 계획하는 것을 돕습니다. 예를 들어, 현금 인출이 자주 필요할 것 같다면, 근처에 ATM이 있는 호텔을 선택하고 싶을 수도 있습니다.

다섯 번째 조언은, 물론, 예산에 따라 선택의 폭을 좁히는 것입니다. 이제 어떤 유형의 호텔을 찾는지 알았으니, 여러분의 가격대에 맞는 호텔을 확인해 보세요. [51]일부 호텔들은 기준에 맞을 수도 있지만, 예산에 맞지 않을 수도 있습니다. 호텔 비용에 대한 예산을 조정지, 선호하는 호텔에 대한 기준을 조정할지의 결정은 여러분에게 달려있습니다.

여섯 번째이자 [52]마지막 조언은 호텔 후기를 읽는 것입니다. 여행 웹사이트에는 종종 투숙객들이 후기를 남길 수 있는 호텔 페이지가 있습니다. 이러한 후기를 읽는 것은 발생할 수 있는 문제를 알게 할 것이고 호텔의 이미지가 실제와 일치하는지 판단하는 것을 도울 것입니다.

그러면 이번 에피소드는 여기까지입니다! 안전한 여행 하시고, 다음 주에 또 청취해 주세요.

어휘 | overseas trip 해외여행 destination [dèstənéiʃən] 목적지, 도착지 essentially [isénʃəli] 본질적으로, 근본적으로 go out 외출하다, 나가다
explore [iksplɔ́ːr] 답사하다, 탐험하다 amenity [əménəti] 편의시설 isolated [áisəlèitid] 외딴, 고립된 tourist attraction 관광 명소
suitable [súːtəbl] 적합한, 적당한 public transportation 대중교통 compensate [kámpənsèit] 보완하다, 보상하다
take note of ~에 주목하다 pharmacy [fáːrməsi] 약국 withdraw [wiðdrɔ́ː] 인출하다 price range 가격대 standard [stǽndərd] 기준
adjust [ədʒʌ́st] 조정하다, 바로잡다 reality [riǽləti] 실제, 현실 tune in (라디오·텔레비전 프로를) 청취하다, 시청하다

주제/목적　담화의 주제　　　　　　　　　　　　　　　　　　　　　　　　난이도 ●○○

What is the topic of the talk?

(a) picking a place to stay on vacation
(b) finding a special hotel deal
(c) choosing the perfect vacation spot
(d) booking an overseas flight

담화의 주제는 무엇인가?

(a) 휴가 때 머무를 장소를 고르는 것
(b) 특별한 호텔 특가를 찾는 것
(c) 완벽한 여행지를 선택하는 것
(d) 해외 항공편을 예약하는 것

◀─○ 정답 잡는 치트키

담화의 주제를 언급하는 초반을 주의 깊게 듣고 전체 맥락을 파악한다.

해설┃ 화자가 'Today, we will be talking about choosing the right hotel when going on an overseas trip.'이라며 오늘은 해외여행을 갈 때 적합한 호텔을 선택하는 것에 관해 이야기할 것이라고 한 뒤, 담화 전반에 걸쳐 휴가 때 머무를 호텔을 선택하는 데 도움이 되는 조언에 관한 내용이 이어지고 있다. 따라서 (a)가 정답이다.

⇄ Paraphrasing
choosing the ~ hotel 호텔을 선택하는 것 → picking a place to stay 머무를 장소를 고르는 것

어휘┃ vacation spot 여행지, 휴양지

---

47 **추론**　특정사실　　　　　　　　　　　　　　　　　　　　　　　　　난이도 ●●○

Why would some travelers want extra amenities at their hotel?

(a) so they can save their money
(b) so they can meet other guests
(c) so they can entertain friends
(d) so they can enjoy staying in

일부 여행객들은 왜 호텔에 있는 추가적인 편의 시설을 원할 것 같은가?

(a) 돈을 절약할 수 있기 위해서
(b) 다른 투숙객들을 만날 수 있기 위해서
(c) 친구들을 즐겁게 할 수 있기 위해서
(d) 머무는 것을 즐길 수 있기 위해서

◀─○ 정답 잡는 치트키

질문의 키워드 extra amenities가 그대로 언급된 주변 내용을 주의 깊게 듣는다.

해설┃ 화자가 'If you're not really interested in exploring the area on your vacation, then a hotel with extra amenities like a pool or a spa will probably suit you more.'라며 만약 휴가 동안 그 지역을 답사하는 데 그다지 관심이 없다면 수영장이나 스파 같은 추가적인 편의시설이 있는 호텔이 아마도 더 적합할 것이라고 한 것을 통해, 일부 여행객들이 머무는 것을 즐길 수 있기 위해서 호텔에 있는 추가적인 편의 시설을 원할 것임을 추론할 수 있다. 따라서 (d)가 정답이다.

어휘┃ entertain [èntərtéin] 즐겁게 하다

---

48 **추론**　특정사실　　　　　　　　　　　　　　　　　　　　　　　　　난이도 ●●○

How, most likely, can one choose a hotel in a safe location?

(a) by staying away from tourist attractions
(b) by sticking to the quiet part of town

안전한 위치에 있는 호텔을 어떻게 선택할 수 있는 것 같은가?

(a) 관광지에서 멀리 떨어져 있음으로써
(b) 마을의 한적한 지역을 고수함으로써

(c) by asking fellow travelers
(d) by choosing a populated area

(c) 동료 여행자들에게 물어봄으로써
(d) 인구가 많은 지역을 선택함으로써

🔑 정답 잡는 치트키

질문의 키워드 safe가 그대로 언급된 주변 내용을 주의 깊게 듣는다.

해설 | 화자가 'you still want to be as safe as possible while you're there ~? Some hotels may be located in isolated areas that don't have many people around, which you may want to avoid if you tend to return to your hotel late at night.' 이라며 그곳에 머무는 동안 최대한 안전하기를 원할 것이며, 일부 호텔들은 주변에 사람이 많지 않은 외딴 지역에 위치할 수 있는데, 늦은 밤에 호텔에 돌아오는 경향이 있다면 피하고 싶을 수도 있다고 한 것을 통해, 인구가 많은 지역에 있는 호텔이 더 안전한 위치에 있음을 추론할 수 있다. 따라서 (d)가 정답이다.

어휘 | stick to ~을 고수하다, 지키다   fellow[félou] 동료인; 동료   populated area 인구가 많은 지역

49 추론   특정사실   난이도 ●●○

Based on the talk, how would having public transportation nearby improve one's vacation?

(a) It will keep one from getting lost.
(b) It will be easier to visit local attractions.
(c) It will be easier to travel to and from the airport.
(d) It will reduce the risk of danger.

담화에 따르면, 주변에 대중교통이 있는 것은 어떻게 휴가를 더욱 좋게 하는 것 같은가?

(a) 길을 잃지 않게 해 줄 것이다.
(b) 지역 명소를 방문하는 것이 더 쉬워질 것이다.
(c) 공항을 오가는 것이 더 쉬워질 것이다.
(d) 위험 부담을 줄일 것이다.

🔑 정답 잡는 치트키

질문의 키워드 public transportation이 그대로 언급된 주변 내용을 주의 깊게 듣는다.

해설 | 화자가 'You'd be surprised at how much exploring you can do when your hotel is accessible to a lot of public transportation!'이라며 호텔에서 다양한 대중교통에 접근할 수 있다면 얼마나 많은 곳을 답사할 수 있는지 놀랄 것이라고 한 것을 통해, 호텔 주변에 대중교통이 있으면 지역 명소를 방문하는 것이 더 쉬워져서 휴가가 더욱 좋아질 수 있음을 추론할 수 있다. 따라서 (b)가 정답이다.

어휘 | improve[imprúːv] 더욱 좋게 하다, 향상시키다   get lost 길을 잃다, 헤매다

50 특정세부사항   Why   난이도 ●●●

According to the talk, why is it important to familiarize oneself with the area around the hotel beforehand?

(a) to avoid asking directions
(b) to find affordable restaurants
(c) to locate important services
(d) to make a detailed itinerary

담화에 따르면, 호텔 주변 지역에 미리 익숙해지는 것이 왜 중요한가?

(a) 길을 묻는 것을 피하기 위해서
(b) 저렴한 식당을 찾기 위해서
(c) 중요한 서비스업의 위치를 찾기 위해서
(d) 상세한 여행 일정을 세우기 위해서

🔑 정답 잡는 치트키

질문의 키워드 area around the hotel이 general area of the hotel로 paraphrasing되어 언급된 주변 내용을 주의 깊게 듣는다.

해설 | 화자가 'check what is in the general area of the hotel. Look at an online map and take note of pharmacies, convenience stores, and banks in the area.'라며 호텔의 주변에 무엇이 있는지 확인하고, 온라인 지도를 보며 그 지역의 약국, 편의점, 은행에 주목하라고 했다. 따라서 (c)가 정답이다.

어휘 | direction[dirékʃən] 길, 방향 affordable[əfɔ́ːrdəbl] 저렴한 itinerary[aitínərèri] 여행 일정(표)

---

51 특정세부사항   What   난이도 ●●○

According to the talk, what should one do if a hotel is out of one's budget?

(a) ask for a special rate
(b) take a shorter vacation
(c) share a room with a friend
(d) decide what is most important

담화에 따르면, 호텔이 예산에서 벗어난다면 무엇을 해야 하는가?

(a) 특별 요금을 요구한다
(b) 더 짧은 휴가를 간다
(c) 친구와 방을 같이 쓴다
(d) 무엇이 가장 중요한지 정한다

○ 정답 잡는 치트키

질문의 키워드 out of ~ budget이 not fit ~ budget으로 paraphrasing되어 언급된 주변 내용을 주의 깊게 듣는다.

해설 | 화자가 'While some hotels might fit your standards, they may not fit your budget. It will be up to you to decide whether you'll adjust your budget for hotel expenses or adjust your standards for your preferred hotel.'이라며 일부 호텔들은 기준에 맞을 수도 있지만 예산에 맞지 않을 수도 있는데, 호텔 비용에 대한 예산을 조정할지, 선호하는 호텔에 대한 기준을 조정할지 결정은 청자들에게 달려있다고 했다. 따라서 (d)가 정답이다.

어휘 | rate[reit] 요금, 가격

---

52 특정세부사항   What   난이도 ●○○

What is the final tip?

(a) to pack as lightly as possible
(b) to read about other people's experiences
(c) to make reservations well in advance
(d) to consult online travel blogs

마지막 조언은 무엇인가?

(a) 가능한 한 가볍게 짐을 꾸리는 것
(b) 다른 사람들의 경험에 관해 읽는 것
(c) 훨씬 미리 예약하는 것
(d) 온라인 여행 블로그를 참고하는 것

○ 정답 잡는 치트키

질문의 키워드 final tip이 그대로 언급된 주변 내용을 주의 깊게 듣는다.

해설 | 화자가 'final tip is to read hotel reviews. Travel websites often have pages for hotels where guests can leave reviews.'라며 마지막 조언은 호텔 후기를 읽는 것이며, 여행 웹사이트에는 종종 투숙객들이 후기를 남길 수 있는 호텔 페이지가 있다고 했다. 따라서 (b)가 정답이다.

어휘 | pack[pæk] 짐을 꾸리다; 짐 in advance 미리 consult[kənsʌ́lt] 참고하다

READING & VOCABULARY

PART 1 [53~59] 인물의 일대기 뉴베리 소설가 어슐러 르 귄

인물 이름	**URSULA K. LE GUIN**	**어슐러 K. 르 귄**

<table>
<tr>
<td>소개
+
유명한
이유</td>
<td>

[53]Ursula K. Le Guin was an American author celebrated for her novels in the fantasy and science fiction genres. She is best known for creating far-flung, unfamiliar worlds, and for using these distant landscapes to explore complex social issues that hit close to home for her many readers.

</td>
<td>

[53]어슐러 K. 르 귄은 판타지와 공상과학 장르의 소설로 유명한 미국 작가였다. 그녀는 멀리 떨어진 낯선 세계를 창조하고, 많은 독자에게 친근하게 다가오는 복잡한 사회 문제를 탐구하기 위해 이러한 먼 지형들을 사용하는 것으로 가장 잘 알려져 있다.

</td>
</tr>
<tr>
<td>어린
시절</td>
<td>

Born Ursula Kroeber on October 21, 1929, in Berkeley, California, Le Guin grew up surrounded by books due to the influence of her parents Theodora and Alfred Kroeber, a best-selling writer and a well-known anthropologist, respectively. [54]As a young girl, Le Guin was fascinated by the Native American myths that her father often told her. She was especially intrigued by the fantastical elements they contained, which [54]soon led her to develop an interest in books that combined fantasy with reality.

</td>
<td>

1929년 10월 21일에 캘리포니아 버클리에서 어슐러 크로버로 태어난, 르 귄은 각자 인기도서 작가이고 저명한 인류학자인 부모 테오도라 크로버와 알프레드 크로버의 영향으로 책에 둘러싸여 자랐다. [54]어린 소녀 시절, 르 귄은 아버지가 자주 들려줬던 북미 원주민 전설에 매료되었다. 그녀는 특히 전설에 담긴 환상적인 요소에 흥미를 느꼈고, [54]곧 환상을 현실과 결합한 책들에 관심을 두게 되었다.

</td>
</tr>
<tr>
<td>업적
시작
계기</td>
<td>

In 1953, Le Guin earned her master's degree in literature from Columbia University and settled in Oregon with her husband soon after. While raising her children at home, [55]she started writing seriously, publishing several poems early on and focusing on fantasy and science fiction stories later. Her first book to attract significant public attention was *A Wizard of Earthsea*, a young adult novel about a boy who joins a school of wizardry and struggles to control his burgeoning power.

</td>
<td>

1953년에, 르 귄은 컬럼비아 대학교에서 문학 석사 학위를 취득했고 얼마 지나지 않아 남편과 함께 오리건주에 정착했다. 집에서 아이들을 키우면서, [55]그녀는 일찍부터 여러 편의 시를 발표하고 나중에는 판타지와 공상과학 소설 이야기에 집중하며, 진지하게 글을 쓰기 시작했다. 상당한 대중의 관심을 끌었던 첫 번째 책인 *A Wizard of Earthsea*는, 마법 학교에 입학한 한 소년이 그의 급성장하는 힘을 통제하기 위해 분투하는 것에 관한 청소년 소설이었다.

</td>
</tr>
<tr>
<td>주요
업적</td>
<td>

[56]Her next book, *The Left Hand of Darkness*, introduced an alien planet in which gender and gender norms do not exist. The book was considered a groundbreaking work of science fiction for its complex analysis of human gender and sexuality. It won Le Guin both the Hugo and Nebula Awards, two prestigious awards for the fantasy and science fiction genres, making her the first female author to receive both prizes for the same novel.

</td>
<td>

[56]그녀의 다음 책인 *The Left Hand of Darkness*는 성과 성 규범이 존재하지 않는 외계 행성을 소개했다. 이 책은 인간의 성과 성적 특질에 대한 복잡한 분석으로 공상과학 소설의 획기적인 작품으로 여겨졌다. 그것은 르 귄이 판타지와 공상과학 소설 장르에서 두 개의 명망 있는 상인 휴고상과 네뷸러상을 모두 수상하여, 같은 소설로 두 상을 모두 받은 최초의 여성 작가가 되었다.

</td>
</tr>
<tr>
<td>작품에
영향을
미친
요인</td>
<td>

[57]In contrast to most science fiction writers at the time, who tended to speculate on the future of natural and physical sciences, Le Guin liked to explore the so-called "softer sciences," like psychology and sociology, in order to confront different aspects of contemporary human behavior. Her father's anthropology career was most

</td>
<td>

[57]당시 대부분의 공상과학 소설 작가가 자연과학의 미래를 추측하는 경향이 있었던 것과 대조적으로, 르 귄은 현대 인간 행동의 다양한 측면을 직면하기 위해 심리학이나 사회학 같은 이른바 "소프트 사이언스"를 탐구하는 것을 좋아했다. 아버지의 인류학 경력은 그녀가

</td>
</tr>
</table>

likely influential in the approach she took with her fiction. She continually [58]tackled sensitive issues such as sexism and racism through her different literary works.

Le Guin died on January 22, 2018. She [59]earned many awards and other distinctions, and her work continues to influence writers both inside and outside the fantasy and science fiction genres.

소설에 취하는 접근 방식에 영향을 미쳤을 가능성이 높았다. 그녀는 다양한 문학 작품을 통해 성차별과 인종차별과 같은 [58]민감한 문제를 지속적으로 다뤘다.

르 귄은 2018년 1월 22일에 사망했다. 그녀는 [59]많은 상과 그 밖의 영예를 얻었고, 그녀의 작품은 판타지와 공상과학 소설 장르 안팎의 작가들에게 계속해서 영향을 미치고 있다.

죽음
+
영향력

어휘 | far-flung adj. 멀리 떨어진 landscape n. 지형, 풍경 explore v. 탐구하다, 탐험하다 surrounded by phr. ~에 둘러싸여 anthropologist n. 인류학자 respectively adv. 각자 be fascinated by phr. ~에 매료되다 myth n. 전설, 신화 intrigue v. 흥미를 끌다 fantastical adj. 환상적인, 기상천외한 contain v. 담다, 포함하다 reality n. 현실 master's degree phr. 석사 학위 settle v. 정착하다 seriously adv. 진지하게, 심각하게 struggle v. 분투하다 burgeoning adj. 급성장하는 alien adj. 외계의 planet n. 행성 gender n. 성 norm n. 규범, 표준, 기준 groundbreaking adj. 획기적인 analysis n. 분석, 해석 sexuality n. 성적 특질 prestigious adj. 명망 있는 speculate v. 추측하다 so-called adj. 이른바, 소위 softer science phr. 소프트 사이언스(정치학·경제학·사회학·심리학 등의 사회 과학·행동 과학의 학문) psychology n. 심리학 sociology n. 사회학 confront v. 직면하다, 맞서다 contemporary adj. 현대의, 동시대의 sensitive adj. 민감한 sexism n. 성차별 racism n. 인종차별

---

53 특정세부사항   유명한 이유   난이도 ●●○

What is Ursula K. Le Guin famous for?

(a) her novels based on explorers' lives
(b) her books set in strange worlds
(c) her articles on social behavior
(d) her illustrations of beautiful landscapes

어슐러 K. 르 귄은 무엇으로 유명한가?

(a) 탐험가들의 삶에 기반한 소설
(b) 낯선 세계를 배경으로 한 책
(c) 사회적 행동에 관한 글
(d) 아름다운 풍경에 관한 삽화

➜○ 정답 잡는 치트키

질문의 키워드 famous가 best known으로 paraphrasing되어 언급된 주변 내용을 주의 깊게 읽는다.

해설 | 1단락의 'Ursula K. Le Guin was an American author celebrated for her novels ~. She is best known for creating far-flung, unfamiliar worlds, and for using these distant landscapes to explore complex social issues'에서 어슐러 K. 르 귄은 소설로 유명한 미국 작가로, 멀리 떨어진 낯선 세계를 창조하고, 복잡한 사회 문제를 탐구하기 위해 이러한 먼 지형들을 사용하는 것으로 가장 잘 알려져 있다고 했다. 따라서 (b)가 정답이다.

⇄ Paraphrasing
unfamiliar worlds 낯선 세계 → strange worlds 낯선 세계

어휘 | based on phr. 기반하여 explorer n. 탐험가, 답사가 illustration n. 삽화

---

54 추론   특정사실   난이도 ●●○

How did Le Guin probably develop her specific taste in reading?

(a) from the myths her father often shared

르 귄은 어떻게 독서에 관한 구체적인 취향을 발전시켰을 것 같은가?

(a) 아버지가 자주 이야기해 줬던 전설로부터

(b) from the books her mother had written
(c) from the stories her grandparents often told
(d) from the books her teachers had assigned

(b) 어머니가 썼던 책으로부터
(c) 조부모님들이 자주 했던 이야기로부터
(d) 선생님들이 지정해 줬던 책으로부터

질문의 키워드 develop ~ specific taste in reading이 develop an interest in books로 paraphrasing되어 언급된 주변 내용을 주의 깊게 읽는다.

해설 | 2단락의 'As a young girl, Le Guin was fascinated by the Native American myths that her father often told her.'에서 어린 소녀 시절, 르 귄은 아버지가 자주 들려줬던 북미 원주민 전설에 매료되었다고 한 뒤, 'soon led her to develop an interest in books that combined fantasy with reality'에서 곧 환상을 현실과 결합한 책들에 관심을 두게 되었다고 한 것을 통해, 르 귄은 그녀의 아버지가 자주 이야기해 줬던 전설로부터 독서에 관한 구체적인 취향을 발전시켰음을 추론할 수 있다. 따라서 (a)가 정답이다.

어휘 | grandparent n. 조부모 assign v. (과제 따위를) 지정하다, 배정하다

55 특정세부사항 When
난이도 ●●○

When did Le Guin first start attracting mainstream attention for her writing?

(a) after releasing her first nonfiction book
(b) before moving to a new state with her husband
(c) after publishing several shorter works
(d) before she earned her master's degree

르 귄은 언제 처음으로 그녀의 글에 관한 주류의 관심을 끌기 시작했는가?

(a) 첫 번째 논픽션 책을 발표한 후에
(b) 남편과 함께 새로운 주로 이사하기 전에
(c) 몇 편의 단편을 발표한 후에
(d) 석사학위를 받기 전에

질문의 키워드 mainstream attention이 significant public attention으로 paraphrasing되어 언급된 주변 내용을 주의 깊게 읽는다.

해설 | 3단락의 'she started writing seriously, publishing several poems early on and focusing on fantasy and science fiction stories later. Her first book to attract significant public attention was A Wizard of Earthsea'에서 르 귄은 일찍부터 여러 편의 시를 발표하고 나중에는 판타지와 공상과학 소설 이야기에 집중하며 진지하게 글을 쓰기 시작했고, 상당한 대중의 관심을 끌었던 첫 번째 책은 A Wizard of Earthsea였다고 했다. 따라서 (c)가 정답이다.

오답분석

(a) 3단락에서 상당한 대중의 관심을 끌었던 첫 번째 책이 A Wizard of Earthsea였다고는 했지만, 이것이 첫 번째 논픽션 책이라고 한 것은 아니므로 오답이다.

어휘 | mainstream adj. 주류의; n. 주류, 대세 nonfiction adj. 논픽션의; n. 논픽션 state n. 주

56 특정세부사항 What
난이도 ●●○

According to the article, what was innovative about *The Left Hand of Darkness*?

(a) It challenged views of the time regarding gender.
(b) It was written as an analytical essay.

기사에 따르면, *The Left Hand of Darkness*에 관해 혁신적인 점은 무엇이었는가?

(a) 성별에 관한 당대의 관점에 도전했다.
(b) 분석적인 에세이로 쓰였다.

(c) It took place on multiple alien planets.

(d) It explored complex human relationships.

(c) 여러 외계 행성에서 일어났다.

(d) 복잡한 인간관계를 탐구했다.

질문의 키워드 *The Left Hand of Darkness*가 그대로 언급되고, innovative가 groundbreaking으로 paraphrasing되어 언급된 주변 내용을 주의 깊게 읽는다.

해설 | 4단락의 'Her next book, *The Left Hand of Darkness*, introduced an alien planet in which gender and gender norms do not exist. The book was considered a groundbreaking work of science fiction for its complex analysis of human gender and sexuality.'에서 르 귄의 다음 책인 *The Left Hand of Darkness*는 성과 성 규범이 존재하지 않는 외계 행성을 소개했는데, 이 책은 인간의 성과 성적 특질에 대한 복잡한 분석으로 공상과학 소설의 획기적인 작품으로 여겨졌다고 했다. 따라서 (a)가 정답이다.

오답분석

(b) 4단락에서 *The Left Hand of Darkness*는 인간의 성과 성적 특질에 대한 복잡한 분석으로 공상과학 소설의 획기적인 작품으로 여겨졌다고는 했지만, 이 책은 에세이로 쓰인 것이 아니므로 오답이다.

어휘 | innovative adj. 혁신적인, 독창적인 view n. 관점, 견해 analytical adj. 분석적인

---

57 특정세부사항   Why   난이도 ●●○

Why was Le Guin considered different from other writers at the time?

(a) She published works in every genre.

(b) She resisted writing about human behavior.

(c) She was heavily influenced by her time spent in nature.

(d) She focused on different branches of science.

르 귄은 왜 당대의 다른 작가들과 다르게 여겨졌는가?

(a) 모든 장르의 작품들을 출간했다.

(b) 인간 행동에 관한 글을 쓰기를 거부했다.

(c) 자연에서 보낸 시간에 영향을 많이 받았다.

(d) 과학의 다른 분야에 집중했다.

질문의 키워드 different from other writers가 In contrast to most ~ writers로 paraphrasing되어 언급된 주변 내용을 주의 깊게 읽는다.

해설 | 5단락의 'In contrast to most science fiction writers at the time, who tended to speculate on the future of natural and physical sciences, Le Guin liked to explore the so-called "softer sciences," like psychology and sociology'에서 당시 대부분의 공상과학 소설 작가가 자연과학의 미래를 추측하는 경향이 있었던 것과 대조적으로, 르 귄은 심리학이나 사회학 같은 이른바 "소프트 사이언스"를 탐구하는 것을 좋아했다고 했다. 따라서 (d)가 정답이다.

어휘 | resist v. 거부하다, 거절하다 branch n. 분야, 부문

---

58 어휘   유의어   난이도 ●●○

In the context of the passage, tackled means _____.

(a) blocked

(b) addressed

(c) ignored

(d) solved

지문의 문맥에서, 'tackled'는 -을 의미한다.

(a) 막았다

(b) 다뤘다

(c) 무시했다

(d) 해결했다

○─○ 정답 잡는 치트키

밑줄 친 어휘의 유의어를 찾는 문제이므로, tackled가 포함된 구절을 읽고 문맥을 파악한다.

해설 | 5단락의 'tackled sensitive issues'는 민감한 문제를 다뤘다는 뜻이므로, tackled가 '다뤘다'라는 의미로 사용된 것을 알 수 있다. 따라서 '다뤘다'라는 같은 의미인 (b) addressed가 정답이다.

---

59 어휘 유의어

난이도 ●●○

In the context of the passage, <u>distinctions</u> means _____.

(a) contracts
(b) elections
(c) approvals
(d) achievements

지문의 문맥에서, 'distinctions'는 -을 의미한다.

(a) 계약
(b) 선거
(c) 승인
(d) 공로

○─○ 정답 잡는 치트키

밑줄 친 어휘의 유의어를 찾는 문제이므로, distinctions가 포함된 구절을 읽고 문맥을 파악한다.

해설 | 6단락의 'earned many awards and other distinctions'는 많은 상과 그 밖의 영예를 얻었다는 뜻이므로, distinctions가 '영예'라는 의미로 사용된 것을 알 수 있다. 따라서 '공로'라는 비슷한 의미의 (d) achievements가 정답이다.

PART 2[60~66] 잡지 기사   CCT 프로그램과 삼림 벌채 비율의 연관성

기사 제목	**INDONESIA REDUCES DEFORESTATION THROUGH CASH INCENTIVES**	**인도네시아가 현금 장려금을 통해 삼림 벌채를 줄이다**
삼림 벌채 비율이 높은 인도네시아	Indonesia is home to the third largest rainforest in the world. However, [60]it also has one of the highest deforestation rates, mainly due to rural farmers who routinely clear the forest for agriculture. Farmers whose harvest is too small, perhaps due to pests or unexpected storms, will often remove trees from the surrounding land so they can plant more crops.	인도네시아는 세계에서 세 번째로 큰 열대 우림이 있는 곳이다. 그러나 [60]주로 농사를 위해 일상적으로 산림을 개간하는 시골 농부들로 인해 삼림 벌채 비율이 가장 높은 곳 중 한곳이기도 하다. 아마도 해충이나 예기치 못한 폭풍으로 인해 수확량이 너무 적은 농부들은 더 많은 작물을 심기 위해 주변 땅에서 종종 나무를 제거할 것이다.
최근의 삼림 벌채 비율 감소	Recently, researchers from Johns Hopkins University have found that Indonesia's average deforestation rate has consistently decreased since 2008. Evidence suggests that [65]the recent reduction in deforestation can be <u>attributed</u> to the Indonesian government's conditional cash transfer (CCT) program.	최근, 존스 홉킨스 대학교의 연구자들은 인도네시아의 평균 삼림 벌채 비율이 2008년 이후 지속적으로 감소하고 있음을 발견했다. 증거에 따르면 [65]최근의 삼림 벌채 감소는 인도네시아 정부의 조건부 현금 이전(CCT) 프로그램 덕분으로 돌려질 수 있다.
CCT 소개	[61]The program, which started in 2008, is meant to give additional money to families living in poverty. Under the program, the government subsidizes $45 to $90 per	[61]2008년에 시작된 이 프로그램은 가난하게 살고 있는 가족들에게 추가적인 돈을 지급하기로 되어 있다. 이 프로그램에 따라, 정부는 등록된 개인들이 매

---

family each year as long as registered individuals fulfill a few conditions, such as receiving yearly medical checkups and keeping children in school until junior high. [61]CCTs are given only to Indonesia's poorest, with the aim of improving the economic condition of over six million residents.

In a 2020 study that examined the environmental impact of the program, [62]researchers analyzed 7,468 rural Indonesian villages where families had received CCTs from 2008 until 2012. It was discovered that deforestation rates in the surrounding areas were 30% lower on average for that time period than they had been in previous years. Further research showed that deforestation rates remained low even after extreme weather events, when strong winds or rains damaged crops and lowered yield for farmers.

Based on these results, researchers theorized that farmers stopped clearing surrounding forestland due to the subsidies they had received under the CCT program. [63]The low deforestation rate even during inclement weather suggested that farmers no longer had to rely on a big harvest for [66]sufficient income, as they now had extra money to support their families.

[64]Indonesia's CCT program has provided some evidence that attempting to reduce poverty may positively affect the environment, despite many policymakers' beliefs to the contrary. Researchers hope that the successful implementation of CCTs in Indonesia and its unexpected influence on the country's high deforestation rate will lead to similar results in other countries with large tropical rainforests.

년 건강 검진을 받고 자녀를 중학교까지 학교에 다니게 하는 것과 같은 몇 가지 조건을 충족하면 매년 가족당 45달러에서 90달러를 보조금으로 지급한다. [61]CCT는 600만 명이 넘는 거주민들의 경제적 상황을 개선하기 위한 목적으로, 인도네시아 최빈층에만 지급된다.

이 프로그램의 환경적 영향을 조사한 2020년 연구에서, [62]연구자들은 2008년부터 2012년까지 가족들이 CCT를 받았던 인도네시아 시골 마을 7,468곳을 분석했다. 그 동안 주변 지역의 삼림 벌채 비율은 예년보다 평균 30%가 낮은 것으로 밝혀졌다. 추가적인 연구는 강풍이나 비가 농작물에 피해를 주고 농부들을 위한 수확량을 낮추는 극단적인 기상 현상 후에도 삼림 벌채 비율은 낮은 상태로 유지되었다는 것을 보여주었다.

이 결과를 바탕으로, 연구자들은 농부들이 CCT 프로그램에 따라 받았던 보조금 때문에 주변 삼림지의 개간을 중단했다고 이론을 세웠다. [63]궂은 날씨에도 낮은 삼림 벌채 비율은 농부들이 이제 가족을 부양할 여분의 돈이 있기 때문에, 더 이상 [66]충분한 수입을 위해 큰 수확에 의존할 필요가 없음을 시사했다.

[64]인도네시아의 CCT 프로그램은 많은 정책 입안자의 반대하는 믿음에도 불구하고, 빈곤을 줄이려는 시도가 긍정적으로 환경에 영향을 미칠 수 있다는 일부 증거를 제시했다. 연구자들은 인도네시아에서 CCT의 성공적인 시행과 인도네시아의 높은 삼림 벌채 비율에 대한 그것의 예상치 못한 영향이 큰 열대 우림이 있는 다른 나라들에서도 비슷한 결과로 이어지기를 희망한다.

CCT의 환경적 영향

CCT의 환경적 영향에 관한 이론

시사점

어휘 | deforestation n. 삼림 벌채 cash incentive phr. 현금 장려금 rainforest n. (열대) 우림 rural adj. 시골의, 지방의 routinely adv. 일상적으로 clear v. (삼림·토지를) 개간하다 agriculture n. 농사, 농업 harvest n. 수확(량); v. 수확하다 pest n. 해충 conditional cash transfer phr. 조건부 현금 이전 poverty n. 가난 subsidize v. 보조금을 지급하다 fulfill v. 충족하다 condition n. 조건 medical checkup phr. 건강 검진 resident n. 거주민 analyze v. 분석하다 extreme adj. 극단적인, 극심한 yield n. 수확(량) theorize v. 이론을 세우다 forestland n. 삼림지 inclement adj. (춥거나 비가 오는 등으로) 궂은 rely on phr. ~에 의존하다 positively adv. 긍정적으로, 적극적으로 policymaker n. 정책 입안자 implementation n. 시행, 실행

---

60 특정세부사항 What

난이도 ●●○

What is the main reason for Indonesia's high deforestation rate?

(a) the need to plant different kinds of crops
(b) the illegal logging done by large companies

인도네시아의 높은 삼림 벌채 비율의 주된 이유는 무엇인가?

(a) 여러 종류의 농작물을 심어야 할 필요성
(b) 대기업들에 의해 행해진 불법 벌목

(c) the frequent clearings of wooded areas by locals
(d) the tourists that hike through the area every year

(c) 현지인들에 의한 삼림 지대의 잦은 개간
(d) 매년 그 지역을 하이킹하는 관광객들

━○ 정답 잡는 치트키

질문의 키워드 high deforestation rate가 그대로 언급된 주변 내용을 주의 깊게 읽는다.

해설 | 1단락의 'it also has one of the highest deforestation rates, mainly due to rural farmers who routinely clear the forest for agriculture'에서 인도네시아는 주로 농사를 위해 일상적으로 산림을 개간하는 시골 농부들로 인해 삼림 벌채 비율이 가장 높은 곳 중 한곳이라고 했다. 따라서 (c)가 정답이다.

⇄ Paraphrasing

forest 산림 → wooded areas 삼림 지대
rural farmers 시골 농부들 → locals 현지인들

어휘 | illegal adj. 불법적인, 위법인 logging n. 벌목 local n. 현지인, 주민; adj. 현지의 tourist n. 관광객

---

61 추론   특정사실   난이도 ●●○

Why, most likely, was the CCT program implemented?

(a) to help students who were failing their classes
(b) to discourage illegal clearing of land
(c) to provide support to struggling schools
(d) to decrease poverty among the country's citizens

CCT 프로그램은 왜 시행되었을 것 같은가?

(a) 수업에 낙제하고 있는 학생들을 돕기 위해서
(b) 불법적인 토지 개간을 막기 위해서
(c) 고군분투하는 학교들에 지원을 제공하기 위해서
(d) 그 나라의 국민들의 빈곤을 줄이기 위해서

━○ 정답 잡는 치트키

질문의 키워드 program implemented가 program ~ started로 paraphrasing되어 언급된 주변 내용을 주의 깊게 읽는다.

해설 | 3단락의 'The program, which started in 2008, is meant to give additional money to families living in poverty.'에서 2008년에 시작된 이 프로그램은 가난하게 살고 있는 가족들에게 추가적인 돈을 지급하기로 되어 있다고 한 뒤, 'CCTs are given only to Indonesia's poorest, with the aim of improving the economic condition of ~ residents.'에서 CCT는 거주민들의 경제적 상황을 개선하기 위한 목적으로 인도네시아 최빈층에만 지급된다고 한 것을 통해, CCT 프로그램이 인도네시아 국민들의 빈곤을 줄이기 위해서 시행되었음을 추론할 수 있다. 따라서 (d)가 정답이다.

⇄ Paraphrasing

residents 거주민들 → citizens 국민들

오답분석
(b) 2단락에서 CCT 프로그램 덕분에 삼림 벌채 비율이 지속적으로 감소하고 있다고는 했지만, 이것은 CCT 프로그램의 시행에 따른 결과로, CCT 프로그램의 시행 목적은 아니므로 오답이다.

어휘 | discourage v. 막다, 낙담시키다 struggling adj. 고군분투하는, 어려워하는 citizen n. 국민, 시민

---

62 특정세부사항   How   난이도 ●●○

How were rural villages in the study affected by the CCT program?

연구에서 시골 마을은 어떻게 CCT 프로그램의 영향을 받았었는가?

(a) They attained the lowest unemployment rates.
(b) They preserved more of their local land.
(c) They increased the sale of natural resources.
(d) They became more resistant to severe weather events.

(a) 최저 실업률을 달성했다.
(b) 지역의 땅을 더 많이 보존했다.
(c) 천연자원의 판매를 늘렸다.
(d) 극심한 기상 이변에 대한 저항력을 높였다.

○ 정답 잡는 치트키

질문의 키워드 rural villages가 그대로 언급된 주변 내용을 주의 깊게 읽는다.

해설 | 4단락의 'researchers analyzed 7,468 rural Indonesian villages where families had received CCTs ~. It was discovered that deforestation rates in the surrounding areas were 30% lower on average for that time period than they had been in previous years.'에서 연구자들은 가족들이 CCT를 받았던 인도네시아 시골 마을 7,468곳을 분석했고, 그 동안 주변 지역의 삼림 벌채 비율이 예년보다 평균 30%가 낮은 것으로 밝혀졌다고 했다. 따라서 (b)가 정답이다.

오답분석

(d) 4단락에서 극단적인 기상 현상 후에도 삼림 벌채 비율은 낮은 상태로 유지되었다고는 했지만, 극심한 기상 이변에 대한 저항력이 높아졌는지는 언급되지 않았으므로 오답이다.

---

63 특정세부사항   How   난이도 ●●○

According to the study, how did the CCT program help farmers?

(a) by enabling them to plant crops in larger areas
(b) by ensuring their crops would survive bad weather
(c) by giving them the means to buy their harvest back
(d) by providing more income during smaller harvests

연구에 따르면, CCT 프로그램은 어떻게 농부들에게 도움이 되었는가?

(a) 더 넓은 지역에 농작물을 심을 수 있게 함으로써
(b) 농작물이 궂은 날씨를 견뎌내도록 보장함으로써
(c) 수확물을 되팔 수 있는 수단을 제공함으로써
(d) 수확량이 적은 동안 더 많은 수입을 제공함으로써

○ 정답 잡는 치트키

질문의 키워드 farmers가 그대로 언급된 주변 내용을 주의 깊게 읽는다.

해설 | 5단락의 'The low deforestation rate even during inclement weather suggested that farmers no longer had to rely on a big harvest for sufficient income, as they now had extra money to support their families.'에서 궂은 날씨에도 낮은 삼림 벌채 비율은 농부들이 이제 가족을 부양할 여분의 돈이 있기 때문에 더 이상 충분한 수입을 위해 큰 수확에 의존할 필요가 없음을 시사했다고 했다. 따라서 (d)가 정답이다.

어휘 | enable v. ~할 수 있게 하다   ensure v. 보장하다   survive v. 견디다, 생존하다

---

64 추론   특정사실   난이도 ●●○

According to the article, what belief about poverty reduction is most likely held by many policymakers?

(a) that it will positively affect population growth
(b) that it can only be achieved through government aid
(c) that it will negatively affect the environment
(d) that it is impossible to manage effectively

기사에 따르면, 많은 정책 입안자가 빈곤 감소에 관해 가지고 있었던 믿음은 무엇인 것 같은가?

(a) 인구 증가에 긍정적으로 영향을 미칠 거라는 것
(b) 오직 정부의 원조를 통해서만 달성될 수 있다는 것
(c) 환경에 부정적으로 영향을 미칠 거라는 것
(d) 효율적으로 관리하기가 불가능하다는 것

○── 정답 잡는 치트키

질문의 키워드 policymakers가 그대로 언급된 주변 내용을 주의 깊게 읽는다.

해설 | 6단락의 'Indonesia's CCT program has provided some evidence that attempting to reduce poverty may positively affect the environment, despite many policymakers' beliefs to the contrary.'에서 인도네시아의 CCT 프로그램은 많은 정책 입안자의 반대하는 믿음에도 불구하고, 빈곤을 줄이려는 시도가 긍정적으로 환경에 영향을 미칠 수 있다는 일부 증거를 제시했다고 한 것을 통해, 많은 정책 입안자는 빈곤 감소가 환경에 부정적으로 영향을 미칠 것이라고 믿고 있었음을 추론할 수 있다. 따라서 (c)가 정답이다.

어휘 | aid n. 원조, 지원 negatively adv. 부정적으로

---

65 어휘   유의어

난이도 ●●○

In the context of the passage, <u>attributed</u> means _____.

(a) returned
(b) released
(c) gifted
(d) credited

지문의 문맥에서, 'attributed'는 -을 의미한다.

(a) 돌려보내진
(b) 방출된
(c) 증여된
(d) 덕분으로 돌려진

○── 정답 잡는 치트키

밑줄 친 어휘의 유의어를 찾는 문제이므로, attributed가 포함된 구절을 읽고 문맥을 파악한다.

해설 | 2단락의 'the recent reduction ~ can be attributed to the ~ program'은 최근의 감소는 프로그램 덕분으로 돌려질 수 있다는 뜻이므로, attributed가 '덕분으로 돌려진'이라는 의미로 사용된 것을 알 수 있다. 따라서 '덕분으로 돌려진'이라는 같은 의미의 (d) credited가 정답이다.

---

66 어휘   유의어

난이도 ●○○

In the context of the passage, <u>sufficient</u> means _____.

(a) valid
(b) enough
(c) enjoyable
(d) taxable

지문의 문맥에서, 'sufficient'는 -을 의미한다.

(a) 유효한
(b) 충분한
(c) 즐거운
(d) 과세할 수 있는

○── 정답 잡는 치트키

밑줄 친 어휘의 유의어를 찾는 문제이므로, sufficient가 포함된 구절을 읽고 문맥을 파악한다.

해설 | 5단락의 'sufficient income'은 충분한 수입이라는 뜻이므로, sufficient가 '충분한'이라는 의미로 사용된 것을 알 수 있다. 따라서 '충분한'이라는 같은 의미의 (b) enough가 정답이다.

지텔프 공식 기출문제집 7회분 Level 2

표제어	**MARDI GRAS**	마르디 그라
정의	Mardi Gras is a holiday most famously held in New Orleans, Louisiana. The celebration features big float parades and an abundance of "throws," trinkets that are traditionally tossed to parade attendees. Due to its festive atmosphere, ⁶⁷Mardi Gras is one of the most well-attended events in New Orleans, drawing thousands of tourists every year.	마르디 그라는 루이지애나주 뉴올리언스에서 가장 유명하게 열리는 휴일이다. 이 기념행사는 큰 장식 차량 퍼레이드와 전통적으로 퍼레이드 참가자들에게 던져지는 다량의 장신구인 "던지기"를 특징으로 한다. 축제 분위기 때문에, ⁶⁷마르디 그라는 뉴올리언스에서 많은 사람들이 참석하는 행사 중 하나이며, 매년 수천 명의 관광객을 끌어들인다.
기원	⁶⁷One theory about Mardi Gras's origin claims that the holiday evolved from the ancient Roman festival that honored Saturn, the god of agriculture. Called Saturnalia, it included extravagant partying and feasting. When Christianity spread to Rome, the festival was incorporated into traditional Christian rituals as a new holiday. ⁶⁸It became a way to indulge oneself before Lent, when ⁷²fasting and silence were commonly <u>observed</u> in religious households.	⁶⁷마르디 그라의 기원에 대한 한 이론은 그 휴일이 농업의 신인 사투르누스를 기리는 고대 로마의 축제에서 발달했다고 주장한다. 농신제라고 불리는, 그것은 사치스러운 파티와 잔치를 포함했다. 기독교가 로마에 퍼졌을 때, 그 축제는 새로운 휴일로 전통적인 기독교 의식에 통합되었다. ⁶⁸이것은 사순절 전에 자신의 욕구를 충족시키는 방법이 되었는데, 사순절은 신앙심 깊은 가정에서 ⁷²금식과 침묵이 일반적으로 <u>준수되었던</u> 때였다.
최초의 기념 행사	The tradition spread throughout Europe where it eventually became known as *Mardi Gras, Mardi* being the French word for "Tuesday" and *gras* for "fat." ⁶⁹The first Mardi Gras celebration in the US was on March 3, 1699, when French explorers camped at a site close to New Orleans. Though the holiday is now celebrated all over the US, New Orleans still hosts some of the most popular Mardi Gras festivities in the world.	이 전통은 결국 *마르디 그라*로 알려지게 된 곳인 유럽으로 퍼져 나갔는데, *마르디*는 "화요일", *그라*는 "지방"을 의미하는 프랑스어 단어였다. ⁶⁹미국에서 최초의 마르디 그라 기념행사는 1699년 3월 3일이었는데, 프랑스 탐험가들이 뉴올리언스 가까이에 있는 장소에서 야영했던 때였다. 비록 이 기념일이 지금은 미국 전역에서 기념되지만, 뉴올리언스는 여전히 세계에서 가장 유명한 마르디 그라 축제를 개최한다.
주요 행사: 퍼레이드	Mardi Gras celebrations in New Orleans start two weeks before the Christian holiday of Ash Wednesday, with the main events of the festival happening during the final week. The exact date of Mardi Gras changes every year, but it always falls between February 3 and March 9. ⁷⁰The biggest events are the parades, where festival organizers showcase elaborate floats based on themes like "Famous Lovers" or "Equality for All."	뉴올리언스의 마르디 그라 축제는 기독교 휴일인 재의 수요일 2주 전에 시작되며, 축제의 주요 행사들은 마지막 주 동안 열린다. 마르디 그라의 정확한 날짜는 매년 변하지만, 그것은 항상 2월 3일과 3월 9일 사이에 해당한다. ⁷⁰가장 큰 행사는 퍼레이드로, 축제 주최 측에서 "유명한 연인" 또는 "모두를 위한 평등"과 같은 주제를 바탕으로 한 정교한 장식 차량을 선보이는 것이다.
주요 행사2: 던지기	During the parade, individuals riding the floats give away trinkets called "throws," generally inexpensive plastic items, to attendees. Throws are usually bead necklaces, souvenir coins, or small toys, and some are even considered collectible items. Eager onlookers can sometimes become very competitive about trying to catch ⁷³these <u>prized</u> trinkets.	퍼레이드 동안, 장식 차를 탄 사람들은 참석자들에게 일반적으로 저렴한 플라스틱 물품인 "던지기"라고 불리는 장신구를 나눠준다. 던지기는 보통 구슬 목걸이, 기념품 동전, 또는 작은 장난감이며, 일부는 심지어 수집품으로 여겨진다. 열정적인 구경꾼들은 때때로 ⁷³이러한 <u>소중한</u> 장신구들을 잡으려고 노력하는 것에 매우 경쟁적으로 될 수 있다.
축제의 효과	⁷¹Much like Saturnalia, Mardi Gras is also known as an opportunity for partying and excessive drinking. Mardi Gras tourism has contributed hundreds of billions of	⁷¹농신제와 마찬가지로, 마르디 그라는 파티와 과음의 기회로도 알려져 있다. 마르디 그라 관광은 지역 사

dollars to New Orleans' economy, significantly boosting local businesses, especially clubs and bars.

업, 특히 클럽과 술집을 활성화하며, 뉴올리언스의 경제에 수천억 달러를 기여한다.

어휘 | float n. 장식 차량 trinket n. 장신구 toss v. 던지다 atmosphere n. 분위기 origin n. 기원 evolve from phr. ~에서 발달하다
Saturn n. 사투르누스, 고대 로마의 농경의 신 Saturnalia n. (12월 17일경의 추수를 축하하는) 농신제 extravagant adj. 사치스러운, 낭비하는
incorporate into phr. ~에 통합시키다 ritual n. 의식, 절차 indulge v. (특정한 욕구·관심 등을) 충족시키다, 탐닉하다
Lent n. 사순절(성회의 수요일(Ash Wednesday)부터 부활절(Easter)까지의 주일(일요일)을 제외한 40일간) fasting n. 금식, 절식
religious adj. 신앙심 깊은, 종교적인 camp v. 야영하다; n. 야영지 festivity n. 축제
Ash Wednesday phr. 재의 수요일(사순절(Lent)의 첫날) showcase v. 선보이다 elaborate adj. 정교한 souvenir n. 기념품
collectible adj. 모을 수 있는 onlooker n. 구경꾼 excessive drinking phr. 과음 tourism n. 관광(업) boost v. 활성화하다, 부양하다

---

67 특정세부사항   What

난이도 ●●○

According to the article, what draws large crowds to New Orleans every year?

(a) a traditional celebration with ancient origins
(b) a chance for an exclusive tour of city landmarks
(c) a nationwide contest for best parade float
(d) a re-enactment of a famous Roman feast

기사에 따르면, 매년 많은 인파를 뉴올리언스로 끌어들이는 것은 무엇인가?

(a) 고대 기원을 가진 전통 축제
(b) 도시 랜드마크의 독점적인 투어 기회
(c) 최고의 행진용 장식 차량을 위한 전국적인 대회
(d) 유명한 로마 축제의 재연

─○ 정답 잡는 치트키

질문의 키워드 draws large crowds가 drawing thousands of tourists로 paraphrasing되어 언급된 주변 내용을 주의 깊게 읽는다.

해설 | 1단락의 'Mardi Gras is one of the most well-attended events in New Orleans, drawing thousands of tourists every year'에서 마르디 그라는 뉴올리언스에서 많은 사람들이 참석하는 행사 중 하나이며, 매년 수천 명의 관광객을 끌어들인다고 한 뒤, 2단락의 'One theory about Mardi Gras's origin claims that the holiday evolved from the ancient Roman festival'에서 마르디 그라의 기원에 대한 한 이론은 그 휴일이 고대 로마의 축제에서 발달했다고 주장한다고 했다. 따라서 (a)가 정답이다.

오답분석
(d) 2단락에서 마르디 그라가 고대 로마의 축제에서 발달했다고는 했지만, 로마 축제의 재연은 아니므로 오답이다.

어휘 | exclusive adj. 독점적인, 유일한 landmark n. 랜드마크, 주요 지형지물 nationwide adj. 전국적인 re-enactment n. 재연

---

68 특정세부사항   Why

난이도 ●●○

Why is Mardi Gras celebrated before Lent?

(a) to encourage fun before a period of self-control
(b) to avoid conflict with other religious holidays
(c) to limit the amount of traffic in the city
(d) to allow tourists to observe both traditions

마르디 그라는 왜 사순절 전에 기념되는가?

(a) 자제 기간 전에 재미를 부추기기 위해서
(b) 다른 종교 기념일과의 충돌을 피하기 위해서
(c) 도시의 교통량을 제한하기 위해서
(d) 관광객들이 두 가지 전통을 모두 지키도록 하기 위해서

─○ 정답 잡는 치트키

질문의 키워드 before Lent가 그대로 언급된 주변 내용을 주의 깊게 읽는다.

해설 | 2단락의 'It became a way to indulge oneself before Lent, when fasting and silence were commonly observed in religious households.'에서 마르디 그라는 사순절 전에 자신의 욕구를 충족시키는 방법이 되었는데, 사순절은 신앙심 깊은 가정에서 금식과 침묵이 일반적으로 준수되었던 때였다고 했다. 따라서 (a)가 정답이다.

⇄ **Paraphrasing**
indulge oneself 자신의 욕구를 충족시키다 → encourage fun 재미를 부추기다

어휘 | self-control n. 자제력 conflict n. 충돌

---

69 특정세부사항   How

난이도 ●●○

How did Mardi Gras end up being celebrated in New Orleans?

(a) It was promoted by a major church in the city.
(b) It spread from other major cities in the US.
(c) It was brought over by world travelers.
(d) It aligned with the state's founding day.

마르디 그라는 어떻게 뉴올리언스에서 결국 기념하게 되었는가?

(a) 그 도시의 큰 교회에 의해서 추진되었다.
(b) 미국 내 다른 주요 도시들에서부터 퍼졌다.
(c) 세계 여행객들에 의해 가져와졌다.
(d) 주의 설립일과 일치했다.

○━━ 정답 잡는 치트키

질문의 키워드 celebrated와 New Orleans가 그대로 언급된 주변 내용을 주의 깊게 읽는다.

해설 | 3단락의 'The first Mardi Gras celebration ~, when French explorers camped at a site close to New Orleans. Though the holiday is now celebrated all over the US, New Orleans still hosts some of the most popular Mardi Gras festivities in the world.'에서 최초의 마르디 그라 기념행사는 프랑스 탐험가들이 뉴올리언스 가까이에 있는 장소에서 야영했던 때였고, 비록 이 기념일이 지금은 미국 전역에서 기념되지만, 뉴올리언스는 여전히 세계에서 가장 유명한 마르디 그라 축제를 개최한다고 했다. 따라서 (c)가 정답이다.

⇄ **Paraphrasing**
French explorers 프랑스 탐험가들 → world travelers 세계 여행객들

어휘 | align with phr. ~과 일치하다, 조화를 이루다

---

70 특정세부사항   What

난이도 ●●○

According to the article, what is a main feature of Mardi Gras?

(a) the chance to wear elaborate costumes
(b) the opportunity to buy collectible items
(c) the concerts organized by festival volunteers
(d) the floats created to reflect certain themes

기사에 따르면, 마르디 그라의 주요 볼거리는 무엇인가?

(a) 정교한 의상을 입을 기회
(b) 수집품을 살 기회
(c) 축제 자원봉사자들에 의해 조직된 연주회
(d) 특정 주제를 반영하여 제작된 장식 차량

○━━ 정답 잡는 치트키

질문의 키워드 main feature가 biggest events로 paraphrasing되어 언급된 주변 내용을 주의 깊게 읽는다.

해설 | 4단락의 'The biggest events are the parades, where festival organizers showcase elaborate floats based on themes like "Famous Lovers" or "Equality for All."'에서 가장 큰 행사는 퍼레이드로, 축제 주최 측에서 "유명한 연인" 또는 "모두를 위한 평등"과 같은 주제를 바탕으로 한 정교한 장식 차량을 선보이는 것이라고 했다. 따라서 (d)가 정답이다.

어휘 | volunteer n. 자원봉사자; v. 자원하다 reflect v. 반영하다

TEST 1
TEST 2
TEST 3
TEST 4
TEST 5
TEST 6
TEST 7

지텔프 공식 기출문제집 7회분 Level 2

71 특정세부사항   What   난이도 ●●●

According to the final paragraph, what does Mardi Gras have in common with Saturnalia?

(a) the negative effect it has on the economy
(b) the time of year it typically takes place
(c) the way it is traditionally celebrated
(d) the contribution it has to local history

마지막 단락에 따르면, 마르디 그라와 농신제는 무슨 공통점이 있는가?

(a) 경제에 미치는 부정적인 영향
(b) 일반적으로 열리는 연중 시기
(c) 전통적으로 기념하는 방식
(d) 지역 역사에 미치는 기여

━○ 정답 잡는 치트키

질문의 키워드 have in common with Saturnalia가 like Saturnalia로 paraphrasing되어 언급된 주변 내용을 주의 깊게 읽는다.

해설 | 6단락의 'Much like Saturnalia, Mardi Gras is also known as an opportunity for partying and excessive drinking.'에서 농신제와 마찬가지로 마르디 그라는 파티와 과음의 기회로도 알려져 있다고 했다. 따라서 (c)가 정답이다.

어휘 | typically adv. 일반적으로   contribution n. 기여, 공헌

72 어휘   유의어   난이도 ●●○

In the context of the passage, underline{observed} means _____.

(a) practiced
(b) serviced
(c) supervised
(d) recorded

지문의 문맥에서, 'observed'는 -을 의미한다.

(a) 준수된
(b) 서비스가 제공된
(c) 감독된
(d) 기록된

━○ 정답 잡는 치트키

밑줄 친 어휘의 유의어를 찾는 문제이므로, observed가 포함된 구절을 읽고 문맥을 파악한다.

해설 | 2단락의 'fasting and silence were commonly observed'는 금식과 침묵이 일반적으로 준수되었다는 뜻이므로, observed가 '준수된'이라는 의미로 사용된 것을 알 수 있다. 따라서 '준수된'이라는 같은 의미의 (a) practiced가 정답이다.

73 어휘   유의어   난이도 ●○○

In the context of the passage, underline{prized} means _____.

(a) useful
(b) expensive
(c) desired
(d) rare

지문의 문맥에서, 'prized'는 -을 의미한다.

(a) 쓸모 있는
(b) 값비싼
(c) 훌륭한
(d) 진귀한

━○ 정답 잡는 치트키

밑줄 친 어휘의 유의어를 찾는 문제이므로, prized가 포함된 구절을 읽고 문맥을 파악한다.

해설 | 5단락의 'these prized trinkets'는 이러한 소중한 장신구들이라는 뜻이므로, prized가 '소중한'이라는 의미로 사용된 것을 알 수 있다. 따라서 '훌륭한'이라는 비슷한 의미의 (c) desired가 정답이다.

수신인 정보

Erwin Todd
839 Park Avenue
Delaware, OH

Dear Mr. Todd:

편지의 목적: 소란에 관한 경고

⁷⁴I am sending this warning letter in response to your ⁷⁹multiple occasions of public disturbance to our community. The behavior of your guests during your frequent late-night parties has resulted in property damage and noise complaints from ⁷⁵your neighbors, several of whom have already approached you on this matter. While your parties temporarily stop after such discussions, they often start up again after a few weeks.

민원 내용1: 음악 소리와 쓰레기 투기

⁷⁶Reports from the community show that this problem does not solely affect your next-door neighbors. Just this week, the Greenbrook Homeowners Association has received six separate complaints from other residents on your street. Each one reported loud music coming from your house from dusk until dawn. Several passersby have also noticed the noise and alerted us to broken bottles and other trash littering the sidewalk in front of your residence.

민원 내용2: 재물 파괴

⁷⁷Just last night, some of your guests sent a baseball flying into the neighbor's house, shattering her window. The neighbor called us shortly afterward to file a complaint. She will be contacting you soon regarding compensation, though I cannot speak to the likelihood of charges being filed against you for destruction of property.

요청 + 끝인사

⁷⁷The association believes that this recent event, on top of a consistent record of public disturbance, ⁸⁰entails serious action on our part. We can no longer let this pass. ⁷⁸Please consider this a formal request to stop disturbing your neighbors and other members of our community. If we receive another complaint, we will be forced to take this matter to the police.

발신인 정보

Sincerely,
Catherine Williams
Catherine Williams
President
Greenbrook Homeowners Association

Erwin Todd
파크 가 839번지
오하이오주 델라웨어

Mr. Todd께:

⁷⁴귀하가 우리 지역사회에 공공연한 소란을 피운 ⁷⁹여러 일에 대응하여 이 경고장을 보냅니다. 귀하의 잦은 심야 파티 동안 손님들의 행동은 ⁷⁵이웃들로부터 재산상의 손해와 소음 민원으로 이어졌고, 그들 중 몇몇은 이 문제로 귀하에게 이미 이야기를 한 적이 있습니다. 이러한 논의 후에는 일시적으로 파티가 중단되지만, 자주 몇 주 후에 다시 시작됩니다.

⁷⁶지역사회의 보고에 따르면 이 문제가 오직 이웃 주민들에게만 영향을 미치는 것은 아닙니다. 이번 주에만, 그린브룩 주택 소유자 협회는 귀하의 이웃 주민들로부터 여섯 건의 별개의 민원을 접수했습니다. 각각의 주민은 해 질 녘부터 새벽까지 귀하의 집에서 시끄러운 음악 소리가 난다고 신고했습니다. 몇몇 행인들도 이 소음을 알아챘고 깨진 병과 그 외의 쓰레기가 귀하의 집 앞 인도에 버려지고 있다는 것을 알려주었습니다.

⁷⁷바로 어젯밤에, 손님 중 몇 명이 야구공을 이웃집으로 날려 보내서, 창문을 산산조각 냈습니다. 그 이웃은 그 후에 즉시 저희에게 전화해 민원을 제기했습니다. 귀하가 재물 파괴로 고소될 가능성에 대해서는 말씀드릴 수 없지만, 그 이웃은 곧 보상과 관련하여 연락을 드릴 것입니다.

⁷⁷협회는 공공연한 소란에 대한 지속적인 기록에 더해, 이번 최근 사건이 저희 측에서도 ⁸⁰심각한 조치를 필요로 한다고 생각합니다. 저희는 더 이상 이 일을 못 본 체할 수 없습니다. ⁷⁸이것을 이웃들과 다른 지역사회 구성원들을 방해하는 것을 중단해 달라는 공식적인 요청으로 여겨주시기를 바랍니다. 만약 또 다른 불만이 접수되면, 이 문제를 경찰에 신고할 수밖에 없을 것입니다.

Catherine Williams 드림
협회장
그린브룩 주택 소유자 협회

어휘 | warning letter phr. 경고장 in response to phr. ~에 대응하여 public adj. 공공연한 disturbance n. 소란, 방해 property damage phr. 재산상의 손해 temporarily adv. 일시적으로 solely adv. 오직, 오로지 separate adj. 별개의 dusk n. 해 질 녘, 황혼 dawn n. 새벽 passersby n. 행인 alert v. 알리다 litter v. (쓰레기 등을) 버리다 sidewalk n. 인도 residence n. 집, 주택 shatter v. 산산조각 내다, 깨부수다 file a complaint phr. 민원을 제기하다 compensation n. 보상 likelihood n. 가능성, 기회 file a charge phr. 고소하다, 고발하다 destruction of property phr. 재물 파괴 let pass phr. 못 본 체하다

Why did Catherine Williams send Erwin Todd a letter?

(a) to inform him of a lawsuit against him
(b) to complain about him destroying her property
(c) to warn him about his behavior toward her
(d) to ask him to stop disturbing his neighbors

왜 Catherine Williams는 Erwin Todd에게 편지를 보냈는가?

(a) 그를 상대로 한 고소를 알리기 위해서
(b) 그녀의 재산을 손상한 것에 관해 불평하기 위해서
(c) 그녀에 대한 그의 행동을 경고하기 위해서
(d) 이웃들을 방해하는 것을 그만두도록 요청하기 위해서

━○ 정답 잡는 치트키

지문의 초반을 주의 깊게 읽고 전체 맥락을 파악한다.

해설 | 1단락의 'I am sending this warning letter in response to your multiple occasions of public disturbance to our community.'에서 지역사회에 **공공**연한 소란을 피운 여러 일에 대응하여 이 경고장을 보낸다고 한 뒤, 심야 파티로 인한 소음, 쓰레기 문제, 새물 파괴를 지적하며 조치하도록 요청하고 있다. 따리서 (d)기 정답이다.

어휘 | lawsuit n. 고소, 소송   disturb v. 방해하다

How did Erwin's neighbors first try to resolve the issue?

(a) by sending him letters of complaint
(b) by speaking with him in person
(c) by contacting an attorney
(d) by pressing charges with the police

Erwin의 이웃들은 어떻게 처음에 이 문제를 해결하려 했는가?

(a) 그에게 항의 편지를 보냄으로써
(b) 그와 직접 이야기를 함으로써
(c) 변호사에게 연락함으로써
(d) 경찰에 고발함으로써

━○ 정답 잡는 치트키

질문의 키워드 neighbors가 그대로 언급되고, issue가 matter로 paraphrasing되어 언급된 주변 내용을 주의 깊게 읽는다.

해설 | 1단락의 'your neighbors, several of whom have already approached you on this matter'에서 이웃 중 몇몇은 이 문제로 Erwin에게 이미 이야기한 석이 있나고 했다. 따라서 (b)가 징답이다.

어휘 | resolve v. 해결하다   in person phr. 직접   attorney n. 변호사   press a charge phr. 고발하다, 고소하다

Why does Catherine believe that Erwin has created a widespread problem?

(a) because guests have destroyed public property
(b) because a number of complaints have been received
(c) because some neighbors have chosen to move away
(d) because people will no longer pass by the house

Catherine은 왜 Erwin이 광범위한 문제를 일으켰다고 생각하는가?

(a) 손님들이 공공 재산을 파괴했기 때문에
(b) 많은 민원이 접수되었기 때문에
(c) 몇몇 이웃들이 이사하기로 결정했기 때문에
(d) 사람들이 더 이상 그 집을 지나가지 않을 것이기 때문에

질문의 키워드 created a widespread problem이 does not solely affect ~ next-door neighbors로 paraphrasing되어 언급된 주변 내용을 주의 깊게 읽는다.

해설 | 2단락의 'Reports from the community show that this problem does not solely affect your next-door neighbors. Just this week, the ~ Association has received six separate complaints from other residents on your street.'에서 지역사회의 보고에 따르면 이 문제가 오직 이웃 주민들에게만 영향을 미치는 것은 아니며, 이번 주에만 협회가 Erwin의 이웃 주민들로부터 여섯 건의 별개의 민원을 접수했다고 했다. 따라서 (b)가 정답이다.

어휘 | widespread adj. 광범위한 pass by phr. 지나가다

---

77 특정세부사항   What   난이도 ●●○

What finally prompted the association to take action?

(a) a report of people trespassing on private property
(b) a call from a concerned community business
(c) a complaint about damage to a residence
(d) a formal request from law enforcement

협회가 마침내 조치하도록 부추긴 것은 무엇이었는가?

(a) 사유 재산에 침입하는 사람들에 대한 신고
(b) 관련된 지역 사업체로부터의 전화
(c) 주거지 파손에 대한 민원
(d) 법 집행 기관으로부터의 공식 요청

○── 정답 잡는 치트키

질문의 키워드 action이 그대로 언급된 주변 내용을 주의 깊게 읽는다.

해설 | 3단락의 'Just last night, some of your guests sent a baseball flying into the neighbor's house, shattering her window. The neighbor called us shortly afterward to file a complaint.'에서 바로 어젯밤에 손님 중 몇 명이 야구공을 이웃집으로 날려 보내서 창문을 산산조각 냈고, 그 이웃은 그 후에 즉시 협회에 전화해 민원을 제기했다고 한 뒤, 4단락의 'The association believes that this recent event, on top of a consistent record of public disturbance, entails serious action on our part.'에서 협회는 공공연한 소란에 대한 지속적인 기록에 더해, 이번 최근 사건이 협회 측에서도 심각한 조치를 필요로 한다고 생각한다고 했다. 따라서 (c)가 정답이다.

⇄ **Paraphrasing**
shattering ~ window 창문을 산산조각 내어 → damage to a residence 주거지 파손

어휘 | trespass v. (남의 땅·집에) 침입하다, (남의 권리를) 침해하다 private property phr. 사유 재산 law enforcement phr. 법 집행

---

78 추론   특정사실   난이도 ●●●

What will probably happen if Erwin does not stop holding loud parties?

(a) The local authorities will get involved.
(b) The association will strip him of community privileges.
(c) The police will evict him from his house.
(d) He will be banned from entertaining guests.

Erwin이 소란스러운 파티를 여는 것을 중단하지 않는다면 무슨 일이 벌어질 것 같은가?

(a) 지역 관계 부처가 개입할 것이다.
(b) 협회는 그에게서 지역사회 특권을 박탈할 것이다.
(c) 경찰이 그를 집에서 쫓아낼 것이다.
(d) 그는 손님을 접대하는 것이 금지될 것이다.

○── 정답 잡는 치트키

질문의 키워드 stop holding loud parties가 stop disturbing ~ neighbors and other members of ~ community로 paraphrasing되어 언급된 주변 내용을 주의 깊게 읽는다.

해설 | 4단락의 'Please consider this a formal request to stop disturbing your neighbors and other members of our community. If we receive another complaint, we will be forced to take this matter to the police.'에서 이웃들과 다른 지역사회 구성원들을 방해하는 것을 중단해 달라는 공식적인 요청으로 여겨주기를 바라며, 만약 또 다른 불만이 접수되면 이 문제를 경찰에 신고할 수밖에 없을 것이라고 한 것을 통해, Erwin이 소란스러운 파티를 여는 것을 중단하지 않는다면 지역 관계 부처인 경찰이 개입하도록 신고학 수밖에 없을 것임을 추론할 수 있다. 따라서 (a)가 정답이다.

⇄ **Paraphrasing**
the police 경찰 → The local authorities 지역 관계 부처

오답분석
(c) 4단락에서 만약 또 다른 불만이 접수되면 이 문제를 경찰에 신고할 수밖에 없을 것이라고는 했지만, 경찰이 어떤 조치를 할 것인지는 언급되지 않았으므로 오답이다.

어휘 | authority n. 관계 부처, 당국 strip v. 박탈하다 privilege n. 특권, 영예 evict v. 쫓아내다, 퇴거시키다
ban from phr. ~하는 것을 금지하다 entertain v. 접대하다, 즐겁게 하다

79 어휘 유의어
난이도 ●●●

In the context of the passage, <u>occasions</u> means _____.

(a) **incidents**
(b) affairs
(c) points
(d) goals

지문의 문맥에서, 'occasions'는 –을 의미한다.

(a) **(일어난) 일**
(b) 사건
(c) 요점
(d) 목표

○ 정답 잡는 치트키
밑줄 친 어휘의 유의어를 찾는 문제이므로, occasions가 포함된 구절을 읽고 문맥을 파악한다.

해설 | 1단락의 'multiple occasions'는 여러 일이라는 뜻이므로, occasions가 '(특별한) 일'이라는 의미로 사용된 것을 알 수 있다. 따라서 '(일어난) 일'이라는 비슷한 의미의 (a) incidents가 정답이다.

오답분석
(b) '사건'이라는 의미의 affair는 주로 공적으로 중요하거나 관심사가 되는 사건이나 일을 의미하므로, 문맥에 어울리지 않아 오답이다.

80 어휘 유의어
난이도 ●●○

In the context of the passage, <u>entails</u> means _____.

(a) prevents
(b) **requires**
(c) limits
(d) protects

지문의 문맥에서, 'entails'는 –을 의미한다.

(a) 막는다
(b) **필요로 한다**
(c) 제한한다
(d) 보호한다

○ 정답 잡는 치트키
밑줄 친 어휘의 유의어를 찾는 문제이므로, entails가 포함된 구절을 읽고 문맥을 파악한다.

해설 | 4단락의 'entails serious action'은 심각한 조치를 필요로 한다는 뜻이므로, entails가 '필요로 한다'라는 의미로 사용된 것을 알 수 있다. 따라서 '필요로 한다'라는 같은 의미의 (b) requires가 정답이다.

MEMO

지텔프 공식 기출문제집 | 7회분 LEVEL 2

초판 2쇄 발행 2024년 11월 4일
초판 1쇄 발행 2024년 1월 8일

지은이	G-TELP KOREA 문제 제공 해커스 지텔프연구소 해설
펴낸곳	㈜챔프스터디
펴낸이	챔프스터디 출판팀
주소	서울특별시 서초구 강남대로61길 23 ㈜챔프스터디
고객센터	02-537-5000
교재 관련 문의	publishing@hackers.com
동영상강의	HackersIngang.com
ISBN	978-89 6965 446-5 (13740)
Serial Number	01-02-01

외국어인강 1위,
해커스인강 HackersIngang.com

해커스인강

- 효과적인 지텔프 청취 학습을 돕는 **문제풀이 MP3**
- 교재의 핵심 어휘를 복습할 수 있는 **지텔프 기출 단어암기장**
- 내 점수와 백분위를 확인하는 **무료 자동 채점 및 성적 분석 서비스**
- 시험 전 꼭 봐야 할 **"딱 한 장에 담은 지텔프 문법 총정리"** 무료 강의

영어 전문 포털,
해커스영어 Hackers.co.kr

해커스영어

- 무료 **지텔프 단기고득점 비법강의**
- 실전을 미리 경험해볼 수 있는 **무료 지텔프 모의고사**
- 지텔프/공무원/세무사/회계사 **시험정보 및 학습자료**